THE AMERICAN CHIEF EXECUTIVE

THE AMERICAN
CHIEF EXECUTIVE

THE PRESIDENCY AND THE GOVERNORSHIP

JOSEPH E. KALLENBACH, *1903-*

The University of Michigan

HARPER & ROW, PUBLISHERS   NEW YORK, AND LONDON

TO

THE FOUR "J's"

JESS, JULIE, JOBY, AND JENNIFER

CONTENTS

PART FOUR
Epilogue

TABLES

PREFACE

The American presidency has for many years been an endlessly fascinating subject for study and analysis by scholars and commentators on public affairs. Along with its counterpart, the state governorship, with which its evolution as an institution has been inextricably intertwined, the presidency has commanded the attention of the public in every period of the nation's history. The never-ending flow of biographical, historical, and analytical studies of the presidency and the attention it receives in the daily and periodical press constantly remind us of the important place the office and its incumbent have in the public eye.

The office of chief executive in the American system of government well deserves the attention it receives from scholars and the public. The presidency has become the focal point of the national government, as has the governorship at the state level. Sooner or later, the chief executive becomes the center of action on every major issue of public policy. There is hardly an area within the whole spectrum of problems of American government studied by political scientists that does not require consideration of the role of the chief executive in the political process. The political scientist may be concerned primarily with public opinion and its formulation, grass-roots politics, political parties and interest groups, the legislative process, the formulation of public policy and public administration, law, or the role of the courts —but always he must give a large share of his attention to the place and function of the chief executive.

Some 20 years ago, I conceived the idea that for more advanced undergraduate college students a course of study organized around the subject of the American Chief Executive would provide an excellent opportunity for exploration into a great many of the problems that challenge the student of American government, whatever his specialized field of interest might be. This book is the outcome of that course. It is an attempt to draw together in one volume most of the materials that make up the core of such a course. This is not, I hasten to add, a "how-to-do-it" book. It does not attempt to probe deeply into the psychological, political, and personality factors that account for the

xi

decisions particular Presidents and governors have to make, or have made. Its purpose is rather to bring together in an organized fashion, from a wide variety of sources, ideas and information that help to explain the office of chief executive as a working element in the American governmental system of today.

In selecting my materials I have tried to keep in view certain aspects of the office of chief executive. One is that the institution of the presidency is the product of growth, conditioned by the political environment in which it has developed. The office of President and the state governorship have a common origin. In their evolution into their present forms they have been shaped by common influences. They have also interacted in their development. Another point of view that I have sought to stress is that the problems confronting Presidents and governors today are not essentially unique. They are merely problems that have presented themselves, in different forms and circumstances, to chief executives before them. If I have given considerable attention to what George Washington or John Adams or Thomas Jefferson or Andrew Jackson did as Presidents, it is merely to show that presidential problems of today are not much different from those of earlier times. Presidents and governors, as well as scholars, can learn from the past.

Another purpose I have kept in view has been to identify, so far as possible, those important points at which the institutional arrangements affecting the office of chief executive today appear to be changing. This is essentially an institutional study. But institutions of government, like giant glaciers, move. It is therefore important to trace the outlines of the forward, "cutting" line of institutional development, to identify those points at which changes are taking place or are likely to take place in the future, and to try to assess their significance.

There are many to whom I wish to acknowledge indebtedness. The students, both graduate and undergraduate, who have studied in my classes have been a never-failing source of inspiration and assistance. My departmental colleagues have given much needed encouragement and advice. I am particularly indebted to my colleagues, Professors Arthur W. Bromage, James H. Meisel, and Norman Thomas, who read parts of the manuscript while it was in preparation and offered valuable suggestions. The Horace H. Rackham School of Graduate Studies of The University of Michigan furnished financial assistance in carrying on some of the preliminary research on the governorship and in getting the manuscript into final shape. Mrs. Jean Martin has given invaluable assistance in putting the manuscript into its final typed form. For any errors of fact or interpretation that may appear, however, I assume full responsibility.

J.E.K.

October, 1965

PART ONE

CONSTITUTIONAL FOUNDATIONS

1

ESTABLISHMENT OF THE OFFICE

OF STATE GOVERNOR

Governmental institutions grow; they are not invented overnight. No other feature of the American system more clearly illustrates this universal principle than the office of chief executive as found in the nation and in the 50 states. The American presidency has been characterized as a modified version of the English monarchy; and so it is. But its line of descent runs back to the kingship through an ancestral tree nurtured in America. It is the product of an evolutionary process that began with the founding of the first English colonies in America. The colonial period, from 1607 to 1775, witnessed significant changes in American thinking regarding the principles that ought to be applied in the organization of a government based on the idea of popular sovereignty. Concepts concerning the nature of executive authority and its place in the governmental scheme were an important part of this evolving philosophy of government.

In the period from 1775 to 1780 pre-existing colonial governments were transformed into 13 governments, organized and limited by the terms of written constitutions. These early state governmental plans were the connecting links between institutions developed in the colonial period under English auspices and the presidency set up by the United States Constitution in 1787. They exhibited many of the characteristic features of the colonial political systems which they displaced, but at the same time they embodied other features deliberately devised to accommodate political institutions to American experience and desires. Out of this experimentation with new forms and formulas came the familiar presidential executive system of the nation and the states.

THE COLONIAL GOVERNORSHIP

The office of colonial governor, from which the state governorship evolved, had progressed through a variety of forms from the beginning of colonization in the early part of the seventeenth century up to the

3

eve of the Revolutionary War.[1] In the earlier colonial period, when settlement was carried forward as a corporate or individual enterprise, the governor was little more than an appointed agent of the corporate directorate or the proprietor, entrusted with local management of the venture. His political functions, vaguely defined and rudimentary, were less significant than his business managerial powers and responsibilities. Later, after the Crown had assumed a more direct control over colonial affairs by substituting a royal provincial form of government for the earlier charter systems in most of the colonies, the royal governor, appointed by the Crown and serving at its pleasure, became the primary political link between the King and his colonial subjects.

By the middle of the eighteenth century eight of the colonies— New Hampshire, Massachusetts, New York, New Jersey, Virginia, North Carolina, South Carolina, and Georgia—had become royal provinces. Pennsylvania, Delaware, and Maryland continued to be proprietary colonies, although they were also made increasingly subject to the home government in political matters as time passed. A position similar to that of the royal provincial governors was held by the governors in the three proprietary provinces, except that they were appointed by the proprietors, subject to the approval of the Crown; they were immediately responsible to the proprietor rather than to the King. In Pennsylvania and Delaware, which had a common proprietor in the Penn family, there was a union of the governorship of the two provinces in one person's hands. The practice of the King's appointing one person to serve as governor of more than one province had been fairly common in the royal provinces also until the 1740s, but this system had finally been abandoned by the Crown as a result of strong local protests against it.[2] In the two remaining colonies, Rhode Island and Connecticut, government continued to be carried on under the terms of the original charters until the outbreak of the Revolutionary War. In these colonies the governor was chosen by the members of the "Company," i.e., the freemen of the colony, from among their own number. The governor held office for a fixed period of time, subject to renewal of his mandate through re-election from year to year.

The political role of the governor in the royal provincial and proprietary colonies was roughly comparable to that of the King in the British system. His powers and duties were outlined in his commission of office at the time of appointment, but over the course of time these commissions had come to follow a common pattern. Royal governors were empowered to appoint and commission major administrative and

---

[1] For an extensive analysis of the development of the colonial governorship and its status in the eight royal provinces and the proprietary provinces at the beginning of the Revolutionary period see Evarts B. Greene, *The Provincial Governor in the English Colonies of North America* (New York: Longmans, Green & Co., Vol. VII, Harvard Historical Studies, 1898).

[2] Greene, *op. cit.*, pp. 52–54.

judicial officers, subject to the approval of the Crown. They were authorized to summon, prorogue, and dissolve the colonial assemblies. The higher administrative officers or "assistants" formed the governor's council, over which he presided. The governor and council together made up the second branch of the legislative body, and the governor presided over its sessions. In some of the colonies the governor and his council also composed the highest court in the colonial judicial system. The governor's assent was required for all legislative measures to become effective: that is to say, he had an absolute power of veto. He also was in command of the colonial militia, and not infrequently took the field in person when it was mobilized for defense against the Indians or forces of hostile colonial powers.

In actual practice the governor's real political power was less than this enumeration of his functions would suggest. Colonial assemblies, emulating the British Parliament in its relations with the King, applied pressure through their control over the purse to exact concession after concession from the governors. Laws requiring the convening of the colonial assemblies at periodic intervals, regulating the manner of administration of laws, and especially, defining and limiting the sources of revenue, were forced upon governors under the threat of denial of necessary money grants. Governors were sometimes placed in the awkward position of having to assent to demands from their assemblies that ran counter to their instructions from the Crown. Attrition of the royal governors' powers in actual practice was well advanced considerably before the events that gave rise to the Revolution.

The governors' position became even more unenviable after 1763, when the home government inaugurated a policy of stricter enforcement of laws and regulations relating to colonial trade and Parliament began to levy taxes directly upon the colonists for the support of British troops garrisoned in the colonies, ostensibly for their defense against the French and Indians. Colonial governors and judges, as the agencies through which these unpopular measures were carried out, were placed in an extremely vulnerable position. In an immediate sense, the Revolution began simply as a protest movement against actions by the royal governors which they had no choice but to take, in view of their status as agents of the home government.

THE TRANSITION FROM COLONIAL TO STATE GOVERNMENT

The processes by which colonial governmental institutions were superseded by new forms during the Revolution varied from state to state. There was no sudden break with the political habits and institutions of the past, but rather a series of adjustments as necessity required. As the regularly established colonial governments fell apart with the ousting of the royal governors and other high administrative and judicial officers who were Loyalist in their sympathies, provisional arrangements were devised to supply appropriate organs for executing the laws, administering justice, and directing military operations. In some cases these *ad hoc* arrangements were legitimized by the enactment of appropriate organic laws; in other cases this was not done. With the change in the character of the struggle in 1776 from an armed protest to a war for independence, these earlier temporary arrangements were supplanted by more complete, formal constitutions, based in theory on the principle of popular sovereignty.

The first step toward reconstructing pre-existing governmental institutions into state governments was the formation of popularly chosen provincial congresses or conventions drawing their support from those elements who objected most strenuously to measures taken by British authorities to suppress what they regarded as incipient rebellion in 1774 and 1775. Although at first these assemblies maintained outwardly the character of regularly constituted colonial legislative bodies, they were actually extralegal if not illegal organs, since they came into being and functioned in defiance of the established colonial executive authority. They became the central agencies through which a protest and resistance movement was organized in the colonies. Through them the Continental Congresses of 1774 and 1775 were set up to coordinate colonial opposition to British policies. When the protest movement became armed rebellion in April, 1775, the provincial congresses or conventions and their central consultative body, the Second Continental Congress, assumed direction of governmental affairs by degrees and as necessities dictated.

In the initial stages of the conflict the administration of measures adopted by these provincial bodies was entrusted to *ad hoc* committees, as was also the practice in the Continental Congress. To administer affairs between sessions it became a general practice to set up a "Committee of Safety," authorized to act for the revolutionary assembly in military matters and to take other needful measures for maintenance of public order. On July 18, 1775, the Second Continental Congress recommended the establishment of such a committee in each colony, a step which had already been taken by many of them.[3] These Committees of Safety acquired in time a semipermanent character and were granted powers of a general executive nature by the revolutionary assemblies. In some cases they assumed such powers without express legislative authorization.[4]

[3] *Journals of the Continental Congress,* Vol. II, p. 189.
[4] Cf. Margaret B. MacMillan, *The War Governors in the American Revolution,* (New York: Columbia University Press, Columbia University Studies in History,

Expedients like these could not long satisfy the public needs, but the course to be pursued beyond these steps was not easily agreed upon. There was sharp division of opinion in the revolutionary assemblies on whether to proceed to a forthright reconstruction of the whole governmental plan or to temporize further in the expectation that the quarrel with the mother country would be amicably resolved. In their perplexity several of the provincial congresses appealed to the Continental Congress for advice. There John Adams took a leading part in urging that the colonies be advised to establish complete new governments through bodies chosen for this purpose, but for some time he was unable to win general acceptance of this view among his colleagues. As early as May 16, 1775, the provincial convention in Massachusetts asked the advice of the Continental Congress on how it should proceed in "taking up and exercising the powers of civil government."[5] It is interesting to observe that the request of the Massachusetts convention was coupled with a declaration of readiness to "submit to such a general plan as you [the Congress] may direct for the colonies."

The idea that the Continental Congress should prescribe a uniform plan of government for the several colonies which were in process of becoming states was advanced in a number of quarters during the early stages of the Revolution. Thomas L. Lee of Virginia advocated this procedure and criticized the Virginia convention for taking independent action in 1776. A mass meeting in Charlotte County, Virginia, adopted resolutions to this effect while the Virginia convention was in the process of drawing up a temporary frame of government for the state.[6] It is unlikely that the principle of a uniform plan of government for the states would have proved acceptable, once the issue had passed beyond the matter of devising temporary governments to function until reconciliation with the mother country might be achieved. John Adams, though recognizing the advantages in setting up a uniform system of government for the states, observed in his *Autobiography:*

> I dared not make such a motion [that Congress prepare a uniform plan of government for the several states] because I knew if such a plan was adopted it would be, if not permanent, yet of long duration, and it would be extremely difficult to get rid of it. And I knew that every one of my friends, and all those most zealous for assuming gov-

Economics, and Public Law, No. 503, 1948), pp. 30–37. See also Agnes Hunt, *Provincial Committees of Safety in the American Revolution* (Cleveland: Winn and Judson, 1904); Allan Nevins, *The American States During and After the Revolution, 1775–1789* (New York: The Macmillan Company, 1924).

5 *Journals of the Continental Congress*, Vol. II, p. 77.

6 See Fletcher M. Green, *Constitutional Development in the South Atlantic States, 1776–1860* (Chapel Hill: University of North Carolina Press, 1930), pp. 52–53; and W. W. Henry, *Patrick Henry: Life, Correspondence and Speeches* (New York: Charles Scribner's Sons, 3 vols., 1891), Vol. I, pp. 407–408.

ernments, had at that time no idea of any other government but a
contemptible legislature in one assembly, with committees for executive
magistrates and judges.[7]

In response to the request of the Massachusetts convention, on
June 9, 1775, the Continental Congress adopted a resolution declaring
that "no obedience being due to the Act of Parliament for altering the
charter of the Colony of Massachusetts Bay, nor to a Governor . . .
who will not observe the directions of, but endeavor to subvert that
charter," the governor and lieutenant governor of the colony should
be deemed "absent." It recommended further that a new assembly and
executive council be elected which should exercise the powers of government "until a Governor, of his Majesty's appointment, will consent
to govern the colony according to its charter."[8] This advice was immediately acted upon by the Massachusetts convention. The 28-member
executive council provided for in its suspended charter remained as
the *ad hoc* executive authority in that state until a formal state constitution was framed and put into operation in 1780.

On October 18, 1775, the delegation from New Hampshire laid
before the Continental Congress instructions from their provincial
convention asking the "advice and direction" of the Congress on what
measures they should take for "administering Justice, and regulating
our civil police." The Congress responded, on November 3, with a resolution advising that a full and free representation of the people be
called by the provincial convention and that those representatives, if
they thought it necessary, should establish such a form of government,
as, in their judgment, would "best produce the happiness of the people,
and most effectually secure peace and good order in the province, during continuance of the present dispute between Great Britain and the
colonies."[9] The next day a similar response was given to a request from
the South Carolina provincial convention for guidance and on December 4 to the Virginia convention.

These recommendations by the Congress, it will be noted, looked
only toward adoption of a temporary expedient, a political modus
vivendi to meet a critical situation arising from a breakdown of the
executive and judicial arms of colonial government. Those who continued to entertain hopes of reconciliation with Great Britain were
still powerful enough in the Continental Congress through the first
year of the war to prevent its taking the bolder line of action that was
urged by John Adams and others. Consequently the adjustments in the
forms of government that followed were, as in Massachusetts, adapta-

[7] *The Life and Works of John Adams,* Charles F. Adams, ed. (Boston: Little,
Brown and Company, 10 vols., 1850–1856), Vol. III, p. 22. (Hereafter cited as
Adams, *Works.*)

[8] *Journals of the Continental Congress,* Vol. II, pp. 83–84.

[9] *Ibid.,* pp. 298, 319.

tions of pre-existing colonial plans to the exigencies of the times, rather than deliberate efforts to create full-fledged, permanent state governments.[10]

A more definitive step toward setting up permanent plans of government in the states was taken by the Continental Congress on May 15, 1776, a year after the fighting phase of the Revolution had begun. At that time a resolution was passed recommending to all the respective assemblies and conventions of the united colonies that they "adopt such government as shall, in the opinion of the representatives of the people, best conduce to the happiness and safety of their constituents in particular, and America in general." The idea that these governments were to be temporary makeshift affairs, it will be noted, was no longer evident in this advice. The preamble to this resolution contained language boldly setting forth a claim to the right of self-government in terms clearly foreshadowing the Declaration of Independence which was to be adopted six weeks later.[11]

This resolution gave encouragement to the states that had not already acted to make plans of governmental reconstruction. As John Adams phrased it, adoption of the Declaration of Independence on July 4, 1776, found the 13 newly fledged states at work erecting governments "as fast as children build cob houses."[12] Rhode Island and Connecticut found it possible to continue their colonial charter forms, under which a system of popular government was already established. Only legislative acts repealing earlier laws referring to the royal authority in oaths and commissions of office and in executive and judicial

[10] Virginia's "temporary" constitution, however, which was put into effect in 1776 shortly before independence was declared, remained as the fundamental law of that state until 1830. Many of the leading citizens of Virginia, among them Thomas Jefferson, James Madison, and George Mason, maintained that this document, having been drawn up by a convention which had no clear popular mandate to do so, was a product of usurped authority. Jefferson played a leading part in unsuccessful movements in 1783 and 1794 to revise it. Green, *op. cit.*, pp. 139–140.

[11] The body of the resolution was adopted on May 10, but final action was deferred until a suitable preamble could be formulated. A committee composed of John Adams, Richard Henry Lee, and Edward Rutledge was named to prepare it. The preamble, which was added to the resolution as passed on May 15, after reciting various grievances of the colonists concluded with the statement that "it is necessary that the exercise of every kind of authority under the said Crown should be totally suppressed, and all the powers of government exerted, under the authority of the people of the colonies, for the preservation of internal peace, virtue, and good order, as well as for the defence of their lives, liberties, and properties, against the hostile invasions and cruel depredations of their enemies." (*Journals of the Continental Congress*, Vol. IV, pp. 342, 357–358.) When James Duane of New York termed the resolution as thus worded "a machine for the fabrication of independence," Adams replied, "it was independence itself, but we must have more formality yet." (Adams, *Works*, Vol. III, p. 46.)

[12] Green, *op. cit.*, p. 56. For a detailed account of the steps by which the original state constitutions were created see W. F. Dodd, "The First State Constitutional Conventions, 1776–1783," *American Political Science Review*, Vol. II (November, 1908), pp. 545–561.

writs and processes were necessary to convert their charters into effective state constitutions. The remaining states, including Vermont, which was in process of establishment as a separate entity, drew up constitutions and put them into operation in due course. Some of the wartime state constitutions were soon subjected to extensive revision; others proved to be relatively long-lived, withstanding efforts to revise them for a generation or longer.[13]

INFLUENCES SHAPING THE CHARACTER OF THE OFFICE OF STATE GOVERNOR

Reconstruction of the scheme of government as it concerned the governorship was at once the most difficult and the most pressing problem confronting the provincial constituent bodies of the Revolutionary War period. It was the most pressing because at an early stage in the struggle, executive authority as represented by the royal and proprietary governors was first successfully challenged and then brought to a practical end by expulsion of the governors from the colony or their removal from office. Unsettled conditions in most of the colonies —where clashes between Loyalist and Revolutionary elements were a continual threat to internal security—demanded a vigilant and effective executive authority to deal with them. These conditions were intensified in those areas, particularly in the middle and southern states, which became the scenes of conflict in the later stages of the war. Successful organization and prosecution of the war effort called for leadership which only a recognized executive head of government could give. Establishing an executive authority to fill these needs proved difficult, however, because the political events leading up to the Revolution had engendered a deep popular distrust of any kind of executive authority. A general tendency to retain colonial political and legal institutions so far as was feasible was manifested in the plans of government drawn up by the Revolutionary state constituent bodies. In arrangements relating to the executive, circumstances and prevailing opinion dictated more radical departures from established practices. On this point, least of all, could the states merely adapt colonial

13 Cf. James Q. Dealey, *The Growth of American State Constitutions* (Boston: Ginn and Company, 1915), pp. 26–30. The following list indicates the dates of adoption of the original state constitutions, with subsequent dates showing when extensive revisions were made before 1860: New Hampshire (temporary plan, 1776), 1784, 1792; Massachusetts (revived charter of 1691, 1775), 1780; Rhode Island (original charter of 1663, 1776), 1842; Connecticut (original charter of 1662, 1776), 1818; New York, 1777, 1823; New Jersey, 1776, 1844; Pennsylvania, 1776, 1790; Delaware, 1776, 1792; Maryland, 1776, 1837, 1851; Virginia, 1776, 1830; North Carolina, 1776, 1835; South Carolina (temporary plan, 1776), 1778, 1790; Georgia (temporary plan, 1776), 1777, 1789, 1795, 1798; Vermont, 1777, 1786, 1793, 1836.

forms to their purposes. Conditions compelled them to strike out along new paths.

It is significant that only in Rhode Island and Connecticut, where under colonial charters the governor was popularly chosen and had no independent veto power, no change in the frame of government was thought necessary. There the locally elected governor could be controlled and even deposed by popular action. This fact, more than any other, explains why seventeenth-century colonial charters were found acceptable as state constitutions in Connecticut until 1818 and in Rhode Island until 1842. In Connecticut, Governor Jonathan Trumbull, who was thoroughly in sympathy with the revolutionists, was continued in office by annual election from 1769 through 1786, when he voluntarily retired. In Rhode Island the colonial governor, Joseph Wanton, was Loyalist in his sympathies and refused to cooperate with the colonial assembly in a resistance program. By action of the assembly he was removed from office on October 31, 1775, and the lieutenant governor, Nicholas Cooke, was elevated to the post of governor. The inference is clear that if all the colonies had had locally chosen, locally responsible governors as these two had, the course of the Revolutionary movement would have been far different. In fact, a protracted war leading to independence might not even have occurred at all.[14]

In the other states, where substantial change in the organization of the executive branch was necessary to give it a popularly responsible character, English and colonial precedents were of varying degrees of importance as guiding principles. Colonial experience was more efficacious in teaching what to avoid than what to provide in its place. Conflict between colonial assemblies and governors had brought into clear view certain elements of the executive power which it was thought necessary to restrict or to assign to the legislative branch. Above all, it had brought into disfavor the colonial governor's powers of prorogation, dissolution, and veto, which permitted him to interfere with the functioning of the legislative branch itself. But it was not clear just how far readjustment should go in strengthening the legislative hand at the expense of the executive. There was a general failure to appreciate the effectiveness of local selection and limited tenure as safeguards against abuse of executive power.

It is not surprising that these first attempts by the states to achieve a more satisfactory institutional relationship between the primary agencies of government led to a variety of interesting experiments. The fundamental problem, as the Revolutionary leaders perceived it, was one of devising a proper balance between the principle of liberty, as represented in a popularly chosen legislative body, and authority as found in an executive arm. Theory was blended with practical ex-

[14] Cf. Nevins, *op. cit.*, pp. 4, 80, 209.

perience to produce some novel arrangements. The more radical departures from colonial precedents did not prove lasting; but the fact that they were made helped to clear the way for the eventual creation of the distinctive type of executive that is now a basic feature of American national and state government. *The pioneering, experimental stage in the development of the "presidential" type of chief executive in the United States was the period from 1776 to 1787.*

The political principles that the Revolutionary state constituent assemblies accepted and sought to apply to the executive can easily be discerned. First, they accepted as axiomatic that the executive should be given a "republican" character by being made directly or indirectly elective from the local citizenry, for a short, fixed term of office. Second, they believed the principle of separation of powers should be adhered to in the sense that the executive should have a status distinct from that of the lawmaking branch itself. Third, it was generally agreed that the role of the executive should be primarily, if not exclusively, that of agent to carry out the legislative will. Whether the chief executive should be personally associated in some manner with the lawmaking and judicial authorities, as were the colonial governors, and—assuming that the executive was to be a single individual—the degree to which he should be subject to control by a council, and how this council should be composed, were matters upon which there was lack of agreement from state to state.

In some of the constituent bodies of the Revolutionary period there was little opportunity for calm study and thorough deliberation. This was particularly true of those that acted before independence was formally declared, since their functioning as constituent bodies was somewhat incidental to their exercise of general managerial functions. After independence was declared, constituent assemblies acted more deliberately in the knowledge that their plans were expected to be permanent. The Massachusetts constitution of 1780, after an earlier one had been rejected through town meetings in 1778, was the first of the completed drafts to be submitted for direct popular approval before being put into operation. In some states before that time, however, indirect popular approval of proposed plans of government had been required through favorable action by a subsequently chosen ratifying assembly.

A common practice in the constituent assemblies was to delegate the responsibility for preparing a draft plan to a committee, and when the draft was brought forward, to subject it to examination and approval section by section. As a rule, only minor alterations were made in committee drafts. Often the work of the committee was entrusted by the committee itself to a subcommittee, so that in some cases the final draft of a constitution became essentially the work of a few men, or even of one individual. Examples of this practice were the New York convention in 1777, in which a committee composed of John Jay, Robert R. Livingston, and Robert Yates was set up to prepare a draft constitution, and the Massachusetts convention that originated the first formal draft constitution in that state. In Massachusetts a drafting committee of 30 members was created, which in turn delegated the actual work of preparing a draft to a subcommittee composed of John Adams, Samuel Adams, and James Bowdoin. Because of the leading roles they took in formulating the first drafts in their respective states, Jay in New York and John Adams in Massachusetts have been credited with having written the first constitutions in these states.[15]

It was a time of considerable popular interest in problems of governmental organization and procedure. The press stimulated popular discussion of issues of this sort, while various individual drafts of plans to be presented to the constituent assemblies brought into view a wide range of ideas. American experience provided the immediate source of most of the plans, but there was also a readily identifiable body of political literature that exercised an influence on the work of the conventions. Some of the leading members of the constituent assemblies were familiar with the concept of government organized on the principle of the separation of powers, as expounded by Montesquieu in his disquisition praising the British system of government, *L'Esprit des Lois,* published some 20 years earlier. Others were familiar with similar principles and theories given currency in Blackstone's *Commentaries on the Laws of England,* published in the decade before the Revolution. As rebels against a governmental authority deemed to have forfeited its right to govern by "a long train of abuses and usurpations" and as advocates of the theories of popular sovereignty, limited government, and legislative supremacy in the formulation of laws, they also drew intellectual sustenance from the Whig "Bible," John Locke's *Two Treatises of Civil Government.*

One of the most influential of the individual plans was contained in John Adams' *Thoughts on Government,* prepared at the request of George Wythe of Virginia, to whom it was addressed as a letter.[16] This

15 See Charles Z. Lincoln, *The Constitutional History of New York* (Rochester: Lawyers Cooperating Publishing Company, 5 vols., 1906), Vol. I, pp. 49ff; Adams, *Works,* Vol. IV, pp. 215–216.

16 Adams, *Works,* Vol. IV, pp. 193–200. Earlier Adams had outlined similar ideas in a letter to Richard Henry Lee. Adams, who had no faith in a governmental plan that concentrated all power in the hands of a "contemptible legislature in one assembly, with committees for executive magistrates and judges," declared he had prepared his plan to counteract the influence of Paine's suggestion of a government of that type in his *Common Sense.* Strangely, though, Adams originally endorsed the idea of a unicameral assembly as the sole governmental organ at the national level. He defended the Congress as a suitable form of government for the nation on the ground that it was "not a legislative assembly, nor a representative assembly, but only a diplomatic assembly," adequately checked by the governments of the

plan, which was presented by Patrick Henry as one of several brought to
the attention of the Virginia convention in 1776,[17] was printed by
Richard Henry Lee in pamphlet form and had a wide circulation. It
proposed a governor, to be chosen annually by joint ballot of a two-
house legislature, who "after being stripped of most of those badges of
domination called prerogatives" should have an absolute veto power
over legislation. It also proposed creation of a council to assist and advise the governor in the exercise of his executive powers. The casual
suggestion by Thomas Paine in his pamphlet *Common Sense* that public
needs required only a democratically chosen unicameral assembly, with
executive functions to be handled through committees responsible to it,
expressed a contrasting widely held view as to the basic plan of governmental organization which the states should adopt. Benjamin Franklin,
who presided over Pennsylvania's constitutional convention, gave
strong endorsement to this idea, and was pleased to see it incorporated
into that state's first constitution.[18] Franklin's idea was, of course, also
given concrete form in the Articles of Confederation plan of national
government drawn up in 1777, wherein all powers were vested in the
unicameral Confederation Congress.

The contrasting ideas of a separate chief executive, popularly
elected or chosen by the legislative organ for a fixed term of office and
armed with a strong veto power, as advocated by Adams, and a plural
executive agency so completely subordinated to the legislature as to
be merely an administrative convenience to it, as suggested by Paine
and Franklin, were the basic alternatives among the many proposals
given serious consideration in the drafting of state constitutions in
the period from 1776 to 1780. The final products represented compromises of one kind or another between these two views. As the business
of constitution-making proceeded, solutions reached on the problem
of the executive in one state exercised an influence on governmental
architects in other states. Thus the principles of the Pennsylvania constitution reflecting Paine's and Franklin's theories reappeared with
only slight modification in the Vermont constitution of 1777; the New
Hampshire constitution of 1784 bore an affinity to the Massachusetts

---

states. He conceded, however, that if the national government should be given additional powers enabling it to act directly on the people, a separate executive should
be created. See his *Preface* to his *Defense of the Constitutions of the United States*,
ibid., p. 584.

[17] Green, *op. cit.*, p. 64. Patrick Henry, Richard Henry Lee, Carter Braxton,
Meriwether Smith, and Thomas Jefferson were the authors of other plans submitted
to this convention. Jefferson's plan was received too late to be of much influence,
although the term "senate" to apply to the upper house of Congress and of state
legislatures was apparently derived from it. Cf. Lincoln, *op. cit.*, Vol. I, p. 503.

[18] Cf. Carl Van Doren, *Benjamin Franklin* (New York: The Viking Press, 1938),
p. 554.

constitution of 1780, which embodied many of Adams' ideas; the Maryland and North Carolina constitutions of 1776 showed evidences of borrowings from the earlier Virginia constitution which was something of an amalgam of the two extremes.

THE EXECUTIVE IN THE ORIGINAL STATE CONSTITUTIONS

No uniform pattern can be discerned in the first state constitutions for the office of state governor. In all cases an official who might properly be termed a "chief executive" appeared, and while his powers and functions were as a rule narrowly defined and in considerable degree subordinated to those of the legislative branch, his position was nevertheless clearly that of a Chief of State and Commander-in-Chief. Beyond this, the provisions were so diverse as to make further broad generalization inaccurate.

State executive arrangements may be classified in four types.[19] In the first category were the "charter" executives of Connecticut and Rhode Island, who as state governors occupied positions identical with those of the colonial governors who preceded them. Though they had no independent veto power and were required to consult executive councils in the performance of their duties, their selection by popular action gave them a certain degree of independence from the legislative branch and gave them some prestige as legislative leaders. In a second group were the relatively strong executives, exemplified by the popularly elected governors in New York under the "Jay Constitution" and in Massachusetts after 1780 under the "Adams Constitution." These governors enjoyed a suspensive veto power as well as a rather extensive appointive authority, along with the powers generally associated with the executive in other states. In a third category were the "Franklin-type" executives, essentially of a plural character, found in Pennsylvania, Vermont, Georgia until 1777, New Hampshire until 1784, and Massachusetts until 1780. Under these systems the "chief" executive was little more than a presiding officer of a council in which executive authority for civil administrative and military purposes was vested. A fourth category was made up of the remaining states, which had legislatively appointed governors of varying degrees of weakness in relation to the legislative branch.

---

[19] The analysis of early state constitutional arrangements that follows is based mainly on provisions found in Francis Newton Thorpe, *The Federal and State Constitutions, Colonial Charters and Other Organic Laws of the States, Territories and Colonies* (Washington: Government Printing Office, 7 vols., 1909).

In keeping with colonial practice the chief executive officer was designated the "governor" in most of the states. Under the first constitutions in Pennsylvania and Delaware and in the temporary plans of government in New Hampshire and Georgia, he was called the "president," while South Carolina's first constitution referred to him as "president and commander-in-chief." These departures from current colonial practice were in part attributable to the fact that under the Pennsylvania, New Hampshire, and Georgia plans the chief executive officer was actually little more than the presiding officer of a conciliar body in which executive powers were lodged. Some of the earlier charter forms had employed the term "president" for the presiding officer in such conciliar bodies, and it was natural to continue to use that title. A wish to avoid the inference that the office being created was intended as a permanent substitute for the governorship may also have been a factor in the choice of the title of president in the temporary plans of government in New Hampshire and Georgia, since these plans were formulated before hope of reconciliation with the mother country had been abandoned. Still another factor could have been the desire to emphasize a fundamental distinction between the new office and the one that in some quarters carried with it unpopular connotations.[20] Subsequent adoption of the Constitution of the United States, in which the term "governor" was used in several passages to refer to the chief executive officer in the states, helped to induce the states to abandon the title of president for this office. By 1792 all the states had adopted the term governor, and it has been used in all states since then.

METHOD OF SELECTION

Devising a new mode of selecting the chief executive officer became an imperative matter in those states which, as colonies, had had governors appointed by the Crown or by the proprietor. Two methods of selection found favor generally with the framers of the original state constitutions. Direct popular election, with possible recourse to legislative election in the event no majority choice emerged from the

[20] In the plan prepared by Thomas Jefferson for presentation to the Virginia Convention of 1776 the title of "Administrator" was proposed for the chief executive. He would have had powers, status and functions roughly comparable to those of a city manager today under the council-manager form of municipal government. W. C. Ford, "Jefferson's Constitution for Virginia," *The Nation*, Vol. 51 (1890), p. 107.

popular vote, was favored in the New England states. Under the Connecticut and Rhode Island charters the freemen of the colony had been privileged to participate in the choice of the governor from among their "Company." This practice was continued in these states after statehood was achieved. A majority vote was required for election; if there was no popular majority the assembly chose the governor. Massachusetts in 1780 and New Hampshire in 1784 also adopted this system, with one refinement: their constitutions provided that in case there was no candidate with a popular majority the choice should be made by the upper house of the legislature from a panel of two selected by the lower house from among the four highest in the popular voting. The New York constitution of 1777 was unique in that it anticipated the modern mode in providing for direct election of the governor by the state's freeholders, i.e., those owning property in land, the candidate with a popular plurality to be deemed elected without further recourse.

In all the states from Pennsylvania and New Jersey southward the principle of legislative appointment was favored. The most common method of choice was by joint vote of the two houses. Ordinarily a majority in the joint vote was required, successive ballots being taken until a majority was mustered for one candidate. The Maryland constitution of 1776 provided that in case there was a tie vote between the two leading candidates after a second ballot the issue should be decided by lot. Under Georgia's constitution of 1777, election of the governor from among its own membership was a function of the unicameral assembly. A variation from the general practice was found in Pennsylvania, where the "president" was chosen annually by the unicameral assembly from among the 12 executive councilmen who were themselves popularly elected for a term of three years.

TERM AND RE-ELIGIBILITY

The idea that executive and legislative officers should hold office for a specific term was accepted without question by the framers of the original state constitutions. In keeping with the aphorism of John Adams in his *Thoughts on Government* that "where annual elections end, there slavery begins," all but three of the original state constitutions gave the chief executive a one-year term. Exceptions were Delaware and New York, with three-year terms, and South Carolina, which allowed a two-year term. The temporary plan of government in effect in Georgia for a brief time in 1776 provided for only a six-month term, but it was replaced the next year by a more complete plan of government under which the chief executive enjoyed a one-year term.

In seven states, all lying from Pennsylvania southward, tenure in office was further limited by various restrictions upon re-eligibility. It should be noted that these were all states in which the principle of legislative election prevailed. Georgia's constitution of 1777 was the most restrictive in that it limited an individual to no more than one one-year term in each three-year period. Despite the further provision obligating a governor through his oath of office "peaceably and quietly" to relinquish his office at the end of one year, that state was the only one to become involved in a squabble over occupancy of the governor-ship during the Revolutionary War period.[21] In the New England states as well as in New York and New Jersey there were no re-eligibility limitations. Continuance of the same person in office for long periods through successive elections was the usual practice in these states both during and after the Revolutionary War. For example, George Clinton was governor of New York for six successive three-year terms from 1777 to 1795; William Livingston, the first governor of New Jersey, served 14 successive one-year terms from 1776 to 1790; Jonathan Trumbull of Connecticut served as colonial governor and state governor from 1769 to 1786; and except for a two-year interlude (1785–1787), John Hancock was governor of Massachusetts from 1780 to 1793.

CONSTITUTIONAL POWERS AND FUNCTIONS

The role assigned the chief executive under most of the original state constitutions, while not an insignificant one in all cases, was considerably less important than that of the colonial governor in the royal and proprietary provinces. The influence of colonial practice was seen in the fact that in every state a conciliar body or bodies was provided to advise, assist, and in some respects restrict the governor in the exercise of certain powers. The agency created took various forms. In Pennsylvania and Vermont and under the temporary plans of government in Massachusetts, New Hampshire, and Georgia, the executive powers were actually in the hands of the executive council itself, rather than in those of the chief executive officer, but under the other forms of government a clearer distinction was made between the chief executive and the body associated with him in the exercise of his powers.

21 Conditions in Georgia were particularly chaotic after British military forces occupied the major portion of the state in 1778. Choice of a successor to the first governor elected under the Constitution of 1777 could not be effected by the new assembly because of British occupation of Savannah, the capital. Rival groups comprised of remnants of the assembly later met and each chose a set of executive officials. For some years there was a succession of rival claimants to the post of governor in that state. See Green, *op. cit.*, pp. 124–126; and Ethel Kime Ware, *A Constitutional History of Georgia* (New York: Columbia University Press, Columbia University Studies in History, Economics and Public Law, No. 528, 1947), p. 52.

EXECUTIVE CONCILIAR BODIES

In the colonial systems the executive council or "body of assistants" to the governor had usually performed a dual or even a triple role. It was associated with the governor as an advisory and controlling agency in his exercise of certain executive powers; it also acted as the upper house of the legislative branch; and in some instances it constituted along with the governor the highest court in the judicial hierarchy. The first of these functions—that of serving as a check upon the exercise of the governor's major executive powers—was assigned to the council in all the original state constitutions, but the definition of the relationships of this agency to the operations of the legislative and judicial branches resulted in arrangements more interesting in their variety and novelty than in their permanence. The judicial function of the conciliar agency was entirely eliminated in most of the states, but there continued to be a joining of legislative and executive responsibilities in it in a number of states. In some states the council was given a status entirely separate from the legislative branch itself, thus emphasizing its purely executive character. In others a conciliar function in executive matters was assigned to the legislature or to its upper house. Arrangements of the latter type proved to be most significant in their impact on later institutional development. *They set the pattern for that familiar feature of the checks and balances system in the nation and in most of the states today under which the upper branch of the legislature serves as a consultative and approving body in the exercise of the chief executive's appointive authority and, in the case of the President, the treaty-making power.*

GENERAL EXECUTIVE AUTHORITY

In assigning general executive authority to the governor the language of the early state constitutions tended to emphasize his subordination to the legislature. Clauses that could be interpreted to extend his authority to cover a wide range of independent executive powers appeared in a few instances, however. The New York constitution vested the "supreme executive power and authority" of the state in him, while New Jersey's declared that the "supreme executive power" should reside in him. Again, the New York constitution, employing phraseology originally found in the Pennsylvania and Vermont constitutions in their definitions of the authority and duties of their plural executive organs, instructed and empowered the governor "to take care that the laws be faithfully executed" and "to expedite all such measures as may be resolved upon by the legislature."

More commonly the language used suggested a dependence of the executive upon the legislative branch in the definition of his powers. For example, the Virginia constitution declared that he should, with the advice of the Council of State, "exercise the executive powers, according to the laws of this Commonwealth," but that he should not "under any pretense, exercise any power or prerogative, by virtue of any law, statute or custom of England." The Massachusetts constitution of 1780 authorized the governor "to hold and keep council for ordering and directing the affairs of the Commonwealth, agreeably to the Constitution and laws of the land." Language of this nature obviously had the effect of emphasizing that the role of the governor and his council was that of an agent executing policies determined by the legislative branch and that the scope of his authority was subject to definition and limitation by laws.

Several state constitutions, recognizing the need for emergency executive action at times when the legislative body was in recess, authorized the governor with consent of his council to interdict trade for a limited period of time. The Pennsylvania and Vermont constitutions authorized the executive councils to lay embargoes or prohibit exports of particular commodities for a period of 30 days during a recess of the legislature. Similar powers were vested in the governor with the advice of his council in North Carolina and South Carolina, while in Maryland this power was in the governor's hands alone. The Maryland constitution also authorized him to compel ships to "ride quarantine" if he deemed it advisable in the interests of public health. These "emergency" executive powers were supplemented from time to time by legislative grants of authority designed to permit him to take needful measures for the maintenance of public peace, safety, and order, particularly when the legislature was not in session.[22] *These concessions of power to the executive were significant in that they reflected a continuing recognition of the necessity for investing the executive with discretionary authority to act when public exigencies require governmental intervention to protect the public interest. At a time when the concept of executive authority was at its nadir in America they preserved, even though in a limited way, the concept of an executive prerogative to act for the preservation of the public good.*

APPOINTMENTS

In many of the states an appointive authority of considerable range was conferred upon the governor, but with few exceptions its exercise was subject to conciliar or legislative approval. State administrative officials other than those concerned with fiscal matters, local administrative officials, judges, and military officials came within the range of this appointive authority in varying measure from state to state. A power to

[22] Cf. MacMillan, *op. cit.*, Chap. V.

fill vacancies occurring in offices filled normally by legislative appointment was also commonly given during a legislative recess. In New York, subject to the approval of a Council of Appointments composed of four senators, the governor filled all offices whose appointments were not otherwise provided for. Included were judges, other state officials with the exception of the treasurer, higher military officers, and local officials other than town clerks, supervisors, assessors, and constables. The Maryland constitution authorized the governor with the advice and consent of his council to appoint "the Chancellor, and all Judges and Justices, the Attorney-General, Naval Officers, officers in the regular land and sea service, officers of the militia, Registers of the Land Office, Surveyors, and all other civil officers of government (assessors, constables and overseers of the roads only excepted)." In contrast with such broad grants of authority as these were the provisions of the North Carolina constitution which gave the governor, with consent of council, only a temporary recess appointive power over civil and military offices, which were filled normally by legislative appointment.

MILITARY POWERS

The early state governor's position in the area of military affairs was a relatively strong one. Conditions existing as a result of the war then in progress as well as colonial precedents account for a willingness on the part of state constituent bodies to entrust the governor with military leadership functions of importance. In every state he was made the commander-in-chief or "captain-general" of the militia and other state military forces. Military leadership of this nature was the main distinction that set off the president in Pennsylvania and the governor in Vermont from their associates on the executive councils in which general executive authority was vested. The "embodiment" of the militia by the governor and his assumption of command over them in the field were usually made subject to conciliar approval. Along with the commander-in-chief function usually went the power to appoint subordinate military officers. The governor's authority in this connection was not all-inclusive, since general officers in the state military forces were in some cases named by the legislature, while the right to select militia officers of lower ranks was often reserved to the militia companies themselves.

LEGISLATIVE POWERS

In the colonial systems the governor had been an integral part of the lawmaking branch of government. His position in relation to the legislative body, particularly in the royal and proprietary provinces, was one closely paralleling that of the King with Parliament. The popularly elected lower branch usually met only at his call, and their sessions were subject to prorogation by him. He possessed the power to dissolve the assembly and call for new elections. At the beginning of a session a formal message from the governor, comparable to the King's "Speech from the Throne," outlined the major matters upon which he desired the assembly to act. He usually presided over the meetings of the council in its deliberations as an upper house of the legislature. Above all, he was armed with an independent power of absolute veto.

Even before the Revolution, colonial assemblies had successfully challenged and limited the governor's actual use of these powers. The threat of refusal of taxes and grants of money had been employed from time to time to compel the governor to assent to measures which gave assemblies greater freedom from executive control. His powers of convocation, prorogation, dissolution and veto, just as the King's, were gradually being reduced to matters of form rather than substance even before 1776.[23] As has already been noted, the resistance movement that culminated in armed rebellion in 1775 was essentially a concerted defiance of the colonial executive authority, which was responsive to directives from the Crown in these matters, by dominant elements in the popularly elected assemblies. Naturally the framers of the first state constitutions believed that the root of their difficulties lay in a system by which the executive could interfere with the functioning of the legislative authority, representative of the popular will. To them it seemed elementary that a government based on the principle of separation of powers must be one in which the legislative branch had independent responsibility for its legislative acts and the executive should be concerned only with the administration of policies embodied in the laws.

Provision for relatively short elective terms for members of the legislative branch, along with an express grant of authority to it to determine the time and duration of its sessions, was generally relied upon in the original state constitutions to give the legislature independence from the executive. In four states—Virginia, South Carolina, Delaware, and Maryland—the chief executive was expressly denied power to "prorogue, adjourn or dissolve" the assembly; but under the Massachusetts and New Hampshire constitutions, in case of disagreement between the two houses on the time of adjournment or prorogation and during a recess, the governor, with consent of his council, might prorogue the legislature for a period not to exceed 90 days.[24] In time of public danger or necessity arising from prevalence of an

23 Cf. Greene, *op. cit.*, Chaps. VIII, IX.

24 The Massachusetts constitutional provisions relating to sessions of the General Court were distinctive in their evident reliance upon colonial forms and procedures. Although regular annual sessions of specified duration were provided for, the formality of a proclamation by the governor to effect an adjournment, prorogation, or dissolution was also required.

"infectious distemper" at the appointed place of assembly, he was also authorized in those states to designate a different place of meeting. Similar provisions giving the governor a hand in determining the time and place of legislative sessions were inserted in the New York constitution. They proved particularly useful because of the uncertainties arising from the presence of British forces in that state during most of the Revolutionary War period.

In all the original state constitutions except North Carolina's the governor was also authorized to assemble the legislature on extraordinary occasions. Approval by the executive council was usually required. In Virginia the governor was obliged to call a special session on application by a majority of the lower house and in Delaware by a majority of either house.

Recommendation of matters for consideration by the legislature was made a constitutional duty of the governor in New York and of the executive council in Pennsylvania and Vermont. Even though not specifically provided for in all state constitutions, the colonial practice of beginning legislative sessions with a message from the executive outlining the state of public affairs and offering suggestions for legislative consideration was generally followed. Personal appearances by the governor before the legislature for the delivery of addresses and reports were sometimes made, but communications were more commonly in the form of written messages. The Georgia constitution explicitly directed that messages from the governor to the assembly be delivered in written form by the secretary of the governor's council, thus by implication forbidding the governor to appear in person before the legislature. Reports, communications from the Continental Congress, and specific recommendations and suggestions for action were transmitted by governors from time to time during legislative sessions. In fact, continual prodding of reluctant and dilatory legislatures by means of executive messages seems to have been the rule then, as it is now.

Direct participation by the governor in the deliberations of the legislature was provided for in three states. The New Hampshire constitution of 1784 made the president of the state the regular presiding officer of the senate and gave him full voting privileges therein, with an extra "casting vote" in case of ties. His position thus was similar to that of the colonial governor, except for a veto power. New Jersey's governor had a similar role, but had only a casting vote. In Vermont the executive council, over which the governor presided, was empowered to examine and make recommendations for amendments to legislation under consideration by the one-house assembly before it was finally enacted, but in Georgia where the executive council had a similar function in relation to the one-house assembly, the governor was excluded from its deliberations when acting in this capacity.

Participation by the governor in the legislative process through use of the veto was provided for only in New York, Massachusetts after 1780, and for a brief time in South Carolina. South Carolina's temporary constitution of 1776 gave the state president and commander-in-chief an absolute veto upon legislation. When in 1778 President John Rutledge vetoed a new organic law designed by the legislature as a permanent state constitution, the reaction was so strong that he was obliged to resign the presidency. The new constitution of 1778, which his successor was willing to approve, deprived the chief executive of his veto power altogether.

Under the New York plan the governor was a member of a "Council of Revision," of which the chancellor and the three judges of the supreme court were also members. The governor with the concurrence of any two members of this body might oppose with a veto any bill "inconsistent with the spirit of the constitution or with the public good" by returning it to the house in which it originated, along with the reasons in writing for disapproving it. By a two-thirds majority vote a vetoed measure could be enacted into law. A period of 10 days was allowed the Council of Revision for action on a bill, and if it failed to express its disapproval within that time the bill would become law. There was no "pocket veto" authority, as all vetoed measures were required to be returned to the legislative branch for consideration. The veto provision of the Massachusetts constitution was similar to that of New York, except that the governor alone exercised this power and he was allowed only five days for consideration. *These veto provisions in New York and Massachusetts proved to be highly significant in American constitutional development. They provided the basic plan and language for formulation of the President's veto power in the United States Constitution and subsequently for the re-establishment of the governor's veto power in the states.*

JUDICIAL POWERS

For the most part the early state constitutions effected a complete separation of the judicial and executive organs of government, except as the executive in some states participated in the selection of judicial officers. Exceptions to the rule of complete separation were found in Pennsylvania and Vermont, where the executive council over which the chief executive presided was to comprise a court of impeachments. When acting in this capacity it was authorized to call upon the supreme court for advice. Other exceptions to the principle of separation were seen in Delaware, where the president was an ex officio member of the court of appeals, the highest court of review in the state; in Massachusetts, where the governor and his council, until the legislature should provide otherwise, handled all marriage, divorce, and alimony cases and all appeals from judges of probate; and in New Jersey, where the functions of chancellor and ordinary or surrogate-general were united with the office of governor, and the governor and his council comprised the court of appeals, the "court of last resort in all clauses of the law." In New York, association of the chancellor and the judges of the supreme court with the governor for purposes of exercising the veto power was a recognition of the quasi-judicial nature of this power when it was exercised against a bill on grounds of alleged conflict with the constitution.

THE PARDONING POWER

The granting of clemency to criminal offenders was a matter of unusual public interest and concern in Revolutionary War times because of the considerable numbers of Tory or Loyalist sympathizers who committed violations of laws enacted for the preservation of public peace and order. Nevertheless, a tendency to entrust to the executive a substantial power of pardon was manifested in many of the early state constitutions. In Georgia the concession of power to the governor went only so far as to give him authority to grant reprieves and suspensions of fines pending final action in each case by the assembly. On the other hand, the constitutions of New York, Maryland, Delaware, and North Carolina vested a general pardoning power in the chief executive alone; while Massachusetts, New Hampshire, New Jersey, and Virginia placed this authority in the governor acting with the advice of his council. The power was limited or qualified in other respects in various states. Impeachments were specifically excluded from the scope of executive clemency in most of the states; pardons prior to conviction were forbidden in Massachusetts and New Hampshire; and in cases of treason and murder only a power to reprieve, subject to final disposition by the legislature, was granted in New York, Vermont, and Pennsylvania.

THE GOVERNORSHIP UNDER THE FIRST STATE CONSTITUTIONS: AN EVALUATION

The observation of Madison in the Convention of 1787 that "the Executives of the States are in general little more than Cyphers; the legislatures omnipotent,"[25] and Jefferson's comment in his *Notes on*

[25] "Debates in the Federal Convention of 1787 as Reported by James Madison," in *Documents Illustrative of the Formation of the Union of the American States,* Charles C. Tansill, ed. (Washington: House Doc. No. 398, 69th Congress, 1st session,

Virginia that under the Virginia constitution of 1776 "all the powers of government, legislative, executive and judiciary result to the legislative body,"[26] so often quoted by historians and commentators, have tended to perpetuate a somewhat inaccurate conception of the position of chief executive as established by the original state constitutions. The governor in Virginia, the state with which Madison and Jefferson were most familiar, was one of the weaker chief executives from the standpoint of constitutional powers. Practically every official action he was authorized to take was subject to approval by an executive council composed of eight individuals chosen by the legislative branch. He himself was elected for only a one-year term by the legislature and could be removed by it. But as has already been pointed out, the position of the governor in the scheme of government varied from state to state. Taking all the state constitutions into account, essentially all the major elements that were later combined in the creation of a strong national chief executive were found in one or more state plans. A one-man executive, a fixed tenure, no limit on eligibility for re-election, executive independence of the legislative branch in the matter of election to the office, an extensive appointive authority, a military commander-in-chief role, a legislative leadership role supported by an effective veto power, a pardoning power of consequence, and the responsibility to act as the agent of the state in its dealings with external sovereignties—all of these elements which contribute to the strength of the presidency can be found in the original constitutional arrangements of one or more states. The governor in New York, in particular, enjoyed a status and powers quite comparable to those given the President by the Constitution.

Furthermore, it should not be forgotten that the state executives of the Revolutionary War period were called upon to serve in times that were far from normal. The disruptions and distractions arising from the war itself placed a strain upon the governmental structure from the outset. Some of the early governors were in the field heading military forces for considerable periods of time. The smouldering conflicts between local Loyalist and Revolutionary elements in the population were a constant threat to internal security. British forces occupied considerable parts of New York and the middle and southern states from 1776 onward, making normal conduct of the affairs of government an impossibility. Two state governors, Thomas Burke of North Carolina and John McKinley of Delaware, were captured by the

Government Printing Office, 1927), p. 398. (Hereafter cited as Madison, "Debates," or Tansill, *Documents*.)

26 *Writings of Thomas Jefferson*, Paul Leicester Ford, ed. (New York: G. P. Putnam's Sons, 10 vols., 1892–1899), Vol. III, p. 223. (Hereafter cited as Jefferson, *Writings*.)

British, and others, among them Thomas Jefferson, narrowly escaped capture. Continual demands by the Continental Congress upon the states for funds, military forces, and supplies were a major concern of the wartime governors.

Under these circumstances it is no less remarkable that the legislatures showed at times a disposition to assume authority properly belonging to the executive or failed to respond to his leadership than that they also exhibited in some cases a willingness to delegate extraordinary "dictatorial" powers to him, particularly during periods of legislative recess. One of the most striking actions of this character occurred in South Carolina. In 1779 the assembly of that state voted to give President John Rutledge and his Privy Council authority "to do everything that appeared to him and to them necessary for the public good," until the assembly should reconvene. The next year, with Charleston already under seige by the British, the assembly upon adjournment vested power in President Rutledge and such of the council as he could conveniently consult "to do everything necessary for the public good except taking away the life of a citizen without a public trial."[27] With the capture of some members of the council by the British soon afterward and the dispersal of most of the rest to remote parts of the state, maintenance of governmental authority in that state became the responsibility of President Rutledge and the remnants of his council for the next two years. When a new legislature was finally called into session by him in January, 1782, it demonstrated its trust and confidence by enacting into law every measure he recommended.[28] While the legislatures of other states showed a reluctance to take such drastic steps as were taken by South Carolina,[29] they did on occasion delegate extensive emergency powers to their governors during legislative recesses. Governors in one state or another were thus authorized to make necessary civil and military appointments; procure and issue military supplies; discontinue or modify trade embargoes; extend time limits upon the service of the militia for various purposes; and vacate individual letters of marque and reprisal.

The lack of a national chief executive to mobilize and direct the nation's energies in the prosecution of the war necessitated great reliance upon the executives of the states to overcome the deficiency.

[27] MacMillan, *op. cit.*, p. 76.

[28] *Ibid.*, p. 233.

[29] Similar proposals were advanced in the Virginia legislature in 1776 when Patrick Henry was governor and in 1781 during Thomas Jefferson's incumbency, but failed to pass. On the first occasion, when fears had been aroused by Lord Dunmore's attempt to return to power with the backing of British guns, intense feeling was aroused over the issue of vesting broad emergency powers in the governor and suspending by legislative act the usual forms of government. Threats were said to have been made on the life of Governor Henry if the bill should pass. MacMillan, *op. cit.*, pp. 79–80; Henry, *op. cit.*, Vol. I, pp. 501–509.

In considerable measure the governors became the local agents of the Continental Congress and of General Washington, serving as the intermediaries through whom liaison was maintained between the central government and the states. Many a governor gave fully as much time and energy to work for the Congress as he did to his constitutional duties.[30] On occasion, resolutions of the Congress conferred specific authority upon state governors in handling the recruitment, supply, and disciplining of Continental troops. Favorable action upon the ratification of the Articles of Confederation by the legislatures of two of the laggard states, New Jersey and Delaware, was largely the result of persistent effort by their executives, William Livingston and Caesar Rodney, respectively. In Maryland, the last state to ratify, Governor Thomas Johnson was chiefly responsible for the successful stand that state took in demanding nationalization of the western territories as its price for ratification of the Articles.[31]

Many of the early state chief executives, especially those in the middle and southern states where constitutional limitations on re-eligibility resulted in frequent rotation in office, failed to achieve national prominence or to make important contributions as leaders in their states. Occupation of much of the Carolinas and Georgia by British troops after 1778 made orderly administration of local affairs by the new governments impossible for considerable periods of time. However, the roster of wartime state chief executives included a number of men who demonstrated a high order of executive ability and leadership. They were not all, to use Madison's term, "mere Cyphers." Among the outstanding governors of this early period were George Clinton of New York, later Vice President of the United States under Jefferson; William Livingston, the first governor of New Jersey; Jonathan Trumbull of Connecticut; John Rutledge, president of South Carolina from 1776 to 1778 and from 1779 to 1782; and Joseph Reed, president of Pennsylvania from 1778 to 1781. By exercise of the power and influence of their positions they contributed much to the successful prosecution of the war for independence. Others among the early governors, including Thomas Jefferson and Patrick Henry of Virginia, John Hancock of Massachusetts, and John Dickinson of Delaware and Pennsylvania, are more remembered for their political contributions to the nation in other capacities.

The most important contribution to the cause of good government made by early state governors was their demonstration that executive power, if placed in the hands of popularly responsible chief executives disposed to recognize and respect constitutional and statutory limitations upon their authority, was not inherently dangerous. The deference shown by them to the legislatures went far toward allay-

---

[30] MacMillan, *op. cit.,* p. 112.
[31] *Ibid.,* pp. 120–123.

ing the deep-lying distrust of executive authority that had developed during the long years of strife between the popular assemblies and provincial governors. At the same time the virulence of factionalism and excesses of narrow self-interest in the legislative branches helped to make clear that unrestrained authority in the hands of a popular assembly could also be dangerous. Thomas Jefferson gave voice to a view that was undoubtedly reflective of a trend in popular thinking when he wrote in his *Notes on Virginia* in 1782:

> The concentrating of [all powers of government] in the same hands is precisely the definition of despotic government. It will be no allevia-tion that these powers will be exercised by a plurality of hands, and not a single one. 173 despots would surely be as oppressive as one.[32]

The conduct of the early governors made possible a reconsideration of the principles that should be followed in organizing a government embodying the idea of balanced powers.

When the Federal Convention met in 1787 and addressed itself to the problem of establishing a governmental plan more suited to the needs of the nation there was a more favorable climate of public opinion toward the executive element in government, growing out of state experience. Experimentation with various forms of governmental organization in the states had provided a rich body of material which the delegates in their collective wisdom were able to draw upon. The lessons to be derived were not lost upon them.

> State experience had taught that executive energy and responsi-bility are inversely proportional to executive size; that, consequently, the one-man executive is best. It taught the value of integration; the necessity of executive appointments, civil and military; the futility of legislative military control. It demonstrated the necessity for the veto as a protective measure. It showed that this power could be utilized as a means of preventing unwise legislation. . . . It demonstrated the value of a fixed executive salary which the legislature could not reduce. It discredited choice by the legislature, though without teaching clearly the lesson of popular choice. . . . And, above all, it assured the ac-ceptance of, if it did not create, a new concept of constitutional govern-ment—the fundamental principles of which were the ruling constitu-tion, the limited legislature, and the three equal and coordinate departments.[33]

The Framers found it politically expedient and feasible to propose a one-man, integrated executive organ for the United States in which were combined most of those features lending greatest strength to the office of chief executive in the states. Subsequent history attests to the wisdom they displayed in their task of synthesis and adaptation.

[32] Jefferson, *Writings*, Vol. III, p. 223.
[33] Charles C. Thach, *The Creation of the Presidency, 1775–1789* (Baltimore: Johns Hopkins Press, Johns Hopkins University Studies in Historical and Political Science, Ser. XL, No. 4, 1922), pp. 52–53.

2

CREATION OF THE OFFICE OF PRESIDENT

When the Federal Convention of 1787 assembled it was practically a foregone conclusion that it would recommend as one major alteration in the Articles of Confederation plan the establishment of a separate executive branch of government. Experience under the Articles had already demonstrated the necessity of permanent administrative departments functioning under the supervision of executive heads responsible to the Congress. The Confederation Congress had adopted ordinances creating departments for administration of foreign affairs, finance, war, and marine affairs, as well as permanent agencies to administer other phases of national government such as the postal service.[1]

These early administrative arrangements were still defective in several important respects. There were no barriers to undue congressional involvement with matters of detail in the operations of the various administrative agencies. Congress was unnecessarily burdened with making decisions that might more properly have been made at the administrative level. Although permanent congressional committees had been established to maintain contact with some of the major administrative departments, there was no single coordinating and superintending authority standing between the administrative departments and the Congress to give direction and energy to the administration as a whole.

Even Thomas Jefferson, whose distrust of a powerful, integrated executive authority was ingrained, was aware of these shortcomings of the existing system. Writing from Paris while the Convention of 1787 was still in session he declared:

> I think it very material to separate in the hands of Congress the Executive and Legislative powers as the judiciary already are in some degree. This I hope will be done. The want of it has been a source of more evil than we have experienced from any other cause. Nothing is so embarrassing as the details of execution. The smallest trifle of that

[1] Cf. Thach, *The Creation of the Presidency,* Chap. 3; Lloyd M. Short, *The Development of National Administrative Organization* (Urbana, Ill.: Institute for Government Research, 1923), pp. 51 ff.

kind occupies as long as the most important act of legislation, and takes place of everything else. Let any man recollect, or look over the files of Congress, he will observe the most important propositions hanging over from week to week and month to month, till the occasions have past them and the thing be never done. I have ever viewed the executive details as the cause of evil to us as if we had no federal head, by diverting the attention of that head from great to small objects; and should this division not be recommended by the Convention, it is my opinion Congress should make it itself by establishing an executive committee.[2]

The Convention itself recognized that the fundamental problem before it was a reconstruction of the machinery of the central government to insure a more energetic performance of those functions already vested in it, rather than the enlargement of the national government's powers and functions.[3] A national administrative branch, directed by a separate, full-time, responsible head and operating directly upon the people independently of state authorities, was widely understood to be a necessary element in such a reorganization.

Developments at the state level in the decade immediately preceding the Convention's meeting, as has been pointed out, had helped considerably to diminish hostility to the idea of a separate executive authority in a system of balanced governmental powers. Locally responsible state executives had demonstrated through direct example that the people had little to fear from an executive deprived of dangerous prerogatives, limited by constitutional rule to a carefully defined range of authority, and accountable to the people or to their representatives for the proper exercise of his powers. Excesses of state legislative bodies in such matters as monetary legislation, debtor laws, and grants of special privilege had convinced many of the propertied element that a check upon the legislative branch in the form of an independent executive veto was essential. Defiance of state authority, as typified in the Shays uprising in Massachusetts, had demonstrated the need for an adequate central government that might be called upon in such emergencies. A national executive authority ready at all times to be summoned to the aid of state governments that had been thus challenged seemed to be the appropriate safeguard. The continuing threat of foreign intervention in American affairs pointed to the same conclusion.

While there was accordingly a predisposition among the framers to favor creation of a separate, permanent executive arm for the na-

[2] Jefferson to Carrington, August 4, 1787; *Writings,* Vol. IV, p. 424. Jefferson was writing from a background of experience as a member of Congress, having served as a Virginia delegate in that body.

[3] Cf. Madison's statement in No. 45 of *The Federalist:* "If the new Constitution be examined with accuracy and candor it will be found that the change which it proposes consists much less in the addition of *New Powers* to the Union, than in the invigoration of *Original Powers.*"

tional government, views on the form it should take varied widely. There was practical unanimity on the point that the executive should have a republican character, but within the limits imposed by this broad principle the range of choice was still extremely wide. When concrete decisions on the form and nature of the executive were actually faced, sharp differences of viewpoint were brought to light. Reaching agreement on the various aspects of the chief executiveship proved to be one of the most difficult tasks of the Convention. The problem of devising an acceptable plan for selection, tenure and re-eligibility of the executive, in particular, proved extremely troublesome. James Wilson declared this to have been the "most difficult" of all the questions the Convention faced.[4]

THE ISSUE: A "STRONG" VS. A "WEAK" EXECUTIVE

In general, two opposed lines of thinking developed in the course of the Convention's deliberations on the executive. On the one hand were those who seemed to have in view an executive who was merely an agent to execute the legislative will. They wished to provide for an officer or a group of officers who would function as the head of the civil and military administration, subject to the overriding direction and control of the legislative branch. Those who advocated an executive of this character tended to favor a plural executive organ, but they were willing to accept a single person at the head of the branch if a powerful council were to be associated with him in the exercise of his powers. A chief executive selected by Congress for a limited term, ineligible for an immediate reappointment, and subject to removal by a procedure in which the Congress would have a dominant role were elements that fitted into this concept. The powers of the executive would, in essence, be those delegated to him by Congress. There would be no executive veto upon acts of Congress; major appointments, both civil and military, would be made by the legislative branch; and the treaty-making and war-making powers would continue to rest in the hands of Congress.

This was a conception of a national chief executive that looked for a model to the weaker executive systems found in most of the state governments of the time. Another source of it may have been the commander-in-chief role, with some civil functions added, that Washington had filled during the Revolutionary War. Typical of this line of thought were the views of Roger Sherman of Connecticut. Outlining his position on the subject at an early stage of the proceedings, he said:

4 Madison, "Debates," p. 664.

He considered the Executive magistracy as nothing more than an institution for carrying the will of the Legislature into effect, that the person or persons ought to be appointed by and acceptable to the Legislature only, which was the depositary of the supreme will of Society. As they were the best judges of the business which ought to be done by the Executive department, and consequently of the number necessary from time to time for doing it, he wished the number might not be fixed but that the legislature should be at liberty to appoint one or more as experience might dicate.[5]

An opposed line of thinking, which might be termed the "quasi-monarchist" viewpoint, looked toward a chief executiveship vested in a single person, chosen by some method other than legislative appointment, with no limitation on eligibilty for reappointment. If a conciliar body was to be provided, its advice should not control his actions, except possibly in the matter of the veto. Associating the higher judicial authorities with him in the exercise of the veto power, as in New York, was advocated by some delegates of the "strong executive" school on the ground that it would add strength to this feature of the checks and balance system. Others preferred to vest an absolute or a suspensive veto power in the chief executive alone. If subject to dismissal at all, the executive should be removable only on specifically enumerated grounds through an impeachment procedure in which the courts or some body other than Congress would render final judgment. The basic powers and responsibilities of the executive should be defined in the constitutional plan so as to place them beyond legislative interference. A broad appointive authority extending to judicial and diplomatic officers, as well as executive participation in the management of foreign affairs including the making of treaties, subject to the approval of Congress, and a pardoning power extending to all offenses against the United States, except possibly in treason and impeachment cases—all these should be included in the assignment of powers to the executive, according to their view.

Advocates of this kind of strong executive saw in the constitutions of some of the states precedents for most of the provisions they favored. In the New York and Massachusetts constitutions, in particular, many of the features they believed should be carried over into the national plan were joined together. Their objective was a national chief executive endowed with sufficient strength and independence to act as a counterpoise to the legislative branch and adequately empowered to give the energy and dispatch to administration that the preservation of the national interest, in both its internal and external aspects, demanded.

Included among the advocates of a strong national executive were a number whose admiration for the British system was so openly

5 *Ibid.*, p. 132.

expressed as to furnish grounds for a suspicion that they would have regarded with equanimity the establishment of a monarchical system modelled after it. In his notable speech before the Convention defending his plan of government, which provided for a "Governour" with broad powers closely resembling those of the British Crown, Hamilton conceded that he had no scruple in declaring that "the British Government was the best in the world." He went on to say that "as to the Executive, it seemed to be admitted that no good one could be established on Republican principles. . . . The English model was the only good one on this subject."[6]

The extent of support among the delegates for the establishment of a limited monarchy, if such a step had been politically feasible, is difficult to assess. The belief that some of the delegates actually desired a monarchy and were covertly laying the groundwork for such a system in the future was entertained by a number of the Convention's members.[7] But no delegate at any time during the Convention's deliberations openly advocated setting up a monarchical system. It was conceded by all that, as Edmund Randolph expressed it, "the fixed genius of the people of America required a different form of government."[8] John Dickinson of Delaware, who agreed with Hamilton that a limited monarchy was "one of the best governments in the world," also recognized that a limited monarchy was "out of the question."

[6] *Ibid.*, pp. 220, 221.

[7] James McHenry, a Maryland delegate, recorded in his *Notes* for August 6 the following incident:

> Saw Mr. Mercer make out a list of the members names who had attended or were attending in convention with for and against marked opposite most of them—asked carelessly what question occasioned his being so particular upon which he told me laughing that it was no question but that those marked with a — were for a king. I then asked him how he knew that to which he said no matter the thing is so. I took a copy with his permission, and Mr. Martin seeing me about it asked What it was. I told him, in the words Mr. Mercer had told me, when he begged me to let him copy the list which I did. (Tansill, *Documents*, pp. 933–934).

During the ratification struggle in Maryland, Luther Martin circulated this list, which contained the names of some 20 delegates alleged to be in favor of a monarchy, in his unsuccessful campaign against ratification of the Constitution. The allegations he made on the basis of it produced a bitter controversy between him and Daniel Carroll, another Maryland delegate, whose name was included in the list as a "monarchist." Cf. Sister Mary Virginia Geiger, *Daniel Carroll: A Framer of the Constitution* (Washington: Catholic University of America, 1943), pp. 144–145; Max Farrand, *The Records of the Federal Convention of 1787* (New Haven: Yale University Press, 4 vols., 1937), Vol. III, pp. 305–306, 319–326. This incident doubtless provided the foundation for Martin's allegation in his *Genuine Information* to the Maryland people that there were three "parties" in the Convention, one of which wished to establish a consolidated national government of a monarchical nature. Farrand, *op. cit.*, Vol. III, p. 179. For Hamilton's answer later to the charge that he had favored the establishment of a monarchical system in the Convention see the exchange of letters between him and Timothy Pickering in 1803. *Ibid.*, Vol. III, pp. 397–398.

[8] Madison, "Debates," p. 132.

"The spirit of the times—the state of our affairs, forbade the experiment, if it were desirable."[9] Yet the Framers could not entirely escape the influence of their British heritage. The presidency they created in some respects bore a resemblance to the kingship, minus the monarchical trappings.

It seems fair to conclude that comparatively few of the delegates had come to Philadelphia prepared to support the creation of a chief executive whose position and powers would approach those of a British King, as they were then commonly understood to be. Major credit for nevertheless evolving a strong executive of that kind must be assigned to James Wilson and Gouverneur Morris of the Pennsylvania delegation; Rufus King and Elbridge Gerry of Massachusetts; Charles Pinckney and John Rutledge of South Carolina; and Alexander Hamilton of New York. To them were joined many others, including Madison of Virginia and Oliver Ellsworth of Connecticut, who recognized that, however dangerous and distasteful a strong executive might appear in their own minds and in the popular thinking of the time, an energetic and powerful head of the administration had to be provided.

As the deliberations proceeded, the idea of a strong, independent chief executive gained more adherents. This result can be ascribed to a number of factors. In the first place, the unspoken thought that the office being set up would be filled in the first instance by Washington—to whom, experience had shown, great power and responsibility could be safely entrusted—helped to dissolve opposition both in the Convention and during the ratification struggle.[10] In the second place, as the Convention proceeded with its work of defining the powers of Congress in far broader terms than those of the Confederation Congress, the conviction that a strong, independent chief executive was needed as a counterpoise grew. A third factor that strengthened the hands of the strong executive advocates was that in pratically every instance the phraseology employed to define the chief executive's powers and functions could be found in language already appearing in provisions for the governorship in the constitutions of one or more states. This was

9 *Ibid.*, p. 143.

10 Writing to Weedon Butler on May 5, 1788, Pierce Butler, who had been a Convention delegate from South Carolina, observed with regard to the office of President:

> Yet after all, My Dear Sir, I am free to acknowledge that His Powers are full great, and greater than I was disposed to make them. Nor, Entre Nous, do I believe they would have been so great had not many of the members cast their eyes towards General Washington as President, and shaped their ideas of the Powers to be given to a President, by their opinions of his Virtue. So that the Man, who by his Patriotism and Virtue, Contributed largely to the Emancipation of his Country, may be the Innocent means of its being, when He is lay'd low, oppress'd. (Farrand, *op. cit.*, Vol. III, p. 302.)

a point upon which Hamilton was to place heavy stress later in *The Federalist* in his defense of the Constitution's provisions on the presidency.[11]

Finally, the records of the Convention's proceedings indicate that in the later stages of its deliberations, an *entente cordiale* or coalition was formed between some of the advocates of a strong, independent chief executive and the small-state delegations. By joint efforts the aims of both were successfully promoted. This was particularly evident in the report of the Committee on Postponed Matters and Unfinished Business made on September 4, on the basis of which final conclusions were reached regarding the mode of electing and removing the President, arrangements for the succession, the President's appointive authority, and his powers in connection with the making of treaties.

In the Committee's report, advocates of a strong executive were successful in getting (1) a recommendation that the President's appointive authority be broadened to include judges and diplomatic officers; (2) that he rather than the Senate should "negotiate" treaties; and (3) that he, along with a Vice President, should be elected by a procedure which in its initial stage, at least, would not involve Congress. As their part of the "deal" the small-state delegates obtained (1) the recommendation that the Senate, in which the states were to be represented equally, should be given the function of serving as the President's council in the making of appointments and treaties, with its consent being required to validate his actions in these matters; (2) a mode of electing the President so devised that if voting by the special electors failed to produce a definitive majority choice, the issue would be decided in Congress by a procedure in which the states would have equal voting power; and (3) a provision making the Senate, rather than the Supreme Court, the trial body in impeachment cases. These recommendations were adopted by the Convention without substantial change. This phase of the Convention's work is one of the prime illustrations of the point that the Framers of the Constitution were practical politicians, willing to "wheel and deal" to achieve their particular objectives, rather than impractical theorists. Whether this be regarded as a fault or a virtue, it is a circumstance for which later generations should be grateful.

BASIC DECISIONS ON THE STRUCTURE OF THE OFFICE

To understand how the concept of the presidential office developed in the minds of the Framers it is necessary to review at some length the evolution of the constitutional phraseology establishing the office

[11] Cf. *The Federalist*, No. 58.

and setting forth its powers, duties, and relationships with the other organs of government.[12] Four distinct stages in the Convention's deliberations as they concerned the office of President may be used as viewing points. The first stage, covering the period from May 30 to July 26, brought the Convention to grips with the problem of the executive through consideration, first in committee of the whole and then through review of the tentative conclusions reached therein, of basic propositions raised by the Virginia Resolutions. During the course of these debates, plans of government submitted individually by Charles Pinckney of South Carolina and Hamilton of New York and a plan submitted by the New Jersey delegation were also brought to the Convention's attention. At the conclusion of this stage, decisions that proved to be lasting were reached respecting the vesting of executive functions in a single officer rather than in a plural executive organ and granting to him a veto power and a general superintending authority over the national administration. Decisions made at that point on the mode of selection, term, re-eligibility, and removal of the executive did not prove to be final.

The second stage came with the setting up of a five-man Committee of Detail on July 26 to incorporate into a tentative draft constitution all decisions reached up to then. To this Committee were referred the resolutions adopted up to that point, along with the Pinckney, Hamilton, and Paterson (New Jersey) plans for reference. The Committee made its report in the form of a tentative draft constitution on August 6. In its Article X appeared for the first time much of the language now found in Article III, Sections 2 and 3, outlining the powers and duties of the President.

When the Convention reached Article X in its review of the Committee of Detail draft, objections were again raised to the arrangements incorporated in it for the mode of selection, as well as other matters. There was also concern over the fact that no executive council had been provided for. Following a procedure it had utilized with good effect for dealing with various other knotty problems that cropped up in the course of its examination of the draft plan, the Convention on August 31 referred these questions, along with other pending and unresolved matters, to a Committee on Postponed Matters and Unfinished Business for further study and report. The Committee consisted of one member from each of the 11 state delegations then in attendance.

The third vital stage in the creation of the executive part of the constitutional plan came when this "Committee of Eleven" made its report on September 4. As indicated above, it proposed a number

---

[12] For a perceptive, detailed analysis of the Convention's deliberations with reference to the executive feature of the constitutional plan see Thach, *op. cit.*

of changes in the system of presidential election as well as in presidential powers in relation to those of the Senate. Consideration of this Committee's recommendations and resolution of the problems to which they related brought the Convention early in September to the final stage of its proceedings. Only when this point was reached did the office of President take on all the basic features ultimately incorporated in the constitutional plan.

The fourth and final stage involved the reference, on September 8, of all the completed work of the Convention to a five-man Committee on Style and Arrangement, headed by Gouverneur Morris, for preparation of the final, definitive draft of the Constitution. At this point the familiar phraseology of the document as it pertains to the presidential office took form. Review of this draft and incorporation of a few relatively minor perfecting amendments brought the Convention to the final step, the signing of the completed document by 39 of the delegates on September 17.

A SINGLE VERSUS A PLURAL EXECUTIVE

Prompt endorsement of the general proposition in the Virginia Resolutions that the form of the national government should be altered to consist of a "supreme legislative, executive, and judiciary" brought the Convention at an early stage to the question of the nature of the executive magistracy to be created. The Virginia Resolutions, which provided the basis for initial discussions on this point, were deliberately vague on the issue. The Virginia delegates themselves were divided in their views. Madison, who had taken a leading role in formulating the Virginia Plan, had no very strong convictions on this important question, while Randolph and George Mason were fearful of investing executive powers in a single individual.[13] Pinckney's plan, offered to the Convention at the same time the Virginia Resolutions were made the basis for discussion, proposed a single executive, as did also Hamilton's outline of a frame of government presented to the Convention near the close of the Committee of the Whole deliberations

    [13] Writing to Washington and Randolph on the eve of the Convention, Madison had declared:

> I have scarcely ventured as yet to formulate my own opinion either of the manner in which it [the executive] ought to be constituted or of the authorities with which it ought to cloathed.

    Two years before the Convention met, in a letter to a Kentucky friend advising him concerning the formulation of a constitution for that state, Madison had likewise been ambivalent in his views on this general question, although he was of the opinion that the executive arrangements in the Virginia constitution were "the worst part of a bad Constitution." *The Writings of James Madison*, G. Hunt, ed. (New York: G. P. Putnam's Sons, 9 vols., 1900–1910), Vol. II, pp. 169–170, 339, 348.

on the Virginia Resolutions. The New Jersey Plan, submitted on June 15 after a tentative decision had already been reached favoring a single executive, proposed a plural executive.

When the Virginia Plan propositions relating to the executive were first taken up on June 1, a motion by James Wilson, supported by Charles Pinckney, that an executive "to consist of a single person" be established precipitated a brief but highly significant debate. The idea of vesting the national executive power in one individual evidently came as something of a shock to some of the delegates. For some moments there was hesitancy even to speak on the proposal.[14] Their reluctance to speak may well have been traceable in part to the unspoken thought that the office to be created would first be filled by the man who was then presiding over their deliberations. A sensitiveness to possible criticism on the ground that they entertained sympathy for a monarchical or quasi-monarchical type of executive may have been another reason for the "shyness" of some delegates in voicing their views. But this hesitancy soon disappeared, and a spirited and remarkably frank exchange of views on the question followed.

The most vigorous opposition to the single executive idea came from Edmund Randolph of Virginia. Asserting that a single executive was but "the foetus of monarchy," he favored instead an executive of three members so chosen as to represent the major sections of the country. He maintained that the temper of the people was "adverse to the very semblance of monarchy"; that a plural executive would be as competent for all the objects of the office as a single person would be; and that public confidence would be lacking in a single officer who would in most instances, for practical reasons, be chosen from the states of the central region.[15] Wilson argued for a single executive as giving the necessary energy, dispatch, and responsibility to the office and as being most conducive to "tranquility" in the government. One fact that had great weight with him, he observed, was that "all the 13 States tho agreeing in scarce any other instance, agree in placing a single magistrate at the head of the Government."[16] Charles Pinckney, Rutledge, and Butler of the South Carolina delegation also

[14] According to Madison's account:

> A considerable pause ensuing and the Chairman asking if he should put the question, Doctor Franklin observed that it was a point of great importance and wished that the gentlemen would deliver their sentiments on it before the question was put.
> Mr. Rutledge animadverted on the shyness of gentlemen on this and other subjects. He said it looked as if they supposed themselves precluded by having frankly disclosed their opinions from afterwards changing them, which he did not take to be all the case. Madison, "Debates," pp. 131–132.)

[15] *Ibid.*, pp. 132, 144.
[16] *Ibid.*, pp. 132, 145.

urged the superiority of the single executive over the plural type.

At Madison's suggestion, action on Wilson's motion was deferred until other questions relating to the method of selection, term, mode of removal, and powers of the executive had been given preliminary consideration. Tentative decisions on these points tended to allay fears that anything resembling an elective monarchy was contemplated by the backers of the single executive idea. When Wilson's motion calling for a single executive was finally put to a test it carried by a vote of seven states to three.[17] This decision made as a Committee of the Whole was accepted by the Convention without further debate on July 17 and was not thereafter seriously challenged. *This was the Convention's key decision on the establishment of the presidential office. It laid the foundation for development of the concept of the President as the Chief of State. By uniting all the powers of the office in one person's hands, it assured that whatever those powers might be, they could be exercised with dispatch and with easily fixed responsibility.*

DESIGNATION OF OFFICE AND TITLE OF ADDRESS

Designation of the chief executive as the "President of the United States" first appeared in the tentative draft reported by the Committee of Detail on August 6. The reason for the choice of this term rather than any one of several others suggested is not altogether clear; but the credit for its selection appears to belong mainly to Pinckney and Wilson.[18] It was accepted by the Convention without discussion.

The draft reported by the Committee of Detail also included a clause stating that the President's title should be "His Excellency." This provision, which was in line with the practice of several of the states with reference to the governorship, was also accepted by the

[17] *Ibid.*, p. 146. State delegations opposing were New York, Delaware, and Maryland. The Virginia delegation was split three to two in favor of Wilson's motion. Madison, Washington, and McClurg supported it, while Randolph and Blair were in opposition. Wythe, who favored a single executive, and Mason, who opposed, were absent. The New Jersey delegation lacked a quorum and therefore did not vote.

[18] In the Pinckney plan, which was submitted to the Committee of Detail for use in preparing its draft, the proposed title of office was "President"; while Hamilton's outline of his ideas, also referred to the Committee for similar use, proposed the term "Governour." The Committee began its work by reviewing a rough outline prepared by Randolph embodying the Convention's decisions up to that point. Manuscript records indicate that in reviewing this rough draft the Committee first inserted the term "Governour of the United People and States of America" as a designation for the office. Farrand, *op. cit.*, Vol. II, p. 145. The Randolph outline was then given over to Wilson for revision and amplification. Substitution of the term "President" for "Governor" was made in Wilson's revision, and this was subsequently approved by the Committee. *Ibid.*, p. 171. Wilson may have taken the term "President" from Pickney's plan, which he used extensively in elaborating the language of the executive article, or from one of the several state constitutions of the time, including that of his own state of Pennsylvania, which he also evidently consulted.

Convention without comment. When the Constitution was put into its final language by the Committee on Style and Arrangement in the closing days of the Convention, however, the phrase about the title of address was omitted. No reason for this was given, nor was it commented upon when the draft of the executive article was reviewed and approved by the Convention. The excision might have been made in the interest of making the new plan more palatable to those who had criticized it as leaning too heavily in the direction of "high-toned" government. More probably it was omitted in the final draft in the expectation that an even more imposing title of address would be prescribed later by legislative act.[19] Whatever the reason for the omission, the unwillingness of Congress later to deal further with the subject had the effect of making the term for the office a title of address as well. The President is addressed simply as "Mr. President."

REJECTION OF AN EXECUTIVE COUNCIL

It is doubtful whether the principle of a single executive could have mustered majority support in the earlier stages of the Convention's deliberations had there not been an expectation by the delegates that a conciliar body would be formed to advise and in some degree control the President in the exercise of his powers. Colonial precedents pointed to such a council, as did the state constitutions of the time. The British Privy Council was likewise an institution familiar to all the delegates and considered by them to be a useful restraining influence on the King. Pinckney's plan for a single executive included a council consisting of the heads of the departments of foreign affairs, war, treasury, and admiralty, who were to be appointed by Congress. Along with the President they were to constitute a council of revision for the exercise of the veto power. The Virginia Resolutions went only so far as to propose the association of a "convenient number of the judiciary" with the executive in the exercise of the veto power. Hamilton's scheme made no provision for an executive council, but it proposed to utilize the Senate as a conciliar body in the making of treaties.

In connection with the council issue the attention of the Convention was first directed toward the Virginia Plan proposal to create a body to share responsibility with the executive in the exercise of the veto power. The council of revision idea, obviously borrowed from the New York constitution, was rejected by the Convention at this stage; consequently, the series of approved resolutions referred to the Committee of Detail on July 26 failed to include a provision for a conciliar body of any kind. The draft reported by this Committee on August 6 therefore made no mention of an executive council.

[19] For an account of the unsuccessful effort in the First Congress to prescribe a more pretentious title of address for the President, see Chap. 8.

Calling attention to this omission some time later, Ellsworth of Connecticut suggested the advisability of establishing a council that should "advise but not conclude" the President in the exercise of his powers. The suggestion was apparently regarded as having merit, for shortly thereafter Gouverneur Morris and Charles Pinckney submitted a formal proposal to create a "Council of State" to consist of the Chief Justice and five designated heads of executive departments.[20] The proposal was referred to the Committee of Detail for consideration. Two days later the Committee made a report favoring the idea. Before consideration was given to this report the Convention voted on August 31 to refer it for study, along with a number of other pending and postponed matters, to the 11-member Committee on Postponed Matters and Unfinished Business.

This group, as has already been noted, proved to be particularly influential in shaping the executive article in the Constitution. The delegates who were appointed by their respective state delegations to serve on it were Gilman of New Hampshire, King of Massachusetts, Sherman of Connecticut, Brearly of New Jersey, G. Morris of Pennsylvania, Dickinson of Delaware, Carroll of Maryland, Madison of Virginia, Williamson of North Carolina, Butler of South Carolina, and Baldwin of Georgia. On the matter of creating an executive council, as suggested, its report was negative. It proposed rather to use the Senate as an advisory and approving body for executive appointments and for treaties. In its report all that remained of the original idea of a Council of State was a clause proposing that the President be authorized to require the opinion in writing of the principal officer in each of the executive departments upon any subject relating to his duties.

The Committee's recommendations about the conciliar problem met with vigorous opposition. Mason of Virginia protested that in rejecting the executive council idea "we were about to try an experiment on which the most despotic government had never ventured," for even "the Grand Signor himself had his Divan." In place of the Senate as a body to approve appointments he proposed instead a council of six members, to be elected by the Senate for six-year overlapping terms from districts representing the three major sectional

[20] Madison, "Debates," pp. 573–574. The Morris-Pinckney resolution provided for an executive departmental organization of five departments. The heads of these departments, whose powers and functions were outlined in some detail, were, together with the Chief Justice, to compose a Council of State "to assist the President in conducting Public affairs" and to furnish him advice upon request. The department heads were to be appointed by the President and were to hold office during his pleasure, but were to be subject to removal also by impeachment. A "Secretary of State," who was to be secretary to the Council and to the President as well, was also provided for in the plan. The resemblance of the proposed body to the Cabinet institution that later appeared is noteworthy.

divisions of the country.[21] Wilson, like Mason, was fearful that the Committee's plan would throw too much power into the hands of an aristocratic, unrepresentative Senate. He maintained that it would violate the principle of separation of powers, diffuse responsibility for appointments, and, along with other provisions already agreed upon, render the President little more than the "Minion of the Senate." He preferred Mason's plan to that of the Committee.[22] Additional support for Mason's council of appointments idea came from Charles Pinckney, Madison, Dickinson, and Franklin.

Despite this array of influential members in opposition, the proposal of the strong executive–small-state coalition to vest a limited conciliar function in the Senate was approved. A last-ditch effort by Mason to instruct the Committee to bring forward a proposal for a six-member executive council to be chosen by Congress or the Senate was rejected, eight states to three. Thus two important elements of the checks and balances system in the final constitutional plan—senatorial controls over executive appointments and treaty-making—grew out of the unsuccessful attempt to create an executive council. Events were to show, however, that the need for an official body of advisers whom the President might consult at his pleasure in connection with major policy decisions was imperfectly met by these arrangements. To fill this need the extralegal institution of the President's Cabinet eventually came into existence.

MODE OF SELECTION: THE ELECTORAL COLLEGE COMPROMISE

The decision of the Convention to place a single officer at the head of the executive branch was only the first step toward creation of a strong, coordinate executive authority. Unity in the headship would have meant little if the chief executive had been made wholly dependent upon congressional favor for his original selection and for continuance in office. A fundamental point of weakness in the state governorship at the time was its dependence in a majority of the states upon the legislative branch in this respect. A method of selection entirely independent of legislative action—popular election by plurality vote—prevailed only in New York. Legislative election in various forms

21 Madison, "Debates," pp. 682–683. The similarity of Mason's plan to the New York Council of Appointments is so close as to suggest that it was based on the New York experience.

22 *Ibid.*, p. 674. It is interesting to note that at an early stage of the Convention's proceedings, Wilson *opposed* the idea of any kind of an executive council on the ground that it served more often "to cover than to prevent malpractices," while Morris had been one of the original *advocates* of an executive council. Observing that "the President by persuading his Council, to concur in his wrong measures would acquire their protection for them," Morris now used Wilson's earlier argument against such a body to attack his later position.

was employed in the middle and southern states, while the four New England states provided for popular election, with legislative selection following in case there was no popular majority choice.

The arrangements for choosing the President finally agreed upon were not regarded by the delegates as a complete rejection of the principle of legislative selection. The electoral vote system, with provision for supplementary action by the House of Representatives if no majority choice emerged from the balloting by the electors, was a compromise on the issue of legislative choice versus an independent mode of selection. But the same issue that proved so critical in setting up the structure of Congress, namely, representation according to population or wealth as against equality of the states as such, proved very troublesome in devising the mode of choosing the President. It was met through an adaptation of the Connecticut Compromise formula to the national governmental plan. Use of an electoral vote distribution formula based on the *total number* of Senators and Representatives tended to favor the more populous states, while the alternative method of choice by the House of Representatives, voting by *state units,* if no electoral vote majority developed, redressed the balance on the side of the less populous states.

The provisions agreed upon for selection and tenure also embodied adjustments of clashing viewpoints in other respects. By leaving the means of choosing electors to the discretion of the several state legisla tures, the decision on whether popular election, legislative appointment, gubernatorial appointment, or some other method should be used was pushed back upon the states.[23] This disposition of the matter left open the possibility of allowing the attitude of the people to be taken into account indirectly in choosing the chief executive, as advocated by some delegates, while at the same time it did not place the actual selection of the President in the hands of the mass of voters, whom other delegates believed totally incompetent to make such an important decision. A four-year term, with no restriction on re-eligibility, represented an adjustment between the views of those who favored a lengthy tenure or even a tenure during good behavior to insure stability and avoid the turmoil of frequent elections and the views of those who desired a shorter term reinforced by ineligibility for re-election as a protection against possible corruptive or tyrannical tendencies.

---

[23] All these methods of choosing the electors were proposed at one time or another during the Convention's deliberations. Long after the Convention had completed its work, Madison declared that most of the delegates, if not all, assumed that the electors would be popularly chosen by districts. Madison to Hay, August 23, 1823, Farrand, *op. cit.,* Vol. III, p. 459. See also the statement of Rufus King to Charles King, September 29, 1823, to the effect that it was not intended by the Convention that the state legislatures themselves should choose the electors. *Ibid.,* Vol. III, p. 459.

Resolution of these issues was achieved by the Convention with great difficulty and only at a comparatively late stage in its proceedings. Repeatedly it appeared to have come to a conclusion on them, only on reconsideration to cast aside the plan agreed on in favor of another. As has been noted, state practice in the selection of the governor followed no common pattern and gave the delegates a variety of procedures to evaluate. Many delegates, perhaps unconsciously, tended to favor adoption of a system modelled after that in their own states.[24] Modes of selection proposed fell under one or another of five major heads: (1) choice by the national legislative body; (2) choice by a special body of electors; (3) direct popular election; (4) choice by the state legislatures; and (5) appointment by the executive authorities of the states. These principal modes of selection were diversified and combined into a bewildering variety of proposed schemes. Legislative election schemes, for example, included one under which the voting in Congress would be by joint vote of the two houses; another under which concurrent action by the two houses, voting separately, would be required; another in which a joint vote of the House and Senate delegations of the respective states would be taken, with each state having one vote; another under which the House would nominate a panel of candidates, from which selection would be made by the Senate; and still another under which a number of members of Congress would be chosen by lot to serve as an electoral body. Altogether, taking the variations on these different basic methods into account, more than 25 different methods of selecting the executive were formally proposed during the course of the Convention.

Inextricably involved in the problem of the mode of selection were the questions of length of term, re-eligibility, and the method of effecting removal.[25] If legislative election was to be the mode, a clause limiting re-eligibility was widely regarded as necessary also, to guard against intrigue by an incumbent executive seeking re-election and to encourage an independent exercise of his powers of office. All but one of the states that provided for legislative selection of their governors also had some kind of restriction on re-eligibility. A limitation on re-eligibility, in turn, pointed toward a relatively long term of office, to insure a reasonable degree of stability in the executive branch. But a long term for the executive could be predicated only on establishment

[24] "The members of the Convention in settling the manner of electing the Executive of the U.S. seem to have been prejudiced in favor of the manner, to which they were accustomed, in the election of the Governor of their respective States." Rufus King to Charles King, September 29, 1823, Farrand, *op. cit.*, Vol. III, p. 459.

[25] "In the debates on the Executive the ball of the length of term bounced on the balls of eligibility and ineligibility for re-election, and they caromed on the method of election." W. Hastings Lyons, *The Constitution and the Men Who Made It* (Boston: Houghton; Mifflin Company, 1936), p. 218.

of a removal procedure which, without rendering the executive wholly
subservient to the legislative branch, would nevertheless afford effective
protection against wrongdoing or lack of ability. On the other hand,
the delegates advocating an independent mode of election emphasized
that it would make possible adoption of a shorter term, diminish or
eliminate wholly the need for a restriction on re-eligibility, and render
less pressing the need for an easily operated removal procedure.

The Virginia Resolutions, which provided a basis for initial discussion of these questions in Committee of the Whole, proposed election
of the executive by the national legislature for a fixed term of unstated
length, with a prohibition against re-election. Discussion of these items
in the Virginia Plan quickly brought into view a sharp cleavage of
opinion on the basic issue of legislative choice versus an independent
mode of selection. Wilson, who sensed from the beginning the incom-
patibility of legislative election with the principle of an effective
separation of powers, took the lead in the attack upon the Virginia Plan
provisions. Although confessing that he was apprehensive that his
suggestion might be regarded as "chimerical," he declared himself in
favor, in theory at least, of election by the people. It was his belief that
the New York and Massachusetts constitutions under which popular
election of governors had proved both convenient and successful were
models that might well be followed. He proposed also a three-year
term with no limitation on re-eligibility, as in New York.

The case for legislative election was first stated by Sherman. In his
opinion it was necessary to make the executive "absolutely dependent
on that body, as it was the will of that which was to be executed." An
executive independent of the legislature would be "the very essence
of tyranny." He approved Wilson's three-year term idea, however, and
opposed the principle of enforced rotation as "throwing out of office
the men best qualified to execute its duties."

Conclusions reached in Committee of the Whole were generally in
accord with the ideas of the advocates of legislative election. First a
preference for a seven-year term, advocated by Pinckney and Mason,
over a three-year term as urged by Wilson was registered. Election by
the legislative branch was then endorsed after rejection of a plan of
choice by popularly chosen electors, which Wilson advanced as a
modification of his original popular-election scheme. Tacitly conceding
that if an incumbent might seek re-election under a system of legislative
selection his independence might be undermined and he would be
tempted to intrigue with the legislature to secure continuance in office,
supporters of this plan rounded it out by winning acceptance of a
prohibition against re-election.

The decisions made in Committee of the Whole on these points
proved to be anything but conclusive. Before they came up for review

by the Convention a development had occurred that was to prove embarrassing to the supporters of the principle of legislative election. This was the acceptance of the Connecticut Compromise by which the principle of state equality was applied in the apportionment of seats in the upper branch of Congress, while seats in the lower branch were to be apportioned according to population. If the upper house was to be given a concurrent and equal voice with the lower in choosing the President, legislative election would have much less appeal to delegates from the populous states. Small-state delegates, on the other hand, regarded legislative election as unattractive if it should be coupled with a system of joint voting by the two houses, which would place the less populous states in a disadvantageous position.

The issue of how Congress should effect a choice of the executive did not finally come to a head until later in the Convention's proceedings, when the Committee of Detail draft came up for review. At that time the problem of how Congress should go about voting in choosing the President proved to be a major factor in inducing acceptance of the compromise plan on presidential election and tenure eventually adopted.

Before then the Convention had revealed uncertainty on the interrelated issues of mode of election, length of term, and re-eligibility by first accepting, then rejecting in favor of an alternative plan of choice by electors,[26] and then reaccepting the recommendations of the Committee of the Whole report on these matters. In accord with this action of the Convention the draft plan subsequently prepared by the Committee of Detail included a clause stating simply that the President was to be "elected by ballot by the Legislature" for a seven-year term, with an incumbent being ineligible for re-election. There was no further specification of the procedure Congress should follow in effecting its choice.

The reason for the Committee's unwillingness to deal with particulars soon became apparent. When this clause in the draft plan came up for review, Rutledge proposed that the word "joint" be inserted before "ballot." The effect of this modification was immediately perceived, and the small-state delegations rose in protest against it. Sherman pointed out that its effect would be to deprive the *states* as

[26] The alternative plan approved tentatively at this stage provided for choice of the President by a body of 25 electors, who would assemble in one national body for this purpose. The states would have from one to three electors depending upon their relative populations at that time. The President would have been chosen for a six-year term, and would have been eligible for an immediate election. Dissatisfaction with this formula on the part of some of the states with small populations and fears that it would prove difficult to induce competent individuals to serve as electors from the more distant states in view of the time and hazard involved in travel to one central meeting place appear to have been major reasons for rejection of the elector plan at that point.

represented in the Senate of equality in voting power in the choice of a President. Soon the argument waxed warm on the question of joint vote versus concurrent voting by the two houses in choosing the President. Ultimately Rutledge's motion to require a joint vote was carried seven states to four, New Hampshire and Delaware deserting the small-state contingent to support it. A proposal advanced by Dayton of New Jersey to follow the principle of state equality in the joint voting was defeated by only the narrow margin of six states to five, however. There was evidently much dissatisfaction among the small-state element with the joint vote system as then accepted.

Seeking to capitalize on this dissatisfaction, Gouverneur Morris once more sought acceptance of a plan by which the President was to be chosen by electors elected by the people of the several states. His motion was lost, but a vote on the abstract principle of choice by electors failed by the narrowest possible margin, four states to four, with two states divided. In this rather unsettled state the matter was passed over for the time being. On August 31 Morris won a technical point when he obtained approval of a motion deleting from the proposed transitional article in the draft plan a clause referring to the time "when a President shall have been chosen by Congress." His supporting statement that this point was not yet finally determined was not challenged. Thus the way was cleared for inclusion of the mode of selecting the President, his tenure, and his re-eligibility among matters to be dealt with by the special Committee on Postponed Matters and Unfinished Business which the Convention set up that day. Morris was named as the Pennsylvania representative on that Committee, and from that vantage point he exerted strong influence in obtaining a revision of the executive article along lines more in accord with his own views.

The Committee's report, presented on September 4, embraced a series of important compromise arrangements on issues relating to the selection and tenure of the President and his relations with Congress. It proposed an elector system as a part of the scheme of selection, with electors to be apportioned among the states in accordance with their total representation in Congress; that is to say, the electors collectively would constitute in their total number a replica of the two houses of congress meeting in joint session. This apportionment plan, which made concessions to both the large-state and small-state elements in some degree, met one of the original objections to the elector plan which had up to that point prevented its acceptance. The electors were to be appointed in a manner to be determined by state law and were to meet in their respective states rather than at one central point (thus eliminating another of the original objections to the elector system) and vote for two candidates for President. A candidate receiving an electoral vote amounting to a majority of the whole number of electors would be deemed elected, but in case of a majority vote tie between the leading candidates or of a failure of any candidate to receive the required majority, the Senate would decide the issue, being limited in its choice to the five leading candidates. The second highest candidate in the electoral voting would become the Vice President, who would be the immediate successor to the presidency in event of a vacancy. The term of office was set at four years, with no limitation on re-eligibility.

So far as it concerned selection and tenure of the President the Committee's compromise plan met with general approval, except for one feature. The proposal to refer an inconclusive electoral choice to the Senate for final disposition was strongly criticized by many of the large-state delegates, including Mason and Madison of Virginia and Wilson of Pennsylvania. They feared that this feature, along with other elements in the compromise scheme, went too far in giving the Senate a position of ascendancy. Various modifications were offered to meet this objection. On the initiative of Rufus King and Elbridge Gerry of Massachusetts, a clause was added making members of Congress and other federal officers ineligible to serve as electors. When Sherman of Connecticut moved that the House of Representatives voting by state units, rather than the Senate, be made the agency for deciding an inconclusive election, another major obstacle to approval was removed.[27] Sherman's suggestion was immediately accepted, and with other minor amendments only, the Committee's plan was adopted.

It is apparent from the debates that most of the delegates believed that the plan they had approved would function quite differently from the way it has in actual practice. They assumed that the electors would serve as a kind of nominating body, with the House making the final choice from the panel of five produced by the votes of the electors. Their mistake, of course, was in failing to foresee the role that political parties would come to play in the selective process. Most of the opposition to the proposal to vest the secondary electoral function in the Senate was predicated on the assumption that final selection would normally be made by it. Mason expressed the belief that "nineteen times in twenty" the President would ultimately be chosen by the Senate.[28] Madison, who apparently shared this view, was apprehensive that the attention of the electors "would be turned too much

[27] Madison, "Debates," p. 678. Shortly before Sherman offered his motion, Williamson of North Carolina had suggested that the two houses of Congress, voting by state units, be the alternative electoral body. Sherman's proposal was obviously a modification of Williamson's idea. Both Sherman and Williamson had been members of the Committee on Postponed Matters and Unfinished Business.

[28] *Ibid.*, p. 663.

to making candidates instead of giving their votes in order to [achieve] a definitive choice," in which case the election of the President would "be consigned to the Senate altogether."[29]

Not all the delegates were of this opinion, however. Morris and Baldwin, both of whom had participated directly in the formulation of the compromise plan, showed an awareness of political implications in the proposed plan which escaped their colleagues. Baldwin pointed out that increasing intercourse among the people of the states would bring "national figures" more and more into the public view; consequently, in his opinion, the votes of the electors would tend to be concentrated upon a few candidates and would be decisive in most cases.[30] Morris agreed, maintaining that in the event an incumbent President sought re-election he would receive the support of a majority of the electors if he had given satisfactory service, and if he had not, "all disliking him would take care to unite their votes so as to insure his being supplanted."[31] The generally held view, however, was that the electoral system would prove to be one in which legislative action would normally be the determining factor.

REMOVAL

Closely involved with the problem of an acceptable plan of selection, tenure, and re-eligibility of the executive was the question of what means should be provided for effecting his removal from office. The principle that the chief executive should be subject to removal for official misconduct was accepted as axiomatic by most of the delegates. Nevertheless, to devise a procedure by which this principle could be effectuated was no easy task. To make the executive's tenure of office depend in any degree upon the favor of the legislative branch was to endanger his independence and risk undermining the principle of separation of powers. To entrust this power to the courts or to some other body of officials, on the other hand, might render it innocuous, particularly if such officials were to be appointed by the President. To make him subject to removal by some state authority would be

---

[29] *Ibid.*, p. 662. Remarks indicating similar views on how the plan would operate were made by Gorham (p. 662), Pinckney (pp. 663, 668), Williamson (p. 663), Wilson (pp. 664, 673), Rutledge (p. 668), Randolph (p. 670), Gerry (p. 673), and Hamilton (p. 675).

[30] *Ibid.*, p. 664.

[31] *Ibid.*, p. 669. Morris's estimation of the impact of the presidential election system on the formation of parties proved to be prophetic. He was so confident of the soundness of his views on this point that he was willing to accept a proposal, offered by Gerry, that if a President seeking re-election did not win a majority of the electors' votes, he should not be eligible for consideration as one of the five candidates from among whom the Senate should make its choice. *Ibid.*, p. 678.

He insisted that if the President were made popularly elective for a two-year term with a possibility of re-election, there would be no need at all for a removal procedure. Morris was supported in these views by Pinckney and King.[35] At this point Morris appeared to be thinking of the President as a kind of elective king who, like his British prototype, would stand above the law in a personal sense and be accountable to the people's representatives only through his ministers.

The willingness of Morris, Pinckney, and King to trust periodic elections as the sole device for holding the executive to account was not shared by many of their fellow delegates. Mason was emphatic in insisting that some punishment be available against even the head of the government for crimes he might commit. He posed the question of how a chief executive who had obtained his election through fraud or corruption might otherwise be dealt with. Franklin dryly observed that if no orderly process of removal were provided, then the only recourse available would be assassination, which would not only deprive the executive of his life but also of the opportunity for rebutting the charges against him. Madison thought that some provision for defending the community against the "incapacity, negligence or perfidy" of the chief magistrate was indispensable, particularly as it had already been decided that the head of the executive branch should be one person. Wilson and Gerry concurred in this view.

Faced with these arguments and realizing, no doubt, that insistence on the nonimpeachability of the chief executive might well defeat efforts to vest strong powers in the office, Morris yielded. Confessing that he was swayed by the reasons that had been offered, he agreed that the executive should be made impeachable for such things as "treachery, corrupting his electors, and incapacity." In the last-mentioned instance, however, he should be punished not as a man but only as an officer by "degradation" from office, and in any case the mode devised should not be one making him unduly dependent on the legislature. "This Magistrate is not the King but the prime-Minister. The people are the King."[36] By this about-face Morris showed a fundamental change in his conception of the office being established. Heretofore he had apparently visualized the office as comparable to the British kingship, shorn of its hereditary aspects, but standing above the law as the fountainhead of authority in the state. He now saw in the national executive rather an enlarged copy of the state governorship. Morris' capitulation sealed the fate of his motion that would have exempted the President from impeachment, and it lost.

Having thus eschewed on the one hand an executive subordinated

[35] Madison, "Debates," pp. 410, 417, 419. Pinckney was aware of South Carolina's experience with the governorship. When Rutledge as governor had exercised the absolute veto power authorized by that state's temporary constitution of 1776, the reaction was so strong he had been forced to resign under threat of impeachment.

[36] *Ibid.*, p. 421.

to the legislative body by being subject to removal at its pleasure and on the other hand an elective, uncrowned monarch standing entirely above the law, the Convention continued on its course of devising a removal procedure that would be available, yet would not dangerously threaten the balance of power between the executive and legislative branches. Substantial progress toward the plan eventually adopted was revealed in the tentative draft of a constitution presented to the Convention by the Committee of Detail on August 6. It proposed to place the sole power to initiate impeachments in the House of Representatives; designated the Supreme Court as the trial body; specified "treason, bribery or corruption" as the grounds upon which the President might be impeached; and limited punishment in impeachment cases to removal from office and possible disqualification from holding any office of trust, honor, or profit under the United States. If impeachment resulted in removal, the officer concerned was to be subject to further punishment under ordinary criminal laws in the regular courts if the grounds upon which he had been removed involved an element of criminal liability.[37]

The most controversial point in this plan was its designation of the Supreme Court as the trial body. Advocates of a strong executive authority desired to vest in the President the power to appoint judges, including members of the Supreme Court. Their case for executive appointment would be materially weakened if, in the event of a presidential impeachment, the trial body were to be made up of his own appointees. An impeachment procedure resting entirely in the hands of Congress, with narrowly defined grounds for action, was a preferable alternative to an executive whose appointive power would not extend to the judiciary. When the clause in the report designating the Supreme Court as the tribunal for impeachment cases came up for consideration, Morris, mindful of these considerations, suggested a postponement. This was agreed to, with the result that this problem also became one of the matters submitted to the Committee on Postponed Matters and Unfinished Business for further study and report.

This Committee's report given on September 4 made this subject part of the package deal concerning the chief executive and his relations with Congress agreed upon by the small-state and the strong-executive groups. It proposed to substitute the Senate for the Supreme Court as the trial body in all impeachment cases, with a two-thirds vote being necessary for conviction. When the President should be on trial it proposed, for obvious reasons, that the Chief Justice, rather than the Vice President, should act as its presiding officer. It proposed further to omit "corruption" as a ground for impeachment of the President. This had been a concession to the strong-executive element, who feared

[37] *Ibid.*, pp. 472, 478–479.

that this term might be construed to include employment of the appointive power for patronage purposes to influence Congress. They
evidently expected the President to use his appointive authority in this
manner, as British kings were generally understood to do.[38]

The Committee's recommendation that the Senate, rather than the
Supreme Court, should be the trial body in all impeachment cases
encountered strong opposition. Wilson objected to the change, as did
Madison, on the ground that together with other parts of the Committee's plan it had a tendency toward dangerous aggrandizement of
the powers of the Senate. The President, in Wilson's words, would
become merely the "minion of the Senate." Madison offered as an alternative a motion reinstating the Supreme Court as the trial body. Answering their arguments, Morris agreed that there was some danger that
the independence of the executive might be impaired by the arrangements proposed by the Committee; he was willing, nevertheless, to trust
the Senate's members, who would be under special oath in such a proceeding, to render a fair judgment on specific charges of crime. The
Supreme Court, he insisted, was too small a body for such a purpose,
and it might more easily be "warped or corrupted." In any event some
body other than the Supreme Court would have to be invested with
power to act as the tribunal in impeachment proceedings when one of
its own members was on trial, he observed. Morris carried his point,
and Madison's motion was defeated, receiving the support of only
Pennsylvania and Virginia.

One further action by the Convention gave final form to the removal procedure as it affected the chief executive. Calling attention to
the language of the Committee's draft that limited the grounds for
impeachment to "treason or bribery," Mason moved to add the word
"maladministration." When Madison objected that the addition of so
vague a term was equivalent to giving the President tenure only during
the pleasure of the Senate, Mason offered as a substitute the term
"high crimes and misdemeanors." In this form Mason's motion was
accepted. Just before conclusion of the Convention's deliberations
Rutledge, with the support of Morris, offered an amendment to the
Committee of Style draft declaring that any officer, if it was voted that
impeachment charges were to be brought against him, should be suspended from office pending the outcome of his trial before the Senate.
Madison and King successfully opposed this amendment as giving the
House, in effect, a power of temporary removal.[39] Thus the impeach-

[38] *Ibid.*, pp. 660–661.

[39] *Ibid.*, p. 721. Strangely enough, later in the Virginia ratifying convention
Madison advanced as an argument in defense of the proposed Constitution the
point that the House of Representatives might "suspend" a President pending
the outcome of an impeachment proceeding. Jonathan Elliot, *The Debates in the
Several States on the Adoption of the Federal Constitution,* 2nd ed. (Philadelphia:

ment clause was given the form it has in the final draft of the Constitution. Removal of the President by action of Congress was made possible, but only through a quasi-judicial proceeding that would make the actual use of this feature of the checks and balances system a most unlikely event.

POWERS AND FUNCTIONS OF THE PRESIDENT

The conception of the President as an officer vested with powers and responsibilities of such scope as to make him a potent force in the governmental scheme matured slowly in the minds of the Convention delegates. In the beginning the prevailing view seemed to be that the head of the executive branch should be little more than a national administrative manager—an instrument for efficient administration of policies determined by the legislative branch. At a relatively early stage in the proceedings, however, a majority had accepted the idea that he should also be equipped with a veto authority to be used to check an impulsive and possibly faction-dominated Congress. As the debates proceeded, the views of such delegates as Wilson, Gouverneur Morris, Hamilton, Charles Pinckney, King, and Gerry, who saw in the executive a symbol of national unity and authority and recognized the necessity of entrusting him with powers commensurate with this role, won wider acceptance. As in the struggle over his selection, tenure, re-eligibility, and removal, the advocates of a strong executive were not successful in winning a complete triumph and they were in the end forced to accept some compromise arrangements on the matter of presidential powers that were not entirely to their liking. But again, the terminology finally agreed upon furnished the foundation for the development of a much stronger executive than was probably anticipated by most members of the Convention.

State constitutional provisions on executive powers and responsibilities provided the delegates with a useful fund of ideas. It is possible to find clauses in one state constitution or another paralleling practically every one of the phrases used in delineating the President's role.[40] The position created was essentially the result of combining selected elements of strength, rather than of weakness, from state constitutional provisions relating to the office of governor. The chief executive's role

J. B. Lippincott Company, 5 vols., 1937), Vol. III, p. 498. (Hereafter cited as Elliot's *Debates*.) The importance of the Convention's refusal to convert the impeachment power of the House into an automatic suspension device was demonstrated when for the first and only time impeachment of a President occurred in Andrew Johnson's administration. Johnson continued to act as President while his trial was in progress.

[40] Cf. Breckinridge Long, *The Genesis of the Constitution of the United States of America*, (New York: The Macmillan Company, 1926), pp. 223–245.

as defined by the Convention had its closest parallels in those of the New York and Massachusetts governors. Wilson, Morris, and, to a lesser extent, Hamilton, all of whom exerted influence in the Convention in the formulation of the article on the chief executive, drew many of their ideas from the New York system. (Morris had been a member of the convention that drafted New York's constitution.) Charles Pinckney, whose constitutional plan as it concerned the executive was largely a combination of elements in the New York and South Carolina constitutions, was another whose influence was considerable. Gerry, King, and Gorham of the Massachusetts delegation contributed ideas definitely traceable to practice in that state. On the important points of the veto power and the appointive authority of the executive, Madison gave his support to those who sought to imitate the New York plan.

The four constitutional plans submitted to the Convention varied considerably in their provisions on executive authority. The Seventh Resolution in the Virginia Plan proposed that the executive should be endowed with "a general authority to execute the national laws" and with "those Executive rights vested in Congress by the Confederation." In addition, according to the Eighth Resolution, the executive and a "convenient number of the National Judiciary" were to be associated to form a Council of Revision which might veto any act of the national legislative body. The Council's veto authority would encompass acts negating state laws thought by the national legislature to be contrary to national laws, treaties, or the Constitution. A veto by the Council of Revision could be overridden by an unspecified majority of the national legislature. These proposals provided the basis for initial decisions by the Convention on the subject of presidential powers.

DECISIONS REACHED IN COMMITTEE OF THE WHOLE

Except for the question of the veto, consideration of the Virginia Plan proposals on the powers of the executive produced little controversy at the Committee of the Whole stage. After the issue of a single versus a plural executive had been taken up and debated inconclusively for some time on June 1, at Madison's suggestion the Convention turned to the matter of the nature of the authority to be given the executive. As a clarification of the somewhat vague clause in the Virginia Resolutions proposing to invest the executive with all the "executive rights vested in the Congress by the Confederation," he moved that the powers of the executive be defined as carrying into effect national laws, the appointment of officers in cases not otherwise provided for, and the execution of such other powers, not "legislative or judiciary in their nature" as might from time to time be delegated by the national legislature. At Pinckney's suggestion the last clause was deleted from his motion on the assumption that its object was already comprehended in the first clause. This rather vague definition of the executive's powers was then accepted by the Convention.

The question of the executive's role in the legislative process was not so easily agreed upon. The absolute veto power of the provincial governors had been one of the most obnoxious features of the colonial governmental systems, and the reactions in the states had carried most of them to the point of denying to the state governors any veto power whatsoever. Some delegates, including Franklin, Sherman, and Bedford, reflected this attitude in their opposition to vesting any veto power in the national chief executive, while Butler of South Carolina proposed that the executive be granted at most only a power to suspend for a limited time the operation of a newly enacted measure as a means of inducing legislative reconsideration.

Those who advocated no veto authority of any kind were distinctly in the minority. Sharp differences of opinion appeared, however, when the Convention undertook to define the nature of the veto. A motion by Gerry to amend the Virginia Plan proposal so as to exclude the judiciary from the revisionary power posed one aspect of this question; a motion by Wilson, seconded by Hamilton, to amend Gerry's motion by making the executive's veto absolute raised another. Aware that his proposal was suggestive of the royal veto prerogative under the British system, Wilson defended it with the arguments that the power would be seldom used, since "its silent operation would . . . preserve harmony and prevent mischief"; that in a period of extraordinary conflict between the executive and legislative branches a qualified veto power would be an ineffective weapon of defense for the executive; and that the exercise of the veto by the executive could never be irresponsible since, being elected for a limited term, he would be answerable to the people.[41]

Wilson was unable to win the support of any considerable number of delegates for his views. Madison's observation that such an executive prerogative, suggestive of the British system, "would certainly be obnoxious to the temper of the country; its present temper at least" was echoed by others. Those delegates who were opposed to the veto principle altogether joined with those who favored only a qualified veto to defeat Wilson's motion by an overwhelming margin. With no recorded vote the Convention then agreed upon a two-thirds majority in each house of the legislature as the number necessary to nullify a veto. The veto clause of the Virginia Resolutions, revised by exclusion of the judiciary from a share in its exercise, was then approved with only two state delegations opposing. By these actions the Convention indicated its preference for a veto plan following the model for the

41 Madison, "Debates," p. 149.

governor in Massachusetts rather than one based on New York's constitution.

This was a decision not altogether pleasing to Wilson and Madison. They feared that a qualified veto power in the hands of the executive alone would prove to be too weak in practice. Associating the judges of the highest court with the executive in the exercise of this power, they felt, would provide a veto authority of such prestige that Congress would hesitate to override its judgments. Madison and Wilson appeared at this time to be thinking of the veto as having essentially the function that judicial review was later to assume. Influenced by such thinking, Wilson moved to reconsider the vote by which the Council of Revision idea had been rejected two days before. Madison vigorously supported Wilson's motion, maintaining that the executive would stand in need of "being controlled as well as supported" in exercising the veto power. Opposing Wilson's motion, Gerry and King of the Massachusetts delegation emphasized the importance of fixing responsibility clearly in the executive for the exercise of this power, as was the case in their state. The upshot was a reaffirmation by the Convention of its earlier rejection of the Council of Revision plan and its support of the independent executive veto.

No material changes were made when these preliminary decisions reached in Committee of the Whole were reviewed by the Convention. Consequently the principles agreed upon relating to the powers of the executive, which were referred on July 26 to the Committee of Detail for preparation of a draft constitution, comprehended a President vested with authority to execute the national laws, to make appointments to all national offices in cases not otherwise provided for, and to veto any act of the legislative body, subject to reversal by a two-thirds majority in each house of Congress.

THE COMMITTEE OF DETAIL DRAFT

Actions taken by the five-man Committee of Detail proved to be of great importance in the evolution of constitutional provisions on executive powers and duties. It had been assumed by the Convention that this Committee, made up of John Rutledge, Edmund Randolph, James Wilson, Oliver Ellsworth, and Nathaniel Gorham, would amplify somewhat the terms defining executive power, particularly the clause in the statement of general principles assigning to the executive the responsibility for executing national laws. To aid the Committee in this phase of its drafting work the Convention referred to it the Pinckney, Hamilton, and New Jersey Plans along with its own resolutions resulting from its deliberations on the Virginia Plan proposals.

Records of the Committee of Detail indicate that it began its work by having Randolph prepare an outline draft embracing the conclusions of the Convention up to that point in the proceedings. Except for the addition of a clause making the President the head of the "militia," Randolph's outline went no further in defining executive powers and duties than the formal actions of the Convention already taken. After reviewing and slightly revising this draft, the Committee then submitted it to Wilson for reshaping. Wilson used this opportunity to enlarge in much greater detail upon the powers and functions of the executive, evidently drawing largely from the Pinckney draft and directly from the New York and Massachusetts constitutions. The report presented by the Committee to the Convention, so far as it concerned the executive, was this draft of Wilson's in slightly revised form.

There appeared in it first the clause that was to prove highly important in the development of presidential authority—the cryptic statement declaring that "the executive power shall be vested in a single person"—the President. There followed an enumeration of various powers amplifying the "execution of the laws" function of the chief executive. Among these were clauses giving the President the role of commander-in-chief of the armed forces of the United States and of the state militia, granting him the pardoning power except in impeachment cases, and making him the authority for commissioning all officers of the United States. Other clauses gave the President the responsibility to report to Congress from time to time on the state of the nation, to recommend measures for its consideration, to call it into session on extraordinary occasions, and to fix a time for adjournment of Congress when the two houses were unable to agree on a specific time. The powers to appoint judicial and diplomatic officers and to make treaties were not included in the Committee's draft. A foundation for assumption of the role of spokesman for the United States government in dealing with foreign powers and the state governments was provided, however, in clauses making the President the agent for receiving foreign ambassadors and for carrying on correspondence with the governors of the several states.[42]

The Committee draft also spelled out in more detail the procedure of legislation so as to make presidential scrutiny of all bills with a view to a possible veto an integral part of the legislative process. The language on this subject in Article VI, Section 13, of the draft constitution was essentially a paraphrase of the corresponding sections of the Massachusetts constitution, which in turn had evidently been adapted from the New York constitution. An important departure from the state models was the inclusion of language in the Commit-

42 The original source of much of this language can be found in Articles XVI, XVIII, and XIX of the New York constitution of 1777.

tee's draft specifically authorizing a veto by inaction—the so-called "pocket veto"—upon bills passed in the closing days of a legislative session.

In the light of later developments the Committee's contributions to the definition of presidential powers were most significant. By outlining in some detail the powers and responsibilities of the executive it provided a basis for his authority in *direct constitutional grant,* rather than leaving it essentially dependent on legislative definition. By stating that "the executive power" was to be vested in the President it provided a plausible basis for later advancement of the contention that *all* powers executive in nature are in his hands. Constitutional *prerogative* rather than legislative *grant* became the fundamental basis of presidential authority. The importance of the Committee's actions in giving the presidency a coordinate status in the scheme of separation of powers can therefore hardly be exaggerated.

Upon reviewing them, the Convention found the recommendations of the Committee of Detail to be acceptable, for the most part. Only relatively minor changes were made in its draft on these points. When the veto power clause came up Madison again attempted, without success, to secure substitution of his Council of Revision idea.[43] As concessions to the views of Madison, Wilson, and others who insisted that the veto in the hands of a legislatively appointed executive might not prove an effective check on the legislature, certain modifications designed to strengthen the veto power were effected by the Convention in the Committee of Detail draft. A proposal by Williamson of North Carolina, that a three-fourths rather than a two-thirds majority in each branch of Congress be required to override a veto was accepted, as was also one extending from seven to ten days the time for presidential consideration of bills.[44] A motion by Madison that the phraseology of the draft plan be altered to extend the veto to all "resolves" of the two Houses, as well as to bills, was at first rejected,

[43] Madison's thinking on this point was influenced by the fact that it was assumed at this stage that the President was to be selected by Congress. In answer to the contention that the Council of Revision as suggested would give the judiciary a preponderant influence in veto actions, Madison offered a modified version of his original scheme. Under his revised plan the executive and the Supreme Court would have exercised the veto power separately. A measure vetoed by only one of the two reviewing agencies could have been overridden by a two-thirds vote in each House, but a veto in which both joined could have been overcome only by a three-fourths majority. This version of his plan attracted the support of three states and was opposed by eight. Madison, "Debates," pp. 547–548. During all the Convention's deliberations Madison appears to have underestimated, if he did not discount altogether, the possibility of a judicial veto upon state and national legislative acts through the exercise of a power of judicial review in actual cases.

[44] *Ibid.,* p. 551. In proposing a seven-day period the Committee of Detail had evidently chosen a middle ground between the New York practice of permitting ten days for consideration and the Massachusetts system of five days.

but on reconsideration the next day in a somewhat revised form it was accepted.

Other revisions in the Committee draft concerned the appointment power and commander-in-chief clauses. The statement vesting in the President a general power of appointment in cases where no other mode of selection was provided was revised slightly to eliminate an implication that the authority to appoint carried with it an authority to create offices by the act of appointment. On Sherman's motion, the commander-in-chief clause was modified to make clear that the presidential power of command over the state militia should take effect only when the militia had been called into the actual service of the United States. A clause in the Committee draft authorizing the President to correspond with the governors of the states was stricken out, on motion by Gouverneur Morris, on the ground that it was unnecessary and might be construed as an implied restriction on his power to correspond "with others." The "others" Morris had in mind presumably included the heads of foreign states.

Approval by the Convention of the Committee of Detail draft, with the modifications noted, was a long step toward agreement on the definition of executive power that was to appear in the completed Constitution. A number of important questions concerning presidential powers and functions were still unsettled, however. The selection, tenure, re-eligibility, removal, and succession issues, events were to show, had not yet been disposed of to the satisfaction of a firm majority of the state delegations. Whether the President should be controlled in his major decisions by an executive council was still undecided. The office of "treasurer of the United States," to be filled by legislative appointment, had been approved as provided for in the draft constitution, but the question of the establishment of other subordinate executive departments and the relationship that should exist between the heads of these departments and the President and Congress had not been dealt with. Under the draft plan as it then stood the authority to appoint judicial and diplomatic officers and to make treaties was to be vested in the Senate.

Postponement of consideration of these latter items at the time of review of the Committee's draft had given evidence of a growing sentiment, reflected by Madison, Wilson, and others, that the President should play a more important role in these matters than was contemplated in the plan under consideration. This was the state of affairs when on August 31 the Convention voted to refer to the special Committee of Eleven for further study and report all pending postponed matters and parts of the Committee's draft plan not yet acted upon. It thus fell to the lot of this Committee to consider and report upon a a number of questions which had vital importance in defining the President's position and powers.

The report of this Committee, made only two weeks before the
Convention was to adjourn, boldly broke new ground on many of the
points at issue. As has already been noted, its recommendations included a series of proposals designed to placate the small-state delegations, along with others desired by the strong-executive group. On the
organization of subordinate executive departments and the relation of
their heads to the chief executive, the Committee's report was brief. No
departmental scheme was proposed, but the creation of departments
was left to be dealt with by legislative act. A clause authorizing the
President to require the written opinions of heads of departments on
matters relating to their duties carried with it the implication that the
President should have a degree of directive power over them and might
resort to them for advice, but they were not constituted an executive
council in the formal sense. The report proposed further that the
treaty-making power be placed in the hands of the President, acting
with the advice and consent of the Senate, and that all treaties must be
approved by a two-thirds majority of the Senate. As for appointments,
it proposed a broadening of the President's power to include judges
of the Supreme Court and diplomatic officers, but the advice and consent of the Senate was made a condition in these cases as well as in all
others where the President was the appointing agent. It proposed also
that the Senate be made the trial body in impeachment cases.

These proposals constituted some shift in power from the legislative branch to the executive, but the Senate, where the states were to
be represented equally, was left in a position where it might exercise
a special degree of influence and control over certain acts of the executive. It was to become, in effect, the President's council in his exercise
of the treaty-making and appointive powers; and in the new arrangements proposed for his selection, it was to have the controlling voice
in the final stages of the elective process. Furthermore, the Senate,
rather than the Supreme Court, was to make the ultimate judgment
in the event of a President's impeachment.

Largely through the efforts of Morris and Sherman, who were the
spokesmen, respectively, for the strong-executive and small-state factions which had negotiated this compromise, the Convention was induced to accept this "package" deal for revision of the executive article,
but not until it had been subjected to some changes. As has been seen,
the scheme of presidential selection was modified by substitution of the
House for the Senate as the ultimate electoral agency. The proposal to
broaden the President's appointive authority to include judicial and
diplomatic officers, with the Senate to serve as a consulting and approv-

ing body, was accepted with surprisingly little opposition. A final effort by Mason to instruct the Committee to bring forward a plan for an executive council chosen by the legislative body on a regionally representative basis to act with the President in appointments was defeated, even though it had the support of such influential men as Wilson, Madison, Franklin, and Dickinson. Two perfecting amendments—one authorizing the President alone to make temporary appointments during a recess of the Senate and the other authorizing him to summon the Senate into special session for the conduct of executive business—were accepted.

The proposed revision on the treaty-making power encountered more opposition. Wilson was unsuccessful in an attempt to associate the House with the Senate on equal terms in this process, but Madison was temporarily successful in obtaining approval of a clause excepting treaties of peace from the requirement that treaties be approved by a two-thirds majority of the Senate. Madison argued that such a majority was too great a hurdle; it might enable the executive to prolong a state of war and thereby continue to enjoy unusual powers. But when Madison sought to follow up this advantage with a proposal to give the Senate exclusive power to make such treaties, he met defeat; the next day, furthermore, on reconsideration of the whole treaty power issue, the Convention voted to adopt the Committee's original proposal without change.

REVISIONS IN THE COMMITTEE OF STYLE DRAFT

These actions of the Convention had the effect of rounding out the general scheme of constitutional provisions on executive powers and functions. Yet even after the Constitution had been given ostensibly its final form by the Committee on Style and Arrangement, review of its draft by the Convention resulted in further changes on the subject of executive powers. The majority required in each house to override a presidential veto was reduced from three fourths to two thirds after a short but intensive debate during which Morris, Hamilton, Gerry, and Madison unsuccessfully opposed the change on the ground that it would dangerously weaken the executive's control over legislation.[45] This slight diminution in the power of the executive was offset somewhat by further changes made in the appointive power and

[45] *Ibid.*, p. 690. The motion to reduce the requirement to two thirds was offered by Dr. Williamson, of North Carolina, who had originally sponsored the three-fourths majority idea. Williamson explained his reversal of attitude by noting that at the time he made his first proposal the Convention had just endorsed the principle of legislative election of the President. Since a mode of independent selection had been subsequently adopted, he declared there was less need for such a strongly buttressed veto power.

by the defeat of an effort to limit the presidential pardoning power in treason cases.

The draft presented by the Committee on Style still carried a clause specifically authorizing appointment by Congress of a "treasurer of the United States." This provision had remained in the constitutional plan despite earlier efforts to eliminate it in favor of presidential appointment. On Rutledge's motion the clause was eliminated in the final review by the Convention, largely on the strength of assertions by Rutledge and Charles C. Pinckney of the South Carolina delegation, both of whom had served as the state's governor, that legislative appointment of the treasurer in that state had proved unsatisfactory in practice.

Another modification in the President's appointing authority was initiated by Morris. The proposed draft defined the President's appointive authority in such a way as to make senatorial approval necessary in *all* appointments. Morris successfully urged a modification permitting the assignment, by law, of the power to appoint "inferior" officers to the President alone, the courts, or the heads of departments. This change not only freed some presidential appointments from the requirement of senatorial approval but also realistically permitted a delegation of powers in this sphere, by legislative act, to subordinate executive officials. The Convention then completed its review of the executive article in the new plan of government by defeating a move by members of the Virginia delegation to exclude treason cases from the President's pardoning power.

THE EXECUTIVE ARTICLE AND STATE RATIFYING CONVENTIONS

As was no doubt anticipated by the Convention delegates, the executive article in the proposed new Constitution became a major target for attack in the ratification struggle. Few of the clauses relating to the executive escaped criticism. George Mason, one of the Philadelphia Convention delegates who had refused to sign the completed instrument, led the fight against ratification in the Virginia convention—the executive article was one of the prime objects of his criticism. Predicting that the proposed Constitution would prove to be a scheme for "an elective monarchy," he saw faults in the proposed method of election, the absence of a clause restricting presidential re-eligibility, the joining of civil and military authority in the President's hands, the failure to provide for an executive council, the scope of the President's pardoning power, and the President's role in treaty-making.[46] Patrick

[46] Elliot's *Debates*, Vol. III, pp. 484–485, 493–494, 496, 507–509.

Henry summed up his views on the subject in the Virginia ratifying convention by declaring that the new plan had an ominous "squint toward monarchy."

Rawlins Lowndes, in a debate in the South Carolina legislature on the question of authorizing the calling of a convention to consider ratification, characterized the new Constitution as "the best preparatory plan for a monarchical government he had read."[47] Similar charges formed a part of the objections advanced in Maryland by Luther Martin, another Convention delegate who refused to sign the completed document. All of the clauses relating to the executive came in for more or less criticism in the Massachusetts convention; in the New York convention the numerous proposals advanced for revision of the executive article indicated much dissatisfaction with the provisions of this part of the new plan.[48]

On the other hand, James Wilson in the Pennsylvania convention noted that "few exceptions were taken to this part of the system," and he was forced into the position of having to defend the new Constitution against the charge "not that [the President's powers] were too many or too great; but to state it in the gentlemen's own language, they are so trifling that the President is no more than the *tool* of the Senate."[49] It will be recalled that in the Constitutional Convention Wilson himself had criticized on these grounds the provisions making the Senate the advisory and approving body for certain presidential actions. The fact that his own strictures against these features of the Constitution were thrown back at him in the Pennsylvania convention debates gives rise to the suspicion that some member of the Pennsylvania delegation must have "tipped off" the opposition regarding Wilson's views as expressed during the supposedly secret debates on the formulation of the constitutional draft.

Yet on the whole it may be concluded from an analysis of the debates in the state ratifying bodies that the executive article, while widely criticized, was less objected to than other features in the Constitution relating to the structure and powers of Congress. The numerous proposals for amendments emanating from various state ratifying conventions and eventually resulting in the addition of the Bill of Rights primarily indicated distrust of the grants of power to Congress, but in some measure they also reflected distrust of the proposed grants of power to the executive. Amendment proposals relating specifically to provisions on the executive included changes to restrict presidential

47 *Ibid.*, Vol. IV, p. 311. In the same vein James Lincoln, another critic of the new plan, asserted, "this mighty, this omnipotent governor-general" may hold office for "fourteen times four years," and "he may hold it so long that it will be impossible without a revolution, to displace him." *Ibid.*, Vol. III, p. 314.

48 *Ibid.*, Vol. II, p. 109; Vol. I, pp. 330–331.

49 *Ibid.*, Vol. II, p. 510.

re-eligibility, to limit the President's pardoning power in treason cases, and to subject his commander-in-chief function to some congressional control. Three conventions proposed adoption of an amendment on the first point, while the New York convention proposed amendments relating to these and other features of the presidential office as well.[50]

Although it reacted favorably to state convention suggestions for a series of constitutional amendments to protect individual and state rights, the First Congress failed to respond to the demands for revision of the executive article. The election of Washington to the post of President had, for the time at least, sufficiently allayed doubts to permit the launching of the new plan of government without alteration of any of the features relating to the executive that had been agreed on in the Constitutional Convention.

Time and experience were to reveal that the Convention had hit upon a successful formula for a truly "balanced" system of executive and legislative powers. Before long the states were applying the lessons learned and revising their own constitutional plans to conform to the federal model. The constitutional foundation for the office of chief executive laid by the Framers proved to be both workable and enduring. Except for changes effected by the Twelfth Amendment in 1804 in the method of chosing a President and the belated acceptance of the principle of limited re-eligibility with the adoption of the Twenty-second Amendment in 1951, the original constitutional design on the executive remains intact. The character of the office and its role in the scheme of government have changed greatly since Washington's time, but the alterations have been achieved through statutory action, interpretation, and practice, rather than through revision of the original phraseology of the Constitution. Drawing upon the experiences of the states as well as upon British practice, the Framers were able to fit together a design for an enduring separation of powers plan uniquely and distinctively American in character.

[50] The Virginia and North Carolina conventions recommended adoption of an amendment providing that no person should be permitted to occupy the office of President for more than eight years in any sixteen-year period; the New York convention proposed an amendment prohibiting a third term altogether. Tansill, *Documents,* pp. 1032, 1042, 1049. The New York convention also proposed that amendments be adopted which would (1) require that the President, Vice President, and members of Congress be natural-born citizens or citizens at the time of achievement of independence; citizens of one of the states; and freeholders; (2) prohibit the President from taking command of the armed forces in the field in person without the consent of Congress; (3) prohibit the granting of pardons in treason cases without the consent of Congress; (4) provide for the trial of impeachments before a Court of Impeachments consisting of the Senate, the judges of the Supreme Court, and the senior judge of the highest court of law in each state, with a majority vote sufficient to convict; and (5) require an oath from all federal officers containing a pledge not to "infringe or violate the Constitutions or Rights of the respective States." *Ibid.,* pp. 1042–1043.

PART TWO

THE STRUCTURE OF THE OFFICE

3

THE SYSTEM OF ELECTION

Strength in the chief executive's office under the separation of powers system depends ultimately upon the principle of independent popular election. More than the other elements in this type of government organization—separate personnel for each of the several branches, constitutionally defined powers and functions for each, power to negate certain acts of another branch—the principle of independent selection of the chief executive gives this system its fundamental distinction from the parliamentary type. Independent popular election provides the chief executive with a mandate to exert leadership in policy matters in the name of the people and, when coupled with partisan choice, of his party or faction. It permits him, within limits, to determine for himself how the powers assigned to him under the constitutional plan shall be used. He alone in the government represents the whole people, in contrast to the individual member of Congress or of the state legislature, whose constituency comprises only a segment of it. By making him a symbol of popular aspirations, values, and beliefs, popular election puts him in a unique position of moral and political leadership.

This principle was not clearly recognized in all the original state constitutions. As was pointed out in Chapter 1, the architects of these pioneering plans for the most part professed adherence to the idea that the executive and legislative powers should be in separate hands. Nevertheless in most of the states they gave the executive branch an unsound foundation from this point of view by providing for legislative selection of the governor. By 1787, when the Framers of the Constitution had to devise a procedure for choosing the President, an appreciation of the importance of an independent method of selection for the chief executive in a viable system of separated powers had penetrated the thinking of a number of influential figures. Only by a somewhat fortuitous circumstance were they successful in getting a scheme of presidential election incorporated into the constitutional plan that could easily be adapted to the idea of indirect popular election. It was mainly because of complications arising from the bicameral structure of Congress and the necessity of adapting the mode of election to federalism that the Convention failed to provide outright for selection of the President by Congress. As it turned out, the scheme agreed upon did not entirely exclude Congress from participation in the process. Not until after the Constitution was put into operation did developments occur that converted the original system into an indirect, but essentially independent, means of popular selection.

Meanwhile, as a result of the same democratizing influences that brought about these developments at the national level, modifications were also effected in state practices in choosing the governor. Direct popular election by a statewide plurality vote—a method only New York among the original states had adopted—eventually became the common practice. These changes were accompanied by a general liberalization of suffrage requirements that strengthened still further the claims of chief executives at both levels of government to the role of chief policy-maker and "tribune of the people." Presidents and governors became major instruments for achieving popular control of government.

A presidential election in the United States—"the most awesome transfer of power in the world"[1]—is now an event unmatched for the popular interest it attracts. Its significance as a demonstration of the democratic process in operation can hardly be exaggerated. In the totalitarian and nondemocratic nations, a head of state suddenly disappears from sight as a political trapdoor controlled by obscure figures working in the secrecy of guarded rooms is sprung; or he is ousted overnight when smouldering discontent suddenly bursts into the flame of a palace revolution or a military coup. But the drama of a presidential election unfolds openly and peacefully before the eyes of the nation and of the world. Millions follow its developments with avid interest, and when the polls have closed on election day, the world waits with eager impatience to learn the results. With its mammoth organization of men and machines for news gathering and dissemination, election night has become the greatest radio and television show on earth. Adding to the drama are the simultaneous contests for the governorship in half or more of the states. When the outcome has become clear the losers congratulate the winners and pledge their patriotic support, and the people heretofore apparently divided in a frenzy of partisan struggle and emotion accept the result and close ranks. These amenities are the outward manifestation of a deep commitment to the ideal of democracy. In devising a workable system through which the people may choose the person who is to occupy the most powerful political office the modern world has known, the American nation has furnished the most striking proof of its capacity for self-government.

[1] Cf. Theodore H. White, *The Making of the President, 1960.* (New York: Atheneum Publishers, 1961), p. 3.

EVOLUTION OF STATE ELECTIVE PRACTICES

Direct popular election of the governor began to be substituted for the system of legislative election soon after the Constitution went into operation. South Carolina, the last state to employ legislative appointment, abandoned it in 1865.[2] The factor that played the leading role in this aspect of state constitutional revision was an undeniable demand for a greater degree of popular participation in government. This was a central element in the Jeffersonian and Jacksonian democratic movement of the early nineteenth century. Other factors were a growing realization of the significance of independent election for the chief executive if a true separation of powers was to be maintained; a decline of confidence in the responsiveness of legislative bodies to popular demands; and a desire to free the elections of state legislative members and the sessions of the legislature itself from the distractions arising from involvement in this electoral function.[3]

The demand for democratization in choosing the governor was, on occasion, successfully resisted. Virginia's constitutional convention of 1829–1830, for example, by a narrow margin and after acrimonious debate, refused to entrust the people with so great a responsibility.[4] But such rebuffs proved to be only temporary setbacks. The principle of indirect election found little favor in the new states admitted to the Union. Only two, Kentucky and Louisiana, failed to provide for direct popular election of the governor, and in these states the earlier plans

---

[2] The dates for the change to direct popular election in the other states which at first employed the legislative appointment principle were as follows: Pennsylvania, 1790; Delaware, 1792; Georgia, 1824; North Carolina, 1835; Maryland, 1837; New Jersey, 1844; Virginia, 1850. Connecticut and Rhode Island adopted a modernized form of direct popular election by revisions of their charters in 1818 and 1842, respectively.

[3] The following editorial in the Savannah *Georgia Journal* of September 30, 1822, published in the course of the agitation for adoption of the principle of direct popular election of the governor in that state, illustrated some of the issues raised:

> The violence of the contest for seats in the legislature, whenever a Governor is to be elected, is to be deprecated. In the midst of it the great interests of the State are lost sight of; and in many instances, men are elected on no other account than because they will vote for some particular individual as Governor. This will continue to be the case as long as this officer is elected by the Legislature. Give his election to the people, and let us have a Legislature elected on account of their qualifications to discharge their duties as law makers.

Cf. Albert B. Saye, *A Constitutional History of Georgia, 1732–1945* (Athens: University of Georgia Press, 1937), p. 175.

[4] Cf. *Proceedings and Debates of the Virginia State Convention of 1829–1830* (Richmond: S. Shepherd and Co., 1830), pp. 464 ff, 709 ff.

of indirect election soon gave way to direct popular election under the plurality rule. Kentucky tried out an electoral vote system modelled after the national plan for choosing the President, but quickly abandoned it.[5]

As they embraced the principle of popular election an accompanying reluctance to accept also the plurality vote rule was manifested in a number of states. Massachusetts' constitution of 1780 had set a pattern for the other New England states in this regard. While providing for a direct popular vote for governor, it specified that in the event no candidate received a majority the issue should be resolved by selection of the governor by the state senate from a panel of two designated by the lower house of the legislature from among the four highest in the popular voting.[6] The other New England states adopted the same or similar provisions for resolving an inconclusive popular contest. When Georgia adopted the popular vote principle in 1824 it also incorporated a majority vote requirement. The Georgia plan, which is still in effect, provides for legislative election of one of the two highest in the popular voting if no candidate has received a majority of the popular vote. A unique system, also still in effect, was incorporated in Mississippi's constitution of 1890. It combines the ideas of a majority popular election and a gubernatorial electoral vote system, with the alternative of legislative election in case no candidate receives both kinds of a majority.[7]

In the course of time the majority popular vote requirement with accompanying provisions for referring an inconclusive popular result

[5] Kentucky's constitution of 1792 provided for election of the governor, as well as the upper house of the state legislature, by a special body of electors chosen by popular vote in the several state legislative districts. This indirect electoral system, somewhat similar to the presidential electoral plan, was abandoned in favor of direct election in 1799. Louisiana's original constitution provided for a direct popular vote for governor, but the popular vote was not conclusive. The ultimate choice was to be made by the legislature as between the two highest in the popular voting. In practice, the legislature regularly elected the candidate receiving the highest popular vote. Cf. *Debates and Proceedings, Louisiana Constitutional Convention, 1845* (New Orleans: Besancon, Ferguson and Co., 1845), p. 200. This plan of a potential legislative veto on the popular choice was discarded in Louisiana in 1845.

[6] Constitution of 1780. Chap. II, Sec. 1, Art. III. The majority rule principle was applied to all popular elections, with various devices, including runoff elections, specified for resolving an inconclusive vote.

[7] Constitution of 1890, Art. V, Secs. 141–142. Under the Mississippi system, which was designed to afford protection of the white racial interest against the Negro element as well as of certain sectional interests against others, to be elected a candidate must receive a popular majority in the statewide vote and also a majority of the gubernatorial electoral votes, which are allotted on the same basis as seats in the state House of Representatives. A popular plurality in a legislative district automatically credits the electoral vote of that district to a candidate. If no candidate receives both a statewide popular and an electoral vote majority, the House of Representatives chooses the governor from among the two highest in the popular voting.

to the legislature fell into general disfavor among the New England states, where it once had its major foothold. Only Vermont still retains it. Experience with the majority vote principle in the New England states came to reveal some of its inherent defects. It was found to endanger the stability of the two-party system by encouraging the casting of votes for third party candidates in the expectation that a strong bargaining position could be attained by a marginal group at the legislative election stage. In one instance in Maine a Democratic party candidate who had finished a rather distant third in the popular voting was elected governor. In other England states there were numerous instances of candidates who had finished second in the popular voting being chosen by the legislature. When elections were thrown into the legislature's hands, intrigues and partisan manipulations were sometimes carried to a point where its usefulness as a legislative organ was impaired. Significantly, abandonment of the system followed in these states soon after one or another of these shortcomings was revealed in practice.

Direct popular election of the governor under a plurality vote rule is now the established practice in 47 states. It should be noted that the three that retain the majority vote requirement—Vermont, Georgia, and Mississippi—are all states in which for many years there has been no effective two-party system. Dominance by one party reduces the likelihood of a nonmajority popular vote for the party's candidate to a minimum.[8] The plurality vote rule, although it has occasionally resulted in the election of a governor who received less than a majority of the popular votes, has generally proved to be sound and satisfactory in practice. It tends to induce voters to fall in line behind one or the other of the two leading candidates and thus becomes one of the prime supports of the two-party system. Debate concerning the relative merits of the majority vote versus the plurality vote principle now has its chief significance in connection with the operation of the direct primary, particularly in the one-party states, and in connection with the electoral vote system by which the President is elected.

EVOLUTION OF THE PRESIDENTIAL ELECTORAL SYSTEM

The method of choosing the President and Vice President, devised by the Convention of 1787 after much debate and vacillation, was generally regarded with satisfaction by the Convention itself and by

[8] Since 1900, four gubernatorial elections—in Vermont in 1902 and 1912, and in New Hampshire in 1906 and 1912—have had to be referred to the legislature for ultimate determination. New Hampshire abandoned the majority vote requirement in 1912; Massachusetts abandoned it in 1855; Maine in 1880; Rhode Island in 1893; and Connecticut in 1901.

delegates to the state ratifying conventions. In the number of *The Federalist* devoted to this feature of the new Constitution Hamilton called the plan agreed upon "excellent if not perfect" and noted that it was "almost the only part of the system, of any consequence, which has received the slightest mark of approbation from its opponents."[9] This was, perhaps, an oversimplification of the matter. What Hamilton failed to emphasize and what Madison, Wilson, Gouverneur Morris, Sherman, and others who had taken a more active part than Hamilton in perfecting the plan of selection fully realized, was that it was made up of a most ingenious series of compromises and adjustments. It was a compromise on the issue of an independent mode of selection versus appointment by Congress; on the question of according to the states equal electoral power or electoral power based on population; and on the question of national control over the procedure as against state control. There was a difference of views among the delegates on how the plan would actually work in practice, after Washington would no longer be available for the post.

THE ORIGINAL PLAN IN OPERATION

In the first two presidential elections the electoral college system functioned in about the way the Framers had anticipated it would, although in neither case was it necessary to refer the election to Congress for final determination. In the election of 1788 only 10 states participated, and four of the electors chosen failed to appear at the appointed time to cast their votes.[10] As was expected for this election, all the participating electors cast one of their votes for Washington. Their second votes were scattered among 11 other persons, of whom

[9] No. 67. Analyzing the plan in some detail, he maintained that its merits were that (1) it made possible the ascertainment of the "sense of the people" in the choice of the President; (2) it placed immediate responsibility for making the choice in the hands of men most capable of making an intelligent, judicious decision; (3) it afforded protection against the dangers of cabal, intrigue, and corruption—since the electors would be chosen anew for each election, no holder of a federal office was eligible to serve as elector, and the electors would undoubtedly be men of high character, "free from any sinister bias"; and (4) it would make the President dependent upon the people for continuance in office, rather than upon some agency he might be tempted to corrupt in order to further his ambition. In short, it was a plan that would insure the "constant probability" that the office of President would be filled by "characters pre-eminent for ability and virtue."

[10] North Carolina and Rhode Island did not choose electors, since they did not ratify the Constitution until after the new government was in operation. The two houses of New York's legislature became deadlocked on the question of the form of a law regulating the selection of its electors. The deadlock failed to be broken in time to permit choice of the eight electors allotted to that state. Two of Maryland's electors and two of Virginia's failed to appear on the day assigned for their meetings at their respective state capitals (February 4, 1789), and their votes were lost. Edward Stanwood, *A History of the Presidency from 1788 to 1897* (Boston: Houghton Mifflin Company, rev. ed., 1928), pp. 22, 27.

John Adams with 34 votes had the highest total, making him the Vice President under the original constitutional arrangement. Somewhat similar results followed in 1792, with Washington again receiving one vote from each of the participating electors in the 15 states of the Union. John Adams again was the runner-up in a field of four candidates and was re-elected Vice President; but there was a suggestion of things to come in the fact that all but five of the electors cast their second ballots either for Adams or for the "Anti-Adams" candidate, Governor George Clinton of New York. The incipient spirit of party was already beginning to manifest itself in the actions of the electors.

By 1796 developments which were to alter profoundly the functioning of the electoral college system began to make themselves even more clearly evident. One development was the injection of frankly partisan considerations into the choice of electors. In the election of that year the competition for these posts was essentially a series of contests between the Federalist and the "anti-Federalist," or Jeffersonian Republican, factions. Another significant development was the giving of pledges in advance by elector candidates that they would cast their votes for designated party leaders. This meant that they no longer considered themselves free agents expected to consult and bargain in casting their votes, but rather as agents bound to carry out the party's will.

Before the choice of electors in 1796 congressional and other party leaders gave out the word that Federalist electors were expected to vote for John Adams of Massachusetts, and Thomas Pinckney of South Carolina. Republican leaders similarly urged that their party's electors vote for Thomas Jefferson of Virginia and Aaron Burr of New York. Party discipline was not yet complete over the electors and there were intraparty intrigues and rivalries which influenced the actions of some of them. Consequently other candidates than the four unofficial nominees received scattered support in the electoral voting. Hamilton allegedly sought to induce some of the Federalist electors not to vote for Adams so as to cause Pinckney to receive a higher vote than Adams, and the presidency. Two Federalist electors of Pennsylvania chosen on the assumption that they would cast their votes for Adams and Pinckney voted a split ticket of Jefferson and Pinckney, as did all eight Federalist electors of South Carolina.[11]

The electoral vote results were extremely close. The 138 electors chosen distributed their 276 votes among 13 different candidates, but

[11] The defection from Adams of the two electors in Pennsylvania led an exasperated Pennsylvania Federalist to write to his newspaper in protest: "What! Do I chuse Samuel Miles to determine for me whether John Adams or Thomas Jefferson shall be President? No! I chuse him to *act* not to *think*." Stanwood, *op. cit.*, p. 51. For an account of Hamilton's machinations in the election see Page Smith, *John Adams* (Garden City, N.Y.: Doubleday & Company, 2 vols., 1963), Vol. II, pp. 902 ff.

Adams received the highest number, 71, which was one more than a bare majority of the number of electors. He was accordingly declared elected by vote of the electors. Jefferson received 68, Pinckney 59, and Burr 30 (the remaining 48 votes were scattered among the nine other individuals). The result was that a President and a Vice President were again selected through action of the electors' votes alone, but there was an unexpected twist to it in that the Federalist, Adams, was chosen President, while his chief rival, Jefferson, was chosen as Vice President to serve with him.

As might have been expected, leaders of both emerging major parties resolved that so anomalous a result would not be repeated in 1800. Plans to this end were perfected by party strategists before that election. The objective of each party was to effect a complete concentration of its electoral vote strength upon the same two individuals. The congressional caucuses of the respective parties became the primary instruments for determining the identities of the party candidates. Through this device the Federalists agreed upon Adams and Charles C. Pinckney of South Carolina; the Jeffersonians upon Jefferson and Burr. A majority of the 138 electors chosen in 1800 were Jeffersonian Republicans, and they all carried out their pledges to vote for their two candidates; but this only served to create another embarrassing situation. Since the 73 Republican electors could not distinguish in their votes their preference between Jefferson and Burr for President, even though it was generally understood that Jefferson was the presidential and Burr the vice presidential candidate, both received the same number and a majority of the electors' votes for President. Thus a majority vote tie was created between them for President.

The original constitutional plan clearly made provision for resolution of a contingency of this kind by placing upon the House of Representatives, voting by state units, the responsibility for deciding between the two for President and Vice President. After an acrimonious struggle lasting until only some two weeks before the time for inauguration of a new President, the Federalist-dominated House, whose members were those chosen in 1798, eventually resolved the issue by designating Jefferson as President and Burr as Vice President. Thus the first of three major crises in the functioning of the electoral college system was surmounted.

THE TWELFTH AMENDMENT

To avert recurrence of another near-fiasco of this kind the Twelfth Amendment was proposed in 1803 and ratified by the necessary number of states prior to the 1804 election. The major change effected by this

Amendment was that presidential electors should henceforth vote separately for President and Vice President, an elector to have one vote in each contest. In each contest a candidate receiving a majority of the electors' votes was to be deemed elected. If no presidential candidate should receive such a majority the issue would still be referred to the House of Representatives, as before; but only the three highest rather than the five highest in the electoral voting would be eligible to be chosen. The "runner-up" rule under which the candidate with the second highest total of electoral votes became Vice President was abolished. If no candidate for Vice President should receive a majority of the electors' votes the Amendment specified that the contest should be referred to the Senate, which might choose one of the two highest in the electoral voting for Vice President.

These changes in electoral procedure enabled the electors to throw their full weight behind both candidates of their respective parties; but it had the not unexpected result of permitting party managers to treat the vice presidential nomination as a kind of consolation prize or makeweight for adding strength to the party ticket. Immediately after adoption of the Twelfth Amendment the Vice Presidency went into a decline in popular esteem and political prestige from which it has only recently shown signs of recovering.

Adoption of the Twelfth Amendment cleared the way for implementation of a new conception of the means of choosing the President. It recognized the injection of partisan considerations into the process. While retaining the electors and the electoral vote distribution formula of the original plan for weighting state influence, it also eased the way for further democratization of the process of selection. Party instrumentalities for naming the candidates were still to be perfected, and state laws had not yet in all cases placed the choice of the electors in the hands of the voters. But it carried with it an implication that the electors had become mere agents of the party's will and that they were no longer expected to exercise discretion.

State legislatures and state politicians thereafter found it impossible to resist for long popular pressure to place the choosing of electors in the hands of the people. With popular election of the electors eventually becoming the established rule in all states, with a national two-party system prevailing most of the time since 1800, and with electors being chosen on a statewide basis by a plurality vote, the electoral vote stage has become decisive, normally, in choosing the President and Vice President. Only one presidential election since 1800, that of 1824, has had to be resolved by vote of the House of Representatives; and only one vice presidential election, that of 1836, by the Senate. Out of the 41 presidential elections from 1804 through

1964, however, there have been 11 others in which more than two candidates received electoral votes for President. In 17 of these contests more than two candidates received electoral votes for Vice President.

THE TWENTY-THIRD AMENDMENT

A further change in the system of choosing the President was effected by adoption of the Twenty-third Amendment in 1961. This Amendment assigned three electors to the District of Columbia, to be elected in accordance with implementing legislation to be enacted by Congress. This constitutional amendment was significant not only in giving the residents of the District of Columbia a voice in the choice of a President; but it also was a breakthrough on the hitherto untouchable system of electing the President. All efforts to revise it in any way by constitutional amendment had been repulsed for a century and a half. The implicit recognition it gives to the idea that the choice of the President is a *national* act by all the people, not a *federal* act in which the states as political entities are the participants, may ease the way in the future for reconsideration and recasting of the machinery by which the President is chosen.

METHODS OF APPOINTING ELECTORS

During the first 30 years of the nation's history under the Constitution, the states experimented freely with various methods of choosing electors. Partisan considerations were a major factor in determining the kind of law each state adopted. State laws were changed frequently. In Massachusetts, for example, the method of choosing electors was changed prior to every presidential election from 1796 to 1828.[12] Methods employed at one time or another have included: (1) choice by the legislature; (2) popular election by special districts; (3) popular election by congressional districts and legislative choice of two from the state at large; (4) popular election at large on a general ticket; (5) and various other combinations of statewide votes, district votes, and legislative appointment.

In time, pressure upon the legislatures to give the voters a direct voice in choosing electors resulted in laws recognizing the principle of popular election in all states; while considerations of state pride and interest as well as partisan advantage led to general acceptance of the statewide general ticket system of election, with a plurality governing

---

[12] H. V. Ames, *The Proposed Amendments to the Constitution of the United States During the First Century of its History* (Washington: Government Printing Office, 1897), p. 85. (Hereafter referred to as Ames, *Proposed Amendments*.)

the result.[13] Acting under authority expressly conferred by the Constitution, Congress in 1845 adopted legislation which is still in force, specifying that electors must be chosen in each state on the Tuesday following the first Monday in November of the year preceding the expiration of an incumbent President's term.[14]

The qualifications for voting for electors are those governing the suffrage generally in each state, with two possible exceptions. By the terms of the Twenty-fourth Amendment, ratified in 1963, a tax-paying requirement for voting in any federal election is forbidden; but a state may retain such a requirement for voting in state and local elections. Four of the five states immediately affected by the Amendment have retained the poll tax payment requirement for state elections; the other, Arkansas, abolished its poll tax requirement altogether in 1964. Consequently, the electorate for choosing presidential electors may include some persons who are not eligible to vote for state and local officers in Virginia, Alabama, Mississippi, and Texas.

A second difference in voting qualifications has been made by a number of states with reference to a minimum period of residence in the state. In 1954 Wisconsin adopted a constitutional amendment under which residents otherwise qualified to vote in that state are exempted from the normal one-year residence rule in connection with voting for presidential electors. The Wisconsin plan has the obvious merit of avoiding disfranchisement of otherwise qualified voters who have moved from another state to Wisconsin shortly before a presidential election. Other states have sought to meet this problem by liberalization of their absentee voting laws so as to permit a departing resident to continue to vote *in absentia* until he has acquired a legal voting status in another state. These ideas have proved popular, and by 1964 some 15 states had taken steps of one kind or another to relax their residence requirements for voters in presidential contests. The problem of the "lost voter," disfranchised in presidential elections by reason of restrictive state residence requirements, is by no means a minor one. It has been estimated that as many as 6,000,000 potential voters are disfranchised by them in presidential election years. The probability that this political injustice will soon be eliminated through state action or by national constitutional amendment fortunately appears to be good.[15]

---

[13] In Georgia a popular majority is still required for the choice of electors. If the popular vote fails to elect a majority of the electors, the legislature appoints them; otherwise, those electors chosen by majority vote appoint the remaining ones. *Georgia Code, Anno.*, (1935) Chap. 34, Secs. 2502–2504.

[14] *United States Code* (1964), Title 3. Sec. 1.

[15] In October, 1964, a suit was launched in a three-judge federal district court in Maryland seeking to have the state's residence requirement for otherwise qualified

It follows from what has been said that there are variations among the several states in requirements for participation in the choice of presidential electors, and through them, of the President. These differences are tending to become less marked; but the point remains that for purposes of filling the highest office in the nation the national electorate is only the sum total of the several variously composed state electorates. With the choosing of electors taking place by popular action throughout the country on the same day, to all appearances and purposes the President is now chosen in a great mass action by the people of the nation. The formal and official election does not come until the electors meet and perform their function and the official national canvass of the electoral votes is made by Congress; but in the popular mind and in a practical sense, the exercise of the franchise by the voters of the nation in November is the "presidential election."

CURRENT STATUS OF THE ELECTOR SYSTEM

The functioning of the electoral college machinery today is a matter of such routine and unnewsworthy nature that it receives little public notice, and the details of the electoral college procedure are a mystery to most citizens. It is generally understood that it is necessary for the presidential electors to go through the motions of recording the popular will in each state, but beyond that the average voter's understanding does not go. The essentially popular character of the presidential selection process rests upon a body of state laws and party usages governing the nomination, election and functioning of the electors.[16]

Nominations of slates of candidates for the elector posts, now regulated by law in most of the states, are usually made by state party conventions or party committees; but in a few states they are nominated at a direct party primary. Some states make provision for nominations of minor party and "independent" slates of elector candidates

---

voters declared void as far as voting for presidential electors is concerned. The effort was unsuccessful. Cf. *Drueding* v. *Devlin,* 234 F. Supp. 721 (1964); 380 U.S. 125 (1965); *The New York Times* March 2, 1965, p. 18. For discussion of the general problem see Morris Ogul, "Residence Requirements as Barriers to Voting in Presidential Elections," *Midwest Journal of Political Science,* Vol. III (August, 1959), pp. 254–262; "The Lost Voter," *National Civic Review,* Vol. LI (October, 1962), p. 480; and the remarks of Senator Keating of New York, and a study by the Legislative Reference Service in the *Congressional Record,* 87th Congress, 1st Session (1961), pp. 8303, 17141. There is a movement under way to deal with this problem by a national constitutional amendment.

[16] For surveys of state practices on this matter see Robert G. Dixon, "Electoral College Procedure," *Western Political Quarterly,* Vol. III (June, 1950), pp. 214–244; and Ruth C. Silva, "State Law on the Nomination, Election and Instruction of Presidential Electors," *American Political Science Review,* Vol. XLIII (June, 1948), pp. 523–529.

by use of the petition device. Pennsylvania has a unique system under which the presidential nominee of a party is required by law to designate the slate of presidential elector candidates for his party—a very logical arrangement in view of the role the elector is expected to play. State laws usually require only that presidential electors be duly qualified voters of the state; but the United States Constitution expressly prohibits any federal officer, including a member of Congress, from serving as an elector. A congressional district residence qualification is usually imposed by state law or by party usage for those electors representing House seats. In a number of states, by law or party usage, a test of party loyalty in the form of an oath concerning the elector's past voting record or party allegiance is imposed.

Until 1917, the complete lists of names of elector candidates appeared on the ballot in all states; in that year Nebraska adopted a "presidential short ballot" law under which the names of the elector candidates are omitted and there appear only the names of the presidential and vice presidential candidates, under the appropriate party caption. A popular vote for the presidential candidate is counted as a vote for his list of pledged electors. This ballot reform found favor rapidly, and now approximately three fourths of the states have adopted it.[17] In those states which still print the electoral candidates' names on the ballot, practice varies as to whether the names of presidential and vice presidential candidates also appear. It also varies with respect to requiring the voter to vote for an entire party slate of electors as a unit or permitting him to vote a split ticket for individual elector candidates. Any voter who votes a split ticket on presidential electors, of course, merely foolishly divides his vote among presidential candidates whose electors he supports in part. In a close popular vote in a state a small number of such split ballots among the elector candidates can result in the election of a politically divided elector delegation, even where the general ticket system is used. This result occurred in West Virginia in 1916, when seven Republican electors and one Democratic elector were chosen. It also occurred in California in the 1912 election, when 11 Progressive and two Democratic electors were chosen. In the 1960 election, only five of the electors running on the Democratic ballot in Alabama were pledged to support the party's nominees for President and Vice President, while six were "unpledged." All 11 Democratic electors were elected. Senator John F. Kennedy received the votes of the five pledged electors, while the six unpledged electors voted for Senator Harry F. Byrd of Virginia. In no state is it

17 *The Book of the States, 1962–1963* (Chicago: Council of State Governments), p. 16. See also L. E. Aylesworth, "The Presidential Ballot," *American Political Science Review*, Vol. XVIII (February, 1923), pp. 89–96; and "The Presidential Short Ballot," *ibid.*, Vol. XXIV (November, 1930), pp. 966–970; S. D. Albright, "The Presidential Short Ballot," *ibid.*, Vol. XXXIV, (October, 1940), pp. 955–959.

possible, however, for a voter to split his ballot by voting for a presidential candidate of one party and a vice presidential candidate of another. He actually can vote directly only for electors rather than for the presidential and vice presidential nominees.

National law now provides[18] that the electors in each state shall meet for the purpose of casting their ballots on the first Monday after the second Wednesday in December following the November election. The actual hour of meeting, as well as the place, which is commonly the state legislative chambers, the governor's office, or the office of the secretary of state, is governed by state law. If there are vacancies in the electoral delegation, a not uncommon occurrence,[19] the laws of most of the states now provide that substitutes may be appointed by those electors present.

A formal procedure, often involving an address of greeting by the governor or the secretary of state, election of officers, adoption of rules, as well as presentation and authentication of credentials, is observed by the elector groups. Several hours may be spent in meeting. The essential function—casting votes for President and Vice President —is the climax of these activities, and is performed in a matter of minutes. No deliberation is necessary. Various methods of balloting— oral voting, voting by signed ballots, voting by unsigned ballots accompanied by oral announcement, or voting by secret written ballot— are used, depending upon the custom or law of the state. An authenticated statement of the ballot result is dispatched to the President of the United States Senate and copies are also sent to the state's secretary of state, to the United States General Services Administrator, and to the federal district court of the district in which the electors meet. In most states a small compensation in the form of a per diem payment ranging from five to twenty dollars, plus a mileage allowance, is paid the electors for performance of these technically important duties. Having performed their essential function, the electors, like the May fly, promptly fade away into the obscurity from which they were called.

It has become one of the great constitutional usages that an elector is honor-bound to vote for the candidates of his party as determined by

18 *United States Code,* (1958), Title 3, Sec. 7. This law was enacted in 1934 following adoption of the Twentieth Amendment to the Constitution which changed the date of the beginning of a President's term of office from March 4 to January 20.

19 In seven of the first ten presidential elections one or more electoral votes were lost by reason of the failure of duly chosen electors to appear and cast their votes. A survey showed that in the 1948 election, one or more substitute electors had to be appointed in at least 18 of the states because of the failure of some of the chosen electors to appear or qualify. Seven substitutes had to be named in Virginia, six in Michigan, and five in Illinois. Dixon, *op. cit.,* p. 219. The presidential elector law of North Carolina provides that any person who, after having been elected to the post of elector, without valid reason fails to carry out his duty shall be subject to a $500 fine. *North Carolina General Statutes* (1952), Vol. 3C, Div. XVIII, chap. 163, Sec. 112.

the national party convention, but this remains only a custom that can be successfully defied by an elector if he so chooses. A number of states have enacted laws which implicitly or explicitly bind electoral candidates, if chosen as members of a party slate, to observe this usage; but these laws are of doubtful validity.[20] The United States Supreme Court has ruled that a state may empower a party instrumentality, such as a state party convention or executive committee, to impose and enforce a test of party loyalty on an individual nominated for presidential elector to insure his casting his votes for the party's official candidates;[21] but this method of compelling observance of the generally respected usage has been demonstrated to be ineffective.

To show his independence in the face of such a restriction, one of the regular Democratic party's slate of electors in 1956 cast his presidential vote for Judge Walter B. Jones of Alabama and his vice presidential vote for Governor Herman Talmadge of Georgia, rather than for the regular party nominees, Governor Adlai Stevenson and Senator Estes Kefauver. Without challenge in the official canvass by Congress his votes were counted as cast. Again in 1960, one of the Oklahoma Republican electors jumped the party traces and cast his presidential ballot for Senator Harry F. Byrd and his vice presidential ballot for Senator Barry Goldwater of Arizona, rather than for the regular nominees, Vice President Richard Nixon and former Senator Henry Cabot Lodge. His votes were recorded as cast, although in accepting nomination as an elector he had pledged himself to vote for the regular Republican nominees.[22] In the 1960 election eight electors

[20] An Alabama statutes of this character enacted in 1945 was held invalid by the Alabama Supreme Court on the ground that the legislature lacked power to control an elector's exercise of power conferred on him by the United States Constitution. *In re Opinion of the Justices,* 250 Ala. 339, 34 So. (2nd) 598 (1948). The statute was not repealed, however, and immediately after the 1948 election in which States Rights electors were chosen on the regular Democratic ballot, an attempt was made by the "loyalist" Democratic faction to enforce it, or the usage it was based upon, by compelling the electors chosen on the Democratic party's ballot to vote for the party candidates nominated by the National Democratic Party Convention. These attempts failed in both federal and state courts. See *State* v. *Albritton,* 251 Ala. 422, 37 So. (2nd) 640, *cert. den.;* 335 U.S. 887 (1948); and *Folsom* v. *Albritton,* 335 U.S. 822 and *Adcock* v. *Albritton,* 335 U.S. 822 (1948).

[21] *Ray* v. *Blair,* 343 U.S. 154, 214 (1952), overruling 257 Ala. 151, 57 So. (2nd) 395. See also *Seay* v. *Latham,* 143 Tex. 1, 182 S.W. (2nd) 251 (1944).

[22] The elector involved, Henry D. Irwin, insisted he had carried out his pledge to vote for the Republican party nominees when he voted for the Republican slate of electors, which included his own name. Irwin's defection was the only result of a bizarre campaign launched by an Alabama lawyer, R. Lea Harris, in the period between the November election and the time of voting by the electors. Harris sent out letters to all the 537 electors, suggesting the advisability of all the Republican electors combining with southern conservative Democratic electors in support of a conservative candidate, such as Senator Byrd or Senator Goldwater, for President. The movement, of course, failed; but Harris and others immediately began to lay plans for electing uncommitted elector slates in a number of states in 1964. An uncommitted slate of electors was nominated in Alabama in the 1964 election, but was

in Mississippi and six in Alabama who were explicitly *not* pledged to vote for any particular candidate for President were chosen in those states. They cast their presidential votes for Senator Byrd, who was not an avowed candidate. In 1964, voters in Alabama had no opportunity at all to vote for a slate of electors pledged to support the Democratic party's nominee, President Johnson.

On the day fixed by national law, now January 6,[23] the President of the United States Senate (i.e., the Vice President), in accordance with the mandate of the Constitution, opens the certificates sent in by the various state groups of electors and in the presence of both houses of Congress the electoral votes are counted. Two tellers from each house, one from each of the two major parties, are designated to examine the lists and compile the totals. Upon completion of the count the result is announced formally by the President of the Senate, and committees of the two houses are named to give official notice of election to the victorious candidates. The announcement, needless to say, comes as no surprise to the candidates or to the nation. If the electoral vote should fail to be conclusive, or if dispute should arise as to the validity of the votes of some of the electors, the formal canvass may become only the prelude to the final drama of the election, in which the members of the House or the Senate become the principal actors.

INCONCLUSIVE AND DISPUTED GUBERNATORIAL ELECTIONS

Popular government depends upon what might be termed "political sportsmanship." Its postulate is that the results of an official canvass in an electoral contest, carried on in conformity with an agreed upon set of rules, will be accepted by all concerned. It assumes that competition for the prize of political office is not a life and death struggle. The competing interests are expected to accept the verdict of the electoral process quietly, if not gracefully. The losers are not to appeal from ballots to bullets and the winners are not to interpret their victory as a mandate to annihilate the opposition.

Through the year 1964, 45 presidential elections and some 2900 gubernatorial elections have been conducted in this country. Three of these presidential elections—those of 1800, 1824, and 1876—produced

---

not elected. For an account of the 1960 episode see *Nomination and Election of the President and the Vice President,* Hearings before the Sub-Committee on Constitutional Amendments of the Senate Judiciary Committee, 87th Congress, 1st Session (1961), Part 3, pp. 562ff.

[23] *United States Code* (1964), Title 3, Sec. 15. In 1957, because January 6 fell on a Sunday, the date was temporarily changed to January 7.

crises in that they required intervention by Congress to resolve the issue. Some 60 gubernatorial elections, all in the New England states, have had to be resolved by the legislature under the rule that if no candidate receives a popular majority, the legislature shall determine the outcome. In the vast majority of instances the verdict as rendered by the people or their agents has been accepted without an appeal to violence. This has been true even when the results have been so close that the victorious candidate has had only a paper-thin margin of victory. One of the most noteworthy instances of acceptance of the popular verdict occurred in Massachusetts in 1839. In that year the Democratic candidate for governor, Marcus Morton, was found on the official canvass to have received a popular majority by only one vote in the statewide voting. Morton was allowed to take office without a challenge.

There have been a number of instances in the choosing of governors in which the officially announced results have been challenged by the losers or the electoral machinery has not been allowed to function in a normal manner. Violent controversies over the outcome of such elections have had a variety of settings and causes. Some have been merely the outward manifestations of deep social and political cleavages which have produced rival governments, each claiming constitutional legitimacy. Such was the nature of the so-called "Dorr's Rebellion" in Rhode Island in the 1840s which for a few weeks threatened to plunge that small commonwealth into bloody civil war.[24] The series of rival state governments, each headed by a governor and complements of other officers, which came into existence during the Civil War in Missouri, Tennessee, Kentucky, Virginia, Louisiana, and other states, also belong in this category. For the states which had been members of the Confederacy, the end of the war brought a temporary suspension in some measure of the normal processes of choosing governors. Governors elected under secessionist auspices were either arrested and removed or forced to resign. Provisional governors appointed by the President and later, in some instances, military governors, took their places. Governors elected under revised state constitutions eventually replaced these appointed military governors. After 1876, following the withdrawal of federal troops from the South, full local control over the choice of governors was restored. Relaxation of national control immediately led to election disputes involving the governorship in three of these states—Louisiana, South Carolina, and Florida. Governors who had been declared elected under federal auspices were ousted in each case.

One of the most violent of these Reconstruction period disputes,

[24] See Arthur M. Mowry, *The Dorr War or the Constitutional Struggle in Rhode Island* (Providence: Preston and Rounds Company, 1901).

known locally as the "Brooks-Baxter War," originated in Arkansas following the 1872 election. Elisha Baxter and Joseph Brooks, the rival Republican claimants for the governorship, and their followers conducted a guerilla war against one another for several months. A score or more persons were killed or wounded.[25]

LEGISLATIVE DEADLOCKS AND DISPUTES

Provisions in state constitutions for majority popular vote requirements, with an alternative of legislative choice in the event the popular vote is not conclusive, have been a fruitful source of difficulty in connection with gubernatorial elections. Clauses imposing on the legislature the duty of canvassing the results of the voting—that is, of serving as the official judge and declarer of the results—have likewise produced conflicts and irregularities. On several occasions in the New England states these provisions have resulted in legislative deadlocks of one kind or another, completely frustrating the elective process. For example, in 1832 and again in 1839 the Rhode Island legislature found itself unable to elect a governor when the choice devolved upon it. In the first instance the officers previously elected were allowed to hold over for another term; in the other the senior senator served as acting governor for a full term. It was against this background of legislative intransigence that the movement for constitutional reform culminating in the Dorr Rebellion took form.

Again in 1892 the two houses of the Rhode Island legislature were unable to agree on a joint meeting to declare the result of the popular election because the lower house insisted upon first unseating certain of its own members, an action which would have had a direct bearing upon the functioning of the two houses as an electoral body. In this contingency the supreme court of the state held that the election had not been consummated. It ruled further that the legislature had been validly adjourned for its entire session by action of the incumbent governor, who continued in office for another full term.[26] In 1890 the popular election result in Connecticut was nullified when one house of the legislature insisted on an investigation of alleged ballot frauds before meeting with the other house for the purpose of declaring the result of the election. The Connecticut Supreme Court ruled that a declaration of the result by the legislature was necessary to give validity to the popular election. Since this had not been made within the time limit prescribed by the state constitution, there had been no election.

25 For detailed accounts of the incident see John M. Harrell, *The Brooks and Baxter War: A History of the Reconstruction Period in Arkansas* (St. Louis: Slawson Printing Co., 1893); and James H. Atkinson, "The Brooks-Baxter Contest," *The Arkansas Historical Quarterly*, Vol. IV, (Summer, 1945), pp. 124–149.

26 *In re the Legislative Adjournment*, 18 R.I. 824, 27 Atl. 324, (1893).

The incumbent governor, who had been defeated on the face of the returns in the popular voting, was allowed to hold over for another term.[27] He governed the state without the assistance of a legislature for the full term.

Constitutional provisions or laws making the state legislature the agency for settling issues arising out of allegations of fraud on the part of one of the contestants have also given rise to a number of bitter controversies. Two of the most notorious contested gubernatorial elections involving the legislature in this fashion were the so-called "Buckshot War" incident in Pennsylvania in 1838–1839, and the "Goebel Affair" in Kentucky at the turn of the present century. The Pennsylvania controversy was bloodless despite the suggestion of sanguinary conflict conveyed by its title.[28] The Goebel incident in Kentucky was much more violent. Goebel, the Democratic candidate whom the legislature insisted upon seating in the governor's chair despite a ruling of the state canvassing board that his opponent had been elected, was assassinated on the steps of the state's Capitol. The Democratic lieutenant governor whom the legislature had installed along with Goebel succeeded to the office. His title to it was upheld by the state supreme court.[29] This incident continued to inflame Kentucky politics for years thereafter.

The most bitter recent controversy arising from a legislature's attempt to intervene in a gubernatorial election arose in Georgia following the 1946 election. In the popular voting a former governor, Eugene Talmadge, who had no regular Republican opposition, received an overwhelming majority of the popular votes, but he died before the official result was received and proclaimed by the legislature as required by the state constitution. In this contingency the legislature asserted a right to elect a governor on the ground that there had been no choice under the majority vote rule. It elected Herman Talmadge, Eugene's son, who had received a few hundred write-in votes at the November election. Eventually the supreme court of the state overruled the legislature's action and held that the newly elected lieutenant governor should act as governor until the next general election, at which

[27] *State ex rel Morris* v. *Bulkeley*, 61 Conn. 287, 23 Atl. 186, (1892).

[28] Cf. William H. Egle, "The Buckshot War," *The Pennsylvania Magazine of History and Biography*, Vol. 23 (1899), pp. 137–156. The incident became known as the Buckshot War because militiamen who had been called into service by the outgoing governor, one of the chief figures in the electoral controversy, were ordered to supply themselves with buckshot ammunition.

[29] *Taylor and Marshall* v. *Beckham*, 108 Ky. 278, 56 S.W. 177 (1900); affirmed, 178 U.S. 548 (1900). Taylor, Goebel's Republican opponent, fled to Indiana to escape prosecution for complicity in the assassination; but Caleb Powers, the Republican secretary of state and one of his aides were indicted for murder. After four trials they were eventually convicted and sentenced to life imprisonment. For an account of the affair see Thomas D. Clark, *A History of Kentucky* (Englewood Cliffs, N.J.: Prentice-Hall, 1937), pp. 605–617.

time a governor should be chosen in the regular manner to fill out the remaining two years of the current term.[30] This disposition of the matter was accepted quietly by the contending interests.

State experience points rather clearly toward the conclusion that there is a considerable risk of partisan political manipulation and frustration of the popular will in entrusting to the state legislature the responsibility for electing the governor when no majority choice has emerged. The same conclusion applies where the constitution invests the legislature with authority to conduct recounts and to make the official determination of the results. The stakes are too high for partisan-oriented state legislators to be expected always to resolve such issues on a fair, impartial basis. If it is deemed essential that a majority popular mandate be given a candidate to make him a winner, it would be preferable to require a runoff election between the two highest candidates in the initial voting rather than to make the legislative body the agency for declaring the public's will. Contested elections involving allegations of fraud in the popular balloting can be better handled through an administrative body functioning under the supervision and control of the courts.

Where the legislature is the vehicle for resolving gubernatorial election contests, state courts have as a general rule taken the position that the conclusions arrived at by the legislature as the head of a co-ordinate branch of government are "political" decisions lying outside the competence of the judicial authorities to review or examine. They have displayed no eagerness to rush into this "political thicket." Thus in the case arising out of the Goebel affair, the supreme court of Kentucky declared:

> The Judiciary have no power to sit in judgment upon the motives of an independent branch of the government, or to deny legal effect

[30] *Thompson v. Talmadge,* 201 Ga. 867, 41 S.E. (2nd) 833 (1947). Article V, Sec. 1, par. IV of the Georgia constitution provides that in the event no candidate is found to have received a popular majority, the legislature shall elect as the governor one of the "two persons having the highest number who shall be in life." Herman Talmadge, who by virtue of his write-in votes was the second highest in number of votes received, maintained that no election by a majority had taken place and that he was one of the two eligibles who might be chosen by the legislature. The legislature agreed and proceeded to elect him. The incumbent governor, Ellis Arnall, refused to recognize the validity of this action by the legislature. Citing another provision of the state constitution that a governor shall hold office "during a term of four years, and until his successor shall be chosen and qualified," he refused to vacate his office at the expiration of his term. For a brief time there were thus three claimants to the office—Herman Talmadge, Arnall, and the newly elected lieutenant governor, Thompson. Talmadge, assisted by some highway patrol officers, forcibly ejected Arnall from his quarters in the Capitol. After a few days Arnall resigned, leaving the issue to be contested in the courts by Thompson and Talmadge.

to the record of its action solemnly made by it pursuant to the Constitution. . . . We have no more right to supervise the decision of the General Assembly in determining the result of this election than we have to supervise the action of the Governor in calling a special session of the Legislature, or in pardoning a criminal, or the action of the Legislature in contracting debts, or determining the election of its members, or doing any other act authorized by the Constitution.[31]

However, state courts do not always stand aloof and let the state legislature work its will in resolving contested gubernatorial elections. In a contest proceeding in Colorado, for example, the state supreme court ruled that the legislature had no power to dispose of the matter before it by voiding the election altogether.[32] The Missouri supreme court acted to forestall a gubernatorial contest proceeding in the legislature following the 1940 election. The official canvass showed that the Republican candidate had received a plurality of 3613 votes over his Democratic adversary; but a petition for a recount had been presented and the Democratic-controlled House had sought to prepare the way for a contest proceeding by instructing its Speaker not to open and publish the results of the popular voting before a joint assembly of the two houses, as required by the state constitution. The court, holding that the Speaker's duty in this regard was purely ministerial, issued a peremptory writ of mandamus to the Speaker ordering him to comply with the constitutional procedure.[33] The contest proceedings were dropped.

In a number of instances state courts have assumed jurisdiction in cases questioning the finality of decisions by state canvassing boards on exclusion or inclusion of certain ballots in the statewide vote totals. They have also acted under laws empowering the courts themselves to conduct recounts. In an early Wisconsin case of this kind the state supreme court entertained a *quo warranto* proceeding against an incumbent governor who had been declared elected by the state canvassing board and had assumed office. On the basis of evidence presented to it, the court overruled the board on the counting of certain questioned ballots, thereby reversing the statewide result. It issued an ouster order against the incumbent in favor of his opponent.[34]

[31] *Taylor and Beckham*, 108 Ky. 278 (1900). For other cases in which state courts refused to interfere with legislative determination of governorship election contests see *State* v. *Baxter*, 28 Ark. 129 (1873) and *Baxter* v. *Brooks*, 29 Ark. 173 (1874); *Ex parte Norris*, 8 So. Car. 408 (1877) and *Ex parte Smith*, 8 So. Car. 495 (1877); *Goff* v. *Wilson*, 32 W. Va. 393 (1889) and *Carr* v. *Wilson*, 32 W. Va. 419 (1899); *State ex rel Morris* v. *Bulkeley*, 61 Conn. 287 (1892).

[32] *In re Senate Resolution No. 10, Concerning Governorship Contest*, 33 Colo. 307 (1905). The legislature subsequently resolved the contest by unseating Alva Adams, the Democratic candidate who had been declared elected on the basis of the official canvass, and seating his opponent, Republican James H. Peabody.

[33] *State ex rel Donnell* v. *Osborn*, 347 Mo. 469, 147 S.W. (2nd) 1065 (1941).

[34] *Attorney General ex rel Bashford* v. *Barstow*, 4 Wis. 567 (1856). The state canvassing board had ruled that William Barstow, incumbent Democrat, had won

Gubernatorial election results as reported and certified by state canvassing boards have been reversed by court action in Florida following the 1876 election;[35] in Arizona (1916);[36] in Rhode Island (1956);[37] and in Minnesota (1962).[37a] In numerous other instances recounts conducted under statutory arrangements making possible ultimate resort to the courts have failed to upset the outcome of elections as determined by administrative authorities.

The key to the problem of resolving such disputes would appear to lie in not assigning to the legislature the role of a residual electoral body; keeping out of its hands the responsibility for resolving disputes arising out of alleged election irregularities; and adopting a code of election administration laws calculated to insure an honest and fair casting and counting of the popular votes. Considerable progress in eliminating fraud, intimidation, and dishonest practices generally in state election law administration has undoubtedly been made since the introduction of the Australian ballot system a half century or more ago; but the ideal of an absolutely honest and accurate poll in the election of governors has by no means been fully attained. It should be observed that the same problems which make for difficulty in assuring fair and honest gubernatorial elections appear also in connection with the choosing of the President. Presidential electors, as well as governors, are chosen by statewide popular vote. The methods employed to insure an accurate poll and canvass in conducting statewide elections for the governorship have relevancy to choosing of presidential electors as well.

Given the elements of possible human error, along with the inevitable partisan and personal interests of officials charged with administration of even the best of election laws in contests where the political stakes are high, no perfect method of attaining an absolutely impartial, honest, and accurate poll may be possible. Even courts are subject to partisan pressure and bias. In a very close statewide election, although the element of deliberate fraud may be reduced to a mini-

---

the election with plurality of 167 votes over Coles Bashford. As a result of the contest proceeding Bashford became the first Republican to be elected governor in Wisconsin.

35 *State ex rel Derw* v. *State Canvassing Board,* 16 Fla. 17 (1876).

36 *Campbell* v. *Hunt,* 18 Ariz. 442, 162 Pac. 882 (1917); and *Hunt* v. *Campbell,* 19 Ariz. 254, 169 Pac. 596 (1917). Hunt, who was ultimately declared to be the winner, served only the last 11 months of the two-year term for which he was elected.

37 *Roberts* v. *Board of Elections,* 129 Atl. (2nd) 330 (1957). The issue turned on the meaning of a constitutional amendment authorizing absentee voting by civilians and members of the armed services. The court held that the legislature had authority to provide for the casting of absentee ballots by civilians only if they were cast on election day. This had the effect of invalidating most of the 8600 civilian absentee ballots which the election board had ordered included in the count, and thereby caused the result of the election to be reversed.

37a *In re Application of Andersen; Rolvaag* v. *Donovan,* 264 Minn. 257, 119 NW (2nd) 1 (1962).

mum, unintentional error or unconscious bias may still be a decisive factor.[38] The outcome of a presidential election nationally may turn on the accuracy of the canvass of the popular votes for electors in a single state. Machinery must be provided through which a review of the official canvass in any state may be had. In the long run the ultimate safeguard against political turmoil in the choosing of chief executives is a willingness of the people to abide by the results of elections, as determined by established rules, imperfect through they may be. Faith in the essential honesty of the elective process is the foundation upon which democracy rests.

INCONCLUSIVE AND DISPUTED PRESIDENTIAL ELECTIONS

Three presidential elections—those of 1800, 1824, and 1876—have been so unusual as to justify reference to them as "election crises." The first two grew out of provisions in the Constitution making the House of Representatives the residual electoral body in the event that voting by presidential electors fails to produce a definitive choice. The 1876 crisis was a result of irregularities in some states in the selection of presidential electors. It raised the problem of the nature of the powers of Congress as the body entrusted by the Constitution with canvassing the votes of the electors and declaring the result. As has been pointed out above, these are the kinds of contingencies which have also caused the states the greatest difficulty in the selection of governors. In each of the presidential election crises, determination of the outcome was delayed until shortly before the term of the incumbent President was to terminate; and the nation faced the possibility of finding itself without a president-elect to take over.

As has been seen, the states have moved toward eliminating the cause of these troubles by changes in the manner by which governors are chosen and the results of elections determined. The role of the legislature as a direct participant in the gubernatorial election process has been eliminated, or practically so, in most of the states. To some extent, the three presidential election crises also produced some remedial action; but the fundamental conditions which gave rise to them still remain. The Congress still has a potentially significant role to play in the presidential election process. The 1800 election crisis, as has been noted above, brought about adoption of the Twelfth Amendment designed to eliminate the particular difficulty involved—

[38] For a detailed study of two recent gubernatorial election recounts in Michigan and the types of counting errors they revealed see Samuel J. Eldersveld and Albert A. Applegate, *Michigan Recounts for Governor, 1950–1952: A Systematic Analysis of Election Error* (Ann Arbor: University of Michigan Press, 1954). Neither recount resulted in reversal of the originally declared result.

the manner of voting for President and Vice President by the electors. The 1824 election crisis was followed by introduction of new devices for effecting party nominations for the presidency and by extension of the principle of popular election in choosing presidential electors into all states. The 1876 crisis was followed by enactment of a federal statute of dubious constitutionality designed to meet the problem of disputes between the two houses of Congress in determining the validity of electoral votes cast by individual states. But the roots of the difficulties still are untouched. The possibility of a shattering dispute over the outcome of a presidential election still remains to haunt the nation.

THE ELECTION OF 1824

The presidential election of 1824 was unusual because for the first and only time after 1800 there was a temporary lapse in two-party competition for the office of President. The Federalist party had disappeared from the scene, leaving the field to the Jeffersonian Republicans. There was no single accepted agency for determining the party's nominees for President and Vice President, although the party's congressional caucus which had more or less fulfilled this role in previous elections continued to function in this capacity. Four candidates, all members of the same party, were put forward by their respective factions, with elector slates pledged to them. They were General Andrew Jackson of Tennessee, John Quincy Adams of Massachusetts, Senator William H. Crawford of Georgia (the congressional caucus candidate), and Henry Clay of Kentucky. It was an independent voter's "dream election"—each candidate ran on a personal platform and a choice among them had to be registered without taking into account his political party.

The electoral college voting gave Jackson 99 votes, Adams 83, Crawford 41, and Clay 37. Under the terms of the Constitution the responsibility for determination of the final outcome fell upon the House of Representatives, with each state delegation voting as a unit. Clay, who as Speaker of the House had great influence and popularity there, might have emerged the victor had he been eligible; but voting in the House had to be confined to the three highest in the electoral voting. Partly because Clay threw his influence behind Adams, the latter was elected.

In the balloting by the House it was necessary for a candidate to obtain the votes of a majority of the states, i.e., 13, to win. Several state delegations were composed of single individuals, giving them equal voting power with those of large delegations from the more populous states. These individual congressmen, particularly those from Illinois and Missouri, were subjected to intense pressure by the backers of Jackson and Adams. Although Missouri's voters had given that state's three electoral votes to Jackson, the Missouri representative, John Scott, was induced to cast Missouri's vote for Adams. For this act of alleged political treachery, he was retired permanently from public life by the voters of his state at the next election.

As the balloting proceeded in the House of Representatives it was expected that the New York delegation of 26 members would be evenly divided between Adams and Crawford, which would nullify the state's presidential vote on the first ballot and prevent the election of Adams, who needed New York's vote for the necessary 13 state votes. The uncertain element in the New York delegation was General Van Rensselaer, an old Revolutionary War veteran who was wavering between Adams and Crawford. If he voted for the latter, the vote of his state would be nullified because of an equal division of the delegation and no choice would be effected on this ballot. If he voted for Adams, New York's vote would go to Adams, and with it, the presidency. A biographer of Jackson has described the dramatic denouement in this fashion:

> State delegations were directed to poll their members. As the New Yorkers' box was passed General Van Rensselaer dropped his head on the edge of his desk in silent appeal to his Maker. Removing his hand from his eyes he saw at his feet a discarded Adams ballot. Accepting this as an answer to his prayer, the old man picked up the ticket and dropped it in the box. This act gave Mr. Adams a majority of one in the New York delegation, and the vote of that state.[39]

This is the way a President may be made by the creaking machinery handed down from a day when faith in the ability of the people to select their President was weak!

Following the 1824 election a number of developments occurred which had the effect of correcting some of the weaknesses revealed by that election. The movement to place the choice of electors in the hands of the voters directly, which all the states had not yet provided for, was carried forward apace. Only South Carolina retained the principle of legislative appointment for long thereafter and that state abandoned the practice after 1865.[40] The significance of this development upon the office of President was profound, as has been noted. Introduction of the national party convention in place of "King Caucus" as an instrumentality for nominating presidential candidates, along with a restoration of two-party competition, was achieved during the 1830s. The triumphant election of Jackson to the presidency in

[39] Marquis James, *The Life of Andrew Jackson* (Indianapolis: The Bobbs-Merrill Company, 1938), p. 439.

[40] In the 1876 election the newly admitted state of Colorado found it necessary to utilize legislative appointment of its electors because there was not sufficient time to enact legislation providing for a popular vote for them in the election of that year.

1828 was a belated reminder that a candidate, even though he was favored by only a national popular plurality, would have been preferable to a candidate who had finished second in the popular voting in 1824. Adoption of the Twentieth Amendment in 1933, which moved forward the date of assumption of office by a newly chosen Congress, looked toward correction of another weakness in the electoral machinery revealed by the 1824 election. Under the new arrangement, choice of a President in the event this responsibility should devolve upon the House of Representatives would be made by members chosen at the same time the presidential electors are chosen rather than by a "lame duck" House elected two years before.

THE PRESIDENTIAL ELECTORAL DISPUTE OF 1876

The election crisis of 1876 clearly proved the determination of the American people to avoid at all costs resort to violence in resolving a disputed election. Even though the issues involved were settled in a way that appeared to many to be a high-handed thwarting of the will of the majority, the settlement was accepted. A candidate who had received approximately a quarter of a million fewer popular votes than his adversary was installed in office by a procedure that carried an aura of legitimacy only under a most generous view of the meaning of that term.

The root of the 1876 electoral dispute difficulty lay in the vagueness of the constitutional provisions regarding the choosing of presidential electors and the manner by which Congress is to conduct the electoral vote canvass. The Constitution in Article II and the Twelfth Amendment merely declares that each state shall "appoint, in such manner as the legislature thereof may direct," its electors. It then goes on to specify that after the electors have cast their votes, certificates of their actions shall be directed to the President of the Senate who shall "in the presence of the Senate and House of Representatives, open all the certificates, and the votes shall then be counted."

These cryptic statements leave unsettled a number of important questions: (1) the authority of Congress, if any, to "go behind" the credentials of any individuals claiming to have authority to act as electors and to examine the regularity of their "appointment" and their eligibility to serve as electors; (2) the details of the procedure by which the official count shall be conducted; and (3) the respective roles and powers of the President of the Senate and of the two houses of Congress in relation to the count. Difficulties involving these points had been encountered in conducting the electoral count on a number of occasions prior to 1876; but as the questioned electoral votes had not been crucial, the controversies had been resolved in ways that permitted Congress to evade the basic issues.[41]

Anticipating that the question would arise whether it should receive and count electoral votes from Tennessee and Louisiana, where there were at the time rival state governments supported by Union and Confederate military forces respectively, prior to the 1864 election Congress passed and President Lincoln reluctantly signed a resolution stating that no electoral votes would be received or counted from these or any of the other nine states of the southern Confederacy in the presidential election of that year.[42] Immediately prior to conducting the count the two houses also adopted the so-called "Twenty-second Joint Rule," which specified that no electoral vote should be received and counted from any state "except by the concurring votes of the two houses."

Shortly before the 1876 election this Twenty-second Joint Rule was repudiated by the Senate; but the two houses had been unable to agree upon a new understanding in its place. Strong doubts were entertained by many members of Congress concerning the power of Congress to act upon the subject at all so as to disfranchise any state in the electoral college. The results of that election presented the whole issue of the manner of conducting the count in such a way that further evasion was impossible.

Upon the basis of electoral vote returns Governor Samuel Tilden of New York, the Democratic candidate, received 184 uncontested electoral votes, with 185 being necessary for a majority. Governor Rutherford Hayes of Ohio, the Republican candidate, received 165 uncontested electoral votes; but dual electoral returns had been received from Florida, with four electors, Louisiana with eight, South Carolina with seven, and Oregon with respect to one of its three electoral votes.[43] If any one of the 20 disputed votes should be assigned to

---

[41] For a detailed account of congressional practice in the counting of the electoral vote up to 1876 see J. Hampden Dougherty, *The Electoral System of the United States* (New York: G. P. Putnam's Sons, 1906), especially Chaps. II–IV.

[42] *Ibid.*, pp. 75–80. The 1864 election was the first one in which Congress excluded the electoral votes of any state. In 1820 the electoral votes of Missouri and in 1836 the electoral votes of Michigan—states which were in process of admission to the Union but had not been finally proclaimed as states prior to the date of the election—were counted "in the alternative"; that is to say, two results were announced, one including the questionable votes and the other excluding them. The same technique of avoidance was employed by Congress after the 1856 election when the Wisconsin electors were prevented by a blizzard from meeting and casting their votes on the specific day prescribed by national law for them to do so. *Ibid.*, pp. 42, 48, 51.

[43] In Florida the Hayes electors had been declared elected by the state canvassing board and had cast their votes on the prescribed day. The Tilden electors, having instituted a contest proceeding in the courts, also cast their votes. The Florida

Tilden, he would have a majority and be elected. If any disputed votes were thrown out so that neither candidate received an electoral majority, the outcome would be resolved by the House, voting by state units. The House was controlled by the Democrats, and it presumably would elect Tilden if given the chance. The Senate was controlled by the Republicans.

Anticipating that difficulty would arise in conducting the electoral count, the two houses soon after they convened in December in 1876 set up a special joint committee to study the problem and propose a procedure for dealing with it. Following the recommendations of the committee, Congress enacted a most extraordinary law on the subject on January 29, 1877, before the count was made. By this Electoral Commission Act a body was set up to be composed of 15 members, of whom five were to be selected by the House from its membership, five from the Senate chosen by it from its membership, and five Justices of the Supreme Court, four of whom were named in the Act.[44] The law provided that any differences between the two houses on the counting

---

Supreme Court eventually sustained the claims of the Tilden electors, as did also the Florida legislature in a recanvass. There was also a question of the eligibility of one of the Hayes electors, who was alleged to have been a United States shipping commissioner at the time of his appointment.

The validity of the vote by the Hayes electors in Louisiana was questioned on the ground that the state canvassing board had thrown out the popular vote in certain parishes so as to diminish the totals for Democratic electors by 13,000 and for the Republican electors by only 2000, and on the further ground that it had counted some 12,000 ballots as cast for all the Republican electors in certain parishes where the ballots bore the names of only three of them. Two of the Republican electors were also alleged to have been ineligible by reason of being federal officeholders at the time of their election. This was the point on which the one Oregon electoral vote was challenged. As in the case of the two challenged Louisiana electors, the Oregon elector in question had been appointed by the other electors to the vacancy created by his own ineligibility; but in the case of the two Louisiana electors it was not clear whether they had in the meantime divested themselves of their federal offices. This the Oregon elector had done.

Double returns came from South Carolina because judicial proceedings had been instituted by the Tilden electors, who maintained that the Hayes electors were improperly certified. It was contended that there had been no valid election because there was no registration law in force at the time of voting and there had been interference with a free expression of the people's will by federal military and civil authorities in the course of the election.

44 The Commission was made up of three Democrats and two Republicans from the House, three Republicans and two Democrats from the Senate, four members of the Supreme Court named in the Act, of whom two were presumed to be Republicans and two Democrats, with a fifth member of the Court to be selected by these four. It was expected that the fifth Supreme Court member would be Justice David Davis, of Illinois, a Union Democrat who had been named by Lincoln to the Court and whose background was such as to suggest that his attitude would be reasonably free of partisan bias; but on January 25, shortly before the Commission was organized, he was elected to the Senate as a Democrat by the Illinois legislature. He promply resigned his Supreme Court seat, and his intended place was filled by Justice Joseph Bradley of New Jersey, an "independent" Republican, who voted with the Republican members of the Commission on all crucial issues.

of any state's electoral votes could be referred to this Commission. Its recommendations would be controlling unless rejected by Congress. This extraordinary piece of temporary legislation, which begged the constitutional question of the powers of Congress in the matter of the electoral count by clothing the Commission "with the same powers, if any, now possessed for that purpose by the two Houses acting separately or together," specified that any finding by the Commission would stand unless rejected by *both* houses.

In each of the four cases the dispute was referred to the Commission. Its findings, which followed partisan lines on crucial issues, were that the votes of the Hayes electors should be received in every instance. Under the terms of the act establishing the Commission the findings of the Electoral Commission stood as the final disposition, despite the fact that the House of Representatives was in disagreement with some of them. This result was confirmed only after certain patronage concessions and a promise of withdrawal of the remaining federal troops from the South had been given to Democratic House leaders by spokesmen for the prospective new Republican administration. Hayes was declared the winner on the basis of an electoral vote margin of 185 to 184. Even though the Electoral Commission Act reserved to the contestants the right to question in the federal courts titles to the offices of President and Vice President if these offices were awarded to their adversaries, neither Governor Tilden nor his vice presidential running mate availed themselves of this opportunity. Thus a crisis that could have kept the country in further suspense while the issue was appealed to the courts, and might possibly have brought about civil strife, was resolved peaceably.

Whether the decisions of the Electoral Commission were in accord with law, political justice, and fairness or were motivated unduly by partisanship continues to be a matter of opinion.[45] The principles by which the majority of the Commission professed to be guided were that it should not go behind the acts of a lawfully constituted state authority deemed to be the appropriate agency for certifying the election of electors, nor should it investigate and resolve any question regarding the eligibility of any elector once his appointment had been certified by proper state authorities and he had cast his vote according to law. On the question of whether Congress had authority to go beyond these limits, the Commission did not vouchsafe an answer.

Following the settlement of the 1876 contest, Congress at once undertook the task of enacting permanent legislation to deal with the

[45] For detailed accounts of the complex circumstances in each case and evaluations of the Commission's judgments see P. L. Haworth, *The Hayes-Tilden Election of 1876* (Cleveland: The Burrows Bros. Company, 1906); Dougherty, *op. cit.,* Chaps. VI–VIII; and C. Vann Woodward, *Reunion and Reaction: The Compromise of 1877 and the End of Reconstruction* (Boston: Little, Brown and Company, 1951).

problem of the electoral count in the future. Again the perplexing constitutional issue of the power of Congress to regulate the electoral voting process and canvass was raised, causing delay and disagreement. It was not until 10 years later that the two houses were able to agree upon the terms of a bill governing the matter. In 1887 it passed the Electoral Count Act. With some later amendments, this embodies the current law on the subject.

The law as revised[46] now provides that if a contest arises over the appointment of electors in a state, it must be decided *in accordance with the law of that state* within not less than six days of the time of meeting of the electors; and all determinations of such contests, as certified by the governor of the state, shall be conclusive upon Congress. If there has been no determination of a contest by a state, but there are electors bearing the certification of the governor, those shall be counted which the two houses acting separately shall agree to receive. If they fail to agree, those bearing the certification of the governor shall be accepted. If there are no electors bearing credentials from the governor and the two houses cannot agree on receiving any of the votes returned from a state, presumably those electoral votes would be lost. A rigid debate limit rule on electoral contest issues is added to prevent the use of the filibuster to frustrate the making of a decision.

The possibility of disputes over state elections of electors and the conduct of the count by Congress remains one of the weak links in the current system of choosing the President. Serious doubt regarding congressional authority to deal with the matter, even in the limited way it has, still persists. One of the objectives of constitutional reform efforts in recent years has been to incorporate language in the Constitution to resolve this doubt, but these efforts have so far proved fruitless.[47] Fortunately, no occasion has arisen since 1887 for testing the practical workings of existing legislation on this subject.

[46] *United States Code* (1964), Title 3, Secs. 5–18.

[47] A constitutional amendment proposal sponsored by Senator George Norris of Nebraska, which was narrowly defeated by the Senate in 1934, contained a clause explicitly conferring authority upon Congress to make provision for cases involving disputed returns or regarding any controversy that might arise in the canvass of the electoral votes by Congress. *Congressional Record*, 73rd Congress, 2nd Session, p. 9127. The opinions of the Supreme Court in *Ex parte Yarborough*, 110 U.S. 651 (1884) and *Burroughs and Cannon v. U.S.*, 290 U.S. 534 (1934) to the effect that any government must be conceded the right to protect elections of its officers against fraud and corruption suggest that the Court might sustain federal legislation of this kind relating to the functioning of the electors and the canvass of their votes, even in the absence of such a clarifying amendment.

ELECTION REFORM ISSUES

As has already been noted, fundamental differences among the states' systems of choosing governors have largely disappeared. State practices for the choice of presidential electors have also fallen into a common pattern. Current issues at the state level affecting the choice of chief executives therefore are mainly related to the conduct of popular elections generally, such as those concerning suffrage qualifications, registration systems, balloting forms and procedures, limitation and control of campaign expenditures, and the timing of elections. Of these the last warrants discussion as having special significance in connection with the choosing of chief executives.

SEPARATE VS. COMBINED STATE AND NATIONAL ELECTIONS

Since governorship contests usually involve candidates backed by the same parties that present candidates for the presidency, alternatives of some consequence in the matter of the election schedule are available to a state. It may conduct its gubernatorial elections at an entirely different time from that on which elections of national officers take place, or it may combine these elections. If it chooses the latter course it has a further choice with regard to the use of a ballot form which permits a voter by one motion to vote for all candidates of a party whose names are on the ballot, or one which requires him to register his choices separately in each contest. If a state has a four-year term for governor and combines its national and state elections it has a further option between choosing its governor in a presidential election year or in the so-called off-year national election when only members of Congress are elected.

These various alternatives present issues of concern to the competing partisan interests as well as to the general public. A completely separate state election has the effect of minimizing the influence of national issues upon the choice of a governor. By focusing attention upon the issues and personalities of the state contest it diminishes the pull of national party loyalties. On the other hand, it places upon the voter the burden of an additional trip to the polls, adds to the public expense of conducting elections, and because of a generally much smaller relative turnout of voters, it tends to exaggerate the influence of a well-organized local majority party "machine." Despite these objections, the authors of the 1963 version of the Model State Constitution recommend an election schedule placing the governor's election on an "odd-year," separate cycle.

Formerly the more common practice was for the states to conduct their elections for state and local officers, including the governor, at times other than when national elections were held. The two-year periodicity of national elections and general adoption by the states of either a two-year or a four-year term for governors have combined to generate pressure for consolidating state and local elections with the national elections. Only a few states have successfully resisted this pressure. At present only five—New Jersey, Virginia, Kentucky, Mississippi and Louisiana—all of which provide for four-year gubernatorial terms of office, choose their governors at elections entirely separate from national elections. In the other 45 states the voters ballot for the governor at the same time they vote for national officers. In all the states that now have a two-year term for governor every other gubernatorial election accordingly coincides with the presidential election. Some having four-year terms for their governors choose them at the off-year national elections, while others choose them when presidential electors are elected. Thus in the off-year national election of 1962, 35 governors were simultaneously elected. In the 1964 presidential election, 25 governors were chosen at the same time. Beginning in 1966 and 1968 these figures will become 36 and 21, respectively, as states continue to tinker with their gubernatorial terms and election schedules.[48]

The extent of the influence of a presidential contest upon the fortunes of the gubernatorial candidates running simultaneously on the respective national party tickets can only be conjectured. It is undoubtedly of some consequence, particularly in improving the fortunes of a gubernatorial candidate of a party that is ordinarily the minority party in a given state.[49] An unusually strong and popular presidential candidate may carry to victory some of the gubernatorial candidates of his party in such states if the competition in the presidential race happens to be fairly close. Likewise, a strong gubernatorial candidate may sometimes enhance the chances of his party's presidential ticket in his state. Presidential candidates have at times shown recognition of this fact by exerting pressure on individuals thought to be strong locally to become candidates for the governorship. For example, Governor Al Smith, the Democratic party presidential nominee in 1928, helped to induce Franklin D. Roosevelt to become the Democratic nominee for governor in New York that year in order to strengthen the party's New York ticket. President Roosevelt, in turn, brought pressure

[48] See Appendix B for a chart showing the election schedules for the governorship in the various states.

[49] Cf. V. O. Key, Jr., *American State Politics: An Introduction* (New York: Alfred A. Knopf, 1956), p. 42.

to bear on New York's Governor Herbert Lehman to seek re-election in 1936 for the same reason.[50]

Gubernatorial candidates, especially in the more closely contested states, ordinarily seek to associate themselves in their campaigns with the personalities and policies of their respective presidential candidates; but occasionally they pursue the opposite course. The 1964 election offered a number of noteworthy exceptions to the general rule. Republican candidates in a number of states maintained an attitude of studied aloofness from the party's candidate for President, Senator Barry Goldwater, whose presence on the ticket they considered to be a "drag." A prime example was Governor George Romney of Michigan. His tactics proved to be well advised—though Goldwater lost the state by a margin of over 1,000,000 popular votes, Romney won re-election by some 380,000 votes.

The influence exerted by the presidential election upon the outcome of gubernatorial contests is most likely to be felt in those years when there is a change in national party control of the presidency. Voter desire for a change tends to carry over into the state contest. If a state employs a type of balloting procedure permitting the straight ticket vote for all candidates of a party by one mark or motion, the "coattail" influence of one candidate on the fortunes of the other tends to be heightened. A system that requires the voter to indicate his choices for each office separately or which provides entirely separate ballots for the state and national contests tends to reduce this influence somewhat.[51]

In spite of this influence, however, enough voters do at times discriminate in their choices so that the electoral votes of a state go to the candidate of one party for the presidency, while at the same time the candidate of the opposing party is elected to the governorship. Even when balloting procedures are designed to encourage straight-ticket voting to the maximum degree, opposing results in this sense

[50] See *The New York Times*, October 3, 1928, and July 1, 1936.

[51] Analysis of a nationwide sample of voters' actions and attitudes in the 1956 presidential election year has shown that in the single-choice ballot states, i.e., those states which permit the voter to indicate a straight party ballot by a single mark, 59 percent of the Eisenhower voters voted a straight party ballot; but in states employing a multiple-choice type of ballot, only 48 percent did so. Among Stevenson voters, 69 percent voted straight party tickets in the single-choice states and 60 percent in the multiple-choice states. Angus Campbell and Warren E. Miller, "The Motivational Bases of Straight and Split Ticket Voting," *American Political Science Review*, Vol. LI (June, 1957), pp. 293–312, at p. 299. It should be emphasized that the split tickets taken into account in this survey did not all necessarily involve differential choices in presidential and gubernatorial contests, since a split between party candidates for *any* office other than president was the criterion used. Furthermore, there were simultaneous *gubernatorial* contests in only about half of the states in that election year.

frequently occur. An analysis of election results in 74 elections in 11 closely contested two-party states over the period from 1928 to 1952 has shown that in 24 instances, or roughly one third of the cases, voters in sufficient numbers split their tickets so as to elect a governor of one party along with electors favoring the other party's presidential candidate.[52]

Other analyses reveal, moreover, that the practice of ticket-splitting as between presidential and gubernatorial candidates is becoming more prevalent. Professor V. O. Key's study of state gubernatorial and presidential voting results in the states outside the South over a 72-year period showed that there was a steady decline in the proportion of elections that produced pluralities for presidential and gubernatorial candidates of the same party in a state when these elections have occurred simultaneously. The figures, by periods, were as follows:[53]

TABLE 1. *State Presidential and Gubernatorial*
Election Results, 1880–1952

Period	Percent with Coinciding Party Results	Percent with Different Party Results
1880–1892	93.1	6.9
1896–1908	89.5	11.5
1912–1924	81.2	18.8
1928–1940	77.8	22.2
1944–1952	75.5	24.5

This trend has become even more pronounced in the 1950s and 1960s. In the 1956–1964 period the percentage of coinciding election results, figured on the same basis as in the table above, was 59.7, with 40.3 percent resulting in the choice of the presidential candidate of one party and the gubernatorial candidate of the other. Even when the four states of the old "Solid South" which elect their governors at the time of the presidential vote are included, the proportion of coincidental results for the 1956–1964 period rises to only 62 percent. Since a coincidental result proportion of 50 percent would represent the number that could be expected to occur under the laws of pure chance, it does not appear that the danger of submerging local issues and gubernatorial candidates by having presidential candidates chosen at the same election is currently a very serious problem, regardless of the balloting forms used. The case for scheduling gubernatorial and

[52] Coleman B. Ransone, *The Office of Governor in the United States* (University, Ala.: University of Alabama Press, 1956), pp. 83–85.
[53] Key, *op. cit.,* pp. 48–49.

presidential elections at different times appears to have been somewhat overstated by its proponents, to judge by these results.

The conclusion seems warranted that coincidental presidential and gubernatorial elections, even when coupled with voting procedures that tend to encourage straight-ticket voting, are by no means an insurmountable obstacle to a discriminating choice by the voters. Against the contention that combining the elections for President and governor has the effect of subordinating to some extent local issues and candidacies to national issues, or in some rare instances, perhaps, has the reverse effect, there are a number of weighty counterconsiderations in its favor. First, it tends to bring a greater proportion of the potential electorate to the polls and thus makes the popular mandate for the successful candidate for the governorship more impressive. Second, it tends to induce greater harmony and identification of interest between the state party organization and its candidates and the national party and its leadership, thus making for a somewhat clearer fixing of party responsibility and a strengthening of party ties generally between national and state elements. A third point in its defense is that it helps the minority party in a particular state to maintain an effective organization and thus tends to strengthen the two-party system generally. Furthermore, many national issues extend into the arena of state politics as well. It is therefore logical, sound policy to encourage voters to take this factor into account in their voting for President and governor. Finally, combining these elections is a measure of economy from the point of view of public expenditures for elections and campaign costs of the parties themselves.

The case for entirely separate gubernatorial elections, or even for timing them to coincide with the off-year national elections, if a four-year term for the governor offers this alternative, can by no means be fully demonstrated by analysis of actual results. The element of advantage or disadvantage to the dominant partisan interest in the light of the local political situation rather than an objective weighing of intrinsic merits of the alternatives is probably the major factor accounting for the kind of election schedule and balloting procedure a particular state employs.

REFORM OF THE PRESIDENTIAL ELECTORAL SYSTEM

Ever since the adoption in 1804 of the Twelfth Amendment through which some changes were made in the operation of the elector system, there has been more or less continuous agitation for further modification of constitutional arrangements governing the election of the President. The issue has been repeatedly raised and debated in

Congress. Every crisis or near-crisis in the functioning of the elector system has been followed by a flurry of congressional and popular interest in proposals for revision of the existing constitutional plan. None of these periods of reforming zeal and interest has resulted in agreement by both houses of Congress upon the terms of a reform amendment; but on five different occasions between 1813 and 1869 the Senate acted favorably on amendment resolutions of this kind.[54] It did so again following the three-way split in the electoral vote in the 1948 election, when reference of the outcome to the House of Representatives for final determination was narrowly averted.

Recent attempts to reform the presidential electoral system have been directed primarily toward bringing the national popular vote results into closer focus upon the outcome of the election. The principle that elevation of the President to his high office should depend upon the suffrage of the people has become firmly embedded in American thinking. The fact that he is the people's choice is the very cornerstone upon which the modern presidency rests. Indeed, the American governmental system may be aptly described as a "presidential democracy." But under the present plan of election the national popular vote totals, *as such,* have no more determinative significance than the Gallup Poll does on the outcome. A candidate's success depends upon obtaining popular pluralities for his slates of electors in a sufficient number of states to produce an electoral vote majority, now amounting to 270 votes. Popular votes cast for elector states of losing candidates in a state contest are not reflected in the national elector vote totals. In the popular vote sense, the presidential election is not a nationwide test of strength by the candidates but a series of statewide contests.

It follows that a candidate may, and often does, amass a winning national *electoral vote majority* while receiving only a *popular vote plurality.* In 10 of the last 27 elections the successful candidate has not had a popular majority—Lincoln in 1860, Hayes in 1876, Garfield in 1880, Cleveland in 1884 and 1892, Harrison in 1888, Wilson in 1912 and 1916, Truman in 1948, and Kennedy in 1960. Indeed, in at least two and possibly three of these instances the winning candidate did not even have a *plurality* of the national popular vote. In the 1876 election Hayes' electors received 4,033,950 votes nationally, while those of Tilden, his defeated opponent, received 4,284,757. In the 1888 election Benjamin Harrison received 5,444,337 popular votes in defeat-

---

54 Amendment resolutions which would have required that presidential electors be popularly chosen by districts were passed by the Senate in 1813, 1819, 1820, and 1822; and in 1869 the Senate approved an amendment resolution which would have given Congress power to prescribe the manner by which electors should be chosen. The House either rejected or failed to consider these resolutions. Ames, *Proposed Amendments,* pp. 81–84, 105.

ing his Democratic opponent. Grover Cleveland, who had 5,540,059. It is uncertain whether electors for Senator Kennedy were favored by more people than were those pledged for Vice President Nixon in the 1960 election. The uncertainty arises from the fact that in Alabama Democratic voters were offered a slate of five "pledged" and six "unpledged" electors, all of whom were elected in that state. The national popular vote totals were very close. Kennedy is credited with 34,221,463 nationwide popular votes and Nixon with 34,108,582 in most calculations, giving the former a nationwide plurality of 112,881. These calculations, however, credit Kennedy with popular votes received by the Democratic electoral slate in Alabama, only five of whom actually voted for Kennedy, with six voting for Senator Harry Byrd of Virginia.

It is also widely recognized that the office of presidential elector has become an unnecessary and, as developments in recent elections have demonstrated, even a potentially mischievous element in the machinery of selection. Unpledged electors or electors who violate their implied pledge to vote for the acknowledged candidates of the national party ticket can frustrate the principle of popular choice in selecting the President. Partisan manipulations at the state level may even deny to the voters of a state the opportunity to vote for electors pledged to the candidates named by the national nominating authority of their party. Nevertheless a few ultraconservatives advocate retention of the electors as officers because, they insist, the electors might be needed to make a choice on their own if a party candidate should die or become incapacitated between the time of choosing the electors and the casting of the electors' votes. It is also argued that keeping the electors as officers tends to discourage the appearance on the ballot of minor party and last-minute "sorehead" or "insurgent" candidacies and thus helps to protect the two-party system. The difficulties of arranging for nomination of a slate of electors in a timely way tend to obviate such last-minute or frivolous candidacies, it is contended. The elector system, these people contend, also helps to keep control over the presidential election system in the hands of the states, where they maintain it belongs.

The majority rule in determining the final electoral vote outcome, with its accompanying provision for election of the President by the House of Representatives wherein each state has one vote without regard to population is another frequently criticized feature of the present system. Under this provision, as the 1824 election demonstrated, it is possible that the presidential vote cast by a state's House delegation may actually be contrary to the recorded will of the voters of that state; for the political complexion of a state's House delegation may be different from that of its winning elector delegation. Furthermore, if a presidential election should be carried to the House stage (or to the Senate stage in the case of the Vice President) the chief executive would owe his election to the Congress. A three-cornered contest for the presidency in the House would be an invitation to political deals and skulduggery on a grand scale; while a two-way contest for the vice presidency would be decided by a Senate only one-third of whose members would have been chosen at the same time the presidential electors were chosen. If the House contest did not result in a prolonged stalemate, the aspirant who emerged successful would undoubtedly have placed himself deeply in political debt to those elements in Congress to whom he owed his election.

While present-day public opinion in this country continues to tolerate the idea of state equality in voting power in one branch of the Congress, it would undoubtedly be shocked violently if occasion should ever arise again for applying the principle of legislative election of a President or a Vice President by politically "equal" states. If a candidate who was the popular plurality choice of the nation as a whole should be passed over by the House in favor of a nonplurality choice, as was the case in 1824, the resulting popular outcry would be formidable indeed. This is a lesson a number of states have had to learn the hard way in choosing their governors. They have responded to it by abandoning the majority vote principle, which is the root of the difficulty, and going over to the principle that a popular plurality in the state at large should govern in choosing the chief executive officer.

Over the years there has been a voluminous literature on the subject of presidential election reform. The ideas advanced with their arguments and counterarguments are too complex to be reviewed here in great detail.[55] Committee hearings, debates and votes in Congress, and comment in the public prints on occasions when amendment resolutions have reached the floor have revealed the difficulty of arriving at a sufficiently broad consensus on the terms of a revisory amendment to bring about its adoption.

Every feature of the present system has its defenders, both in Congress and outside it. When the operations of the present system are analyzed in the light of past election results it can be demon-

---

[55] Extensive committee hearings have been conducted on the subject in nearly every Congress since 1949. For an earlier comprehensive study of the subject see Dougherty, *op. cit.* See also *Nomination and Election of President and Vice President*, Hearings before the Sub-Committee on Constitutional Amendments of the Committee on the Judiciary, United States Senate, 88th Congress, 1st Session (1963). Senator Estes Kefauver's "The Electoral College: Old Reforms Take on a New Look," *Law and Contemporary Problems* (Spring, 1962), pp. 188–212, is a good brief analysis of various reform proposals which have been advanced recently in Congress and of the arguments for and against them. See also the *Congressional Quarterly*, February 17, 1961, pp. 279–288 for a similar analysis of current electoral reform proposals.

strated that one feature or another tends to give an advantage to this or that state, sectional, partisan, or group interest. Each of these interests—be they the "liberals," the "conservatives," Republicans, Nothern Democrats, Southern Democrats, spokesmen for urban or for rural interests, "states rights" advocates, advocates of a "weak" executive, "independents," defenders of the two-party system, spokesmen for minor parties, or whatnot—find something in the present system they like because it protects in a special way values they regard as important. Each interest tends to resist any change it believes will weaken *its* particular position of advantage or supposed advantage; but naturally enough its spokesmen express a willingness to change the system in ways which might have the effect of diminishing or eliminating a supposed advantage of *opposing* interests. Politicians who have become expert in manipulating the present system and who know how it works are loath to see modifications which would change the environment in which they must function. Consequently the result of reform efforts to date has been a kind of stalemate; the conclusion has been to let well enough alone rather than to adopt any change in the rules of the great game of national presidential politics.

In recent years Congress has centered its attention upon constitutional amendment proposals of four basic types. One suggested approach is to abolish the office of elector as such, but retain all or most of the other features of the elector system. A second type of proposal is directed toward imposing upon the states a requirement that electors be chosen from separate electoral districts within each state, rather than all from the state at large as is now the uniform practice. Another type of proposal looks toward abolishing the office of elector as such while retaining the present electoral vote distribution formula for weighting a state's influence, but awarding to the several presidential candidates electoral votes from a state in the same proportion as they receive popular votes therein. Finally, there have been proposals designed to sweep away the electoral vote system entirely and elect the President and Vice President on the basis of the nationwide popular votes. Plans embracing these various basic approaches have differed on the point of whether a majority or a plurality vote nationally shall determine the ultimate result, and on the method of resolving an inconclusive election in case a majority is required and no candidate receives the necessary majority on the first round.

1. ABOLITION OF THE OFFICE OF ELECTOR

The idea of abolishing the *office* of presidential elector as a functioning element in the elective plan while retaining the other main elements of the present system is by no means new. In his first annual message to Congress in 1829 Andrew Jackson recommended adoption of a constitutional amendment which would "preserve to each state its present relative weight in the election" of the President—that is, retain the electoral vote formula for weighting state power, and award a state's electoral votes automatically to the candidate winning the popular vote contest in the state. In the event no national electoral vote majority resulted, he would have had the amendment provide for a runoff election on a state-by-state basis between the two leading candidates.[56] In 1934 a somewhat similar amendment proposal sponsored by Senator George W. Norris of Nebraska came within a few votes of receiving the necessary two-thirds majority for passage in the Senate. Unlike Jackson's proposal, Norris's would have retained the current system for resolving an election when no candidate receives a national electoral vote majority.[57]

While he was a Senator from Massachusetts, President John F. Kennedy strongly urged adoption of an amendment proposal of this general character; but his proposed amendment would also have altered the current method of resolving an inconclusive electoral vote for President or Vice President by placing this function in the hands of a joint meeting of the two houses of Congress. Each Senator and Representative would vote individually in such a proceeding, rather than have each state delegation cast one vote; and a majority of the entire joint body would be necessary to resolve a contest. In a message to Congress on February 1, 1965, President Lyndon B. Johnson gave his endorsement to a proposal following the lines of the Kennedy plan.[58]

The arguments in favor of a constitutional revision along the lines of the Kennedy-Johnson proposal are obvious. Since it does not basically alter the current method of voting for President on a state-by-state electoral vote basis, it does not raise the fears that other more far-reaching proposals engender. It would resolve the troublesome problem of the "unpledged," nonfunctioning or malfunctioning elector, which recent elections have demonstrated can be potentially inimical to the principle of popular choice of the President. At the same time a popular plurality in a state would control the disposition of the entire bloc of that state's electoral votes, as is now usually the

---

56 James D. Richardson, *A Compilation of the Messages and Papers of the Presidents, 1789–1897* (Washington: Published by authority of Congress, 10 vols., 1900), Vol. II, pp. 445–446. (Hereafter cited as Richardson, *Messages and Papers of the Presidents.*)

57 Cf. Joseph E. Kallenbach, "Recent Proposals to Reform the Electoral College System," *The American Political Science Review*, Vol. XXX (October, 1936), pp. 924–929.

58 *Congressional Record*, (89th Congress, 1st Session, Daily, February 1, 1965), pp. 1589–1590.

case. In the event no candidate receives a national electoral vote majority the issue would be resolved by a system of voting in Congress more defensible from the popular representative point of view than the current "one state, one vote" method.

On the other hand it is also obvious that the Kennedy-Johnson proposal fails to come to grips with some of the aspects of the present system which many critics condemn most strongly. It leaves untouched the state "unit" or "bloc" vote system under which all of a state's electoral votes are normally given to the candidate who receives a popular plurality therein. The national popular vote total a candidate receives would be no more accurately reflected in his electoral vote total than it now is. The proposed plan would preserve the special importance attaching to the contest in the 12 or so large and populous "pivotal" states at the expense of voters who happen to reside in the less politically critical states.[59] Indeed, by its proposed change in the method of resolving an inconclusive nationwide electoral vote result it would actually enhance the potential influence of those states. The possibility would remain that a nonplurality President might be chosen through either the electoral vote or action by Congress. The proposal's underlying theory is that the President should be the choice of the people of the *states* as separate political units, rather than of the people of the *United States*. It would therefore do nothing to strengthen the claim of the President to speak and act in the name of a truly *national* political party.

2. THE STATE-DISTRICT ELECTOR SYSTEM

The idea that electors should be chosen by the people voting in constituencies paralleling those from which members of Congress are chosen or from specially drawn single-member districts in each state is as old as the Constitution itself. During the early years of the nation's history a number of states employed various types of district systems for electing some or all of their electors, thus facilitating the choosing of a "split" elector delegation from a given state. Indeed, there is nothing in the Constitution as it now stands to prevent a state from choosing its electors in this manner; but considerations of state pride, the desire to enhance the state's influence to the utmost in the presidential contest, and the immediate self-interest of the dominant party or of the two major parties have combined to induce every state to adopt a "winner-take-all" general ticket system for choosing its elec-

---

[59] For an analysis of this well-understood feature of the present system see Joseph E. Kallenbach, "Our Electoral College Gerrymander," *Midwest Journal of Political Science,* Vol. IV (May, 1960), pp. 162–191.

tors.[60] No state is inclined to adopt a district plan for choosing its electors as long as all other states cling to the general ticket method.

The district electoral vote idea, whose most energetic recent champion in Congress has been Senator Karl Mundt of South Dakota, is defended on a number of grounds as being preferable to the present system. If, as is commonly proposed, one presidential elector is elected by the voters from each congressional district and two from each state at large, the constituencies from which presidential electors are chosen would parallel those from which members of Congress are elected. The electoral college would thus be a specially chosen replica of a joint meeting of Congress. Every voter in the nation, regardless of his state of residence, would participate in the choosing of only three electors. This would correct an imbalance of the present system under which voters in the very populous states, such as New York, Pennsylvania, Illinois, Texas, or California, may participate in choosing relatively large blocks of 25 to 40 or more electors while voters in the less populous states, like Alaska, Delaware, or Wyoming, may participate in the election of only three.

Under the district system, it is further argued, the proportion of the national popular vote received by a presidential candidate would tend to be more closely approximated by his proportion of the total electoral vote; and the likelihood that a presidential candidate might win a majority of the electoral votes nationally without having received also a plurality of the national popular vote would be somewhat lessened, although it would not be entirely eliminated. Since the successful presidential candidate's electoral constituency would be similar to that of Congress collectively it could be assumed that his views and program and those of his party in Congress would be more likely to coincide than is now normally the case. At present the special importance attaching to the voters holding the balance of power between the two major parties in the pivotal states tends to cause a President—whether he is a Republican or a Democrat—to be more sensitive to their demands than is his party's membership in Congress as a whole. By leaving untouched the electoral vote distribution formula for weighting state power in the choosing of the President and Vice President this plan would presumably be more acceptable to the

60 Prior to the 1892 presidential election in Michigan the state legislature, which had temporarily fallen under the control of the Democrats who were then the minority party in the state, passed a statute providing that the people in each congressional district should choose one elector, with two electors at large being chosen by the voters of the entire state. This method of electing the state's electors was held by the United States Supreme Court to be within the competence of a state to adopt under existing constitutional arrangements. Cf. *McPherson* v. *Blacker*, 146 U.S. 1 (1892). Under this arrangement the Democrats won 5 of the 14 electoral votes in Michigan in 1892.

smaller and medium-sized states than other proposed plans involving a departure from the electoral vote idea.

Objections to the district electoral vote concept are most strongly voiced by representatives of the populous states in which urban influence is dominant. They contend that breaking up their bloc vote in the electoral college would weaken the influence of their states and of the urban interest generally. They point out that it would increase the temptation to gerrymander congressional districts by rural-dominated state legislatures, since not only congressional seats but electoral votes would be at stake. Instead of the national outcome of the election depending primarily on the popular voting in about a dozen pivotal states, as is now the case, the result would depend upon the vote in these states plus approximately 100 congressional districts scattered throughout the country where the major party voting strength is relatively close. It is contended that there might actually result a greater discrepancy between the total national popular vote and the number of electoral votes a candidate receives, and the possibility of a nonplurality choice might even be greater than at present. In this connection it is noted that if the state-district electoral vote system had been in effect in the 1960 election Vice President Nixon rather than Senator Kennedy would have won the presidency. The district system of choosing electors, it is further contended, would give encouragement to third parties and increase the probability that the electoral votes would be split among more than just the two major party candidates, thus requiring that more elections be decided by Congress.[61] Altogether, it is a plan which would weaken the present influence of the populous, urbanized areas and increase the influence of the smaller, more sparsely populated states and areas. It would unduly enhance the strength of the more conservative rural elements in national politics by making the President more responsive to their views, according to its critics.

3. THE PROPORTIONAL ELECTORAL VOTE SYSTEM

The thought that the electoral vote of a state should be made to correspond more closely to its popular vote is a natural consequence of the practical political fact that a President is actually chosen by the *people, through* the electors. It has therefore long been contended that it would be logical to require that the electoral votes of a state be

[61] Recognizing the validity of these objections, Senator Mundt, in the most recent versions of his plan, has incorporated provisions calculated to minimize the dangers of runaway gerrymandering in laying out electoral districts and providing for reference of the election to a joint session of Congress, rather than to the House voting by states, in case the electoral vote is inconclusive.

divided among the various candidates for the presidency in the same proportion as the popular vote. In 1950 an amendment resolution incorporating this idea was passed by the Senate by a 64 to 27 majority. The resolution had the bipartisan backing of Senator Henry Cabot Lodge, Republican, of Massachusetts and Representative Ed Gossett, Democrat, of Texas. However, strong opposition to it on partisan and sectional grounds developed in the House, and it was rejected by that body by a vote of 210 to 134.[62]

As passed by the Senate the Lodge-Gossett Resolution provided for (1) abolition of the *office* of elector but retention of the electoral vote formula for weighting state voting power in presidential elections; (2) distributing a state's electoral votes automatically to the candidates in the same proportion as they receive popular votes therein; (3) making an electoral vote *plurality* in the nation determinative of the result, provided that the leading candidate's plurality amounts to at least 40 percent of the total electoral vote; and (4) in the event no candidate receives that electoral vote plurality, referring the issue to a joint meeting of the Congress where a choice between the two highest in the electoral vote would be decisive. The plan did not explicitly state that candidates on the same party ticket for President and Vice President would be presented to the voters as inseparable pairs, but it was assumed that this would be the case.

Backers of the Lodge-Gossett approach advanced a number of weighty arguments in support of their proposal. It would have abolished the "fifth-wheel" office of presidential elector and its potential dangers to the principle of democratic choice; but by preserving the *electoral vote principle* in weighting state influence it would have bypassed one of the major obstacles to change from the present system. In effect, it was a proposal for direct popular election, but with the proviso that the relative weight of each state's popular vote should be measured through the electoral vote formula and translated by it into a common coin for national counting purposes. It would not completely eliminate the possibility that a nonplurality candidate might be chosen but it would minimize the chances of this happening. Election of the President would become dependent upon the will of the voters of the nation in a much more direct sense than is the case at present. There would be an incentive for parties in every state to marshal their support to the utmost, regardless of their minority or majority status in their state; for the effect of every popular vote would be carried forward to the final stage in the electoral contest—that is, to the national level. A President would become the spokesman for a *national* political party, rather than continue to be a feudal party chieftain representing a loose coalition of state parties bearing the

62 *Congressional Record,* 81st Congress, 2nd Session (1950), pp. 1278, 10427.

same name. There would be an incentive for each political party to organize and campaign for what might prove to be marginal vote strength in *all* parts of the country rather than to concentrate attention and favors on the marginal voters in a relatively few close states.

Despite these arguments in its favor, strong opposition to the proposal was voiced in some quarters. Many Republican members of Congress believed on the basis of application of the new formula to past election results that it would make it more difficult for a Republican to win the presidency. This would happen, it was claimed, because the expected gains of electoral votes by Republican candidates in the states of the Solid South would not compensate for the losses of Republican electoral votes in the more closely contested states elsewhere in the country. It was even claimed that the Lodge-Gossett plan might relegate the Republican party permanently to the status of a minority party.[63] Because it ignored developments already under way which have transformed the states of the Solid South in recent elections into hotly contested battlegrounds between the two major party candidates for President, this reason for Republican opposition was subsequently proved to be badly out of focus. Ironically, if the Lodge-Gossett plan had been in operation in 1960 and the popular vote had been cast as it was, Nixon rather than Kennedy would have won the presidency; while the impressive Eisenhower electoral sweeps of 1952 and 1956 would still have occurred.

Northern Democrats were also induced to believe that their influence in Democratic presidential contests would be diminished. They argued that a Democratic presidential candidate could expect to get a greater relative margin of electoral votes in southern states than in more closely contested ones elsewhere; consequently he would feel more indebted to conservative political interests in the South than is now the case. This line of thinking overlooks the obvious fact that under the distributive electoral vote plan it would be the *total number* of Democratic electoral votes in the nation at large which would be decisive in electing a Democratic President, not his relative margin of victory in particular states. In order to win, a candidate would have to have a general *national* appeal to partisanly marginal voters everywhere, not just to those in states where he is the popular majority choice.

Another argument of dubious validity against the plan was that the distributive electoral vote system might endanger the two-party system and lead to the formation of many splinter parties, because votes cast for minor party candidates would be reflected in the final electoral vote totals. This argument, plausible enough at first view, fails to recognize that under it the national contest would doubtless

[63] Cf. Ruth Silva, "The Lodge-Gossett Resolution: A Critical Analysis," *American Political Science Review*, Vol. XLIV (March, 1950), pp. 86–99.

still be one in which two major party contestants would be the primary factors. The great mass of the nation's voters would feel impelled to support one or the other of them as they do in similar contests on a statewide basis for governor or Senator wherein a *plurality* governs the outcome. Voters would have no added incentive to throw away their votes on certain losers. Indeed, it might well be that third party or minor party candidates would have even less chance to influence an election under the Lodge-Gossett plan than under the present system. Now a minor party can hope to be a decisive influence in a presidential election by holding a balance of power between the two major parties in a *single state*; whereas under the distributive electoral vote system it could have this kind of decisive influence only if it achieved a balance of power position in the *whole nation*.

4. DIRECT POPULAR ELECTION FROM THE NATION AT LARGE

Most authorities on the presidential electoral system have assumed that the idea of having the President chosen by direct national election from the nation at large has a great deal of sound logic behind it, but that it is "impractical," given the conditions that now prevail. Recent votes in the United States Senate when this kind of an electoral reform amendment has been brought forward have shown that only a minority of some 15 to 20 Senators are willing to support such a plan. The unwillingness of the states to surrender the guaranteed weight in a presidential contest which the elector system provides, the implication that a uniform national system of suffrage requirements would be necessitated, and the change in philosophy from the present *federalized* scheme into a truly *national* type of election are all pointed to as impassable barriers to establishment of a national direct popular vote system.

These are, of course, formidable obstacles to adoption of such a mode of election. Yet when one surveys the developments that have come about in connection with American electoral processes generally, the prospect for adoption of a presidential election reform amendment of this kind is far less chimerical than when it was first suggested and so characterized by James Wilson in the deliberations of the Constitutional Convention. First of all, the idea that the *people* should elect the President—an idea which George Mason dismissed in the Convention as being "as unnatural . . . as to refer a trial of colors to a blind man"—is now basically a part of our scheme of government. Disparities among the states in the matter of qualifications for voting in national elections are becoming less pronounced. Not only do the Fifteenth, Nineteenth, and Twenty-fourth Amendments reflect a growing insistence on more uniform suffrage requirements in the several states, but passage of the Civil Rights Acts of 1957, 1960, and 1965 represents an increasing direct concern and involvement by the national government in the character and administration of state suffrage laws. The Twenty-fourth Amendment established a new principle when it abolished tax-paying as a requirement for voting in *national* elections but not necessarily in *state* elections; while the Twenty-third Amendment, by enfranchising the people of the District of Columbia for presidential elections, recognized that a voice in the choice of President need not be based upon state residence and state representation in Congress. The recent trend through voluntary state action toward relaxation of state residence requirements for voting in presidential elections, noted above, is another straw in the wind indicating a popular willingness to accept the fact that the choice of the President is a *national* act to be performed without too technical a regard for the usual state voting qualifications.

The recent series of Supreme Court decisions upholding the principle of "one man, one vote" in the layout of congressional and state legislative districts is another indication that districting schemes resulting in disparites in voting power by people based upon the accident of their place of residence similar to those fostered by the electoral college system are indefensible under modern democratic dogma. Furthermore, it should be noted that direct popular election of the President from the nation at large is squarely in line with the views of a great many authorities who urge strengthening the President's hand as the leader of his party. His position as the leader and spokesman for his party would be immeasurably stronger if he could point to the fact that he was the choice of the people of the nation speaking directly through a *national* party without regard to state lines, and not through the intermediary of a series of state-based parties.

The prospect for eventual adoption of a presidential election reform amendment embracing the direct election principle may therefore not be so remote as some authorities assume. In any case it may be confidently predicted that if there is ever again a crisis in the operation of the present system brought about by the failure of the machinery to produce a choice through the electoral vote alone or through elevation to office of a President who is clearly not the choice of a plurality of the voters of the nation, the resulting popular outcry will force Congress to act in some manner to correct the generally recognized deficiencies in the current system. In that event it would not be at all unlikely to see it sweep away all the impedimenta of the electoral college procedure and go over to some form of direct popular election. A system based on the principle of "one man, one vote" is the only one that is immune to charges that it would favor some special interest over another in the selection process. It would favor only *one* interest, that of the people in the nation as a whole.

4

THE NOMINATION PROCESS

Presidential elections and, in most of the states, gubernatorial elections, are contests in which competition by organized political parties reaches its highest intensity. The point that the primary objective of a party is to capture control of the presidency and the governorship goes far toward explaining why the American party system has evolved into its present form. With its great potentiality for shaping public policy and dispensing patronage, the office of chief executive quickly became a prize of the first order in the partisan struggle. Political parties adapted their organization and strategies to this fact of political life. At the national level the major political parties can best be described as loose federations of state party organizations, held together by the common goal of capturing and maintaining control of the presidency.[1] Within the ranks of each major party a wide diversity of political views and objectives is to be found, its presidential candidate being the unifying force. Similarly at the state level by rallying around its candidate for the governorship a party is able to give the illusion of being a united body, however heterogeneous the interests, objectives, and political ideologies represented in its membership actually may be.

Since 1800, presidential elections, with only a few exceptions, have been contested on fairly even terms by two major parties which between them have attracted the support of the greater part of the national electorate. Since the 1870s an even balance has been maintained between the two major parties with respect to the presidency. In the last 22 presidential elections Republicans have triumphed on 11 occasions and Democrats on 11.

National parties have always sought to extend their influence into state government as a secondary base of support. The parties which compete for the presidency appear on the battle lines in state elections as well. The two-party struggle is not always carried on with equal vigor at the state level, however. Even though gubernatorial elections now generally pit Republican and Democratic party candidates against one another, the competition in some cases is perfunctory and unequal. In some southern states the Republican party in recent years has not

[1] Cf. A. W. MacMahon, "Government—United States," *Encyclopedia of the Social Sciences* (New York: Macmillan Company, 1937), Vol. IV, p. 19.

even troubled to present an official candidate for the governorship.[2] However, developments since 1960 indicate that a viable two-party system at the state level may be developing in that region as a complement to the national two-party trend evident there in the last four presidential elections. Final partisan contests for the governorship have also sometimes been obviated by endorsement of the same individual as a candidate by both major parties. For example, in 1946 Governor Earl Warren of California, under the peculiar cross-filing system authorized by that state's primary laws at that time, won both the Republican and Democratic nominations and was unopposed by a major party candidate in the general election. In 1952 Governor Allan Shivers of Texas, the Democratic nominee for re-election, announced his support of General Eisenhower, the Republican candidate for President. The Republicans did not nominate a candidate to oppose him in the general election, choosing to endorse him instead.

Third parties have at times successfully competed with the major parties in governorship races or have joined forces with one of them to install a candidate in office. During the 1830s, although the Whigs and Democrats were the major national parties at the time, the Anti-Masonic party was victorious in a number of gubernatorial elections in the northeastern section of the country, either independently or on a fusion basis with one of the major parties. The Free-Soil and the American ("Know-Nothing") parties were similarly successful on a number of occasions in that area during the late 1840s and the 1850s. After the Republican and Democratic parties had become the major contenders in national politics in a new party alignment following the Civil War, the Greenback party edged into the governorship in a number of western states during the 1870s and 1880s, as did also the Populist party in the 1890s.[3] A People's Independent party elected a governor in cooperation with the Democrats in Nebraska on several occasions between 1912 and 1920.

The most recent minor party successes in governorship contests occurred in the 1930s. From 1930 to 1936 four consecutive governorship elections in Minnesota were won by candidates of the Farmer-Labor party, which has since fused with the Democrats. The Wisconsin Progressive party, which has since disbanded, sent Philip F. La Follette to the governor's chair in that state in 1934 and 1936. Most unusual,

---

[2] Recent examples have been gubernatorial elections in Georgia in 1946, 1948, 1950, and 1954; in Louisiana in 1948 and 1956; in Mississippi in 1951 and 1955; and in Tennessee in 1950 and 1954.

[3] On third parties and their fortunes generally see Fred E. Haynes, *Third Party Movements Since the Civil War* (Iowa City: State Historical Society of Iowa, 1916); William B. Hesseltine, *The Rise and Fall of Third Parties* (Washington: Public Affairs Press, 1948); and Howard P. Nash, Jr., *Third Parties in American Politics* (Washington: Public Affairs Press, 1959).

perhaps, were insurgent movements during the 1930s in Oregon and North Dakota which resulted in the choice of nominally "Independent" governors. Actually these candidates were backed by a Republican faction which refused to go along with the regular nominee.[4]

During the past 50 years in about a third of the states Republican and Democratic candidates have contested for the governorship on fairly equal terms, and the outcome has usually been doubtful from election to election. In another category, comprising about 20 states, the party normally in the minority has won the governorship at relatively infrequent intervals and the element of effective interparty competition has sometimes been lacking. In still another category, including most of the southern states, one major party has held the governorship uninterruptedly for the past 60 years or longer. Strong two-party competition has been so lacking as to warrant classifying them as essentially one-party states so far as the governorship is concerned.[5] Yet even in these states gubernatorial elections during the past decade have in some cases been closely contested, and the prospect of effective two-party competition in governorship contests throughout the nation is continuing to improve.

Whatever the degree of intensity of competition may be, the point is clear that before the door of the White House or the governor's mansion opens to a successful aspirant he must have first emerged the victor in an intraparty contest for nomination as its official candidate. This step in the selective process often involves a more strenuous struggle than the final election itself. It is a contest that in some states is tantamount to election for the victor. Even where the final election remains a major hurdle, by narrowing the choice to the two individuals who will have major party backing the nominating procedure is a fundamentally important part of the process through which an individual is elevated to the office of chief executive.

---

4 In the 1930 Oregon election the Republican nominee, George Joseph, died of a heart attack about a month after winning the nomination. As a "Progressive" Republican he had been at odds with the regular party organization leaders on a number of issues, including public power policies. The Republican State Committee named a conservative Republican as a replacement candidate, whereupon the erstwhile supporters of Joseph bolted and named Julius Meier, a close friend of the deceased candidate, to run as an Independent. Meier won the ensuing election by a large margin, receiving more votes than the combined totals of his two major party opponents. He thereby achieved the distinction of being one of the first two persons of the Jewish faith to be elected to a governorship.

In North Dakota, where the Republican party had for years been split into two strong factions, the Non-Partisan League and the regular Republicans, former Governor William Langer, with Non-Partisan League backing, was defeated for the Republican nomination in the 1936 primary. His name was placed on the ballot by petition as an Independent, and he was elected.

5 Appendix B indicates the outcome of party voting on the governorship, state by state, since 1900.

EVOLUTION OF PARTISAN NOMINATING PROCEDURES:
THE CONVENTION SYSTEM

The American habit of leaving matters in the sphere of politics to pragmatic improvisation is well illustrated in the evolution of partisan nominating procedures. Arrangements through which parties nominate their candidates were left in the hands of party managers for the first century of the nation's existence, with practically no interference or control by government. The idea prevailed that a political party was something on the order of a private club or association, free to manage its affairs for itself. In the very early years when legislative election of the governor was the rule in a majority of the states, selection of the candidate to be backed by a particular party or faction naturally was assumed by that party's influential members in the legislative body. Aspirants for the office sometimes openly sought the backing of their party colleagues; others, no less eager perhaps, merely made known that they were receptive to the honor; while still others had to be persuaded to accept the role of candidate. On at least one occasion the eventual choice fell upon an individual who was so far from being an aspirant for the governorship that he refused to serve after being elected. When he was named to the governorship in Georgia in 1788, James Jackson, modestly citing his youth and inexperience (he was 30 at the time), refused to serve. Later, in 1795, he was again elected and served as governor for three one-year terms.

Where popular election was the mode various methods of nomination, such as informal meetings and understandings by prominent party members, the legislative party caucus, and endorsements by local gatherings and rallies, were employed to bring forward candidates. These devices were eventually displaced by assemblages of legislative party leaders and appointed delegates which in time took on the character of "mixed" state party conventions.[6] By the 1820s state party conventions made up mainly or exclusively of emissaries representing local party member groups had become the most widely used method for naming candidates for the governorship.

The evolution of practices in naming presidential candidates followed somewhat similar lines. Endorsements of candidates at local gatherings of the party faithful, by state legislative party caucuses, by state legislatures, and eventually by state delegate conventions were

---

[6] Stanwood, *A History of the Presidency from 1788 to 1897*, (rev. ed. 1928), pp. 170–171, credits the Jeffersonian Republican party in Pennsylvania with being the first to develop and use a "mixed" type of state delegate convention for nominating candidates for state office.

all methods used to bring forward candidates for the first 10 presidential elections.

In the 1800 election the congressional party caucuses made their appearance as agencies for focusing support upon designated candidates. In a number of succeeding elections this body enjoyed an ascendancy in the nominating processes of the Jeffersonian Republican party, for it was able to speak for the party nationally with a semblance of representativeness and authority. The Federalist party, as its congressional membership dwindled steadily after 1800, could not continue this practice. In both the 1808 and 1812 elections secret meetings of Federalist leaders in and out of Congress were held to agree on campaign strategy and candidates. These gatherings have been credited by some historians with being the seed from which the national party convention system eventually grew.[7]

There was always a certain amount of objection by local party groups to alleged dictation by the Republican party's congressional caucus in presidential nominations. In the 1824 pre-election maneuverings, the pro-Jackson element boycotted the party's congressional caucus and insisted on presenting him as their candidate independently. Backers of other candidates also offered their favorites as nominees. When the congressional caucus choice, Senator William H. Crawford, finished a rather distant third in the electoral voting, the caucus ceased to be a significant factor in the naming of presidential and vice presidential candidates. This was a development of much consequence to the presidency; for it meant that the successful aspirant to the office would no longer be indebted to his party colleagues in the legislative branch. Indeed, with the decline and eventual demise of the Federalist party in the period from 1800 to 1820 the Jeffersonian Republican congressional caucus, in effect, had appointed presidents.

Late in 1831, imitating the example of the Anti-Masonic party which earlier year had assembled a national delegate convention to formulate a statement of its principles and to settle upon a presidential nominee, the National Republican (Whig) party resorted to the same device for naming Henry Clay as their candidate for the 1832 election. The Democrats, under the urging of President Jackson, who wished to give the prestige of national party endorsement to his personal choice as his running mate, Martin Van Buren, also held a national party convention. A Democratic convention was held again in 1836; but the Whigs did not hold one, preferring the strategy of presenting several candidates with sectional appeal in the hope of throwing the election into the House of Representatives. Both major parties nominated their candidates at national conventions in the

[7] Cf. V. O. Key, Jr., *Politics, Parties and Pressure Groups,* 5th ed. (New York: Thomas Y. Crowell Company, 1963), p. 397.

1840 election. Since that time the national convention has been a regular part of the machinery by which a party reaches agreement on the makeup of its ticket and on a statement of the principles of public policy it pledges itself to carry out if placed in power.

Indicative of the informality and looseness with which these early national conventions were assembled and conducted is an account of the 1836 Democratic convention which met in Baltimore:

> Twenty-two States and two Territories—Michigan and Arkansas —were represented. No delegates were present from Illinois, South Carolina, or Alabama. . . . A list of those who took part contains 626 names. Of these, 422 came from the states of Maryland, Virginia, New Jersey, and Pennsylvania. Maryland is mentioned first because it contributed 181 members. The [Maryland] state convention, called to select delegates, was apparently unwilling to deny any of its own members an opportunity to take part, and accordingly resolved that all of them should be delegates. Virginia sent 108, New Jersey 73, and Pennsylvania 60, being two contesting delegations of 30 each. On the other hand, Tennessee sent no delegates; but a citizen of the State who would vote for Van Buren, chancing to be in Balitmore, presented himself, was admitted, and cast the fifteen votes allotted to Tennessee. His name was Rucker; and he achieved fame through the verb, "to ruckerize," which was coined at the time, a political piece of slang long since forgotten.[8]

State and national party conventions were based, in theory, upon the concept of representative democracy. Their authority to speak and act for the party derived by delegation from the party membership meeting in local caucuses. Impulses and desires generated at that level were presumed to be transmitted by delegate spokesmen to the state and national party assemblages through a hierarchy of conventions. In practice, this pyramidal convention structure did not always function in the expected representative democratic fashion. Apathy on the part of the rank and file party membership permitted actual power and control to be seized by self-interested cliques and machines often motivated more by the prospect of spoils and political influence than by principles.

Left entirely to self-regulation in such matters as apportionment of delegate strength, the time and manner of selecting delegates, and the internal organization and procedure of delegate meetings, the convention system proved susceptible to abuses. In the struggles for control of the party machinery and especially for nominations for public office, sharp practices of one kind and another appeared—corrupt bargains, "steamrollering" and other more crude methods of manhandling minority dissenters, exercise of influence by business corporations and unsavory social elements with important financial interests at stake in public policies, and so on. The convention system fell into

[8] Stanwood, *op. cit.*, pp. 181–182.

such disrepute in the latter decades of the nineteenth century that a demand for reform of nominating practices through public action was generated. This reform movement brought into existence a still-growing body of state legislation regulating state and local party conventions. It also produced in the form of the direct primary a new type of partisan nominating procedure.

THE DIRECT PRIMARY

The direct primary system was first adopted on a statewide compulsory basis for major parties in Wisconsin in 1903. The idea did not originate in that state, for it had been employed by parties on a voluntary or optional basis elsewhere for a number of years. It was first used by Democrats in Crawford County, Pennsylvania, during the 1850s, giving rise to its being called the "Crawford County System." Before 1900 it was being used on an optional basis in many parts of the country, particularly in the West and South.[9] Wisconsin was merely the first state to embrace it as a basic feature of public policy.

The central idea of the direct primary system is that major political parties should be required, or at least permitted, to use the regular public election machinery of the state at public cost and under public supervision for polling its membership to determine its candidates for office, to select individuals to hold certain party offices including convention delegate posts, and to resolve other issues arising in the conduct of party affairs. After its adoption in Wisconsin, the direct primary gained favor very rapidly in other states. Within a few years it had largely displaced the convention as a nominating procedure in connection with the governorship. The direct primary has in most states become a preliminary intraparty election, carried on under public auspices, having the effect ordinarily of narrowing down the voter's choice in the general election to the two individuals who as the major party candidates will receive the bulk of the popular vote. In states where one party is dominant, the primary of that party becomes for all practical purposes the significant part of the popular election process. The fact that one major party or the other had come to dominate state elections in a majority of the states during the 1900–1920 period tended to further the acceptance of the direct primary idea.

This does not mean that the state convention has been entirely supplanted by the direct primary. It continues to be used for such purposes as drawing up platforms, appointing various party function-

9 The early history and development of the direct primary movement is reviewed in detail in Charles E. Merriam and Louise Overacker, *Primary Elections* (Chicago: University of Chicago Press, 1928), Chap. V.

aries, selecting delegates to the national convention, and making some nominations for public office. Newly formed parties and minor parties continue to use the convention device for selecting their candidates. In two states—New York and Indiana—both major parties still nominate their gubernatorial candidates at state conventions. In Maryland, candidates are also nominated at state conventions; but state law requires that the delegates cast their votes automatically for the candidate who receives a plurality of the popular votes in a direct primary contest in their respective counties or legislative districts. The candidate receiving the highest number of such directed delegate votes is nominated, even though he may not have received the largest total statewide popular vote in the primary.[10] Until 1964 Georgia employed a somewhat similar system. A party nomination for statewide office was conferred automatically upon a candidate who won a majority of the "county unit" votes with which he was credited by obtaining a popular plurality in a county. This system was invalidated by the United States Supreme Court in 1963 on the ground that it violated the principle of equal protection of the laws.[11]

In still other states, as will be noted later, the convention continues to play a role in the nominating process. In some states it serves as an agency for mobilizing support behind a particular candidate or candidates before a direct primary is held. In others it is empowered to make the ultimate decision on a nomination in the event the direct primary has not produced a definitive choice by the party membership.

EVALUATION OF THE DIRECT PRIMARY

The relative merits of the direct primary and the convention systems of nominating gubernatorial candidates are difficult to assess. Whether the direct primary produces a "better" candidate than the convention system is incapable of proof. Any conclusion on this point can only be a subjective judgment. The avowed purpose of the direct primary has been to democratize the nominating process. It has un-

10 *Flack's Annotated Code of Maryland* (1951), Art. 33, Sec. 68. In 1950 Governor William P. Lane was renominated as the Democratic party candidate by 84 votes to 68 in the party convention, even though he had received some 17,000 fewer popular votes in the statewide primary than his opponent, George P. Mahoney. Lane was subsequently defeated in the general election by his Republican opponent, T. R. McKeldin. In the light of recent Supreme Court pronouncements this nominating scheme may well be held unconstitutional. A movement is under way to replace it with a direct primary in Maryland.

11 *Gray* v. *Sanders*, 372 U.S. 368 (1963). Counties were allotted from one to three unit votes, which had the effect of discriminating against voters residing in the heavily populated urban counties. A new primary law was enacted by the Georgia legislature in 1964 providing for a statewide direct primary, with a runoff between the two leading candidates if no one receives a majority on the first try. *Georgia Laws, Extra Session,* 1964, Sec. 34–1514.

doubtedly resulted in greater popular participation in nominating procedures; but experience has shown that it does not necessarily insure elimination of party organization influence upon the results. Political party machines and other power elites have demonstrated a great capacity to adapt their techniques to the climate of public control as exemplified in direct primary and other types of party regulatory measures. One recognized authority not only has questioned whether the direct primary has achieved its objective of democratizing party nominating procedures, but he goes further to question whether the whole concept of a "party" as consisting of all the voters who support its candidates is not based on a false conception of the nature of parties and their function in a democratic system.[12] This view is receiving increasing support among close students of the political process in the United States.

The case against the direct primary is built largely around the proposition that it has had a disruptive effect upon the two-party system and therefore, upon responsible party government. It has had some impact upon the power structure within the parties and upon the party system generally; but there are complicating and variable factors from state to state that make it difficult to assess the extent and nature of this impact.[13] Whatever its shortcomings may be, there has been no general movement by the states away from the direct primary system. It has apparently won such a large measure of popular acceptance that its continuation in one form or another appears assured for some time to come.

The direct primary has its greatest justification for existence in those states where one party dominates the political scene. In this situation, where the final election is practically a formality and the real contest is the one for recognition as the nominee of the dominant party, the direct primary serves the purpose of a popular elective process. But at the same time its tendency to induce most of the voters to classify themselves as members of the dominant party in order to preserve their right to participate in its decisive primary hampers efforts to organize an effective opposition party. The direct primary system coupled with a scheduling of gubernatorial elections in the off years or the odd years thus tends to perpetuate such one-party situations, with all of the disadvantages that accompany the absence of effective interparty competition. It is significant that those southern states which

12 E. E. Schattschneider, *Party Government* (New York: Holt, Rinehart and Winston, 1942), pp. 57ff.

13 For a most thoughtful and informative analysis of the impact of the direct primary upon state gubernatorial politics see V. O. Key, Jr., *American State Politics: An Introduction* (New York: Alfred A. Knopf, 1956), particularly Chaps. IV and V.

elect their governors in presidential years include most of those which have displayed greatest promise of developing an effective two-party system.

In states where there is effective competition between major party candidates in the final election the direct primary has other kinds of effects upon the party system and upon responsible party government. A common problem is the invasion of one party's primary by adherents of the opposition or by independents, with the result that the integrity of the nominating process as a strictly intraparty affair is impaired. The primary laws of a number of states, in effect, condone and encourage this kind of independency of party by voters. One state, Washington, employs a unique type of "consolidated" primary ballot which deliberately invites a voter to participate in those intraparty contests of either party as he prefers. A voter can participate in the nomination contest of only one party for a particular office; but as he proceeds from office to office in marking his ballot he may shift from one party primary to another. About a half dozen other states have the so-called "open" primary system, under which any qualified voter receives the primary ballots of all major parties and selects in the secrecy of the polling booth the ballot of the party in whose primary he chooses to participate. Election officials make no attempt to limit participation in a party's primary to its acknowledged members.[14] Until 1959 California achieved a somewhat similar result by permitting a candidate to cross-file for nomination by more than one party for a designated office. It was under this system that Governor Earl Warren won both the Republican and Democratic nominations for governor in 1946.

Even though the laws of most of the states provide for a "closed" type of partisan primary under which participation in a particular party's primary is limited to those voters who have made some form of public acknowledgement of their adherence to it, there is no completely effective system of insuring that those who take a hand in the nominating processes of a party are "members" in the full sense of the term. It should be noted, in passing, that the problem of preserving the integrity of the party nominating process is not confined to the direct primary. It presents itself under the convention system as well. For example, participation by large numbers of "Eisenhower Democrats" in Republican party caucuses in Texas in the initial stages of the 1952 preconvention struggle for the presidential nomination gave rise to a controversy in the Republican National Convention over

[14] Open primary states in 1962 were Alaska, Hawaii, Michigan, Minnesota, Montana, Utah, and Wisconsin, along with, of course, Washington. Hawaii uses a modified form of the Washington "wide open" primary. *Book of the States, 1962–1963* (Chicago: Council of State Governments, 1962), p. 22.

the seating of rival pro-Taft and pro-Eisenhower delegations from that state.[15]

In addition to the charge that the direct primary impairs the integrity of party nominations, critics maintain that it tends to weaken the party system in other ways. They point out that it sometimes produces candidates who will not work in harmony with the party organizations which must sponsor them; it intensifies the spirit of factionalism and perpetuates personal rivalries within the ranks of a party to a degree destructive of party unity and responsibility; and, if the nomination contest is governed by the plurality vote rule, it may force upon the party a candidate who represents a point of view untypical of the general party attitude. These complaints have had a foundation in gubernatorial primary results on a number of occasions. Above all, critics emphasize that it fails to provide opportunity for consultation, consideration of alternatives, and compromise in resolving intraparty disputes and differences, as the convention system does. Consequently one of the vital elements in the process of party government is lost.

DIRECT PRIMARY REFORMS AND MODIFICATIONS

The weight of these strictures against the direct primary has been recognized by its defenders. This is evidenced by the variety of attempts through state legislation as well as through informal party practice to minimize or correct these faults. So far as nominations for the governorship are concerned, four general types of approaches have been tried to this end: (1) establishment by law or by party rule of some sort of preprimary sifting or endorsing procedure permitting the state convention or some other party organ to designate one or more favored candidates in order to provide leadership and guidance to the party's voters at the primary; (2) referring a nomination contest for final resolution to the state convention when no candidate emerges from the primary with a strong plurality; (3) using a preferential voting system in the primary; or (4) setting up a majority vote requirement for deciding a primary contest, with a second or runoff primary being held between the two leading contenders in the event no candidate obtains a majority in the regular primary.

1. THE PREPRIMARY ENDORSEMENT SYSTEM

Various forms of preprimary endorsement systems have been adopted through state legislation. A plan of this kind has been used in Colorado since 1910. In that state any major party candidate who

---

15 Cf. Paul David, Malcolm Moos, and Ralph M. Goldman, *Presidential Nominating Politics in 1952* (Baltimore: The Johns Hopkins Press, 5 vols., 1954), Vol. I, *The National Story*, pp. 50, 53, 69–85, 87, 167.

receives the support of 20 percent or more of the delegates at a state party convention is entitled to have his name placed on the primary ballot, the names of all such candidates being listed in the order of the convention support they received. Other candidates can obtain placement on the ballot by petition; but candidates who fail to receive the necessary convention support usually, but not always, drop out. In 1918 a candidate who failed to win convention endorsement by the Republican convention nevertheless succeeded in winning the party's nomination in the primary. He was eventually elected governor. Since 1947 Utah has employed a somewhat similar system; but in that state only the names of the two leading candidates in the convention voting appear on the primary ballot.

Connecticut in 1956 modified its convention procedure of nomination by providing that an unsuccessful candidate at the convention may challenge the convention's choice in a direct primary by filing a petition with a specified number of signatures and depositing a sum equal to 15 percent of the annual salary of the office sought. If the challenger does not secure at least 15 percent of the primary vote, his deposit is forfeited. Rhode Island has also recently abandoned the convention system in favor of the direct primary for gubernatorial nominations, with the proviso that the state central committee of a party may officially endorse a favored candidate to give guidance to primary voters. Massachusetts adopted a similar law in 1953, with the designation of an approved candidate being made by the state party convention. Minnesota authorizes endorsement of candidates by the state party conventions, but no official indication of an endorsement appears on the ballot by the candidate's name. In a number of other states, even though no official endorsement by a state convention or party committee is authorized by law, support of a particular candidate by the organized party leadership or by a considerable segment of it may be the decisive factor in a direct primary contest. In California and Wisconsin voluntary associations within the parties have made their appearance and by giving their endorsements to favored candidates have influenced the outcome of primary contests.[16]

These various formal or informal attempts to amalgamate the convention system and the direct primary so as to realize the advantages of both are still in the experimental stage. Under them the direct

[16] Cf. Hugh A. Bone, "New Party Associations in the West," *American Political Science Review*, Vol. XLV (December, 1951), pp, 1115–1125; Frank J. Sorauf, "Extra-Legal Political Parties in Wisconsin," *ibid.*, Vol. XLVIII (September, 1954), pp. 692–704. In the 1956 Republican gubernatorial primary in Michigan the state party organization more or less openly threw its support behind one of the candidates, Mayor Alfred E. Cobo, of Detroit, but it did not officially endorse him. Cobo won the nomination easily. Similar informal endorsements of favored candidates by party organization elements are usually made in Illinois.

primary becomes a kind of "gun behind the door," an instrument for ratifying or rejecting nomination recommendations made by the party convention or some other party agency. Whether this kind of hybrid nominating system will win general acceptance in the two-party states remains to be seen. Abandonment of the preprimary convention idea in several states after trial suggests that popular hostility to bossism and other alleged evils of the convention system is still strong.[17] Continuing popular distrust of the motives and standards of those who constitute the "organization" in a party will no doubt make difficult even this type of partial restoration of authority to it in effecting party nominations for so important an office as governor.

2. THE POSTPRIMARY CONVENTION SYSTEM

Two states, Iowa and South Dakota, have approached the problem of associating the convention with the direct primary from the side of making the convention an alternative agency for resolving an inconclusive primary result. The primary laws of those states specify that if no candidate receives a plurality amounting to at least 35 per cent of the total vote, the nominee shall be chosen by the state party convention from among the leading contenders in the primary. Recourse to the convention for settling nomination contests is very rarely necessary. One instance occurred in South Dakota in 1948 when a candidate who had received less than the required 35 percent plurality in the Republican primary was nominated by convention. He was subsequently elected.

In this connection it should be noted that the laws in most of the direct primary states provide that vacancies on the party ticket occasioned by death or withdrawal of the chosen candidate shall be filled through action of the party's state central committee or the party's state convention. Recent successful contenders for state governorships who received their nominations from their party's state central committee after the regularly nominated candidate died include Dan Thornton, Republican of Colorado, in 1952; and Guy Park, Democrat of Missouri, in 1932. Replacement candidates were named by the Republican state committee in Oregon in 1930, in North Dakota in 1934, in Massachusetts in 1958, and by the Democratic state committee in Illinois in 1952 and 1956; but the candidates so nominated were defeated in the general election.

---

[17] States which have abandoned the preprimary convention after varying periods of trial are South Dakota, Nebraska, and New Mexico. Massachusetts dropped it after a five-year trial in 1937, but readopted it in 1953. Cf. Adam C. Breckenridge, "Pre-Primary Trial Dropped," *National Municipal Review*, Vol. 43 (April, 1954), pp. 186–191.

3. THE PREFERENTIAL VOTE SYSTEM

Two states, Florida and Alabama, have experimented briefly with the idea of permitting voters in a primary to indicate a series of alternative choices among the various candidates after marking their first choice for the nomination. The basic purpose of this plan is that if the first choice results do not produce majority support for one candidate, then second, third, and fourth choices and so on will be taken into consideration until one candidate has amassed majority support. Voters quickly learned that by lending their support to second and third choices on their ballots they were weakening the chances of their first choice to win; hence many of them expressed only a first choice, expecting secondary support for their candidate from other sources to put him over the top. On the three occasions when this system was used to decide gubernatorial nominations in Alabama, a candidate won by an outright majority on the first choice ballots once, and on the other two occasions the one who had received a plurality on the first round was the eventual winner. In Florida the candidate who received a first choice plurality was the eventual winner on all three occasions this system was used in the Democratic primary.[18] The preferential vote system was thereupon abandoned in favor of a runoff primary plan. It was discontinued in Florida in 1929 and in Alabama in 1931.

4. THE RUNOFF OR "DOUBLE PRIMARY" SYSTEM

A majority vote requirement for nomination at a primary, with recourse to a runoff between the two leading contenders in the event of an inconclusive result in the first primary, has found favor almost exclusively in the South, where it is now generally in effect. States using this device as of 1962 were Alabama, Arkansas, Florida, Georgia, Louisiana, Mississippi, North Carolina, Oklahoma, South Carolina, Texas and Virginia. The only states outside the South to experiment with the double primary have been Utah, which adopted it in 1937 but abandoned it in 1947, and Kentucky, which used it in 1936 but abandoned it the next year.

The peculiar conditions prevailing in southern gubernatorial elections until recently have given the double primary a justification which is lacking for the most part in other sections of the country. Final elections have sometimes not even been contested by a regular Republican party candidate in Mississippi, Georgia, and South Carolina;

[18] Cf. Alexander Heard and D. S. Strong, *Southern Primaries and Elections, 1920–1944* (University, Ala.: University of Alabama Press, 1950).

and occasionally this has been true in other southern states as well. Even when a Republican candidate has been put forward, the final election contest has been a perfunctory affair.[19] Since 1952 there has been a noticeable change in this regard in some southern states. Final gubernatorial elections have been rather hotly contested on occasion in a number of them. Results in the last four presidential elections as well as in congressional and senatorial contests indicate that an effective two-party system is in the process of being established in most parts of the South. If this proves to be the case it will no doubt bring about a re-evaluation of the gubernatorial nominating methods now being employed in that area.

Under the double primary system many of the weaknesses of the majority vote rule in final elections—a rule that has been abandoned by practically all states that have tried it—have made themselves manifest. Southern Democratic gubernatorial primaries have tended to be dual-factional or multi-factional affairs, with the nominal party organization forces remaining in the background or dividing their support among the various candidates.[20] Constitutional restrictions on re-eligibility eliminate the incumbent governor as a possible candidate for renomination in most of these states, and uncontested nominations are accordingly quite rare. One of the effects of the double primary appears to be encouragement of multiple candidacies. Fewer nominations by majority vote are made at the first trial, as compared with states using a single primary system wherein a plurality vote is conclusive. In southern gubernatorial primaries about one-half of the initial contests progress to the runoff stage where one is provided for. In roughly two cases out of three the individual receiving a plurality in the first primary is successful in the runoff. It thus appears that the runoff system has the effect of causing the nomination to go to the individual finishing second in the first primary in only about one case out of six.[21] Considering the additional costs involved, the inconvenience to the public in making an extra trip

19 In the 11 states making up the ex-Confederate South, plus Oklahoma, in 134 gubernatorial elections from 1919 to 1952, only one Republican governor was elected. This was in Tennessee in connection with the Harding landslide of 1920. Coleman B. Ransone, Jr., *The Office of Governor in the United States* (University, Ala.: University of Alabama Press, 1956), p. 13. A Republican governor was chosen in North Carolina in 1896 when a Populist candidate cut into the normal Democratic vote rather heavily. Oklahoma elected a Republican governor in 1962.

20 An analysis of the various one-party situations in the southern states is given in Ransone, *op. cit.*, pp. 29ff. For a more extended treatment of the conditions that affect gubernatorial nominations in individual southern states see V. O. Key, Jr., *Southern Politics in State and Nation* (New York: Alfred A. Knopf, 1949). Changes in the political, economic, and racial basis of politics in the South during the 1950s and 1960s have been so great, however, as to make these analyses somewhat out of date.

21 These conclusions are based on an analysis of gubernatorial primary election results in 11 southern states from 1919 to 1949 as presented in Heard and Strong, *op. cit.*

to the polls, the tendency to encourage frivolous and "strategic" candidacies that prevent a majority choice in the first instance, and the effect it has in helping to perpetuate a one-party system, it is by no means clear that the merits of the double primary system clearly outweigh its disadvantages. In view of recent developments suggesting that the two-party system is on the way toward becoming a more firmly established feature of southern politics it may be expected that the double primary will be subjected to searching re-examination in that area in the years to come.

Viewing the country as a whole, the pattern of nominating practices followed by major parties in gubernatorial contests is thus quite varied. Two states cling to the convention system even for the major parties. Two others use the convention as a "back-stop" to the direct primary. In some 10 or 12 others the party convention, a state party committee, or some other party organ in an official or unofficial capacity exercises considerable influence on nominations, with party voters acting through the direct primary being relied upon to make a final judgment on candidates. In the remaining states the direct primary is employed, with a plurality vote being controlling in over two-thirds of this group. This means that in about three fourths of the states the direct primary, operating under the plurality vote principle, is the method used for naming major party candidates.

Whatever the method used, the importance of the nominating process as a phase of the process of selecting state chief executives cannot easily be overemphasized. The route to the governorship in every state necessitates successful traversing of the quicksands of preferment by a major party as its candidate. Conditions differ greatly from state to state, not only in the procedure to be followed in obtaining official party endorsement but also with respect to the complex of local political forces and factors that affect the outcome. An aspirant who is successful in being nominated by a major party will necessarily have demonstrated a considerable degree of political acumen and campaigning skill. In reaching this stage he will already have been tested for many of the extralegal "political" attributes and qualities demanded for final election to the office of governor.

PRESIDENTIAL NOMINATIONS: THE NATIONAL CONVENTION SYSTEM

The procedures by which parties select presidential nominees are no less significant today as a part of the system of choosing the national chief executive than are partisan nominating processes in the election of state governors. As has already been pointed out, one of the keys to understanding the nature of political parties and the role they play in American government is found in the partisan struggle for control of the presidential office. At four-year intervals the presidential contest draws state and regional groups that make up the two major parties into their most intensified and united effort as national instrumentalities. Differences within the ranks of a party tend to be submerged or ignored in this supreme common enterprise. No person, no matter how personally popular or well-regarded he may be, has a chance of receiving the electoral votes necessary to place him the presidential chair unless he is presented to the voters as the official candidate of a major party. The procedures by which agreement is reached on candidates are therefore significant not only as a vital part of the electoral process, but also as an element giving stability to the two-party system.

Although the states have experimented freely with various devices in connection with partisan nominations of gubernatorial candidates, the presidential nominating system has remained basically unchanged over the past century or more. The national convention, brought into being by voluntary action of the parties in the 1830s and still resting essentially on a foundation of party rules and usages, continues to be used for this purpose. During the past half century partial statutory control over it has developed in the form of state laws regulating the choice of convention delegates. The role of the national convention as a nominating agency has also been implicitly recognized in state legislation governing the nomination and election of presidential electors in that they are expected to support the nominee chosen by their respective national party conventions. But no state, for obvious reasons, can regulate the national party convention as a complete entity; and Congress also apparently lacks constitutional authority to legislate directly upon the presidential nominating process. As a consequence the movement for popularization of partisan nominating procedures which has resulted in the displacement of the party convention by the direct primary in most of the states has so far failed to bring about any fundamental change in the presidential nominating system. Except for new procedures imposed by law concerning the manner of choosing national convention delegates in some states, the most significant changes in the national convention system have been instituted voluntarily by party rule and practice.

Although they differ in certain relatively minor respects in organization and procedures, the national conventions of the two major parties today operate in a generally similar manner and perform the same functions. The initial moves in assembling a convention are made by a party's National Committee, which issues the call to the heads of the several state and territorial units of the party organization. The call indicates the time and place for holding the convention and specifies the number of delegates each unit will be entitled to select under prevailing party rules. Local arrangements, the preparation of a temporary roll of delegates as reports are received from the states regarding the results of their selective procedures, and the naming of a slate of temporary convention officials are other matters handled by the National Committee before the convention.

DELEGATE APPORTIONMENT PRACTICES

Originally both major parties followed the rule of allocating convention delegate strength to state units in accordance with the formula governing representation in Congress. It also early became the practice in both parties to allocate some representation to the major territories, even though these areas, having no electoral votes, exercised no direct voice in the election of the President. Allocation of delegates solely on the basis of congressional representation emphasizes the federal character of parties; but it produces inequities in representation of the party's membership according to their numbers. Regular adherents of the major parties are not distributed evenly through the nation. Assignment of delegates on the basis of the number of Senators and Representatives therefore produces wide disparities from state to state in the ratio of party voters to delegates votes. The failure of the Republican party to establish and maintain itself as an effective major party in the South after the Reconstruction period made this "federal representation" rule of delegate apportionment work particularly unfairly in its convention. A southern state with only a sprinkling of Republican voters was allowed the same number of delegate votes as a northern or western state with possibly 10 or 20 times the number of Republican voters, but with the same number of congressional seats.

These disparities between numbers of party voters and delegate votes in the Republican National Convention were brought dramatically to national attention in the Taft-Roosevelt contest in 1912. A considerable part of President Taft's delegate support was found to lie in the patronage-controlled, overrepresented southern state delegations; while most of Roosevelt's delegate support came from the more Republican, relatively underrepresented states elsewhere in the country. The bitter convention struggle, the subsequent party split into two camps, and the resulting loss of the presidency to the Democratic opposition set in motion a movement in the party for a revision of rules on delegate apportionment. It had as its objective the equating of delegate strength more nearly with Republican voting strength. Beginning with the 1916 convention revised delegate distribution formulas have been applied by that party to realize this objective.[22] The Democratic party, with its adherents more evenly distributed throughout the 50 states, has been under less pressure to revise its apportionment practices. Eventually in 1940, following abolition of the two-thirds rule for deciding nomination contests, its national convention also took steps to revise party rules on this subject.

Current Republican rules allocate delegate strength according to the following formula:[23]

(a) 1 delegate vote for each United States Senator and Congressman-at-large.

(b) 1 delegate vote for each congressional district casting at least 2000 Republican votes for President or Representative at the last election.

(c) 1 additional delegate vote to each congressional district casting 10,000 or more Republican votes for President or Representative at the last election.

(d) 6 "bonus" delegate votes for each state that voted for the Republican candidate at the last election or which has elected a Republican Senator or governor since the last national convention was held.

(e) territories: District of Columbia, 9; Puerto Rico, 5; Virgin Islands, 3.

From 1940 through 1960 the Democratic party used various allocation schemes also designed to equate delegate strength more closely with actual party strength. The rules for apportionment in its 1964 national convention were as follows:[24]

(a) 3 delegate votes for each electoral vote in a state and the District of Columbia.

(b) 1 additional delegate vote for each 100,000 popular votes or major fraction thereof cast for the Democratic candidate for President at the last election.

(c) 10 "bonus" delegate votes for each state that cast its electoral votes for the Democratic candidate for President at the last election.

(d) 1 delegate vote for each National Committeeman and Committeewoman.

(e) territories: District of Columbia, 16; Canal Zone, 5; Guam, 3; Puerto Rico, 8; Virgin Islands, 5.

[22] In 1952 the Republican National Convention also initiated a change in long-established rules respecting representation on the party's National Committee. Originally each state and major territory had one representative on this committee. In the 1920s, following the advent of women's suffrage nationally, both parties had added a woman representative from each state and major territory, thus doubling its size. The 1952 Republicn convention provided that the state party chairman in each state casting its electoral votes for the Republican candidate at the last election should have a seat and full voting power on its National Committee. Ironically, the effect of this rule in view of the 1964 presidential election results will be to increase the weight of the erstwhile Solid South states of South Carolina, Georgia, Alabama, Mississippi and Louisiana in Republican party councils.

[23] *Congressional Quarterly Convention Guide Supplement*, 1964 (Washington: Congressional Quarterly, Inc., 1964), pp. 1125–1126.

[24] *Ibid.*, pp. 1140–1141.

Application of these formulas in 1964 produced a delegate convention of 1308 votes in the case of the Republicans, and 2316 in the case of the Democrats. The actual number of delegates exceeded this number of votes in the Democratic convention, however, in view of the widespread practice of that party's state units in splitting their at-large seats among larger numbers of delegates and giving them fractional votes.

While current delegate apportionment practices do not achieve a distribution of delegate votes, state by state, in an exact ratio to party voting strength, they give more recognition to this principle than the simple rule of apportionment according to the federal representation formula applied prior to 1912. Inasmuch as the electoral vote system for choosing the President allocates voting power to the states according to their congressional representation rather than in strict accordance with numbers of actual voters, there is some logic in basing convention representation on a rule which recognizes also in some degree this aspect of state power in presidential elections.

CONVENTION VOTING RULES AND PROCEDURES

Another difference in party convention practices of some consequence, but of diminishing importance, is the use by the Democrats of the "unit rule" in connection with voting by state delegations. Under this rule, which again emphasizes the federalized character of the national party, all members of a state delegation may be required to vote as a majority of its members do if its state convention has so directed or if the delegation, by unanimous consent, has imposed the rule upon itself. It is not applied on delegates who have been elected at a direct primary if the effect is to cause them to violate pledges to their constituents in the course of being elected to their seats; and a self-imposed unit rule can always be abrogated by a majority of the delegation itself. Republican practice, on the other hand, permits each delegate to act individually on all ballots. Generally only one-fourth or less of the delegations in a Democratic convention are actually governed by this rule. Abolition of the two-thirds majority rule for deciding nominating contests has weakened considerably the case for its retention.

The two-thirds majority rule for deciding nominations, which until recently afforded another illustration of a major difference in Republican and Democratic convention practice, was introduced at the first Democratic convention and followed uniformly by that party until 1940. It was adopted originally to give the appearance of greater solidarity in support of the party's nominees. It was also defended as a safeguard against sectional or minority domination of party nominations, particularly as application of the unit rule might mean that some votes cast for a candidate might not necessarily represent true delegate preference for him. From the beginning the Republican practice has been to apply the ordinary majority vote rule.

The impact of the two-thirds rule on Democratic nomination contests while it was in operation is somewhat difficult to assess. An implicit understanding that any candidate who achieved a majority would be given the necessary two-thirds majority was usually observed; but on two occasions this unwritten corollary to the rule was not respected. In 1844 former President Martin Van Buren obtained a majority vote in the Democratic convention but was denied the party nomination, which went eventually to James K. Polk; and in 1912 House Speaker Champ Clark attained a majority on eight consecutive ballots, but was finally passed over in favor of Woodrow Wilson. Both Polk and Wilson were subsequently elected. In view of the already visible split between the Progressive and Regular wings of the Republican party in 1912, when the Democratic convention was held, nomination was recognized as almost certainly insuring election. Thus the two-thirds rule might be considered to have been responsible for putting Wilson rather than Clark in the White House. Whether it was responsible for making Polk, rather than Van Buren, the President in 1844 is not clear in view of the issues at stake and the extreme closeness of the ensuing election.

The fact that protracted nominating contests have been more common in Democratic conventions than in those of the Republicans may also be attributed in some degree to the two-thirds rule. Presumably it gave encouragement to supporters of dark horse candidates to continue steadfast ballot after ballot in the hope that a deadlock between the leading candidates might eventually be resolved by a resort to a compromise candidate. The first candidate to deserve characterization as a "dark horse," James K. Polk, was nominated on the ninth ballot as a direct result of the two-thirds rule. He had received no votes on the first ballot, and actually at the outset was hoping only to become the vice presidential nominee.

Fifteen of the 32 Democratic conventions since 1840 and 10 of the 28 Republican conventions since 1856 have required more than one ballot to select the presidential nominee. There have been seven Democratic conventions but only two Republican ones in which 10 or more ballots have been required to select a presidential nominee. Both the Republican conventions eventually named "dark horse" candidates in the persons of James A. Garfield (1880, 36 ballots) and Warren G. Harding (1920, 10 ballots). Democratic conventions which could be said to have nominated candidates of this type were those of 1844 (Polk, nine ballots), 1852 (Pierce, 49 ballots), 1868 (Horatio

Seymour, 22 ballots), and 1924 (John W. Davis, 103 ballots). Since abolition of the two-thirds rule only one Democratic convention has required more than one ballot to name a presidential candidate.

"LOYALTY" OATHS

A problem that has arisen to plague the Democratic party's national convention in recent years has been the question of how to insure that the delegates permitted to participate in its deliberations are loyal to its aims and principles. In 1948 a number of southern delegations "bolted" the convention when it became evident that a platform unsatisfactory to them in a number of respects, particularly on civil rights issues, would be adopted and that President Truman would be renominated. They subsequently joined in a dissident States Rights Democratic party movement which nominated Governor J. Strom Thurmond of South Carolina as its candidate for President and Governor Fielding Wright of Mississippi for Vice President. In some of the southern states the States Rights presidential electoral slates were presented to the voters at the 1948 election under the Democratic party emblem, and the regular Democratic electors were forced to appear, if at all, under some other label. No elector slate pledged to vote for the regular Democratic party nominees was offered in Alabama.

In the 1952 convention the issue of party loyalty arising out of these events came to a head. A resolution was presented to the convention to bar delegates who refused to give assurance that, as a condition of being allowed to participate in the proceedings, they would exert every effort to insure that the candidates named would be presented to the voters in their respective states as the official candidates of the Democratic party. This loyalty resolution threw the convention into an uproar and threatened to bring about another walkout by some southern delegations, against whom it was obviously directed. The matter was finally settled by the seating of the protesting delegations; but an understanding was reached that the matter would be studied further as a prelude to action at the next national convention. The issue was studied by an advisory committee set up by the Democratic National Committee before the 1956 convention. The committee's report, which was accepted, recommended that the issue be resolved by a compromise "gentlemen's agreement" approach. Under the plan as approved each state party organization in presenting credentials to its delegation would assume responsibility for seeing that the candidates nominated by the convention would be presented to the voters as the Democratic candidates in their states.[25]

[25] See "The Democratic Party's Approach to Its Convention Rules," *American Political Science Review*, Vol. L (June, 1956), pp. 553–568.

This was not the end of the matter, however. Despite such assurances given by the Alabama party organization prior to the 1960 convention, in the presidential election a slate of Democratic electors, five of whom were pledged to vote for the convention's nominees and six who were "unpledged," was offered to Alabama's voters. As it turned out all of them were elected; but the unpledged electors did not vote for the regular Democratic nominees. Prior to the 1964 convention the Democratic party in Alabama had voted to present a complete slate of unpledged electors on its ticket for the forthcoming election. Statements by some Democratic leaders in Mississippi had indicated that they did not consider themselves bound to support the party's candidates; but the Mississippi party convention had taken steps to see that a slate of pledged Democratic electors would be offered to the voters.

In the light of these developments the 1964 Democratic National Convention's credentials committee determined that a personal affirmation of loyalty to the party should be required of delegates from these states as a condition of their being seated. This was too much for a number of the delegates from Mississippi and Alabama, who thereupon walked out. A few members of these delegations indicated their willingness to take a party loyalty pledge of the sort demanded and remained to participate in the convention's proceedings.[26] The problem will undoubtedly appear again at the 1968 Democratic convention.

REFUSALS OF NOMINATIONS AND CANDIDATE VACANCIES

As yet no individual has ever refused a major party's nomination for the presidency when actually tendered; but on several occasions potential nominees have effectively put a check upon preconvention activities by their supporters which may well have amounted to renunciation of the nomination in advance. Vice presidential nominations have been rejected in at least three instances after being formally offered. Senator Silas Wright of New York rejected the Democratic nomination for Vice President in 1844. The party convention then chose George M. Dallas, who was subsequently elected. In 1860 Benjamin Fitzpatrick of Alabama refused to accept the Democratic nomina-

---

[26] Cf. *The New York Times*, August 24, 25, and 26, 1964. A resolution offered by the credentials committee was adopted by the convention. It authorized the chairman of the National Committee to appoint a special committee prior to the 1968 election to aid state Democratic parties in meeting their responsibilities and assurances that voters in a state shall be given an opportunity to participate freely in the choice of electors pledged "formally and in good conscience" to the election of the Democratic party's presidential and vice presidential nominees, under that party's label and designation. *Ibid.*, August 26, p. 31.

tion on the ticket with Stephen A. Douglas, and Hirschel V. Johnson of Georgia was selected as a replacement by the party's National Committee. In 1924 former Governor Frank Lowden of Illinois rejected the Republican nomination for Vice President as President Coolidge's running mate. The party's national convention, which had remained in session, proceeded to name Charles G. Dawes, who was subsequently elected. The current practice in both major parties is for its convention to remain in session until both the presidential and vice presidential nominees appear and accept their nominations in person. This leaves in their hands the selection of a replacement in the event the nomination is refused.

No major party's presidential nominee has died during the course of a presidential campaign; but in 1912 former President Theodore Roosevelt, running as the Progressive party's candidate, narrowly escaped assassination while making a campaign speech in Milwaukee. In that same campaign the regular Republican nominee for the vice presidency, James Sherman, died shortly before the November balloting for the electors. The Republican National Committee had been empowered by the national convention to fill candidate vacancies on the party ticket, but because of the shortness of time before the election it could not be assembled for this purpose. After the election, upon a suggestion from the White House, presumably with the defeated President Taft's blessing, the eight Republican electors chosen at the November election cast their vice presidential ballots for President Nicholas Murray Butler of Columbia University, as a complimentary gesture. It has become the regular practice in both major parties to empower the National Committee to fill a vacancy on the party ticket before the November election. The Republican rule authorizes the National Committee to reassemble the national convention for this purpose if time permits.[27] The Democratic party rule awards to each National Committee member as many votes as his state had votes in the last national convention, if they should have to name a replacement candidate.

Since the 1912 convention the nearest approach to a situation requiring a national party committee to name a replacement candidate occurred in the 1952 campaign. Revelations about the existence of an "office expense fund" contributed by wealthy constituents to the Republican vice presidential candidate, Senator Richard M. Nixon, gave rise to a demand from some quarters in the party that he be forced to resign the nomination. The crisis quickly subsided when

[27] For a discussion of the problem of candidate vacancies, see "Legal Tangle If Presidential Candidate Dies," *Congressional Quarterly Weekly Report,* Vol. XIV (February 17, 1956), pp. 190–191; and "If a Presidential Nominee or President-Elect Dies," *ibid.,* Vol. XXII (October 16, 1964), p. 2466.

Nixon went before a nationwide television audience and in his famous "Checkers" and "respectable Republican cloth coat" speech turned the incident into an asset for himself.[28]

SELECTION OF CONVENTION DELEGATES

Of crucial importance in giving the convention system a representative democratic character is the manner of selecting delegates. A convention may be conceived of as a gathering of party leaders and "bosses," each intent upon manipulating the nominating and party management processes for ends and interests that have little to do with the actual wishes of the party membership; or it may be regarded as a representative assembly of trusted spokesmen for their several party constituencies, who as responsible agents seek to carry on the processes of party government in a democratic manner. Neither of these conceptions is wholly accurate. But it can be said that the capacity and willingness of a convention to act responsibly depends in great measure upon the nature of the procedures through which the delegates are invested with their office and upon there being means by which their constituents may express their will on matters of party management and policy, particularly with regard to candidates to be nominated.

Selection of convention delegates takes place in the four or five months immediately preceding the national conventions, which meet in midsummer of the presidential election year. A rather confusing variety of selective practices is used. Not only are there variations in procedures from state to state, but there may also be differences within a given state between the major parties. Methods employed may differ within a party in a given state from election to election. Adding to the confusion is the fact that state laws on the subject are still in a process of evolution and there is usually a change in some of them from one election to the next.

Originally the national party organizations let the state party units decide how to select their respective delegations. A number of methods of appointing them, such as choice by state legislative party caucuses, by local mass meetings, by state party committees, or by state and district delegate conventions came into use under local party auspices. In time, the national party conventions undertook to establish general party rules on the subject, but for the most part these rules merely confirmed existing practices. Eventually, during the later decades of the nineteenth century, regulatory state laws began to appear as a part of the general movement for reform and public control of nomi-

[28] For a full account of the incident, see Eric F. Goldman, *The Crucial Decade: America, 1945–1955* (New York: Alfred A. Knopf, 1956), pp. 225–231.

nating practices. This regulatory legislation, however, not infrequently took the form of optional rules, binding the parties only if their governing authorities decided to conform to them.

The direct primary movement, beginning shortly after 1900, brought into being a new type of state law designed to give party rank and file members the opportunity, under public supervision, to elect national convention delegates at a direct primary. Some states also adopted laws to permit party voters to express a preference on potential presidential candidates as a guide or instruction to delegates at the national convention. By 1920 nearly half of the states had adopted some form of "presidential primary" or "presidential preference primary" law of this kind. Thereafter a reaction occurred and a number of states repealed their laws on this subject. Currently some 20 states have optional or mandatory laws of this type.

State laws differ in a variety of respects, such as their mandatory or optional character; the time of conducting the primary; whether participation in it is restricted to registered party members or not; the procedures by which delegate slates pledged to a particular candidate are placed on the ballot; the procedure by which presidential aspirants' names are placed on the presidential preference ballot; whether all delegates or only district delegates, or no delegates at all are elected directly by the party voters; whether voting for pledged or unpledged delegates is on a statewide slate basis, or otherwise; and the extent to which delegates are bound to act in the convention in accordance with their proclaimed pledges of support for a particular candidate or with the revealed preference of the party voters. A detailed state-by-state analysis of current provisions on these points would be unduly tedious; but in general, four types of systems may be distinguished.[29]

1. Choice of national convention delegates by the state party convention, with a statewide presidential preference vote being taken to guide or instruct them. This makes the presidential primary vote little more than a popularity contest among the aspirants for the nomination, inasmuch as the delegates are not bound to support the winner of the preferential vote.

[29] Cf. Key, *Politics, Parties and Pressure Groups*, 5th ed., for an analysis of state presidential primary systems. For a detailed description of the methods used to select and popularly advise delegates to the 1952 party conventions see *Manner of Selecting Delegates to National Political Conventions*, compiled by the Senate Library, (Washington: Government Printing Office, 1952), pp. 81. The actual workings of the delegate selecting process, state by state, for that election are described and analyzed in David, Moos, and Goldman, *op. cit.* The early history of the presidential primary movement and of state practices in the selection of delegates when the movement was at its height are presented in detail in Louise Overacker, *The Presidential Primary* (New York: The Macmillan Company, 1926). The presidential primary system is analyzed critically in Paul David, Ralph Goldman, and Richard Bain, *The Politics of National Party Conventions* (Washington: Brookings Institution, 1960), Chap. 10.

2. Election of delegates by popular vote, with delegates indicating the candidates they expect to support, coupled with an opportunity for voters to express their preference on presidential candidates. Aspirants for delegate seats may if they choose run as "unpledged" delegates, or in some cases merely indicate the candidate they are "favorable to" without pledging themselves to vote for him.

3. Direct election of a slate of pledged electors, but with no preferential vote on presidential candidates as such. In some states the entire slate is voted for on an at-large basis as in the case of presidential electors; in others there is a combination of statewide and district voting procedures, as in the manner of electing Senators and Representatives.

4. Direct election of convention delegates, but with no formal expression of delegate preferences on candidates being indicated on the ballot and no popular preferential vote being taken.

It should be emphasized that the existence of presidential primary legislation on the statute books of a state does not automatically insure that the voters of that state will be given an opportunity to express their views, directly or indirectly, on prospective nominees. Whether such a test of voter sentiment is actually conducted depends not only on the terms of state laws, but also upon the willingness of presidential aspirants to submit their candidacies to the hazards of a primary contest. This in turn may depend upon their ability to attract sufficient local backing to place their names and/or a slate of delegate candidates favorable to them upon the ballot in a given state. The problem of financing a campaign for delegate support by a presidential aspirant is a formidable one, and he can hardly be expected to wage an intensive campaign in every state where action by the party voters may be taken. Strategic considerations may dictate that he stay out of a state where there is strong support for a "favorite son" candidate, to avoid giving offense to that candidate's followers in the hope of receiving their support later during the convention's proceedings. He also must consider the possible effect upon his candidacy of a defeat in a pitched battle against other major contenders. A poor showing in only a few states may create the impression that he is not an attractive candidate and cause the convention to pass him by.

Recent presidential nominating campaigns have demonstrated that the course of the campaign may be drastically affected by the outcome of presidential primary contests in only a very few states. In 1944 Wendell Willkie gave up his effort to win a second Republican nomination when he made a poor showing in the Winconsin primary. General Eisenhower suddenly emerged as a formidable candidate for the Republican nomination in 1952 when 100,000 voters in Minnesota took the trouble to write in his name on the presidential primary ballot. Senator John F. Kennedy demonstrated by his victory over Senator Hubert Humphrey in the West Virginia primary in 1960 that he could win popular support in an overwhelmingly Protestant state. His victory there gave his candidacy an impetus that carried him through to nomination. Senator Goldwater's triumph over Governor Nelson Rockefeller in the California primary in 1964 practically assured his nomination by the Republican convention. The presidential primary thus has a significance that reaches beyond the numbers of delegates actually chosen.

Currently three general types of procedures are employed in choosing national convention delegates. The most widely used method is appointment by state party conventions or by a combination of state and congressional district conventions. This type of selection procedure is used by the major parties in more than half the states. It accounts for about half the delegates making up a convention. Direct election of delegates through some form of the presidential primary is employed in about a third of the states, accounting for slightly less than half the total number of delegates. In a few states the state executive committee or council of the party appoints the delegates.

Viewing the national scene as a whole, contemporary processes of delegate selection undoubtedly give to the national conventions a more representative character than was the case a half-century or longer ago. Apathy on the part of the vast majority of rank and file party members and their failure to participate actively in the processes of party management and decision-making at the grass roots level, of course, often leaves in the hands of the active few selection of many of the delegations at a national convention. Nevertheless, convention delegates, regardless of the manner by which they have attained their posts, cannot be wholly unmindful of the sentiments of their constituents. Delegates are party members of some standing, discernment, and influence. They realize that only at their party's peril may they ignore the drift of opinion on potential presidential nominees as revealed to them by personal contacts, informal polls, petitions, and other such means of communication. The results of presidential primaries, spotty and inconclusive though they may be, guide and inform all delegates in their deliberations.

REFORM OF THE PRESIDENTIAL NOMINATING SYSTEM

It would have been surprising indeed if the revolt against the convention system which brought the direct primary into general use in the states had not carried over into the field of presidential nominations. Criticisms applied to the convention system at the state level were applicable to the national party conventions as well. In fact, the familiar charges of bossism, corruption, unsavory deals, and perversion of the democratic process raised against party conventions generally have had added potency against the national convention because of the wider public interest attaching to it. The knowledge that it continues to rest in large measure upon a foundation of local delegate bodies and caucuses in which relatively few participate gives color to the charge that the national conventions themselves must necessarily be undemocratic and irresponsible. The noisy, circuslike atmosphere in which the convention conducts its business, the unwieldiness of the body as the numbers of delegates have grown to unmanageable proportions, and the increasing influence of an incumbent President over its decisions through use of federal patronage are pointed to as features making it an unsatisfactory instrument for presidential nomination purposes.

These strictures against the system were probably more valid for the decades immediately following the Civil War than for the period since 1900, after many of the states had instituted statutory controls over party procedures in the selection of convention delegates; but these reforms at the state level have by no means silenced the barrage of criticism. The dictation by Theodore Roosevelt of the nomination of William H. Taft as his chosen successor in 1908; the apparent denial of the will of the party majority in Taft's renomination in 1912; the delegate "slush fund" scandals traced to supporters of Governor Frank Lowden in the 1920 convention and the ultimate bestowal of the nomination in that year upon a relatively obscure Senator from Ohio, Warren Harding, at the behest of a few party leaders meeting in a "smoke-filled room"; and the capture of the party nomination in 1940 by a financially well-backed political newcomer, Wendell Willkie, who had not deigned to enter the state primaries against his better-known opponents, are all comparatively recent incidents on the Republican side cited to the discredit of the convention system. The triumph of Senator Barry Goldwater in the Republican convention in 1964 in the face of public opinion polls showing him to be less favored among Republican voters than several other prospective nominees was another demonstration of the shortcomings of the convention system, according to some observers.

The bitter, ruthless, and sometimes demoralizing struggles carried on by contending elements in some of the recent Democratic conventions have repelled some people. Behind-the-scenes maneuverings and deals, such as those which produced the Roosevelt-Garner ticket in 1932, are also pointed to on the Democratic side as evidence of need for further improvement in party nominating procedures. When Senator Estes Kefauver of Tennessee, who had made the best showing of any of the aspirants entering the state primaries was denied the Democratic nomination in 1952 through the opposition of President Truman and various other important state figures whom Kefauver had allegedly offended by his crime-investigating activities, another exhibit was added to the collection of the critics of the convention system. Senator Kefauver's later characterization of the national nominating convention as "a mockery of our democratic processes—an easy tool for the political bosses, the slick manipulators and the unscrupulous kingmakers"[30] is one that continues to strike a responsive chord in the thinking of many.

For the most part, advocates of reform have taken their cues from experiments conducted by the states. As has been seen, the states have not been lacking in ingenuity and willingness to try out new methods in this field. Numerous proposals have been introduced in Congress for the establishment of a nationwide direct primary system under which the nominating function would be taken entirely out of the hands of the party convention and given to the rank-and-file voters of the party, as is now the practice in most of the states in the choice of gubernatorial candidates. Other suggestions look toward combining the direct primary idea with the convention system, as some states do, by referring only an inconclusive popular vote in the primary to the national convention for ultimate decision; or by providing that a primary be resorted to only when the convention is unable to agree on a nominee on the first, second, or third ballot.

Another type of proposal is one that would leave the nominating function in the hands of the national convention, but would employ national power to further state adoption of presidential preference primary laws having some degree of binding effect upon the delegates. From still another quarter have come proposals that the parties themselves take the initiative in overhauling their convention machinery and convert them into a kind of modern version of the earlier type of "mixed" convention. By reducing the number of participants involved and by officially injecting all elements of the national party leadership into the nominating process, it is urged, parties could give their convention procedures a more truly deliberative character and advance the cause of democratic, responsible party government.[31]

[30] See the article by Senator Kefauver, with Sidney Shallet, "Why Not Let the People Elect Our President?" *Collier's,* January 31, 1953. For other critical comment see Kefauver, "Indictment of the Political Convention," *The New York Times Magazine,* March 16, 1952; and James Reston, "The Convention System: A Five-Count Indictment," *ibid.,* July 11, 1948.

[31] The most thorough recent analysis and evaluation of current proposals for reform of the presidential nominating process is presented in David, Goldman, and Bain, *op. cit.*

PROPOSALS FOR A PRESIDENTIAL DIRECT PRIMARY SYSTEM

Adoption of a compulsory nationwide direct primary as a nominating device supplanting the national convention, most of its advocates concede, would necessitate an amendment to the Constitution. This type of reform proposal was first brought prominently to national attention during the 1912 campaign, after the developments at the Republican convention had revealed in dramatic fashion some of the weaknesses of the convention as a nominating agency. Both the Democratic and the Progressive party platforms carried planks advocating presidential nominating system reform.[32] The next year President Wilson in his first annual message to Congress urged adoption of a national direct presidential primary law.[33] Despite his expressed hope that the matter could be handled "promptly and without serious controversy," nothing came of his suggestion, although several bills on the subject were introduced.

Thereafter the direct presidential primary idea found a champion in Senator George Norris of Nebraska, who kept it alive in subsequent sessions of Congress. Later its most active and persistent congressional advocate was Senator William Langer of North Dakota. Regularly he introduced an amendment proposal joining the idea of nominating presidential and vice presidential candidates by a nationwide direct primary to that of electing them by a direct vote of the people.[34] More recently Senator Margaret Chase Smith of Maine has sponsored an

[32] The Democratic party platform carried an endorsement of state presidential primary laws and directed the National Committee to require the use of the primary system for choosing and pledging delegates where state laws did not so provide. The Progressive platform favored "nation-wide direct primaries for candidates for the presidency." Kirk H. Porter and Donald B. Johnson *National Party Platforms 1840–1956* (Urbana: University of Illinois Press, 1956), pp. 170–176.

[33] *Congressional Record*, 63rd Congress, 2nd Session, (1913), p. 44. Wilson apparently assumed that the matter could be dealt with by an ordinary statute, without the necessity of a constitutional amendment. As governor of New Jersey he had led a successful fight for adoption of a direct primary law in that state two years earlier.

[34] Under the Langer plan the names of aspirants for a party nomination would be placed on the primary ballot by petitions signed by a number of qualified voters constituting one-tenth of one percent of the total who voted for President at the most recent election (approximately 70,000 as based on the 1964 election). Voting would take place on the first Monday in June throughout the country in the presidential election year, with voters being eligible to participate in the primary of a party only if they have been registered members of it for at least six months prior to the primary. A plurality of the primary votes in the country at large would be sufficient to nominate. Vice presidential candidates would be presented to the voters and nominated in the same way as presidential candidates. "Independent" candidates could be placed on the general election ballot by petitions signed by a number of voters equalling one-half of one percent of the total vote for President at the last election (approximately 350,000 at present).

amendment proposal providing for a direct presidential primary incorporating the runoff primary idea in case no candidate receives a
popular majority on the first try. Still another type of direct primary
proposal is illustrated by one offered by the late Senator Kefauver. His
proposed amendment would merely grant broad powers to Congress to
"provide for nominating of candidates for President and Vice President by primary election." It was so flexible in its terms that it could
have eventuated in any of the kinds of primary already described, or
some totally novel system.[35]

Although the idea of nominating presidential candidates through
some form of nationwide direct primary appears to have strong popular
support,[36] the prospects for its adoption are remote. It is unlikely that
the parties will take the initiative in developing any kind of practicable
nationwide direct primary system for themselves; and the special
majorities required for use of the national constitutional amending
process to achieve this objective by national law interpose an apparently
insuperable barrier. There is a measure of support for a direct primary
law or constitutional amendment in Congress, and considerable study
has been given the matter by congressional committees in recent years;
but no amendment proposal of this kind has progressed beyond the
committee stage.

Problems and issues that have had to be met by the states in connection with their direct primary laws would be magnified manyfold
in a national presidential primary system. With nominees being
chosen at a national direct primary, lengthy and expensive campaigns
by individual aspirants for a nomination would have to be carried on
throughout the country. The question of how such campaigns might be
financed without placing the candidates irretrievably in the political
debt of their backers looms large. The rules adopted for determining
eligibility to seek a party's nomination, for determining voters' eligibility to participate in a particular party's primary, and for placing
the names of independently sponsored and party insurgent group

[35] For an outline of the type of implementing statute which he favored in
the event of adoption of his amendment proposal, see the statement of Senator
Kefauver in *Hearings on S.J. Res. 3*, etc., before the Senate Judiciary Committee's
Sub-Committee on Constitutional Amendments, 84th Congress, 1st Session (March–
April, 1955), pp. 110–114. The plan he outlined would have required that delegates
be chosen in each state through a presidential primary similar to that provided for
by the current Wisconsin presidential primary law. It would leave the nominating
function in the hands of the national convention, but would require delegates elected
under a pledge of support to a specified candidate to continue to vote for that
candidate on successive ballots until released by him or until his total delegate
vote falls below 10 percent in the convention.

[36] According to a statement by Senator Kefauver, an Institute of Public Opinion (Gallup) poll taken in July, 1952, showed 73 percent of those queried as favoring
nomination of presidential candidates by a direct primary vote, 16 percent opposed, and 11 percent undecided. *Ibid.*, p. 14.

candidates on the final election ballot would carry with them serious implications with respect to maintenance of the integrity of party nominations and continuance of the two-party system. Whether voting power should be allotted to the party electorate of a state according to some fixed formula, or whether the total vote in the nation at large should be controlling would invite controversy, as it has in connection with presidential election reform. The manner of dealing with the vice presidential nomination and with possible candidate vacancy problems are other questions that would have to be resolved. Whether agreement could be reached in Congress on solutions to these questions is most doubtful.

Substitution of some form of direct primary for the present system would have a considerable impact upon the party system and on the type of candidate selected. The nature of this impact cannot be predicted with complete assurance; but it would doubtless have a number of more or less foreseeable results. The "availablity factors" governing the disposition of the nomination would undoubtedly be altered to some extent. The influence of mass communications media in building up prospective candidates would be enhanced. Because they occupy places of advantage from which to attract national attention, members of the House and Senate who are in posts of leadership, and high-ranking officials in the executive branch would probably become more formidable competitors for the presidential nominations; while by the same token, governors of the large pivotal states, who have been prime presidential nominee material for both major parties in recent decades, for the same reason would become less likely prospects. Experience in public office as a test of fitness for the nomination would probably have less importance. Individuals such as business executives, labor leaders, military figures, journalists, and other professional people who have achieved national prominence in fields other than public service might become more likely prospects than they are at present.

The reluctant candidate who has the nomination thrust upon him by a real or simulated draft at the last moment would probably become a thing of the past, since it is inconceivable that any individual would be entered in a primary without his sanction. The "dark horse" candidate, brought forward as a compromise when powerful factions have reached a deadlock in the convention balloting, would be eliminated. The practice of using the vice presidential nomination as a counterpoise to the presidential nomination would also be ended unless the candidates for the two offices were required to present themselves in pairs at the primary. Whether the national two-party system could even survive under a nationwide direct primary is questioned by some authorities. Altogether the long-range effects of a direct primary system on the type of candidate selected and the reallocation of power and influence within the existing parties, to say nothing of its possible effects on the two-party system as presently constituted, would be so far-reaching that the chances of favorable action upon such a proposal by national and state legislative bodies dominated by existing major party interests appear very slight.

PROPOSALS TO IMPROVE THE NATIONAL CONVENTION SYSTEM

While it is improbable that the movement to adopt a direct primary for nominating presidential candidates will bear fruit, there is more promise of success for efforts to bring about improvements in the national convention as the party organ for this purpose. As has been noted, on their own initiative the parties have been developing new rules governing delegate apportionment which are intended to make their conventions more representative of actual party membership. Another approach toward the same end is to be seen in recent efforts to encourage wider use of state-administered presidential primaries. Still another approach being urged upon the parties is a rather drastic overhauling of the convention itself in the direction of making it a smaller body wherein major decisions on platforms and candidates can be arrived at by a consultative process involving the party leadership in a more open, responsible fashion.

Following the 1956 presidential campaign, Senator Paul Douglas of Illinois and Representative Charles Bennett of Florida advanced a proposal designed to bring about more uniformity in state presidential primary laws. The central idea of a bill sponsored by them jointly was the offer of a subsidy of up to 20 cents per vote cast to help states meet administrative costs for holding an approved type of presidential primary. The assumption was that the offer of financial aid would not only induce more states to adopt presidential primary laws but that it would also cause states that have such laws to adapt them to a common pattern.[37] If the resulting more widespread primary voting re-

[37] The Douglas-Bennett Bill proposed the establishment of a bipartisan, five-member presidential nominations commission to be appointed by the President for overlapping terms, to which petitions submitting the names of presidential candidates to the voters of their respective parties would be presented. A nominating petition would have to bear the names of at least 1000 voters in each of four or a minimum of three-fourths of the participating states. A candidate so designated would have a limited time in which to withdraw his name from consideration; if he failed to ask that it be withdrawn, it would be certified to the participating states and would appear on their presidential preference ballot. The law would apply only to nominations by parties for whose candidates at least 10,000,000 popular votes were cast at the last presidential election.

To be eligible for the federal financial aid authorized by the plan, a state would have been required to have a presidential preference primary law under which only the names of prospective candidates whose names are certified by the commission appear; to limit participation in a party's primary to those qualified

vealed a clear-cut popular preference, a party convention would be placed under strong pressure to implement it. Even the mild degree of interference by the national government involved in the Douglas-Bennett approach on a matter heretofore left exclusively to the states and state party organizations stirred strong opposition, and it failed to progress beyond the committee stage. Its sponsorship was taken over by other members of Congress in subsequent sessions; but its chances of passage remain very remote.

Approach to the reform of presidential nominating procedures through voluntary change in party rules and usages governing the structure, organization, and procedures of national nominating conventions has been urged for some time. When President Wilson recommended to Congress the enactment of a presidential primary law in 1913 he coupled with it a suggestion that the national party convention, which he said should be retained only for platform-making purposes, be reconstituted. He suggested that the conventions should consist not of delegates chosen for this purpose, but of the nominees for Congress, the nominees for vacant seats in the Senate of the United States, the Senators whose terms have not yet closed, the National Committees, and the candidates for the presidency themselves, "in order that platforms may be framed by those responsible for carrying them into effect."[38] Nothing came of his proposal.

More recently a Committee on Political Parties of the American Political Science Association advanced a series of recommendations for alteration of the scheme of party government in the United States.[39] With regard to presidential nominating practices the Committee proposed to leave the nominating function in the hands of the national convention; but it suggested that the conventions be drastically altered in composition. The number of members should be reduced to about 500 to 600. Some 300 to 350 of them would be elected delegates, while the remainder would be made up of the congressional, National

---

voters who are registered members of the party; its primary would have had to be held within a specified period of time (April 1 to July 31); and its law would have had to make the results of the preferential primary binding on delegates "to a reasonable extent," a phrase which the commission was authorized to define by appropriate rules. Cf. the remarks of Senator Douglas, *Congressional Record,* 85th Congress, 1st Session (1957), p. 2221.

[38] *Congressional Record,* 63rd Congress, 2nd Session (1913), p. 44.

[39] Report of the Committee on Political Parties, "Toward a More Responsible Two-Party System," *American Political Science Review* (Supplement), Vol. XLIV (1950), p. 10. This recommendation was only a part of a plan for a more unified and better disciplined type of national party. It should be pointed out that the Report does not represent the official point of view of the American Political Science Association as a body. For critical reactions to it see Austin Ranney, "Toward a More Responsible Party System: A Commentary," *American Political Science Review,* Vol. XLV (June, 1951), pp. 488–492; and Julius Turner, "Responsible Parties: A Dissent from the Floor," *ibid.* (March, 1951), pp. 144–145. However, neither of these writers was critical, specifically, of the committee's recommendation regarding reconstitution of the national convention.

Committee, and other party leadership elements, along with a few others from the nation at large. It would meet biennially rather than only once in four years. The Committee's report has been studied by the national party organizations; but there is no indication as yet that either major party intends to move along the lines suggested.

Reforms in presidential nominating procedures in the immediate future are most likely to be made through improving the convention system rather than by substituting some radically different mode of nomination. The advent of radio and television has placed the national conventions and their proceedings in the spotlight of public observation. This has already proved to be a factor impelling the parties to put their houses in better order with regard to the conduct of convention business. A by-product has been a great increase in public knowledge of the workings of the system and greater public concern over how delegates are selected. Even without the stimulus of a federal subsidy of the sort proposed in the Douglas-Bennett Bill the states appear to be undergoing a revival of interest in presidential primary legislation. In the past decade a number have enacted laws of this kind, while others have revised and improved existing laws.[40] Both the National Municipal League and the Council of State Governments have initiated studies for the purpose of drafting model laws for the guidance of state legislators.

THE NATIONAL CONVENTION: AN EVALUATION

While a plausible case can be made against the convention system and there is undoubtedly much room for improving convention procedures, this institution has served the country well over the years and gives promise of continuing to do so. James Bryce in his famous chapter on "Why Great Men Are Not Chosen President" laid a major share of the blame for this alleged fault on the convention system and the factors affecting its operation.[41] The conditions he described three quarters of a century ago still persist in some measure. To the casual

[40] Since 1948 Minnesota, Wisconsin. New Hampshire, Nebraska, and New Jersey have revised their presidential primary laws; and Indiana, Montana, and Nevada have adopted new ones. Congress also adopted such a law for the District of Columbia. The Nevada statute, however, was repealed in 1955. A good summary of recent developments in the field of state primary legislation, together with concrete suggestions for improvements, may be found in Manning J. Dauer, William A. F. Stephenson, Harry Macy, and David Temple, "Toward a Model State Presidential Primary Law," *American Political Science Review*, Vol. L (March, 1956), pp. 138–153. In 1952 over 13,000,000 voters participated in presidential primaries in 15 states; and in 1956 over 11,000,000 in 17 states. See the *Congressional Quarterly Weekly Report*, Vol. XIV (June 15, 1956), p. 690, for state-by-state and party summaries.

[41] James Bryce, *The American Commonwealth* (New York: The Macmillan Company, 3 vols., 1888), Vol. I, Chap. VIII.

observer today a national convention with its noise, contrived demon-
strations and confusion is not an edifying spectacle when it is recalled
that from this body a most momentous decision affecting the fate of the
nation and possibly of the world must emerge. To the somewhat more
sophisticated it is no less disquieting to know that negotiations among
influential party figures operating behind the scenes in hotel room
conferences and convention hall lobbies may actually be shaping
the course of the convention's actions.

Over against these considerations must be measured the discipline
exerted by public opinion upon conventions and their leadership. The
relatively even balance of strength between the two major parties
nationally makes each a threat to the other. Party leaders realize that
to ignore popular opinion is to risk the loss of control of the presidency.
They are concerned, first of all, with winning the election. As shown at
the Republican convention in 1952 when it nominated General Eisenhower over Senator Taft, the party organization may sometimes pass
over a candidate it really prefers as the party standard-bearer in favor
of one whose popular backing is so strong that the party would be
running a grave risk of defeat in defying it. The reluctant acceptance
of Herbert Hoover by the Republican party organization leaders in
the 1928 convention affords another example of the operation of this
rule. Viewed over the years, the convention system as tested by results
has by no means been a failure. After all, as has been said, "it works."[42]
While it has spawned some mediocrities as candidates, it has also given
the nation Abraham Lincoln, Theodore Roosevelt, Woodrow Wilson,
and Franklin D. Roosevelt; and who is so say that some of the unsuccessful nominees it has produced would not have achieved high distinction if they had been elevated to the presidency?[43]

The party convention, moreover, plays an important role in helping to maintain the American two-party system. The two-party system,
by its very nature, depends upon the "politics of moderation." The
platform of a major party and its presidential candidate's views must
reflect an attitude near the middle of the political spectrum presented
by its varied membership. For him to represent the views of either the
extreme right or the extreme left wings of the party is to court disaster.

---

[42] Cf. James M. Burns, "The Case for the Smoke-Filled Room," *The New
York Times Magazine*, June 15, 1952. See also Fletcher Knebel, "One Vote for the
Convention System," *ibid.*, August 23, 1964. Herbert Eaton, *Presidential Timber:
The Story of How Presidential Candidates Are Nominated* (New York: The Mac-
millan Company, 1964) recounts in lively fashion the history of the major party con-
ventions from 1868 to 1960.

[43] For an interesting study of the men who as major party candidates failed
to reach the presidency and an estimate of how they might have performed in that
office, see Irving Stone, *They Also Ran* (Garden City, N.Y.: Doubleday & Company,
1943).

This was a lesson which had to be relearned by the Republican party through its landslide defeat in the 1964 election.

The convention system for settling upon a candidate tends to further, although it does not necessarily guarantee, this kind of decision·making process. It fosters negotiation and compromise among the various sectional, social and economic interests that associate them-selves under one party's banner. The instinct of the party leadership is to avoid extremism in the choice of the nominee for President. By a process aptly termed "co-ordinate factionalism,"[44] responsible party leaders seek to identify in their candidate and their platform the areas of agreement within the party and to minimize the areas of disagree-ment. As a standard-bearer they prefer one to whose support there will be a minimum of difficulty in rallying the party faithful, along with a goodly share of the "independents."

After the battle for the nomination is over the pledges of sup-port to the successful candidate and other visible evidences of en-thusiasm with which the convention closes are a demonstration that a process in party self-government has been successfully completed. Now that national convention proceedings are broadcast by radio and television throughout the country, they serve as an energizing and activating force within the party's ranks everywhere. Some of the fizz and froth, the hyperbole and high-sounding oratory can be under-stood as merely a calculated effort to arouse and intensify feelings of loyalty among all who have an inclination, latent or otherwise, toward the party. Well-informed people among the general public understand this and look upon such doings with tolerant and amused smiles. The convention provides tangible evidence that a party is self-disciplined, truly national in its composition and outlook, and worthy of being entrusted with control of the executive branch of the government without endangering the stability of the political system. An institu-tion that contributes to this kind of result, as the national party con-vention does, should not be lightly discarded.

[44] Malcolm Moos, "New Light on the Nominating Process," in *Research Fron-tiers in Politics and Government* (Washington: Brookings Institution, 1955), p. 138.

5

THE CONDITIONS OF
ELIGIBILITY AND TENURE

From the time of its establishment in America the office of chief executive has been based upon the "republican" principle. The Founders of the Republic accepted as axiomatic that preservation of liberty requires not only that those entrusted with high public office be recruited from among the populace served, but that their mandate have a fixed time limit. These cornerstone principles of republican government were solemnly proclaimed in the Massachusetts Bill of Rights in these words:

> In order to prevent those who are vested with authority from becoming oppressors, the people have a right, at such periods and in such manner as they shall establish by their frame of government, to cause their public officers to return to private life; and to fill up vacant places by certain and regular elections and appointments.[1]

As a further measure for insuring wise, beneficent, and restrained government, the Founders deemed it essential to place in the constitutions and laws safeguards against elevation of the unfit to public office. Definitions of eligibility both general and specific should be prescribed, they believed, lest the people or their agents betray the public interest by investing with the dangerous authority of the state those who are unworthy of public trust. These principles as applied to the office of state governor were accepted by the architects of the office of President. Although the terms of national and state constitutions have been modified from time to time, these principles continue to characterize constitutional arrangements at both levels of government.

[1] Constitution of 1780, Part I, Art. VIII. The Bills of Rights of the first constitutions of Virginia, Pennsylvania, and Maryland contained similar statements of these fundamental principles.

CONSTITUTIONAL AND LEGAL QUALIFICATIONS FOR CHIEF EXECUTIVES

ORIGINAL STATE CONSTITUTIONAL PROVISIONS

The framers of the original state constitutions displayed some diversity of thought on what special qualifications, if any, should be set for their governors. A special qualification in the form of property ownership was imposed in some states. Maryland's constitution required that the governor own real and personal property to the value of £5000, including £1000 in real estate; South Carolina's, a freehold to the value of £10,000 "free of debt"; North Carolina's and Massachusetts', a freehold in lands and tenements above the value of £1000; and New Hampshire's an estate to the value of £500, of which at least one-half must be a freehold. Even in a society where land-owning was much more widespread that it is at present, qualifications such as these indicated an intent to restrict eligibility to those who possessed a substantial economic stake in that society.

Reflecting the importance of religious orthodoxy in the thinking of the times were provisions in several state constitutions prescribing a qualification in the form of religious belief.[2] New Hampshire required that the governor be a Protestant, while Massachusetts more broadmindedly required only that he be a Christian. Delaware required of him an oath "professing belief in God, the Father, in Jesus Christ, and the Holy Ghost," and an acknowledgement that the Holy Scriptures were of "divine inspiration." New Jersey specified that he be "some fit person," but then went on to limit office-holding generally to "members of a Protestant sect who shall demean themselves peaceably under the government, as hereby established." North Carolina disqualified any person who denied the being of God, the truth of the Protestant religion or the divine authority of either the Old or the New Testaments, or who held religious principles incompatible with the peace and safety of the state. Maryland required that the governor be a person of "wisdom, experience and virtue"; but while forbidding any religious test for office-holding other than belief in the Christian religion, its constitution went on to require a test of that kind of every officeholder.

Minimum age and local residence requirements, both types of

[2] Religious qualifications for office-holding in these early instruments of government may also have been intended to give effect to the old common law rule that only believers in God and a future state of rewards and punishments could give a valid oath. Cf. Frank Swancara, "The Surviving Religious Test," *St. Louis Law Review*, Vol. 18 (February, 1933), pp. 105–116.

qualifications which were in time to become common in the states, were also prescribed in some cases. Representing the more liberal approach to the whole matter were Virginia's constitution, which laid down no special eligibility requirements for the governor; New York's, which required only that he be a "wise and discreet freeholder"; and Rhode Island and Connecticut, whose converted charters specified only that he be a "freeman of the Company."

CONSTITUTIONAL QUALIFICATIONS OF THE PRESIDENT

In view of the concern exhibited in most of the states to limit office-holding to persons of orthodox religious views with a sufficient property interest to insure their devotion to the established order, the fact is noteworthy that the Constitutional Convention of 1787 prescribed no qualifications for the office of President except those concerning age, natural-born citizenship, and residence in the United States. An attempt to establish a property ownership qualification for federal officeholders, including the President, was made in the Convention, but the effort failed. This question was posed by Charles Pinckney of South Carolina who, though maintaining that he was opposed to the establishment of an "undue aristocratic influence in the Constitution," thought that members of all three branches of the government should be "possessed of competent property to make them independent and respectable." Accordingly he offered as an amendment to the Committee of Detail report on this point a proposal that a property ownership qualification of not less than $100,000 be set for the President, with lesser amounts for members of the other two branches. His motion was opposed by Ellsworth and Franklin. The former called attention to the disparities in distribution of wealth from state to state which would make agreement on a common standard difficult; while Franklin made the point that wealth was no criterion of virtue and that "some of the greatest rogues he was ever acquainted with, were the richest rogues." These observations seemed to carry weight with the delegates; for Pinckney's motion was voted down, being rejected by "so general a *no,* that the States were not called."[3]

This was the end of the effort to place in the Constitution a property qualification for the President. The qualifications eventually prescribed—a minimum age of 35, natural-born citizenship or United States citizenship at the time of adoption of the Constitution, and 14 years of residence in the United States—were recommended as a seeming afterthought in the report from the Committee on Postponed Matters and Unfinished Business near the end of the Convention's

[3] Madison, "Debates," pp. 511, 512–513.

deliberations. They were accepted without debate or explanation. The citizenship and residence qualifications were obviously calculated to offset fears that a President unduly subject to foreign influence might be selected, a fear which had been frequently expressed during the debates in the Convention. It has been suggested that the citizenship and residence qualifications actually originated with John Jay, who was not a member of the Convention, and that he had in mind particularly the exclusion of General von Steuben from the presidency.[4] The German-born General had been sympathetic to the army veteran followers of Daniel Shays in the Massachusetts uprising of 1786 and had been suspected of intrigues with Prince Henry of Prussia regarding the latter's assumption of the American crown. The issue of a religious test for the President was disposed of by inclusion of the clause in Article VI prohibiting the imposition of such a test for holding any office under the United States; while the special oath of office prescribed for the President in Article II was designed to give further assurance of his attachment to this country and its form of government under the Constitution.

These restrictions have been of very slight significance in actually limiting the range of choice in the selection of the President and Vice President. Few individuals have acquired sufficient national prominence before reaching the age of 35 to warrant serious consideration as candidates for the presidency or the vice presidency. A few prominent persons not of American birth may have been affected by the natural-born citizen requirement. A possible instance occurred in 1872. Senator Carl Schurz of Missouri, who was a prominent leader and organizer of the Liberal Republican party, might have been nominated instead of Horace Greeley as the Liberal Republican-Democratic coalition candidate to oppose President Grant for a second term had he been eligible as a natural-born citizen. Schurz, who was of German birth, had achieved fame in the publishing field as well as in politics, and later served as Secretary of the Interior under President Hayes from 1877 to 1881.

Questions of interpretation have arisen in connection with both the 14-year residence rule and the meaning of the phrase "natural born citizen." When Herbert Hoover was brought forward as the Republi-

4 Charles C. Thach, in *The Creation of the Presidency, 1775–1789* (Baltimore: Johns Hopkins University Press, Johns Hopkins University Studies in Historical and Political Science, Ser. XL, No. 4, 1922), at p. 137, notes that in a letter to Washington on July 25, 1787, Jay had written:

> Permit me to hint whether it would not be wise and seasonable to provide a strong check to the admission of Foreigners into the administration of our national Government, and to declare expressly that the Command in chief of the American army shall not be given to, nor devolve upon, any but a natural born citizen.

can candidate for President in 1928, it was pointed out by some constitutional purists that he had not been a resident of the United States for all of the immediately preceding 14 years. The issue was not seriously pressed.[5] This precedent provides some support for the conclusion that the 14 years of residence need not necessarily be the 14 years immediately preceding a President's assumption of office. But it should be noted that one of the objectives of the Framers in inserting the 14-year residence rule evidently was to bar, temporarily at least, those Americans of Tory sympathies who had fled the country during the course of the Revolutionary War. To achieve this objective the phrase would have to be construed to mean the years immediately preceding election.

The question of the meaning of "natural born citizen" has been raised most seriously in connection with the presidential or vice presidential eligibility of persons born outside the United States to American parents. It was raised when Franklin D. Roosevelt, Jr., was touted for the vice presidential nomination on the Democratic ticket in 1952 and again when Governor Christian Herter of Massachusetts was proposed for the vice presidency in an abortive "dump Nixon" movement in the Republican party in 1956. Roosevelt was born at Campobello Island, New Brunswick, and Herter was born in Paris. The issue will also arise again if Governor George Romney of Michigan, who was born of American parents in Mexico, should become a contender for the Republican nomination for President or Vice President. Are such persons "natural born citizens" or does the phrase cover only persons born within the United States who become citizens by reason of the operation of the rule of *jus soli?*

The common sense view would seem to be that persons acquiring American citizenship by reason of being born abroad to American parents should be considered natural-born citizens within the context of this clause. In the first act passed by Congress soon after the Constitution went into effect the term was assigned this broader meaning,[6] and

---

[5] Edward S. Corwin, in *The President: Office and Powers,* 4th ed. (New York: New York University Press, 1957), p. 330, n. 7, points out that former Attorney General Wickersham defended the eligibility of Mr. Hoover in an elaborate opinion published in *The New York Times* for December 20, 1927. Wickersham stressed the point that during his absences abroad before 1920 Hoover had retained his legal domicile in the United States as well as his American citizenship.

[6] Act of March 26, 1790, 1 *Stat.* 415. It stated:

> The children of citizens of the United States that may be born beyond sea, outside the limits of the United States, shall be considered as natural-born citizens of the United States; provided that the right of citizenship shall not descend to persons whose fathers have never been resident in the United States.

The essence of this provision has been continued in later nationality legislation, although the specific reference to persons acquiring citizenship through parentage

this early usage carries great weight as a contemporary interpretation of it. The alternative of being a citizen at the time of the adoption of the Constitution has ceased, of course, to have any significance. It was important for a time in that none of the first seven Presidents was a natural-born American citizen at birth. They were all born British citizens. The first President who could claim American citizenship by reason of being born in the United States was Martin Van Buren, who was born in New York in 1782.

CURRENT QUALIFICATIONS FOR THE GOVERNORSHIP

As the older states proceeded with revisions of their constitutions and as new states reflecting the more democratic conceptions of the frontier became members of the Union, the categories employed by the United States Constitution in defining eligibility requirements for the President supplied the pattern for the new states in setting qualifications for their governors. Qualifications based on property ownership were eliminated and those based on religion were either eliminated or watered down so as to exclude only atheists. In the light of the Supreme Court's 1961 ruling in the case of *Torcaso* v. *Watkins*,[7] wherein the Court struck down as violating the constitutional guarantee of religious liberty a Maryland statute requiring of all officers an oath declaring a "belief in the Christian religion" or in the case of Jews "belief in a future state of rewards and punishments," these remaining religious qualifications for the governorship are no doubt unconstitutional.[8]

Specific eligibility requirements for governors in the form of a minimum age, United States citizenship, and state citizenship or state residence have become standard provisions of state constitutions. All but eight states set special age requirements above the normal voting age minimum, most commonly 30 years. United States citizenship is a

---

as natural-born citizens has been eliminated. The nationality laws now refer to them as "citizens at birth." Cf. *United States Code* (1964), Title 8, Sec. 1401. During the 1964 presidential campaign suits were launched in state courts in California and New York seeking to bar the candidacy of Senator Goldwater for the presidency on the ground that he was not a natural-born citizen of the United States because he was born in Arizona Territory, three years before Arizona became a state. The suits were properly dismissed as raising no valid constitutional issue. Cf. *The Ann Arbor News,* September 26, 1964.

[7] 367 U.S. 486 (1961).

[8] Art. IV, Sec. 3 of the South Carolina constitution specifically excludes from the governorship anyone who "denies the existence of the Supreme Being." Art. 19, Sec. 1 of the Arkansas constitution sets up as a general requirement for office-holding in that state belief in "the being of a God." Art. IX, Sec. 2 of the Tennessee constitution similarly excludes those who deny "the being of God, or a future state of rewards and punishments." These provisions are probably intended not so much to make atheists ineligible for public office as to give effect to the old common law rule regarding capacity to give a valid oath.

specifically mentioned requirement in about three-fourths of the states and is indirectly called for by the others. A few of the older states at one time or another have required that the governor be a native-born United States citizen, but this qualification no longer is found.[9] The United States citizenship requirement in about one-fourth of the states carries with it a specification of the number of years, ranging from five to twenty, that the individual must have been a citizen. Residence within the state, or state citizenship, or both, for a minimum number of years ranging from one to ten, with five being the most common, is a qualification specifically prescribed by the constitutions of all but eight states and indirectly by the others. The constitutions of Kansas, Ohio, Rhode Island, Vermont, and Wisconsin are the most liberal in that they provide no specific qualifications for the governorship beyond those imposed on voters generally. Attachment to the Constitution and to the principles of government it embodies is required by the oath prescribed for all federal and state officers in Article VI of that instrument.

SPECIAL DISQUALIFICATIONS

In addition to the specifically enumerated qualifications for the governorship there are other restrictions which afford grounds for exclusion of certain individuals from this office. Under a long-standing rule of the common law the holder of one public office may not simultaneously hold a second office carrying with it duties and responsibilities that are incompatible with the first. Most state constitutions reinforce this rule by declaring that a governor may not at the same time be a member of the state legislature or hold another state office or an office under the United States, including a seat in Congress. The United States Constitution only goes so far as to prohibit a person holding any office under the United States from being at the same time a member of Congress. By executive and legislative action this principle has been supplemented so as to prohibit federal officers from holding state office simultaneously.[10] Provisions such as these not

---

[9] The last state to impose such a requirement was Maine. In 1955 a constitutional amendment was adopted in that state substituting a 15-year period of United States citizenship for the natural-born citizenship requirement. See *Laws of Maine,* 1955. Chap. 100, p. 1001, and the *National Municipal Review,* Vol. XLV (January, 1956), p. 21.

[10] In 1873 President Grant issued an executive order, which was continued with certain modifications by later Presidents, stating that acceptance by a federal officer of a state or territorial office was to be deemed a surrender of the federal office. Beginning with legislation enacted in 1894 Congress has prohibited holders of federal offices carrying a compensation of $2500 or more per year from being appointed to or holding any other office to which compensation is attached unless authorized by law. The statute, with modifications, remains in force. Cf. *United*

only support the system of separation of powers but they also prevent the joining of state and national offices in the same hands.

These restrictions are of considerable consequence in view of the fact that not infrequently state governors are elected or appointed to national office during the course of their term. In such a case a governor must relinquish the governorship upon accepting the national post. The question whether a governor might continue in that capacity after accepting a federal office was posed at an early date when John Sullivan, the President of New Hampshire, refused to vacate that post after accepting an appointment from President Washington as a federal district judge in 1789. Sullivan's term as governor did not have long to run and the issue was not pressed. When the New Hampshire constitution was revised in 1792, however, a clause was inserted forbidding this type of dual officeholding.

It should be noted that these general restraints do not necessarily prevent an individual from offering himself as a candidate for two different offices at the same election, nor from seeking another elective office while holding on to one he already has. His right to seek two elective offices simultaneously depends upon the provisions of the election laws of his state. Thus in 1932, John N. Garner, who was Speaker of the United States House of Representatives, ran for re-election to Congress while at the same time running for Vice President. He was elected to both offices and resigned his House seat upon becoming Vice President. A similar maneuver was employed by Lyndon B. Johnson when he was the Democratic candidate for Vice President in 1960. He was at the same time re-elected to the United States Senate, where he had been the floor leader of his party. The Arizona legislature obligingly changed the election laws at that state to permit Senator Goldwater to run for re-election to his Senate post in 1964 while also running for the presidency; but he resigned his candidacy for the Senate as soon as he was nominated for President by his party. Governor Adlai Stevenson likewise resigned his candidacy for re-election to the governorship in Illinois when he accepted the Democratic nomination for President in 1952. There have been numerous instances, however, of "holdover" United States Senators' accepting party nominations for President or Vice President without resigning their Senate seats. Senator Truman became a candidate for the vice presidency in 1944 while retaining his Senate seat, as did Senators Barkley in 1948, Sparkman and Nixon in 1952, Kefauver in 1956, and Humphrey in 1964. Senator John F. Kennedy made the race for President in 1960 while retaining

---

States Code (1952). Title 5, Sec. 62. On the general subject see Joseph F. Barbano, "Dual Office Holding—Federal, State and Municipal," *St. John's Law Review*, Vol. X (December, 1935), pp. 83–92; and G. B. Conklin, "Plural Office Holding," *Oregon Law Review*, Vol. 28 (June, 1949), pp. 332–361.

his Senate seat; and Governor Dewey conducted his campaigns for the presidency in 1944 and 1948 while retaining his post as New York's governor.

The problem of dual officeholding has presented itself most seriously when governors who have been elected to the United States Senate have delayed giving up the office of governor until some time after their senatorial term has begun. One of the most spectacular cases of this kind occurred in Louisiana in the early 1930s. When Governor Huey Long was elected to the Senate at the November, 1930, election, his term as governor had a year and a half to run. Unwilling to resign his gubernatorial post because the lieutenant governor who would succeed him, Paul Cyr, had become an opponent of his regime and could be expected to take steps to wreck the Long machine if he became governor, Long refrained from taking the oath of office and accepting the salary of a Senator when his term began on March 4, 1931. However, he was assigned office space in Washington and began enjoying other perquisites of his senatorial post at that time.

After waiting in vain for seven months for the mantle of the governorship to fall on his shoulders, on October 13, 1931, Cyr took matters into his own hands. He had himself sworn in as governor, maintaining that under the terms of the Louisiana constitution forbidding dual officeholding, Long could not lawfully retain the governorship. For a time it appeared that there might be violence when Long, fearing a coup d'etat by Cyr and his supporters, called out a detachment of the militia to prevent seizure of the capitol and the executive mansion. Cyr instituted an intrusion into office suit against Long and the matter was left to the courts for decision. A district court ruled that Cyr had no cause for action since he was not the governor. The Louisiana Supreme Court sustained this ruling.[11] Long eventually was sworn in as a Senator on January 25, 1932, some three months before his term as governor expired and over ten months after his term as a Senator had begun. The president pro tem of the state senate, a Long partisan, finished out the term as acting governor, Cyr having conceded that his action in taking the oath as governor had severed his connection with the lieutenant governorship. The incident was not without its comic aspect when in the midst of the controversy an unemployed citizen, one Aldrich, also set up a claim to the governorship on the ground that it was "abandoned property," and took the oath of office.

11 *State ex rel Cyr* v. *Long,* 174 La. 170, 140 So. 13 (1932). Later the Louisiana courts were called upon to determine whether a member of Congress was eligible to seek the Democratic nomination for governor while still retaining his seat in Congress. A clause of the state constitution provides that no person "who holds office under the United States at the time of his election" is eligible for the governorship. It was held that membership in Congress is not an "office under the United States" within the meaning of this clause. *Grace* v. *Boggs,* (La. App.) 55 So. (2nd) 45 (1951).

Under the constitution or laws of some states a conviction for certain types of crimes, including perjury, embezzlement of public funds, bribery or attempted bribery of public officials, and "corrupt practices" as defined by laws regulating campaign fund sources and expenditures, carries with it ineligibility to hold public office thereafter. Reflecting a problem posed by the "code of honor" of an earlier day a number of the older state constitutions specifically exclude from public office participants and seconds in duels. The requirement of an oath of fidelity to the Constitution of the United States imposed by Article VI of that instrument upon all legislative, executive, and judicial officers of the states sets up another type of test which governors must meet. In recent years special loyalty oath statutes and constitutional provisions designed to exclude from office those who have engaged in variously defined forms of subversive activity have been added by some states to the list of legal barriers intended to enforce political orthodoxy and prevent the governorship from falling into untrustworthy hands.[12]

The utility of detailed enumerations of tests and elgibility requirements as a means of preventing election as chief executives of persons unworthy of public trust is open to serious question. Most, if not all, of the current eligibility requirements for chief executives could no doubt be eliminated without lowering the standards actually applied in their choice. It is rather futile in any case to seek to prevent a miscarriage of the selective process by disqualifying various categories of unworthy individuals so long as reliance is placed upon popular election as the method of choice. The mass of eligibles from which the public may choose necessarily includes a large proportion of persons unfitted for high public office, and an unwise or dangerous choice must always remain a possibility. Detailed eligibility requirements stand as a rather meaningless testimony to lack of faith in the democratic process.

ENFORCEMENT OF ELIGIBILITY RESTRICTIONS

Incorporation in constitutions and laws of detailed eligibility requirements for chief executives not only gives rise to questions of interpretation in borderline cases but it also presents the difficult problem of how the requirements shall be enforced. Shall such issues be treated as political questions which the legislative branch of the government shall resolve, using its inquisitorial and impeachment powers, or are they justiciable controversies falling within the province of the courts? The problem presented is similar to that involved in the disability issue, discussed in the next chapter. An auxiliary question is whether the legislative branch may, in effect, add to prescribed constitutional eligi-

12 Cf. Osmond K. Fraenkel, "Law and Loyalty," *Iowa Law Review*, Vol. 37 (Winter, 1951), pp. 153–174; and the note "Loyalty Oaths . . . How Far?" *Albany Law Review*, Vol. 17 (June, 1953), pp. 266–282.

bility requirements by declaring by law that certain acts or crimes shall carry with them disqualification from officeholding. The problem is a particularly delicate one under a separation of powers system. It involves the nature of the authority of one of the coordinate branches to set limits and inquire into the legitimacy of a person's claim to be the head of another coordinate branch—the branch, moreover, in which reside the civil and military arms of the government ordinarily depended upon to enforce the legislature's acts and judgments of the courts.

Fortunately, the nation has been spared serious controversy over the meaning and application of terms of the United States Constitution and laws defining eligibility for the presidency; but governorships have been involved in disputes of this kind. The judicial branches of the states have accepted jurisdiction in several cases raising the issue of the eligibility of an incumbent governor or candidate for the office; but they have done so with evident reluctance, and they have been careful to point out that their ruling upon the issue should not be construed as depriving the legislative branch of its constitutional authority to act in the premises.[13] Judicial rulings resulting in the unseating of incumbent governors have been made in three such cases, and in each of these instances the governor concerned more or less quietly accepted the court's judgment. In view of the highly charged political atmosphere in which the rulings have been made this is a remarkable testimony to the strength of the ideal of government by law, however questionable the rulings of the courts concerned may have been from the standpoint of sound reasoning and freedom from political bias or pressure.

The first of these cases arose in Nebraska following the 1890 election. James E. Boyd, a conservative Democrat, was elected to the governorship over his Farmers Alliance (Populist) and Republican opponents in an extremely close contest. After Boyd had taken office following a recount, the outgoing governor, John M. Thayer, a Repub-

---

[13] In the case of *Cyr* v. *Long, supra,* note 11, the Louisiana Supreme Court was particularly troubled by the question of its right to inquire into the legitimacy of Long's claim to the governorship. It ruled that Long was not a Senator so long as the United States Senate, which was the "sole judge" in such a matter, failed to recognize him as a member; but that if Long was, in fact, an intruder into the office of governor and a dual officeholder, the Constitution of Louisiana prescribed the exclusive method by which he could be removed, i.e., by impeachment.

In the case of *Dickson* v. *Strickland et al,* 114 Tex. 176, 265, S.W. 1012 (1924), the Supreme Court of Texas took a similar ambivalent position in ruling upon the question of the eligibility of Mrs. Miriam A. Ferguson for the governorship. Mrs. Ferguson, whose husband had been impeached and removed from the governorship earlier, had won the Democratic nomination for governor in 1924. In this suit her right to be certified as the Democratic candidate was questioned on the grounds that her sex, her married status, and her being married to a husband who was disqualified from holding public office made her ineligible. The Court overruled these contentions, but at the same time insisted that the ultimate authority to pass upon the eligibility of a governor-elect rested with the legislature.

lican, instituted a *quo warranto* suit against Boyd, contending that Boyd was ineligible because he had not been a citizen of the United States and of the state for two years prior to his election, as required by the state constitution. Thayer as the outgoing governor asked that the court recognize his own right to continue to hold the office under another provision in the constitution fixing the term of the governor at two years "or until a successor has qualified." A majority of the Nebraska Supreme Court upheld Thayer's contentions, and ordered Boyd to vacate the office in Thayer's favor.[14] Boyd did so, but appealed to the United States Supreme Court on the point of his United States citizenship status. That body reversed the Nebraska Supreme Court on this aspect of the case,[15] and Thayer promptly surrendered the post to Boyd again. After reflection, Thayer concluded he had acted too precipitately and sought to reopen the issue before the Nebraska Supreme Court; but this time it rebuffed him and the issue remained settled.[16] In this merry-go-round of litigation Boyd occupied the office of governor from January 15, 1891, to May 5 of that year; Thayer held office from that date to February 8, 1892; and Boyd was in again from then until the end of the term in January, 1893.

An even more remarkable and dramatic series of events involving eligibility requirements and the governorship occurred in North Dakota in 1934 and 1935. Two elected occupants of the governorship in succession were ousted as a result of court proceedings raising questions concerning their eligibility; and in the space of a little more than six months four different individuals occupied the governor's chair. First, William Langer, who had already won renomination as the Republican candidate in a bitter intraparty struggle, was declared by the North Dakota Supreme Court to have lost his eligibility by reason of his indictment and conviction on felony charges in a United States district court.[17] Langer sought to assemble the state legislature to secure from it an independent investigation of and ruling upon the

[14] *State ex rel Thayer* v. *Boyd*, 31 Neb. 682, 48 N.W. 739 and 51 N.W. 602 (1891). Boyd had been born in Ireland and had been brought to this country at the age of 10 by his father, who had settled in Ohio. The elder Boyd had taken out his first naturalization papers, but had not completed the process of naturalization immediately. James Boyd had moved to Nebraska at the age of 22 and had lived there continuously thereafter. He had not gone through a formal naturalization procedure on his own behalf, although he had voted and held office there.

[15] *Boyd* v. *Nebraska ex rel Thayer*, 143 U.S., 135 (1892).

[16] *State ex rel Thayer* v. *Boyd*, 34 Neb. 435, 52 N.W. 964 (1892).

[17] *State ex rel Olson* v. *Langer*, 65 N. Dak. 68, 256 N.W. 377 (1934). Langer had been convicted on charges of conspiracy to defraud the United States in connection with the administration of federal public works and relief programs. Ole Olson, as lieutenant governer, initiated a *quo warranto* suit maintaining that Langer's conviction on the felony charge had the effect of disqualifying him as an elector. This in turn, it was maintained, made him ineligible for the governorship under a provision of the state constitution which specified that the governor must be a "qualified elector of the state." The state supreme court upheld these contentions.

charges against him. When it proved impossible to assemble a quorum he relinquished the office of governor to his constitutional successor, Lieutenant Governor Ole Olson. Langer resigned the Republican gubernatorial nomination as well; but he sought exoneration at the hands of the people by inducing the Republican state committee to nominate Mrs. Langer as his replacement on the party ticket for governor. She was defeated in the ensuing election by her Democratic opponent, Thomas L. Moodie.

As soon as Moodie was installed in office early in 1935 a *quo warranto* suit was begun by the attorney general of the state against him, questioning his eligibility under the clause in the state constitution requiring the governor to have been a resident of the state for five years immediately preceding his election. While the state courts were dealing with the case, the state legislature held in readiness an impeachment resolution against Moodie to use in the event the court action failed to result in his being ousted. The North Dakota Supreme Court found that Moodie did not in fact meet the residence qualification prescribed by the constitution. It ruled that the office should be vacated by Moodie and that the newly elected lieutenant governor, Walter Welford, should fill out the remainder of the term.[18] Moodie quietly surrendered the office.[19]

Other facets of the problem of eligibility are presented by the enactment of statutes enlarging upon the constitutional definitions of eligibility to public office, and by the imposition of a penalty of disqualification as the consequence of an impeachment proceeding carried on by the legislative body. May Congress or a state legislature, for example, prescribe disqualification from officeholding as one of the penalties for violation of laws relating to subversive activities or prohibiting

---

[18] *State ex rel Sathre* v. *Moodie*, 65 N. Dak. 340 258 N.W. 448 (1935). The North Dakota Supreme Court, which by consent of the parties was authorized to make a finding of fact as well as of law, found that within the prescribed five-year period Moodie, in carrying on his newspaper publishing business, had resided for more than a year in Minnesota and had voted in that state.

[19] As a postscript to this series of political ups and downs it should be added that Langer's conviction on the fraud charges was set aside on appeal and the charges were eventually dropped. He was defeated in the Republican primary for the nomination for governor in 1936, but ran as an "independent" candidate and was elected. He was elected to the United State Senate in 1940, but his right to a seat in that body was challenged on the basis of allegations of acts of "moral turpitude" growing out of his conduct as governor and as a candidate for the Senate seat. He was seated tentatively while an investigation of the charges was carried on by the Senate Committee on Privileges and Elections. It reported a resolution declaring that Langer was "not entitled to be a Senator of the United States from North Dakota"; but after lengthy debate the resolution denying him a seat was rejected by the Senate on March 27, 1942, by a vote of 52 to 30. *Congressional Record*, 77th Congress, 2nd Session, p. 3065. This had the effect of confirming him in his seat. He continued to represent his state in the Senate until his death in 1959.

variously defined corrupt practices in connection with the use of money in elections? Cases have arisen in Texas and Wisconsin touching upon the authority of the legislature to thus add, in effect, to the constitutional qualifications for the governorship. While the state courts in both instances were emphatic in declaring that the legislature lacked power to impose qualifications beyond those outlined by the state constitution, their rulings nevertheless left open the door for the legislature to bar an individual it finds to be disqualified.[20] The South Dakota legislature has even gone so far as to set up what amounts to a two-term limit upon governors by legislative act.[21] A ruling of the Texas Supreme Court supports the proposition that the courts may not review an impeachment trial judgment of the state senate removing a governor from office and declaring him ineligible to hold office under the state in the future.[22] In a later case the same court ruled that the legislature by passing a joint resolution could not subsequently cancel the disqualification thus established.[23] Georgia's legislature has enacted legislation making itself the sole judge of whether a governor-elect possesses the prescribed constitutional qualifications for his office.[24]

Whether the legislature or the courts have the ultimate authority to pass upon the eligibility of the chief executive is not clearly established under the system of separation of powers. There is a possibility of a clashing of views between them on this point. The courts in some

[20] *Dickson* v. *Strickland*, 114 Tex. 176, 265 S.W. 1012 (1924); *State ex rel La Follette* v. *Kohler*, 200 Wisc. 518, 228 N.W. 895 (1930), and 202 Wisc. 352, 232 N.W. 842 (1930).

[21] *South Dakota Code of 1939 (1952 Supplement)*, Sec. 16. 0208. The provision, which was part of a general revision of the state's direct primary law, states that "no person shall be nominated under the provisions of this chapter for election to the office of Governor for a third successive term."

[22] *Ferguson* v. *Maddox*, 114 Tex. 85, 263 S.W. 888 (1924).

[23] *Ferguson* v. *Wilcox*, 119 Tex. 280, 28 S.W. (2nd) 526 (1930). The case also presented the question whether a still later action of the legislature cancelling the earlier cancellation of the disqualification was valid; but the court found it unnecessary to follow the gyrations of the legislatude that far in disposing of the case.

[24] Following the ousting of Herman Talmadge from the governorship in Georgia in 1947 as a result of the election controversy of that year. *supra*, p. 89. Talmadge was elected governor in 1948 to complete the last two years of the term for which his father had been elected in 1946. The Georgia constitution prohibits a person from being elected to an immediately succeeding term. In 1949 the Talmadge-controlled legislature passed two laws, one of which placed in the hands of the state executive committee of a party sole power to determine all questions relating to the qualifications of a candidate for state office at its primary, including his eligibility for the office sought. The other made the General Assembly the sole judge of the eligibility of the governor-elect under the terms of the constitution. See *Georgia Laws* (1949), pp. 967, 1948. The effect of these laws was to remove from the courts authority to pass upon the question of Talmadge's eligibility to be elected for a succeeding full term in 1950 under the provision of the state constitution forbidding an immediate successive elective term. Talmadge was elected to a full term in 1950 and was permitted to serve without a judicial examination of his eligibility.

states have accepted the responsibility for making rulings on this type of question; but as in instances where they have intervened in election disputes, these precedents do not fully establish the principle that such questions shall be treated as justiciable. As in the ancient fable about belling the cat, such questions can be embarrassing to the judiciary. For obvious reasons, state courts have hesitated to take a position on gubernatorial eligibility that might place them in opposition to the dominant element in the legislature or to a governor already in office. They are under strong pressure to treat this as a political question and wash their hands of it. What would happen if this kind of issue should be pressed on the national courts with reference to an incumbent President or Vice President is hazardous to predict. So far the nation has been spared this kind of crisis.

EXTRALEGAL QUALIFICATIONS OF CHIEF EXECUTIVES

Of far greater significance than constitutional and legal definitions of eligibility requirements are those imposed by practical political considerations. The factors that shape political availability for prospective Presidents and state governors cannot be blueprinted with exactitude. They are subject to change with the times and with the vagaries of popular mood and opinion. Nevertheless it is evident that certain "laws of natural selection," as they have been aptly termed,[25] give direction to and set limits upon the processes of popular choice. These "laws" have their origin and basis in the political sociology and psychology of the American people, the character of the party system, and the nature of the election system by which chief executives are chosen. They are enforced by the people themselves through the machinery of the parties and the ballot box. Their total effect is to narrow the field of actual choice at a given election to only a handful of politically eligible people.

PRESIDENTIAL "AVAILABILITY" FACTORS

An outline of the political qualifications for the presidency as shaped by the demands of practical politics may be drawn from a composite portrait of the 35 individuals who have achieved the distinction of being elevated to this high office. This portrait is that of a white, male citizen of Protestant faith who can trace his lineage back to pre-Revolutionary American origins. At the time of his first election

---

[25] Sidney Hyman, *The American President* (New York: Harper & Row, 1954), p. 183. Chap. 10 in that work is a perceptive treatment of the political factors governing the choice of the President.

he is in the 45 to 65 age bracket, generally in his 50s. He is a resident of one of the populous, politically doubtful states. He has had prior experience in public office or has distinguished himself as a military leader. He has associated himself with one of the major parties, at least to the extent of accepting nomination by it and becoming its spokesman in the campaign. His educational background and training have brought him into contact with the great cultural heritage of the nation. His studies have included the field of law. The class and economic status of his family are not in themselves important, but he himself has displayed the virtues, tastes, and standards expected of the materially successful, upright citizen. Sufficient wealth of his own or enough financial backing of supporters has been available to him to carry on a successful campaign for the nomination. No scandal in his public or private life or evidence of undue subservience to any special class or sectional interest has marred his career. If he inherited wealth, his sense of social obligation and zest for action have been strong enough to cause him to renounce the life of quiet ease his economic status would permit; if brought up under conditions making him dependent upon his own economic resources, he has demonstrated an ability to improve his status in this respect. He is a person of a gregarious bent, a "joiner" of numerous social, fraternal, and civic uplift organizations. In his pursuit of his goals and in his enjoyment of power, recognition and preferment by his fellows he has shown himself to be an "uncommon" man, a member of the aristocracy of ability, talent, and material success.

Each of the elements in this composite portrait has its explanation, if not its justification, in the nature of American society itself. They reflect its mores and values, its standards of judgment, its prejudices and enthusiasms. If the portrait fails to include necessarily those qualities that conceivably should characterize the ideal President—intellectual genius, genuine humility, compassion of soul, moral and spiritual qualities towering far above the average—the fault must be attributed to the people themselves and to the system of popular choice.

1. RACE, ANCESTRY AND SEX

The minority status of nonwhite elements in American society, together with feelings of racial prejudice still prevalent among many segments of the white population, automatically excludes any individual not a member of the white majority. The political emancipation of women has not yet progressed so far as to bring about the nomination of a woman for President or Vice President; but the serious candidacy of Senator Margaret Chase Smith of Maine for the Republican nomination in 1964 suggests that the time may not be too distant when a woman may be nominated by a major party for one of these offices.[26]

Twenty-nine of the 35 individuals who have occupied the presidency have been able to trace their ancestries back to pre-Revolutionary British origins, and five of the six others could trace theirs to Dutch or German-Swiss immigrant origins antedating American independence. This almost total exclusion of descendants of more recent Central and Southern European and Irish immigrants shows signs of giving way, however. The assimilation of these elements into the political life of the nation has been proceeding apace. The nomination in 1928 of Alfred E. Smith, who had an Irish immigrant background, and in 1940 of Wendell Willkie, whose German forebears reached this country in the mid-nineteenth century, were unsuccessful challenges to this English-Dutch tradition. The election in 1960 of John F. Kennedy, of Irish immigrant origins, was a breakthrough. The nomination of Senator Barry Goldwater, whose paternal grandfather was a late nineteenth-century Polish Jewish immigrant, by the Republicans in 1964 was another strong indication that the English ancestry tradition is fading.

2. RELIGION

With regard to his religious beliefs, at least until recently political expediency has dictated that the President be a Protestant, preferably a member of one of the older, larger sects, such as the Episcopalian, Presbyterian, or Methodist denominations. Although Roman Catholics comprise the largest single Christian denomination in the country they have until recently been excluded from the presidency. When the Democrats dared to challenge this tradition in 1928 and again in 1960 by nominating a Roman Catholic, latent religious prejudices were resurrected and fanned into flame to a dismaying degree in some sections of the country.[27] The election of Senator Kennedy, a Catholic, coupled

---

26 At the 1952 Democratic National Convention the names of two women, Mrs. India Edwards, vice chairman of the Democratic National Committee, and Judge Sarah T. Hughes of Texas were placed before the convention as candidates for the vice presidential nomination. Their candidacies were not seriously pressed, and their names were withdrawn before the actual balloting. *The New York Times,* July 20, 1952, p. 28; and July 27, 1952, p. 1. The first woman to be formally nominated by any party for the presidency was Victoria Claflin Woodhull, who was nominated by a militant women's suffrage "Equal Rights" party in 1872. This party also nominated woman candidates in the 1884 and 1888 elcetions.

27 There is no very reliable way of measuring the extent to which anti-Catholic feeling was responsible for the defeat of Alfred E. Smith in 1928 or the near defeat of John F. Kennedy in 1960; but it was undoubtedly a factor in causing defection of large numbers of normally Democratic voters, particularly in the South and Border State regions. These defections were to some extent offset by gains for these candidates in the centers of Catholic concentration, particularly in the urban areas of the Northeast and Middle West. For studies of this aspect of presidential elections see Edmund A. Moore, *A Catholic Runs for President— The Campaign of 1928* (New York: The Ronald Press Company, 1956); Ruth Silva,

with his demonstration while in office that a Catholic President will not necessarily function as a vassal of the Pope in political matters, appears to have laid to rest this anti-Catholic tradition.

It is interesting to note that two recent presidential campaigns—those of 1928 and 1960—have pitted a Roman Catholic against a Quaker. It is a testimony to the growth of religious toleration in the United States that members of these two faiths, against both of whom strong prejudices have been held in some quarters in the past, could be named as major party candidates. The country seems now about ready to put fully into practice the principle spelled out in Article VI of the Constitution, viz., that "no religious test shall ever be required as a qualification to any office or public trust under the United States."

Whatever his religious affiliation may be, a President is expected to display a tolerant and broad-minded attitude toward all faiths. Religious militants of whatever stripe are politically unacceptable as presidential material. He may even be a Christian who strays so far from the paths of Christian orthodoxy as not to be a member of any church, as in the case of Lincoln; or he may hold religious views that place him on the fringe of the mainstream of Christian thought, as was the case with Jefferson with his deistic philosophy or William H. Taft with his Unitarian faith. In any case his religious background must not be one that offends too deeply the orthodox Christian majority.

3. STATE OF RESIDENCE

A presidential candidate's state of residence is a matter of consequence from the standpoint of his political eligibility, primarily because of the electoral vote system. If a candidate is a "native son," or at any rate an "adopted son" of a populous, politically doubtful state, the assumption is that he will be more likely to receive its large block of electoral votes, which may possibly be decisive in a close election. Residents of the smaller or politically sure states, having no political asset of this kind to reinforce their claims for consideration, are usually passed over at the nominating stage. Although the validity of this particular rule of political availability is somewhat questionable inasmuch as a candidate sometimes fails to win the electoral votes of his state of residence it continues to carry weight in the naming of major party nominees.

Rum, Religion and Votes: 1928 Re-examined (State College: Pennsylvania State University Press, 1962); Berton Dulce and Edward J. Richter, *Religion and the Presidency* (New York: The Macmillan Company, 1962); John H. Fenton, *The Catholic Vote* (New Orleans: Hauser Press, 1960); and Theodore H. White, *The Making of the President, 1960* (New York: Atheneum Publishers, 1961).

Its effect can be seen in the fact that a relatively few states have had a near-monopoly on presidential nominees. Since the Civil War New York or Ohio has been the state of residence of the winning candidate in 17 of the 25 elections held. One or the other of these states has also been the residence of 13 of the defeated major party candidates over that period. Only two successful presidential candidates during this period have come from other than a northeastern or middle western state. The exceptions were Hoover (California) in 1928 and Lyndon B. Johnson (Texas) in 1964.

4. PRIOR PUBLIC SERVICE

Prior public service, especially in an elective post, is practically an indispensable requirement for the presidency. Anyone who aspires to be a statesman, it has been said, must first prove he can perform successfully as a politician. There is no substitute for active engagement in politics as a means of gaining valuable experience for the presidency. As Woodrow Wilson observed while serving as governor of New Jersey:

> Some gentlemen . . . seem to have supposed that I studied politics entirely out of books. Now, there isn't any politics worth talking about in books. In books everything looks obvious, very symmetrical, very systematic, and very complete, but it is not the picture of life and it is only in the picture of life that all of us are interested.[28]

All successful aspirants and most unsuccessful major party nominees, except for a few military hero candidates, have been tested for their capacities as politicians in high civil office. Horace Greeley, the Liberal Republican-Democratic fusion nominee in 1872, and Wendell Willkie, Republican nominee in 1940—both of whom were defeated—have been the only notable exceptions to this rule since the Civil War. The collective experience of Presidents has included a wide variety of civil office positions ranging from local office up through the state services to Congress, the diplomatic service, Cabinet and lesser federal administrative posts, and the vice presidency.

Over the years the category of public office providing the most promise of immediate advancement to the presidency by election has shifted from time to time. When John Adams followed Washington from the vice presidential post and was succeeded in turn by Jefferson, who had occupied that post under him, it appeared that the vice presidency might prove to be the immediate stepping-stone to the presidency. Indeed, under the original plan of filling these two posi-

28 Editorial on "The Teacher Politician," *National Municipal Review*, Vol. XLVI (January, 1957), quoting from a speech made by Wilson at St. Patrick's Hall, Jersey City, on January 5, 1911.

tions, this appeared to be a most logical and expected development. Adoption of the Twelfth Amendment in 1804 and abolition of the rule of conferring the vice presidency on the runner-up in the presidential contest relegated the vice presidency to the status of a pawn in the political chess game and cut short this usage. Since then only one Vice President, Martin Van Buren, has risen to the presidency by election. However, each of the last four who succeeded to the top post upon the death of the elected incumbent has gone on to win a successive full term in his own right. Furthermore, Vice President Nixon's success in winning his party's nomination for the presidency from this post in 1960 may be a portent of things to come with regard to the vice presidency and the presidency.

The election of James Madison, Secretary of State under Jefferson, as the latter's successor signalized a shift in the line of political succession to this Cabinet post; both Monroe and John Quincy Adams advanced from it to the presidency. This development was checked by the election of Andrew Jackson in 1828, who was known primarily as a military hero. However, both Martin Van Buren and Henry Clay, rivals in the 1836 election, had served earlier as Secretary of State. For the next 40 years presidential candidates were chosen mainly from among those whose claims to fame rested on service in Congress or on their military records. Another route to the White House emerged in the 1876 campaign when both major parties named candidates whose main claim to preferment lay in service as governors of their respective states. For the next three-quarters of a century the state governorship supplied a large proportion of the presidential and vice presidential candidates, particularly in the case of the "out" party. Candidates who used the state governorship successfully as a springboard for the presidency included Hayes (1876), Cleveland (1884), McKinley (1896), Theodore Roosevelt (1900, via the vice presidency), Wilson (1912), Coolidge (1920, via the vice presidency), and F. D. Roosevelt (1932). Unsuccessful candidates of this category included Tilden (1876), Cox (1920), Smith (1928), Landon (1936), Dewey (1944 and 1948), and Stevenson (1952).

The explanation for the emergence of the governorship as a stepping-stone to the presidency is to be found in a number of factors. Increased influence of governors as party leaders in their respective states has given them a stronger bargaining position in the maneuverings at the national convention. To a considerable degree the political leadership qualities demonstrated by a successful performance in the office of governor in a large state are those desired in a President. Governors today have improved opportunities to obtain national attention from their state posts through the press, television, and political tours and speeches in other states. Moreover, they have an advantage of sorts over high officials at the national level in that they may be able to steer clear of having to commit themselves definitely on national issues that may sharply divide some segments of their party nationally.

The last four or five presidential elections suggest, however, that the pendulum is swinging back toward Congress as the most promising place for the nurture of presidential ambitions. President Truman and Johnson reached the presidency from the Senate, via the vice presidency. Two major party nominees, John F. Kennedy in 1960 and Barry Goldwater in 1964, were Senators at the time of their nomination. Every major party nominee for the vice presidency since 1948, with one exception, has been a United States Senator or Representative. Probably the greater importance attaching in the public's estimation to foreign policy matters, about which members of Congress have a better opportunity than do governors to acquire firsthand knowledge, accounts for this change in presidential recruitment practice.[29] If this is so, it may be expected that a public service record in Congress or in the national administration will again become the preferred admission card to the White House.

5. PARTY STATUS

A President must have status as a member of one of the major political parties, at least to the extent of being willing to identify himself with it by accepting its backing for the office. The concept of the President as a nonpartisan of such high principle and purity of motive that he should not stoop to engage in the intrigues, dissimulations, and compromises of partisan politics went out the window at an early date in the history of the Republic, despite Washington's attempt to set such a pattern.

Ordinarily a President has been a lifelong member and has participated actively in public affairs as a member of the party whose nomination he receives; but there have been a number of exceptions to this rule, particularly in the case of the military hero type of candidate. General Zachary Taylor, whose political principles and party identification were quite vague, was courted by both major parties as a possible candidate in 1848. When a definite approach was made to him by Whig leaders with regard to his becoming the candidate of that party in 1848, after mulling the matter over for some time he announced that he was "a Whig but not an ultra Whig" and indicated his willing-

[29] For discussions of this aspect of the presidency see Russell Baker, "Best Road to the White House—Which?" *The New York Times Magazine,* November 22, 1960, pp. 22ff; David S. Broder, "What's the Best Road to the White House?" *ibid.,* September 22, 1963, pp. 28ff; and Paul David, Ralph Goldman, and Richard Bain, *The Politics of National Party Conventions* (Washington: Brookings Institution, (1960), pp. 145–163, 485–488.

ness to accept the nomination on those terms. General Grant, the Republican nominee in 1868 and 1872, had not participated in partisan affairs before his rise to prominence as a Civil War general; in fact, he had voted only once for President, in 1856, and had then supported the Democratic nominee. General Eisenhower's party status was so ambiguous that in 1948 unsuccessful movements were launched in both of the major parties to make him the party nominee. Herbert Hoover's party status was also so anomalous that he was boomed in each major party for its nomination in 1920. His later service in a Cabinet post under two Republican Presidents had disposed of the question of his party allegiance when he was named as the Republican candidate in 1928. Another exception to the usual rule of early party identification was Wendell Willkie, who had been an active member of the Democratic party until a few years before becoming the Republican candidate for President in 1940.

6. WILLINGNESS TO CAMPAIGN

A successful candidate for the presidency must be willing not only to involve himself in partisan politics to the extent of appearing before the people as the spokesman and protagonist of a political party; he must also frankly avow his status as an office seeker. The axiom that "the office should seek the man and not the man the office"—a myth that was cultivated and nurtured for many years and is still paid a semblance of lip service—has given way to a much more frank approach. The nominations by the Democrats of the weeping Governor Horatio Seymour ("Pity me, Harvey, pity me.") in 1868 and Governor Adlai Stevenson in 1952 appear to have been the only cases of genuine "drafts" of unwilling candidates during the past century."[30]

No longer does an aspirant for a party nomination, unless he is an incumbent President whose nomination for a second term is practically assured, content himself with a few discreet public addresses and unobtrusive contacts with key supporters and advisers. He joins actively with his supporters in "beating the bushes" for delegates favorable to his candidacy, and through numerous speaking engagements, conferences with local party chieftains, appearances at public rallies and a well-planned nationwide publicity campaign, strives to build up popular support for himself. When the national convention assembles for the climactic moment of the partisan stage of the selective process, it is now customary for each aspirant for the nomination to establish a headquarters near the convention site and to appear there in person ready to take an active hand in wooing delegates, conferring with key members of state delegations, and directing the convention floor

[30] Cf. Eaton, *op. cit.,* pp. 17, 456ff.

strategy of his forces. Once the nomination has been won the candidate takes the leading role in reorganizing the top echelons of the party, mapping campaign strategy, and carrying on the canvass for popular support for his electoral slates. All of this means that a prime condition imposed by the political facts of life is that only those otherwise politically eligible individuals who genuinely desire the office and who are willing to make that fact known and to give unstintingly of their energy and talent can ordinarily be included in the list of eligibles.

7. PHYSICAL STAMINA

The strenuous effort that must be made to win the office suggests another kind of qualification—an unusual endowment of physical stamina. Even more than the physical demands laid upon a candidate by the necessities of modern-day campaigning is the burden of the office itself. Half a century ago Woodrow Wilson observed that the physical demands of the office had grown to an unbearable point and that "men of ordinary physique and discretion cannot be President and live." If ways could not be found to relieve the presidency of some of its burdens and tensions, he added, "we shall be obliged always to be picking our chief magistrates from among wise and prudent athletes— a small class."[31]

Since then, despite innovations designed to relieve the President of some of his tasks, the burden of the office has continued to mount as its responsibilities have multiplied on a score of fronts. Only a person of unusual physical stamina can withstand for long the grueling daily round of activities and decisions fraught with enormous consequence to the nation and the world. This has the practical effect of prescribing a fairly limited age range for Presidents as well as unusual physical and spiritual vigor for those falling within this range. On the one hand the amount of prior experience in public affairs needed to acquire stature as a national figure and to establish confidence in a candidate's maturity of judgment rules out the relatively young man; on the other hand a man well past the prime of life cannot carry the burden of the office. The youngest man to hold the presidential post was Theodore Roosevelt, who succeeded to the office at the age of 42. The youngest to be elected was John F. Kennedy, who was 43. The oldest man to be elected was William H. Harrison, who was 68 at the time of his inauguration; he died only 31 days after taking office. A minimum age limit of approximately 45 and a maximum of approxi-

[31] Woodrow Wilson, *Constitutional Government in the United States* (New York: Columbia University Press, 1908) pp. 79–80. For an informed analysis of the medical history of Presidents from Washington to F. D. Roosevelt, see Dr. Rudolph Marx, *The Health of the Presidents* (New York: G. P. Putnam's Sons, 1960).

mately 65 set the bounds of the age group from which the President is likely to be chosen.

8. PERSONAL QUALITIES AND TRAITS

Primarily because he must fill the role of Chief of State, a number of other qualities and attributes of a more personal sort are required of a President. He and his family occupy a place similar in some respects to that of the royal family under a monarchical system. The President not only personifies in himself the dignity and power of the government he heads, but his family must fit the popular image of what the nation's First Family should be. In their relationships, their manners and conduct, their tastes and interests, they are expected to display the qualities highly esteemed in the mores of the nation. A happily married status and children, while not absolutely essential, enhance the political eligibility of a prospective candidate. A divorce puts him under an apparently insuperable handicap.[32]

The President himself should present a dignified, if not an imposing appearance; but he should not be so aloof as to destroy his image as a "man of the people." If he can become familiarly and affectionately known to them as "Old Hickory," "Honest Abe," "Teddy," "FDR," or "Ike," so much the better; but he should not carry his informality to the point of clownishness and undue display of wit and levity. The warning of Senator Thomas Corwin, onetime governor of Ohio and United States Secretary of the Treasury, to young James A. Garfield that "if you would succeed in [political] life you must be solemn—solemn as an ass," was no doubt an overstatement of the point; but it is true that there is a certain antipathy in the public's mind to the idea of a man of wit and humor in the White House—stories of Lincoln's humor to the contrary notwithstanding.[33] Governor Adlai Stevenson's propensity for sophisticated humor, sometimes when discussing the graver issues of the day, was considered by some commentators to have been a factor in his defeats in 1952 and 1956. On the other hand, President Kennedy's witty, self-depreciating humor was generally viewed as one of the personal attributes that enhanced his popular appeal.

[32] Three Presidents—Jefferson, Jackson, and Van Buren—were widowers at the time of taking office; and two—Buchanan and Cleveland—were bachelors. Two candidates who had been divorced have been nominated—James M. Cox in 1920 and Adlai Stevenson in 1952 and 1956. The extent to which their divorced status contributed to their defeats can only be conjectured, but it was undoubtedly a disqualifying factor. Governor Nelson Rockefeller's divorce and subsequent remarriage to a divorcée which occurred not long before he became an active candidate for the Republican nomination in 1964, was a factor in his failure to achieve his goal.

[33] Cf. Richard Strout, "Foe of the Bon Mot: Politics," *The New York Times Magazine*, April 22, 1956.

He need not be especially endowed with oratorical talent, but it is an advantage if he is an able speaker. The advent of television as a campaigning device has no doubt given oratorical talent increased importance, as it has also personal charm, poise, and magnetism. Television is credited by many astute observers with having made John F. Kennedy President in 1960. A candidate's avocational and recreational tastes and interests should be of a sort that are looked upon with favor, or at least with indulgence, by the public. An active interest in an outdoor sport such as fishing, hunting, sailing, riding, or golf is regarded as most appropriate.

Finally, the successful aspirant for the presidency must be a person who combines in his makeup a number of more or less intangible qualities which set him apart from the mass. One of these is a capacity to enjoy possession of power and of being the center of attention. He must relish a life of action and being a major actor in the political drama of the world of his time. He must have a genuine belief in his capacity to serve the nation well as a leader and as a shaper of its destiny. This means that he must be something of an egotist, even to the point of having a messianic complex. He must have more than the common man's share of driving ambition and self-confidence. At the same time he must be able to mask or subdue his love for preferment, power, and esteem to the point that it does not become, or appear to become, a consuming passion. Along with his pride, self-confidence, and ambition there must be a certain admixture of humility, genuine or assumed. He must be able to give his aspiration for the office the appearance of a call to duty rather than the fulfillment of a long and carefully nurtured program of self-advancement.

Above all, he must have good fortune on his side. He must get the breaks. Adventitious circumstance plays a greater part in the selection of Presidents than is commonly recognized. The roll call of able and illustrious men who might have served the nation well but who were denied this opportunity by fate or circumstance is a long one. The stars that guide the affairs of men and of states must be on the side of the survivor of the selective process. The man and the forces and events of his time must be in happy conjunction for him to rise to the pinnacle of his political ambition.

Over the years there have been few exceptions in the operation of these "laws of natural selection" in the choosing of Presidents. Whether they will continue to have the same force in future years cannot be foretold. For the time being a prospective candidate who does not measure up well under them has no chance of being seriously considered. Whether these rules are wholly valid and defensible in every particular or not, political managers whose voices count heavily in party councils attach weight to them. Their effect is to cut down to a relatively small number the individuals who in a given election year are actually eligible in a political sense. On their validity depends in large measure the successful operation of the process of popular selection.

GUBERNATORIAL "AVAILABILITY" FACTORS

As in the presidential selective process, there are political mores, traditions, and factors in each state that condition the functioning of the electorate and in a practical sense pare down the lists of legally qualified individuals who can be given serious consideration as gubernatorial material. However, the laws of natural selection affecting the choice of governors, viewed collectively, are considerably less exacting than those governing the choice of the President. In part this is a result of differences in the nature of the nominating and elective systems at the two levels of government. The direct primary system of nominating candidates and election by direct popular vote on a plurality rule basis provide a different setting for the development and maintenance of established rules of selection. The way is more open to continual challenge of traditions and precedents at every election; consequently the validity of established patterns and the force of precedent and political habit are not so great in the choice of governors.

No individual state's electorate is an exact microcosm of the nation's electorate as a whole. It varies from the national pattern in such respects as its ethnic and religious elements, major economic interests, popular prejudices, standards of value, and attitudes on political affairs generally. Differences in the nature of the partisan balance at the two levels and in the popular estimate of the importance attaching to the offices of governor and President are other factors accounting for variation between national and state usages in filling these positions. Extralegal availability factors that loom large in the selective processes of one state may be unimportant in another. For example, a two-term limit may be inviolably observed in one state, but have no significance in a neighboring state. The kind of background that would enable an individual to become a formidable contender for the governorship in an agricultural state such as South Dakota or Kansas might involve features that would place an individual with the same characteristics out of consideration in an urban, industrialized state such as Connecticut or Massachusetts, and vice versa.

The extralegal, implicit rules that are operative in each state in the selection of its governor can be discovered only through an analysis of the sociological, economic, and cultural attributes of its electorate and the political habits and traditions that have evolved from this social base. Detailed analyses of this kind for each state cannot be attempted here;[34] but an insight into the results of these political conditions and traditions can be gained by surveying the characteristics of the individuals who have emerged from the gubernatorial selective processes over a number of years.[35] On the basis of this kind of evidence some of the more significant and interesting similarities and differences in the laws of natural selection governing the choice of Presidents and governors may be noted.

1. ANCESTRY

As might be expected, the rule of selecting chief executives only from ancestral strains representing pre-Revolutionary and Western European contributions to the makeup of American society has not been strictly adhered to by the states. The more recent migrations from Germany, Scandinavia, Southern Ireland, Hungary, Poland, and Italy have had their representatives in gubernatorial chairs in recent decades. Even the fact of foreign birth has not been an absolute barrier to the governorship, as indicated by the election of a number of such persons in the period from 1915 to 1940.[36] Although no representative of the nonwhite racial minority groups has reached the governor's chair since the turbulent days of Reconstruction in the South, it is obvious that the record of the states in selecting governors demonstrates the capacity of the nation to assimilate varied nationality and ethnic strains into its political life to a greater degree than its political mores have permitted so far in the choosing of Presidents.

[34] For studies bearing on this general subject see V. O. Key, Jr., *Southern Politics in State and Nation* (New York: Alfred A. Knopf, 1949); and *American State Politics: An Introduction* (New York: Alfred A. Knopf, 1956); Duane Lockard, *New England State Politics* (Princeton: Princeton University Press, 1959); John H. Fenton, *Politics in the Border States* (New Orleans: Hauser Press, 1956); Frank H. Jonas, ed., *Western Politics* (Salt Lake City: University of Utah Press, 1961); Warren Moscow, *Politics in the Empire State* (New York: Alfred A. Knopf, 1948); and Leon D. Epstein, *Politics in Wisconsin* (Madison: University of Wisconsin Press, 1958); Herbert Jacob and Kenneth N. Vines, eds., *Politics in the American States: A Comparative Analysis* (Boston: Little Brown and Company, 1965).

[35] Studies have been made covering most of the state governors who have served from 1900 to 1940. See Austin F. MacDonald, "American Governors," *National Municipal Review*, Vol. 16 (November, 1927), pp. 715–719, covering the 187 men who held this office from 1900 to 1910; Samuel R. Solomon, "American Governors Since 1915," *ibid.*, Vol. 20 (March, 1931), pp. 152–148, covering 209 of the 232 who served between 1915 and 1930; and John A. Perkins, "American Governors, 1930–1940," *ibid.*, Vol. 29 (March, 1940), pp. 178–184, covering the 178 individuals who served during the 1930 decade. Cortez A. M. Ewing, "Southern Governors," *Journal of Politics*, Vol. 10 (May, 1948), pp. 385–409, gives more data on the 46 men who occupied the governorship in 12 southern states from 1938–1948.

[36] Perkins, *op. cit.*, notes that three individuals of Canadian, one of English, one of German, and two of Scandinavian birth were chosen to state governorships during the 1930 decade. Solomon, *op. cit.*, lists two of English, two of German, one of Welsh, and one of Norwegian birth in the 1915–1930 period.

2. RELIGION

In the matter of religious affiliation of governors the states have likewise demonstrated less rigid adherence to the extralegal qualification of Protestantism than the nation has in choosing Presidents. Numerous instances of elections of Catholics can be cited, not only in states such as Massachusetts, Rhode Island, New York, New Mexico and others where members of that faith comprise a very substantial if not a preponderant element in the population, but also in many other states where Protestantism predominates very heavily. Oregon and New Mexico in 1930 were the first to elect Jewish governors, and five states altogether have done so. New York's election of a Catholic, an Episcopalian, and a Jew in succession in the period from 1926 to 1932 is a striking illustration of the degree to which the religious factor has been de-emphasized in the politics of that state. In 1957 the roster of the 48 governors represented nine different faiths. The count was 13 Methodists, 8 Baptists, 7 Episcopalians, 6 Presbyterians, 5 Roman Catholics, 4 Lutherans, 2 Congregationalists, 1 Mormon, 1 Jew, and one who had no religious affiliation.

3. SEX

In still another interesting respect the states have deviated sharply from the national pattern in choosing chief executives. The barrier of sex has been broken in two states by women governors, and in two other instances women candidates have received major party nominations but have lost in the final election.

The successful women candidates were Mrs. Nelle Tayloe Ross of Wyoming, in 1924, and Mrs. Miriam A. Ferguson of Texas, in 1924 and 1932. Mrs. Ross was named as a candidate by the Democratic party convention when her husband, the incumbent governor, died shortly before the middle of his four-year term and a special election was held to elect a successor for the last two years. Mrs. Ferguson won the Democratic nomination in a regular primary contest in 1924 after her husband, who had been removed from office in 1917 in an impeachment proceeding, was declared ineligible to run. The unsuccessful women candidates were Mrs. William Langer of North Dakota, who was named as a replacement candidate on the Republican ticket after her husband, the incumbent governor, was found to be ineligible; and Mrs. Anastasia Frohmiller of Arizona, who was the Democratic nominee in 1950. Mrs. Frohmiller, who had served for 24 years in the elective post of auditor-general of the state and had been a widow for 20 years, was the only one of the four whose nomination was clearly a personal victory, unrelated to her husband's political career. She lost in the general election by about 3000 votes.

4. PARTY STATUS AND PLACE OF RESIDENCE

As has been pointed out in Chapter 3, third party and independent candidates have won election to gubernatorial posts on occasion. The place of residence of a candidate within a state does not have the same significance as that of the presidential candidate within one of the states of the Union. This is, of course, because the whole state is treated as one single constituency in casting up the votes for governor, while in the electoral vote system of choosing the President the outcome depends upon the popular voting considered on a state-by-state basis. The place of residence of a gubernatorial candidate within his state has significance only to the extent that it may be affected by sectional rivalry or by a conflict of interest between the chief urban center or centers and the rural areas. It is interesting to note that the constitution of Maryland carried a unique provision from 1837 to 1846 under which there was an enforced rotation of the office of governor among residents of different areas of the state. The state was divided into three districts and the governor was required to be chosen from each of them in turn. This was Jacksonian "rotation in office" with an extra spin added!

5. PRIOR PUBLIC SERVICE, AGE AND OCCUPATION

As it is for the presidency, prior public service of some kind is an almost indispensable political qualification for the state governorship. Approximately 95 percent of the individuals who occupied this office from 1915 to 1940 had previous experience in a public post. Positions previously held covered a very wide range of local, state, and federal offices, with mayorships, legislative and administrative offices at the state level, the lieutenant governorship, and membership in the United States House of Representatives being the offices most frequently included. Whereas only five of the twelve Presidents since 1896 had previously held congressional office, nearly two-thirds of the governors in the same period have had experience in state legislative posts. A seat in the state legislature, the lieutenant governorship, or a seat in the lower house of Congress has been the office most commonly used as the immediate stepping-stone to the governorship; but the patterns of political pathways to this position vary considerably from state to state.[37] One

[37] A comprehensive study of the public office backgrounds of state governors from 1870 to 1950 is found in Joseph A. Schlesinger's *How They Became Governor* (East Lansing: Government Research Bureau, Michigan State University, 1957).

individual, Sam Houston, has had the distinction of having served two states, Tennessee and Texas, as governor.

The fact that the governorship usually comes to an individual who has already achieved a record of some distinction in the public service has the effect of imposing, in practice, a minimum age requirement considerably above that set by constitutional rule. The age brackets of the 40s and 50s supply the greater part of them, as in the case of the presidency; but there is a larger proportion of successful gubernatorial aspirants in their 40s and even some in their 30s.

Again as in the case of Presidents, a majority of governors have had training and practice in the law; but the ranks of governors in recent years have included individuals from many walks of life ranging through various types of business, manufacturing and trade occupations, farming, newspaper work and the professions. Even such occupations as "laborer," "clerk," "electrician," "livestock auctioneer," and "housewife" are to be found in the listings of the governors of recent years. While economic status ranges widely, any aspirant must be assured of sufficient financial means of his own or from his backers to meet the costs of conducting a successful campaign for the nomination, if he is to be a serious contender.

Although the governorship is generally regarded as the topmost position in the political hierarchy of a state, and, as in the case of the presidency, carries with it a certain representational function and dignity, the extralegal qualifications demanded of governors on that account are considerably less exacting than those required of presidential aspirants. The ranks of the governors of the past half century have included individuals whose personal eccentricities and showmanship antics would have been considered entirely out of place for an occupant of the presidential post.

TERM OF OFFICE AND RE-ELIGIBILITY

A condition of tenure universally imposed upon national and state chief executives is a term of office of fixed duration. Reinforcing this rule of a fixed term are constitutional provisions and usages less generally prevalent prohibiting an immediate re-election or limiting

He finds that out of 995 governors covered, all but 88 had previously held some sort of public office. The last public office held before reaching the governorship was a state legislative office in 200 cases; a law enforcement office (prosecutor, judge, sheriff, etc.) in 162 cases; a statewide elective office, including the lieutenant governorship, in 157 cases; an appointive administrative office in 136 cases; a federal elective office (usually Representative in Congress) in 112 cases; and local elective office, 74 cases. More than half the governors had served in the state legislature at some time. *Op. cit.,* p. 11.

the number of terms that one individual may serve. Both types of restrictions reflect a distrust of executive authority, a feeling which grew out of pre-Revolutionary War American experience. While the distrust of executive power has been overcome to the extent of permitting a revision of original state constitutional provisions setting up extremely short terms for chief executives, less progress has been made in the direction of general relaxation of re-eligibility restrictions. The proportion of states having such rules has not altered greatly since 1789; while the adoption of the Twenty-second Amendment in 1951 establishing a two-term limit for the presidency indicates that hostility to the idea of long continuance of the same individual in office has by no means abated.

TERM OF OFFICE

The pattern set by the original state constitutions with respect to the term of office of the governor did not prevail for long. Ten of them provided for a one-year, one for a two-year, and two for a three-year term. The establishment of a four-year term for the President in the United States Constitution set up a norm which the states over the years have been gradually adjusting to by revision of their constitutions on the matter of the governor's term of office. The first state to imitate the federal Constitution in this respect was Kentucky, which entered the Union in 1792 with a constitution providing for a four-year term for its governor. It was followed by Louisiana in 1812, Illinois in 1818, and Missouri in 1820, with constitutions having a similar provision. No new states except Vermont, with a constitution formulated during the Revolutionary War period, followed the one-year term example of the majority of the original states.

During the nineteenth century, two-year, three-year, and four-year terms vied for favor in the states. The two-year periodicity of national elections has been a powerful factor in inducing the states to adopt either a two-year or a four-year term for the governorship. By 1900 the one-year and three-year plans had all but disappeared.[38] A steady progression from the two-year to the four-year term has been in evidence during the past 60 years. Only one state, New Mexico, has abandoned the four-year term in favor of a shorter one during this time,[39] while

[38] The last states to employ the one-year term were Rhode Island, until 1911, and Massachusetts, until 1918, both going over to the two-year term in the years indicated. Seven states have used the three-year term system: Delaware from 1776 to 1831; Pennsylvania from 1790 to 1873; New York from 1777 to 1821 and from 1874 to 1894; Maryland from 1837 to 1851; Indiana from 1816 to 1851; Virginia from 1830 to 1850; and New Jersey from 1844 to 1947. All these states now have a four-year term.

[39] New Mexico entered the Union in 1912 with a constitution providing for a four-year term but very shortly thereafter amended it to provide for a two-year

approximately one third of the states have moved from a shorter term to the four-year plan. The progress of the states toward a longer term for the governor is indicated in the following tabulation:

TABLE 2. *Length of Term of State Governors, 1780–1964*

Year	No. of States	1-Year Term	2-Year Term[a]	3-Year Term	4-Year Term
1780	13	10	1	2	0
1820	24	10	6	4	4
1860	34	5	16	2	11
1900	45	2	21	1	21
1940	48	0	24	1	23
1964	50	0	15	0	35

[a] Three states, Massachusetts, Michigan, and Nebraska, will change from the two-year to the four-year system in 1967. They are counted in the two-year category in the table.

A longer term for the governor is one of the elements in state governmental revision plans looking toward strengthening the chief executive's hand in policy-making, legislative leadership and administrative management. The current and continuing debate on the respective merits of the two-year and four-year term moves along familiar lines. Advocates of the two-year term bear down heavily on the theme that it is more democratic to subject a governor's performance to the test of popular approval at more frequent intervals. They voice the fear that a four-year term will increase an incumbent's opportunity to build up a machine to perpetuate himself in power. They also point out that a shorter term does not necessarily imply frequent turnover of personnel in the office; for a satisfactory performance can be rewarded by re-election, giving the incumbent a fresh mandate for continuation of his policies.

The counterargument for a four-year term emphasizes the drain upon the time and energy of a governor necessitated by his having to campaign for re-election within two years, and the greater handicap a two-year-term governor has in dealing with legislators or subordinate administrative officers whose terms of office may overlap his. A four-year term, it is argued, is necessary to give a governor the opportunity to develop a program and make a record on which his performance may be fairly judged. Another point stressed by advocates of the longer term is that it permits the scheduling of every gubernatorial election

term. An amendment proposal to make the governor's term four years, with a prohibition on an immediate re-election, was rejected by New Mexico's voters in 1948. *New Mexico Statutes Anno.* (1949 Supp.), Vol. I, p. 13.

at the off-year general election, thereby eliminating the influence of presidential voting on the choice of the governor.

The original constitutional provision for a four-year term for the President has withstood all efforts to change it. There has been little demand for reducing the term to a lesser number of years, particularly as there is an opportunity for the people to express indirectly their approval or disapproval of a President's administration in the midterm congressional elections. In 1913, the year after former President Theodore Roosevelt's unsuccessful attempt to win what some considered to be a third term had aroused popular interest in the question of presidential tenure, the United States Senate passed an amendment resolution sponsored by Senator John D. Works of California proposing a presidential term of six years and forbidding election to a second term.[40] The resolution did not come to a vote in the House, and interest in the question soon subsided. On the whole there has been much more congressional and popular interest in the idea of limiting presidential tenure to one term or two terms than in revision of the four-year-term system.

Implicit in the fixed term principle is the problem of the timing and the means for the turning over of administration to a new incumbent by the outgoing President or governor. The common practice in the states that hold their gubernatorial elections in November is to have the new governor take office on the first day of the following January or shortly thereafter. This allows approximately two months for any election contests or recounts to be settled and gives the governor-elect a breathing space for making preliminary decisions on major appointments, planning his legislative program, etc. One difficulty with this schedule is that the preparation of the budget for the next fiscal year, which in many cases must be submitted to the legislature in January, must go forward under the auspices of the outgoing governor. For this reason the suggestion has been made that the new governor be installed in office sooner, so that he, rather than a "lame duck" governor, can assume the responsibility for this important phase of policy initiation. Both Hawaii and Alaska responded to this suggestion when preparing their first state constitutions by moving up the time for inauguration to a date in December.

Under the terms of the Twentieth Amendment a newly elected President takes office on the following January 20. The problems of transition found at the state level are multiplied manyfold at the

---

[40] The resolution passed by a bare two-thirds majority vote of 47 to 23. *Congressional Record,* 62nd Congress, 3rd Session, p. 2420. The Democratic party platform in the 1912 campaign had contained a plank favoring a single four-year term for the President, with a prohibition against re-election. It might be noted that the constitution of the southern Confederacy established a six-year term for the presidency.

national level. In time of crisis, as in 1861 when the Union began breaking apart even before Lincoln assumed office, or in 1933 when the country's economy had reached a perilous state of disorder, the need for cooperation between the outgoing and incoming administrations becomes imperative. In 1952 President Truman and again in 1960 President Eisenhower, recognizing this need, took steps to make the transition as smooth as possible by inviting the incoming Presidents to designate in advance a number of their key officials, including their prospective Director of the Budget, so that liaison could be established between them and their outgoing counterparts.

In 1964 Congress passed legislation designed to facilitate this process. It enacted a Presidential Transition Act[41] authorizing the incoming President to designate an administrator to whom $900,000 in public funds would be made available to provide suitable office space, staff, travel expenses, etc., required in setting up the new administration. The Act provides further that 10 percent of the funds allocated need not be accounted for to the General Accounting Office, so as to give the new administration more freedom from governmental scrutiny in these operations. Public funds were also made available to the outgoing President for six months after his leaving office in order to meet special expenses he might have in winding up his official business in Washington. This constructive piece of legislation may be expected to make the inevitable interregnum period less hazardous for the nation than it has been in the past.[42]

RE-ELIGIBILITY LIMITATIONS

Closely involved with the duration of term question is the matter of the propriety of prohibiting a chief executive's seeking an immediate re-election or, if he is allowed to do so, of specifying a limit on the number of terms. As has already been pointed out, restrictions of this kind relative to the governorship were placed in the constitutions of about half of the original states and the advisability of prescribing a similar limitation upon presidential eligibility was a hotly debated question in the Constitutional Convention of 1787 and in the state ratifying conventions.[43] Although a decision was reached at that time that no clause of this kind should be placed in the Constitution, the issue has continued to be a matter of controversy. Washington's volun-

[41] 78 *Stat.* 153, *P.L.* 88–277.

[42] An exhaustive and authoritative treatment of this problem is Laurin L. Henry's *Presidential Transitions* (Washington: Brookings Institution, 1960). See also Henry F. Graff, "Problem of the Interregnum," *The New York Times Magazine*, October 2, 1960, pp. 15ff.

[43] Chap. 2, pp. 45–49, 65–67.

tary retirement after two terms and Jefferson's discountenancing, for reasons of principle, of efforts to re-elect him for a third term laid the foundation for a two-term tradition that was observed in practice for nearly a century and a half. Even a one-term tradition seemed in process of becoming established during the 1840s and 1850s, but it was ended with the election of Lincoln to a second term in 1864. Although he accepted and won re-election to a second successive term President Jackson repeatedly urged Congress to submit an amendment to the states limiting presidential tenure to one term of four or six years. Most of the amendment proposals designed to limit presidential tenure introduced in Congress from 1825 to 1860 were directed to this end.

Eventually the two-term tradition was successfully challenged by the renomination and re-election of Franklin D. Roosevelt for a third successive term in 1940 and for a fourth term in 1944. In the reaction following his death in 1945 agitation was renewed for a re-affirmation of the two-term tradition through a specific constitutional provision. An amendment proposal to this effect was submitted to the legislatures of the states by Congress in 1947 and was incorporated into the Constitution as the Twenty-second Amendment in 1951.[44]

The states have followed their separate ways in dealing with the re-eligibility problem in connection with the office of governor. State practice on this point has undergone a rather remarkable series of ups and downs. Changes and trends have corresponded in some degree with the trend of national practice relative to presidential re-eligibility.[45] During the past three-quarters of a century a number of states have added specific constitutional limitations on gubernatorial re-eligibility, as has been done also at the national level in the adoption of the Twenty-second Amendment; but one state, Idaho, has gone in the opposite direction by repealing in 1956 an existing restriction of this kind, while Missouri in 1965 substituted a two-term for a one-term limit. A factor of some importance affecting state practice has been the tendency to lengthen the term of office of the governor. In some cases where a longer term has been established by constitutional revision, a price has been paid in the form of a restriction upon an immediate re-election or a limit on the number of successive terms a governor may serve.

[44] For a consideration of the background circumstances that gave rise to the Amendment see P. G. Willis and G. L. Willis, "The Politics of the 22nd Amendment," *Western Political Quarterly*, Vol. 5 (September, 1952), pp. 469–482.

[45] Cf. Joseph E. Kallenbach, "Constitutional Limitations on Re-eligibility of National and State Chief Executives," *American Political Science Review*, Vol. XLVI (June, 1952), pp. 438–454, for a fuller treatment of this subject. See Appendix B for data on current state practice.

At the present time 23 states impose by specific constitutional rule re-eligibility restrictions of one kind or another on their governors; while one additional state, South Dakota, achieves the same result by a statutory restriction. All but two of the states with specific limitations are four-year-term states. Fourteen four-year-term states prohibit an immediate re-election, but permit an unlimited number of non-successive terms; seven permit two successive four-year terms, followed by a four-year interval of temporary ineligibility; and one, Delaware, permits two four-year terms, followed by perpetual ineligibility, as in the case of a two-term President under the Twenty-second Amendment. New Mexico and South Dakota permit two successive two-year terms, followed by a temporary two-year period of ineligibility.

The advisability of incorporating into constitutions specific re-eligibility limitations on chief executives continues to be a subject of controversy. Modern defenders of the principle of limited tenure are still able to capitalize upon the traditional popular distrust of the executive and the fear of "Caesarism" growing out of American colonial experience. The current trend toward stronger executive authority at both the national and state levels helps to keep these fears alive. Advocates of tenure limitation advance the arguments that it prevents prostitution of official powers by an executive to insure his continuation in office; frees him from personal interest and narrow partisan considerations; prevents the retention in office of a personally popular incumbent after he no longer has the physical vigor and energy to carry out his duties efficiently; and clears the way for the rise of new political leadership.

Supporters of the no-limitation principle point out that there is sufficient protection against dictatorship by a fixed term of office for the chief executive. Written constitutional limitations circumscribing his powers, providing for separation of powers and a checks and balances system, and guaranteeing civil and political liberties are adequate safeguards, it is argued. They also insist that the possibility of obtaining a vote of confidence through re-election gives an executive an added incentive to conduct himself with rectitude and attention to the public needs; that tenure limitation may deprive a state or the nation of the services of a tried and able leader, perhaps at a time of crisis when his experienced hand is most needed; and that a prohibition against re-election may weaken unduly the chief executive in his functioning as legislative leader and head of his party, particularly when his forced retirement draws near. They also contend that a limitation of this kind is essentially illogical and undemocratic, for by preventing the re-election of an executive whom the people on the basis of his performance desire to continue in office, it in effect penalizes by disqualification a *successful* and *satisfactory* discharge of official duties.[46]

Where the true course of wisdom and sound public policy lies as between these two opposing viewpoints cannot be determined with complete assurance and finality for all time and circumstance. It should be recognized that much of the debate on the subject over the years has been colored by partisanship and considerations of immediate political expediency. The views of some members of the legislative branches of government must be discounted to a considerable extent for this reason. Hostility to long continuance of the same person in power as the head of the executive branch comes easily and naturally to members of that branch deliberately designed to act as a check upon him. A forced rotation in that office may merely be a gimmick to clear the way for advancement of ambitious members of the legislative branch themselves to the executive chair.

The practices of the states and the provisions of the Twenty-second Amendment raise two subordinate issues of some importance, if it be conceded that a tenure limitation of some kind should be imposed upon the chief executive. Should an immediate re-election be prohibited altogether, as the constitutions of a majority of the states having such limitations provide, or should an incumbent be allowed to seek *one* successive term, as permitted by the restrictive provisions of other states and by the terms of the Twenty-second Amendment? If the primary object of a tenure limitation clause is to prevent misuse of executive powers to obtain renomination and re-election, it misses its mark if an incumbent may seek an *immediate* successive term. But if it is proper to permit him to seek *one* successive term on the basis of his performance in office, why not permit him to seek an unlimited number of successive terms on the same basis?

Another question posed is whether an executive, having served the permissible number of terms, should be barred perpetually or only temporarily from that office; that is, should he be consigned to a political "hell" or a political "purgatory." The Twenty-second Amendment and the constitutional provision in Delaware make the ineligibility perpetual; but in the other 23 states having specific limitations, one who has held the office of chief executive for the permissible number of terms may regain his eligibility after a short lapse of time. His having served one or two terms does not bar him forever from the office he once filled satisfactorily. Re-election of a number

[46] Hamilton in Number 72 of *The Federalist* explored thoroughly the issues involved in the re-eligibility question. Little has been added in subsequent debates to what he stated there regarding the objectionable aspects of a policy of tenure limitation. Fred Rodell, *Democracy and the Third Term* (New York: Howell, Soskin and Company, 1940) presents a good analysis of the issue in the light of American practice before 1940.

of governors to a second, but nonsuccessive, term in those states which impose temporary ineligibility after one term demonstrates that the people upon occasion may wish to avail themselves again of the services of a tried and experienced chief executive.[47]

Although the proposition is not susceptible to absolute proof, re-eligibility limitations probably have the overall effect of reducing in some measure the political influence of a chief executive within his party and with the legislative branch. When an irrevocable terminal date is set upon his tenure he no sooner is installed in office than he becomes a special kind of political "lame duck." In this circumstance some of the incentive for his followers in the legislative branch to remain loyal and responsive to his leadership must surely evaporate. Would-be successors are placed on notice that they are free to plunge into the scramble for political advantage in the next contest for the leadership post. While denial of the privilege of seeking re-election may remove the temptation for a chief executive to give in to pressures he might otherwise surrender to in order to insure his re-election, it is no cure-all against possible misuse of his powers for personal or political reasons. He may seek to advance the cause of a chosen successor, or in the case of a governor, he may use his position to promote his own advancement to another political post, such as a senatorship or even the presidency. As witnessed by the "Byrd machine" in Virginia, the "Long machine" in Louisana and the "Talmadge machine" in Georgia, some of the most powerful, long-lived, personally directed political organizations built up by governors have appeared in states that have the supposed protection of a one-term tenure limitation on their governors.

The long-range effect of the Twenty-second Amendment on the presidential office cannot yet be fully assessed. President Eisenhower, the only President to be affected by it to date, was re-elected under circumstances that raised the question of his physical fitness to withstand the rigors of even a second term of office. The likelihood of his running for a third term would have been extremely remote, even if the Constitution had not made him ineligible. But he perceived the implications of the inflexible rule, as indicated by his comment shortly before his re-election in 1956 in which he characterized the

---

[47] In recent years, governors who have been returned to office after periods of enforced ineligibility are Robert E. Pattison and Gifford Pinchot of Pennsylvania; A. Harry Moore of New Jersey; Olin Johnston of South Carolina; David Bibb Graves and James Folsom of Alabama; Theodore Bilbo and Hugh White of Mississippi; Earl Long and James H. Jones of Louisiana; Phil Donnelly of Missouri; Frank Clement of Tennessee; Henry Schricker of Indiana; and A. B. Chandler of Kentucky. An interesting earlier case is that of James B. McCreary, governor of Kentucky from 1875 to 1879. After an interval of 32 years, during which he served in both houses of Congress, he was elected for a second gubernatorial term in 1911 at the age of 73.

Amendment as being "not wholly wise." President Kennedy observed that the end of his eligibility under the Twenty-second Amendment, if he should serve two terms, would find him at "the awkward age— too old to begin a new career and too young to write my memoirs." Nevertheless he expressed the view, after two years in the office, that "eight years is enough."[48]

In 1957 a campaign to bring about submission of an amendment repealing the Twenty-second Amendment was launched in Congress by Representative Stewart Udall of Arizona. A survey of scholarly opinion made by Senator Kefauver on the subject showed a substantial majority of those consulted were opposed to the Amendment; but no action on the repeal proposal has been taken by Congress.[49] The general public appears to have accepted the idea of limiting a President to two terms, and there is no strong popular demand for a change.[50] Prospects for repeal of the Amendment are dim.

Be that as it may, it would seem that a limitation on executive re-eligibility founded on a healthy tradition is preferable to one spelled out in inflexible terms by constitutional language. Such traditions are not entirely without force. The presidential two-term tradition withstood all challenges until 1940, and it was successfully challenged then largely because the extraordinary crisis in world affairs was believed by many to justify a continuance of the incumbent president in office.[51] Limitations on gubernatorial tenure resting only upon usage are still observed in a number of states. In view of the fact that an individual rarely reaches the presidency until he is fairly well advanced in years, to say nothing of the killing burden of the office, it is unlikely that the nation would have been required on many occasions to face the question of continuing a President in office for a third term, even if the Twenty-second Amendment had never been incorporated

---

[48] *Public Papers of the Presidents of the United States* (1961), p. 86; *ibid.* (1962), p. 892. Kennedy as a Representative had voted for the Amendment.

[49] Of 62 political scientists who replied to Representative Udall's questionnaire, 53 favored repeal, 8 were opposed and one was ambivalent. See Sub-Committee of the Senate Committee on the Judiciary, *Hearings on S.J. Res. 11, Presidential Term of Office,* Part II, 86th Congress, 1st Session (1959), p. 1–35.

[50] A survey of attitudes of 1350 voters in Detroit in 1963 showed that 11 percent thought an anti-third term limit for the President was "bad"; 66.4 percent thought it was "good"; 19.2 percent thought it was both "good" and "bad"; while 6 percent had no opinion. Roberta S. Sigal and David J. Butler, "The Public and the No-Third Term Tradition: An Inquiry into Attitudes Toward Power," *Midwest Journal of Political Science,* Vol. VIII (February, 1964), pp. 39–54.

[51] For accounts of the circumstances leading up to F. D. Roosevelt's decision to seek a third term see James M. Burns, *Roosevelt: The Lion and the Fox* (New York: Harcourt, Brace & World, 1956), pp. 408ff; and P. H. Appleby, "Roosevelt's Third-term Decision," *American Political Science Review,* Vol. XLVI (September, 1952), pp. 754–765.

into the Constitution. While a tenure limitation resting on the foundation of usage and enforced only through public opinion does not have the force and finality of one based on explicit constitutional rule, it has the advantage of flexibility in meeting an extraordinary crisis or situation. At the same time in his relations with his party, his administrative colleagues and subordinates, and the legislative branch of government, the chief executive is not deprived of the advantage implicit in the possibility that he may be continued in his post of party leadership beyond his current term of office.

COMPENSATION AND EMOLUMENTS OF OFFICE

A condition of some consequence in the selection of chief executives and in maintaining the republican character of the office involves the financial arrangements attached to it. If the compensation and other emoluments are fixed at so low a level that they fail to cover the actual costs entailed in holding the office, undesirable consequences follow. An individual without independent financial means is denied the opportunity to seek the post of chief executive unless he is willing to place himself in the debt of financial "angels" who may well have ulterior motives in placing a protégé in office. An impecunious aspirant, if successful in attaining his objective, is placed under heavy temptation to prostitute his office for financial gain. On the other hand, if the financial rewards of the office are made so great as to make it attractive for the opportunity of enrichment it affords, it may on this account become the goal of those whose objective renders them unworthy of it. Moreover, if an incumbent is not given security in the salary and perquisites of his position for the period of his incumbency and is made dependent upon the whim of the legislative branch for the level of and continuance of his salary, his independence can be undermined and he can be forced into a position of disadvantage in his dealings with the controllers of the purse strings.

American experience with colonial governors had taught some of these lessons; but the provisions of the original state constitutions on the point of compensation of public officers, including the governor, reflected appreciation of different facets of the problem. A few made no special provision on the subject; a number of others followed the example of the Virginia constitution in specifying merely that "an adequate, but moderate salary shall be settled on him during his continuance in office." The Massachusetts constitution, probably reflecting the views of John Adams, emphasized the importance of assuring to the governor an "honorable" and "fixed" salary; while the

Pennsylvania and Maryland constitutions placed emphasis upon the necessity for keeping proper limits upon the sources of financial gain for public officers, including the governor.[52]

The question of what provisions should be included in the United States Constitution on the matter of the salary and emoluments to be attached to the chief executive's office was posed early in the proceedings of the Constitutional Convention. The Virginia Resolutions proposed that the executive to be established should receive "punctually at stated times, a fixed compensation for services rendered, in which no increase or diminution shall be made so as to affect the Magistracy existing at the time of the increase or diminution." Similar language was found in the New Jersey Plan submitted later.

The proposal to include such a clause in the Constitution encountered no opposition except for a frontal attack by Franklin on the fundamental proposition of attaching any salary at all to the office of chief executive. Franklin's argument, centering around the proposition that the love of money is the root of all political evil, was listened to respectfully; but consideration of his substitute proposal to permit the executive to receive "no salary, stipend, fee or reward" beyond that required to defray the necessary expenses of his office was postponed and conveniently forgotten. Franklin was successful later, however, in bringing about the adoption of a limiting amendment to the compensation clause so as to prohibit a President from receiving "any other emolument from the United States or any of them" in addition to his regular fixed salary.[53]

The principles incorporated in the federal Constitution on the subject of the compensation of the chief executive were in time imitated by the states, but with special attention being given in some

[52] Section 36 of the Pennsylvania constitution of 1776, reflecting the views of Franklin on this point, stated:

> As every freeman to preserve his independence, (if without a sufficient estate) ought to have some profession, calling, trade or farm, whereby he may honestly subsist, there can be no necessity for, nor use in establishing offices of profit the usual effect of which are dependence and servility, unbecoming freemen, in the possessors and expectants; faction, contention, corruption, and disorder among the people. But if any man is called into the public service, to the prejudice of his private affairs, he has a right to a reasonable compensation: And whenever an office, through increase of fees or otherwise, becomes so profitable as to occasion many to apply for it the profits ought to be lessened by the legislature.

[53] Madison, "Debates," p. 731. As a matter of fact, Franklin's idea of making the President's office solely one of honor and not of profit was realized in Washington's administration. In his inaugural address Washington declared that the "high light" in which he contemplated his duty required that he renounce "every pecuniary compensation," and that appropriations for his office be limited to such actual expenses as the public good may be thought to require. He declined as inapplicable to himself any share in personal emoluments included in a permanent provision for the executive office.

instances to a rigorous delimitation of the sources from which a governor may receive income while in office. With changing times and with increasing importance of the position, salary scales for chief executives at both levels have been adjusted upward. First fixed at $25,000 annually, the President's salary has been adjusted upward by that amount in successive stages until, beginning in 1949, it reached $100,000. In addition he is granted a tax-free official expense account of $50,000, a grant of $40,000 for travel, and the use of the White House as his official residence with a liberal allowance for maintenance and staff.[54] A majority of the states now fix the governor's salary within the range of $15,000 to $25,000. At the top of the list are New York, with an annual salary of $50,000, California $40,000, Pennsylvania, $35,000, and New Jersey, Michigan, and Illinois, $30,000. In addition to the basic salary most states supply an executive mansion and an adequate official expense and travel allowance.

In view of the great responsibilities which have come to be associated with the office of chief executive, these levels of remuneration can hardly be assailed as making it an office of enrichment. Taking into account the cost of campaigning for nomination and election and the requirements of maintaining the dignity of the position, as well as the fact that these official salaries are subject to income taxes, the levels of remuneration are not calculated to meet more than the necessary costs of serving the public. The occupant of the office must expect his chief reward in the opportunity to help shape the course of public policy, in the power and prestige of the position, and in his sense of pride and satisfaction in performing an onerous public duty. For some who occupy it the office of governor offers the prospect of advancement to public office at the national level, particularly a seat in the Senate; for others it may be followed by lucrative private employment in which they may capitalize in some degree upon the contacts and fame they have achieved in the post. But the chief executiveship marks the end of the political road for most occupants of the office. The distinction of having held high office may be all they carry away from it.

The role of "elder statesman" to which a President inevitably succeeds upon leaving the White House is one that has always carried with it a certain degree of public responsibility. A few ex-Presidents have later served in public office. Only one was successful in a comeback effort to regain the presidency—Grover Cleveland in 1892. Three other ex-Presidents—Martin Van Buren in 1848, Millard Fillmore in 1856, and Theodore Roosevelt in 1912—made unsuccessful bids for the presidency as third party candidates. John Quincy Adams subsequently served with distinction for a number of years in the House

[54] *United States Code* (1958), Title 3, Secs. 102–103.

of Representatives; while Andrew Johnson was later elected to the United States Senate. William H. Taft was appointed Chief Justice of the United States Supreme Court. Herbert Hoover served in the Truman and Eisenhower administrations as chairman of special commissions set up to study the problems of federal administrative reorganization and intergovernmental relations.[55]

In recent years the idea has been advanced that ex-Presidents should be given honorary seats in the United States Senate along with the salary and emoluments of a Senator. This, it is urged, would not only assist them in meeting some of the financial burden imposed by their status as public figures, but it would also make possible the utilization of their knowledge and talents in public affairs. In 1958 Congress passed a Presidential Retirement Act[56] which carried this idea into effect, in part. The Act extends to ex-Presidents a $25,000 annual allowance, plus up to $50,000 per year for maintaining an office staff. It also makes provision for suitable office space and extends the franking privilege. Widows of former Presidents are given an allowance of $10,000 annually under the terms of the Retirement Act. These perquisites when established were comparable to those of a United States Senator while in office.

On October 1, 1963, the United States Senate completed the process of making ex-Presidents honorary members of the Senate by adopting an amendment to its rules, sponsored by Senator Claiborne Pell of Rhode Island, giving to ex-Presidents the privileges of the Senate floor.[57] What may prove to be a historic moment occurred on May 8, 1964, when former President Truman appeared in the Senate and for a time occupied the seat he had formerly sat in while he was a member of that body. It was his 80th birthday, and his brief appearance provided an opportunity only for a sentimental display of respect and affection for him by his former colleagues. But it is not difficult to imagine some future ex-President, still in the vigor of his years, making a regular practice of appearing on the Senate floor, participating in the debates on the issues of the day, and giving the country the benefit of his wisdom and experience.

[55] The subsequent careers of former Presidents are reviewed in an interesting fashion in Asa E. Martin, *After the White House* (University Park, Pa.: Penn Valley Publishers, 1951).

[56] Act of August 25, 1958, 72 *Stat.* 838; P.L. 85–745. In 1961 after President Eisenhower retired Congress restored his rank as a 5-star General of the Army, but allowed him to retain the benefits of the Presidential Retirement Act. 75 *Stat.* 5; P.L. 87–3.

[57] *Congressional Record*, 88th Congress, 1st Session (Daily, October 1, 1963), p. 17554.

6

VACANCIES IN OFFICE AND
THE SUCCESSION

Under the separation of powers system special importance attaches to arrangements for maintaining continuous occupancy of the office of chief executive. A vacuum in this part of the governmental mechanism cannot be tolerated for long. Like a ship at sea, the Ship of State must have a first mate ready to take over if the captain should be stricken. The exercise of executive powers, particularly by the chief officer in the department in which those powers are vested, must be continuous. The machinery of administration can function on its own momentum for a time and in many routine respects needs little direction from above; but there must ultimately be decisive action at the top where the final authority resides. Given the hierarchical pattern of the administrative structure and the nature of the administrative process itself, energy, direction and coordination must be supplied from this source. Planning and execution of policy cannot be allowed to come to a standstill for long. Consequently there must be a resource readily available to fill the post of chief executive if a vacancy should exist.

The need for a plan to meet the problem of vacancies in the office of chief executive was recognized explicitly in all the original state constitutions. In this matter recourse was had to the concept of a "deputy" governor, with which Americans had become familiar during the colonial period. Various arrangements were devised to establish such a post. Most commonly a designated member of the governor's council or the presiding officer of the upper house of the legislature was named as the officer upon whom the powers and duties of the governorship or "presidency" would devolve in the event of a vacancy. In describing the conditions under which the succession rule should operate the language of the original state constitutions was in some cases quite vague, in others more specific.

In making provision for a succeeding officer for the President, the Convention of 1787 at first accepted the idea that the presiding officer of the Senate should be so designated. This was logical enough so long as the principle of legislative appointment of the President had the tentative approval of the Convention. When this principle was eventually rejected in favor of his selection, at least in the first stage, by a body of specially chosen electors in order to insure his greater independence of the legislative branch, the idea of designating as Vice President and potential successor the runner-up in the presidential contest was brought forward. This proposal, which originated with the Committee on Postponed Matters and Unfinished Business at a relatively late stage in the Convention's proceedings, was accepted with little objection. The recommendation of the Committee that the Vice President thus chosen should serve ex officio as the presiding officer of the Senate also encountered little opposition.

In making this type of provision for an immediate successor to the President the Framers chose to follow most closely the model of the New York constitution. In that state a lieutenant governor who served ex officio as the presiding officer of the state senate was elected by popular vote in the same way as the governor. The Framers specified that the powers and duties of the presidential office were to devolve upon the Vice President in the event of the removal, death, resignation, or inability of the President. With the exception of the substitution of "inability" for "absence from the state," the terms describing the contingencies under which the powers of the President were to devolve on the succeeding officer also followed quite closely the terminology of the New York constitution. It thus appears that New York's original constitution not only had great influence in shaping the Convention's decisions on the outlines of the presidential office, but that its provisions on the lieutenant governorship supplied a model for the office of Vice President as well.

SUCCESSION CONTINGENCIES

Many sorts of contingencies may cause the succession rule to become operative. Not every conceivable situation which might give rise to a question of succession has been provided for in the national and state constitutions. Some matters have been left to be filled in by statute. Pronouncements of the courts have resolved other issues in this area; while still others have been resolved by usage and practice. It is perhaps impossible to foresee every possible contingency and problem that may arise and provide in advance a clear rule of law to govern each of them. But in the light of national and state experience more should be done than has been in most jurisdictions to establish clearly defined rules and procedures for resolving some of the subordinate issues.

Application of succession rules may be necessitated by (1) death, (2) resignation, (3) impeachment, (4) removal, (5) absence, (6) inability, or (7) disqualification of incumbent chief executives. The succession issue has also presented itself at the state level through (8) refusal of an elected governor to qualify or serve, (9) death of the governor-elect, and (10) failure of the selective process to produce an acknowledged successor to an incumbent at the end of his term. Taking both national and state experience into account, the number of instances wherein rules of succession have become operative is probably greater than is generally realized.

With regard to the presidency, death has been the only factor actually bringing into operation the constitutional rule of succession. Eight of the 31 individuals who have been elected to this office have failed to live out their terms, with the result that the presidential chair has had to be filled by a succeeding Vice President. For approximately 24 years out of the 176 (to 1965) since the presidency has existed—roughly one year out of every seven—a successor elected as Vice President has exercised the powers of the presidency. Four Presidents died at the hands of assassins. Several others, including Andrew Jackson, Franklin D. Roosevelt, and Harry S. Truman, had narrow escapes from death from this cause. No President has been removed, although Andrew Johnson, after he had succeeded to the presidential office, was brought to trial under the impeachment process in 1867 and escaped removal by the margin of only one vote in the Senate.[1] No President has resigned the office; but at least one, Woodrow Wilson, apparently seriously considered doing so.[2] No President has relin-

---

[1] Cf. Howard M. DeWitt, *The Impeachment and Trial of Andrew Johnson* (New York: The Macmillan Company, 1903). The first impeachment resolution to be directed against a President was introduced in the House during President Tyler's administration in 1842.

[2] Wilson used the threat of a resignation and an "appeal to the country" in 1913 in order to mobilize his party's support in Congress for repeal of the exemption of American vessels from payment of tolls through the Panama Canal; and again in 1917 when he successfully opposed passage of the McLemore Resolution warning American citizens against travelling on armed vessels of belligerent powers prior to our involvement in World War I. Cf. Wilfred E. Binkley, *President and Congress* (New York: Alfred A. Knopf, 1947), pp. 207–208. Just how he expected to carry out his "appeal to the country" in the event Congress proved recalcitrant, Wilson did not say. Wilson also reputedly contemplated resigning in 1916 in the event of Hughes' winning the election, in order to permit the new administration to assume responsibility of office as soon as possible in a time of international crisis. Wilson's thought was that, after Vice President Marshall should have given his resignation, he himself would resign after having appointed Hughes to the post of Secretary of State. Under presidential succession legislation then in effect Hughes would then have become Acting President some four months before the date of his regular inauguration as President. Cf. Edward S. Corwin, *The President: Office and Powers*, 4th ed. (New York: New York University Press, 1957), pp. 358–359, n69.

According to a statutory provision originally included in the Presidential Succession Act of 1792, a resigning President would tender his resignation to the Secretary of State. The provision now appears in *United States Code* (1958), Title 3,

quished the powers and duties of his office under the disability provision; but again in three administrations—those of Garfield, Wilson,
and Eisenhower—situations have given rise to serious consideration of
this aspect of the succession arrangements. On two occasions, in 1800
and 1876, election deadlocks and disputes have threatened to leave the
nation with no successor chosen at the conclusion of the outgoing
President's term; but both of these crises were resolved in time for a
new President to be sworn in on the regular inauguration date. Although eight Presidents have died in office, and seven Vice Presidents
have also failed to live out their terms and one has resigned, on no
occasion have vacancies developed in both offices simultaneously so as
to cause the succession to run beyond the vice presidency.[3]

As might be expected, the states, considered collectively, have not
been as fortunate as the nation in having the contingencies other than
death bring into play their succession arrangements. In the period
from 1900 through 1957 some 716 different individuals were elected
to one or more gubernatorial terms in the several states. Eighty-five
of them did not serve out full terms. Of these, 35 died in office, 43
resigned, four were removed through the impeachment process and
one by popular recall, and two were ousted through judicial findings
that they were constitutionally disqualified. Three others were ousted
following election recounts and two governors-elect died before they
could be inaugurated. Only 14 states escaped having a permanent
vacancy in the office for one or the other of these reasons over this
period; and in some of these 14 states there were temporary devolutions
of the powers of the governorship upon a succeeding officer by reason
of the governor's absence from the state. Permanent successions running
beyond the first successor have occurred in several instances; and in a
large number of instances successions running beyond the first officer
in the line have occurred on a temporary basis.

Resignations of governors over this period were most commonly
occasioned by their having been chosen to seats in the United States
Senate. Other resignations were caused by acceptance of federal administrative positions or federal judicial posts. One governor, Woodrow Wilson of New Jersey, resigned to become President of the United
States; another, Earl Warren of California, to become Chief Justice
of the United States Supreme Court; and another, Harold Stassen of
Minnesota, resigned to enter the United States Navy as a commissioned

---

Chap. 1, Sec. 20. See the note by Everett S. Brown in the *American Political
Science Review*, Vol. 22 (August, 1928), pp. 732–733, for an account of the origin
of this provision.

[3] The Vice Presidents who died in office were George Clinton (1812), Elbridge
Gerry (1814), William R. King (1853), Henry Wilson (1875), Thomas A. Hendricks
(1885), Garrett A. Hobart (1899), and James S. Sherman (1912). John C. Calhoun
resigned the vice presidency in 1832.

officer during World War II. Two resignations were induced by illness, and two were forced by the threat of removal. The 10 cases of actual removal occurred in seven different states.

In addition to the 85 instances in which the governorship was vacated permanently over the 1900–1957 period by reason of death, resignation, removal, or disqualification, there were numerous other temporary devolutions of the governorship upon succeeding officers because of absence of the governor from a state. There were also eight temporary devolutions of power because of the illness or incapacity of the incumbent governor. All in all, the experience of the states and the nation in maintaining continuity of occupancy in the office of chief executive serves to bring into view a number of aspects of the succession problem, not all of which are adequately provided for by current arrangements.

REMOVAL PROCEDURES AND PROBLEMS

A basic problem in the organization of a government based on the separation of powers is to devise an appropriate procedure for effecting the removal of a chief executive from office before expiration of the term for which he was elected. The concept of government by law requires that some measure short of violence or revolution be constitutionally recognized and made available for cutting short the tenure of an executive who has proved to be corrupt, incompetent, or dangerous to the liberties and security of the people. At the same time the political independence of the executive from the other two branches must be protected to insure that he does not become the mere tool and servant of either of them. As has already been shown in Chapter 2, this aspect of the problem of creating a properly balanced organization of government authority gave the Framers of the Constitution much anxious concern.

REMOVAL PROCEDURES AVAILABLE

In the original state constitutions a procedure for effecting removal of an unsatisfactory head of the executive department was not explicitly provided in every instance. Some state plans authorized an impeachment type of removal process in specific terms, while others left the matter to implication. The fact that in a majority of the states the governor owed his elevation to office to the legislature carried with it the idea that the legislative branch might effect his removal, if necessary, even though no special procedure for doing so was provided.

With reference to the President the Framers of the Constitution, after wrestling with this problem at some length, devised a carefully circumscribed version of the impeachment process. The sole power of impeachment was vested in the House of Representatives and it was given the authority to bring to trial under this process the President, the Vice President, and all civil officers of the United States on charges of "treason, bribery, or other high crimes and misdemeanors." The Senate was made the trial body in all such cases, with a two-thirds majority being necessary to convict. Its judgment in impeachment cases could extend no further than removal from office and disqualification from holding any office of honor, trust, or profit under the United States thereafter.[4]

The constitutions of all states except Oregon now provide for removal of the governor by an impeachment procedure patterned in most cases after the national constitutional model. Variations from the normal pattern are found in Nebraska, where the unicameral legislature is the impeaching body and the trial is conducted before the state supreme court;[5] and in New York, which has retained its original constitutional plan of joining the membership of the highest state court with the state senate to constitute the trial body. Impeachment is specifically forbidden by the Oregon constitution; but in that state the governor and other public officers are made amenable to trial in the regular courts on charges of "incompetency, corruption, malfeasance or delinquency in office." A trial is initiated and conducted in the same manner as in ordinary criminal offenses; but the charges, if proved, carry with them the penalty of removal from office as well as other penalties which may be prescribed by law.[6] Impeachment provisions of state constitutions in some cases vary from the national constitutional pattern on such points as the vote necessary in the lower legislative house to initiate proceedings; the grounds upon which an impeachment action may be based; and on suspending the accused from office pending the outcome of his trial.

Removal procedures other than impeachment are provided by the constitutions and laws of some states, or have been resorted to

[4] The Convention's deliberations on the question of a removal procedure applicable to the President are treated in more detail in Chap. 2, pp. 50–56.

[5] The Nebraska provision making the Nebraska Supreme Court the trial body was not, as might be supposed, an accommodation introduced after adoption of the unicameral type of legislature in that state in 1936. It was made a part of the constitution of 1875 following the impeachment and removal of Nebraska's first governor, David Butler. The extreme partisanship exhibited by the state senate in his trial brought about a revulsion from the idea of entrusting this judicial function to that body. Cf. C. F. Potts, "Impeachment as a Remedy," *St. Louis Law Review*, Vol. 12 (1927), p. 36.

[6] Oregon constitution, Art. VII, Sec. 6. This provision has been a part of Oregon's constitution since the admission of the state in 1857. Proposals have been advanced recently to substitute an impeachment procedure of the usual type.

in actual practice. Twelve states, most in the western section of the country, make available popular recall as a removal device against governors.[7] In some states conviction for certain types of disqualifying crimes may also cause forfeiture of office. Forfeiture of office through court action is provided for in a few states in connection with laws regulating the use of money in elections.[8] A *quo warranto* suit instituted by a succeeding officer or by the state itself through its appropriate law enforcement officer has also been used to effect removals of governors under the terms of constitutional provisions defining qualifications for the office.[9] Under the extraordinary conditions brought on by the Civil War, removals of governors were effected in some instances by resort to extraconstitutional measures involving exercise of sovereign power by a convention acting in the name of the people.[10] As the war progressed, governors elected under Confederate auspices were deposed through force and supplanted by military governors appointed by the President as their states fell under the sway of Union forces.

IMPEACHMENT AND ITS USE

The most serious and disruptive type of contingency creating a vacancy in the chief executiveship is that occasioned by exercise of the removal process. The relatively infrequent resort to the removal procedure demonstrates that it is an extraordinary remedy to be resorted to only when popular confidence in the integrity of the chief executive has reached a very low ebb and the normal relationship between the executive and legislative branches has become strained to an intolerable degree. Actual use of constitutionally prescribed procedures for removal of chief executives began with the Civil War era. The first governor to be brought to trial under the impeachment procedure was Charles Robinson of Kansas, in 1862. Along with two

[7] These states, with the dates of their adoption of popular recall, are Oregon (1908), California (1911), Arizona (1911–1912), Colorado (1912), Idaho (1912), Nevada (1912), Washington (1912), Michigan (1913), Kansas (1914), Louisiana (1914), North Dakota (1920), and Wisconsin (1926).

[8] For example see West's *Wisconsin Statutes Anno.* (1957), Vol. 2, Sec. 12.24. The validity of this type of restriction and the manner of its enforcement was upheld in a case involving the governorship in Wisconsin, but for technical reasons the governor involved was not removed. *State ex rel. La Follette* v. *Kohler,* 200 Wisc. 518, 228 N.W. 895 (1930), and 202 Wisc. 352, 232 N.W. 842 (1930).

[9] See Chap. 5, pp. 166–168.

[10] At the beginning of the conflict Governor Claiborne Jackson of Missouri, whose sympathies lay with the South, was foiled in his effort to lead that state into secession. He was eventually deposed by a convention assembled originally to determine whether the state should adopt an ordinance of secession. On the other hand, Governor Sam Houston of Texas, who refused to go along with the more extreme Secessionist element in his state, was forced to relinquish the governorship by a state convention called originally to consider the question of secession.

other state executive officers he was impeached on charges of irregularities growing out of the marketing of a state bond issue. Robinson was acquitted, but the other two officials were found guilty and were removed.[11]

The decade immediately following the Civil War witnessed a rather widespread use of the impeachment device. The establishment in the southern states of regimes lacking the political support of a large part of the white population was a major factor in bringing on political struggles between dominant legislative factions and the executive in those states; but the generally low tone of public morality and the inevitable reaction against arbitrary use of executive power which the war had induced also accounted to some extent for use of the removal process in a number of states.

For a time immediately following the Civil War the impeachment device seemed to be in process of developing into a major instrument for holding chief executives to account and for subordinating them politically to the controlling faction in the legislative branch. During this period not only was a President for the first and only time brought to trial before the Senate, but in seven other instances this procedure was invoked against state governors and in one case against a United States Cabinet official. The impeachment of President Johnson, which had as its underlying cause basic differences between him and the Radical Republican element in Congress over Reconstruction policies, failed to result in his removal from office; but the Cabinet official, President Grant's Secretary of War, William W. Belknap, avoided removal under charges of bribery and corruption only by resigning.[12] In three instances the impeachment device was invoked successfully during this period to oust state governors and in another to force a governor to resign. The three removed were Governor William Holden of North Carolina, in 1871; Governor David Butler of Nebraska, in 1871; and Acting Governor Alexander H. Davis of Mississippi, in 1876. Governor Adelbert Ames of Mississippi was impeached in 1876, but was allowed to resign to escape trial. Three other southern governors—Harrison Reed of Florida, Powell Clayton of Arkansas, and Henry Warmoth of Louisiana—were impeached during the Re-

[11] Roger Foster, *Commentaries on the Constitution of the United States* (Boston: Boston Book Co., 1895), pp. 705–707. Chap. III of this treatise presents an illuminating analysis of impeachment in American practice. An appendix, pp. 633–713, presents a brief account of all state impeachment proceedings up to 1895.

[12] Cf. DeWitt, *op. cit.*; and Foster, *op. cit.*, pp. 546–566. Belknap resigned before he was formally impeached; but the charges were nevertheless preferred by the House and he was tried by the Senate. A majority of the Senate short of the necessary two-thirds judged him guilty. The fact that he had already resigned his office was evidently the decisive factor in the Senate's failure to find him guilty by a sufficient majority to impose the penalty of disqualification.

construction period, but were not removed from office inasmuch as their trials were not carried through.

More recently the impeachment process has been successfully invoked to bring about the removal or resignation of governors in New York, Texas, and Oklahoma. Governor William Sulzer of New York was impeached and removed from office in 1913 on the basis of a number of charges growing out of his uncooperative and allegedly contemptuous attitude toward the state legislature.[13] In 1917 Governor James E. Ferguson of Texas was impeached on charges involving misuse of his appointive, pardoning, and financial administrative powers. He attempted to circumvent being removed and disqualified from office by resigning the day before judgment against him was pronounced by the Texas state senate; but this maneuver was later held by the Texas Supreme Court not to have deprived the senate of its authority to remove and disqualify him from holding office in the future.[14]

During the 1920s two Oklahoma governors were removed from office by the impeachment process. In 1923 Governor John C. Walton, who had incurred the active hostility of the Ku Klux Klan and other elements because of his use of the militia and martial law measures to suppress Klan activities, was impeached and removed. Six years later Governor Henry S. Johnston, who had Klan support, was impeached on a variety of charges. He was exonerated on all the specific charges of misfeasance and malfeasance, but was found guilty on the general charge of "incompetency."[15] The only governor in recent years successfully to withstand a formally presented impeachment was Huey P. Long, the self-styled "Kingfish" of Louisiana. In 1929 the lower house of the Louisiana legislature voted to impeach him and advanced a series of charges alleging attempted suppression of freedom of the

[13] See Jacob A. Friedman, *The Impeachment of Governor William Sulzer* (New York: Columbia University Press, 1939). The charges followed Sulzer's break with the Tammany Hall leadership in the Democratic party. He was alleged to have violated provisions of the state corrupt practices law in his campaign for election.

[14] *Ferguson v. Maddox*, 114 Tex. 85, 263 S.W. 888 (1924). This case arose when Ferguson attempted to enter the Democratic primary as a gubernatorial candidate in 1924. He not only questioned the authority of the senate to pronounce judgment on him in 1917 in view of his resignation, but also contended that his trial was improper because he had been impeached at a session of the legislature called by him for another purpose; that some of the offenses with which he was charged were not indictable offenses; and that his trial was concluded at a session of the senate other than the one in which it began. The Texas Supreme Court overruled his contentions on all points. For accounts of the circumstances of his impeachment and removal and a consideration of some of the constitutional issues raised by it see the note, "Impeachment of Governor Ferguson," *American Political Science Review*, Vol. 12 (February, 1918), pp. 111–115; and Frank M. Stewart, "Impeachment in Texas," *ibid.*, Vol. 24 (August, 1930), pp. 652–658.

[15] Cf. Cortez A. M. Ewing, "Impeachment of Oklahoma Governors," *ibid.*, pp. 648–652.

press, bribery, misuse of appointive and removal powers, and intimidation of members of the legislative branch. Two days after his trial began in the Louisiana senate the charges were suddenly and rather mysteriously dropped. Subsequently an attempt was made to launch a recall movement against him but this likewise proved abortive.[16]

Experience with impeachment as a means of removing chief executives has served to reveal some of its shortcomings as well as to raise a number of issues relative to its use, application, and effect. It is ponderous and slow in operation. As James Bryce once observed:

> Impeachment . . . is the heaviest piece of artillery in the congressional arsenal, but because it is so heavy it is unfit for ordinary use. It is like a hundred-ton gun which needs complex machinery to bring it into position, an enormous charge of powder to fire it, and a large mark to aim at.[17]

It is also expensive;[18] and because legislative bodies are not continuously in session, it is not always readily available. Its British antecedent was a special type of judicial proceeding which could be used to administer punishments, including fines and forfeitures, imprisonment or death, to persons, whether public officers or not, who were found guilty of political crimes of particular gravity. Impeachment has disappeared in British practice, having been supplanted by the principle of ministerial responsibility to Parliament as a means of holding executive officers to political account and by trial in the ordinary courts for criminal offenses. In American practice it retains its judicial form, with the impeaching body acting as investigator and accuser in much the same manner as a grand jury and the trial body functioning as a court. "Managers" representing the accusing body present the evidence and argument in support of the charges, and the accused is represented by counsel.

Because it retains the character of a special quasi-judicial proceeding for punishment of alleged criminal offenses, a variety of issues and problems of procedure are presented by the impeachment process. What does the term "high crimes and misdemeanors" mean? Does it include executive shortcomings outside the range of indictable offenses, such as mere incompetence, insolence, neglect of duty, lack of prescribed qualifications, or physical or mental incapacity? May an officer be impeached for criminal acts not related to his conduct

---

16 See Harnett T. Kane, *Louisiana Hayride: The American Rehearsal for Dictatorship, 1928–1940* (New York: William Morrow and Company, 1941), pp. 70–76.

17 *The American Commonwealth* (New York: The Macmillan Company, 3 vols., 1888), Vol. I, p. 283.

18 On the basis of special appropriations made to finance the legislative sessions involved, the Ferguson impeachment and trial in Texas cost $325,000; the Walton impeachment and trial in Oklahoma about $150,000; and the Sulzer trial in New York $246,000. Potts, *op. cit.*, p. 34, n. 64.

in office? At his trial may he be compelled to be a witness against himself? May he invoke "executive privilege" to prevent legislative prying into state secrets and highly privileged confidential exchanges between himself and his subordinates? Since a possible penalty is disqualification from future officeholding, may he be impeached, tried, and disqualified after he has left office? May the penalty upon conviction be less than removal, e.g., a formal censure or reprimand, or a suspension from office for a specified period?

Upon presentation of the charges should the accused be automatically suspended from office until he is acquitted or found guilty, or should he be allowed to hold his office unless and until he is found guilty? If the voting of impeachment charges in itself results in his automatic suspension how can he be assured of a speedy trial when the objective of the impeaching body is already served by his suspension? Are the proceedings of the trial body, as a special court, reviewable by the regular courts? May the legislature subsequently remove the penalty of disqualification by a later act of remission of punishment?[19] Does the legislative body have power to convene itself in special session to initiate an impeachment proceeding when the constitution prescribes no method for assembling it other than by call of the chief executive? The constitutions of more than half of the states authorize the chief executive calling a special legislative session to limit the agenda of that session to subjects specified by him. May the legislature nevertheless take up an impeachment matter in a special session, possibly one involving the chief executive himself, and appropriate funds for that purpose, even though these are matters not covered in the call?[20]

At first glance these may appear to be technical questions of interest only to constitutional lawyers; but they are practical problems that have actually arisen. They help explain why impeachment has never developed into a useful device for resolving political disharmony between the legislative branch and the chief executive. It is a heroic

[19] The authority of the state legislature to remit, by joint resolution, the punishment of disqualification from officeholding was denied by the Supreme Court of Texas in the case of *Ferguson* v. *Wilcox*, 119 Tex. 280, 28 S.W. (2nd) 526 (1930), *supra*, Chap. 5, p. 169; but the constitutions of a number of states expressly permit this to be done. Cf. Maurice R. Van Hecke, "Pardons in Impeachment Cases," *Michigan Law Review*, Vol. 24 (May, 1926), pp. 657–674.

[20] The question of the authority of the legislature to assemble itself for the purpose of conducting an impeachment proceeding or to engage in such a proceeding when called by the governor for other purposes was involved in the Ferguson and the Walton impeachment cases. For a discussion of the point see Potts, *op. cit.*; Stewart, *op. cit.*; Ewing, *op. cit.*; and Maurice T. Van Hecke, "Impeachment of Governor at Special Session," *Wisconsin Law Review*, Vol. 3 (April, 1925), pp. 155–159. For discussions of legal questions involved in impeachments generally see Alex. Simpson, Jr., "Federal Impeachments," *University of Pennsylvania Law Review*, Vol. 64 (May, June, 1916), pp. 651–695; and Robert S. Rankin, "Is There a Time Limit for Impeachment?" *American Political Science Review*, Vol. 28 (October, 1934), pp. 866–872.

remedy which, if successfully invoked, involves branding a chief executive, technically at least, as a criminal. Except by subterfuge it cannot be used to resolve an ordinary political deadlock between the policy-making branches of government. Under the separation of powers system the impeachment device is an ultimate weapon to be resorted to only when relations between the legislative and executive branches have degenerated to the point of political war to the death. While it is not a mere "scarecrow" as Jefferson scornfully dubbed it when its limitations as an instrument for controlling the federal judiciary were demonstrated during his administration, it has a very limited utility.

In view of the fact that the chief executive as the head of the state's or the nation's law enforcement machinery can hardly be expected to bring down the penalties of the law on his own head (he might issue himself a pardon before conviction!) there is some logic in preserving the device as a special procedure for calling him to account for his acts in his capacity as a public officer; but even this reason loses some of its force in the case of governors. Their official position does not grant them immunity from criminal prosecutions under federal laws, and their removal or resignation may be forced by conviction for crime in a federal court. In 1924 Governor Warren T. McCray of Indiana was forced to resign after his conviction in a federal district court on charges of using the mails to defraud; and in 1939 Governor Richard Leche of Louisiana resigned after inquiries were launched by federal and state grand juries into some of his financial affairs and manipulations. He was subsequently convicted on mail fraud charges and imprisoned. Conviction on federal charges while in office also supplied the reason for the removal of Governor Langer of North Dakota by state court action in 1934.[21]

POPULAR RECALL

Recognition of the unsatisfactory nature of impeachment as a means of holding chief executives to account is reflected in the advancement of other types of removal procedures. One that has won a degree of acceptance is the popular recall device. Along with several other "direct government" reform measures which included the direct primary, the legislative initiative and referendum, and the constitutional initiative, popular recall was widely proclaimed by its advocates at the beginning of the present century as a panacea for most of the ills of American democracy. Within the space of a few years it was adopted in a dozen states on a statewide basis. Under it a governor is made subject to removal from office at a special election called for that purpose through popular petition.

21 See Chap. 5, pp. 167–168.

In practice, popular recall so far as it concerns the governership has proved to be as difficult and cumbersome as impeachment, even though it eliminates the constricting criminal proceeding aspects from the removal process. To secure the necessary number of petition signatures for a gubernatorial recall election is laborious and expensive, particularly as the number of required signatures has to be set at a relatively high level—from 10 to 25 percent of the state's active electorate —in order to prevent its use by political malcontents for mere harassment purposes. The recall election itself also involves a considerable drain on the public treasury when conducted on a statewide basis, as it must be in the case of a governor. The mechanics of the system for naming a successor present a special difficulty in the case of a chief executive. Although several abortive recall movements have been launched against governors, in only one instance has such a movement advanced to the point of bringing about a recall vote and a removal. This was in North Dakota, where a recall election directed against Governor Lynn J. Frazier and several of his administrative associates in 1921 resulted in his removal.[22]

The idea of applying the popular recall device to the presidency has received some support. At the height of the movement for its adoption in the states proposals were advanced in Congress directed to this end. In 1913 in the course of Senate consideration of the Works Resolution proposing a single six-year term for the President, Senator Joseph W. Bristow of Kansas offered as an amendment to the resolution a clause authorizing Congress "to provide for the recall of the President by a popular vote at any biennial election." It received the support of only 10 Senators.[23] Practical difficulties in implementing a presidential recall plan would appear to be even greater than those which have made the device of little value as a means of removing governors.

LEGISLATIVE OR INDIRECT POPULAR RECALL

Still other types of proposals have been advanced from time to time for resolving political conflicts between the chief executive and the legislative branch by cutting short the appointed term of the former. One such proposal is the "legislative recall," under which the execu-

---

[22] The recall movement was inspired by factional strife within the Republican party, of which Frazier was a member, and was directed particularly toward rebuking him for his allegedly "socialistic" policy experiments in the fields of banking, insurance, and grain elevator operation. See *The New York Times*, October 30, 1921, p. 1, and October 31, 1921, p. 1.

[23] *Congressional Record*, 62nd Congress, 3rd Session, pp. 2266, 2274. Senator Bristow indicated that he intended by his proposal to give Congress the power to arrange for election of a successor in the event a recall of the incumbent should be voted; but this point was not specifically covered by the language of his amendment.

tive can be removed by a two-thirds vote of the legislature for any reason it deems proper, after giving him due notice and opportunity for defense, but without resort to a formal trial as in an impeachment. This idea, reminiscent of earlier plans of removal of officers by "legislative address," received the endorsement of the committee of political scientists that drew up the 1926 version of the Model State Constitution; but it failed to attract favorable attention and was discarded in later versions of that document.

More recently Senator J. W. Fulbright of Arkansas, after the 1946 congressional elections had brought a switch in party control of both houses of Congress in the middle of a presidential term, suggested that President Truman appoint a Republican Secretary of State as his immediate successor and then resign. In this way, he pointed out, an apparently impending political guerilla war between the two policy-making branches could be avoided and one party could be held clearly responsible for the conduct of national governmental affairs for the next two years.[24] In the next Congress he introduced a constitutional amendment resolution designed to implement his suggestion.[25] It failed to attract favorable public attention and was buried in committee.

In 1954 the 1946 situation was repeated by the election of a Congress controlled by the party in opposition to the President's; but there was no revival of interest in suggestions for resolving the expected political impasse by requiring the President to resign in the face of a national popular repudiation of his party. When in 1956 the people re-elected President Eisenhower and at the same time gave him a Congress controlled by the opposition party, they seemingly placed their stamp of approval on continuation of divided partisan responsibilty in the operation of the national government. Midterm congressional elections have resulted in the choice of a House of Representatives under the control of the party in opposition to the President on 16 of the 44 possible occasions from 1790 through 1962.[26] The occasions when the President's

24 *The New York Times*, November 7, 1946, p. 3. President Truman took no official notice of the statement, but obviously disapproved of and was irked by it.

25 S.J. Res. 29, 80th Congress, 1st Session. Senator Fulbright's amendment would also have provided concurrent six-year terms of office for the President, Vice President, and Representatives. Their terms could be terminated within the six-year period and new officers chosen for six-year terms by an election called by a concurrent resolution of Congress or by an executive order of the President. For a defense of his proposal, which was obviously an attempt to graft a basic feature of the parliamentary system into the American constitutional plan, see his remarks on August 6, 1948, *Congressional Record*, 80th Congress, 2nd Session, p. 9997.

26 On this general subject see Pearl Olive Ponsford, *Evil Results of Mid-Term Congressional Elections and a Suggested Remedy* (Los Angeles: University of Southern California Press, University of Southern California School of Research Studies, No. 16, 1937). The "remedy" she proposed was a four-year term for members of the House.

party has strengthened its hold on the House at the midterm election have been extremely rare. At the state level, situations of divided partisan control of the policy-making branches of state government have been even more common than at the national level;[27] but recent anti-gerrymandering rulings of the United States Supreme Court may be expected to reduce this kind of political schizophrenia somewhat.

Proposals like Senator Fulbright's involve taking a long step in the direction of a parliamentary type of relationship between the chief executive and the legislative branch. They strike at the very heart of the scheme of balanced powers underlying the structure of government in the United States. On the whole it may be concluded that the American people are generally content with current constitutional arrangements for security of tenure for the chief executive, even if they do produce situations of political disharmony between the policy-making branches from time to time. They do not consider a more readily available method for removing a President or governor before the end of his regular term to be necessary. There has been much discussion and theorizing regarding the need for new institutional arrangements to resolve partisan disharmony between the chief executive and the legislature. It is unlikely that any new constitutional formulas will be put into operation to meet this alleged weakness in the separation of powers system at either the national or the state levels. A frequently mentioned scheme to obviate political disharmony between the President and Congress is to make the terms of Senators and Representatives four years and to elect them all at the same time the President is elected. While this would tend to minimize the chance that control of the Congress and the Presidency would be in the hands of different parties, it would not eliminate the possibility entirely.

It must be kept in mind that in a system of balanced powers some friction between the political arms of the government is to be expected and tolerated. This is a deliberately planned feature of the basic organizational scheme.[28] A system of checks and balances in which the checks do not operate is an anomaly. Moreover, it is well to keep in

27 An analysis of state legislative and gubernatorial election results with respect to the matter of divided partisan control of the two branches is presented in V. O. Key, Jr., *American State Politics* (New York: Alfred A. Knopf, 1956), Chap. 3. Excluding the 14 consistently one-party states and the two states which elect their legislators on a nonpartisan basis, he found that in the remaining 32 states over the period from 1931 to 1952 at least one house of the legislature was controlled by the party in opposition to the governor's after approximately one out of every three elections. Governors with four-year terms in the politically competitive states lost partisan control of the lower house of their legislatures at midterm in approximately one case out of five.

28 For a most thoughtful and penetrating analysis of the American governmental system and the operational theory underlying it the author commends to the reader Professor Arthur N. Holcombe's *Our More Perfect Union* (Cambridge: Harvard University Press, 1950).

mind that when the legislative and executive branches are pulling at cross-purposes, by and large it is an indication that there has not developed a popular consensus or clear majority view as to what course of action should be pursued. Whenever that consensus is present the fact that the two branches are controlled by different parties proves to be no obstacle to action—provided, of course, the legislative branch is set up and organized on a basis that gives it a fairly representative character. Constitutional provisions assuring tenure to a chief executive for a fixed period of time lie at the very heart of the American governmental mechanism. There is no quicker way to upset that mechanism than to tinker with its arrangements for removing or compelling the resignation of the chief executive in order to resolve political differences between him and the legislative branch. If harmony between the executive and a majority in the legislature should always be assured, then a frank endorsement of the parliamentary system would offer the way to move.

OTHER CONTINGENCIES INVOLVING SUCCESSION

The contingencies of death, resignation, or removal of an incumbent chief executive are similar in that they all create a permanent vacancy. When they occur the previously designated official successor has no choice but to assume the powers and duties of the chief executive's office. An exception to this general rule should be noted in case a removal is effected by popular recall. Some states having this device provide for the selection of a potential successor to complete the regular term at the same time the recall question is voted upon. Others provide for holding a subsequent special election to choose a successor in the event the incumbent governor is recalled. Some provide that the governor being subjected to the recall vote may be a candidate to succeed himself in case the recall vote is positive; others do not.[29] Ambivalence of the states on these matters serves to illuminate one of the fundamental difficulties in the recall device: how to make the recall vote purely a vote on removal of the incumbent for alleged shortcomings or transgressions, rather than simply a contest between him and a potential replacement candidate.

When there has been an irrevocable removal of an incumbent from office either by death or resignation, there is no uniformity in state and national practice with regard to whether the succeeding officer assumes the title to the office along with its emoluments and

[29] In the one instance in which a governor was removed from office by popular recall, in North Dakota in 1921, a successor was chosen at the same election to complete the regular term. The removed governor, Lynn J. Frazier, was elected to a seat in the United States Senate the next year.

perquisities. There is also diversity of practice on whether he sur-renders the post from which he succeeded to the duties of the chief executive and on whether he serves out the full term for which his predecessor was elected. When succession occurs for reasons that may prove to be transient and the role of the succeeding officer is obvi-ously that of a temporary fill-in, the question of his tenure and status becomes even more complex. Contingencies which may give rise to temporary devolution of the powers of the chief executiveship upon a substitute include impeachment charges against the incumbent, his absence, or his inability for physical reasons to exercise the powers and duties of his office. Another type of contingency in this category is one arising through failure of the selective process for one reason or an-other to produce an **available regular** successor at the end of an in-cumbent's term of office.

INCONCLUSIVE ELECTIONS AND THE SUCCESSION

The circumstance of no duly elected successor being at hand to take over as chief executive at the beginning of a term has arisen very in-frequently. This may occur in the unlikely event of refusal of the elected successor to qualify and serve. Actually it has come about only because of an election deadlock or dispute or through the death of the executive-elect before his induction into office. In general, two different approaches have been followed toward filling the vacancy under these circumstances. One has been to apply a holdover rule, i.e., to extend the term of the outgoing chief executive beyond its normal limit until a successor has been declared elected and "qualifies" by pre-senting himself and taking the oath of office. A second approach has been to follow the normal rules of succession, with the appropriate officer taking over the powers and duties of chief executive at the beginning of the new term and serving until a duly chosen successor appears.

State experience has produced instances of the use of both these approaches at the beginning of a gubernatorial term;[30] but no con-

[30] An inconclusive gubernatorial election in Connecticut was followed by application of the holdover rule in 1890, as were also deadlocked elections in Rhode Island in 1833 and 1893. The effect in these cases was to give the incumbent governors full additional terms of office, since the election disputes were never resolved, *Supra,* Chap. 3, p. 88. The holdover rule was also held applicable in a contested gubernatorial election in West Virginia in 1888, *Carr* v. *Wilson,* 32 W. Va. 419, 9 S.E. 31 (1889) and *Goff* v. *Wilson,* 32 W. Va. 393, 9 S.E. 26 (1889); in Nebraska in *State ex rel Thayer* v. *Boyd,* 31 Neb. 682, 48 N.W. 739 (1891); and in the election dispute in Georgia in 1947 arising out of the death of the governor-elect, Eugene Talmadge. *Thompson* v. *Talmadge,* 201 Ga. 867, 41 S.E. (2nd) 883 (1947), *supra,* Chap. 3, p. 89. In the Georgia case, however, the holdover governor, Ellis Arnall, resigned after a few days of his extended term and was succeeded by the newly-elected lieutenant governor. The holdover rule has been held to be

tingency has yet called for application of the rules of the United States Constitution and laws governing the point. Prior to the adoption of the Twentieth Amendment in 1933 and the Presidential Succession Act of 1947, there was some uncertainty about what officer would assume the duties of the presidency in the event neither a President-elect or a Vice President-elect was on hand at the start of a term. The Constitution carries no clause that could be construed as granting the incumbent the right to hold over; indeed, the language of Aritcle II appears to negate such a construction.[31] It was accordingly assumed that the Secretary of State of the outgoing administration, being the officer next in the line of succession after the Vice President under the Presidential Succession Act of 1886 and having been appointed for an indeterminate term of office, would take over the presidency until a new President or Vice President should appear. The language of the Twentieth Amendment, supplemented by that of the Presidential Succession Act of 1947, has partially eliminated uncertainty on this point.

Section 3 of the Twentieth Amendment declares that if the President-elect shall have died before taking office, the Vice President shall *become* the President; and that if no President-elect shall have been chosen or shall have qualified by the time for the beginning of a new term, the Vice President-elect shall *act* as President "until a President shall have qualified." Under an express authorization of this section of the Amendment Congress made further provision on this point in the Presidential Succession Act of 1947. It imposed upon the officers in the order named in the statutory line of succession the duty of acting as President when neither a President-elect nor a Vice President-elect shall have qualified at the beginning of a term.[32]

An uncertainty still remains as to when an officer has attained the status of "President-elect" or "Vice President-elect" in view of the

---

applicable in Ohio. *Ops. Atty. Gen.* (Ohio), 1947, pp. 53–66. In 1942, when the Wisconsin governor-elect died before his installation in office, the lieutenant governor-elect was permitted to serve out the full two-year term as acting governor. Cf. *State ex rel Martin* v. *Heil*, 242 Wisc. 41, 7 N.W. (2nd) 375 (1942). An unusual situation developed in Alaska at the beginning of its statehood in 1960 in that the first elected governor, William A. Egan, was unable because of illness to assume the governorship at the beginning of his term. The secretary of state as the officer named by the Alaska constitution as the next successor took over and served as acting governor until Egan recovered and took the oath of office.

[31] Article II, Section 1, declares that the President "shall hold office for the term of four years," which eliminates any possibility of a holdover period of incumbency. It might be observed that the Twentieth Amendment, by changing the date for the beginning of the President's term from March 4 to January 20, had the effect of shortening the first term of F. D. Roosevelt to some six weeks less than four years. President Washington also actually had a shortened first term, since he did not assume office until April 30, some eight weeks after his term began on March 4, 1789.

[32] *United States Code* (1958), Title 3, Chap. 1, Sec. 19.

peculiar nature of the electoral college selective process. By popular usage, the successful candidate becomes the President-elect from the time the results of the popular voting for the electors in November are known. In the strict and legal sense of the term, however, he does not achieve this status officially until the electors have met and cast their votes in December and the official canvass of their votes has been made and the result proclaimed before a joint meeting of Congress on the following January 6. There is accordingly a hiatus in the constitutional and statutory arrangements in that they do not cover the possibility of the death or disqualification of a presidential or vice presidential candidate before the electoral vote count has been officially determined by Congress. In view of the nature of the elector system by which these officers are still elected, it is doubtful whether Congress has the authority to fill this void in the present arrangements. Section 4 of the Twentieth Amendment authorizes Congress to provide by law for the case of the death of one of the candidates for President or Vice President when the choice shall have devolved upon the House or the Senate, as the case might be. To date there has been no legislation enacted by Congress covering this point as well.

The principle of temporary succession applied by the United States Constitution and laws for filling a vacancy at the beginning of a President's term is to be preferred to the holdover rule in that it eliminates the temptation for an outgoing President, or for his partisans in Congress, to manipulate the elective process so as to prevent a choice of a successor and thus to continue himself in power. Present arrangements could, however, result in a prolonged period of temporary occupancy of the presidency, pending the resolution of an election deadlock, by a succeeding officer whose tenure would be uncertain and who would lack the prestige of having been elected in his own right.

SUSPENSION BY IMPEACHMENT

The language of some of the original state constitutions clearly indicated that upon the voting of impeachment charges against a governor he should be considered as having been temporarily suspended from his office. Executive powers would devolve upon the succeeding officer, with the outcome of the impeachment trial determining whether the governor resumed his office or not. In at least 15 states the language of the state constitution now clearly indicates or has been construed to mean that such a temporary devolution of powers upon the succeeding officer must follow the voting of impeachment charges against the governor.[33] The Model State Constitution also carries a clause indicating that this rule is to be observed.[34]

Debates in the Constitutional Convention of 1787 reveal clearly that it was not the intention of the Framers to confer power upon the House of Representatives to suspend the President from office by the mere act of preferring impeachment charges against him.[35] The wisdom of the observation of Madison, who opposed giving the House such a power on the ground that "they could at any moment, in order to make way for the functions of another who will be more favorable to their views, vote a temporary removal of the existing Magistrate," was amply demonstrated when President Andrew Johnson was impeached in 1867. Had it been within the power of the Radical Republican element in Congress to do so, they would undoubtedly have been content to have suspended Johnson from office by impeaching him and by dragging out his Senate trial to keep his hands tied until the end of his term. Such tactics were attempted in two of the post-Civil War cases involving use of the impeachment power against governors in southern states.[36] Denial of the power to suspend as part of the impeachment device against the President and the governor in most of the states helps to explain why this method of legislative control over chief executive officers has not developed into a significant feature of the American separation of powers system.

ABSENCE

In the minds of the framers of the original state constitutions absence of the chief executive from the seat of government was a matter of prime concern in devising arrangements to insure continuity in the exercise of the executive powers. Not only were they

[33] For cases thus construing the language of state constitutions see *State ex rel Trapp* v. *Chambers*, 96 Okla. 78, 220 Pac. 890 (1923); *People ex rel Robin* v. *Hayes*, 149 N.Y. Supp. 250 (1914); *Opinion of the Judges*, 3 Neb. 463 (1873); *In the Matter of the Executive Communication Filed the 17th Day of April, A.D., 1872*, 14 Fla. 289 (1872); and *State ex rel Marr* v. *Stearns*, 72 Minn. 200, 75 N.W. 210 (1898).

[34] *Model State Constitution*, 6th ed., (1963), Art. V, Sec. 5.08 (b).

[35] *Supra*, Chap. 2, p. 55.

[36] In 1872 the Florida Legislature used the automatic suspension rule to deprive Governor Harrison Reed of his powers of office for a year by impeaching him. His trial was begun before the senate but the senate adjourned without rendering a judgment in his case. He resumed his office after the expiration of the one-year time limit allowed by the state constitution for completion of the trial aspect of the impeachment proceeding, having been neither convicted nor acquitted of the charges brought against him. In 1871 the Arkansas House of Representatives attempted to use the same tactics against Governor Powell Clayton. He defied their efforts to enforce the suspension rule against him and eventually the impeachment charges were dropped. Cf. Powell Clayton, *The Aftermath of the Civil War in Arkansas* (New York: Neale Publishing Co., 1915), p. 319.

familiar with the problem presented by absentee governors during the colonial period, but the conditions engendered by the Revolutionary War reminded them that the governor might be called away as head of the military forces of the state or might even fall into enemy hands as a prisoner, as two Revolutionary War governors did. Consequently in devising succession rules most of the original state constitutions placed emphasis upon absence of the governor.

The Framers of the United States Constitution were also mindful of this problem. In the original version of the succession clause considered and approved by it, absence of the President was specifically mentioned as one of the conditions under which the powers and duties of his office would devolve upon the succeeding officer. This term was subsequently omitted from the succession clause by the Committee on Style and Arrangement; but whether this was done in the belief that it was redundant as being comprehended in the broader phrase "inability to discharge the powers and duties of the office" or was dropped in order to eliminate it as a basis for calling the succession rule into play is not clear.

Current interpretation of the Constitution's phraseology on this point is the product of evolution and usage. During his two terms as President, Washington made a series of tours and "progresses" about the country to show himself to the people, consult with local officials, and acquaint himself with the state of popular feeling about the new plan of government. His absence from the seat of government did not give rise to a demand that the Vice President be considered as having become temporarily invested with the powers and duties of the presidential office. Thus the precedent was established that mere absence from the seat of government should not bring into operation the succession rule. Whether for reasons of political expediency or because he believed that his departure from the territorial limits of the nation might temporarily deprive him of his powers of office, however, Washington pointedly refrained from entering Rhode Island as long as that state had not become a member of the new Union under the Constitution.

During Grant's administration Congress grew restive about his long and frequent absences from Washington. On April 3, 1876, the House of Representatives, then under control of the Democrats, passed a resolution requesting information from him regarding what executive acts, offices, and duties had been performed by him "at a distance from the seat of Government established by law, and for how long a period at any one time, and in what part of the United States." The resolution went on to demand an answer to the question "whether any public necessity existed for such performance, and if so, of what character, and how far the performance of such executive offices, acts or duties at such a distance from the seat of Government established by law was in compliance with the act of Congress of the 16th day of July, 1790."[37]

Grant replied with a sharp statement declining to supply the information requested on the ground that the House had no authority to require of the executive an account of his discharge of his appropriate and purely executive offices, acts, and duties, "either as to when, where, or how performed." If such information was sought in view or in aid of the power of impeachment, he declared, it was asked in derogation of his constitutional right not to be made a witness against himself. Insisting that his absences from the seat of government in no wise prevented his exercising the powers and duties of his office, he appended a memorandum noting the number of days his predecessors from Washington to Buchanan had spent away from the seat of government during their terms of office.[38]

For many years Washington's precedent of refraining from leaving the territorial limits of the United States was observed by his successors. This helped to give currency to a belief that if a President should do so, he would automatically become divested of his powers of office. The tradition was first broken by Grant, who vacationed briefly in Mexico during his term as President.[39] Presidents Benjamin Harrison, Theodore Roosevelt, and William Howard Taft also sojourned briefly outside the continental limits of the United States. It remained for Wilson to set at rest all doubts on the point. Soon after the end of World War I in 1918 he announced that he would attend the Paris Peace Conference as the head of the United States delegation. He carried through his announced plan and was abroad for two considerable periods of time during the course of the next few months. His decision to leave the country, particularly at a time while Congress was in session, stirred up considerable critical comment in the press and elsewhere; but in the end no formal challenge to his position in the matter was made.[40] Since that time numerous absences by Presidents from the country on official diplomatic and military business have established firmly the constitutional usage on the point.

Although this liberalized interpretation of the Constitution is

[37] *Congressional Record*, 44th Congress, 1st Session (1876), p. 2158.

[38] Richardson, *Messages and Papers of the Presidents*, VII, pp. 361 ff. The data indicated that Washington had been away from the seat of government 181 days; John Adams, 385 days; Jefferson, 796 days; Madison, 637 days; Monroe, 708 days; John Quincy Adams, 222 days; and Jackson, 502 days.

[39] Ruth C. Silva, *Presidential Succession,* (Ann Arbor: University of Michigan Press, 1951), p. 93.

[40] A few members of the political opposition in Congress questioned the right of the President to leave the country without permitting the Vice President to act in his stead, but no concerted effort was made to challenge his position. Silva, *op. cit.,* pp. 93–97. For a defense of the President's interpretation of the Constitution on the point see David Hunter Miller, "Some Legal Aspects of the Visit of President Wilson to Paris," *Harvard Law Review,* Vol. 36 (November, 1922), pp. 51–78.

probably not in accord with the original understanding and intent of the Framers, its wisdom and practicability can no longer be questioned. Under modern conditions of travel and communication, absence, per se, from the seat of government is not a seriously inconveniencing or disabling matter. Moreover, the demands placed upon a President by his roles as Chief of State and Commander-in-Chief of the armed forces may well require his presence abroad. If a stricter view were taken, he would be unduly hampered in the full use of the power and prestige of his office.

An indication of the difficulties that would be encountered by him if this were the rule is afforded by the experience of governors who must automatically surrender their powers of office upon leaving the territorial limits of the state. Currently the constitutions of some 30 states explicitly or implicitly provide for temporary devolution of gubernatorial powers upon the succeeding officer in case of absence from the state. If there is a lack of political harmony between the governor and his immediate successor in these states, as is not infrequently the case, the governor may find himself a kind of political "prisoner." His duties and responsibilities may require his presence outside the state —to confer with federal officials in Washington, to attend a conference of state officials, or to attend a political meeting in his capacity as an important party figure of his state—yet he may feel a constraint not to leave lest his temporary successor seize the opportunity to sign a bill, issue a pardon, make an appointment or perform some other official act contrary to his policies.

For example, in 1935 Governor Ruby Laffoon of Kentucky was in Washington conferring with federal officials about certain work relief projects affecting his state when Lieutenant Governor A. B. Chandler seized the occasion to call a special session of the legislature to consider enactment of a compulsory primary law. Laffoon rushed back to Kentucky and immediately upon crossing the state line issued a proclamation rescinding the special session call. Some of the legislators assembled anyway and instituted court tests of the validity of Governor Laffoon's proclamation. Rulings were obtained in a district court holding invalid and ineffective the rescinding order, and these rulings were sustained by the Kentucky Court of Appeals by a four to three vote.[41]

Under modern conditions of travel and communication the ab-

[41] Cf. *Royster, Clerk* v. *Brock;* and *Laffoon, Governor* v. *Rankin,* 258 Ky. 146, 79 S. W. (2nd) 707 (1935). The special session was held and passed a compulsory primary law under which Chandler subsequently won nomination and was later elected governor. An incident similar to the Kentucky affair occurred in Nebraska in 1872. In litigation arising out of it, the Nebraska Supreme Court, by a two to one vote, held that the proclamation of the governor (who was himself only an acting governor because the regularly elected governor had been removed from office) rescinding the special session call had the effect of cancelling it. *People ex rel Tennant* v. *Parker,* 3 Neb. 409 (1872).

sence of the chief executive from the seat of government, at least for relatively brief periods of time and for the purpose of performing normal duties, should not be made a cause of automatic application of the succession rule. The provisions of the Alabama constitution specifying that the powers of the governorship shall devolve upon a successor by reason of the governor's absence only after he has been absent for at least 20 days continuously points to one type of reasonable solution for this problem. Another more reasonable approach is one suggested by a constitutional amendment adopted in New Hampshire in 1956 providing that a governor "absent from the state on official business . . . shall have the power and authority to transact such business."

DISABILITY

The Constitution of the United States and practically all of the state constitutions contain language indicating that the succession rule shall operate in the event of circumstances rendering the chief executive unable to exercise the powers and duties of his office.[42] Provisions of this kind have caused a number of difficulties and questions relative to the succession. For the most part they leave unsettled such questions as what constitutes "disability," who shall determine it, and what shall be the status of a succeeding officer who assumes the powers and functions of chief executive under this type of circumstance.

Although no temporary succession to the office of President has taken place under the inability provision of the United States Constitution, on a number of occasions succession to the governorship has come about under similar clauses in state constitutions. These state experiences throw some light on the questions that may be raised with regard to implementation of constitutional clauses of this nature. The fact that in more than half of the states absence of the governor is treated as a special form of inability which results in an

---

[42] Article II, Sec. 1, of the Constitution employs the phrase "inability to discharge the powers and duties of the said office" to describe this type of contingency. With reference to the gubernatorial succession eight state constitutions describe this contingency in similar language; 34 refer directly or indirectly to "disability" of the governor as a succession contingency; while five others use such phrases as "or otherwise," "other disqualification," "any cause whatsoever," etc., in a context which presumably covers the inability concept. The term "disability" is also used in some states in a context suggesting lack of legal or constitutional qualifications. Only Tennessee's constitution fails to carry any language that could be construed as covering physical inability of the governor as a contingency bringing into play the succession rule. Cf. *Presidential Inability*, House Judiciary Committee Print, 84th Congress, 2nd Session (1956), pp. 66–74, for a brief analysis of state constitutional provisions and laws on the matter of gubernatorial disability.

automatic devolution of his powers temporarily upon the succeeding officer has, perhaps, conditioned the people and officialdom of those states to the idea of temporary transfers of gubernatorial powers. It is not viewed with the doubts and apprehensions that have so far paralyzed national action on this point. A governor's powers and duties, while similar to those of the President, are not so awesome and far-reaching in their scope and potential as are the latter's. Consequently a temporary devolution of powers does not excite the fears and apprehensions regarding possible repercussions that can be conjured up in contemplation of a temporary exercise of the great power of the presidency by a substitute.

Since 1900, instances of temporary devolution of gubernatorial powers because of inability have occurred in Alabama (twice), Alaska, Iowa, New Hampshire, Oregon, Illinois, and Louisiana. Also during this period the Ohio Supreme Court was called upon to make a ruling on the question of a governor's inability by reason of illness. It found the evidence insufficient to prove that executive power had devolved automatically upon the lieutenant governor because of the incumbent's illness.[43]

Both the Illinois case, which occurred in 1940, and the Louisiana incident, in 1959, brought on controversies of a rather serious sort over application of the succession rule. The Illinois controversy involved Governor Henry Horner and his lieutenant governor, John Stelle. Horner was stricken with a severe heart attack in 1938, midway in his second term. He recovered partially, but was forced to forego full activity for a time, spending several months in Florida to recuperate. Stelle acted as governor during his absence. In April, 1940, after returning to Illinois and resuming his office, Horner suffered another attack. Alleging that the powers of the office were being exercised by a "bedside cabinet," Stelle issued a proclamation declaring that he was assuming the powers and duties of the governorship. The other elected state officials refused to recognize Stelle's claim to the office; and after some 20 days of controversy Stelle gave up his attempt to take over the governorship. Later in the year Horner suffered

---

[43] Governor John M. Pattison was inducted into office on January 8, 1906. He became ill shortly thereafter and finally succumbed on June 18 of that year. A case was brought testing the validity of a liquor licensing bill which became law without his signature during his illness, the contention being advanced that the bill had not been presented to the officer actually entitled to exercise the powers of the governorship, i.e., the lieutenant governor, inasmuch as Governor Pattison was allegedly incapacitated during the 10 days allowed for executive consideration of it. The Ohio Supreme Court refused to go behind the record in the official journal of the governor's office showing the bill had been received. *Wrede* v. *Richardson*, 77 Ohio St. 182, 82 N.E. 1072 (1908). In a similar situation that developed near the end of President Wilson's administration in 1919–1920, 28 bills became law without scrutiny by the President because of his illness.

still another attack and fell into a coma. His secretary finally issued a statement announcing to the secretary of state and the state auditor that Horner was unable to act as governor, and suggesting that they ask Lieutenant Governor Stelle to assume the powers of the office. This was done. Horner died shortly thereafter and Stelle completed the term as acting governor.[44]

The Louisiana case in 1959 was a lurid affair involving a series of attempts, with the collaboration of Mrs. Long, to have Governor Earl K. Long committed to a mental hospital, first in Texas and later in Louisiana. Long successfully resisted the attempts through court actions and served out his term. During his temporary confinement in a hospital in Louisiana while these joustings were going on the lieutenant governor, acting on advice of the state's attorney general, hesitantly took over the duties of the governorship. Long died the next year after having won nomination for a seat in Congress.[45] During the same year Governor Ralph G. Brooks of Nebraska suffered a disabling stroke; but despite his incapaciting illness and frequent absences from his job, he held on to the office for the next year and a half until his death in August, 1960.[46]

The principle generally recognized in cases of incapacity of state governors because of illness has been that whenever a governor himself issues an official declaration that he is under a physical disability which prevents his exercising the powers and duties of his office, his legal successor must assume them, but that a governor may resume his official powers by a statement that his disability has been removed. Two governors since 1900, James K. Toole of Montana and Beauford Jester of Texas have resolved disability crises by resigning their offices. A troublesome aspect of the problem is how a chief executive who is unable or unwilling to recognize his own disability can be forced to relinquish his office temporarily. Five states—Alabama, Mississippi, Michigan, North Carolina, and New Jersey—have adopted constitutional provisions setting up special procedures for determining the fitness of the governor if there is a question about his physical or mental ability; while a number of others, including Oregon, have enacted laws setting up special medical boards that can be convened to give opinions in this kind of emergency. In none of these states have these procedures been called into play.

Presidential disability crises of serious proportions have arisen in three different administrations. The first was brought about by the assassination of President Garfield in 1881. After being shot on July

44 Cf. C. F. Snider, "Gubernatorial Disability," *University of Chicago Law Review*, Vol. 8 (April, 1964), pp. 521–529.

45 Cf. Richard H. Hansen, *The Year We Had No President* (Lincoln: University of Nebraska Press, 1962), pp. 101–102.

46 *Ibid.*, p. 102.

2 he lingered in a more or less critical and incapacitated condition until his death on September 20, some 80 days later. Congress was not in session at the time, but his inability came at a critical juncture when his new administration was just getting under way. The second crisis occurred during the last year and a half of President Wilson's second administration. Wilson collapsed on September 26, 1919, while in the midst of a cross-country tour to carry his fight for ratification of the Versailles Treaty to the people. Shortly thereafter, on October 2, he suffered a stroke that completely incapacitated him for several weeks. He eventually made a partial recovery, but did not resume meetings with his Cabinet until April 13, 1920, and never regained his full vigor during the remainder of his term.

A third disability crises, or series of crises, came during President Eisenhower's tenure. On September 24, 1955, over a year before the end of his first term, he suffered what his physicians described as a "moderate coronary thrombosis" while vacationing in Colorado. His recovery from his attack came gradually and after some 20 weeks of convalescence, part-time activity, and physical checkups, he was pronounced fully recovered. In February, 1956, he announced his willingness to be a candidate for the presidency again; but in June of that year he was forced to undergo a serious abdominal operation for ileitis. His recovery from this illness was sufficiently rapid to permit him to accept his party's renomination in August and he went on to win re-election by a large majority. Again, in November of 1957 he was temporarily incapacitated by a minor cerebral hemorrhage, but he was able to attend a conference of North Atlantic Treaty Organization heads of government in Paris some two weeks after his seizure.

In none of these cases did the Vice President actually move to assume the powers and duties of the presidential office. Doubts regarding the location of authority to decide the question of the President's incapacity, as well as uncertainty regarding the effect of a Vice President's assumption of presidential powers upon the status of the disabled President and his right to resume those powers after his recovery, proved to be insurmountable barriers to action. A major stumbling block has been a certain confusion as to the nature of the problem itself. A procedure by which a *temporary voluntary* devolution of the powers of the office upon a successor may be effected when there are reasonable grounds for belief that the disability may prove to be transitory is one aspect of it. A procedure for effecting an *involuntary suspension* of an incumbent for reasons of physical or mental incapacity is another. In the latter case the problem is similar to one of removal from office; conceivably it could be met by making available the normal removal procedures for this kind of purpose. The difficulty arises in devising a procedure adaptable for use in either of these contingencies.

The problem of presidential inability has continued to receive much study and attention. It has been thoroughly explored in congressional committee hearings and in scholarly literature and comment in recent years.[47] On April 1, 1957, Attorney General Herbert Brownell, responding to an invitation from the House Judiciary Committee to present the Eisenhower administration's views on the problem, submitted a plan for dealing with it. It was in the form of a proposed constitutional amendment providing that : (1) a Vice President who succeeds to the powers and duties of the presidency because of the death, resignation, or removal of the President should "become" the President for the remainder of the full term; (2) a President might voluntarily declare his own inability and thereby cause presidential powers, but not the office itself, to devolve upon the Vice President temporarily; (3) if the President should be under a disability preventing his making a declaration to that effect, the Vice President, with the approval of a majority of the Cabinet, should assume the role of Acting President; and (4) the President by declaring in writing that his disability had ended could reassume the powers and duties of his office.[48]

While congressional committees continued to wrestle with the problem, President Eisenhower revealed at a press conference late in February, 1958, that he had reached an understanding with Vice President Nixon regarding the procedure they would follow if circumstances necessitated resort to the disability clause of the Constitution. Details of their agreement, released to the press several days later, showed that it incorporated substantially the modes of action outlined in the amendment proposal urged by the administration in 1957. The agreement specified that if the President gave notice in writing

[47] Hansen, *op. cit.,* is a comprehensive review and analysis of the problem of executive inability which takes into account both national and state experience. See also Silva, *op. cit.;* also her "Presidential Inability," *University of Detroit Law Journal,* Vol. XXXV (December, 1957), pp. 139–173; and "Presidential Succession and Disability," *Law and Contemporary Problems* (Duke University School of Law, Autumn, 1956); Silva and Everett S. Brown, "Presidential Succession and Inability," in *The Presidency in Transition,* (R. S. Rankin, ed.), *Journal of Politics,* Vol. II (February, 1949), pp. 236–256; John D. Feerick, "The Problem of Presidential Inability—Will Congress Ever Solve It?" *Fordham Law Review* (October, 1963), pp. 73–134; and James M. Burns, "Let's Stop Gambling with the Presidency," *Saturday Evening Post,* January 25, 1964, pp. 12–16.

Comprehensive studies of the problem are presented in House Committee on the Judiciary, *Presidential Inability,* House Committee Print, 84th Congress, 2nd Session (1956); *Presidential Inability,* Hearings before the Sub-Committee on Constitutional Amendments, Senate Judiciary Committee, 85th Congress, 2nd Session (1958); and *Presidential Inability, ibid.,* 88th Congress, 1st Session (1963).

[48] For an exposition and defense of the plan by Attorney General Brownell see *The New York Times,* April 2, 1957, pp. 1 and 20; and *Hearings on Presidential Inability,* Special Sub-Committee on Presidential Inability, House Judiciary Committee, 85th Congress, 1st Session (April 1, 1957).

to the Vice President that he was under a disability preventing his exercise of presidential powers, the Vice President would become Acting President until the inability of the President had ended. The determination of the President's inability would be made by the President "if possible"; but in case of a disablement which would prevent the President from informing the Vice President of it, the Vice President would make the determination "after such consultation as seems to him appropriate under the circumstances." The President himself would determine when his inability had ended and at that time would resume the full exercise of the powers and duties of his office.[49]

Although only a kind of informal modus vivendi, binding only on the principals of the administration in which it appeared, the Eisenhower-Nixon Agreement may have cut the Gordian knot on the question of implementing the constitutional clause on presidential inability. President Kennedy and Vice President Johnson entered into a similar understanding soon after they assumed office in 1961; and after President Kennedy's death President Johnson reached understandings of the same nature with his potential successors.

President Kennedy's assassination on November 22, 1963, once more brought to the attention of Congress and the nation the need for remedial action on a number of problems relating to the presidential succession. Under existing succession legislation assumption of the presidency by Vice President Johnson had the effect of bringing into the immediate line of succession after him 72-year-old Speaker John McCormack of the House of Representatives, and after him Senator Carl Hayden, the 87-year-old President pro tem of the Senate. At last the Senate was moved to action. On September 29, 1964, near the end of its session, the Senate passed by a vote of 65–0 a constitutional amendment proposal. It was not taken up in the House because of lack of time in the closing days of the session. But in 1965, after a request from President Lyndon B. Johnson for congressional action, the two Houses agreed upon the terms of a constitutional amendment resolution and in July of that year it was submitted to the states for ratification.[50]

Major credit for passage of the proposal is due to Senator Birch Bayh of Indiana, who, as Chairman of the Senate Judiciary Committee's Sub-Committee on Constitutional Amendments, had conducted lengthy hearings on the problem during the 88th Congress, and to Representative Emanuel Celler of New York, Chairman of the House Judiciary Committee, who had concerned himself with

[49] See *The New York Times,* March 4, 1958, p. 1.
[50] The resolution was passed in its original form in the Senate by a vote of 72–0 and in the House by 368–29.

this matter during recent Congresses. The Bayh-Celler Amendment proposal[51] incorporates the basic approach of the Eisenhower-Nixon Agreement in dealing with the problem of temporary inability; it also includes an important clause concerned with filling a vacancy in the vice presidency. If this office should become permanently vacant either by operation of the succession rule or for any other reason, the President is authorized to nominate a new Vice President who would take office upon being confirmed by a majority vote in both Houses of Congress. Thus under the proposed amendment's terms it would be rather unlikely that the actual succession would ever progress beyond the vice presidency. The proposed amendment would also give constitutional support to the usage that in case of a permanent succession a Vice President *becomes* President; it makes clear also, however, that in case of a temporary succession because of a disability of the incumbent President, he serves only as *Acting* President.

It is to be hoped that this action by Congress will break the impasse and that the proposed amendment will soon become a part of the Constitution. It embraces a number of commendable features; but it can legitimately be criticized on its provision that the President

[51] The amendment proposal reads as follows:

Section 1. In case of the removal of the President from office or of his death or resignation, the Vice President shall become President.

Section 2. Whenever there is a vacancy in the office of the Vice President the President shall nominate a Vice President who shall take office upon confirmation by a majority vote of both Houses of Congress.

Section 3. Whenever the President transmits to the President pro tempore of the Senate and the Speaker of the House of Representatives his written declaration that he is unable to discharge the powers and duties of his office, and until he transmits to them a written declaration to the contrary, such powers and duties shall be discharged by the Vice President as Acting President.

Section 4. Whenever the Vice President and a majority of either the principal officers of the executive departments or of such other body as Congress may by law provide, transmit to the President pro tempore of the Senate and the Speaker of the House of Representatives their written declaration that the President is unable to discharge the powers and duties of his office, the Vice President shall immediately assume the powers and duties of the office as Acting President.

Thereafter, when the President transmits to the President pro tempore of the Senate and the Speaker of the House of Representatives his written declaration that no inability exists, he shall resume the powers and duties of his office unless the Vice President and a majority of either the principal officers of the executive departments or of such other body as Congress may by law provide, transmits within four days to the President pro tempore of the Senate and the Speaker of the House of Representatives their written declaration that the President is unable to discharge the powers and duties of his office. Thereupon Congress shall decide the issue, assembling within forty-eight hours for that purpose if not in session. If the Congress, within twenty-one days after receipt of the latter written declaration, or, if Congress is not in session, within twenty-one days after Congress is required to assemble, determines by two-thirds vote of both Houses that the President is unable to discharge the powers and duties of his office, the Vice President shall continue to discharge the same as Acting President; otherwise, the President shall resume the powers and duties of his office.

shall fill by appointment a vacancy in the office of Vice President, subject to confirmation by both houses of Congress. The provision concededly is in harmony with recently developed practice under which the presidential candidate of a major party imposes upon his party's national convention his choice for the vice presidential spot on his party ticket.[52] But the President's choice of his vice presidential successor under the Bayh-Celler proposal could conceivably run into difficulty in winning the approval of both houses of Congress if one or both of them should be in the control of the opposition party, particularly in view of present statutory arrangements governing the succession beyond the Vice President. For example, consider the situation that would have resulted if this amendment provision had been in effect during the second half of President Truman's first term when the House and Senate were controlled by the Republican party. Under the terms of the Presidential Succession Act in force then, as well as now, the next officer in line for the presidency after Vice President Truman was House Speaker Joe Martin, a Republican. It seems unrealistic to assume that the Republican-controlled Congress would have approved President Truman's nomination of a Democrat to the vice presidency, thus removing Martin from the post of immediate heir apparent. It probably would have stalled on approving his choice until the end of the presidential term in 1949. The same political situation in reverse prevailed during the last six years of President Eisenhower's administration. This potential flaw in the Bayh-Celler Resolution's arrangements could be eliminated if the 1947 Succession Act were amended to remove the Speaker and the President pro tempore of the Senate from the line of succession entirely; thus the succession would remain in the executive department of the government exclusively. The 1947 Act is an unwise and possibly unconstitutional piece of legislation as it now stands, in any case.[53]

Another point in the Bayh-Celler proposal that might be criticized is its stipulation that a majority of the heads of the executive departments is not the only group able to assume, with the Vice President, the responsibility to act when the President is unable or unwilling to declare his own inability or insists that his disability has been removed. The Cabinet group may be bypassed by "such other body as Congress may by law provide" in bringing about a congressional determination of the President's inability. Presumably, "other body" is intended to mean a special medical board of some kind by whose expert opinion Congress might be influenced; or the object might be to permit

[52] Cf. Chap. 9, pp. 302–304.

[53] Cf. Joseph E. Kallenbach, "The New Presidential Succession Act," *American Political Science Review*, vol. XLI (October, 1947), pp. 931–941; and Ruth C. Silva, "The Presidential Succession Act of 1947," *Michigan Law Review*, vol. 47 (February, 1949), pp. 452–476.

some official organ of the President's political party to take action. Rather than making provision in the amendment proposal itself for creation of such a body to serve as a check upon the Acting President and/or his department heads, it would be simpler to leave this question to the initiative of the Vice President and a majority of the Cabinet, subject to their being supported in their judgment by a two-thirds majority vote of both Houses of Congress; also, Congress should itself be authorized to take the initiative in making such a determination. What is being sought is a method for *suspending* a President from exercising the powers and duties of his office when he is unable or unwilling to recognize his physical or mental incapacity himself. In any such proceeding one would assume that the Acting President, his principal executive subordinates, and Congress itself would wish to be guided by the opinions of medical experts. Provisions could be adopted by law for making technical advice available to them without placing such a body in a position to initiate or block consideration of the question by Congress.

Meanwhile, until the necessary number of states acts favorably on the proposed constitutional amendment, informal understandings based on the Eisenhower-Nixon Agreement should prove to be a partial solution to the problem of presidential disability. By challenging directly the stultifying theory that a Vice President cannot "act" as President without "becoming" President and thus ousting the incumbent permanently, this formula makes the disability clause of the Constitution a meaningful part of the presidential succession plan. It is in line with the actual experience of the states in dealing with this problem in connection with the governorship. A President suffering a possibly transitory physical disability will have a course available other than resigning his position or pursuing a policy of drift and inaction. In accepting the proposition that the responsibility for making an initial judgment in a disability contingency rests upon the officers charged by the Constitution with the exercise of executive powers—the President normally and the Vice President contingently—the Eisenhower-Nixon arrangement is in accord with a common-sense construction of the Constitution on this important point.

CHIEF EXECUTIVES BY SUCCESSION: STATUS AND POWERS

A number of other questions are presented by national and state succession systems involving the chief executiveship. What officer or officers shall be formally named by constitutional provision or law as being in the line of executive succession? What is the official status and scope of powers of a chief executive by succession? If the vacancy such an officer is filling is permanent, what shall be the duration of his term of office? In answering these questions considerable diversity of practice prevails among the states and in the nation.

THE OFFICIAL LINE OF SUCCESSION

Following the model set by the United States Constitution, all but 12 of the states now provide for a popularly elected lieutenant governor as the first successor in the gubernatorial line of succession. The chief significance of this office, like that of the vice presidency, derives from its place in the succession scheme. Except in one state having an officer with this title,[54] lieutenant governors are elected in the same manner and from the same constituency as the governors in their respective states; but they are not always members of the same political party. In 1953, New York adopted a constitutional amendment which provided that the governor and lieutenant governor candidates of the same party must be voted upon as an inseparable pair by the voters. This has the obvious advantage of giving assurance that they will always be of the same political party, as is normally the case with the President and Vice President.[55] The idea has found favor in other states as well; the principle is now also followed in Connecticut, Michigan, and Alaska. In eight of the states lacking an independently chosen lieutenant governor the president of the state senate or the speaker of the lower house, a member elected to this post by his colleagues, is named as first in line of succession for the governorship; and in the remaining four the popularly chosen secretary of state occupies this position.

Further provision by statute on the line of presidential succession is authorized by the United States Constitution; and the constitutions of the states, in some cases supplemented by statute, extend the line of gubernatorial succession well beyond the first-named officer. In

---

[54] In Tennessee the presiding officer of the senate has been given the title of lieutenant governor ex officio, thus reversing the usual relationship between these two offices. He obtains his post by being elected to it by the Senate from among its members. Cf. *Tennessee Code, Anno.* (1955), Secs. 8–201, 8–202.

[55] It should be noted that it is still possible under present arrangements that a President of one party and a Vice President of another party could be chosen if some of the electors failed to go along with the previously named candidates of their respective parties. This situation could also result if a failure of the electoral vote to produce a majority choice caused the election of a President to be put into the hands of the House of Representatives and of a Vice President into the hands of the Senate. There also remains the possibility that a party may nominate a "fusion" ticket, with a presidential candidate of one party and a vice presidential candidate of another. This, in a practical sense, was what happened in 1840 when the Whigs named an anti-Jackson Democrat, John Tyler, as Harrison's running mate; and in 1864, when the Republicans named a Union Democrat, Andrew Johnson, to run with Lincoln.

recent years some 14 states have adopted "disaster" succession laws making provision for assumption of executive powers by a lengthy line of public officials in the event of a dislocating event such as a nuclear war. In carrying out its responsibility on this point Congress has displayed some ambivalence. In the first Presidential Succession Act, passed in 1792, the President pro tem of the Senate and the Speaker of the House were named, in that order, as successors beyond the Vice President. This arrangement was superseded by the terms of an 1886 law under which the major department heads, beginning with the Secretary of State, were named as potential successors. Then in 1947, following a recommendation made by President Truman shortly after he succeeded to the presidency in 1945, Congress again altered the line of succession by reinserting the positions of Speaker of the House and President pro tem of the Senate, in that order, immediately after the Vice President and ahead of the Cabinet members.[56] This move was in general accord with the practices of the states, most of which place the presiding officer of either the upper or lower house next to the lieutenant governor, or if there is no such officer, next in line to the governor. No succession to the presidency has yet progressed beyond the vice presidency; but a number of permanent successions to the governorship running beyond the first successor in the official line have occurred.

A number of issues are posed by these succession arrangements. First of all there is the fundamental question whether provision should be made at all for the post of Vice President or lieutenant governor, positions that at least until recently have had little power or prestige beyond the possibility that the rules of succession may elevate the incumbent temporarily or permanently into the chief executive's chair. If such a position is established, the further question arises, what regular duties and powers should be given this officer. Beyond that is the question of the propriety of placing legislative officers in the line of succession in view of the philosophy underlying the separation of powers system.

The advisability of electing a spare President or governor in the person of a Vice President or lieutenant governor has long been debated. The vice presidency has been looked upon by many as a position of little importance and has been made the object of numerous jokes and lampoons. Incumbents in the office themselves have contributed to this popular image. John Adams was temporarily successful in making the vice presidency a position of some power; but later in a letter to his wife he complained, "My country has in its wisdom contrived for me the most insignificant office that ever the invention

---

56 Cf. Kallenbach, "The New Presidential Succession Act," *loc. cit.*, for an account of the political circumstances leading up to enactment of the 1947 law.

of man contrived or his imagination conceived."[57] When the question of his running for Vice President in 1944 was first broached to the future President Truman while he was a member of the Senate, in his earthy manner he characterized the office as "useless as a cow's fifth teat." Vice Presidents Thomas R. Marshall and Alben Barkley were fond of telling the story: "A farmer had two sons. One of them ran off to sea; the other was elected Vice President. Nothing was ever heard of either of them again."[58] When Lyndon Johnson was considering Senator Kennedy's urging that he accept second place on the Democratic ticket in 1960, the story has it that Johnson called former Vice President John N. Garner to ask his advice on what to do. Garner reportedly told him to turn it down, saying, "Lyndon, the vice presidency isn't worth a pitcher of warm spit." In the light of history, these low estimates of the importance of the office seem rather misplaced. Eleven Vice Presidents have become Presidents—eight by succession and three by using the post as the immediate stepping-stone to reach the presidency by election.

Abolition of both the offices of Vice President and of lieutenant governor has often been seriously urged.[59] The dispensability of the latter is said to be proved by the fact that 12 states now find it possible to get along without such an officer. The latest version of the Model State Constitution makes no provision for the office of lieutenant governor. Moreover, when the vice presidency had been vacated by death or resignation or when the Vice President has been called upon to assume the post of President his position as Vice President is deemed to be vacated but no one is elevated to it.[60] This would, of course, no longer be the case if the Bayh-Celler Amendment were adopted.

Despite the barrage of criticism and disparagement directed against these offices, they survive. Indeed, the trend during the past half century appears to be in the direction of making the vice presidency and the

[57] Edgar W. Waugh, *Second Consul: The Vice President* (Indianapolis: The Bobbs-Merrill Company, 1956), p. 38.

[58] *Ibid.*, p. 166.

[59] During the debate in the House of Representatives on the resolution which eventually was adopted as the Twelfth Amendment to the Constitution, a proposal to abolish the vice presidency was seriously urged. The proposal was defeated by a vote of 85 to 27. Waugh, *op. cit.*, p. 164.

[60] In that event the President pro tem of the Senate, who becomes the regular presiding officer of that body, succeeds to the salary and other perquisites of office of the Vice President, but not the title. *United States Code* (1964), Title 2, Sec. 32. When a vacancy occurs in the office of lieutenant governor by reason of death or resignation, in some states the position is filled by appointment or by special election. Cf. *People ex rel Lynch* v. *Budd,* 114 Calif. 168, 45 Pac. 1060 (1896); and *State ex rel Martin* v. *Ekern,* 228 Wisc. 631 280 N.W. 393 (1938). In others the next officer in the line of succession, usually the president pro tem of the Senate, is regarded as lieutenant governor ex officio in this type of situation. In still others the post is left vacant, as in the case of the vice presidency.

lieutenant governorship more important parts of the governmental machinery. Since 1900 three states—Alabama, Arkansas, and Georgia—which previously did not provide for a separately elected lieutenant governor have established the office. There is a noteworthy trend toward giving both the Vice President and the lieutenant governor official duties in the executive branch. There is need for careful reconsideration of the place these officers should have in the governmental scheme.[61] Since a Vice President or lieutenant governor may at any time be called upon to fill the post of chief executive, he should be elected along with the chief executive as a member of his administrative team. He should be shorn of his traditional ex officio function of serving as the presiding officer of the Senate—a post carrying with it comparatively little power and, in the case of the Vice President at least, an office to which he devotes little time—and freed to participate in the executive councils and to accept such administrative and representational duties as the chief executive might choose to assign him. Former President Hoover suggested that there be two Vice Presidents, one a "legislative" Vice President who would function ex officio as the presiding officer of the Senate and the other an "administrative" Vice President assigned ex officio to the job of supervising certain phases of general administration. It has been suggested that he be made ex officio the Director of the Budget or a kind of general administrative manager; but this is not advisable for a number of reasons. The character of his duties should be kept flexible. He should become a sort of "minister without portfolio" subject to assignment to such duties as the President may direct. This would not only insure that he would function in a subordinate administrative capacity to the President (or to the governor in the case of the lieutenant governor) and not be tempted to become a rival. It would also make possible an adjustment of his duties to his particular talents. A series of different assignments over a period of time would

61 Greater appreciation of the importance of the offices of Vice President and lieutenant governor is attested by the number of recent studies of them. Cf. Louis C. Hatch and Earl L. Shoup, *A History of the Vice Presidency* (New York: The American Historical Society, 1934); Waugh, *op. cit;* Irving G. Williams, *The American Vice Presidency* (Garden City, N.Y.: Doubleday & Company, 1954); and *The Rise of the Vice Presidency* (Washington: Public Affairs Press, 1956); Klyde Young and Lamar Middleton, *Heirs Apparent* (New York: Prentice-Hall, 1948); Clinton Rossiter, "The Reform of the Vice Presidency," *Political Science Quarterly*, Vol. LXII (September, 1948), pp. 383–403; Lucius Wilmerding, Jr., "The Vice Presidency," *ibid.,* Vol. LXVIII (March, 1953), pp. 17–41; Donald Young, *American Roulette: The History and Dilemma of the Vice Presidency* (New York: Holt, Rinehart and Winston, 1965); Robert E. Patterson, *The Office of Lieutenant Governor in the United States* (Vermillion: University of South Dakota, Government Research Bureau, 1944); and Warren R. Isom, "The Office of Lieutenant Governor in the States," *American Political Science Review*, Vol. XXXII (October, 1938), pp. 921–926. For an interesting evaluation of the performance in the presidency by the first seven Vice Presidents who succeeded to that office see Peter R. Levin, *Seven by Chance* (New York: Farrar, Straus & Cudahy, 1948).

enable him to acquire a wider knowledge of the operations of the government as a whole. In this way he could be given a better opportunity than at present to prepare himself for the responsibility of serving as chief executive in case fate should thrust that role upon him.

STATUS AND POWERS

National and state practice are in agreement on the point that an officer succeeding to the chief executiveship, either temporarily or permanently, comes into possession of the whole power of the office. There can be no partial devolution of its constitutional powers.[62] On the question of whether the succeeding officer becomes invested with the office itself, as well as the title and emoluments thereof, practices vary somewhat. When in 1841 John Tyler became the first Vice President to assume the powers and duties of the presidency, there was some uncertainty as to whether he should be considered thereafter as the "Vice President acting as President" or as the "President." He soon resolved the matter by taking the oath of office as President and laying claim to the office, its title, and all its emoluments. Congress acquiesced in this disposition of the matter.[63] The usage thus established was continued in the seven other cases when Vice Presidents succeeded to the presidency upon the death of the incumbent—they are placed in the list of the "Presidents of the United States." This usage in time helped to support the proposition that no Vice President might act as President without "becoming" President, a view which has proved to be a serious stumbling block in the way of implementation of the disability clause.

An examination of comparable state practices shows that they have not fallen victim to this inhibitory view of the status of a succeeding officer. Numerous temporary successions by reason of the absence or disability of the incumbent governor have made clear that a temporary successor may exercise the powers and duties of the chief executive's office without having to surrender his original office or having to "become" governor in the sense of ousting the incumbent. In such cases his position is clearly that of an acting governor in law as well as fact, even though he may be entitled to the salary attached to the position of governor during the time he performs the duties of that office. Even

[62] State cases supporting this principle include *Walls* v. *Hall*, 202 Ark. 999, 154 S.W. (2nd) 573 (1941) (the veto power); *McCluskey* v. *Hunter*, 33 Ariz. 513, 266 Pac. 18 (1928) (the appointive power); *State ex rel Attorney General and Carey* v. *Barrow*, 29 La. Ann. 243 (1877) (the removal power); *Royster, Clerk* v. *Brock*, and *Laffoon, Governor* v. *Rankin*, 258 Ky. 146, 79 S.W. (2nd) 707 (1935) and *People ex rel Tennant* v. *Parker*, 3 Neb. 409 (1872) (power to call special legislative session); *Montgomery* v. *Cleveland*, 134 Miss. 132, 98 So. 111 (1923), *Ex parte Crump*, 10 Okla. 133, 135 Pac. 428 (1913), and *Ex parte Hawkins*, 10 Okla., Cr. 396, 136 Pac. 991 (1913) (the pardoning power).

[63] Cf. Silva, *Presidential Succession*, pp. 14–24; and Herbert W. Horwill, *The Usages of the American Constitution* (Glasgow: The University Press, 1925), pp. 58–87, for accounts of the events leading up to this disposition of the question.

where the succession is for the residue of the term, in most states the successor is still regarded as an "acting governor"; but in a few jurisdictions he is considered as having "become" the governor in this type of circumstance.

TENURE OF A SUCCEEDING OFFICER

A further issue arises in connection with the status of a succeeding officer who is called upon to fill the post of chief executive when there has been a permanent vacation of that office. Shall he be permitted to serve out the regular term or shall arrangements be made for selecting a new chief executive in the regular manner? This becomes a question of some weight when the vacancy occurs at the beginning or in the early part of a regular four-year term, or when the succession runs beyond the first successor in the regular line.

On this point again there is some diversity in national and state practices. The United States Constitution indicates that a Vice President who may be called upon to act as President in this circumstance shall continue to do so until the end of the term. This practice lends supports to the usage of considering him to have "become" President.[64] But the Constitution also clearly indicates that Congress may provide by law for the election of another President, presumably for a full term, in case a permanent succession should run beyond the Vice President. The 1792 Succession Act took this into account by authorizing the setting in motion of the electoral college machinery for choosing another President in the event the office should devolve upon one of the legislative officers named in the statutory line of succession; but the 1886 law backed away from this arrangement somewhat. It specified merely that if the responsibility of acting as President should devolve upon one of the officers named in the statutory line of succession, he must assemble the Congress within 20 days if it was not already in session, presumably to give it opportunity to provide for election of a new President should it see fit to do so.

One of the stated objectives of President Truman, when in 1945 he suggested that existing presidential succession legislation be revised, was to make such a special election mandatory if the succession should run beyond the vice presidency in the first half of a presidential term. Congress saw fit to ignore this aspect of his proposal for introducing more "orderly, democratic government" into the succession arrange-

---

[64] The Twentieth Amendment makes clear, however, that a new Vice President who is called upon to exercise the powers of the presidency at the beginning of a term because of an inconclusive presidential election shall merely *act* as President until the electoral deadlock is resolved. The Bayh-Celler Amendment, *supra*, p. 228, also contemplates a Vice President who may be called upon to serve as an "Acting President" for an indeterminate period.

ments and it became lost from view. Instead, the legislation finally enacted closed the door to any possibility of choosing a successor, either by a special election or indirectly through the choice of a new Speaker of the House as determined by the outcome of the midterm congressional election.

Inasmuch as Congress followed President Truman's suggestions in part by naming the Speaker as the next successor after the Vice President, it could have made possible a kind of national referendum on the choice of an Acting President for the last two years of a presidential term by attaching this role inseparably to that of the speakership. A change of party control of the House as a result of a midterm election would then have been reflected in a change in the identity of the person acting as President for the last two years of a presidential term. There would have been a reversion to the idea of legislative choice of the President. President Truman may have had this objective in mind when he recommended putting the Speaker next in line after the Vice President. But by providing that the person acting as President must *surrender* the post by virtue of which this duty falls upon him, Congress eliminated this possibility. It apparently felt that the language of the Constitution forbidding a member of Congress to hold "any office under the United States" while remaining a member of Congress foreclosed this kind of arrangement. The main justification for placing legislative officers in the line of succession at all is that these officers, having been chosen by a majority vote of the members of their respective houses, have the support of the currently dominant party in these bodies. But the ill-advised 1947 Act failed to carry through on this point. It should be noted that in a number of states which place the duty to act as governor in one of the presiding officers of the legislative branch, a new election resulting in a change in the occupancy of the presiding officer post produces a change in the acting governor post as well.[65]

When a vacancy occurs in the second half of a four-year term, and no general election intervenes before election of a chief executive for the next full term, there would appear to be little reason for holding a special election to choose a successor for the remaining part of the term; but when the vacancy comes about early in a term and no officer has been elected with the particular thought in view that he shall be the successor if a vacancy should occur, the case for a new election becomes very persuasive. About one third of the states with four-year terms for their governors permit or require election of a successor if a permanent vacancy in the governship occurs early enough for this to

[65] Cf. *Futtrell* v. *Oldham*, 107 Ark. 386, 155 S.W. 502 (1913); and *People ex rel Parks* v. *Cornforth*, 34 Colo. 107, 81 Pac. 871 (1905). See also *Clifford* v. *Heller*, 63 N.J.L. 104, 42 Atl. 155 (1899).

be done at the next midterm election. Eight states without lieutenant governors provide for a special election under these circumstances.[66] Four states with lieutenant governors provide for election of a successor for the second half of a term. In Maryland, which has no lieutenant governor, the legislature elects a successor as soon as it can be assembled. In California and Virginia a special election must be held if the succession goes beyond the lieutenant governorship, and in Alaska if it goes beyond the elected secretary of state, the next officer in the line of succession in that state.

There are, of course, special obstacles in the way of holding a special election to fill a vacancy in the office of President at midpoint in a term. They arise from the unique method of electing a President. Nevertheless, as the power and prestige of the office of President have grown the need for insuring that the person filling it has a popular mandate becomes correspondingly stronger, regardless of the nature of provisions that may be devised to cover the point of immediate succession. A re-examination of this aspect of succession arrangments relating to the presidency would seem to be highly in order. The provision in the Bayh-Celler Amendment permitting a succeeding Vice President to be named proposes to meet this problem by insuring that there will always be a Vice President available to take over. By requiring that the person so designated be confirmed by both houses of Congress, an element of indirect popular control is introduced into the process of selecting a successor. This is a commendable feature. But if the cumbersome machinery of the electoral college could be thrown into the ashcan where it belongs, it would be feasible to provide for the election of a new Vice President for the last two years of a presidential term whenever a vacancy has developed in the offices of President or Vice President during the early part of the term. Whatever the method of selection may be, it is important that the person who may be called upon to exercise the powers of the presidency through succession have the strongest possible evidence that he has a mandate from the people to exercise the powers of this great office.

---

[66] In Oregon and Washington state constitutional amendments were adopted requiring the holding of special elections to fill out the second half of gubernatorial terms, after there had been judicial rulings holding that this was not provided for in the state constitution. In *State ex rel Ayres* v. *Gray*, 69 So. (2nd) 187 (1953), the Florida constitution was held to require such an election. In *State ex rel Lamey* v. *Mitchell*, 97 Mont. 252, 34 Pac. (2nd) 369 (1934), the Montana Supreme Court held that such an election was not required.

PART THREE

EXECUTIVE POWERS AND FUNCTIONS

7

THE ROLE OF THE CHIEF EXECUTIVE:

A GENERAL VIEW

The presidency and the state governorship have come over the years to conform to a common basic institutional pattern. They are fundamentally similar not only in their place in the governmental structure but also in their powers, responsibilities, and functions and in the qualities called for from those who seek to fill them. Collectively the governorships and the presidency exemplify the classic form of the presidential system of executive organization in government. This is not to say that this system as now found in the United States had its character irrevocably fixed by the terms of the United States Constitution as it came from the hands of the Founders in 1787. That document set up a basic framework, to be sure; but the presidency and the governorship of the 1960s are the products of an institutional growth that has altered their character very materially. They differ in many important respects from the chief executiveship as conceived by the generation which established them.

A general trend toward enhancement of the power, influence, and importance of the chief executive has characterized constitutional development at both the national and state levels since 1789. This has not been a uniformly continuous trend, however. Recurring periods of political crisis and calm, differences in personal attributes and attitudes toward their office by individuals who have filled these posts, and the varying moods of the public, the legislative branches, and the courts toward the assumption of a stronger role by the executive have helped or retarded, as the case might be. The process of change has been spasmodic rather than continuous. Forward surges have been followed by limited retreats and reactions; but the overall trend has been in the direction of aggrandizement, in a relative sense, of the chief executive's place.

Interaction and imitation have played a part in bringing about institutional changes in the offices of governor and President. Practices at one level of government have seeped over into the other level. By and large, since 1789 the national constitutional pattern relative to the chief executive's role has had a greater impact upon state practice than the latter has had on the former; but there has been interaction in both directions. The national constitutional model has contributed most significantly, perhaps, to strengthening the governor's constitutional powers in relation to the legislative process. On the other hand, certain state governors—most notably the two Roosevelts and Woodrow Wilson—have, as Presidents, expanded the president's role as legislative leader by methods learned while serving as governors. Experimentation in one state in the organization of the governorship, when the results have proved satisfactory, has also had an impact upon practices in other states. Changes in the manner of selection of governors, for example, reflect in great measure this willingness of states to learn lessons from one another.

Differences of detail in institutional arrangements still remain, of course, as between the presidency and the state governorship. Because of the vital role it plays in the political affairs of the nation, the former overshadows the latter. The office of governor is not so much in the public eyes as the presidency. Problems relating to it do not command as much attention generally from scholars. Complicating study and understanding of it is the fact that executive arrangements still differ from state to state on a variety of points, and it is easy to lose sight of fundamental features of the office in detailed analysis of these differences. As a matter of fact, fundamental variations in the organizational pattern and role of the chief executive were wider and more significant among the original 13 state governments than they are now, taking the presidency and all 50 governorships into account. The differences that remain are significant enough, however, to make comparative analysis of executive arrangements at the two levels instructive. They present common problems, constitutional developments and practice with respect to them have followed similar lines, and their political relationships have become closer.

CONDITIONING FACTORS AND INFLUENCES

Influences on the evolution of the executive office have been varied and complex. To analyze them fully the political history of each state and of the nation would have to be reviewed in detail and depth. Without undertaking such detailed review it is possible to identify a number of factors that have helped to shape the course of constitutional development insofar as the office of chief executive is concerned. For the most part these factors have operated at both levels of government. They include: (1) the tendency to broaden the democratic base of government; (2) vagueness in the constitutional phraseology defining executive powers and duties, with the result that occupants of the office have had considerable leeway to apply their own interpretations; (3) recurring conditions of crisis and emergency; (4) the expanding role of government generally; and (5) the rise of the United States to the status of a world power.

BROADENING OF THE DEMOCRATIC BASE OF GOVERNMENT

No factor has more profoundly affected the character of the offices of President and governor than extension of the principle of popular election to these offices, accompanied by a broadening of the electoral base on which this choice depends. The effect has been nothing less than revolutionary. Democratization of the method of nominating and electing chief executives has given them the right to claim a popular mandate for their policies. It has given substance to their assertion that they are spokesmen for their party and for the people as a whole. This is the main foundation of the chief executive's vastly strengthened position in relation to legislation; and it tends to reinforce his authority to act as a policy-maker generally. Public confidence in the capacity and willingness of individual members of legislative bodies to act responsibly in the general interest has declined as they have shown themselves to be highly responsive to local constituency interests and pressures. Being popularly elected from a constituency which combines the constituencies of all the legislators, the chief executive has been enabled to assume the role of legislative leader. This, in turn, has given him more potency in all his official functions.

Giving the office a popular base through making it popularly elective has not been wholly on the plus side so far as making the chief executive stronger is concerned. It has exposed him to new kinds of pressures. Because he has become a popularly chosen and popularly responsible official, he must choose courses of action that will presumably command political support from the critical elements in his constituency. A leader without a following is powerless. The popularly chosen chief executive becomes something of a prisoner of the political forces which have thrust him into his high position. His constituency pressures differ only in composition and character from those that bear upon the individual legislator or administrator. And so it is with other accretions of powers and responsibilities by chief executives generally. Each new power or function has usually brought built-in checks, limits, and conditions that make it something less than an unalloyed gain. What he has gained often turns out merely to be a broadened opportunity to use the arts of persuasion, influence, and bargaining, rather than the power to command.

LOOSE CONSTITUTIONAL PHRASEOLOGY

Another factor of importance in making possible an enlarged field of action for chief executives is the vagueness of the constitutional language defining their role and powers. The origins of this part of the United States Constitution have been examined in some detail in Chapter 2. The conclusion was reached that the terminology adopted was drawn in an immediate sense from language found in the various state constitutions of the time; and that behind it all was a conception of the executive office and function leading back to colonial and British practice. Whatever its origins were, the essential point is that the language employed, perhaps with some deliberate intent, left considerable room for interpretation.

This fact was quickly demonstrated in a number of instances during Washington's administration. His adoption of the course of enunciating on his own a foreign policy position through the Neutrality Proclamation in 1793; his conversion of his department heads into a collective political advisory body, the Cabinet; and his espousal before Congress of a specific program of economic and fiscal measures formulated by his Secretary of the Treasury were all examples of uses that could be made of the rather vague wording of the Constitution. His successors have made similar contributions while building on the precedents established by their predecessors.

Writing in 1840 in the light of Andrew Jackson's vigorous assertions of executive independence of the other two branches of government and in criticism of Justice Story's advocacy of a broad, loose interpretation of executive powers, Able P. Upshur, later to serve as President Tyler's Secretary of State, observed:

> The most defective part of the Federal Constitution, beyond all question is that which relates to the executive department. It is impossible to read that instrument without being forcibly struck with the loose and unguarded terms in which the powers and duties are pointed out. So far as the Legislature is concerned, the limitations of the Constitution are perhaps as precise and strict as they could safely have been made; but in regard to the Executive, the Convention seems to have studiously selected such loose and general expressions as would enable the President, by implication and construction, either to neglect his duties or to enlarge his powers. We have heard it gravely asserted in Congress that whatever power is neither legislative nor judicial is, of course, executive, and as such belongs to the President under the Constitution. Be this as it may, it is a reproach to the Constitution that the executive is so ill-defined as to leave any plausible pretense, even to the insane zeal of party devotion, for attributing to the President of the United States the powers of a despot—powers which are wholly unknown to any limited monarch in the world.[1]

[1] *A Brief Enquiry into the True Nature and Character of our Federal Government* (Petersburg, Va.: E. & J. C. Ruffin. 1840), pp. 116–117; quoted in Edward

It follows that a chief executive's own conception of what his duties are in the light of the conditions confronting him has a great deal to do with what they are in practice. Presidential interpretation of the Constitution as it bears on his office becomes highly important in giving it actual meaning.[2] Woodrow Wilson, writing as a scholar before he became President, may have overstated the point somewhat when he asserted that the President "has the right, in law and conscience, to be as big a man as he can" and that "only his capacity will set the limit";[3] but there is certainly a large measure of truth in his statement. While state constitutions are somewhat more circumspect in outlining the executive's powers and functions than the United States Constitution is, they contain the same general, loose phraseology on some points.

As among the three branches of government in the tripartite separation of powers system, the courts by laying claim to and being accorded the power of judicial review have acquired in fullest measure authority to define their own role in the governmental system. But as between the executive and the legislative branches, the former has been more successful than the latter in this regard. In one sense the executive is in an even stronger position in this respect than the courts; for the courts restrict their own role in that they follow various self-limiting rules in exercising the power of judicial review. The Supreme Court has conceded to the executive the ultimate authority to determine for himself how his powers shall be applied in various situations heavily freighted with implications for the public welfare. Moreover, the courts restrain their own freedom of choice, as a general rule, by respecting the principle of *stare decisis;* and they act only in retrospective fashion on cases brought to them for the most part through the initiative of the executive branch or of private parties. The executive, on the other hand, can take the initiative in making determinations respecting his powers and role; he is not bound by precedent; and his actions may have a prospective application. Many of his interpretations are never passed upon by the courts. Indeed, Presidents have on occasion even dared to challenge or to ignore judicial pronouncements on matters touching their official powers and duties. Andrew Jackson in his famous Bank Bill Veto Message insisted that his own views, and not the Supreme Court's, were controlling upon himself on the question of the validity of legislation establishing a United States Bank. Lincoln instructed a military officer holding a civilian in custody by executive directive to

---

S. Corwin, *The President: Office and Powers,* 4th ed., (New York: New York University Press, 1957) p. 22.

2 On this aspect of the presidential office see Norman J. Small, *Some Presidential Interpretations of the Presidency* (Baltimore: Johns Hopkins Press, 1932); and Arthur Bernon Tourtellot, *The Presidents on the Presidency* (Garden City, N.Y.: Doubleday & Company, 1964).

3 Woodrow Wilson, *Constitutional Government in the United States* (New York: Columbia University Press, 1908), pp. 202–205ff.

ignore an order for a return on a *habeas corpus* writ issued by Chief
Justice Taney. Neither Jackson's veto nor Lincoln's directive was
successfully challenged.

Building on the foundations laid by Jackson and Lincoln, Theodore Roosevelt enunciated a broad view of presidential powers and
functions which has tended to set the mode for most of his successors.
Writing in his *Autobiography,* he set forth his "stewardship theory" of
the office in these terms:

> My view was that every executive officer, and above all, every ex-
> ecutive officer in high position, was a steward of the people bound
> actively and affirmatively to do all he could for the people, and not to
> content himself with the negative merit of keeping his talents undamaged
> in a napkin. I declined to adopt the view that what was imperatively
> necessary for the nation could not be done by the President unless he
> could find some specific authorization to do it. My belief was that it
> was not only his right but his duty to do anything that the needs of
> the Nation demanded unless such action was forbidden by the Consti-
> tution or by the laws. Under this interpretation of executive power I
> did and caused to be done many things not previously done by the
> President and the heads of departments. I did not usurp power, but I did
> greatly broaden the use of executive power. In other words, I acted for
> the public welfare, I acted for the common well-being of all our peo-
> ple, whenever and in whatever manner was necessary, unless prevented by
> direct constitutional or legislative prohibition. I did not care a rap for
> the mere form or show of power; I cared immensely for the use that
> could be made of the substance.[4]

Viewing the matter in retrospect, as he was when he wrote those
lines, Roosevelt may have made his point a bit too strongly. Certainly
he failed to note that the mere possession of constitutional power to act
is not the true measure of its actual use; for practical political considerations may impose limits falling far short of those set by constitutional
definition. Indeed, the Rooseveltian conception of the scope of presidential power was challenged by his immediate successor, William
Howard Taft. "The true view of the Executive functions," Taft insisted
in a series of lectures on the presidency, "is that the President can exercise no power which cannot be fairly and reasonably traced to some
specific grant of power or justly implied and included within such grant
as proper and necessary."[5] But later, as Chief Justice, Taft was to write
the Court's opinion in the *Myers* case,[6] wherein the doctrine was set
forth that the President is invested with constitutional authority

---

[4] Theodore Roosevelt, *An Autobiography* (New York: The Macmillan Company, 1916), p. 372.

[5] William Howard Taft, *Our Chief Magistrate and his Powers* (New York:
Columbia University Press, 1925), pp. 139–140.

[6] *Myers* v. *United States,* 272 U.S. 52 (1926). See Chap. 12 for a fuller discussion of the case. As President, Taft had also continued Roosevelt's practice of
withdrawing public lands from sale without express legislative authorization, a

to remove subordinate officers in the executive branch by virtue of implications drawn from the "executive power" and the "take care" clauses.

Even cautious Calvin Coolidge, whose conception of the President's role was considerably short of Rooseveltian, refused to allow himself to be pinned down on the broad question of the scope of the President's powers and duties. Writing after he had left the office, he stated in his *Autobiography*:

> The Constitution specifically vests him [the President] with the executive power. Some Presidents have seemed to interpret that as an authorization to take any action which the Constitution, or perhaps the law, does not specifically prohibit. Others have considered that their powers extended only to such acts as were specifically authorized by the Constitution and statutes. This has always seemed to me to be a hypothetical question, which it would be idle to attempt to determine in advance. It would appear to be the better practice to wait to decide each question on its merits as it arises.[7]

A chief executive's conception of his role, coupled with his boldness and ingenuity in devising means for discharging it any given time, thus becomes a key factor in giving content to the executive function. For this reason Woodrow Wilson, writing as a President-yet-to-be but with the examples of Theodore Roosevelt, McKinley, and Cleveland immediately before him, observed: "It is easier to write of individual Presidents than of the presidency itself."[8] As one individual follows another in it the office itself undergoes change. Sometimes the change has been quite marked, as when Lincoln, who took a broad view of his powers and responsibilities in the face of the challenge of state secession, succeeded Buchanan, whose conception of his proper role in this type of situation was limited; or when the thoroughly politically minded Franklin D. Roosevelt, whose views on the scope of presidential powers were perhaps in some respects even broader than his distinguished cousin's, succeeded Herbert Hoover, who entertained a more limited view of the constitutional functions of the President and of the propriety of governmental intervention in an economic crisis.

Not only do the actual powers and responsibilities of the office depend in considerable measure upon the individual who occupies it, but the personal factor is important in giving an emphasis to one aspect of his role over another. A politically oriented modern-day chief executive will devote a far larger proportion of his effort to his legislative leadership function than another who may concern himself more with

practice which the Supreme Court upheld in *United States* v. *Midwest Oil Co.,* 236 U.S. 459 (1915).

[7] Calvin Coolidge, *The Autobiography of Calvin Coolidge* (New York: Cosmopolitan Book Corporation, 1929), pp. 198–199.

[8] Wilson, *op. cit.,* p. 57.

purely administrative responsibilities. One President, by choice or necessity, may give priority to foreign policy, leaving the formulation of policy on the domestic front largely to other hands; while another may reverse this emphasis. In similar fashion state chief executives may choose to place major emphasis upon their administrative leadership and supervisory role or upon their political and legislative leadership functions, depending upon their particular talents and inclinations. National and state chief executives acting in the area of legislation may secure quite different results from those achieved by others occupying the same offices and enjoying the same constitutional powers. Like violin players of varying degrees of musical taste and talent playing the same Stradivarius, they evoke quite different tones and harmonies from the same instrument.

All this is not to say that change in basic laws has played no part in the expansion of executive power. Changes in constitutional language as well as statutory elaborations tending to strengthen the chief executive as policy-maker and administrative head of government have also been significant in giving shape to the modern conception of the office. Constitutional revision by formal methods has been important, particularly in redefinition and amplification of the powers and functions of the governor; while to a very great extent the modern-day role of the President finds authorization and confirmation in statutes enacted by Congress.

CONDITIONS OF CRISIS

Executive power thrives and is magnified under conditions of emergency. The first resource of government in dealing with widespread emergencies is the capacity of the executive to take immediate steps to relieve distress, to maintain the authority of the law, and to rally the people to a common effort to meet a danger. Such dangers may be posed by war or threats of war, insurrection, severe economic distress, pestilence, flood, drought, and other kinds of natural disasters. In situations of this kind the people turn instinctively to that element in the government which symbolizes its capacity to act—the executive. They demand from him a plan of action and the measures necessary for relief, either through legislation or, if the emergency is sufficiently great, through independent executive action. Though the executive may wish to do so, he cannot pass this responsibility on to others. He must act.

Great emergencies in the life of the nation have stimulated exercise of executive power and leadership to the maximum extent when they have occurred during the administrations of Presidents who viewed their responsibilities broadly and had faith in the efficacy and propriety of governmental intervention to restore the normal order. It reached its greatest heights during the crises of the Civil War, World War I, the depression of the 1930s, and World War II because the Presidents in office during these emergencies—Lincoln, Wilson, and Franklin D. Roosevelt —assumed responsibility for action beyond that which other Presidents had assumed in crises before them. Crises of this kind also provide state governors with challenges. There must be a proper coincidence in the man and his times to call forth a maximum exertion of executive power and leadership. Some Presidents and governors, it is true, have managed to play a strong role in the affairs of their time in the absence of conditions of serious crisis; but this has been done, as was the case with Theodore Roosevelt to a considerable degree, by their seizing vigorously upon opportunities afforded by relatively minor crises to display executive leadership.

A characteristic feature of the impact of crisis conditions upon the role of the executive has been a marked reaction against executive pretensions to power and authority, once the crisis has been alleviated. The public seems to welcome a return to "constitutional" habits and attitudes after a period of vigorous exercise of executive power. The legislative branch enjoys a resurgence of prestige, and even the courts on occasion have joined in the effort to cut back executive authority to its previously conceived dimensions. The heights in executive power and independence reached under Andrew Jackson, for example, were followed by a succession of one-term Presidents who were overshadowed by such figures as Webster, Clay, Calhoun, and others in Congress or in their administrations. The great issue of the years leading up to the Civil War—the extension of slavery into the territories—did not lend itself to ready solution through executive initiative. When the crisis of threatened disunion over it finally came, Lincoln formulated and acted upon a conception of the war powers of the President never before advanced. But he was followed by Andrew Johnson who barely managed to withstand an effort to subordinate his office completely to the legislative will, and by Supreme Court rulings in the *Milligan* and *Lee* cases[9] repudiating much of the Lincolnian theory regarding the scope of presidential war powers.

Woodrow Wilson's vigorous leadership in domestic and foreign affairs was followed by a return to "normalcy" in presidential-congressional relations under Harding and Coolidge. The extension of presidential influence to new heights under F. D. Roosevelt during his first term was temporarily checked by a rebellious Congress in his second term, only to be resumed again during World War II. In some respects his successor, Harry S Truman, pressed still further the claims to presidential authority and initiative. But these advances in turn

---

[9] *Ex parte Milligan,* 4 Wallace 2 (1866); *United States* v. *Lee,* 106 U.S. 196 (1882). See Chap. 16 for a fuller discussion of these cases.

brought on a reaction expressed in a variety of ways. The Twenty-second Amendment limiting presidential tenure to no more than two terms was adopted in 1951. Congress asserted its independence of the chief executive by passing a number of major statutes, including the Taft-Hartley Act, the McCarran-Wood Internal Security Act and the Walter-McCarran Immigration and Nationality Act in defiance of presidential vetoes. Congress stepped up its investigative probes into the conduct of administration. In the *Steel Seizure* case[10] the Supreme Court joined in the fray by delivering a lecture to the President on the limits of executive prerogative. Eventually, by the election of General Eisenhower who was pledged to restore "constitutional" government and harmony between the two political branches of government, the reaction ran its course. Unfortunately for him, as it turned out, the continuation of extreme international tensions as well as new economic and political crises on the domestic front during the 1950s served to demonstrate rather quickly that a complete retrogression to pre-1930 conceptions of the President's role was politically impossible, even under a President reluctant to exploit the full potential of his office.

This political pendulum effect in the relations between the executive on the one hand and the legislative and judicial branches on the other undoubtedly reflects underlying changes in popular mood and opinion on executive ascendency. It is no doubt a politically healthy thing in that it tends to maintain as a long-range proposition the basic conception of balanced powers. But it is significant that the claims to authority put forward and established by the executive in one period of crisis tend to become the bench marks from which new assertions of authority are made in the next emergency. Confronted by open defiance of federal authority in the Little Rock crisis in 1957, President Eisenhower responded in the tradition of Washington, Jackson, and Lincoln when confronted by similar crises. His vigorous reaction, without prior consultation with or approval by Congress, to British, French, and Israeli resort to military force in the Suez Crisis of 1956 was in the tradition of the two Roosevelts, Wilson, and Truman in the realm of foreign affairs.

THE EXPANDING ROLE OF GOVERNMENT

Evolution of the role of chief executives in the United States has also been profoundly affected by economic and social changes which have drastically altered the character of American society, bringing in their train a new emphasis on the place of government in it. As the society and the economy have changed, government has by popular

10 *Youngstown Sheet and Tube Co.* v. *Sawyer,* 343 U.S. 579 (1952). See Chap. 16.

demand been required to assume a wider range of regulative and service functions. The "regulative state," the "service state" and the "welfare state" concepts have necessitated the establishment of a far-ranging bureaucracy; and as that bureaucracy has burgeoned, the responsibility for its direction and supervision has fallen in great measure upon the head of the executive branch in which it finds a place.

To be sure, the legislative branch exercises a large share of this responsibility also; and as the administrative establishment grows in size and complexity, the chief executive's job of supervising every part of it becomes more and more impossible. His headship becomes more nominal than real. Nevertheless, the chief executive is expected to devise methods of coordinating administration where various governmental activities impinge upon one another. Long-range planning and programming, and implementation of accepted programs by appropriate legislation and provision for financial support become imperative. As head of the administration and as the leader of a party pledged to particular lines of action, the President or the governor must assume a major part of the job of engineering the legislature's consent and of injecting energy into the administration of an ever-changing body of measures designed to attain economic justice, prosperity and full employment, and social well-being generally. Compelled to be both legislative leader and economic planner, he is expected to employ his constitutional powers as well as extraconstitutional means adaptable to his ends in discharging his function as political head of the government. So fundamental a part of the chief executive's office has this aspect become that his reputation with the public as a successful President or governor turns largely upon the extent to which he originates and obtains legislative approval of economic and social welfare programs of lasting benefit.

EMERGENCE OF THE UNITED STATES AS A WORLD POWER

The rise of the United States to a position of political, economic, and military leadership in the Western community of nations may well prove to have been the factor having the most profound effect of all upon the office of President.[11] The constitutional language defining the powers and responsibilities of the President in the conduct of foreign relations remains as it came from the hands of the Founding Fathers; but its significance has been greatly altered by the problems confronting the United States in the modern world. As the chief spokesman of the leading power in a coalition of free nations resisting the

---

[11] On this general aspect of the evolution of the presidency see the excellent study by Sidney Warren, *The President as World Leader* (Philadelphia: J. B. Lippincott Company, 1964).

challenge of Communist imperialism, the President carries a responsibility to the world as well as to the nation. He is "President" of more than the United States, in a sense; his constituents include peoples of many foreign lands. They have no direct voice in his election, but they observe his course of action with avid interest. In the area of foreign policy he must be particularly mindful of public opinion throughout the free world; for "when he falters, free people everywhere grow faint; when he creaks, they groan; when he slips, they fall; when he stands firm and acts with assurance, they feel braced."[12]

A condition of relentless "cold war" dating from shortly after World War II has given modern diplomacy new political, psychological, and economic dimensions. International Communism and the democratic way of life are locked in a deadly competition for the hearts and minds of humankind the world over. Ours has become an era in which the instruments of warfare, readied by modern science, are continually poised for instant, devastating combat. We live in an era in which the interests of the nation may be involved in events occurring almost anywhere on the globe. Maintenance of national security dictates that policy-making and decision-making authority be consolidated in the President's hands to a degree never before approached. The fateful decision on "when to use the bomb," if ever that awful moment should come again has to be placed in his hands.

The responsibility of the office is truly staggering. To be sure, the President's responsibility is shared by Congress and by those in high executive office upon whom he depends for information and advice; but as the organ of communication with other governments, and as the head of a diplomatic, intelligence, and military network that circles the globe, the President is in a position to commit the United States to courses of action upon which the fate of the nation and, indeed, of all humankind, may turn.

EXECUTIVE FUNCTIONS

From what has been said, it is obvious that the office of chief executive is a many-faceted job, not susceptible to neat blueprinting and clear-cut definition. It is a job calling for many different kinds of talents. To conceive of the chief executive's function in civics-textbook terms as merely that of "seeing that the laws are executed" or "carrying out the policies set by the legislative branch" falls far short of the mark. More properly the executive function may be thought of as simply a convenient term for describing everything the chief executive is ac-

[12] Sidney Hyman, "What Makes a 'Strong' President?", *The New York Times Magazine*, December 13, 1953, p. 1.

tually expected to do. He performs an "executive" function no less when he recommends a tax revision plan for consideration of Congress, dedicates a national monument, pardons a convicted violator of federal law, or participates in a "summit" conference with heads of other governments, than when he issues a directive to the Department of Justice or to the Internal Revenue Service on some matter involving the administration of federal laws.

A political chief executive, it has been frequently said, wears a good many different hats. His office may more readily be understood if conceived of as several offices, tied together by being vested in the same person. Yet the fact that several different offices are in one man's hands does not mean that his function can be viewed accurately as merely the sum total of these separate, discrete parts. His various powers and duties are intermingled and complement one another in such fashion that the totality of his office amounts to something more. If he wears many hats he "wears them all at once."[13] His performance in one phase of his office is affected by the fact that he has to keep the other phases in mind. There is an inner core, an essence, to his office in its totality that arises from the joining of the various identifiable elements in one person's hands. It is the wise use of *all* his constitutional, statutory, and political powers and influence to foster public morale, to define goals, and furnish the necessary leadership in attaining them that unites the several parts of his job into a whole totaling more than the sum of the parts. His office is not merely a collection of powers or tools; it also involves political artistry in their application.[14]

That is no doubt what Franklin D. Roosevelt had in mind when, shortly after his election to the Presidency in 1932, he indicated his conception of the office he was about to occupy in these terms:

> The Presidency is not merely an administrative office. That is the least of it. It is pre-eminently a place of moral leadership.
>
> All of our great Presidents were leaders of thought at times when certain historic ideas in the life of the nation had to be clarified. Washington personified the idea of Federal Union. Jefferson practically originated the party system as we know it by opposing the democratic theory to the republicanism of Hamilton. This theory was reaffirmed by Jackson.
>
> Two great principles of our government were forever put beyond question by Lincoln. Cleveland, coming into office following an era of great political corruption, typified rugged honesty. Theodore Roosevelt and Wilson were both moral leaders, each in his own way and for his own time, who used the Presidency as a pulpit.
>
> That is what the office is—a superb opportunity for reapplying,

[13] Richard E. Neustadt, *Presidential Power: The Politics of Leadership* (New York: John Wiley and Sons, 1960), p. viii.
[14] Cf. Sydney Hyman, *The American President*, (New York: Harper & Row, 1954), Chap. 4.

applying to new conditions, the simple rules of human conduct to which
we always go back. Without leadership, alert and sensitive to change,
we are bogged up or lose our way.[15]

THE "CHIEFSHIPS" OF THE CHIEF EXECUTIVE

A commonly used method of viewing the dimensions of the office
in its modern-day form is the so-called "taxonomist" approach, i.e.,
describing its facets and component parts as seen from different angles
and vantage points. This method of analysis is unsatisfactory in that
it tends to obscure the point that it is the practical *use* of its powers,
prestige, and influence to produce a whole result rather than the separate powers themselves that constitutes the office in a real sense. Nevertheless, the piecemeal analytical approach has the merit of highlight-
ing some of the major contours of the office and identifying the points
where these contour lines are not firmly fixed and clearly drawn.

Moreover, major similarities and differences in the offices of
President and state governor become more obvious when both are
subject to this kind of rough job analysis. Of course, the President's
powers are necessarily of a grander, more impressive sort than those
of a governor in every respect because of the wider stage on which
the former performs his various roles. As the constitutional lines defining the respective spheres of operation of the national and state
governments have become blurred in the "New Federalism," the
activities of the national government have come to occupy a greater
importance than those of the states in the thinking of the people.
Furthermore, the central government has always had a monopoly in
managing foreign affairs and insuring national security—functions
which have become of such transcendant concern in the mid-twentieth
century as to overshadow all other aspects of government and public
policy. The President and his policies have been thrust into the
foreground of popular attention, with the governors and the state
governments they head playing distinctly secondary roles.

Consequently, in the analysis of executive powers and functions
that follows in the succeeding chapters, primary attention will be given
to the presidential office as typifying the chief executive's place in the
system of separated powers. Reference to the office of governor will
be made for the most part only to call attention to notable dissimilar-
ities and innovations which may point the way toward future developments.

The several facets of the chief executive's job have been categorized
in various ways. For example, Rossiter in his excellent portrait of the
modern-day presidency identifies five "constitutional" chiefships of the

---

[15] *The New York Times,* November 13, 1932, VIII, p. 1.

President, viz., "Chief of State," "Chief Executive," "Chief Diplomat," "Commander-in-Chief," and "Chief Legislator." He ascribes to the President in addition five other extraconstitutional roles—those of "Chief of Party," "Voice of the People," "Protector of the Peace," "Manager of Prosperity," and "leader of a Coalition of Free Nations."[16] The range of activities of the post is so great that one might go even further in identifying its distinctive elements to show its full impact upon Amercan political, socal, and economic life. In a similar vein, for example, Hyman has enumerated the President's various roles as follows:

> [He is] Chief of State, the Chief of Government, the Chief of Party, the chief organ of foreign affairs, the chief admiral and general, the chief administrator, the source of appointments and removals, the ultimate source of clemency and discipline, the chief social worker, the chief banker and insurance agent, the keeper of the conscience, the guide and interpreter of public opinion, the prophet of warning and encouragement, the manager of social justice and prosperity, and manager of the search for peace.[17]

The main dimensions of the office at both levels of government can be made sufficiently clear through an analysis which, by a somewhat arbitrary classification, distinguishes its component elements under the following "chiefship" headings: (1) Chief of State; (2) Party Chief; (3) Chief Legislator; (4) Chief of Administration; (5) Conservator-in-Chief of the Public Peace and Order; (6) Manager-in-Chief of External Relations; and (7) Commander-in-Chief. In the chapters that follow this approach will be used.

THE "INSTITUTIONALIZED" OFFICE OF CHIEF EXECUTIVE

The foregoing observations should not be allowed to obscure another aspect of the office of chief executive which has become more and more apparent in recent years. Constitutional theory calls for a concentration of responsibility upon one man; expediency requires that in practice this responsibility be diffused in considerable degree among those upon whom the chef executive must rely for assistance in discharging his manifold duties. No President or governor can be expected to attend personally to every matter which is placed in his hands by constitutional directive, by statute, or by usage. He must be able to delegate authority and permit others to perform acts in his name. He must have at his command the services of a staff to assist him in discharging his duties. He must have at his disposal information

---

16 Clinton Rossiter, *The American Presidency,* 2nd ed. (New York: Harcourt, Brace & World, 1960), Chap. 1.
17 Hyman, "What Makes a 'Strong' President?", *loc. cit.*

and advice of experts and specialists in particular phases of governmental policy and operation to enable him to reach informed and intelligent decisions thereon.

In earlier times when the range of governmental activities was
relatively restricted, Presidents were able to perform the functions of
their office with a small number of such aides. With the assistance of a
secretary or two they could maintain direct personal contact with all
major administrative subordinates, with legislative leaders, and with
those upon whose cooperation and advice they might have to rely.
Down to the time of Grover Cleveland presidents carried on much of
their correspondence personally, in longhand. But the need for an advisory staff was felt from the start. It was met in part through the
establishment of regular Cabinet meetings—consultations by the
President with his department heads as a group—through which he
might seek their advice collectively upon whatever matters he chose to
lay before them. This had become a regular practice by the end of
Washington's administration.

With the expansion of the functions of government to embrace a
constantly widening and deepening front of activities, the pressures
upon the chief executive have multiplied to the point where an expanded staff for the executive office itself has become imperative. This
need has been met through establishment of the Executive Office of
the President as a formal part of the administrative structure in the
national government. Brought into existence by an executive order
of President F. D. Roosevelt in 1939 following a recommendation of
the President's Commission on Administrative Management in 1937,
this nerve center of the federal administrative system now embraces
the major staff agencies upon which the President relies in an immediate sense for assistance in carrying out his constitutional duties.
The units which make up the Executive Office of the President reflect
the vast extensions of presidential responsibility and authority in
policy-making, planning, and coordination that have come about in
recent decades. Through them the powers and responsibilities of the
President have, to a degree, been diffused among many hands. His office
has become "institutionalized" in its administrative procedures and
its decision-making processes. The presidency has become, in effect,
"many men"; the "men around the President," not the President alone,
discharge its functions. A similar evolution in the operational side of
the office of governor is discernible, most particularly in the populous,
industrialized states.

This is not to say, however, that the American chief executiveship
is on its way toward becoming collegial in character. Basic constitutional arrangements stand in the way of such a fundamental change.
However far the concept of the staff system may be carried, ultimate

responsibility remains with the chief executive. Final decisions on matters entrusted to him are his to make or to assume the responsibility for making. As former President Truman spelled out the point: "The President must make his own decisions. He cannot pass the buck up or down."[18] Institutionalization is a necessary response to the cumulation of tasks beyond one man's capacity to give them all his immediate, personal attention. But it cannot alter the fundamental character of the office itself, as shaped by the Constitution and by the image of it as conceived by the public it serves.

"JOB QUALIFICATIONS" OF THE OFFICE

Before proceeding to a closer examination of the major component elements of the chief executive's functions and powers, it is appropriate to point out in general terms the kind of qualities called for in a successful discharge of them. In Chapter 5 the constitutional, legal, and political qualifications for the offices of President and governor were surveyed. An ability to win election to the office, while demonstrating that the successful aspirant possesses at least some of the essential qualities required in a chief executive, does not furnish final proof of executive talent. That comes only by a performance test in the office itself. Incumbents fulfill the job requirements of the post with varying degrees of success, depending upon their possession of qualities and talents that can be described only in somewhat vague, general terms. Their application to the performance of an individual in office necessarily involves a large element of subjective judgment. Some of the indices by which performance of executives in government may be evaluated are the same as those applicable to the measurement of executive performance in the business world. But it is a mistake to assume that qualifications demanded of business executives are identical with those making for successful performance by a political chief executive. The most reliable index for judgment of the competence of a business executive—a balance sheet showing a high level of financial profit—is inapplicable in the case of a President or governor, since government is not a profit-making enterprise. The milieu in which a political chief executive must operate, the kinds of pressures that play upon him, and the goals he must aim for are so different from those of a business executive that the criteria by which their respective performances must be rated are quite different.

Any attempt to list all the desirable personal qualities a political chief executive should have tends to produce a mere catalogue of practically all the human virtues. An illustration of this point is

18 Harry S Truman, "The Day Ike Snubbed Me," *Look*, May 24, 1960, p. 32.

afforded by a summation of views of five authorities, including one of
the nation's leading political scientists, a United States Senator, and
three noted American historians, on the personal qualities demanded
for a successful performance in the office of President.[19] A compilation
of the qualities mentioned by them includes, in addition to "all those
virtues celebrated in the New Testament, 'The Compleat Gentleman,'
'The Way to Wealth' and the handbook of the Boy Scouts of America,"
(1) political skill, (2) political experience, (3) "bounce," (4) cunning,
(5) a sense of history, (6) a sense of humor, (7) imagination, (8) ability
to inspire others, (9) gravity, (10) self-possession, (11) moral courage,
(12) patience, (13) kindness, (14) objectivity, (15) warm-heartedness
(16) initiative, (17) leadership, (18) physical courage, (19) self-dis-
cipline, (20) creativeness, (21) vitality, (22) curiosity, (23) "nerve," (24)
faith, (25) a commanding personality, (26) a sense of direction, (27)
flexibility, (28) ability to play, (29) toughness, (30) tirelessness, (31)
dedication, (32) energy, and (33) an ability to make decisions. Another
astute scholar has attempted to subsume all the desirable attributes
of a chief executive under the rubric of the "twelve C's," namely,
consciousness, conviction, command, creativity, courage, conciliation,
cleverness, coherence, constancy, charm (or captivation), conscien-
tiousness, and constitution.[20] Without gainsaying the judgments of
these eminent authorities one may venture to detail another list of
human qualities that have special applicability in evaluating the performance of a political chief executive. They include the following:

1. ABILITY AS A JUDGE OF MEN

No President or governor can personally make the myriad of day-
to-day decisions that must be made on the executive side of government. He must therefore be able to select as his aides men and women
of capacity, to delegate to them in clear terms a share of the heavy
burden he bears, and to hold them accountable for their acts. Though
the office of chief executive has become institutionalized, he is the
prime architect of the institution itself. He must select the parts and
fit them together. To use the current hackneyed expression, he and
his aides must function as a team; but it is he who must be the
manager, who must be the judge of individual talents and capacities
and assign to its members their appropriate positions and roles.

He must be inflexible in demanding of them the high sense of

19 "The Right Man for the Big Job," *The New York Times Magazine,* April 3,
1960, pp. 27 ff. The participants in the symposium included Professsors Clinton Rossiter, Arthur Schlesinger, Jr., Richard Hofstadter, and Allan Nevins, and Senator
Margaret Chase Smith of Maine.

20 Herman Finer, *The Presidency: Crisis and Regeneration* (Chicago: University
of Chicago Press, 1960), Chap. III.

devotion to duty and the public interest which he demands of himself. The injection of personal friendship considerations in choosing his subordinate staff, or an attitude of easygoing good fellowship and an unquestioning trust toward them, has proved to be a vulnerable point in the administrations of more than one chief executive. A weakness on this score accounts for the low rating generally given the administrations of Presidents Grant and Harding in comparison with those of other Presidents. A shortcoming in this regard need not be exhibited with respect to a relatively large number of appointments to amount to a serious flaw; only a few scalawags and incompetents may give an administration a bad name.

2. ABILITY TO MAKE HARD DECISIONS AND ASSUME RESPONSIBILITY

A capacity to reach decisions upon questions posing difficult alternatives is an essential quality in any executive. A political chief executive's job consists in large measure of making difficult choices among alternative courses of action. He cannot avoid having to make them, however unpleasant the implications and consequences may be. Often the course of taking no action at all involves the making of a choice that may bring unhappy results. Theodore Roosevelt was reputed to have said that the first and most essential requisite of the job of being President was "to be able to make decisions and be right part of the time."

An individual who finds it a trying ordeal to resolve competing considerations and settle upon a course of action, or who after having done so remains unconvinced of the rightness of his decision, is temperamentally unfitted for the post of chief executive. It is no post for a Hamlet. An element in the tragedy of Lincoln was that, a most sensitive and humane man, he was condemned for the duration of his administration to contemplate the bloody results of a momentous decision that was forced upon him at the outset. Although he never wavered from his aim of preserving the Union at all costs, the terrible burden of responsibility for having to act as a principal in events which produced the carnage weighed heavily on Lincoln's mind and soul. At times, according to his biographers, he was driven to contemplation of suicide. The brooding passages in his Second Inaugural Address attributing the misery, suffering, and bloodshed of the Civil War to the judgment of a just God upon a nation which had tolerated human bondage reveal an anguished soul seeking to find some release from its own moral burden.

Any President or governor is confronted by a never-ending series of crises and issues to be resolved. The road he walks is a lonely one. He cannot escape his burden of responsibility. He must be able to proceed from one critical decision to the next, confident in his belief that having given an issue the most careful and intelligent consideration permitted by the time and means available to him and having reached a conclusion, the matter is closed. Like a highly competent athlete, he must be able to relax between plays, forgetting the mistakes or bad breaks of the last one, while he concentrates on the next.

Along with this capacity of decision should go a readiness to assume responsibility for his own decisions and those of subordinates to whom he delegates authority. A President or governor, of course, cannot properly be held responsible for the misdeeds and errors of judgment of every obscure administrative official. In an immediate sense, responsibility for their acts rests upon subordinate executives in the higher echelons of the administrative hierarchy. These higher subexecutives may not themselves be amenable to the directives of the chief executive. In the states independently elected department heads and local officials administer some of the most important phases of state policy and the governor may have no very effective way of enforcing accountability upon them. The administrative bureaucracy the President heads has become so vast that presidential responsibility for the manner in which particular elements of it may function tends to be more a matter of theory than practical reality. Nevertheless, within the area of decision-making and action where he can enforce accountability the chief executive must be willing publicly to assume the ultimate responsibility for his own actions as well as those of his subordinates to whom he entrusts power to act in his name.

A President who fully appreciated his responsibility in this sense was President Truman. He expressed his views on the point in these terms:

> . . . The President has an executive job that is almost fantastic. There has never been one like it. I think no absolute monarch ever had such decisions to make or the responsibility the President has. After all, every final important decision has to be made right here on the President's desk, and only the President can make it. Nobody else can do it for him, and his decisions affect millions not only in his own country but throughout the world. No one man can really fill the Presidency. The President has too many and too great responsibilities. All a man can do is to try to meet them. He must be able to judge men, delegate responsibility and back up those he trusts.[21]

President Truman's conduct in office amply demonstrated his recognition of this principle. His removal of Secretary of Commerce Henry A. Wallace when an internal schism in his Cabinet over foreign policy threatened to create confusion; his removal of General Douglas

[21] Quoted in William Hillman, *Mr. President* (New York: Farrar, Straus & Cudahy, 1952), p. 10.

MacArthur as head of the United Nations forces in Korea when in the President's judgment the General was following a political course at odds with that of the administration; his removal of Attorney General J. Howard McGrath when a shadow of suspicion was cast regarding his involvement in favor-seeking scandals—all were evidence of his regard for the principle of presidential responsibility for the actions of his subordinates. On the other hand a widely noted phenomenon of the subsequent administration of President Eisenhower was a seeming public indifference toward holding him personally accountable for a wide range of policy decisions in such areas as foreign affairs, agriculture and conservation, fiscal policy, personnel management, party management, and party campaign techniques. The general inclination of the public seemed to be to hold members of his team responsible rather than the President himself. He was reelected in 1956 by an overwhelming majority; yet in that election as well as in both midterm congressional elections of his administration, his party was denied control of both houses of Congress in what could only be construed as a vote of lack of confidence in its administration of public business under his leadership.

3. POLITICAL SENSITIVITY AND TIMING

Another mark of a successful chief executive is his ability to gauge public opinion, to sense its force, depth, and direction and to distinguish underlying trends among the seemingly confused crosscurrents and conflicts. His success in achieving election will have demonstrated his possession of this talent in some degree; but as his term in office progresses new problems and issues will arise to test his ability to sense the popular mood and shape his course accordingly. His capacity to move forward toward his policy objectives is dependent in great measure upon the degree of popular support he can muster for them. As Lincoln was said to have put it, "With public sentiment everything is possible; without public sentiment nothing is possible."

A successful chief executive must be equipped with political antennae of unusual sensitivity. The means by which he arrives at his conclusions as to the state of the public mind are various. He may depend upon the press, key advisers in or out of public office, political commentators, opinions expressed on the floor of Congress, or other sources to furnish the evidence from which he draws his conclusions; but in any event he must have a kind of sixth sense that enables him to draw the right conclusions most of the time. Time after time in the conduct of his office he is faced with situations calling for application of the Bismarckian adage that "politics is the art of the possible." The state of the public mind in the final analysis determines the limits of the possible in a democracy.

Along with his political sensitivity should go a feeling for appropriate timing of his moves and a sense of drama which enables him to present his programs in terms which will be understood and accepted by the man in the street. He must appear to be neither so far in advance of public opinion as to have no substantial popular support for his stand, nor so far behind it as to create the impression that he is being pushed into action. For example, Franklin D. Roosevelt's 1937 "quarantine the aggressors" speech in which he attempted to arouse public support for a more active role by the United States in opposing the aggressive moves of the dictatorial leaders of Japan, Germany, and Italy fell upon deaf ears and failed temporarily. But as soon as the state of the public mind permitted, after the outbreak of World War II, he pushed ahead rapidly on a program for readying the country's resources for defense. He sensed and acted in accord with a stiffening public determination to prevent an Axis victory at any cost.

As it is with other aspects of his office, a chief executive's judgment regarding the state of the public mind and his use of public relations techniques to influence it and to bring it to bear upon those whose cooperation he must have can be strengthened by the quality of his staff of experts in this area. But in the final analysis his own skill and talent are the ultimate measure of his success in this aspect of his job. He must be his own public relations expert. He must develop the "newspaper habit," and cultivate sources of opinion and information outside his immediate staff. He must be able to draw conclusions on the state of the public mind and probable reactions to his moves for himself. Again we have the testimony of President Truman on the point:

> You hear people talk about the powers of the President. In the long run, his powers depend a good deal on his success in public relations. The President must try to get people to do things that will be best for the most people of the country. . . . The President of the United States represents 154,000,000 people. Most of them have no lobby and no special representation. The President must represent all the people.
>
> Therefore the President must be a sort of super public relations man. His powers are great, but he must know how to make people get along together.[22]

This sense of being able to feel and interpret the variety of impulses that animate the public mind and employ them for constructive ends, it should be observed, must extend not only to inter-

22 Hillman, *op. cit.*, p. 11.

pretation and translation of public desires to those in positions of power. There are also "governmental publics" with which the President must deal, made up of the elements in the bureaucracy and in the legislative branch with their various competing interests and desires. The President has the ultimate responsibility of receiving and evaluating the expressions of sometimes conflicting desires and viewpoints among these centers of influence as well as those outside the government, and of reacting intelligently to them.

4. POLITICAL AUDACITY AND ZEST FOR COMBAT

The conclusion should not be drawn from what has just been said that the single and overriding aim of a chief executive should be to function merely as a political weathervane, following changes in public opinion wherever they may lead. He should be something more than a reflector and transmitter of the popular mood; something more than a mediator among conflicting interests. He should not be content to permit public affairs merely to drift with the tide. As captain of the Ship of State he should set a course; and while he may have to tack or change sail in response to vagaries of the political weather, he should not lose sight of his ultimate objective. Political opposition to his programs and policies will always be forthcoming from some quarters. He should welcome it as a means of testing and refining his own ideas, but not be awed or intimidated by it.

He must be willing to lead, at times, in causes which for the moment may appear to be unpopular and unfeasible, under the firm conviction that time and events will prove him to have been right. Jackson began his war on the United States Bank at a time when the prevailing opinion in Congress and perhaps in the country was against him. After first joining in the cry for harsh treatment of the defeated South, Andrew Johnson espoused the cause of moderate treatment of the ex-Confederate states in the face of a widespread feeling in the North and in Congress that the "rebel" states should be dealt with harshly and their leaders punished severely. Theodore Roosevelt challenged the opposition of a considerable segment of his own party in advancing his "trust-busting" program in 1904, as did Harry S Truman in espousing his 10-point civil rights program in 1948. A President or a governor who does not relish the give and take of political combat, who is unwilling to put to the test his popularity and his reputation as a farsighted statesman, will fail in his duty. He will never win the accolade given to Cleveland by one of his enthusiastic followers—"We love him for the enemies he has made."

Again a caveat should be entered, however. While a chief executive should be a fighter, and while he should strive to shape events and not merely react to them, he should not allow his combative instinct to convert him into a frustrated, querulous champion of unpopular causes. The line between futile bullheadedness and praiseworthy bull-dog tenacity is a fine one, but he must be able to preceive it. He must have the sagacity to recognize when the attainment of an objective has become impossible, or when he must be content with a compromise falling short of his goal. He must not be so prideful as to refuse to listen to counsels of moderation. Instances of excessive tenacity by executives striving for unattainable goals abound in the pages of history. Woodrow Wilson's standing among the Presidents will always be impaired by the fact that he was so determined to obtain the Senate's unqualified approval of the Versailles Treaty and its League of Nations provisions that he refused even the least offensive face-saving compromises in its terms. His intransigence only served to put his nobly conceived plan for organizing the world for peace under a fatal handicap from the start. Andrew Johnson's shrill and intemperate challenge to the dominant thinking in Congress on issues growing out of Reconstruction and his unwillingness to compromise led to his own political downfall and brought the presidency to one of its lowest ebbs in history. Governor Sulzer's refusal to make any sort of deal with the Tammany influence in his party on the distribution of patronage in New York only brought about his repudiation by dominant elements in his own party and his subsequent impeachment and removal.

5. ABILITY TO INSPIRE CONFIDENCE AND LOYALTY

One of the most intangible and elusive qualities that distinguishes a successful chief executive is his ability to attract and hold the loyalty and confidence of those who work with him or come within the range of his voice, his personality, or his messages. His leadership is measured by the character and devotedness of his "followership." Any successful aspirant usually begins his term with an immense backlog of popular acclaim and goodwill. He can count on the unquestioning support and faithful echoing of his ideas from thousands or even millions of the party's rank and file, regardless of how well he may actually discharge the duties of his office. Blinded by partisanship, their eyes can perceive in him no wrong. He can ordinarily expect to enjoy a political "honeymoon" when goodwill dominates and criticism is muted, for at least several months following his inauguration.

He must have a capacity to command support beyond this, after the going gets rough. He must be able to retain the support and confidence of those who are most closely associated with him as well as that of a significant segment of the general public who are not merely blinded by hero-worship and extreme partisanship. His staff must be willing to concede to him unquestioningly the role of "chief," even though this may entail political sacrifice and unrecognized, unrewarded toil and effort for them. Seeing and recognizing his human frailties, they must nevertheless feel impelled through a sense of personal loyalty he has generated in them to render the support he requires to accomplish his objectives.

The foundation of this quality undoubtedly lies in the chief executive's confidence in himself, in his mission, and in the soundness and rightness of his actions. But beyond his own self-confidence there must be an ability to transmit to others an impression of his own sincerity, vision, and devotion to the public weal. By whatever name it may be called—personal charm, magnetism, charisma, savoir faire in human relations—he must be able to command the unwavering support and allegiance of others. If he can extend this sense of personal allegiance beyond the circle of those who are most important to him and who know him through direct daily contact, his path will be smoother; but first he must be able to command at all times a feeling of personal loyalty within his official household before he can expect it from the general public. Whatever dangers to the democratic system lurk in charisma, a chief executive without the ability to invoke a feeling of hero-worship among those who fall under his personal influence is lacking in one of the essential qualities of leadership.

6. SENSE OF PROPORTION AND PERSPECTIVE

Another essential qualification of the job is an ability to apply a proper scale of values to the many demands, pressures, and responsibilities. The chief executive must be able to take a long-range view of himself and his job. He must have the gift of seeing himself and the events of his administration in their proper historical perspective. A thorough knowledge of political history is an indispensable asset. It enables him to be guided in his own judgments by the experience of the past, to make the most of precedents established by his predecessors, and to see in the problems confronting him replicas of problems confronting chief executives in the past, with only relatively minor differences in form and emphasis. Lincoln drew sustenance from Jackson's vigorous response to the challenge to national authority in the South Carolina tariff nullification controversy of 1832 when he faced a similar challenge of state secession in 1861. Wilson reshaped his own ideas regarding the political leadership role of the President in the light of the examples afforded by Cleveland, McKinley, and Theodore Roosevelt. Franklin D. Roosevelt applied lessons learned from all of these outstanding predecessors. Not only will a knowledge of history furnish clues as to what a chief executive's course should be, but it can give him increased confidence that, whatever the contemporary judgment and reaction may be toward him and his measures, time will vindicate him.

7. ABILITY TO WITHSTAND UNFAIR CRITICISM

Whatever the rewards and satisfactions of serving as chief executive may be, immunity from criticism and calumny is not one of them. The conditions of political life in the United States seem to be deliberately calculated to make the chief executive the natural and obvious target of attack—his elevation to office through a partisan contest in which tempers and emotions are aroused to a high pitch; a separate, independent legislative body that is prone to look upon his acts with suspicion; a latent, easily aroused public distrust of executive "dictatorship"; and the constitutionally ordained periodicity of elections which causes aspiring politicians to seek every advantage for their own interests in the light of the soon-to-be-renewed struggle for the top job in the political hierarchy. Every President, from Washington on, has been exposed to faultfinding, questioning of motives and integrity, and ridicule, most of it quite vicious and unfounded. This is an ordeal which no occupant of the office can avoid, and he must be able to withstand it.[23]

Washington, dubbed by his critics "the American Caesar," was accused of desiring to become a king. Borne down by the slanderous attacks and charges of his political opponents, Jefferson characterized his office as a "splendid misery," a sentiment later to be echoed by Jackson for similar reasons. One of the milder epithets hurled at Lincoln by his critics was "baboon." Hoover complained of the "hair shirt" a President is condemned to wear and referred to his job as a "compound hell." To some of his critics, Franklin D. Roosevelt was "that megalomaniac cripple in the White House." "Liar," "idiot," "crook," "thief," "traitor," "dictator," "adulterer," "butcher," and "drunken beast" have been terms used to describe various occupants of the White House by their political enemies. Any President or governor quickly becomes a favorite target for the circulators of unprintable locker-room humor.

Unless a chief executive can adopt a tolerant or indifferent attitude toward these countless annoyances and prickles, his tenure in office can become a nightmare to himself and his family. President Jefferson's solution was simply to avoid reading the opposition news-

---

[23] David Cushman Coyle's *Ordeal of the Presidency* (Washington: Public Affairs Press, 1960) is a compendium of the criticisms, slanders, and vituperative attacks Presidents and presidential candidates have been forced to endure.

papers, an expedient to which some of his successors have resorted. In a sense this is unfortunate, for a chief executive is thereby deprived of an opportunity to learn what his opposition is saying, which may be useful to him in gauging public opinion. Lincoln's tolerant attitude was exemplified in his observation: "Let them talk: it seems to do them some good and it doesn't hurt me any." President Truman's succinct comment on the point was, "If you can't stand the heat, stay out of the kitchen." President Kennedy declared there was "a terrific disadvantage [in] not having the abrasive quality of the press applied to you daily." A sense of humor and proportion permits a chief executive to place personal vilification and mere carping criticism in their proper perspective and to direct his energies toward matters more deserving of his attention. He may even be able to turn some of it to his political advantage, as illustrated by F. D. Roosevelt's 1944 campaign remarks in defense of his devotion to his dog Fala.

"STRONG" AND "WEAK" CHIEF EXECUTIVES

The above list of job qualifications is far from being an exhaustive one. There are many other attributes that go toward making an incumbent chief executive's performance successful; but those mentioned undoubtedly stand high on the list. They serve to suggest the difficulty inherent in drawing a judgment upon the performance of any individual who has occupied such an office. The standards are not only elusive and inexact; but their application to the record of any individual chief executive's performance involves the reaching of conclusions so subjective in character as to render the relative ratings produced highly questionable. Nevertheless, a favorite occupation of political commentators and historians is to attempt to apply the very elastic and inexact available measuring sticks to the records of particular Presidents and to come up with conclusions on whether they were "strong," "weak," "great," "near-great," "mediocre," or otherwise rateable chief executives.[24]

Characterization of chief executives as "strong" or "weak" or somewhere between the extremes should not be governed by certain extraneous factors that have relevance only to their popularity with the people. Success in winning re-election, for example, does not in itself constitute evidence of much value in reaching a conclusion. It demonstrates an incumbent's capacity to maintain his footing in the

[24] For examples of such evaluations see Rossiter, *op. cit.,* especially Chaps. 3 and 5; James Fort Milton, *The Use of Presidential Power, 1789–1943* (Boston: Little, Brown and Company, 1945); Norman J. Small, *op. cit.;* and J. C. Long, *The Liberal Presidents* (New York: Thomas Y. Crowell, 1948).

shifting sands of politics and to secure a contemporary popular endorsement of his record; but his being returned to office may have depended upon circumstances having little to do with whether he should be regarded as a "strong" or "weak" executive. James Monroe won re-election by a near-unanimous electoral vote and his administrations were characterized by an absence of extreme partisan rancor and conflict to such a degree that this period has been called the "Era of Good Feeling"; yet Monroe is not generally regarded as deserving of rank among the strongest Presidents.

On the other hand, while most strong executives have been quick to resist what they regarded as attempts by the legislative branch to usurp their prerogatives and have promptly reacted against efforts by insurgent elements within the party to challenge their leadership, an administration punctuated by repeated battles between a President and his Congress and by bitter factional struggles within his party is not necessarily the hallmark of a strong executive. John Tyler, Andrew Johnson, and Chester A. Arthur—all "accidental" Presidents by rule of succession, it may be remarked—were Presidents whose administrations were rocked by struggles of this kind; yet they are not generally considered to be among the strong or great Presidents.

Possession in marked degree of most or all the talents described above and their successful application to achieve solutions for the problems of their day are the criteria by which strong Presidents and governors are distinguished. A chief executive who rightfully deserves this rating will have displayed ingenuity and boldness in exploiting to the fullest the potentialities of his office. He will have impressed upon it meanings and interpretations from which his successors have derived strength to accomplish their objectives more easily and fully. In the policies he has espoused and brought to realization the strong executive will have had a profound impact upon the events of his time. He will have sensed and given expression to the mood and spirit of his times by serving as a catalyst for the inchoate aspirations of the people. In a word, he will have supplied *effective leadership*.[25] Historical perspective is needed to reach even an approximation on the rating that should be given a particular occupant of the office of President or governor; and even for those who can be evaluated in the more detached and objective fashion which historical perspective makes possible, the verdicts of competent analysts are continually

[25] Cf. Sidney Hyman "What Makes a 'Strong' President?" *supra*. For a criticism of this standard of judgment see Curtis A. Amlund, "President-Ranking: A Criticism," *Midwest Journal of Political Science*, Vol. VIII (August, 1964), pp. 309–315. He suggests therein that instead of rating Presidents as "strong" or "weak" it might be more appropriate to rate them in terms of their possesssion of the quality of "adaptability." He defines this as their "capacity to meet changes by maintaining a policy equilibrium between power and ideological centers both within and without our society."

being revised as new insights are gained into the records of men and their times. Contemporary judgment upon a man who has occupied the office of chief executive is particularly likely to be badly out of focus and distorted by the political myopia of the evaluator.

A rating of the Presidents which has received considerable publicity is one published in 1962 through the initiative of Professor Arthur M. Schlesinger, Sr., of Harvard University. It embodies the composite views of 75 eminent American historians and commentators on public affairs. The results were as follows:[26]

GREAT PRESIDENTS
1. Lincoln   2. Washington   3. F. D. Roosevelt   4. Wilson   5. Jefferson

NEAR-GREAT PRESIDENTS
6. Jackson   7. T. Roosevelt   8. Polk   9. Truman   10. J. Adams
11. Cleveland

AVERAGE PRESIDENTS

12. Madison	15. McKinley	18. Monroe	21. Arthur
13. J. Q. Adams	16. Taft	19. Hoover	22. Eisenhower
14. Hayes	17. Van Buren	20. B. Harrison	23. A. Johnson

BELOW AVERAGE PRESIDENTS
24. Taylor   26. Fillmore   28. Pierce
25. Tyler   27. Coolidge   29. Buchanan

FAILURES
30. Grant   31. Harding

The game of rating the Presidents, of course, is one in which any number may play. Another group of 75 eminent people in another field of endeavor, such as business or the law, would probably reach different conclusions from those of the authorities consulted by Professor Schlesinger. No attempt will be made here to give comparative ratings to the individuals who have occupied the office of President, much less to the more than 2000 persons who have served the states in the office of governor. In the pages that follow the more frequent mention of certain Presidents as major contributors to the evolution of the office into its present form will inevitably serve to identify some of the outstanding occupants of the office. Washington, Jefferson, Jackson, Lincoln, Theodore Roosevelt, Wilson, and Franklin D. Roosevelt each made major contributions in this respect.

[26] "Our Presidents: A Rating by 75 Historians," *The New York Times Magazine,* July 29, 1962, pp. 11 ff. Presidents William Henry Harrison and James A. Garfield were omitted from the list because their tenure in office was too short to afford a basis for rating them. President John F. Kennedy's name was also omitted because he had not served long enough at the time the ratings were made to provide a proper basis for judgment.

Among governors a constantly growing number since the turn of the present century have had a similar strong influence on the evolution of the office of governor in their own states, and by example, in others. Any listing of the outstanding governors of the first three or four decades of the century would undoubtedly include, among others, Robert M. La Follette of Wisconsin; Hiram Johnson and Earl Warren of California; Charles Evans Hughes, Alfred E. Smith, and Herbert Lehman of New York; Gifford Pinchot of Pennsylvania; Harry Byrd of Virginia; Frank O. Lowden of Illinois; and Albert C. Ritchie of Maryland. In terms of the impact he had upon the politics and public policies of his state, Huey P. Long of Louisiana would also deserve mention, however questionable his political ethics may have been. A careful and unbiased examination of the political history of each state over this period would reveal many others entitled to be rated as outstanding or strong governors.

A heartening conclusion that follows from an examination of the performance of all the occupants of the presidency is that the challenge of the office has seemed to bring forth their best efforts, within the limits imposed by their personal political philosophies and abilities. Men of ordinary talents have been, at least, dignified by it; men of extraordinary talent have been raised to greatness by its challenge. No President has been wanting in patriotism, personal integrity, or in devotion to the best interests of the nation as he saw them. If some of them have aggrandized their office, it has not been through mere lust for power and a place in the sun, but for the achievement of objectives proper for them to seek. In a sense they have been compelled, willy-nilly, by the exigencies of government in modern society to assume a more active, positive role. As one competent observer has pointed out:

> The American Presidency is an endlessly fascinating and instructive institution. One of the many things to be learned from it is that the Actonian doctrine of power as an inevitably corrupting force, and a force that corrupts in direct ratio to its magnitude, is something less than a universal law. Generally speaking, in our society, the insolence of office is most frequently encountered among those of severely limited authority. The worst tyrants are to be found in sheriffs' offices, the worst moral rot in city councils and state legislatures. Our presidents, far from having been corrupted by the power given them as a rule have been elevated by it. We have never had a truly corrupt president—a president, that is, who either used the office for purely personal gain or sought to broaden his powers merely for the satisfaction of their exercise. On the contrary, the lesson of experience is that men increase in stature in the White House.[27]

[27] Richard Rovere, *The Eisenhower Years* (New York: Farrar, Straus & Cudahy, 1956), pp. 369–370.

Presidents have displayed differences in virtues and talent; but the range has been from the more able to the less able, not from the paragon to the scoundrel. Even the most successful have had human faults which have at times betrayed them in their conduct of the public business; and the least successful have had their virtues. They form collectively a company of notables; and in joining such a company no newly chosen President can fail to be impressed and stimulated to his highest endeavors by being privileged to be numbered with it. As the office of state governor continues to grow in power and prestige, undoubtedly it will come to exert in increasing measure the same kind of influence on those chosen to occupy it.

8

CHIEF OF STATE

The President, as well as every state governor, plays a role in the governmental scheme that can best be described by the term "Chief of State" or "Head of Government." Neither of these terms is used in the national or state constitutions in defining the position; and in a sense, to ascribe to the chief figure in one of the three coordinate departments of government the role of "head" of the whole governmental organization is a contradiction in terms. Yet the very nature of government itself seems to call for the identification of one figure in it as the ultimate symbol of authority and head of the political system.

This function can be assigned to an office which may or may not carry with it great political power. In some constitutional monarchies, of which Great Britain is the prototype, the wearer of the crown is the Chief of State in the full sense of the term; yet the British monarch's position has become one of little real political power. He "reigns but does not rule." He is the symbol of authority rather than the actual possessor of it. His ministers, his Parliament, and his judges exercise the powers of government in his name. In some modern republics with cabinet-type executives, as in France during the Fourth Republic or in the Western German Republic, the presidential office likewise finds its chief significance in its representational and symbolic functions. Under the terms of the 1958 "De Gaulle" Constitution, however, the vesting of political powers of potentially great magnitude in the French presidency has given this office more of the character of the chief executive under the American presidential system. Indeed, in an emergency the French President can invoke constitutional powers reaching even further than those of the American President. He can assume on his own initiative the position of a constitutional dictator.[1]

---

[1] Cf. Stanley H. Hoffman, "The French Constitution of 1958: The Final Text and Its Prospects," *American Political Science Review,* Vol. LIII (June, 1959), p. 332; and Martin Hoffman, "The French Experience of Exceptional Powers: 1961," *Journal of Politics,* Vol. 25 (February, 1963), pp. 139–168. Article 16 of the 1958 constitution reads:

Attachment of the function of acting as Chief of State to an office in which even in normal times very substantial powers over the formulation of legislation, execution of the laws, command of the military forces, and supervision of the conduct of external relations are also vested gives to the office of chief executive in the American system its distinctive character. No other aspect of the office more clearly demonstrates its lineal descent from the British kingship of the seventeenth and eighteenth centuries through the connecting links of the colonial and early state governorships. The American presidency embodies certain features of the modern British kingship, joined with other features of the prime ministership; but the President is both something more and something less than either the King or the Prime Minister. In his role as the acknowledged Chief of State he is the counterpart of the King, minus, of course, the trappings of monarchy and the hereditary feature; but the President is vested with direct and substantial powers over policy-making and administration which in the British system are exercised in the name of the King by his ministers with the assent of Parliament.

By reason of being the chief executive officer and legislative leader, the President is more strongly placed than the British Prime Minister in some respects. The President is secure in his post for a fixed period of time regardless of the political complexion of the legislative branch; and his powers, in part at least, have a foundation beyond the reach of the legislative branch. On the other hand the President lacks some of the means available to a Prime Minister for exerting direct leadership over the legislative body. He is not a member of it, as the Prime Minister is; and the President does not enjoy the disciplinary powers over his fellow party members in the legislative branch that a Prime Minister has over his parliamentary party group. An American Congress or state legislative body cannot force the resignation of an American chief executive by a vote of lack of confidence or by failure to support a key element of executive policy, as can the House of Commons with a Prime Minister. On the other hand an American chief executive cannot employ the threat of dissolution as a means of inducing support of his policies; and he may on occasion be confronted by a legislative body of which one or both houses are under the control of an opposition party.

When the institutions of the Republic, the independence of the nation, the integrity of its territory, or the fulfillment of its international commitments are threatened in a grave and immediate manner and when the regular functioning of the constitutional government is interrupted, the President of the Republic shall take the measures commanded by these circumstances, after consultation with the Premier, the Presidents of the Assemblies, and the Constitutional Council.

FOUNDATIONS OF THE CHIEF OF STATE ROLE

TITLE OF ADDRESS

A President or state governor, as befits the republican principles of government to which the American people are attached, is not surrounded with the pomp, ceremony, and deference to his person that are accorded a royal head of state. He bears no official title of address other than that of the office he occupies. In a few of the older states the use of "His Excellency" as a title of address for the governor, a carry-over from colonial practice, has survived; but the practice has not been adopted generally. This title of address for the President was proposed in the draft constitution as it came from the hands of the Committee of Detail in the Convention of 1787; but it was excised during the course of the Convention's deliberations. Antimonarchists charged that the change was acceded to by the strong-executive advocates only in the hope that a more pretentious title would be provided by law later.

At the outset of Washington's administration Vice President Adams energetically sought to induce the Congress to adopt a special title of address for the President. "His Highness the President of the United States and Protector of the Rights of the Same" was the title he favored. The idea was considered by a joint committee of the two houses in connection with several other matters of procedure and protocol prior to Washington's inauguration; but in the end nothing was done about it.[2] The President's title of address is, simply, "Mr. President," and nothing more. Nevertheless, a pre-eminence is extended to him in his capacity as Chief of State that sets him out from among his fellow citizens. The distinction accorded him, as well as the protocol which recognizes it, is almost entirely the product of usage and circumstance.

THE INAUGURAL CEREMONY AND ITS SIGNIFICANCE

Following precedents set in Washington's administration, the beginning of a President's term of office is signalized by an inaugural ceremony that is not without considerable political significance. In compliance with the Constitution's directive that a President must,

[2] Vice President Adams wished titles to be provided by legislative act for both the President and the Vice President. The House members of the joint committee indicated that they preferred no titles other than the designations of office set forth in the Constitution. Unwilling to let the matter drop, Adams induced the Senate to set up a committee of its own to consider the matter. It proposed the title of address for the President which Adams favored, but after some rather bitter controversy the

as his first act upon assuming office, take the oath of fidelity therein set forth,[3] he performs this duty in a public ceremony. The oath is customarily administered by the Chief Justice of the Supreme Court. The oath-taking is made the occasion for delivery of an inaugural address in which he outlines his conception of the commanding issues of the day and the approach he expects to follow in trying to resolve them. Afterward there is a public reception where he meets as large a number of the assembled officialdom and citizenry as time and space permit.

An inauguration is a ceremony suggestive of the coronation of a king—the oath-taking in the presence of the notables, the declaration of faith, the hailing by the multitudes, and the receiving of pledges of loyalty and support from the lords of the realm. More than that, it symbolizes also acceptance of the principle of peaceful transfer of political power in accordance with constitutional process—the corner-stone upon which republican government rests. By custom the retiring chief executive accompanies the President-elect to the inaugural ceremony and remains in the background during its progress. He signifies by his presence his acquiescence in the quiet transfer of power from himself to his successor.

On a number of occasions these amenities signifying willing acquiescence in the transfer of power have not been observed to the letter. In 1801 the retiring President, John Adams, smarting under the political vituperation that had been hurled at him in the heat of the preceding campaign, hastily vacated the executive mansion at an early hour and failed to appear at Jefferson's inauguration. In 1829 his son, John Quincy Adams, likewise failed to remain to participate in Jackson's inaugural, a coolness having developed between the two because of Jackson's failure to respond to Adams' earlier polite overtures relative to the change of occupancy of the executive mansion. In 1869 President-elect Grant refused to ride to the inaugural ceremonies with outgoing President Andrew Johnson. The two were not on speaking terms because of bitterness arising out of the attempt by Johnson to remove Edwin Stanton as his Secretary

---

issue was dropped after the House refused to change its attitude. During the controversy some anti-Federalist members of the Senate suggested privately in derision as a suitable title for the Vice President, "His Superfluous Excellency" or "His Rotund Highness." For an account of the matter see James Hart, *The American Presidency in Action, 1789,* (New York: The Macmillan Company, 1948), pp. 34–40.

[3] Art. II, Sec. 1, par. 7: "Before he enter on the execution of his office, he shall take the following oath or affirmation:—'I do solemnly swear (or affirm) that I will faithfully execute the office of President of the United States, and that I will to the best of my ability, preserve, protect and defend the Constitution of the United States.' "

of War and replace him with General Grant as a means of providing a court test of the constitutionality of the Tenure of Office Act. Johnson had charged that Grant double-crossed him in the affair.[4]

The most recent of these coolnesses was in 1953. President-elect Eisenhower refused to leave his car and enter the White House to be greeted by President Truman at the beginning of the inaugural parade; but the two rode together in the procession to the Capitol. According to President Truman, General Eisenhower had taken umbrage at the President's order that the General's son, John, who was serving as an officer with the American forces in Korea, should be given leave so that he might attend his father's inauguration. During the preceding campaign General Eisenhower had pledged that his first act, if he was successful in winning election, would be to go to Korea to survey conditions there with a view to putting a stop to a fruitless war and bringing American troops home. Immediately after the election, President Truman had offered him the use of the President's official plane for this purpose "if he still wished to go." The offer was refused. This marked the beginning of the coolness between the two which persisted throughout President Eisenhower's administration.[5]

Inaugural ceremonies similar to those at the national level are usually observed in the states. A Vice President succeeding to the presidency by reason of the death of the incumbent, following the precedent set by John Tyler, takes the oath of office at the earliest feasible time; but there is no formal inaugural ceremony in such cases, nor has the Tyler precedent of the presentation of an inaugural address to the people via Congress always been followed. The fact that Tyler saw fit to take the oath of office as President on assumption of the duties of the office, it might be observed, has helped to provide a basis for the contention that the Vice President cannot "act" as President without "becoming" the President. It is argued that by taking the oath the Vice President "becomes" the President. This in turn has proved to be a stumbling block to efforts so far to carry out the consti-

---

[4] Cf. Joseph Bishop, *Presidential Nominations and Elections* (New York: Charles Scribner's Sons, 1916), pp. 195–199.

[5] Cf. Harry S Truman, "The Day Ike Snubbed Me," *Look* (May 24, 1960), pp. 25–33; and his *Mr. Citizen* (New York: Popular Library, 1961), Chap. 1, for his version of the matter. According to President Eisenhower's account: "The only comment of any consequence that I can recall during the short ride to the Capitol was asking the President the identity of the person who had ordered my son back from the combat area of Korea to be present at the inauguration. The President replied, 'I did,' and I thanked him sincerely for his thoughtfulness." Dwight D. Eisenhower, *Mandate for Change, 1953–1956* (Garden City, N. Y.: Doubleday & Company, 1963), p. 101.

tutional arrangements for temporary succession of a Vice President when the President is disabled.

Oath-takings by Vice Presidents on the occasion of sudden accession to office by reason of the death of the incumbent President have supplied some of the dramatic highlights of the history of the office. In 1923 when Vice President Coolidge learned of the death of President Harding, he was vacationing at the Vermont farmhouse of his father. The oath of office was administered by his father, a justice of the peace, in a kerosene-lighted room at 2:43 in the morning. However, ever cautious on the point of the legal proprieties, Coolidge secretly took the oath again upon his return to Washington, this time from a justice of the Supreme Court of the District of Columbia.[6] In 1963, Lyndon Johnson took the presidential oath in the presidential plane at Dallas, Texas, moments before it took off for Washington bearing the body of the assassinated President Kennedy. The oath was administered by United States District Judge Sarah Hughes, with the late President's widow standing courageously by the new President's side.

SYMBOLIC AND REPRESENTATIONAL ASPECTS

Save for a passage in the Constitution stating that the President shall "receive ambassadors and other public ministers" of foreign countries—a function which Hamilton in one of *The Federalist* essays characterized as "more a matter of dignity than authority" and mistakenly predicted would have nothing more than a ceremonial significance[7]—there is little in it that would indicate directly that the President should be regarded as the "head" of government. During his incumbency, Washington set a pattern of conduct and established a tone of dignity that made the Chief of State function one of the essential elements of the office and added much weight to its political prestige and influence. Under him the national habit of looking upon the President as embodying the dignity and authority of the government over which he presides took root. State governors of the Revolutionary period, notwithstanding the fact that their positions were not posts of great power, had been popularly regarded as the official heads of their respective governments, personifying the organized authority of their states. This was one of the attributes of the colonial

---

[6] Edward S. Corwin, *The President: Office and Powers,* 4th ed. (New York: New York University Press, 1957), pp. 347–348.

[7] *The Federalist,* No. 69. The phrase came later to be regarded as a significant constitutional basis for the President's exercise of power to extend formal recognition to foreign governments and to serve as this country's official spokesman in international communications. See Chap. 15.

governorship which had been passed on to the state governors without question. It thus came easily to a people who held their great war hero in highest esteem to accept him in the newly created position of President as the Chief of State. To them he personified the new political system and the high hopes they had that it would prove to be a success.

Although superficially the Chief of State role might appear to be of little political significance, it is an attribute of his office that lends material strength to a President's or a governor's constitutional powers. It contributes immeasurably to his political influence. As the Chief of State he can command respectful attention. This in turn affords him the opportunity to exert influence upon the popular mind and attitudes, and through them, to bring the force of public opinion to bear in support of his policies. When the President addresses the Congress on the state of the Union and recommends measures for its consideration, or when he takes into his own hands negotiations with a foreign power, the knowledge that he speaks not only in his capacity as a constitutional partner of Congress in legislation or as his own minister of foreign affairs but also as the Chief of State adds force to his words. Particularly in times of crisis the chief executive speaks for the whole political community when he acts as Chief of State. He becomes a symbol of unity, of the people's will to surmount the difficulties that threaten them.

From the time of his election until he leaves office, a chief executive can never divest himself of his character as Chief of State, even for a moment. It colors his every action, public or private. It requires that he weigh carefully every public statement he makes. As President Truman put it, "Every word he utters weighs a ton." President Coolidge's taciturnity in his conversations with visitors, in his press interviews, and even with persons whom he met in lighter social contacts caused the name of "Silent Cal" to be bestowed upon him by his more or less friendly critics; but we have his own testimony that this was owing in part, at least, to his keen appreciation of the dangers inherent in undue loquacity for one in his position. "The words of the President have enormous weight, and ought not to be used indiscriminately" summarized the rule by which he felt he should be guided.[8] A chief executive must also be mindful of the danger of over-

[8] Calvin Coolidge, *Autobiography* (New York: Cosmopolitan Book Corporation, 1929) p. 184. During the 1932 presidential campaign, Coolidge, in explaining his refusal to take a stand on an issue which had developed, defended his refusal in these terms: "Theodore Roosevelt was always getting himself in hot water by talking before he had to commit himself upon issues not well-defined. . . . It seems to me public administrators would get along better if they would restrain the impulse to butt in or to be dragged into trouble. They should remain silent until an issue is reduced to its lowest terms, until it boils down into something like a moral issue." William Allen White, *A Puritan in Babylon* (New York: The Macmillan Company,

exposure through too many public statements and appearances. As Shakespeare expressed it through one of his characters, too much speaking will cause him to become "as the cuckoo is in June, heard, not regarded."[9]

The restraints which bear upon a President or a governor by reason of his Chief of State function extend beyond him to his family and immediate associates. Like royalty, he and his family lose their private status and become in a sense hostages to the office he fills. They are continually in the public view whether they want to be or not.[10] Their doings are daily grist for the newspapers, radio, and television newscasters. They live, as it were, in a glass house. Whether it be an evening's diversion at the theater, a shopping tour, an afternoon on the golf links or the beach, or a dinner with guests, whatever the President or his family does is a matter of public interest. His wife is the "First Lady" of the land and his family the nation's "First Family." They must live up to the standards of the station he occupies or bring upon him reproaches from a possessive public.

Viewed from another angle, the public attention given the chief executive affords him an opportunity to have a considerable influence upon the manners, tastes, and attitudes of the people. He and his family become pacesetters and arbiters of fashion in many matters beyond the realm of political affairs. They help to shape the national culture in countless ways.

A prime example of this was Theodore Roosevelt. Advocate of the "strenuous life," an amateur naturalist, a historian of some parts, ex-soldier and amateur military strategist, an ex-Wild West cattle rancher and cowboy, an ex-police commissioner, an explorer, a lover of sports, he filled his spare time in pursuit of a dozen varied interests with an avidity that set a standard for others to imitate. A preacher of the virtues of family living, and of the "full baby carriage," during his occupancy of the White House, he and his six very active offspring gave it the character of a typical American home, with a family-oriented manner of life. The ever popular children's "teddybear" doll was named in his honor. His daughter Alice gave the world of ladies' fashion a new term in color—"Alice blue." Concerned about the excessive roughness and near-mayhem displayed in the increasingly popular sport of football, Roosevelt served notice on the leading figures in the collegiate sports world that unless something was done about this, the game would have to be abolished. The result was an

1938), p. 433, quoted in James E. Pollard, *The Presidents and the Press* (New York: The Macmillan Company, 1947), p. 733.

[9] *King Henry IV* (First Part), Act III.

[10] Cf. Eric F. Goldman, "Can Public Men Have Private Lives?" *The New York Times Magazine,* June 14, 1963, p. 13.

opening up of the game by introduction of the forward pass, thus making him indirectly one of the prime contributors to the development of this crowd-pleasing American sport. But even a Theodore Roosevelt could attempt too much in the way of trying to dictate American tastes and preferences, as evidenced by the failure of his lifelong efforts to make simplified spelling acceptable.

Other Presidents or "First Ladies" have left their imprint on American culture and habits in one way or another. Mrs. Rutherford B. Hayes, an ardent prohibitionist, forbade the use of spirituous liquors at all White House functions. She helped in this way to give publicity and support to the prohibition movement which in time culminated in adoption of the Eighteenth Amendment. Her attitude also won from her critics the sobriquet of "Lemonade Lucy" and gave rise to one of the widely circulated jokes of the time concerning a guest who reportedly was heard to say after attending a White House affair, "It was a gay party; buttermilk flowed like wine." Mrs. Franklin D. Roosevelt was a dynamo of energy in the White House, lending her prestige and active support to countless causes for human betterment. Setting a new pattern for participation by women in public affairs, she became a political force in her own right during and after her husband's presidency. President and Mrs. Kennedy, with their urbanity, culture, and appreciation for the arts gave distinctive tone and "style" to White House living during their tenure.

During the course of a term a chief executive in his capacity as Head of the Government has numerous opportunities to participate in various kinds of ceremonial and representational undertakings having political implications. In recent decades goodwill visits to foreign states have become an important device for cultivating friendly relations. Receiving official visitors and distinguished figures from abroad, entertaining formally the officials representing the other branches of the national government, appearing before gatherings of state and local officials such as the Governors' Conference or the Conference of Mayors, participating in dedicatory ceremonies for new public works, and "inspecting" military establishments are examples of official activities that have a semipolitical aspect.

Beyond such activities as these lie others having as their purpose the stimulation of loyalty, patriotism, and religious faith. Supporting by public endorsement such benevolent undertakings as Red Cross or Community Fund drives, lighting the "Nation's Christmas Tree" on the White House lawn, participating in the opening day festivities at the beginning of the professional baseball season, and extending greetings to national meetings of war veterans are illustrative of modes by which a President expresses approval of activities deemed commendable. Proclamation of special "days" or "weeks" in furtherance of generally approved objectives is another way in which the chief executive may use his influence as Head of Government. Establishment of the nationally observed Thanksgiving Day, first proclaimed by Washington and eventually developed into an annual event since Lincoln's administration, shows how the nation's chief executive can affect custom in this manner.

Even after he has ceased to occupy the presidency, a certain aura of pre-eminence continues to attach to a former President as one who has filled the nation's highest office. The public continues to follow his career and give him respectful attention. His status confers on him certain privileges and public responsibilities, even in retirement, a fact which Congress has seen fit to recognize by granting him a lifetime annuity of $25,000, together with a generous allowance for maintaining an office staff and free use of the mails.[11]

His status as a retired Chief of State, however, also imposes on him obligations and restraints. Though the standards governing the conduct of an ex-President are vague, he is free to pursue only those activities that will be in keeping with the dignity of the role he once filled. He must avoid giving an impression of trying to "cash in on" the enormous prestige he still has. Standards have changed since the days when former President Benjamin Harrison saw nothing out of order in affiliating himself with a law firm and pursuing actively the interests of clients before the courts, some manned by judges whom he had appointed. He commanded such handsome fees for his services that his income was said to be one of the highest in the country.[12] Lecturing on public affairs, writing, and participating in political activities appropriate to his status as elder statesman are the outlets regarded as most suitable for one who has once been hailed as Chief of State.

A former occupant of the governorship may with greater freedom than an ex-President resume an ordinary vocation or seek a federal office. If not excluded by age, ineligibility, or physical infirmity, he may even be a serious contender for the office of governor again. Unless he continues his career in public life and achieves even higher office, however, the unofficial title of address as "Governor" is likely to be his for the rest of his life as evidence that his name and person continue to be associated in the public mind with the office he once occupied.

[11] See Chap. 5, p. 198.
[12] Asa E. Martin, *After the White House* (University Park, Pa.: Penn Valley Publishers, 1951), p. 351.

PROBLEMS INHERENT IN THE CHIEF OF STATE ROLE

Fulfilling the obligations of a Chief of State presents problems
for a chief executive. Not the least is the sheer physical burden imposed by his duties. Countless invitations pour in to give addresses,
attend social events, and otherwise lend the prestige of his office to
the support of one kind of undertaking or another. Even though by
temperament and inclination he may find these duties not unpleasant
and may even relish the acclaim that accompanies them, he cannot
respond to all such requests; most of them, in fact, must be refused.
Fortunately, a refusal on the ground of pressure of other business
is accepted in good faith by most initiators of such invitations; and
he can gracefully delegate to members of his entourage some of the
unavoidable chores of this kind. A notable development in recent
years has been the increased use of the Vice President as the President's
stand-in on various occasions. Presidents Truman, Eisenhower, and
Kennedy employed their Vice Presidents even in the important matter
of making good-will visits to other countries. Some of the burden of
acting as an offcial greeter or representative can also be shifted to department heads and other members of the official staff.

A matter of some political delicacy inherent in the discharge of
this function is one of judgment in the selection of those causes and
occasions that are deemed worthy to receive the Chief of State's notice
and inferential approval. He must always be mindful of the implications that will be drawn from his actions as well as his words. Cour-
tesies must be extended with an even hand toward visiting official
dignitaries, lest unintended offense be given. In his appearances to
make speeches, too close an identification with one interest group,
or with a restricted category of them, to the exclusion of opposing
interests will quickly undermine the popular impression of him as
impartially dispensing the patronage and official favor of his presence
and good will. A politically astute President understands that he
must achieve some semblance of balance in making appearances before national meetings representing the great interest groups in the
fields of business, banking, communications, the professions, farming,
and organized labor.

A President or governor must also understand that implications
will be drawn from the character of the people to whom the hospitality
of the executive mansion is extended. Even a social invitation can
be used as a political gesture, as it was undoubtedly meant to be
when Theodore Roosevelt set tongues wagging by inviting the famous
Negro educator, Booker T. Washington, to breakfast at the White

House. Coming in an era when the color line was far more sharply drawn than it is now, the significance of the event was not overlooked by the public. In his *Autobiography* Calvin Coolidge summarized his appreciation of the importance of this aspect of the presidential role in these terms:

> Everything that the President does potentially at least is of such great importance that he must be constantly on guard. This applies not only to himself, but to everybody about him. Not only in all his official actions, but in all his social intercourse, and even in his recreation and repose, he is constantly watched by a multitude of eyes to determine if there is anything unusual, extraordinary, or irregular, which can be set down in praise or in blame. Oftentimes trifling incidents, some insignificant action, or unfortunate phrase in an address, an injudicious letter, a lack of patience towards some one who presents an impossible proposition, too much attention to one person, or too little courtesy towards another have been magnified into the sensation of the hour. While such events finally sink into their proper place if they occur frequently they create an atmosphere of distraction that might seriously interfere with the conduct of public business which is really important.[13]

Still another problem is posed by the showering of gifts and honors upon the Head of Government as a gesture of esteem, gratitude, or affection. If such gifts are proffered by another government they cannot be accepted as personal gifts by the President unless Congress grants its approval, in view of the constitutional restrictions applicable in such matters.[14] He may, however, accept them on behalf of this government, in which case they become public property to be disposed of as the President or Congress sees fit. Sometimes the dilemma is presented of refusing the gift and risking offense, or accepting it and risking embarrassment from another direction, as when Lincoln was offered as a gift a breeding stock of elephants from the King of Siam in token of that monarch's esteem for a fellow Chief of State. Lincoln politely demurred on the matter of accepting the elephants and dumped the "puzzlement" of what to do with other gifts from the King in the lap of Congress.[15]

Even more troublesome is the problem posed by those who wish to show their good will and incidentally reap some favorable publicity, if nothing more, by making the Head of Government the object of their generosity. The drawing of a proper line between the favors, gratuities, and hospitality that a President or governor can accept

[13] *Op. cit.,* p. 184.

[14] Article I, Sec. 9, of the Constitution states: "No title of nobility shall be granted by the United States; and no person holding any office of profit or trust under them, shall, without the consent of Congress, accept of any present, emolument, office, or title, of any kind whatever, from any king, prince, or foreign State."

[15] Richardson, *Messages and Papers of the Presidents,* Vol. VI, p. 66.

with propriety and those he should refuse because of the unfavorable implications that might be drawn from his accepting them is not always easy. Few Presidents or governors have escaped criticism, justified or otherwise, on the score of the company they have kept and the gifts, hospitality, and other favors they have accepted.

In some instances an inability to assess properly the motivations of others and to appreciate the public's reactions in such matters can lead a personally honest chief executive into indiscreet acceptance of favors so as to damage seriously the reputation of his administration. This was undoubtedly the case with President Grant,[16] even though it could be said in his defense that he was merely following the generally accepted standards of public morality of his time. Critics of President Truman made much of the disclosure of gifts of deep freezes and mink coats to members of his official staff. The stocking and equipping of President Eisenhower's Gettysburg farm by grateful admirers provided occasion for unfavorable gossip from opposite quarters. One of the unwritten qualifications for the chief executive would seem to be a kind of cynicism and worldly-mindedness that leads him to adopt a somewhat suspicious view of the motives of "exhibitionists" who like to "preen themselves in public," as President Hoover expressed it,[17] by giving the impression they are closely placed and privy to his councils. He is doubly wise to be wary of people who seek to put him in their debt by making him the object of their generosity in a material sense.

[16] "Grant in the Presidency supplied a good example of how men suffer from the kind of company they keep. Personally the President was democratic but wealth and creature comforts dazzled him and his family. In all, he accepted three homes as the gifts of grateful citizens. . . . He had eighteen horses, all but two of which were said to be gifts. He consorted continually with the rich. After his retirement, Grant accepted without question the fruits of a campaign begun in 1880 by the *New York Times* to raise a fund of $250,000 to insure for him a life income of $15,000 a year. The same year another group of friends raised $100,000 which was finally used to buy for him a house in New York City." (Pollard, *op. cit.*, pp. 437–438.)

[17] Gridiron Club speech, December 12, 1931. *State Papers and Other Public Writings of Herbert Hoover*, William S. Myers, ed. (Garden City, N. Y.: Doubleday & Company, 2 vols., 1934), Vol. II, p. 87.

9

PARTY CHIEF

No aspect of the modern chief executive's position more clearly reflects the change from the eighteenth-century conception of his office than his present-day role as the leader of his political party. Of all the various chiefships ascribed to him, this is, perhaps, the most elusive of exact delineation. While it has its foundation in the manner by which he is elected and is supported by the totality of the constitutional and statutory provisions defining his official powers, this is a role which rests essentially upon usage and practice. It is not necessarily inseparably associated with his office, but attaches only loosely and conditionally to it. Whether he makes it a significant part of his official functions depends in part upon his personal qualities, capacities, inclinations, background, and experience, and in part upon the political milieu in which he must operate. His making it an important attribute of his office may depend upon circumstances not always within his control.

Association of the party leadership function with the chief executive, who as has just been pointed out also is expected to serve as the unpartisan Chief of State—the representative and spokesman for *all* the people—presents one of the great anomalies of the American presidential system. The chief executive is asked to fill two essentially incompatible roles. He must function as chief and spokesman for the "government party" as opposed to the "government opposition" in much the same way a Prime Minister does in Great Britain. At the same time he is expected to serve as the symbol of political unity and public authority, standing above party, as the British monarch does.

In this combination of roles is to be seen a fundamental contradiction in the presidential scheme of governmental organization. A President or governor must constantly concern himself with maintaining a proper balance between, or a proper blend of, the two functions of his office. In this he is not always successful to his own satisfaction. As President Taft once observed:

> I am afraid I am a constant disappointment to my party. The fact of the matter is, the longer I am President the less of a party man I become.

> . . . it seems to me to be impossible to be a strict party man and
> serve the whole country impartially.[1]

President Eisenhower likewise found it difficult to descend from the
lofty heights of the nonpartisan Chief of State role into the hurly-
burly of the partisan struggle. Looking back over his experience as
President he regretted that he had not from the beginning taken a
more active hand in Republican party leadership in order to bring
more younger people into the party organization and give it a new
image.[2]

The conflict of interest inherent in thrusting both roles upon the
chief executive is one that will not yield to any solution short of a
basic change in the constitutional plan upon which the national and
state governmental systems rest. Such a change, involving a break with
long-standing tradition and practice, is highly unlikely to be sanctioned
by American public opinion in the foreseeable future. And so it is
that American chief executives must face their dilemma and try as
best they can to find a workable formula for harmonizing the two
inconsistent roles that are entrusted to them.

Even before attaining the office itself a party's candidate for
President or governor acquires presumptively the status of party
leader by being put forward as his party's nominee for the highest
office. Election confirms his title to the position of party leader and
spokesman. His de facto status as party leader may even survive for
a time his leaving the office, or his unsuccessful effort to attain it. The
post of "titular leader" of his party falls upon the defeated candidate,
pending arrival on the scene of the next duly chosen candidate; but
unfortunately it is ordinarily a position of little power or significance.
The suggestion has been advanced that a defeated major party's
candidate for the presidency be given a seat in the Senate for the
next four years, where he can continue to speak and act in the public
limelight as the spokesman for his party. Legislative bodies to date
have shown little interest in advancing such a scheme.[3]

---

[1] Arthur Bernon Tourtellot, *The Presidents on the Presidency* (Garden City,
N. Y.: Doubleday & Company, 1964), p. 387, quoting Archie Butt, *Taft and Roosevelt* (Garden City, N.Y.: Doubleday & Company, 2 vols., 1930), Vol. II, p. 645.

[2] CBS–TV interview, as reported in *The New York Times*, October 13, 1961, pp.
1, 71; and October 15, 1961, pp. 1, 56.

[3] Cf. Clinton Rossiter, "Yet's Not Lose the Losing Candidate," *The New York
Times Magazine*, November 6, 1960, p. 24. Professor Rossiter endorsed a plan of giving each losing candidate for the presidency who received at least 25 percent of the
popular vote a seat as a senator-at-large for the next four years. This idea was embraced in a constitutional amendment introduced during the 86th Congress by
Representative Udall of Arizona. It should be noted that a seat in either house of
Congress could be given a nonmember, but without voting privileges, without resorting to constitutional change. For a discussion of the "titular" leadership role of a
defeated party candidate for the presidency, see Paul David, Ralph Goldman, and
Richard Bain, *The Politics of National Party Conventions* (Washington: Brookings
Institution, 1960), pp. 75 ff.

A candidate who has been successful in his campaign may not choose to perform in full measure the functions normally associated with the position of Chief of Party. He may prefer to delegate or leave by default to others most of the responsibilities in the sphere of party affairs. In this event a President or governor quickly finds that there are others within the party hierarchy, especially among those in the legislative branch, who will move in to fill the vacuum. Indeed, there will often be some party figures entrenched in positions of power in the legislative branch or in the local organizations who acknowledge his position of primacy grudgingly or not at all; their attitude toward him may range from mere tolerance to overt hostility. Nevertheless, the position of the chief executive is so important to the operation of the party mechanisms that his party associates can refuse to acknowledge him as chief and spokesman only at some peril to their own political fortunes and their party's welfare. A party's interest, like that of an army's, does not thrive when there are too many generals and not enough followers.

EVOLUTION OF THE PRESIDENT'S PARTY LEADERSHIP ROLE

Association of the party leadership function with the presidency, and in a less generally inclusive sense with the governorship, has been a more or less inevitable consequence of the injection of partisan considerations into the process of choosing these officers. As has already been noted, partisan competition in the choice of the President had become clearly evident by the time of the election of Jefferson in 1800. The two parties that appeared on the national scene during the 1790s—the Jeffersonian Republicans and the Federalists—extended the conflict into state electoral contests as well.

The quiet but nonetheless revolutionary transformation of the presidential electoral system—so carefully designed by the Framers to eliminate the "spirit of faction" in choosing the President—into an instrument of partisan choice was accomplished in the face of earnest warnings by Washington. In his Farewell Address, delivered during the course of the 1796 presidential campaign when there was already beginning to be apparent a polarization of elements into Federalist and anti-Federalist ("Republican") camps, Washington deplored the rising spirit of partisanship. Warning his countrymen against its "baneful effects," he enumerated the mischiefs that would flow from the injection of the spirit of party into the conduct of government:

> It serves always to distract the public councils and enfeeble the public administration. It agitates the community with ill-founded jealousies and false alarms; kindles the animosity of one part against another;

foments occasionally riot and corruption, which finds a facilitated
access to the government itself through the channels of party passion.
Thus the policy and the will of one country are subjected to the policy
and will of another.[4]

Noting that there was an opinion that parties in a free government
were a "useful check upon the administration of government" and
that they served "to keep alive the spirit of liberty," he conceded that
this might be true within limits, particularly in monarchical systems;
but in a popular type of government, the partisan spirit should not
be encouraged lest its flames "instead of warming . . . should con-
sume."

John Adams, victor over Jefferson with only one electoral vote
to spare in the closely contested election of 1796, echoed the sentiments
of Washington. In his inaugural address he pointed to the danger to
our liberties "if anything partial or extraneous should infect the purity
of our free, fair, virtuous, and independent elections," particularly
when an election might be determined by a majority of a single vote
"and that can be procured through artifice or corruption . . . [by]
. . . a party for its own ends."[5] His attempt to carry on in the office
of President along the lofty, unpartisan line suggested by these sentiments proved notably unsuccessful. A strong-minded, rather combative individual himself, he drove the opponents of his policies into
an opposing coalition. Party alignments in Congress became more
clearly drawn than ever. The unwillingness of Adams to assume frankly
the status of party leader, he discovered to his dismay, did not prevent
injection of partisan considerations into the presidential election of
1800. Jefferson's triumph after an extremely bitter campaign raised
fears in the minds of many Federalists that the dire predictions of
Washington were on their way to fulfillment. Taking cognizance of
these fears, Jefferson on assuming office was careful to assure his erstwhile opponents that the spirit of partisanship would be kept within
proper bounds. While maintaining that differences of opinion must be
expected and tolerated in a popular system of government, he went on
to say:

> But every difference of opinion is not a difference of principle.
> We have called by different names brethren of the same principle. We
> are all Republicans, we are all Federalists.[6]

Spokesman of a party group that entertained views on a number
of matters of public policy at variance with those of the administration
leaving office and pledged to carry those views into effect, Jefferson
inevitably gave a new dimension to the presidency. He did so by exer-

4 Richardson, *Messages and Papers of the Presidents,* Vol. I, pp. 218–219.
5 *Ibid.,* p. 230.
6 *Ibid.,* p. 322.

cising consciously and deliberately, if not openly, the functions of party leader. As Vice President during Adams' administration Jefferson had felt some constraint in assuming outwardly the role of leader of the party in opposition to the administration. Nevertheless he had been the actual source and instigator of much of the critical comment on the policies of the Adams administration. Working through his cohorts, particularly Madison, who served as a kind of chief of staff for the Republican element in Congress, he had seen to it that his point of view found public expression. He had encouraged the founding of newspapers dedicated to the party's viewpoint, and inspired the publication of critical letters and pamphlets and seemingly spontaneous resolutions from state legislatures where his followers were in control.

Dominating by the force of his intellect the faction on whose shoulders he had ridden into power, Jefferson as President proceeded by adroit influence over his followers in Congress to implement his policy programs. Outwardly deferential to Congress—he deliberately discontinued the practice of delivering the annual messages to it in person on the ostensible ground that it smacked of monarchical practice—he worked closely with his party colleagues in that body to shape the course of its action. During his incumbency the foundations for party control of the House machinery were laid through the establishment of standing committees, the institution of the party caucus, and informally, the party post of Floor Leader. Utilizing the party caucus and committee chairmen as points of contact, Jefferson helped to mould the legislative product, even to the point of assisting in preparing the original drafts of bills. So effective was he in exercising his influence that never once during his eight years in office did he feel the necessity of using his veto power.

Jefferson's activities as party leader extended even beyond the legislative halls. By a judicious use of the removal power he cleared the way for filling what he regarded as a fair proportion of the administrative offices with faithful party henchmen. Likely party prospects were encouraged through letters from him to aspire for seats in Congress when vacancies appeared. When John Randolph, Chairman of the Ways and Means Committee, opposed an appropriation of $2,000,000 desired by Jefferson for his projected purchase of Florida from Spain, the President encouraged another Republican to run for Randolph's seat in the next congressional election.[7] The maneuver, which, incidentally, did not prove successful, was the first of similar attempted "purges" of disloyal party followers to be initiated by later Presidents.

[7] W. F. Binkley, *The Man in the White House* (Baltimore: The Johns Hopkins Press, 1958), p. 17.

Jefferson had succeeded in giving the Presidency a new look, but his immediate successors, Madison and Monroe, while willing and eager enough to emulate his example, never rose to a comparable position of dominance in party affairs. Politically indebted to the members of the party caucus in Congress for nomination as their party's candidates, they were not in a strong position to direct the course of congressional action. Moreover, the disappearance of the Federalist party as an effective opposition force following its ill-advised, ill-timed threats against national unity during the second war with Great Britain eliminated the incentive for party cohesion among the Republicans and ushered in a period of jockeying for personal power within their ranks. Temporarily the party leadership function of the presidency was obscured. Disdaining the role of a "politician," John Quincy Adams preferred to try to maintain the stance of "a man of the whole country" just as his father had, but he met with equal lack of success. With the election of Andrew Jackson in 1828 the conditions were set for the reappearance of a two-party alignment in national politics. It soon manifested itself in the formation of the National Republican (Whig) party, with the remaining Jeffersonian Republicans assuming the name of the Democratic party. As leader of the latter faction, Jackson by personal force and adroitness fashioned the "Democracy" into a powerful instrument for achieving presidential aims.

Jackson not only resurrected the party leadership role that Jefferson had pioneered, but he also found ways of strengthening it. Unable to bend Congress entirely to his will during his first administration, he made use of the veto power to an unprecedented degree to give focus to the issues upon which the presidental campaign of 1832 was fought. Making use of the power of appointment and removal frankly for partisan ends, he strengthened his control over both Congress and the administration. Emulating Jefferson, he built up support for himself and his party by working with "Jackson men" in posts of power in the state governments, welding his western frontier following and elements of the emerging proletarian class in the East into an effective national party machine.

The introduction of the national party convention as the nominating agency for presidential and vice presidential candidates during Jackson's administration proved to be a master stroke in facilitating party leadership by the chief executive. Jackson did not actually originate the idea of the nominating convention, but he was quick to perceive the advantage of the plan, already in use in some states, in freeing the selection of presidential nominees from domination by the congressional leadership. With the aid of his leading New York henchman, Martin Van Buren, Jackson engineered the calling of the first Democratic party convention in 1832 to ratify and give standing to his personal choice, Van Buren, as his running mate in that election. He thereby humiliated the dwindling opposition within his own party's ranks and had the satisfaction of imposing upon the Senate as its presiding officer a man whose nomination for the post of minister to Great Britain the Senate had refused to confirm a short time before. In 1836 he completed the rout by employing the convention device to bestow the party nomination for President upon Van Buren. He then had the personal satisfaction of witnessing the administration of the oath of office of President to Van Buren by another of his appointees, Chief Justice Taney, whom the Senate had on two occasions refused to confirm as his nominee to high public office.

Jackson's accomplishments in assimilating the party leadership function to the President's office had a profound effect upon it. Few, if any, of his successors have been as successful as he was in building a party in his own image and moulding its philosophy and program to his desires. But the pattern and habits of thinking for others to try to follow had been set. For this reason, as well as others relating to his conception of the office, Jackson well deserves the title sometimes given him, "the first modern President." *In his hands the office became a major instrument for achieving popular control over governmental policy.*

Like those who followed Jefferson, Jackson's immediate successors proved to be comparatively unsuccessful, if not complete failures in their attempts to give concrete form to this aspect of the office. A number of factors militated against assumption of a strong party leadership role by the eight occupants of the presidency from 1837 to 1861. The persistent problem of slavery was a divisive influence in both major parties during this period. In an era when the idea of rotation in executive office was in the ascendancy—an idea endorsed by Jackson himself, but not followed by him in that he accepted an immediate, successive term as President, it might be observed—none of the eight served more than one term. Only one, Van Buren, was even nominated by his party to succeed himself.

The two Whig Presidents, William Henry Harrison and Zachary Taylor, both failed to live out their terms. They belonged to a party that had its strongest and most politically experienced leaders in the legislative branch. The Whig party, moreover, with its virulent opposition to "Jacksonism" was committed to the idea of a President subordinated to Congress and pledged not to seek a second term.[8]

8 The main reason for the party leadership's willingness to accept the name of "Whig" was that they perceived their major objective to be similar to that of the old British Whig party which had opposed the pretensions of the Crown in eighteenth-century England. Their bête noire was the man they dubbed "King Andrew I."

John Tyler, Harrison's vice presidential successor, was actually an anti-Jackson Democrat who had been teamed with Harrison on a coalition ticket for political expediency. He soon broke with the Whig leaders in Congress and in his Cabinet on a number of basic policy issues and was disowned by his nominal party allies. Perhaps the most successful of the lot during the pre-Civil War period from the standpoint of effective party leadership was James K. Polk; but he was a compromise, relatively unknown, "dark horse" party standard-bearer; he lacked personal magnetism and color; and he continued to be harassed during his term by the growing division in his party over the issue of slavery. Pledged to hold office for only one term, he refused to become a candidate to succeed himself. His death very soon after leaving office terminated the possibility of his fully living up to his sobriquet of "Young Hickory" in terms of party leadership.

Abraham Lincoln, chosen in 1860 as the candidate of the only third party in United States history to become one of the two major parties, possessed qualities that might well have enabled him to raise the party leadership function of the President to the level it had attained under Jackson; a number of factors, however, combined to direct him instead into the paths of national leadership rising above narrow partisanship. He began his first term under the handicap of being a minority President chosen on a party platform cleverly designed to hold together a number of disparate elements—high tariff industrialists, antislavery moderates from the dissolving Whig and Democratic parties, "free homestead" advocates, midwestern farmers and new settlers interested in internal improvements, former "Free Soilers," and zealous abolitionists—whose only area of agreement was opposition to expansion of slavery into the new territories.

Confronted immediately by the threat of dissolution of the Union, he responded by attempting to unite behind him a following whose central concern was preservation of the Union. Subordinating all other considerations to this fundamental goal, he set up a coalition Cabinet and proceeded to carry on war operations with a minimum of reliance upon congressional support. In his successful campaign for re-election in 1864 Lincoln insisted on presenting himself before the country as the candidate of the "National Union" party and emphasized this point by helping to bring about the nomination of a Union Democrat and former slaveholder, Andrew Johnson of Tennessee, as his running mate. Lincoln's untimely death at the hands of an assassin left unresolved the question whether he would have successfully maintained his position as the leader of his fellow Republican party members in Congress, who had begun to grow increasingly restive about Reconstruction policies he was espousing. The open conflict that soon developed between Johnson and the Radical Republican element in

Congress on this point soon made it clear that a majority of the congressional Republican party membership refused to accept as a party leader the "accidental" President Johnson.

For the next 20 years control and initiative in shaping party programs tended to fall more or less completely into the hands of congressional party leaders, entrenched in power through operation of the senority rule, the standing committe system, and the increasing authority of the House speakership. Observing this state of affairs as a student of political philosophy at Johns Hopkins University in 1884, the young Woodrow Wilson was constrained to advocate in his *Congressional Government* a reformation of congressional organization and procedure in the direction of a parliamentary form of government so as to provide within Congress a strong, responsible leadership. The President's role, as he saw it then, should be that of a chief administrator and little more. He thought it a "rational tendency" that Presidents should be chosen from among the governors of the states, for the presidency was "very much like a big governorship," and "training in the duties of the one fits for the duties of the other." As for his duties, these were mainly "mere administration, mere obedience of directions from the makers of policy, the Standing Committees." Except that his power of veto made him a part of the legislative authority, he "might not inconveniently, be a permanent officer." He was a "part of the official rather than the political machinery of government."[9]

Wilson wrote these words at a time when the political leadership role of the President was at a low ebb. Andrew Johnson had not only failed in his efforts to lead the Republican majority in Congress, but had barely averted removal from office through impeachment. Grant had come into office innocent of political experience, a weakness which party colleagues in Congress and elsewhere were quick to convert to their own advantage. His successor, Hayes, was a compromise candidate whose title to office was clouded and who was continually harassed during his term by factionalism in his own party and by a Congress controlled by the opposition party during the second half of it. Garfield, a "dark horse" candidate, had failed to survive long enough to display his talent as a party leader, and his vice presidential successor, Arthur, had lacked the confidence of important elements of his party.

Later, after observing the relative success of Presidents Grover

[9] Woodrow Wilson, *Congressional Government* (Cleveland: The World Publishing Company, Meridian Books; originally published in 1884), p. 253. On the evolution of Wilson's ideas regarding the presidency see A. J. Wann, "The Development of Woodrow Wilson's Theory of the Presidency: Continuity and Change," in *The Philosophy and Policies of Woodrow Wilson*, Earl Latham, ed., (Chicago: University of Chicago Press, 1958), pp. 46–66.

Cleveland, William McKinley, and Theodore Roosevelt—all Presidents, it might be noted, who had acquired political leadership experience in the office of governor before reaching the presidency—Wilson drastically revised his views on the President's obligation to supply needed party leadership. Roosevelt in particular had demonstrated to Wilson the potentialities of the office in this respect. Writing in 1907 Wilson outlined his more matured conception of the presidential role in these frequently quoted words:

> He cannot escape being the leader of his party except by incapacity and lack of personal force, because he is at once the choice of the party and of the nation. He is the party nominee, and the only party nominee for whom the whole nation votes. Members of the House and Senate are representatives of localities, are voted for only by sections of voters, or by local bodies of electors like the members of the state legislatures. There is no national party choice except that of President. No one else represents the people as a whole, exercising a national choice; and inasmuch as his strictly executive duties are in fact subordinated, so far at any rate as all detail is concerned, the President represents not so much the party's governing efficiency as its controlling ideals and principles. He is not so much part of its organization as its vital link of connection with the thinking nation. He can dominate his party by being spokesman for the real sentiment and purpose of the country, by giving direction to opinion, by giving the country at once the information and the statements of policy which will enable it to form its judgments alike of parties and of men.[10]

This is the classic statement of the twentieth-century conception of the President's position in relation to his party. It is Jackson's "tribuneship" theory of the presidency restated. With his elevation to the presidency in 1913, after he had himself acquired some practical political leadership experience as governor of New Jersey, Wilson was afforded the opportunity to give concrete expression to these views. This he did vigorously and with notable success, setting a standard of effective political leadership of Congress during his first term which few Presidents since his time have equalled.

Leadership of his party has become an inescapable function of the modern President. As demonstrated in the case of President Eisenhower, whose personal popularity transcended party lines and who apparently would have preferred to act as a President above party as Washington had sought to do, practical considerations compel a President to assume the role of party leader, manager, and spokesman, whether he wants to or not.[11] If he fails in this he fails to realize the full potential of his office. While some of his party colleagues in Con-

---

[10] Woodrow Wilson, *Constitutional Government in the United States* (New York: Columbia University Press, 1908).

[11] Cf. William S. White, "Evolution of Eisenhower as a Politician," *The New York Times Magazine*, September 23, 1956, pp. 11 ff.

gress and elsewhere may balk under his leadership, they find it difficult if not impossible to challenge successfully his claim to speak for the party as its national head.

GOVERNORS AND PARTY LEADERSHIP

As has been pointed out, development of the role of party leader by state governors has contributed in some measure to assumption of this function by the President. The injection of partisan considerations into the choice of the governor has imposed upon governors in the populous, two-party states a function of leadership roughly comparable to that of the President's; but the extent to which governors actually play a primary role in party affairs varies considerably. While the comparatively even balance of strength between the two major parties nationally induces a relatively high cohesion within each of them in the competition for the presidency and enhances the prestige of the presidential candidate as national party spokesman and leader, the parallel does not necessarily hold true in all cases at the state level.

In a number of states, most notably in the South, and in some New England and midwestern areas, two-party competition is so lacking that the major parties, as rivals for power, are not subject to the constant discipline derived from the danger of losing on the one side, or the likelihood of winning on the other.[12] Success is assured, or practically so, for the one party and defeat for the other most of the time. Consequently the contest for the governorship is determined by the outcome of a bifactional or multifactional struggle within the ranks of the regularly dominant party, rather than by a clear-cut interparty fight. In these states, independents and even considerable numbers of voters who consider themselves to be members of the opposition party in national politics enroll themselves as members of the dominant local party in order to participate in its direct primary, the instrument most widely used for nominating gubernatorial candidates.[13] In such one-party situations the successful candidate cannot assert and maintain his claim to act and speak as the acknowledged head of all members of his "party" within the state. Rather he speaks and acts as the leader of a successful faction or coalition of factions within it, made up of whatever elements he can attract to his support.

[12] *Supra,* Chap. 4, pp. 118–120. See also Coleman B. Ransone, Jr. *The Office of Governor in the United States* (University, Ala.: University of Alabama Press, 1956), pp. 149 ff.

[13] Cf. Seymour M. Lipset, *Political Man: The Social Bases of Politics* (Garden City, N. Y.: Doubleday & Company, Anchor Books, 1963), pp. 322 ff.

Fortunately for the cause of responsible party government, the number of genuine one-party states in the nation appears to be on the wane as revealed by state election results during the last decade.

These conditions that characterize the American party system help to throw light on the relationship between a President and state governors of his party. State party alignments represent, outwardly at least, an extension of the same alignments that have formed in the competition for the presidency; and even though presidential two-party politics tends to produce state two-party politics ultimately, the several state segments which in their totality comprise the national party sometimes represent philosophies and programs in state affairs at variance with those presented by it nationally. As a consequence a governor may well find himself the nominal head of a party organization for his state which presents a somewhat schizophrenic aspect to the public. The policies the party ostensibly supports in the person of the presidential candidate may well be quite at variance with those espoused by it in the person of its candidate for the governorship. The loyalty of a governor to the presidential candidate of his party tends to be based upon institutional rather than ideological considerations. It is a feudal relationship arising out of mutual interests, rather than one of obligation enforced by cumpulsion of an inferior to obey the dictate of a superior. Governor-led rebellions against the national leadership disturbed Democratic party harmony during the Roosevelt, Truman, Kennedy, and Johnson administrations. A half-century earlier, rebellious Republican governors supplied much of the political pressure which erupted in the Progressive ("Bull Moose") revolt in the Republican party in 1912. Governor-led forces have supplied much of the strength of the anti-Goldwater movement in the Republican party since the 1964 presidential election.

A number of other factors growing out of the governmental structure at the state level also militate against a governor's becoming the generally acknowledged head of his party in the same degree that a President may be regarded as the head of the national party. A governor has as potential rivals for the role one or both of the United States Senators from his state. They are elected from the same statewide constituency as he, so that he, unlike the President, lacks the uniqueness of being the only elected officer of the constituency from which he is chosen. If a Senator's party is in power nationally he will usually have control over a considerable amount of federal patronage within his state. Not infrequently he will himself have moved to the Senate from the governorship and will have retained in some measure the base of personal political support he built up during his tenure as governor. Uninhibited by limitations on tenure in the senatorial post, in contrast to the enforced rotation system to which governors in almost half the states are subjected, a United States Senator—particularly one who has advanced to the Senate from the governorship—is in a strong position to make himself the dominant figure in state party affairs and cause the party organization to look to him for its cues, rather than to the governor.

Illustrations of the continued ascendancy of ex-governor Senators in state political affairs in recent years are found in the domination of the Democratic party in Virginia by Senator Harry Byrd; in Georgia by Senators Herman Talmadge and Richard Russell, and, in the Republican party, by the late Senator Styles Bridges in New Hampshire. Earlier instances were Senator Huey Long, who remained the primary figure in Louisiana Democratic politics after his transfer to the United States Senate in the early 1930s; Senator Hiram Johnson, who dominated Republican politics in California for many years after his elevation to the Senate; and Senator Robert M. La Follette of Wisconsin, who remained the most powerful figure in Wisconsin Republican party affairs until his death. The strength of an incumbent Senator's position in the party is shown in another way by the relatively few instances of a state governor's successfully contesting with an incumbent Senator for the party nomination for the senatorship when concurrent expiration of their terms of office coupled with a re-eligibility limit on the governorship has induced the governor to try for the Senate.

A governor not only has to fear the rivalry of a Senator for the role of party leader in his state, but there are other elective officers chosen on a statewide basis who have considerable patronage at their disposal and sometimes can challenge his primacy. Even the State Chairman, the national party Committeeman, or a party boss who operates from outside the formal party structure may be so securely entrenched in power within the party organization that a governor may find his position of party leader far from unchallengeable. Occasionally a state governor may obviate potential rivalry for leadership of his party from the National Committeeman or state party Chairman by occupying one of these posts himself while serving in the governorship; but this method of forestalling other figures is foreclosed to him in the case of a Senate seat, since state constitutions prohibit a governor's holding a seat in the national Congress and the governorship simultaneously.

With due allowance for the considerations just noted, the general proposition still stands that the importance of the governorship today, like that of the presidency, has come to depend in increasing measure upon the fact that a governor is chosen as a representative of a partisan point of view and that he is expected to, and does so far as circumstances permit, assume the status of leader of his party in his state. His official duties are political as well as administrative, and in discharging them he exerts influence through and upon his party colleagues. In some matters of party management his influence is very likely to be dominant. Depending upon his skill in this sphere of his operations, his official role, like that of the President, takes on added weight and broader dimension. As head of an important dukedom in the party's feudal structure he may have reason to hope that he can eventually elevate himself to the top place itself—the presidency.

PARTY LEADERSHIP AND MANAGEMENT FUNCTIONS OF THE CHIEF EXECUTIVE

The ultimate results of a chief executive's operations as a party leader will be found in the public policy products of his administration. The extent to which his policy programs take form and are implemented through exercise of his influence as a partisan leader is difficult to measure with any degree of exactitude, however. His role as a partisan tends to color all his official actions and to be involved in the exercise of all his constitutional authority, more or less; but it is difficult, if not impossible, to make an accurate assessment of the impact of this element of his authority in particular situations. The party chieftainship role, whatever its implications may be, is blended with his office in its totality. It is usually most clearly manifested in the discharge of his official responsibilities in the field of legislative action. The party tie is one of the invisible cords that bind together the legislative and executive branches of government. As policy-making has become more prominent in the administrative process, the leadership role of the chief executive necessarily has taken on great significance in administrative management and direction as well. *Who* administers policies and *how* they employ the wide discretionary powers vested in them become matters of as great concern as who the lawmakers are and how they exercise their policy-making authority.

As with other powers and functions associated with his office, the chief executive's position as the top man in the party hierarchy adds to the influence of his office and at the same time imposes restraints upon his freedom of choice and initiative. He is the leader of his party; but in a sense he is also its prisoner. The need to preserve party harmony, or at any rate an outward semblance of it, imposes a constant constraint upon him. He is under a compulsion not to undertake a course of action likely to seriously disrupt his party following in the face of a strong, well-organized opposition. Under the pressures of opposing interests within his own party he must seek to strike a balance between what he may personally feel the public interest requires and what can be achieved, given the conditions imposed by the necessity of maintaining a substantial degree of unity of support among his party followers.[14]

The price of attaining one objective, as Franklin D. Roosevelt once observed, often may be the sacrifice of others. In choosing appointees for the major posts within his administration, for example, a chief executive may desire to recruit an administrative corps made up of "the best brains in the country," one in complete harmony with his own philosophy in all respects; but he finds his freedom of choice is limited by the need to give representation to the various sectional and group interests within his party's ranks. He may even feel a compulsion to woo friendly elements of the opposition party by giving a Cabinet post to one of them. To ignore such considerations involves a risk of offending some powerful segment of party support whose assistance may be needed in a future contest over a matter of public policy. And so it goes with all his other official powers and duties. The implications of his official acts in terms of party politics must ever be kept in view.

TECHNIQUES OF PARTY LEADERSHIP

Campaign speeches and "position papers," legislative messages, public addresses, press conferences and press releases, and open letters are the vehicles by which the chief executive commonly makes known to the public his views on party policy questions. Although in the form of communications to the general public, they are meant for the eyes and ears of his party supporters as well. Messages meant for his party subordinates alone are transmitted more privately through personal contacts, letters, and directives, or through trusted emissaries in the legislative body, the administrative branches, or in the party organization. This process of giving form and expression to the party line and program, of course, is by no means a one-way operation. Leadership involves consultation, exchange, and accommodation of views. Counsel given by party lieutenants and reactions to conflicting pressures from various interests and centers of influence within the party must always be taken into account by a chief executive determining a course of action to which he commits himself and, by implication, his party. A President or governor cannot afford the luxury of continual fighting with his party's subordinate leadership. Leadership involves more than just giving orders.

[14] For an excellent analysis of a number of presidential campaigns showing how the practicalities of party politics compelled certain Presidents, including Lincoln, Jefferson, Jackson, Wilson, Theodore Roosevelt, F. D. Roosevelt, and Eisenhower, to pursue particular courses of action, see Binkley, *op. cit.*, Chap. V.

In the area of party management and government per se, the hand of the chief executive is most likely to be seen in (1) the formulation and elucidation of the party platform—the statement of principles and objectives by which the party proposes to be guided if it is given a mandate by the voters; (2) the designation of party nominees for public office; (3) the selection of key figures in the party organizational scheme; and (4) the determination of campaign strategy and tactics. His authority in these matters rests mainly upon party usage and practice and is dependent upon variable factors of one kind or another to such a degree, however, that it may be great, or little, or even nonexistent.

1. PARTY PLATFORM-MAKING

If the nominee has been designated before the platform has been adopted, or if his nomination is assured even though it has not yet been officially made before the platform is drafted, the platform statements on the major issues of the day will usually be cleared with him unofficially before adoption. An incumbent President or governor about to be renominated by his party can thus assume a major share of direct responsibility for what is proposed as a program of party action.

Even if the identity of the nominee has not been determined before the platform has been formulated—as is usually the case in an open presidential nomination contest, since the regular order of business in both major party national conventions now is to choose the nominee after the platform has been adopted—the nominee may still have the final word on some matters dealt with in the platform. The platform drafting committee in such a contingency will ordinarily include one or more spokesmen for each of the major potential candidates. Through these emissaries the leading contenders can be kept informed of developments and can make their influence felt. Often the resulting statements of the party's position on some issues are designedly vague or ambiguous, in order to bridge over some wide gulf of disagreement among party elements or potential candidates; or the platform may be entirely silent on some major question for a similar reason. The apogee of evasion was reached by the Whig party in 1848. Split by the burning issues arising out of the slavery question they made only a vague reference to the party's "principles," trusting that their popular war hero candidate, General Taylor, would be elected by "spontaneous combustion." They were not disappointed.

When the platform-makers leave to the candidate the responsibility of spelling out in clear terms the meaning of the platform, it becomes possible for the candidate to become in effect the declarer of the party's position on major issues. In fulfilling this function he may even go so far as to modify or disavow entirely the position the convention has endorsed on a particular point. If he does so, the public is inclined to accept his view rather than that of the platform as the party's official stand. Thus the carefully drawn statement in the Democratic party platform of 1904 straddling the currency issue was disavowed by its candidate for President, Judge Alton B. Parker, who made it clear he was an uncompromising gold standard man. The equivocal statement in the 1928 Democratic platform on the prohibition issue which stopped short of outright advocacy of repeal of the Eighteenth Amendment was promptly consigned to the wastebasket by the nominee, Governor Alfred E. Smith, who favored repeal. Similarly Governor Alfred M. Landon, the Republican nominee in 1936, made clear that he would not consider himself bound in all particulars by platform statements on the currency question and the matter of public regulation of wages and hours of labor.

Gubernatorial candidates, who for the most part are now nominated through the direct primary, not infrequently find themselves at odds with the platform-makers of their parties. They likewise feel free on occasion, as did Governor Earl Warren, the Republican candidate in California in the 1950 election, to endorse a proposed course of action differing markedly from that of the official party declaration.

2. SELECTION OF CANDIDATES

Under the conditions of partisan nominations there is little or no opportunity for a President or a governor in his capacity as party leader to designate directly the candidates who will be presented to the public under the party's banner. This is reserved by law or by party practice to the party membership operating through the direct primary or to party conventions or caucuses. Decentralization and democratization of control over nominations is the object sought through current nomination procedures. So highly are these principles esteemed by a considerable part of the public that "anti-bossism" becomes a potent rallying cry for those who would resist selection of candidates by the central leadership element in the party.

An open attempt on the part of the chief executive as party leader to discipline a recalcitrant member of his party by employing influence to cause his rejection as a candidate very likely will be resented by the local party constituency. As often as not the "rebel" will be returned in triumph to carry on his campaign of resistance to executive "dictatorship." Nevertheless, by a judicious use of the patronage at his disposal, by quietly letting the word be spread regarding his desires among those party members faithful to his cause, and by other more subtle means, a chief executive can sometimes make his influence felt effectively in the nominating procedures of his party.[15] Even a purge effort that fails in its immediate objective may have a sobering effect on other members of the chief executive's party who have not been giving him and his policies strong and faithful support generally.

In 1950 President Truman's open intervention in the Democratic primary for a nominee in the President's home congressional district in Missouri resulted in the rejection of the incumbent Democrat, Roger C. Slaughter, who as a member of the House Committee on Rules had made himself particularly obnoxious to the President by helping the opposition prevent consideration of measures supported by the President. President F. D. Roosevelt's attempted purge of several prominent Democratic members of Congress in the 1938 primaries was so generally unsuccessful that it is frequently cited as evidence of the unwisdom of a President's open interference in congressional primaries of his party. However, Roosevelt's efforts were successful at that time in bringing about the elimination of a Democratic Representative from New York, John J. O'Connor, who had been an obstructionist against the President's program from his post on the House Committee on Rules; and the long-range objective of the President which gave rise to the purge effort—a change in the course of Supreme Court interpretation of the Constitution—was eventually attained.

Probably the most significant development in the matter of the chief executive's influence in the naming of party nominees has occurred in connection with the designation of the vice presidential nominee. Since 1940, when President F. D. Roosevelt imposed upon a somewhat reluctant Democratic convention his choice of Secretary of Agriculture Henry A. Wallace as the party's vice presidential nominee, it has been the practice for conventions to nominate the presidential candidate's expressed choice or to choose one of several persons from a "preferred' or "acceptable" list drawn up by him. In 1944 President Roosevelt's inclusion of Senator Truman's name on his list of preferred vice presidential nominees was instrumental in giving Truman the nomination, and, as later events proved, the presidency itself. In 1948 Governor Thomas E. Dewey, the Republican nominee, brought strong pressure to bear upon an erstwhile rival for the presidential nomination, Governor Earl Warren, to accept the vice presidential nomination and had no difficulty in getting the convention to agree to his choice. A similar move in the 1944 convention had resulted in Dewey's being paired with Governor John W. Bricker of Ohio.

[15] For a more extended discussion of attempts by Presidents to influence congressional nominations see William H. Riker, *Federalism: Origin, Operation, Significance* (Boston: Little, Brown and Company, 1964), pp. 96–101.

Senator Richard M. Nixon received the Republican nomination for Vice President in 1952 when his name was included on a short list of acceptable candidates approved by General Eisenhower, the presidential nominee. Before the 1956 Republican convention, when a movement was launched by former Governor Harold Stassen of Minnesota and other party members to "dump" Nixon as the vice presidential nominee, a statement from President Eisenhower that he considered him to be an eminently satisfactory man for the job caused the movement to collapse. Vice President Nixon, who became the presidential nominee in 1960, selected Ambassador Henry Cabot Lodge as his vice presidential partner; while in that same year Senator John F. Kennedy, the Democratic nominee, settled upon his major rival for the presidential nomination, Senator Lyndon Johnson, for this post. Their choices were agreed to by the respective party conventions in perfunctory fashion, despite evidences of strong preferences by some delegates for other candidates. Again in 1964, the party conventions deferred without demur to the wishes of their respective presidential nominees in naming their vice presidential running mates. In fact, the only instance since 1940 of a convention's being allowed a free choice in naming a vice presidential candidate occurred in 1956. Governor Stevenson, the Democratic presidential nominee, invited the convention to make its own choice. It selected Stevenson's major rival for the presidential nomination, Senator Kefauver of Tennessee, for the vice presidential place after a sharp, spirited contest between Kefauver's backers and supporters of Senator John F. Kennedy of Massachusetts.

Whether for good or ill these recent developments suggest the establishment of a new usage in presidential politics that could have great significance for the future of presidential selection.[16] Two of the vice presidential candidates designated by the presidential candidate of a party since 1940 have succeeded to the presidency through the death of the incumbent President. Another has used the vice presidency as a springboard to the presidential nomination of his party. The practice gives evidence of developing into a procedure through which, in some cases at least, the mantle of party leadership is passed on by the party leader of the moment to an heir apparent of his own choosing. The Bayh-Celler Amendment, discussed in Chapter 6, would extend this principle into the area of filling vacancies that may occur in the office of vice president itself. There are objections to this convention practice from some quarters on the ground that it involves concentration of too much political power in one person's hands. In rebuttal it is pointed out that recent developments in connection with the vice president—his closer association with the

[16] For a discussion of this trend in national convention nominating practice and its implications see David, Goldman, and Bain, *op. cit.*, pp. 59–62.

administration of which he is a part, the practice of assigning to him political, administrative, and representational functions of one kind or another, and the consequent need for assurance that the President and Vice President will work well together—justify deferring to the presidential candidate's wishes in determining who will be associated closely with him if the party is successful in the presidential contest.

In states which still employ the convention for nominating gubernatorial candidates and other party nominees for statewide elective office, a similar tendency to defer to the gubernatorial candidate's wishes in filling out the ticket may be noted. In New York, for example, where the gubernatorial candidate is nominated in convention, his wishes about the nominations for the other elective offices of lieutenant governor, attorney general, and comptroller carry great weight. In Michigan, where party candidates for governor are nominated at a direct primary, the gubernatorial candidate's wishes about nominations for other statewide elective posts, including the lieutenant governorship, if he cares to make them known, will ordinarily be carried out at the state convention which makes up the rest of the slate of nominees.

In some southern states where candidates for the offices of governor and lieutenant governor are nominated by direct primary, candidates for these nominations sometimes campaign in pairs, each partner attempting to convey to the other his popular support. If the maneuver is successful it has, of course, an effect similar to the practice previously noted in connection with the presidency and vice presidency in that it places the lieutenant governor in some debt to the governor, tends to improve the chances of harmonious relations between them, and gives the former a place of vantage as heir apparent from which to compete for the top spot at the next election. This becomes particularly important in states having re-eligibility limitations forcing the governor to step down after one term.

A President or governor may also use his influence directly in choosing the party nominee to succeed himself. If he wishes to succeed himself, his position in the party organizational scheme has become so strong as to enable him usually to bring about his own renomination. During the past three-quarters of a century, every incumbent President who sought renomination at the hands of his party has gained it. Presidents Taft in 1912 and Truman in 1948 both achieved renomination in the face of massive revolts within their own parties. The reason for this is not far to seek. It is not merely to be found in the great amount of patronage at a President's disposal which enables him to exercise an influence upon the selection of convention delegates, although this is, of course, a factor. A more fundamental explanation is that, if the opposition party poses a real threat to the party in power, the President's party can repudiate him as its leader only at the gravest risk of losing the ensuing election. It must contend on the basis of its record under his leadership or, to all intents and purposes, forfeit the contest. The 1962 gubernatorial election in New Hampshire illustrated the point. In the Republican primary of that year the incumbent governor, Wesley C. Powell, sought renomination for a third term. He was defeated in the party's primary. Incensed at this rejection of his leadership, Governor Powell threw his support to the Democratic nominee, with the result that a Democratic governor was elected in that state for the first time in some 30 years.

If an incumbent chief executive is not himself a candidate for renomination, his support of a favored candidate may well become a decisive factor in the choice of a successor. During the nineteenth century incumbent Presidents, with the notable exception of Andrew Jackson in the 1836 campaign, publicly maintained a posture of neutrality in the nomination contests of their respective parties. This view that a President should remain aloof and above the struggle over the succession to his post of leader appears now to be undergoing change. An incumbent has a personal stake and interest in trying to insure continuance of the policies he has pursued as a party leader, and it is natural that he should use the influence accruing to his office to bring about that result.

Thus in 1908 President Theodore Roosevelt gave his endorsement to his Secretary of War, William H. Taft, as his successor, and his positive support was probably decisive in causing Taft to become the Republican nominee. Woodrow Wilson's health prevented him from taking an active hand in the Democratic nomination contest in 1920; but he insisted on a candidate who would carry on the fight for American participation in the League of Nations. Franklin D. Roosevelt was apparently prepared to throw his support to his Secretary of State, Cordell Hull, for the Democratic nomination in 1940, but the outbreak of war in Europe and the deepening international crisis that followed led him to accept renomination himself for a third term. President Truman's preference for Governor Adlai Stevenson over his chief competitor, Senator Estes Kefauver, was instrumental in causing the Democratic nomination to be given to the former in 1952, even though in the President's estimation Stevenson seemed reluctant to allow the impression to be created that he owed his selection in any way to the President's support.[17] President Eisenhower reverted to the earlier practice of not designating a favorite candidate as a successor in 1960; he had contributed, however, to enhancing Vice President Nixon's national stature by assigning him

---

[17] For President Truman's version of the matter see his *Mr. Citizen* (New York: Popular Library, 1961), pp. 43 ff.

functions that brought him to public attention and enabled him to lay claim to the succession on the ground of experience in dealing with national problems. At an early stage in that campaign, when Governor Nelson Rockefeller of New York, Vice President Nixon's chief rival for the nomination, discovered that Nixon had the support of the party organization regulars as well as the President's tacit approval, he withdrew from the contest.[18]

In the states, even though the direct primary system used generally in the selection of party nominees for the governorship is deliberately designed to counteract the power of the party organization and its leaders in the selection of party candidates, the influence of the outgoing governor in naming a candidate has by no means been completely discounted. His support is a significant asset for a candidate to have in the intraparty primary contest, and is eagerly sought.

In this connection another dimension of the relationship between the party leadership role of the President and that of governors should be brought to mind again—the increasing influence of state governors in the selection of presidential candidates. As governors have established themselves more openly and firmly as the recognized heads of their party organizations in the states, their influence in the selection of the presidential candidate has grown stronger. One indication of their growing influence is seen in the number of them who participate as delegates in the national nominating conventions. In the 1860 campaign only one governor was a member of either the Democratic or the Republican national convention. In later conventions the number who have participated as delegates has grown steadily larger. In the 1956 conventions 20 of the 27 Democratic governors and 15 of the 21 Republicans were members of their party delegations.[19] In about three cases out of four where a governor was a member of his state delegation, he served as delegation chairman. Depending on the situation in which their party finds itself at the time of the presidential nominating contest, the influence of governors, particularly those in the populous, pivotal states, can be of crucial importance. In an open contest for the presidential nomination the support of these local party chieftains is eagerly sought by aspirants for the nomination, and their success in amassing delegate strength through enlistment of party governors as supporters sometimes proves decisive. State governors proved to be key factors in swinging their party nominations to Governor Dewey in 1948, to General Eisenhower in 1952, and to Senator Kennedy in 1960.

In the earlier stages of a presidential nominating contest governors with a tight grip on the votes of their delegations are in a strong

[18] *The New York Times*, December 27, 1959.
[19] David, Goldman, and Bain, *op. cit.*, p. 98.

bargaining position either to advance the interests of some favored candidate or to promote the cause of one of their own number. A common maneuver for a governor is to advance himself as a "favorite son" candidate for the nomination until the issue clears and he can decide whether to make an outright bid for the nomination for himself or to join forces—sometimes for a price in the form of a future patronage concession—with some other candidate. The impressive list of individuals who have vaulted from a state governorship directly to the status of party nominee for President or Vice President since 1900 is a testimonial to the strong leverage that can be exerted in national party affairs from this post.

3. SELECTION OF PARTY OFFICERS

From their position in the party, chief executives in their capacity as party candidates are usually able to exert a strong influence in the selection of others to certain posts of management in the party hierarchy; but again the decentralized, informal character of party organization in the United States generally militates against their acquiring and exercising much direct control in this area. A presidential candidate's wishes about who will head the National Committee of his party have come to be regularly respected, so that this post, although filled nominally by action of the Committee itself, lies within his control. Through him the candidate may exert influence upon the selection of other major figures in the party campaign organization. In similar fashion in states where a viable two-party system prevails the post of state party chairman is ordinarily filled by an individual who is the choice of, or is at least acceptable to, the party candidate for the governorship.

During the course of an election campaign these party officials are closely associated with the candidate for the post of chief executive and serve, in effect, as campaign managers and organizers under his direction. The need for harmony between the candidate and the party chairman is self-evident, and this need is recognized in these practices. In filling other positions in the party hierarchy, however, the influence of a candidate for the chief executiveship will usually be exerted through counsel, persuasion, and the use of governmental patronage if it is available. The National Committee itself is made up of individuals in whose choice the presidential candidate has no direct voice; and the state and local party committee members will also ordinarily have been selected by processes outside the direct control of the candidates for state executive office.

For the sake of maintaining a semblance of party harmony a chief executive candidate in his role as party head must perforce tolerate a great deal of indifference or even hostility toward himself as the party leader by some occupants of such posts. Few Democrats, for instance, who used their positions within the congressional and state party organizations to furnish leadership for the 1948 States Rights party defection in the presidental contest were ostracized and stripped of their party posts as a penalty for their actions. The conditions of American political conflict tend to dictate a strategy of leaving out the welcome mat for strayers from the party fold, even in the face of utmost provocation.

In the legislative party organization the chief executive likewise does not usually have a controlling voice in the naming of individuals to posts of influence. Such matters are left to the party legislative caucus and its leadership, operating under the rules and usages in the context of the situation confronting them as they choose to apply them. The chief executive may use his influence behind the scenes quietly or through indirect pressure; but even in doing this much he runs some risk of criticism by his party colleagues in the legislative branch, who tend to resent any intrusion into affairs they consider to be their own business. When President F. D. Roosevelt intervened directly in a contest over the filling of the post of party Floor Leader in the Democratic Senate caucus in 1937 and indicated through an open letter his preference of Senator ("Dear Alben") Barkley of Kentucky over his chief opponent, Senator Pat Harrison of Mississippi, there was much criticism by some Democratic senators. The President's intervention was successful in that Barkley was chosen by a single vote, but the animosity engendered by this allegedly unwarranted intrusion in a matter of internal business of the senatorial wing of the party was one of the contributing factors to Roosevelt's loss of influence with some of his party colleagues in that and subsequent Congresses.

On the other hand, House Republican Floor Leader Joe Martin of Massachusetts attributed his ouster from his post in 1959 to President Eisenhower's unwillingness to use influence on his behalf. Confronted by a somewhat similar situation in 1961 when the death of House Speaker Sam Rayburn created a vacancy in that important party post, President Kennedy elected to maintain a strictly hands-off attitude in the choice of a successor by the Democratic House caucus (though for a number of reasons he was believed to prefer someone other than the person eventually selected, Representative John McCormack).

4. DECISIONS ON CAMPAIGN STRATEGY AND TACTICS

As already pointed out, defining his party's position and program on some of the basic issues of the day is a function that falls upon a candidate in his capacity of party leader. This is only one aspect of his job as supreme director of the party's campaign strategy in the election contest in which he is the featured candidate. To him will also be referred for his advice a host of subordinate matters connected with the campaign. What particular issues shall be highlighted? What slogan or slogans shall summarize the basic appeal for popular support? What type of program shall be devised for raising campaign funds? How shall the available funds be allocated by area and among the various objects of expenditure so as to obtain maximum results? To what extent and in what manner shall there be a concentrated, organized effort to attract the support of special groups of voters, such as women, racial and nationality minority groups, union members, farmers, intellectuals, independents, and potential defectors from the opposition party? How shall the tempo of the campaign be timed or paced so as to realize the maximum support on the crucial day when the voters go to the polls? What party figures shall be called upon to carry the brunt of the campaign speech-making chores? Should the candidate for the chief executive's post attempt to induce the public to support not only his own candidacy, but that of his party colleagues as well, some of whom he may already have discovered, to his dismay, to be very unreliable allies? Above all, what shall be the nature and extent of the candidate's active participation in the effort to bring his candidacy and his party's appeal directly to the attention of the electorate?

These are problems of political organization, strategy, and logistics similar to those confronting a general planning a military operation. There must be a careful and accurate analysis of one's own position, assets, and liabilities and a similar analysis of the strengths and weaknesses of the opposition. A basic plan of combat must be devised in the light of these estimates, and tactics must be employed to meet the exigencies of the moment as the campaign unfolds. The outcome of the campaign may well depend upon choice of the right course of action in these particulars.

This is not the place to recount in detail the history of presidential or gubernatorial campaigns of the past. Every such campaign has its own exciting story.[20] It suffices to point out here two developments of note that reflect change in the relationship of the candidate

[20] For vivid and informed accounts of the presidential campaigns of 1960 and 1964 see Theodore H. White, *The Making of the President, 1960,* and *The Making of the President, 1964* (New York: Atheneum Publishers, 1961 and 1965). Theodore Sorenson's *Kennedy* (New York: Harper & Row, 1965), Chap. IV–VIII, gives an "inside" account of the Kennedy campaign of 1960. Arthur M. Schlesinger's *The Age of Roosevelt: Politics of Upheaval* (Boston: Houghton Mifflin Company, 1960), Part IV, is an equally interesting account of the presidential campaign of 1936. See also Nelson W. Polsby and Aaron B. Wildavsky, *Presidential Elections: Strategies of American Electoral Politics* (New York: Charles Scribner's Sons, 1964).

for executive office to this phase of the political process. One is the increasing involvement of the candidate himself in bringing his candidacy and proposed program to the attention of the electorate; the other is the broadening of the base of his appeal to reach the great mass of the voters directly through modern-day facilities of mass communication and rapid transport—the daily newspaper, radio, television, and jet airplane transportation.

Until near the end of the nineteenth century, it was the usual practice for a presidential candidate to leave the speech-making in a campaign mainly or even entirely to his supporters. His activity in this connection was confined to short talks to visiting delegations to his home, the sending of open letters to supporters outlining his position on specific topics, and the occasional releasing of statements to newspapers for publication. Sometimes he even chose the course of making no comments at all on the issues as they developed in the campaign, preferring to let his record speak for itself. For example, in the exciting campaign of 1860, in which the question of eventual disunion and possibly war hung in the balance, Lincoln decided to remain in Springfield, Illinois, leaving the speech-making to his supporters.[21] He was not to be lured away from this course even though his opponents, particularly Stephen A. Douglas, engaged in active speech-making campaigns throughout the country.

The famous "Free Silver" campaign of 1896 brought with it something of an innovation in presidential campaigning when the Democratic candidate, William Jennings Bryan, undertook to bring his appeal directly to the people by a series of nationwide, whirlwind speaking tours. Realizing that he was relatively unknown to the national electorate and having faith in his uncommon oratorical skill, the "Silver-tongued Orator of the Platte" logged over 13,000 miles of travel by train in the course of two and a half months, visiting 29

---

[21] Lincoln's very brief speech of acceptance, given at a rally in Springfield on August 8, 1860, forecast his campaign of silence. Speaking to his enthusiastic supporters he said: "It has been my purpose, since I have been placed in my present position, to make no speeches. . . . I appear upon the ground here at this time only for the purpose of affording myself the best opportunity of seeing you and enabling you to see me. You will kindly let me be silent." Bruce Catton, *The Coming Fury* (New York: Doubleday & Company, 1961), p. 91.

Later, taking the position that anyone seeking light on his position on the issues could look at the Republican platform and at what he had already said in his speeches and statements before his nomination, he had his secretariat prepare a form letter to be sent to such inquirers. It read as follows: "Your letter to Mr. Lincoln, of —, and by which you seek to obtain his opinion on certain political points, has been received by him. He has received others of similar character; but he also has a greater number of the exactly opposite character. The latter class beseech him to write nothing whatever upon any point of political doctrine. They say his positions were well known when he was nominated, and that he must not now embarrass the canvass by undertaking to shift or modify them. He regrets that he cannot oblige all, but you perceive that it is impossible for him to do so." *Ibid.*, p. 93

of the 45 states, giving as many as 20 separate speeches in a 24-hour stretch, and addressing in person an estimated 5,000,000 people—all in a losing cause, it should be added. But he had set a new fashion in presidential campaigning.

Although some candidates thereafter continued to follow the style of Bryan's opponent, William McKinley, by conducting stay-at-home "front porch" campaigns in the older form, by the 1920s the energetic campaign in which the rival candidates tour the country and engage in a great amount of speech-making, attendance at party rallies, conferring with local party leaders and candidates, and so on, had become the rule. The presidential campaign of 1928 brought the first extensive use of radio speech-making on nationwide hookups, bringing candidates' voices to millions of voters who were given a sense of personal contact with the nominees. Television, first used on a nationwide scale in the 1952 campaign, added a new medium of personal contact. In 1960 in addition to a number of televised speeches by each candidate, four joint debates by Senator Kennedy and Vice President Nixon were televised to national audiences numbered in the millions.[22]

One might reasonably suppose that with radio and television as means of access to the nation's ears and eyes, presidential candidates might well deem it less necessary than before to travel about, show themselves to the people, and address them in person. Yet this has not been the case. Modern campaign strategy has dictated on the contrary that the candidate take advantage of improved means of transport to bring himself even more into direct contact with the people. In his speech of acceptance to the Republican convention in 1960 Vice President Nixon pledged himself to carry his campaign in person to "every one of the 50 states between now and November eighth." He kept his promise. By November seventh he had flown 65,500 miles, appeared in 188 cities at least once, made over 150 major speeches, and had been seen by an estimated 10,000,000 people.[23] Senator Kennedy engaged in an equally strenuous schedule. Truly it can be said that if the candidates for the office of chief executive now are the generalissimos of their respective armies of followers in a campaign, they are generals who conduct their battles in the front lines, where the strife is the hottest—and they do not spare themselves.

OBSTACLES TO EFFECTIVE PARTY LEADERSHIP

The environment in which an American chief executive must operate as party leader is by no means conducive in every respect to an effective discharge of this responsibility. Indeed, the cards seem

[22] Cf. Sidney Kraus, Ed., *The Great Debates* (Bloomington: University of Indiana Press, 1962) for a complete analysis of this new technique.
[23] White, *The Making of the President, 1960,* pp. 263, 317.

stacked heavily against him on this score. Though he is regarded as the leader, his following is far from being a highly disciplined, loyal army. As he surveys its motley ranks he may well be justified in echoing the sentiments of the Duke of Wellington, who in reply to a question from a subaltern on his reactions after conducting his first review of the ill-equipped, poorly drilled Peninsular Army, answered: "Sir, I cannot say if they would frighten the enemy; but by G–d, they frighten me." Persuasion, bargaining, compromise, indirect pressure, and cajolery must be the chief executive's methods of control, rather than direct orders reinforced by a strong disciplinary authority.

While it admires strong party leadership in a chief executive, the American public also tends to be suspicious of party bossism; and the distinction between them is by no means always easy to make. The independent-minded legislator who stands ready to challenge alleged dictation by the party machine may become a hero in the minds of some people. He is praised for being "his own man," as "one who puts principle above expediency," who "refuses to be a rubber stamp," and so on. As party leader the chief executive sometimes finds himself in a position somewhat similar to that of the lion tamer who confronts a collection of caged beasts armed with only a chair and a pistol loaded with blanks. The general public sits and enjoys the spectacle; while it admires his mastery over the snarling beasts, at the same time it may subconsciously hope that one of them will rebel and make a real fight of it. Newspapers and news commentators are always ready to do their part by playing up any story that suggests an intraparty squabble. Intraparty fights make news; as a rule, disciplined responses to executive leadership do not.

The factors that make it difficult for a chief executive to impose his will consistently upon his party followers are manifold. They arise from the kind of governmental institutions the nation has designed for itself, from the nature of the party system, and from the underlying conditions that generate the dynamics of American politics. In the case of the presidency the federalized character of the national parties, party nomination practices, and the peculiar character of the elective process by which the President is elevated to the party leadership post are the root of many of his difficulties. He may influence, but not command, the nomination of candidates favorable to the programs he espouses. The statewide bloc system of choosing the presidential electors through whose accumulated votes he is elected tends to make a President more sensitive to the demands of the potential "swing" voters in the populous, pivotal states and induces him to advance party programs sometimes at variance with those his followers in the legislative branch, considered collectively, will readily support. In the states the very considerable degree of autonomy enjoyed by local governmental units and the heterogeneity of interests included within any party having a sufficiently widespread appeal to have captured the governorship results in a similar difference of outlook as between the party leader in the person of the governor and the party membership in the legislative branch. Presidents and governors must recognize that to a certain extent they have attracted the popular support needed to place them in office through their personal appeal and magnetism rather than because of their party's programs and records.

By its very nature the system of separation of powers throws formidable obstacles in the way of a chief executive who seeks to establish and exercise authority as party leader. Under it the chief executive and his party allies in the legislative branch not only represent different types of constituencies, but they are independent of one another in the matter of their tenure in office. The "presidential" political party and the "congressional" political party of the same name are not necessarily in agreement on all major points of public policy, because they are responsible to different groupings of interests.[24] Similarly in the states the "gubernatorial" and "legislative" political parties of the same name may answer to disparate political pressures and interests. Indeed, in the one-party states, to say nothing of those in which the legislators are chosen on a nonpartisan basis— Nebraska and Minnesota—the party leadership role of the governor becomes one of leadership only of a loosely defined pro-executive faction lacking the formal organization of a party.

Beyond these differences in political pressures which play upon the executive and the members of the legislative branch the structure of American legislative bodies poses still other obstacles to effective leadership by the chief executive. The fact that the Congress and all the state legislatures (except that of Nebraska) are set up on a bicameral basis adds to the difficulty a chief executive has in maintaining an effective liaison with his party or factional following in the legislative branch. His influence as leader may be strong in one branch but count for little in the other.

Nonconcurrence of the President's term of office with that of members of Congress adds to the hazards confronting him in maintaining party leadership in that body. A newly chosen President is usually able to carry into office with him a party majority of the House and Senate, even though only one-third of the latter are elected at the same time.[25] Since 1888 there have been only two occasions when a

24 See on this general subject the very illuminating study by James M. Burns, *The Deadlock of Democracy: Four-Party Politics in America* (Englewood Cliffs, N.J.: Prentice-Hall, 1963), especially Chap. 10. See also Willmoore F. Kendall, "The Two Majorities," *Midwest Journal of Political Science*, Vol. IV (November, 1960), pp. 317–345; and Polsby and Wildavsky, *op. cit.*, Chap. V.

25 The extent to which a presidential candidate is able to transfer his personal

President failed to carry into office with his election a majority in the House of Representatives. During the same period there was only one instance when he failed to carry with him a party majority in the Senate. The Eisenhower election of 1956 was the first in over a century in which the party that won the presidency failed to obtain a majority in either house of Congress. As a general rule, the President's party suffers a loss of congressional strength as a result of midterm elections; and not infrequently this erosion of strength goes so far as to put the opposition party in control of one or both houses. In seven of the nineteen midterm Congresses from 1890 to 1962 the President's party lost or failed to regain control of the House of Representatives; and in five of these elections his party lost or failed to regain control of the Senate. President Wilson in the second half of his second term (1919–1921), President Truman in the second half of his first term (1947–1949), and President Eisenhower during the second half of his first term and throughout his second term (1955–1961) were all confronted by Congresses controlled in both houses by the opposition party.

Conditions faced by many state governors in their partisan relations with their legislative bodies are, if anything, even more difficult than those faced by Presidents. This is true despite the fact that in about one third of the states one party is so dominant that undisputed control of the legislative branch by the governor's party is assured and despite the further fact that the two-year term for the governor still employed in some states eliminates the problem of change in the composition of the legislature during the course of a governor's term.

In some northeastern and midwestern states, because of gerrymandering practices tending generally to favor rural areas as against urban areas in the layout of legislative districts and a consequent imbalance in partisan composition of the legislature in relation to statewide partisan strength, a situation in which the governorship is controlled by one party and the legislature in whole or in part by the opposition has been almost chronic. In New York, for example, over the period from 1900 to 1950 the Democratic party controlled the governorship for 26 years and the Republicans for 24 years. Yet the Democratic governors had party majorities in both houses of the legislature during only two of their 26 years in office and control of one house for four other years.[26] In Michigan from 1933 to 1963, the Democratic party controlled the governorship 20 years in the 30-year

---

popularity to others running on the same ticket is questionable; but it is commonly assumed that such a transfer of support does occur. For an interesting analysis of election results suggesting that this assumption has less validity than has been generally accepted see Malcolm C. Moos, *Politics, Presidents and Coattails* (Baltimore: Johns Hopkins University Press, 1950).

[26] Ransone, *op. cit.*, p. 87.

span; but their governors had a party majority in both houses for only two years and a majority in one house for two additional years.

Taking all states into account in the period from 1930 to 1950, state governors had a party majority in both houses of their legislatures only about two-thirds of the time. Democratic governors tended to fare worse than their Republican counterparts in that they found themselves opposed by a partisan opposition majority in one or both houses of their legislatures about four times as often as Republican governors did.[27] It may be confidently expected that one of the major results of recent Supreme Court rulings holding that the Fourteenth Amendment requires observance of the principle of population equality in the layout of legislative districts[28] will be to reduce substantially the likelihood of partisan political disharmony between the executive and legislative branches at the state level. By putting checks on the gerrymandering of congressional districts the Court's rulings will also tend to produce a United States House of Representatives more amenable to presidential leadership by reducing the overall disparity between his constituent interests and those of the House membership, considered as a whole. When the impact of the Court's rulings in this sphere can be fully assessed it will no doubt be recognized that the "one man, one vote" principle enunciated by it was one of the most significant steps ever taken toward advancing the cause of responsible party government in the United States.

PROPOSED REFORMS OF THE PARTY SYSTEM

In view of the many obstacles confronting an American chief executive who seeks to exercise in full the functions of a responsible party head, the question inevitably arises whether changes in the system of party government should be introduced looking toward a more responsive, responsible, and disciplined type of party under the leadership of the chief executive. Students of the American party system have devoted much attention to this subject in recent years. In general, two opposing schools of thought seem to have emerged. On the one hand there are those who accept as fundamental the views on the nature of politics set forth by Madison in his famous Number 10 of *The Federalist* essays. According to this view it is necessary in a

[27] *Ibid.*, pp. 188–189.

[28] *Baker* v. *Carr*, 369 U.S. 186 (1962); *Gray* v. *Sanders* 372 U.S. 368 1963); *Reynolds* v. *Sims*, 377 U.S. 533 (1964) and accompanying cases. In *Wesberry* v. *Sanders*, 376 U.S. 1 (1964), the Court held that the principle of popular representation prescribed by Article I, Section 2, of the Constitution requires that members of the United States House of Representatives be elected from districts substantially equal in population.

republic with as many and as varied interests as there are in the United States to devise a system of representation, with built-in checks and counterchecks, in order to avoid the virulence of faction and the oppression of minorities by the stronger factions. According to these thinkers the essence of party government lies in obtaining a consensus on public policy issues by a process of debate, compromise, and accommodation of competing interests. The two-party system, with major parties made up of a wide variety of disparate interests bound together into loose coalitions, is the natural counterpart of an environment in which this set of conditions prevails.

Indeed, as one advocate of this school of thought has observed, one of the elements in the American system that has never been fully explored and appreciated is its built-in negative features; that is to say, its mechanisms for *avoidance* of action.[29] One of the secrets of success of the American democracy, according to his view, is its means for temporarily smothering demands for action on an issue upon which there is no workable compromise attainable for the moment because of extreme tensions. There must be ways by which political leaders and men in public office can avoid a tough problem and at the same time conceal the fact that they are doing so. The heterogeneous character of our two major parties and their lack of disciplined cohesiveness permit this to be done with some grace.

On the other side, political parties are viewed as vehicles for achievement of policy goals held in common by their respective members. Advocates of this point of view look to Thomas Jefferson and his theories of the political process for their inspiration;[30] but whether admittedly or not, their concept of party is akin to the ideologically based, policy-oriented parties along the lines of European models. According to this view, a political party is simply an instrument or vehicle for attaining agreed-upon public policy goals, but within the limits imposed by the democratic dogmas of respect for the rights of opponents or dissidents to organize, propagandize, and pursue their objectives also by peaceful persuasion. It follows that there should be a process within the party through which policy goals are agreed upon and a hierarchy of leadership through which discipline and cohesiveness is imposed upon those in posts of responsibility who may be reluctant to go along with the agreed-upon party line.

It is not the purpose here to explore the ramifications of this continuing debate about the nature of the American party system and American politics and what, if anything, should be done about it.[31]

[29] Charles S. Hyneman, "The American Lesson in Democratic Government," in *Government and the World Crisis* (Knoxville: University of Tennessee Press, 1962), pp. 18–19.

[30] Cf. Burns, *op. cit.*, Chap. 2.

[31] In addition to the works previously cited in footnotes 24 and 29 above,

The conclusion appears warranted, however, that reforms designed to strengthen the hand of the chief executive in his capacity as a responsible party leader, if they are to be realistic, must go beyond mere party government and institutions and reach into the fundamentals of the scheme of governmental organization itself. Proposals for changes touching only party organs and party practices do not go to the heart of the matter. So long as the present basic patterns of governmental structure are retained, chief executives will never be able to act in the full sense as responsible, fully effective party leaders. Federalism, separation of powers, bicameralism, the electoral college system, plurality elections, and checks and balances—devices which Madison viewed as necessary to enable the government to control itself —are the basic substructure for the system of party government also. The legislative committee system and a complex system of legislative rules and usages which fragment political power in legislative bodies reinforce this system of checks upon a majority. As they serve to diffuse responsibility in government itself, so do they serve to weaken and diffuse responsibility in party government and management as well. A unified, hierarchical pattern of party government built on the concept of highly ideologically oriented political parties simply does not fit in with the institutions of government presently found in this country.

Another consideration that must be weighed carefully before endorsing schemes for reform of party government by strengthening the role of the chief executive is the inherent conflict that exists between his roles of Chief of State and Party Chief. As Chief of State he has an obligation to serve as a symbol of unity, to speak and act for all the people without regard to party. His functioning as the head of a faction in competition with an opposing segment of political society is obviously incompatible, in some degree at least, with his role as Chief of State. But at the same time, the joining of these two roles in the same person's hands has an element of safety in it, for it tends to inhibit the carrying of either role to dangerous extremes. So long as there is a recognition that the Chief of State is also a party leader, with an opposition party or parties which he must tolerate and whose leaders in turn feel free to criticize and question his policies and acts, the likelihood that a power-hungry Chief of State might seek to con-

see on the general subject *Toward a More Responsible Two-Party System,* a Report of the Committee on Political Parties of the American Political Science Association (1950); E. E. Schattschneider, *Party Government* (New York: Holt, Rinehart and Winston 1942); Stephen K. Bailey, *The Condition of our National Political Parties* (New York: Fund for the Republic, 1959); Austin Ranney and Willmoore Kendall, *Democracy and the American Party System* (New York: Harcourt, Brace & World, 1956); and Austin Ranney, *The Doctrine of Responsible Party Government* (Urbana: University of Illinois Press, 1954).

vert his office into a disguised dictatorship based upon some kind
of mystical *fuehrership* concept is minimized. A Chief of State exposed
to the slings and darts of an opposition party is not likely to develop
megalomania or become a demigod in the eyes of the public. His feet
of clay are always kept exposed by the opposition.

On the other hand, the realization that as Chief of State he has an
obligation to the whole state or nation transcending mere partisan
ends tends to temper his acts as Party Chief. He must be ever mindful
of his actions in terms of maintaining the integrity of the social and
political fabric he represents. For example, Woodrow Wilson's pre-
election appeal to the nation in 1918 to return to Washington a
Democratic Congress to support his hand in the impending peace
negotiations did his own party and the nation a disservice. It caused
much resentment among Republicans and independents who had
loyally supported his war measures and aims. When the people returned instead a Congress controlled in both branches by the opposition party the conditions were set for repudiation, on mere partisan
grounds, of the President's leadership in negotiating a satisfactory
peace settlement. A less doctrinaire, less partisan attitude on his part
might have averted an impasse that proved fateful to the nation and
the world.

Party government in a representative democratic system such as
ours is founded on the proposition that progress should be sought
through evolutionary processes, discussion and, frequently, compromise. The mandate given a chief executive and his party in the light
of all the issues that influence voter attitudes in an election is by no
means always clear.[32] A party leader may be in the situation an earnest
but simpleminded, uneducated farmer found himself in. He thought
he had received a call from on high to enter the ministry when he saw
illumined in the sky the letters "GPC," which he interpreted to mean,
"Go Preach Christ." A friend to whom he revealed his vision, knowing
his actual talents and shortcomings, asked "Are you sure about this?
Perhaps the letters meant 'Go Plow Corn.' "

Too complete a concentration of the powers of party leadership
in the hands of one man or a few men, along with too intense an
absorption in promoting what *he* or *they* perceive to be the party's
program, can inhibit the process of adjustment of conflicting points
of view. Democracies as well as dictatorships may suffer from a "cult
of personality." Party government, if it is to serve the ends of democracy, must itself be democratic. While fulfilling his role as Party Chief,
a chief executive will be wise to keep in mind his other roles as well.
As Woodrow Wilson put it before he became President, he should
stand "a little outside party" and insist upon recognition for the

[32] Cf. Polsby and Wildavsky, *op. cit.*, pp. 193–198.

"general opinion" as well.[33] He should not expect his own views or will always to be regarded as law within the councils of his party; nor should he assume that his party's having been given a mandate to govern necessarily means that every item in its platform has been given equal and specific endorsement by a majority of the voting public. In government under the two-party system there must always be room for difference of opinion and give-and-take compromise within a party itself on what its mandate to govern means.

[33] Woodrow Wilson, *Constitutional Government in the United States* (New York: Columbia University Press, 1908), p. 69.

10

LEGISLATOR-IN-CHIEF (PART 1)

Of the many hats the modern President or governor wears, in the general public's view that of "Legislator-in-Chief" stands out above all others. Informed popular judgments on the rival candidates are strongly influenced by the public policies they pledge themselves to carry out; and policy-making in large part involves action on the legislative front. Popular judgment on an incumbent's performance is based mainly upon the legislative product of his administration. Without fine discrimination and with a tendency to overlook or discount the difficulties under which the chief executive labors in trying to obtain legislative support for the measures he espouses, the public considers him to have been a successful chief executive if he has been able to translate into affirmative legislation programs calculated to serve the public interest and welfare.

The "strong" Presidents and governors, particularly those who have merited this designation since the turn of this century, have been those who have sensed this public mood and have sought with relative success to respond to it in discharging their duties. Theodore Roosevelt's success in obtaining enactment of a number of his "Square Deal" progressive economic and social regulatory measures, Woodrow Wilson's leadership in piloting through Congress the "New Freedom" measures of his first administration, and F. D. Roosevelt's initiation of his "New Deal" program of economic reforms would have warranted characterizing them as strong Presidents even if they had not used their powers in other ways to justify such an evaluation. President Lyndon Johnson's remarkable success during his first two years in office in obtaining legislative implementation of his "Great Society" program of domestic reforms has already assured him rating as a "strong" President, regardless of the rating his performance during the rest of his administration may warrant.

CONSTITUTIONAL FOUNDATIONS OF THE LEGISLATIVE LEADERSHIP ROLE

The modern conception of this aspect of the chief executive's role is a far cry from the views on his functions generally held when his office first took shape in the Revolutionary War-time state constitutions. A primary objective of early state constitution-makers was to establish the supremacy and independence of the legislative body. Its dependence upon the executive in any degree was thought to be dangerous to liberty. The result was an almost total exclusion of the executive from legislative affairs in the original state governmental plans. Except in New York and Massachusetts where a limited veto power was permitted to rest in the executive the position of the pre-1789 chief executive in legislative matters was largely that of a friendly bystander.

Adoption of the United States Constitution in 1789 heralded the beginning of a change in this generally held attitude of hostility toward executive participation in the legislative process. In line with practices then generally observed with reference to state governors, the Constitution placed upon the President the responsibility of giving Congress from time to time "information on the state of the Union" and recommending to its consideration such measures as he should deem "necessary and expedient." He was also authorized to convene both houses of Congress, or either of them singly, on "extraordinary occasions"; and in case of disagreement between the two houses on a time for adjournment, to "adjourn them to such time as he shall deem proper." Most important of all, he was made a direct participant in the legislative process by being given a qualified veto power over every "bill, order, resolution or vote to which the concurrence of the Senate and House may be necessary," except as to the time of adjournment.[1] Inclusion of a suspensive veto power was thought by the Framers to be a necessary and salutary check on a Congress which, in its popular branch particularly, might prove susceptible to factional pressures operating against the general interest. It was to be purely an instrument of negation, however, not a weapon for imposing the executive's will on Congress.[2]

These provisions, which have continued unchanged in the Constitution to the present, established the basic formula defining executive-legislative relationships in the legislative process under the separation of powers system. They have become a model for state governmental arrangements as well. Soon after adoption of the federal Constitution a trend began to incorporate similar provisions on this subject in state constitutions. By 1812, nearly one-half the states had adopted the idea of the executive veto; by 1860, 25 of the 33 states had adopted it; and by 1900, all but three of the 45 states had accepted it.[3] Currently only

[1] Art. I, Sec. 7.

[2] *Supra*, pp. 58–61. "The Superior weight and influence of the legislative body in a free government, and the hazard to the executive in a trial of strength with that body," predicted Hamilton, "afford a satisfactory security that the negative would generally be employed with great caution; and there would oftener be room for a charge of timidity than of rashness in the exercise of it." (*The Federalist*, No. 73.)

[3] Frank W. Prescott, "The Executive Veto in American States," *The Western Political Quarterly*, Vol. III (March, 1950), pp. 97–99.

North Carolina is without an executive veto provision in its constitution.

Inclined at first to include a weaker veto authority than was found in the federal model, during the last 75 years or so the states have exhibited a tendency to revise their original constitutional language in the direction of giving the governor a more powerful veto. In a number of states this trend has carried beyond the terms of the national model so as to make the governor's veto power even stronger than the President's in some particulars. Along with these changes there has been general acceptance of the other elements in the national constitutional formula for defining the executive's role in legislative matters. With reference to making legislative recommendations and exercising control over legislative sessions, governors in some states have been given an even stronger authority than that vested in the President.

Formal constitutional phraseology provides only the foundation upon which executive power in shaping the legislative product now rests. Here as in so many aspects of the office of chief executive constitutional prescriptions fall short of explaining the functioning realities. What the Framers perceived as a relatively minor role of the President has become one of his major roles. Formal constitutional language, to be sure, has been liberally construed by executives toward giving a wider range to their authority in this field; and legislative bodies themselves, as well as the courts, have acquiesced in these broad constructions for the most part. Legislatures have even reinforced and extended by statutory provisions the constitutional arrangements in some respects. Budgetary legislation placing in the executive's hands the responsibility for originating taxing and appropriations measures is an example. But the constitutional phraseology encompasses only some of the avenues and procedures through which a chief executive goes about discharging his duties and responsibilities as a Legislator-in-Chief. As much depends upon his use of the extralegal means available to him for shaping legislation as in his manipulation of the constitutional and statutory powers at his command. His role in this area, as in other phases of his office, is shaped and governed ultimately by his capacity to exert *influence* as well as by his exercise of prescriptive *power*. His ability to employ effectively the art of persuasion rather than of command, to mobilize and use the force of public opinion, to bargain and deal with individual legislators for their support, and, in general, to generate political energy and harness it to his objectives is the final measure of his success as a Legislator-in-Chief.

FILLING VACANCIES IN LEGISLATIVE SEATS

American chief executives have not been invested with a power comparable to that of the British King, who by conferring certain offices or titles upon those who have official favor can make them members of the House of Lords. The President has no constitutional authority to fill seats in Congress. Such influence as he has in this connection arises from his party leadership function. Under the terms of the United States Constitution as implemented by state legislative acts, state governors may, however, exercise powers of some significance in this area. The Seventeenth Amendment provides for issuance of writs of election by the state executive to fill vacancies in his state's representation in the Senate; but it contains the further proviso that "the Legislature of any State may empower the Executive thereof to make temporary appointment until the people fill the vacancies by election as the Legislature thereof may direct." Since House vacancies can be filled only by the elective process, the governor's authority over them reaches only to the question of deciding whether, in view of the time remaining in the expired term, it is expedient to call a special election for that purpose. State law may limit closely his discretion in this regard.

In filling Senate vacancies the power of the governor is a matter of some consequence. The usual practice in the states has been for the legislature to authorize the governor to make a temporary appointment to a vacant Senate seat, effective until the time of the next regular election, when a popular election for the unexpired portion of the term is made. If the governor is a member of a party other than that of the previous holder of the seat, his appointment of a temporary successor can cause a switch in party control of the seat and thereby conceivably affect the course of legislation in the Senate, particularly if there is a close party division there.

Moreover, by choosing a compliant temporary successor who agrees beforehand not to contest for the seat when the subsequent election is held, a governor who is ambitious for himself may facilitate his own eventual election to the post. On occasion, by prearrangement with their own potential successors in office, governors have resigned and accepted appointment to a vacant Senate seat at the hands of the succeeding governor. This maneuver sometimes backfires. There is a certain measure of popular resentment against a governor's elevating himself to the Senate by his own political bootstraps, so to speak. For example, Wyoming's Governor Hickey, a Democrat, resigned the governorship in 1960 and was immediately appointed by the succeeding governor to a vacancy in the Senate caused by the death of the Republican senator-elect. Hickey was defeated in a contest for the unexpired portion of the Senate term at the next election. Again, in 1963 Governor Edmondson of Oklahoma elevated himself to the Senate in this manner, but he was defeated in his party's primary in 1964 when he sought to win election to the Senate in his own right. Some states attempt to foreclose this use of the governorship as a springboard to the Senate by making a governor ineligible for election or appointment to the Senate during the term for which he was elected as governor and for a period of time thereafter. Such state laws or constitutional provisions are of doubtful constitutionality, since they seek to add to the provisions laid down by the United States Constitution defining eligibility for the Senate.[4]

In the states the general practice is to require that special elections be held to fill vacancies in state legislative seats. In a few instances, however, the governor may be authorized to make a temporary appointment, pending the election of a replacement. In Vermont (until 1961, when the system was changed) the governor could fill vacancies in the lower house of the legislature by appointment.

CONTROL OVER LEGISLATIVE SESSIONS

Current state and national constitutional provisions defining executive authority over the time of meeting of the legislative body represent the residue of powers originally vested in the British King with regard to sessions of Parliament. Colonial governors under the royal provincial and proprietary forms of government were given the authority to assemble, prorogue, and dissolve the colonial assemblies. But just as the King's powers to control sessions of Parliament had begun to be curtailed by law and usage following the seventeenth-century struggles between the Crown and Parliament, so had colonial governors' pore in this field suffered serious erosion through the enactment of colonial laws regulating the time of legislative sessions and requiring periodic assembly elections. The first state constitutions completed this process of legislative emancipation. Characteristically they included clauses requiring the election of members of the legislature at regular intervals and establishing the principle that it should meet periodically. Recognizing that emergencies might arise during a recess of the legislative body necessitating its reassem-

---

[4] The ruling of the Senate on August 13, 1964, upholding the seating of Pierre Salinger as a Senator from California by appointment of the governor would appear to be controlling. Salinger did not possess certain qualifications prescribed by California law for a Senator, but he met the standards prescribed by the United States Constitution.

bling before the appointed time, however, most of the Revolutionary War-time instruments of government conferred authority upon the governor, acting usually with the advice and consent of his executive council, to assemble the legislature in special session.

The arrangements incorporated into the United States Constitution on the matter of sessions of Congress were little more than an adaptation of current state constitutional plans to national practice. The Constitution specified that Congress was to meet at least once every year, on the first Monday in December unless the Congress should by law designate a different time for meeting. Beyond this, the President was authorized to convene the two houses on "extraordinary occasions." Even though the Senate was given the status of an executive council to advise with him on certain executive matters, its advice and consent was not made a condition for his exercise of this authority. He was explicitly empowered to assemble either house of Congress independently of the other if he so desired, an arrangement which has permitted him to convene the Senate alone from time to time to consider executive appointment and treaties.

USE OF SPECIAL SESSION CALLING AUTHORITY

In actual practice the President's power to convene both houses in special session has been employed relatively infrequently, even though the concept, an "extraordinary" occasion, is obviously elastic and interpreting it is left to the President's unfettered discretion. Up to 1964 this power had been employed 27 times. It was first used by President John Adams in 1797. Three weeks after taking office he issued a call for Congress to meet. He reported to it a rupture in diplomatic relations with the revolutionary government in France and recommended a number of measures intended to strengthen the land and naval forces of the country. Before 1861, when President Lincoln reluctantly assembled Congress for the momentous special session that began on July 4, only eight special sessions of Congress had been called.[5]

Following the Civil War use of the special session device became somewhat more frequent. One reason was that as originally arranged the time of regular congressional sessions did not permit a newly chosen President and his Congress to begin work immediately to implement the policies the electorate had endorsed in the election.

[5] In addition to the 1797 meeting in Adams' administration, there had been two sessions initiated by Jefferson, two by Madison, and one each in the administrations of Van Buren, Tyler, and Pierce. The call for the special session in Tyler's administration was actually issued by President W. H. Harrison, who died before Congress met. The total of eight special sessions does not include a number of special sessions of the Senate alone to consider executive business.

Their terms of office began on March 4 of the year following the November election, but since the regular annual sessions began on the first Monday in December, a newly chosen Congress ordinarily began its actual deliberations some 13 months after the voters had registered their verdict at the polls. In view of this circumstance, Presidents began to speed up action on major parts of their legislative program by assembling the new Congress in special session soon after the March 4 inauguration date.

From 1909 on the assembling of Congress in special session soon after a newly chosen President took office had become a regular practice. Presidents Taft in 1909, Wilson in 1913 and 1917, Harding in 1921, Hoover in 1929, and F. D. Roosevelt in 1933 all called special sessions to meet within a short time after they had taken office. Some of these sessions were particularly noteworthy in their results. In his first special session in 1913 Wilson set Congress to work immediately on such major tasks as tariff revision, currency and banking reform legislation, and strengthening the antitrust laws. By the end of the session through exercise of iron discipline over his party majority in Congress he had made substantial progress toward achievement of all his major objectives. His 1917 special session received his message asking for a declaration of war on Germany and at his behest began immediately to enact a sweeping program of war measures. The 1933 special session called by President Roosevelt—the famous "Hundred Days" session—resembled the 1913 Wilson session in its ready and rapid response to executive leadership; it began the New Deal program of major fiscal and economic reform that will always be associated with Franklin D. Roosevelt.

Adoption of the Twentieth Amendment in 1933, moving forward the beginning of the terms of office of members of Congress from March 4 to January 3 and specifying that the annual sessions of Congress shall begin on that day unless otherwise directed by Congress, has relieved a newly elected President of the necessity of exercising his authority to assemble Congress in special session to permit it to begin deliberations on his legislative program immediately. By the terms of the Amendment the time of induction into office of a President was also moved forward, from March 4 to January 20. Consequently, a newly inaugurated President now finds the Congress elected concurrently with him already in session and organized, ready to receive his recommendations.

By the same token, the Twentieth Amendment has deprived the President of the opportunity to refrain from using his session-calling power at the outset of his administration so as to leave himself free to set a policy to meet an emergency situation without reference to Congress. This strategy was employed by Lincoln when, confronted immediately by the secession crisis which he hoped to resolve by measures short of war, he delayed calling Congress into special session for three months. During this time the course of events dictated that he take the irrevocable step of meeting armed rebellion with force; and when Congress finally was convened the nation was already committed to war. President Andrew Johnson, who succeeded to office in 1865 shortly after Lincoln's second term had begun, attempted the same strategy of delay in the hope of using executive initiative to set a policy for reconstruction of the former Confederate states. Unlike Lincoln's 1861 Congress, Johnson's 1865 Congress when it ultimately met in December insisted upon undoing much of what he had done. It proceeded to enact, over his objections, a reconstruction program of its own devising. By adopting a new statute regulating the time of its meeting so as to hold itself technically in continuous session, the Congress, moreover, effectively deprived Johnson of further opportunity to carry on the government free from congressional supervision for the remainder of his term.[6]

However salutary they may be, the changes introduced by the Twentieth Amendment have by no means deprived of all significance the presidential power to call Congress into special session. It remains a potent threat in the President's hands to keep Congress at work and to compel it to make a record on the proposals he advances for consideration. The continuing potentialities of the power in the hands of a President willing to run the political risks of its use were well demonstrated during Truman's administration. In the November, 1946, midterm election of his first administration a host of frustrations and discontents engendered by the war resulted in a political reversal for the President's party. The Republicans gained control of both houses of the 80th Congress, which began its work in January, 1947. The President presented to it a many-sided economic and social reform program of domestic legislation, his so-called Fair Deal program; but the Congress was generally cold to these proposals. It recessed in late summer, subject to recall by the presiding officers and majority leaders of the two houses, without taking action on most of the items in his program. The President then used his authority to assemble Congress in extraordinary session beginning on November 17, 1947. His avowed purpose was to afford Congress an early start on its agenda of unfinished business so as to permit it to complete its work before adjournment in mid-1948 in time for the national party conventions and the presidential campaign.

Again the Congress showed little interest in taking affirmative action on his domestic reform proposals. Stalled in the legislative mill

[6] Wilfred F. Binkley, "The President as Chief Legislator," *The Annals of the American Academy of Political and Social Science,* Vol. 307 (September, 1956), p. 101.

when it again recessed in midsummer of 1948, subject to recall by the congressional leadership, were bills relating to such matters as broadening the social security system, a national health and medical care plan, federal aid to education, agricultural policy changes, new housing and resources conservation legislation, and a comprehensive civil rights program. The Republican convention met and nominated Governor Dewey of New York on a platform that promised action on these and other matters.

Meeting in convention in an atmosphere of division and defeatism, the Democrats nominated President Truman as their candidate. In his speech of acceptance in the early morning hours of July 15, he electrified what had been up to that point a dull and dispirited gathering of delegates by announcing dramatically his intention of calling Congress back into session. His purpose, he said, was to give the opposition party an opportunity before the 1948 election to enact at least a part of the program it had endorsed in its recently adopted platform. This, he maintained, could easily be done in a few weeks and would demonstrate whether the Republican congressional majority and its candidate were acting in good faith.[7] The ensuing July 26 ("Turnip Day") short session of Congress, as the President had shrewdly conjectured, failed to produce any significant legislative results. Thus the stage was set for the presidential campaign of 1948. Touring the country by train in a whistle-stop campaign, Truman hammered again and again on his themes—the insincerity of the campaign pledges of the opposition party and the "do-nothing" 80th Congress. The calling of the session of Congress was unquestionably a key move in the President's plan to highlight the issues of the campaign. The upset victory he achieved the following November was traceable in great measure to the bold use he had made of his power to put the opposition party in a difficult spot by keeping the nation's attention centered upon its congressional performance.

GOVERNORS AND SPECIAL LEGISLATIVE SESSIONS

All states vest in their governors a power to call extraordinary sessions of the state legislature; and in general the positive or negative use of this power is governed by the same kinds of considerations that apply in the case of the President and Congress. There are a number of differences between the governor's position in this matter and the President's that are worthy of note. Inasmuch as it is the usual state practice to provide by constitutional rule for the assembling of a newly chosen state legislature in January following the November elections and the meeting of the new legislature takes place at ap-

[7] *The New York Times,* July 15, 1948.

proximately the same time a newly elected governor takes office, the problem that was resolved by adoption of the Twentieth Amendment at the national level has not developed in the states. In adopting this Amendment, the nation was simply taking advantage of experience at the state level by eliminating the hiatus between the beginning of the chief executive's term and the initiation of his legislative program.

With regard to convening the legislative body in special session a variation of note from national practice is the explicit provision in the constitutions of a number of states vesting in the legislative membership concurrent power with the governor to reassemble the legislature before its regularly appointed time.[8] This "self-starting" arrangement has the obvious purpose of preventing the governor from keeping the legislature inactive for a time by not using his power to call a special session.

Taking its cue from this kind of state practice, Congress has sought to devise means for reassembling itself without having to depend on the President. Mindful of the precedent set in the Reconstruction era, the Republican-controlled 80th Congress under President Truman, fearing that some unexpected emergency might arise and that the President might refuse to reconvene Congress before the next regularly scheduled meeting time of January 3, terminated its first annual session of 1947 by recessing until January 2, 1948, rather than adjourning sine die. By the terms of the recess resolution the two houses could be reconvened by joint action of their presiding officers and the majority Floor Leaders.[9] As matters turned out it was President Truman rather than the congressional leadership who determined that Congress should reconvene before the next regularly scheduled meeting time. As already mentioned, he issued a call for a special session to meet in November, 1947. The opposition party leadership did not challenge his authority to reconvene the two houses; but resumption of its meeting by Congress gave rise to a technical question of some constitutional significance, that is, was the November, 1947, resumed meeting a termination of the recess by presidential request and a continuation of the same session; or was it a separate, "special"

8 In New Jersey a petition signed by a majority of the members of both houses may cause the legislature to assemble in extraordinary session. Similar plans under which a three-fifths majority of its members may cause the legislature to be reassembled are found in Georgia and New Mexico; and in Alaska, Arizona, and Louisiana a two-thirds majority of the members may do so. Hawaii's consitution has a unique provision under which the members of the legislature may reconvene to consider repassage of measures over the governor's veto following the end of a session, if they choose to do so. The *Model State Constitution* (6th ed., 1963) provides that a petition signed by a majority of the members of the legislature may cause the legislature to be convened in special session.

9 *Congressional Record,* 80th Congress, 1st Session, p. 10521. Inasmuch as the office of Vice President was vacant temporarily, the regular presiding officer of the Senate was its President pro tem, Senator Vandenberg of Michigan, a Republican.

session; or was it a "special" session called within the duration of a regular session? After some study the officers of the two houses decided that the resumption of meetings was a continuation of the original session, and not a separate, special session.[10]

This episode left unresolved the question whether the two houses, by recessing themselves for an indefinite period subject to recall by the presiding officers and/or the floor leadership of the majority party, can constitutionally reduce to a concurrent power, or even nullify altogether, the exclusive authority of the President to determine if conditions warrant reconvening Congress before its regularly appointed time. In any event the Congress always has the choice of nullifying the President's special session-calling authority by remaining continuously in active session throughout the year. This was the course the 78th Congress took during 1943 and 1944. It was in session continuously from January 3 until late in December each year, with only brief recesses for the November elections of 1944 and the usual holiday periods.

EXECUTIVE CONTROL OF THE LEGISLATIVE AGENDA

The most important difference from national practice in the matter of executive control over special sessions of state legislatures is in the constitutional provisions of about half the states that declare that when the legislature has been called into special meeting by the governor (or in some instances where there is a regular off-year session, normally limited to voting on budget matters) it may consider only those items of legislative action specified in his call. This type of provision is modified in a few states by an escape clause granting to the legislature the authority in such a case—by a special majority vote, usually two thirds of each house—to introduce items not mentioned in the governor's call. With or without such an escape clause, such provisions enhance a governor's authority over the legislature's agenda.[11]

---

[10] The President's proclamation concerning Congress was in the form of a conventional call for a special or "extraordinary" session. Cf. *Congressional Record,* 80th Congress, 1st Session, p. 10564. The ruling that the November meeting should be regarded as a resumption of the regular session, rather than a special session, was based upon an opinion by the Federal Law Section of the Library of Congress. *Ibid.,* p. 10576. The rationale of the opinion was that to regard the resumed meeting as a separate, special session would amount to a concession of power to the President to convert a recess of Congress into an adjournment, since he can initiate a new session only after termination of another. The same issue was involved when the July, 1948, pre-election short session was called by President Truman.

[11] Court rulings in two states have construed the legislative agenda-limiting authority of the governor authorized by the state constitution as not extending to the matter of impeachment and trial of the governor at a special session called by him for other purposes. See *Ferguson* v. *Maddox,* 114 Tex. 85, 263 S.W. 888 (1944) and *People ex rel. Robin* v. *Hayes,* 82 Misc. 165, 143 N.Y.S. 325, 163 App. Div. 725, 149

In any case it reinforces the influence the executive has over the business of a special session by spotlighting its purposes and bringing the force of public opinion into play to an unusual degree. A President who calls Congress into special session must take his chances on whether it will confine its attention to the matters he has in mind.

This agenda-setting authority of the governor assumes even greater significance if a state provides in its constitution a time limit on the duration of regular legislative sessions, or discourages lengthy sessions by providing for diminution or discontinuance of the per diem compensation of legislators after a specified number of days in regular, and, in some instances, in special, sessions. Resort to the special-session device more frequently than would ordinarily be the case is induced by such limitations on the legislature's freedom. This is especially so if the state constitution also provides, as approximately two thirds of them do, for only biennial regular sessions of the legislature. Under such conditions the agenda-limiting power of the governor over special sessions can become a powerful weapon in his hands. For a considerable part of the time the legislature finds itself working under a rule which permits the governor to confine its attention to tasks he sets for it. He cannot, of course, compel it to follow his recommendations; but he can force the legislature to go on record on particular issues in the full glare of public view.

A governor may even call a number of special sessions in succession, feeding each session only one item for consideration at a time and holding it in session until it has produced the desired result or has placed its members on record on the issue. For example in 1950 Governor Folsom of Alabama called five special sessions in the course of seven weeks in an attempt to induce legislative action on a number of measures, including legislative reapportionment.[12] Reactions of state legislators to such "strong-arm" tactics by governors have been understandably resentful. This has been a major factor accounting for successful legislative efforts in some states in recent years to bring about adoption of state constitutional amendments providing for regular annual sessions and removing limits on the duration of sessions. Annual sessions of indeterminate length not only give the legislature more time to deal with the increasing volume of business, free of the constrictive effects of the governor's agenda-setting authority. They also open the way for circumventing the governor's special session-calling power entirely by permitting the legislature to recess, subject to reconvening at the call of the legislature's leaders rather than to adjourn sine die. This device has been employed on several

N.Y.S. 250 (affirmed); 212 N.Y. 603, 106 N.E. 1041 (1913) (appeal dismissed). In both instances the governor involved was removed from office.
    [12] *The New York Times,* August 5, 1950, p. 28.

occasions by the Michigan legislature since 1950 when the governor-ship and the legislature have been under the control of opposing parties.

TERMINATION OF LEGISLATIVE SESSIONS

The authority of executives to resolve disagreements between the two houses of the legislative branch on the time of adjournment has proved to be of little consequence in American governmental practice. The presidential power of arbitration in this regard has never been used, but it remains in the background as a threat to make the two houses resolve differences that might arise on this point. President Jackson once vetoed a bill fixing the length of sessions of Congress, the veto in part being based on the point that the proposed statute, which would have required adjournment of the first, "long" session of Congress on the second Monday in May in the even numbered years, would infringe upon this constitutional prerogative of the President.[13]

Gubernatorial authority on this matter has likewise proved to be practically a dead letter, though it has been used in a few instances. In 1893 the governor of Rhode Island used his authority to adjourn the legislature for its entire term of one year as a result of an electoral dispute in which the governor himself was involved.[14] More recently, in 1949, Connecticut's Democratic governor, Chester Bowles, issued a proclamation terminating a special session of the legislature which he had called to consider certain taxation measures. The senate, which was controlled by the governor's party, had adopted an adjournment resolution; it abided by the governor's directive. The Republican majority in the house defied his proclamation and met in a "rump" session thereafter, attended by only the opposition members plus one member of the governor's party; it adopted a resolution condemning the governor's action as illegal. After taking action on other matters, it then adopted a resolution recessing the house indefinitely, subject to recall by its speaker. The issue did not reach the courts.[15] A somewhat similar affair occurred in Illinois in 1963. When Governor Kerner, a Democrat, issued a proclamation terminating a session of the legislature, the senate refused to comply for a time. The 34 Re-

[13] Cf. Richardson, *Messages and Papers of the Presidents,* Vol. III, p. 231.

[14] The legislature was required to meet for the purpose of canvassing the result of the previous year's elections. One of the two houses refused to convene, contending there had been fraud in the election. The governor adjourned the session of the house which had met, and his action in so doing was sustained by the Rhode Island Supreme Court. *In re the Legislative Adjournment,* 18 R.I. 824, 27 Atl. 324 (1893).

[15] Cf. *The New York Times,* July 1 and 7, 1949.

publican members of that body continued in a "rump" session and transacted further business, including the killing of a bill relating to harness racing that it had previously acted on favorably.[16] These episodes serve as reminders that executive-legislative conflicts of the sort that led to dissolution of parliamentary sessions by military force during the regimes of Charles I and Cromwell in seventeenth-century England may not have been entirely obviated by American constitutional arrangements.

MESSAGES AND RECOMMENDATIONS

The President's constitutionally imposed duty to report to the Congress from time to time on the state of the nation and to recommend legislation thought by him to be necessary and expedient embodies a practice of long standing with American chief executives. Under the colonial forms of government the governors exercised a similar function. Their addresses to their legislative bodies, in turn, were modelled upon the British King's "Speech from the Throne" delivered traditionally upon the assembling of a new session of Parliament. These contacts with the legislatures continued to be the practice after independence was declared, even though not specifically provided for in all the original state constitutions. The Framers of the Constitution had no qualms about including this duty in their outline of the constitutional functions of the President. Their decision to do so has had tremendous implications for the development of the modern conception of the President's office. Of all the Constitution's provisions aimed at defining the chief executive's relationship to the legislative organ of government, this one implies most directly that he should exercise an active, positive leadership role in the legislative process. If the term Legislator-in-Chief can now be properly applied to the President, it is largely because of the superstructure of usage and practice that has been erected on the foundation of this clause of the Constitution.

The manner in which the President should go about implementing this phase of his official duties was left by the Founders to the President's discretion. Writing on a clean page in this matter as in so many others, President Washington chose to keep his relationship with Congress on a somewhat distant, formal plane. On the occasion of his first inauguration, before a joint assembly of the two houses of Congress, he combined in one address his inaugural speech and a message to Congress. His recommendations for legislative action were very general in character, leaving to the good judgment of Congress

16 *The Detroit News,* June 30, 1963.

how it should go about implementing the new design of government under the Constitution.[17] Thereafter he established the practice of delivering in person an annual State of the Union address before a joint assembly of Congress at the outset of each regular session. Other written messages were directed to the respective houses from time to time dealing with more or less routine questions as they came up. A rather formal protocol was followed in connection with the annual message during the Washington and Adams administrations. After receiving the President's personally delivered report on the state of the Union, the two houses retired to their respective chambers and each proceeded to adopt a formal "Address in Reply" to his message, indicating its reaction to the President's comments. A committee was then selected by each House to present its "Reply" to the President, who then responded to each "Reply" with one of his own.

This elaborate protocol, reminiscent of British royal practice, was promptly discarded upon Jefferson's accession to office. Distrustful of high-toned practices which had been taking root under his Federalist predecessors, he chose to dispatch his first annual message in written form to be read before the respective houses. In an accompanying letter to the presiding officers he asked that the formality of a reply be dispensed with, pointing out as his reasons for the change his "regard to the convenience of the Legislature, to the economy of their time, to their relief from the embarrassment of immediate answers on subjects not yet fully before them, and to the benefits thence resulting to the public affairs."[18]

Jefferson's example was followed by his successors in the presidency, and for more than a century Presidents communicated officially with Congress only by written messages. But this usage was shattered in 1913 when President Wilson, having called a special session soon after his inauguration, startled Congress and the nation by appearing in person to deliver his message outlining his purposes in calling the legislators into session. Wilson was an admirer of Jefferson and entertained generally a Jeffersonian view of the legislative branch as the residing place of ultimate power in the American governmental sys-

---

[17] Richardson, *op. cit.*, Vol. I, pp. 52–53.

[18] Richardson, *op. cit.*, Vol. I, p. 325. Jefferson possessed a poor speaking voice and it is believed by some historians that his realization of that fact might have been a factor in his decision to resort to the written message. Whatever his reasons, he was very pleased with his idea. Writing to Benjamin Rush on December 20, a few weeks after the session of Congress began, he declared: "By sending a message instead of making a speech at the opening of the session I have prevented the bloody conflict to which the making of an answer would have committed them. They were consequently able to set into real business at once, without losing ten or twelve days in combatting an answer." Bernard Mayo, *Jefferson Himself* (Boston: Houghton Mifflin Company, 1942), p. 229.

tem. He explained his seemingly un-Jeffersonian act in terms indicative of a matured philosophy of the executive-legislative relationship which he was soon to apply in other ways as well:

> I am very glad indeed to have this opportunity to address the two houses directly, and to verify for myself the impression that the president of the United States is a person, not a mere department of the government hailing Congress from some isolated island of jealous power, sending messages, and not speaking naturally and with his own voice, that he is a human being trying to cooperate with other human beings in a common service. After this first experience I shall feel quite normal in all our dealings with one another.[19]

Later in the same session he addressed the two houses personally on other occasions for the purpose of presenting his views on particular subjects of legislation. Wilson's successors saw fit to follow his lead; personal delivery of the annual message as well as special messages, on occasion, has become an accepted feature of presidential behavior.

Where Wilson got the inspiration for his innovation is an intriguing question. The idea was, of course, entirely in keeping with his "prime ministership" conception of the President's role which he had espoused earlier in his Columbia University lectures on *Constitutional Government in the United States*. Yet nowhere in his writings before his assumption of the presidency had he advanced this particular thought. Wilson did not use the personally delivered message while governor of New Jersey, although he attended party legislative caucuses. A former Princeton student of his maintained that a newspaper reporter, Oliver P. Newman, suggested the idea to Wilson after his election.[20] Another possible source of inspiration was the example of Governor Robert La Follette of Wisconsin. At the beginning of his first term in 1901 La Follette had read his message to the legislature in order to "invest the whole matter [of his proposed legislative program] with a new seriousness and dignity that would not only affect the legislators themselves, but react upon the public mind."[21] Until revision of the New York constitution in 1821 the governors of that state delivered their messages to the legislature in person.[22] Whatever the source of the idea. Wilson was pleased with it. Later, having in mind his erstwhile rival who had himself raised the legislative leader-

---

[19] *Congressional Record,* 63rd Congress, 1st Session (1913), p. 130.

[20] David Lawrence, *The True Story of Woodrow Wilson* (New York: Doubleday & Company, 1924), pp. 81–83.

[21] Robert M. La Follette, *Autobiography* (Madison: Robert M. La Follette, 1913), p. 243; quoted in Leslie Lipson, *The American Governor: From Figurehead to Leader* (Chicago: University of Chicago Press, 1939), p. 51.

[22] See *Speeches of the Different Governors to the Legislature of the State of New York* (Albany: J. B. Van Steenburgh, 1825).

ship role of the President to new levels, he remarked gleefully to a friend that he had "put one over on Teddy."[23]

CURRENT SIGNIFICANCE OF EXECUTIVE MESSAGES AND
RECOMMENDATIONS

Superficially, Wilson's revival of the personally delivered communication to Congress was not of great consequence. Whether the President's messages are read by him in person or are read by a legislative clerk does not, in itself, give them a different content or make their reasoning more or less convincing. In what it symbolized, however, the personally delivered message was an important innovation. It was a highly visible milestone marking the line of progress of presidential participation in the legislative process.

First of all, it underscored in an arresting way the point that the President had come to play a positive role in planning and initiating a legislative program. It emphasized that from his position as head of the administrative bureaucracy with access to expert knowledge of the nation's condition, and in his capacity as spokesman for the people and of his party, he had ideas to which the legislative branch should pay heed. An increasing degree of involvement of the chief executive with legislative planning and leadership had been discernible on both the state and national fronts for some time before Wilson's historic break with precedent. His move served to direct attention to a constitutional development that had been gathering force under Presidents Cleveland, McKinley, and particularly Theodore Roosevelt. This was a development that had its counterpart at the state level in the same decades through the positive legislative leadership activities of state governors such as La Follette of Wisconsin, Hughes of New York, Johnson of California, and Wilson himself in New Jersey.[24]

In the second place, Wilson's innovation underlined another current aspect of the message device. This was that a presidential message is directed to the public at large, not merely to the members of the legislative branch. It is a report to the people on the state of the public welfare, an account of successes and failures in the government's policies, a description of the dangers and problems that lie ahead, and a suggestion of ways for meeting them. It seeks to inform, persuade, and arouse and, through the force of public opinion, to bring influence to bear upon legislators to support the President's proposals. This, again, was not a new view of its uses. Executive mes-

23 Richard P. Longaker, "Woodrow Wilson and the Presidency," in *The Philosophy and Policies of Woodrow Wilson*, Earl Latham, ed. (Chicago: University of Chicago Press, 1958), p. 73.
24 Cf. Lipson, *op. cit.*, pp. 50–55.

sages to the legislative branch have always had in some measure the character of appeals for public support. They have been instruments for public persuasion, even in written form; for they have usually been given widespread notice in the public press. But President Wilson's delivery of his message in person gave it a heightened effect in its impact on the public mind and in stimulating public discussion and debate. By defining more sharply in the public mind his party's policy program, the President was able to make a more effective appeal for rank-and-file party support for it. Later, the use of radio and, still later, of television in the presentation of the President's messages, giving him a listening and viewing audience of millions, added still more potency to the personally delivered message as an instrument of legislative leadership.

President Wilson's resort to the oral message device was accompanied by another consequential change of technique. Before his administration it had been the practice of the President to include in his annual message mention of all his major legislative recommendations for the year. With the expansion of the President's concern into many new sectors of the nation's economic and social life, the annual message had become a voluminous, scissors-and-paste catalogue of recommendations. It suffered because of its diffusiveness. President Taft had perceived this weakness and had sought to meet it by more extensive use of special messages to amplify his general recommendations in his annual messages.

Wilson, however, carried the matter a step further. He chose to shorten the annual message still more in the direction of making it a general statement of the lines along which he proposed to move. He then followed the annual message with a series of special messages, each devoted to a single major proposal. Thus each special message signalled the start of intensive effort toward a particular legislative goal, and as soon as one enterprise was fairly embarked on its way through the legislative course, another was launched. With each major proposal highlighted by a detailed message setting forth the President's ideas on how he wished to have Congress deal with a problem and answering objections in advance, the President was able to give a primary impetus to each major item on his legislative agenda.

This refinement of the message technique also facilitated resort by President Wilson in a more open manner to still another practice— the introduction of bills, drafted under presidential supervision, designed to carry out the chief executive's policies. In consultation with his party lieutenants in Congress, Wilson participated in formulating bills to carry out his major proposals. Participation by the chief executive in drafting bills was by no means a new idea when Woodrow Wilson assumed the presidency. In Washington's administration his

Secretary of the Treasury, Alexander Hamilton, who liked to think of himself as the administration's spokesman and as Washington's "prime minister," had, with his chief's blessing, collaborated directly with friendly members of Congress in planning measures to carry out policies favored by the administration.

Later Presidents, their departmental subordinates, or other trusted advisers and representatives had participated from time to time in the drafting and sponsorship of bills on major matters of public policy. Even Thomas Jefferson, who was critical of executive interference in the work of Congress and professed to believe that legislators should be left to carry out their responsibilities free from executive pressure, belied his own theories in practice. He sat in on party legislative caucuses and conferences and assisted in drafting bills. For example, the measure eventually adopted by Congress setting up the first civil government in the new Louisiana Purchase territory followed closely the outline of a Jefferson draft.[25] At the conclusion of the first session of Congress in his administration Jefferson was pleased to record that "The Legislature . . . have carried into execution, steadily almost, all the propositions submitted to them in my message."[26] In subsequent administrations the office of the Attorney General came to be relied upon particularly heavily by Presidents for assistance in drafting bills to implement their legislative recommendations.

Before Wilson's administration the tendency to broaden the President's function of recommending measures into a bill-originating prerogative had received its most powerful impetus under Theodore Roosevelt. One bill after another emanating from administration sources and bearing the President's seal of approval fell into the legislative hopper. Many of them were passed with little or no change. Commenting on this point during the course of debate on the Hepburn bill for amending the Interstate Commerce Act in 1906, Senator Dolliver of Iowa pointed out that there had been "at least five acts of legislation, all of them referring to this and similar questions, that were put through both houses of Congress in the last five years, practically without change, as they came from the office of the Attorney General."[27] What President Wilson did in originating drafts of bills embodying the administration's viewpoint was merely to do more openly what chief executives at both levels of government had been doing for some time. As governor in New Jersey he had partici-

25 George Fort Milton, *The Use of Presidential Power, 1789–1943* (Boston: Little, Brown and Company, 1945), p. 63.

26 Letter to Joel Barlow, May 3, 1802; quoted in Mayo, *op. cit.*, p. 230.

27 *Congressional Record*, 59th Congress, 1st Session (1906), p. 4777; quoted in Edward S. Corwin, *The President: Office and Powers*, 4th ed. (New York: New York University Press, 1957), p. 268.

pated actively in the formulation of a number of bills embodying his legislative program. The fact that the chief executive and his department heads lack the authority actually to introduce their draft bills formally into the legislative mill has never proved to be an obstacle of consequence, for friendly members of the legislative branch are always available to serve as "godfathers" for administration bills.

As might well be surmised, reactions of individual legislators to the chief executive's conversion of his message-giving authority into a legislative planning and bill-originating function have by no means been universally favorable. Appearance of a measure known to have originated in the administration tends inevitably to sharpen the antagonism of opposition party members to it. Indeed, under a system of responsible party government it is the duty of opposition party members, within reasonable limits, to oppose and criticize and thereby expose the weaknesses in measures proposed by the administration.[28] They tend instinctively to view an administration bill with suspicion. It "draws the party line," and in so doing it may easily suggest to them executive interference with the "constitutional" processes of law-making contrary to the traditions of the separation of powers system. Records of congressional debates abound with criticisms of executive "usurpation of legislative prerogatives," "dictatorial methods," and "bullying tactics."[29] Even the chief executive's own party colleagues have sometimes joined the chorus of disapproval.

Here again Wilson's administration was something of a watershed on the point of legislative reaction to executive initiation of measures. While legislative hostility to the idea by no means came to an end, it began to abate. To be sure, the succeeding administrations

[28] Recognizing the value of an alert opposition in the legislative process, Jefferson made the following observation in a letter to Joel Barlow on May 2, 1802, following the end of the first session of Congress in his administration: "Our majority in the House of Representatives has been about two to one; in the Senate, eighteen to fifteen. After another election it will be two to one in the Senate, and it would not be for the public good to have it greater. A respectable minority is useful as censors. . . ." (Quoted in Mayo, *op. cit.*, p. 230.)

[29] Typical of opposition party reactions to Theodore Roosevelt's aggressive tactics in legislative matters were the turgidly sarcastic remarks of Senator Rayner of Maryland in 1907: "Here we were day after day struggling with questions of constitutional law, as if we really had anything to do with their settlement, laboring under the vain delusion that we had a right to legislate; that we were an independent branch of the Government; that we were one department, and the Executive another, each with its separate and well-defined distinctions, imagining these things, and following a vision and a mirage, while the President was at work dominating the legislative will, interposing his offices into the law-making power, assuming legislative rights to a greater extent than he could possibly do if he were sitting here as a member of this body; dismembering the Constitution, and . . . adopting a system that practically blends and unites legislative and executive functions, a system that prevailed in many of the ancient governments that have forever gone to ruin. . . ." (*Congressional Record*, 59th Congress, 2nd Session [1907], p. 2008.)

of Harding (the advocate of a return to "normalcy" in the operations of government), Coolidge, and Hoover were characterized by a somewhat less aggressive performance than Wilson's had been. But with the passage of the Budgeting and Accounting Act of 1921 the Congress imposed upon the President the duty of presenting to Congress a comprehensive plan of proposed expenditures for the executive agencies, together with proposals he might think necessary for financing the government's operations. Similar "executive" budget systems began about the same time to be set up in the states, and by 1950 42 of the states either by law or constitutional provision had imposed this kind of duty on the governor. Since most substantive policy programs require fiscal support sooner or later, the concession of a fiscal planning responsibility to the executive has as a practical matter signified legislative acquiescence in executive initiation of substantive policy measures of national significance also. Enactment of the Full Employment Act of 1946,[30] which imposed on the President the responsibility for a coordinated plan of measures to keep the nation's economy in a state of good health, was a further concession by Congress that the President should take an active hand in proposing legislation.

So far has the attitude of legislators changed on the point of the executive's responsibility to initiate legislative proposals that a President or governor is now more likely to be criticized for failing to advance proposals than for doing so. For example, when President Truman assembled Congress in session in November, 1947, to ask for anti-inflation legislation, opposition members in Congress who had previously been in the forefront among critics of his predecessor for seeking to "usurp" legislative functions changed their tune and upbraided President Truman for not bringing forward a draft bill to carry out his recommendations. "If the President wants to tell the people that he stands for a certain thing," commented Senator Ferguson of Michigan, "he ought to come out with his proposal. He ought to come to the House and Senate with a message. And he ought to provide a bill if that is exactly what he wants."[31] In 1953 at the outset of the Eisenhower administration the Republican chairman of the House Committee on Foreign Affairs reportedly admonished an administration witness before his Committee, "Don't expect us to start from scratch on what you people want. That's not the way we do things here— *you* draft the bills and *we* work them over."[32]

[30] 60 *U.S. Stat. L.* 23. Section 3 (a) of the Act requires the President to submit an "Economic Report" within 60 days after the beginning of each regular session of Congress together with "such recommendations for legislation as he may deem necessary or desirable."

[31] Bertram M. Gross, *The Legislative Struggle* (New York: McGraw-Hill Book Company, 1953), p. 189; quoted from Homer Ferguson, "What is Your Congress Doing?" *University of Chicago Round Table*, No. 483, 1947, p. 4.

[32] Richard E. Neustadt, "Presidency and Legislation: Planning the President's Program," *American Political Science Review*, Vol. XLIX (December, 1955), p. 1015.

CENTRAL CLEARANCE OF LEGISLATIVE PROPOSALS

Assumption of responsibility by chief executives to initiate legislation has been accompanied by two other noteworthy developments in national administrative organization and procedures since 1920, namely, elaboration of executive staff personnel to facilitate this process and the establishment of machinery for central clearance of legislative proposals emanating from the executive branch.[33] A foundation for these developments at the national level was laid by the Budget and Accounting Act of June 10, 1921, recognizing the principle of executive responsibility for initiating a fiscal expenditures program each year. A Bureau of the Budget, functioning under a Director appointed by and accountable to the President, was created by this Act to carry out the task of budget preparation. On December 19 of that year President Harding, in a move suggested by the House Committee on Appropriations, issued Budget Circular 49. It directed in rather sweeping language that all agency proposals for legislation or expression of views on pending legislation that, if adopted, would create a charge upon the public treasury or commit the government to obligations which would later require appropriations, be submitted to the Budget Bureau before presentation to Congress. Subsequent modifications of this directive recognized the right of agencies to respond to congressional requests for "technical drafting services" without first obtaining Bureau clearance, it being understood that agency assistance rendered in this manner in connection with bill-drafting would carry with it no official endorsement of the measure concerned. This new system of central clearance of legislative proposals did not become fully operative until the Coolidge administration, and even then central clearance was conceived to be primarily an adjunct to the budgetary control function of the President.

Under President F. D. Roosevelt expansion of central clearance procedures to include review of agency proposals covering all matters of substantive policy was decreed. This was a step of vital significance, for by it the President made clear his intention "to protect not just his budget, but his prerogatives, his freedom of action, and his choice of policies, in an era of fast growing government and of determined presidential leadership."[34] In actual practice the system of central clearance fell short of the President's declared purpose, since a number of the really important Roosevelt administration bills, to say nothing of many minor ones, failed to pass through Budget Bureau clearance

[33] Cf. Richard E. Neustadt, "The Presidency and Legislation: The Growth of Central Clearance," *American Political Science Review*, Vol. XLVIII (September, 1954), pp. 643–644.

[34] *Ibid.*, p. 650.

machinery. President Roosevelt himself was partially responsible for this, since he utilized his own staff, particularly his Special Counsel, Judge Samuel Rosenman, to formulate some of his major proposals through channels bypassing the Budget Bureau machinery. Yet a major step had been taken. The point was further emphasized when the Budget Bureau, previously attached nominally to the Treasury Department, was made an integral part of the newly established Executive Office of the President by executive order in 1939. In that year the Legislative Reference Division of the Bureau processed agency reports on 2448 pending public bills during the course of only the first session of the 76th Congress.[35]

The exigencies of World War II caused these central clearance procedures to be temporarily suspended in part, but during the Truman and Eisenhower administrations they were re-established on a firmer basis than ever before. Adoption of the Full Employment Act of 1946 provided an added incentive for a more closely coordinated system of central legislative clearance. Beginning with preparations for the first session of the 80th Congress in 1947, President Truman gave the Legislative Reference Division of the Budget Bureau, working in close cooperation with presidential staff aids, the task of reviewing and coordinating into a comprehensive program all agency suggestions and recommendations. Formulation of a presidential legislative program thus became the end product of a careful audit of agency plans, reviewed and reduced into an integrated scheme conforming to the basic policy guidemarks set by the President himself. With his commitment to the "staff" system of operation arising from his military experience, President Eisenhower gave further support to the system of central review and clearance of his legislative program.[36] It would appear from these developments that the process of "institutionalization" of presidential functions, so characteristic of the mid-twentieth-century presidency generally, has been extended permanently into this area of operation of his office. The President's recommendation of measures to Congress has become the final, visible part of a vast and complicated bureaucratic operation involving many minds and reacting to a variety of conflicts and pressures emanating from within as well as from outside the administration.

ASSESSMENT OF RESULTS

The tangible results of executive initiation of legislation in terms of finished legislative product are not susceptible to exact measure-

35 *Ibid.*, p. 653.
36 See Neustadt, "Presidency and Legislation: Planning the President's Program," pp. 980–1021, for an analysis of developments in the first two years of the Eisenhower presidency.

ment; but the conclusion seems incontrovertible that executive influence is very great, at both the national and state levels.[37] A rough measurement of an executive's success in winning legislative support for his recommendations is often made by compilation of a "box score" at the end of a legislative session, showing the proportion of executive requests acted upon favorably as compared to those rejected or not acted upon.[38] "Box-score" averages of 90 percent success or higher have been achieved by governors in some states for a session's product, and achievement ratios of 50 percent or better are common. Such figures can be deceptive, however, in that they measure results quantitatively rather than qualitatively. All measures are counted as having equal weight in arriving at the final percentage; yet it may well be that relatively few of them constitute the major items in an executive's program.[39]

Again, not all administratively originated measures are promoted with the same degree of urgency by the chief executive. Even the bills to which the executive attaches the "must" label do not all have the same degree of high priority. Moreover, it is difficult to determine whether a particular bill passed, which may have been altered considerably during the course of its progress through the two chambers, reflects in its final form a victory for the executive even though it deals with a subject upon which he asked the legislature to act. For example, President Truman at the outset of the Korean War in 1950 asked Congress in a special message to strengthen national laws against espionage and to grant the Attorney General authority to exercise stricter control over aliens subject to deportation. Congress responded by passing the McCarran-Wood Act, which went much further than the President desired in tightening national internal security legislation. The President felt obliged to veto the measure. It was then passed by Congress over his objections. Should this bill have been counted in the "won" or "lost" column of Truman's record? Even if the executive approves a bill in its final form it may represent something quite different from what he desired.

Translation of an idea into a finished product in the form of a

[37] For an analysis of presidential influence upon the legislative product over the period from Theodore Roosevelt to F. D. Roosevelt see Lawrence H. Chamberlain, *The President, Congress and Legislation* (New York: Columbia University Press, 1946).

[38] *The Congressional Quarterly Almanac,* for example, in recent years has published regular analyses of the performance of Congress in response to presidential requests for legislation.

[39] Coleman B. Ransone, Jr., *The Office of Governor in the United States* (University, Ala.: University of Alabama Press, 1956), p. 79, notes, for example, that a recent governor of Vermont declared he had been successful on 22 of 27 recommendations for a session, but that the five measures defeated embraced the most important items in his program.

legislative enactment is a long and involved process. A multiplicity of complex, interacting pressures affects the fate of a bill embodying such an idea, of which support by the chief executive is only one.[40] A measure may have been proposed by the executive (as is often the case with individual legislators also) primarily for its political "window-dressing" effect, to cultivate favor with an interest group. Again, a bill on a given subject may be made a part of the executive's legislative program in the interest of political education and to stimulate public discussion. Approval is not expected to be obtained immediately. It is the planting of a seed that will not bear fruit until sufficient political pressure has been generated over a period of time, which may cover several years. Indeed, most measures of major importance usually have a gestation period of four or five years or even longer. For example, President Truman's ten-point civil rights program which he launched in 1948 was enacted in piecemeal fashion by laws passed in 1952, 1957, 1958, 1959, 1960, 1964 and 1965. A "medicare" plan tied to the Social Security system included in a program of public health measures recommended by him in a special message in 1945 was eventually enacted by Congress under President Lyndon Johnson's leadership in 1965.[41] A final judgment on whether a particular proposal from the executive branch will be given life in the form of legislation or will be buried forever cannot always be rendered at the end of the legislative session in which it first appeared.

Taking into account all these inadequacies of the "box score" as an accurate measurement of the results of executive initiation of legislative proposals, the actual figures are nevertheless impressive. The authority of the chief executive to "recommend such measures he deems necessary and expedient" has been translated into an important dynamic force in the scheme of executive-legislative relationships. From his position as the head of a vast "administrative lobby," in daily contact with individual members of the legislative body, its leaders, and its committees, the chief executive can exert strong influence in promoting or opposing legislative measures, as dictated by the policy objectives he has espoused. Through his power to recommend measures, he has become an influential working part of the legislative machinery.

[40] Cf. Gross, *op. cit.*, pp. 100–105, and William J. Keefe and Morris Ogul, *The American Legislative Process* (Englewood Cliffs, N. J.: Prentice-Hall, 1964), Ch. 11, for general appraisals of the executive's position in relation to legislation.

[41] See *The New York Times*, November 20, 1945, p. 20, for the Truman program. In a gesture of recognition of former President Truman's contribution to the final result, President Johnson carried out the signing ceremony at Truman's office in Independence, Missouri, and presented to him the pen used.

11

LEGISLATOR-IN-CHIEF (PART 2)

THE VETO POWER

The ultimate weapon in an American chief executive's legislative arsenal is his power to withhold his assent to measures passed by the legislative branch. The language of the Constitution defining the President's authority on this point was viewed with some doubts by many members of the 1787 Convention. On the one hand there were those, including Madison and James Wilson, who feared the power conferred would prove to be a nullity because either a President would lack courage to interpose his will against the formally expressed views of a majority of both houses or the legislators would pay scant regard and overpower him if he did so intervene. Others, such as Franklin, viewed the veto power with misgivings because they saw in it a revival of an executive prerogative shown by English and colonial experience to be susceptible to the uses of despotism.[1] In actual practice the President's veto power has proved to be a more potent instrument than Madison's doubts suggested; but at the same time it has not developed into the serious threat to democratic self-government that Franklin feared. It has been accepted as an essential element in the scheme of checks and balances, as shown by its eventual inclusion in the constitutional plans of all but one (North Carolina) of the 50 states.

THE VETO PROCESS

The phraseology of the United States Constitution was deliberately made quite specific on the manner of operation of the veto system. Within a 10-day period (Sundays excepted) following presentation of a measure to the President he must exercise any one of three options. He may (1) sign the measure, thus making it a law; (2) he may disapprove it by withholding his signature, that is, he may "veto" it; he then returns it to the house in which it originated, along with a message stating the reasons for withholding his approval,

[1] Chap. 2, pp. 58–61.

in which case if the two houses after reconsideration repass it by a two-thirds majority vote the measure becomes law despite his disapproval; or (3) he may do nothing about the measure, neither signing or disapproving it. In this event it becomes law without his signature at the expiration of the 10 days, if Congress is still in session. If it has adjourned in the meantime, so as to prevent his returning the measure to the house of origin with an expression of disapproval, his inaction causes it to be killed without further recourse, i.e., it is said to have been "pocket vetoed."

In actual practice, the exercise of this power is a more complicated process than the Constitution's language suggests. Although the time for presidential consideration of a measure officially begins with the delivery of the enrolled bill to his office, the actual process of study may well have begun long before. If it is a bill upon which the administrative clearance procedure outlined above has taken place a dossier will have been accumulated on it in the Legislative Reference Division of the Bureau of the Budget at the time of introduction. The President will have been kept apprised of its progress in Congress through direct contacts with party lieutenants there as well as through information supplied by members of his own staff assigned to legislative liaison duties.

In any event, receipt of the measure at the White House sets in motion a round of surveys of administrative reactions and opinion on it by interested agencies. Until the F. D. Roosevelt administration this was somewhat of a hit-and-miss operation, carried out under the President's immediate supervision or by a presidential staff aide acting more or less under presidential direction. Beginning with the Roosevelt administration steps were taken in the direction of placing this responsibility on the Legislative Reference Division of the Budget Bureau. Under Presidents Truman and Eisenhower this procedure became standard practice. After the solicited reactions and comments have been collected, Legislative Reference collates and summarizes the assembled materials and presents them to the President for his information and guidance. In the meantime the President himself, if the bill is controversial and of major importance, will have been subjected to a bombardment of views and opinions from various interest groups through telegrams, personal contacts by their representatives, letters, and editorials. The decision he finally renders reflects a judgment, based upon advice, solicited or unsolicited, from a host of people both within and without the administration as well as Congress. He sits, as it were, at the center of a hearing proceeding not unlike that conducted by a legislative committee.

The ultimate judgment must, of course, be his own; but to the extent that he is guided in it by his immediate staff, other trusted advisers, and the administrative agencies consulted, the decision to sign or veto may well reflect a collective administrative judgment rather than his own independent opinion. If his decision is to veto, the preparation of a draft veto message setting forth the grounds for disapproval is also usually a collective effort. Institutionalization of the veto authority has become a fact of political life in the operation of the presidency in much the same way the formulation of the President's legislative program has become a collective act.[2] Formalization of the process of veto clearance through the Budget machinery was carried to its ultimate height under President Eisenhower. To a much greater degree than his predecessors, Eisenhower was inclined to be guided on his use of the veto by the advice he received from his administrative team. The power was in his hands, but how it was used was largely governed by men who commanded his confidence and were highly placed in his councils.

SCOPE AND MANNER OF USE

Despite the careful attention given by the Convention of 1787 to the phrasing of the Constitution on the subject, a number of questions were left unresolved regarding the scope and nature of the President's power of negation over congressional acts. Most of the major ones have been resolved by usage, supported in some instances by Supreme Court rulings; others have not. The general trend has been in the direction of making the veto power a more potent instrument of legislative control than it might otherwise have been, but some of the omissions supplied have run in the opposite direction.

Two actions taken in the first Congress assembled under the Constitution which have become established practice looked in the direction of diminishing the presidential veto power. In deciding on the form of the enactng clause introducing every bill as proposed legislation, Congress adopted the form "Be it enacted by the Senate and House of Representatives of the United States of America in Congress Assembled" rather than a form which included reference to the President as a part of the lawmaking authority. This decision by Congress, while it has not prevented the President from becoming an effective part of the machinery through which legislative proposals become law, was nevertheless indicative of a jealous regard by Congress for its prerogatives. It was a congressional prejudgment on the place the

---

[2] Cf. Richard E. Neustadt, "Presidency and Legislation: The Growth of Central Clearance," *American Political Science Review*, Vol. XLVIII (September, 1954), pp. 654ff.

President's assent or disapproval was expected to have in the legislative process.

Of more lasting significance was the decision of the First Congress to exclude presidential participation in the formal submission of constitutional amendment proposals. Concerned that the Congress might seek to evade the presidential veto by resorting to some technical subterfuge, Madison at a late stage in the 1787 Convention's deliberations had sponsored the addition of a supplementary clause to Section 7 of Article I to make clear that the veto should apply to "every order, resolution or vote to which the concurrence of the Senate or House of Representatives may be necessary (except on a question of adjournment)." In spite of his precautionary move, the veto authority has been construed to apply to a somewhat more limited range of matters than this language would indicate.

Congress normally uses four types of vehicles for transaction of its business: (1) House and Senate "bills," for ordinary legislative acts, public and private; (2) "joint resolutions," which are used for dealing with legislative items of an unusual nature but have the same effect in law as do bills upon completion of the enacting process; (3) "concurrent resolutions," which deal with matters of organization, procedure, and opinion of concern to the two houses only, but which must have the assent of both houses to become effective; and (4) "House resolutions" and "Senate resolutions," dealing similarly with matters of concern to only one of the houses. House resolutions and Senate resolutions are required to have the approval only of the body wherein they are introduced. Such resolutions, as well as concurrent resolutions, have never been considered as falling within the range of the veto power, even though the latter are measures requiring the concurrence of both houses to become effective. All bills and joint resolutions are submitted to the President for approval or rejection, except for joint resolutions proposing constitutional amendments.

The bypassing of the President's veto authority on constitutional amendment proposals despite their being cast in the form of joint resolutions which require the concurrence of both houses was established during Washington's administration. None of the perfecting amendment proposals submitted to the states in 1790 out of which emerged the first 10 Bill of Rights amendments to the Constitution was submitted to President Washington for his approval. He made no protest himself, but the propriety of exempting this type of measure from the executive veto as applied to adoption of the Eleventh Amendment was questioned in the early case of *Hollingsworth* v. *Virginia*. Taking the view that the Congress in submitting amendment proposals was acting in its capacity as a constituent body rather than performing an ordinary legislative function, the Supreme Court refused to find the short-circuiting of presidential scrutiny of such measures to be unconstitutional.[3]

Other early understandings regarding the limited scope of veto authority of the President have not proved to be lasting. The view advanced in some congressional quarters that the veto power could reach only public, as opposed to private, bills was successfully challenged by President Grant, who vetoed 29 bills of the latter kind during his tenure, and by President Cleveland, most of whose more than 500 vetoes during his two terms were directed against individual pension and relief bills.[4] On the theory that levying taxes and appropriating money for public purposes are peculiarly legislative prerogatives—the "power of the purse"—some members of Congress have at times contended that all revenue and appropriation bills should be immune from the veto. This attempt to graft a limitation on the veto power by implication has not proved successful. Presidents Madison, Monroe, and Jackson all vetoed on constitutional grounds bills authorizing expenditures for various internal improvement projects, while President Hayes became the first President to veto a general appropriation measure on policy grounds. President Tyler vetoed two tariff revision bills during his administration, setting a precedent for executive veto of this type of revenue measure. President F. D. Roosevelt's veto of a general internal revenue revision bill in 1944 consigned to limbo the remaining vestige of this doctrine of implied limitation on the veto power.

This particular veto had important repercussions in another way. The strong language of President Roosevelt's veto message, in which he charged that in some of its parts the bill seemed to be designed to provide tax relief "not for the needy but for the greedy," stirred up a storm among members of Congress, particularly in the Senate. Senate Majority Leader Alben Barkley resigned his post in protest after a speech advocating passage of the bill over the veto. The bill was repassed by the necessary constitutional majorities in each house and became law. After the President had sent Barkley a letter explaining that he had not meant to impugn the integrity of any Senator and expressing confidence in Barkley's leadership, Senator Barkley permitted himself to be triumphantly re-elected to his post by his Democratic colleagues. His triumph may have been a costly one for him, however, for his short rebellion against his party chief eliminated

[3] Dallas 378 (1798). This early ruling was reaffirmed in a later decision of the Court, *Rhode Island* v. *Palmer*, 253 U.S. 350 (1920), relative to adoption of the Eighteenth Amendment. For some reason, however, the joint resolution that eventually became the Thirteenth Amendment was submitted to President Lincoln for his approval, and he signed it. Cf. Edward C. Mason, *The Veto Power* (Boston: Ginn and Company, Harvard Historical Monographs No. 1, 1890), p. 117.

[4] See Clarence A. Berdahl, "The President's Veto of Private Bills," *Political Science Quarterly*, Vol. LII (December, 1937), pp. 505–531. Presidents Madison and Buchanan had each vetoed two private bills earlier.

him as a possible vice presidential running mate with Roosevelt in the ensuing fall election. As events turned out Barkley, rather than his colleague, Senator Truman, might have become Roosevelt's successor in the presidency the next year.[5]

Opposed to the usages and interpretations that have had the effect of diminishing the scope of the presidential veto power stand a number of others that have given it increased strength. The proposition that the two-thirds majority required for overriding a presidential veto means two thirds of the members present and voting, provided they compose a quorum, rather than two thirds of the entire elected membership of each house, has been sustained by the Supreme Court as the constitutional rule on the basis of long-continued practice and understanding.[6] Nevertheless, comparatively few vetoes are ever overridden.

The constitutional requirement of a two-thirds majority vote in each house is a double barrier that is difficult to surmount. More often than not no attempt is even made in Congress to repass a bill over the President's veto. Up to the time of Lincoln's administration, it was the practice in Congress to put the question of repassage of every vetoed measure to a vote in the house to which it was returned. One measure vetoed by Lincoln was allowed to die with no further action, and from that time on the procedure of referring a vetoed bill to committee where in most cases it is pigeonholed became standard practice. No veto was overridden until a relatively innocuous bill relating to the construction of two revenue cutters was passed over President Tyler's objection in 1845. Less than 6 percent of all direct vetoes—73 out of a total of 1278 up to the end of 1963—have been overridden. It should be noted, however, that many of the bills that have been enacted over express presidential objection have been public bills of major significance. Included in this category have been such important measures as the Burnett Immigration Control Act of 1917 and the Volstead (National Prohibition) Act of 1919 passed over President Wilson's veto; the Soldiers' Bonus Payment Act of 1931, enacted over President Hoover's objection; the Taft-Hartley Labor Relations Act of 1947, the McCarran-Walter Immigration and Naturalization Act of 1952, and the McCarran-Wood Internal Security Act of 1950, all passed over President Truman's veto; and a series of acts dealing with reconstruction in the South, the admission of Nebraska as a state, the President's removal power, and the size and jurisdiction of the Supreme Court, all enacted over vetoes by President Andrew Johnson in 1866–1869.

A development of considerable consequence has been a broaden-

[5] Cf. Jack Bell, *The Splendid Misery* (Garden City, N.Y.: Doubleday & Company, 1960), p. 435.
[6] *Missouri Pacific Ry. Co.* v. *Kansas*, 248 U.S. 276 (1919).

ing of the potential scope of the pocket veto authority of the President. From the beginning, the power of the President to veto by inaction any bill presented to him within 10 days of an adjournment of Congress has been construed to apply at the end of *any* session, rather than only the end of the *last* session of a Congress. The understanding that the pocket veto does so apply was eventually challenged. The contention was made before the Supreme Court that a bill passed by Congress in 1926 and permitted to die by President Coolidge through a pocket veto had became law because of his inaction. The theory advanced was that since the same Congress that had passed the bill was to reconvene for another session, the President had not been prevented by adjournment from returning it unsigned to the house of origin, with his objections, if he wished to veto it. Since he had not done so, it was argued, the bill had become law without his approval. This contention was not accepted by the Court. It held that, in the light of long-established practice and understanding, adjournment of *any* session of Congress, not merely a final adjournment terminating the two-year existence of a Congress, brought into play the pocket veto authority of the President.[7] This construction of the constitutional language has had the effect of converting the veto authority into an absolute veto power over a considerable part of the legislative product, since no opportunity to override a pocket veto is given Congress. This is a matter of some consequence in view of the fact that of the approximately 2200 vetoes from 1789 to the end of 1963 more than 40 percent have been of the pocket variety.

Another comparatively recent constitutional interpretation giving the President more freedom in exercising his veto power is one relating to the 10-day period permitted him for consideration of bills. Before Wilson's administration it was the common practice for a President to sign all the measures he intended to approve before the end of the session in which they were passed. To facilitate presidential action on bills passed near the end of the session as well as to enable the President to be readily available for consultation with legislative leaders regarding last-minute decisions on pending bills, it was customary for the President to go to the Capitol on the last day of a session, where he stationed himself in the "President's Room" near the legislative chambers.

Feeling this practice was too constricting, President Wilson asked his Attorney General for an opinion on whether he might approve a bill within the specified 10-day period, even though he signed it after

[7] *Okanogan Indian Tribe v. United States,* 279 U.S. 655 (1929). A memorandum submitted by the Department of Justice in connection with the case revealed that up to 1928 there had been more than 400 instances of the use of the pocket veto, of which 119 came at the end of a session other than the final session of Congress. The pocket veto was first used by President Madison, it should be noted.

Congress had terminated its session. His Attorney General ruled in an opinion that he might.[8] Wilson applied this new rule, without challenge, on a number of bills at the end of the 1920 session of Congress. When President Hoover did the same thing after receiving an opinion from his Attorney General supporting his authority to do so, his action was questioned in a case brought to the Supreme Court. Observing that "no public interest would be conserved by the requirement of hurried and inconsiderate examination of bills in the closing hours of a session," the Court upheld his authority to so act.[9]

Also, the official time limit for presidential consideration of measures has been made more flexible by the practice of marking the beginning of the 10-day period from the time an enrolled bill is officially received at the White House, rather than from the day it is given final enrolled form by Congress and is signed by the presiding officers of the two houses. In 1919, when President Wilson left Washington to attend the Paris Peace Conference while Congress was in session, an adjustment was agreed upon to suit his convenience. Signatures were temporarily withheld from passed bills by the presiding officers in Congress until his return at midpoint of the Conference when the bills were then signed by them and presented for his consideration in the regular way. Congress was no longer in session when he returned to Paris for the final stages of the Conference. During the time of Wilson's temporary disablement by a severe stroke in 1919–1920, however, no adjustment of this kind was made; a total of 28 bills became law without the President's signature during this period through operation of the 10-day rule.

A very unusual procedure was involved in a veto by President Lyndon Johnson in 1964. On August 24 he returned to Congress with

---

[8] *Ops. of the Atty. Gen.*, Vol. 32, p. 225 (1920). It should be noted that President Lincoln had once signed a bill passed just before the expiration of his first Congress in March, 1863. He signed it on March 12, 1863. This was within the 10-day limit, but 8 days after the Congress which had passed it had gone out of existence. In the next Congress the House Committee on the Judiciary after making a study of the problem at the direction of the House concluded he had no authority to act affirmatively on bills after the expiration of a Congress. Cf. Charles F. Zinn, *The Veto Power of the President*, House Judiciary Committee Print (Washington: Government Printing Office: 1951), p. 19.

[9] *Edwards v. U.S.*, 286 U.S. 482 (1932). President Hoover's postsession signing of the bill in question, as in the case in Lincoln's administration, came after the Congress which had passed the bill had gone out of existence. The issue presented was therefore somewhat different from that raised by Wilson's signing of bills in 1920, since the Congress there involved was to meet again for its final regular session. According to a memorandum submitted by the Attorney General in connection with the *Edwards* case, between February 28 and March 4, 1931, 269 bills were presented to the President for his consideration, of which 184 were presented during the last 24 hours of the session. For comment on the problem see Zinn, *op. cit.*, pp. 19–20; and Lindsay Rogers, "The Power of the President to Sign Bills after Congress has Adjourned," *Yale Law Journal*, Vol. XXX (November, 1920), pp. 1–22.

a memorandum of "pocket veto," a bill sponsored by Senator Everett Dirksen of Illinois that authorized the United States Court of Claims to hear and resolve a specifically described suit against the government. The President's memorandum cited constitutional grounds for his refusal to sign the bill. On August 26, however, the President changed his mind (he wished to give the courts an opportunity to pass on the constitutionality of the act); he therefore "recalled" his veto and signed the bill. He had been able to consider the veto to be of the pocket type because Congress was in temporary recess from August 21 to 31 to permit its Democratic members to attend the party's national convention.

While these incidents demonstrate that the Congress by following a course designed to suit the convenience of the President or by not doing so may affect his opportunity to use the veto authority, a number of important procedural questions remain unsettled. It has been suggested by a close student of the problem that Congress should resolve these questions by adoption of a clarifying statute spelling out in detail its view of how the constitutional phraseology should be applied in relation to them.[10] So far this suggestion has fallen on deaf ears.

THE VETO AS AN INSTRUMENT FOR SHAPING POLICY

Undoubtedly the most notable development in connection with the veto power has been the change in presidential attitudes toward the purposes for which the President may interpose objection against a measure through a veto, or a threat of it. The first six Presidents employed the veto power very sparingly, and in some cases not at all. Washington vetoed only two bills, Madison seven, and Monroe one, while the two Adamses and Jefferson vetoed none. In the eyes of these

[10] Cf. Zinn, *op. cit.*, for a detailed analysis of procedural problems which remain unsettled. Among the questions he suggests should be clarified by such an implementing statute are: What shall constitute an official "presentation" of a measure to the President? How does the 10-day rule operate when there has been a change during the 10 days in the person occupying the presidency, as, for example, on January 20 at the beginning of a new President's term of office? What time limit, if any, shall govern the taking up of a vetoed bill for reconsideration in Congress? The Supreme Court has held that a temporary recess of the house of origin is not an "adjournment" preventing the return of a vetoed measure, if that house has designated an officer thereof to receive messages from the President during its recess. *Wright* v. *United States*, 302 U.S. 583 (1938). May the two houses acting in concert in this manner nullify the President's pocket veto authority altogether by regularly taking a recess of more than ten days immediately before a final adjournment? This is a procedure regularly followed by legislatures in some states, including Michigan and Kansas, to assure legislative opportunity to repass any bill vetoed by the governor. Frank W. Prescott, "The Executive Veto in American States," *The Western Political Quarterly*, Vol. III (March, 1950), p. 104. For other comment on questions relative to the presidential veto see Edward S. Corwin, *The President: Office and Powers*, 4th ed. (New York: New York University Press, 1957), pp. 280–281.

Presidents the veto was an instrument to be used to guard against infringement of constitutional limitations and guarantees rather than a means for imposing presidential public policy views on Congress. "From motives of respect to the Legislature (and I might add from my interpretation of the Constitution)," Washington wrote to Edmund Pendleton, "I gave my signature to many bills with which my judgment is at variance."[11] Jefferson was of the opinion that "unless the President's mind, on a view with everything which is urged for and against the bill, is tolerably clear that it is unauthorized by the Constitution— if the pro and con hangs so evenly as to balance his judgment—a just respect for the wisdom of the Legislature would naturally decide the balance in favor of their opinion."[12]

With Andrew Jackson the veto power began to take on a different character. He used the veto more frequently than any other President up to his time—he vetoed 12 bills in eight years, as compared with a total of 10 for all his six predecessors. Furthermore, by buttressing his objections not only with arguments derived from "constitutional principles" but also upon considerations of what he conceived to be sound public policy, he maintained that the veto authority gave the President a right and a responsibility to interpose his own judgment against that of Congress. So far as constitutional issues were concerned, moreover, he maintained that he was not even obliged to accept the pronouncements of the Supreme Court as binding. His famous Bank Veto Message of 1832, while it heavily emphasized alleged constitutional grounds for his disapproval, also advanced considerations of social and economic justice in defense of his action. It was a powerful appeal to the citizenry of the country for their support, a masterful campaign document for the forthcoming presidential election.

Jackson's "tribunative" view of the veto authority has been espoused and acted upon by most Presidents since his time. President Polk, faced by an increasing congressional restiveness reflected in a series of unsuccessful attempts to adopt a constitutional amendment weakening the veto or eliminating it altogether, felt it necessary to devote a considerable part of his last annual message to a defense of the Jacksonian concept of the veto as a viable element in the system of checks and balances.[13] It has come to be generally so regarded since that

11 Bertram M. Gross, *The Legislative Struggle* (New York: McGraw-Hill Book Company, 1953), p. 407, quoting Jared Sparks, *Writings of George Washington* (Auburn, N.Y.: Derby and Miller, 1851), Vol. X, p. 371.

12 Jefferson, *Writings,* Vol. V, p. 289.

13 Richardson, *Messages and Papers of the Presidents,* Vol. IV, pp. 662–670, and Leonard D. White, *The Jacksonians: A Study in Administrative History, 1829–1861* (New York: The Macmillan Company, 1954), pp. 28–33. Abraham Lincoln's view of the veto power and of authority to recommend legislation was in line with the earlier Washingtonian view. He declared: "By the Constitution the executive may recommend measures which he may think proper, and he

TABLE 3. *Presidential Vetoes, 1789–1963*

President[a]	Regular Vetoes	Pocket Vetoes	Total Vetoes	Vetoes Overridden
Washington	2	—	2	—
Madison	5	2	7	—
Monroe	1	—	1	—
Jackson	5	7	12	—
Tyler	6	3	9	1
Polk	2	1	3	—
Pierce	9	—	9	5
Buchanan	4	3	7	—
Lincoln	2	4	6	—
A. Johnson	21	8	29	15
Grant	45	49	94	4
Hayes	12	1	13	1
Arthur	4	8	12	1
Cleveland	304	109	413	2
B. Harrison	19	25	44	1
Cleveland	43	127	170	5
McKinley	6	36	42	—
T. Roosevelt	42	40	82	1
Taft	30	9	39	1
Wilson	33	11	44	6
Harding	5	1	6	—
Coolidge	20	30	50	4
Hoover	21	16	37	3
F. D. Roosevelt	372	261	633	9
Truman	180	70	250	12
Eisenhower	73	108	181	2
Kennedy	12	9	21	—
L. B. Johnson	0	2	2	—
Totals	1278	940	2218	73

[a] Presidents John Adams, Jefferson, John Q. Adams, Van Buren, Taylor, and Fillmore vetoed no bills during their terms; and Presidents W. H. Harrison and Garfield had no opportunity to exercise this power.

SOURCE: R. D. Hupman (compiler), *Presidential Vetoes, 1789–1961*, Office of the Secretary of the Senate (Washington: Government Printing Office, 1961), p. iv. Data on vetoes by Kennedy and L. B. Johnson are from the *Congressional Almanac*, 1963, p. 1020; *ibid.*, 1962, p. 923.

may veto those he thinks improper, and it is supposed that he may add to these certain indirect influences to affect the action of Congress. My political education strongly inclines me against a very free use of any of these means by the executive to control the legislation of the country. As a rule I think the Congress should originate as well as perfect its measures without external bias." John G. Nicolay and John Hay, *Complete Works of Abraham Lincoln* (New York: F. D. Tandy Company, 12 vols., 1905) Vol. I, p. 697. The two Whig Presidents, Taylor and Fillmore, did not exercise the veto power at all, and Lincoln vetoed only six measures.

time, as indicated by its general acceptance in state plans of government.

As shown by the accompanying table, the veto has been used with increasing frequency, particularly in recent years. Presidents F. D. Roosevelt (633), Truman (250), and Eisenhower (181) have accounted for approximately half the total number since 1789. They rank, respectively, first, third, and fourth in the list of Presidents in frequency of use of the veto, being approached or surpassed only by President Cleveland (583), who built up his unusual record largely by vetoing a great number of private pension and relief bills. The increase in recent years is partially accounted for, of course, by the greater number of bills that now reach the President, but the primary explanation is to be found in a changed attitude of Presidents toward the purposes the veto should serve. It should be pointed out that Eisenhower, who on most matters had a more limited "Whig" view of executive authority than his two immediate predecessors, had no reservations about using this instrument of executive power to promote those objectives of public policy he favored. At a press conference in 1959 he made the following revealing observation:

> By the Constitution, I am part of the legislative process. I think that the American public expects its President always to exercise his best judgment in giving his approval or disapproval or qualified approval or disapproval in such cases. That's exactly what I do. . . . I think it is a disservice to veto anything merely because it has failed in some detail to go along with the expressed views of the President. On the other hand, as quickly as it gets out of line I think the President is not doing his duty unless he does express disapproval.[14]

THE "QUALIFIED" VETO

Along with its forthright endorsement of the Jackson-Polk representative-at-large view of the President's responsibility in his use of his veto authority, President Eisenhower's statement suggests, by implication, other facets of this power which should be noted. Faced with an actual decision whether to sign or disapprove a measure, a President has a limited choice. He must go all the way in one direction or the other. Yet he may find a bill to be unsatisfactory only in part. As President Eisenhower put it, he may desire to give it only "qualified approval or disapproval." In this case he must weigh the risk of a veto and the likelihood of getting no legislation at all on the subject against the "half a loaf" of imperfect legislation at hand.

If his conclusion is that the shortcomings of a bill outweigh its merits so that a veto is called for, the procedure set up by the Con-

[14] Press Conference Transcript, June 17, 1959. *Public Papers of the Presidents: Dwight D. Eisenhower* (1959), p. 468.

stitution offers some further recourse. In returning the vetoed bill he must accompany it with a message stating the grounds for his disapproval. In the event the veto prevails, his message has pointed the way through which the two houses, by passing a new bill with the objectionable features altered or eliminated, can obtain presidential approval. Occasionally a veto message thus finally results in legislation that the President will accept. For example, in 1956, when President Eisenhower vetoed a farm price support bill and suggested in his veto message compromise terms between the policy he favored and that desired by the congressional majority, Congress eventually passed a measure that he could approve. On the other hand the President may choose to return a "hard" veto message, so sweeping in its condemnation as to offer no hope of compromise. In this event the veto message is likely to be addressed not so much to Congress as to the general public, in the expectation that it will draw the line on a basic issue of public policy. Jackson's veto of the Bank Bill was of this kind, as were Truman's vetoes of the 1946 Price Control Bill and the Taft-Hartley Labor Relations Bill of 1947. Eisenhower's veto of the Federal Employee Pay Raise Bill of 1960, one of the two vetoes of his administration to be overridden, was also of this character.

In this connection a recent resurrection of an earlier practice connected with pocket vetoed bills should be noted. The first two Presidents to use the pocket veto, Madison and Jackson, sent messages to Congress to be spread on its journals indicating their reasons for allowing bills to die by inaction at the close of sessions. This practice in time fell into disuse, beginning with the Lincoln and Grant administrations; F. D. Roosevelt, however, influenced no doubt by the practice of governors in New York with which he was familiar, reverted to it on occasion.[15] The advantage in his doing so is obvious. Even though the Congress has no opportunity to try to pass the bill over his objections, the "memorandum of disapproval" furnishes the legislators with guidance in the same way a regular veto message does, in case they should attempt to act again on the same subject.

When presented with a bill, if the President decides to sign it in spite of various objections he may have to parts of it, he may affix his

[15] In New York governors usually return all bills vetoed after adjournment of the legislature with either a "memorandum of disapproval" or a notation "veto without memorandum," depending on whether they wish to elaborate on their reasons for withholding their approval or not. Cf. Prescott, *op. cit.*, p. 104. President Roosevelt accompanied his first "memorandum of disapproval" in June, 1934, with a public statement saying that he had instituted the practice because he felt he should "take a more affirmative position" by giving his reasons for disapproval, rather than to allow the question to pass by default. Cf. R. D. Hupman, compiler, *Presidential Vetoes, 1789–1961*, Office of the Secretary of the Senate (Washington: Government Printing Office, 1961), p. 107. See also Clement E. Vose, "The Memorandum Pocket Veto," *Journal of Politics*, Vol. 26 (May, 1964), pp. 397–405.

signature (or let it become law without his signature if the time element permits) and at the same time issue a public statement or dispatch a message to Congress placing his reservations on record. Thus in signing the Emergency Housing and Rent Control Act of 1947, President Truman sent to Congress a message stating his belief that "its rent control provisions are plainly inadequate" and criticizing its housing provisions for veterans. "Had I withheld my signature," he continued, "national rent control would die tonight. . . . I have chosen the lesser of two evils."[16] Both Presidents Truman and Eisenhower carried the matter of qualified approval one step further. In signing the Hobbs Anti-Racketeering Act in 1946 and again, the Portal-to-Portal Pay Act of 1947, President Truman issued statements declaring that he had done so with the understanding, upon advice of his Attorney General, that the acts in question would not be given interpretations hostile to the legitimate interests and rights of labor.[17] His actions in these instances were not without precedent, as both Jackson and Tyler had expressed reservations in attaching their signatures to bills; they had, however, drawn critical comment from a House committee for doing so.[18] As noted elsewhere,[19] President F. D. Roosevelt in signing the Lend-Lease Bill of 1941 prepared a memorandum not made public at the time pointing out that he regarded certain provisions of the bill to be void on constitutional grounds.

Undoubtedly the most striking instances of presidential signature of bills with accompanying reservations and "advance interpretations" occurred in Eisenhower's term. When he signed the Mutual Security Act of 1959, which contained a clause requiring that any documents relating to the functioning of the Office of Inspector General and Comptroller, created by the Act, be furnished to the General Accounting Office or "to any duly authorized committee or subcommittee of Congress," he issued simultaneously the following statement:

[16] Gross, *op. cit.*, p. 405.

[17] *Ibid.*, p. 404.

[18] In 1830 Jackson interpolated a note over his signature to an internal improvements bill calling attention to his earlier communication to Congress on the subject. The message to which he referred explained that he wished to be understood as having approved the bill with the reservation that a road authorized by one section of the bill would not be extended beyond the limits of the Territory of Michigan. Later, after President Tyler had signed a bill and had sent to Congress a message explaining his reasons and understanding regarding it, a select committee of the House made a report (*House Report No. 909*, 27th Congress, 2nd Session) that was highly critical of the actions of both Presidents. It declared that President Jackson's action was in substance an approval of a bill together with an objection to one section of it, and was therefore unconstitutional. It also declared Tyler's attempt to qualify his signature to be unwarranted by the Constitution. Cf. Zinn, *The Veto Power of the President*, pp. 23–24.

[19] See Chap. 13, p. 430.

> I have signed the bill on the express premise that the three amend-
> ments relating to disclosure are not intended to alter and *cannot alter
> the recognized constitutional duty and power of the executive with
> respect to the disclosure of information, documents, and other materials.*
> Indeed, any other construction of these amendments would raise grave
> constitutional questions under the historic separation of powers doc-
> trine.[20]

A similar reservation of freedom of action relating to executive prerogative in maintaining secrecy of information in the public interest
accompanied Eisenhower's signature of the Availability of Information
Act of 1958.[21] The President's stated reservation in the latter instance
had the effect of reducing the Act itself to a mere pious wish, since its
whole object was to give by inference a right of access by Congress
to information in the hands of the chief executive's subordinates.

Whether the courts would feel obliged to attach weight to such
executive advance interpretations of legislative acts on the ground that
they form part of the legislative history of the acts remains to be seen.
It would appear to be impossible for them to discount such expressions
of presidential views entirely.[22] In any event, such statements qualifying presidential approval have a political value in that they place a
President on record and stake out for him a position for defense in case
of future attack.

THE THREAT OF VETO

A veto is negative in its effect so far as legislative action is concerned. When actually used it can only further a policy of inaction. It
maintains the status quo in terms of declared policy. Yet it also has

[20] *Public Papers of the Presidents: Dwight D. Eisenhower* (1959), p. 549.
(Italics added.)

[21] *Ibid.*, 1958, p. 601.

[22] Corwin, *op. cit.*, p. 283, advances the view that the courts will attach no
weight to such presidentially expressed reservations. His argument in support of
this view—that the President cannot "foist upon the houses intentions they never
entertained and thereby endow him with a legislative power not shared by Congress"—is equally valid as against assigning weight to statements made by any individual member or committee of Congress who may have voiced opinions on a
measure during the course of its passage. Members of Congress who vote for a
measure do not all necessarily entertain the same views on what its language
means. Zinn is of the opinion that such executive views expressed in connection
with the signing of a bill "would not be as persuasive as regular items of legislative
history but might be helpful as cumulative evidence of legislative intent if not
inconsistent with statements in the committee reports and other elements of the
history, including any Executive communication transmitting the proposed legisla-
lation to the Congress." *Op. cit.*, p. 24. The Supreme Court, it might be added, has
long since concluded that "the President when approving bills may be said to
participate in the enactment of laws." *La Abra Mining Co.* v. *United States,* 175
U.S. 423 (1899).

a positive side in helping to shape the legislative product. In its total effect upon legislation it may be compared to an iceberg. The visible part represents the instances of actual use. The submerged, invisible part, many times greater in bulk and importance, represents the influence exerted positively by the veto power upon the legislative product. The veto power complements and reinforces a President's authority to propose, with authority to reject. His messages permit him to place before the legislature affirmative suggestions and proposals defining the nature of the measures he desires and will approve. By telling Congress in advance what will cause him to use the veto weapon, he can define as closely as he thinks appropriate the limits beyond which he will not go in collaborating with Congress. Drawing a line in advance by a statement of what he will not accept by way of legislation on a given subject can thus positively affect legislative deliberations. The veto power can in this way be turned into a creative force.

Use of the threat of a veto to compel revision of legislative measures while they are in the formative stage has become a familiar feature of executive-legislative relations under the separation of powers system. The executive's anticipated response conditions legislative action throughout its range. "What will the President think of this idea?" is a question legislators must continually raise, and the answer does not always have to wait until the finished measure is presented to him for approval or rejection. An alert executive concerned about the legislative product will see to that. Warnings, implicitly or openly expressed by the President himself or conveyed through trusted spokesmen, can guide a measure into safe channels so as to avert executive disapproval. This advance voicing of disapproving views by the executive has become the inevitable result of wider choice in the exercise of the veto power just as the practice of submitting administrative drafts of bills has evolved from a practical view of the power to recommend measures for legislative consideration.

The threat of veto is a delicate and sensitive bargaining tool, however. It must be used with political skill if it is to produce the positive results desired by the executive. Unless a President is willing to allow an issue to advance to a showdown between himself and Congress, he will not box himself in by taking too uncompromising a stand on pending legislation. The legislative process involves reconciliation of opposing viewpoints at all stages, and a President must be willing to participate in a give-and-take way. The veto as a threat is usually most effective if it is voiced quietly and informally, through trusted emissaries, rather than openly and in public view.

The veto, or a threatened one, may even be used obliquely to produce a result desired by the executive; that is to say, he may use it as a punitive instrument to influence the vote of a wavering member of Congress on measures the executive thinks are of primary importance. By vetoing or threatening to veto relatively minor bills important to an individual legislator because of their local significance, the executive may seek to bring him into line on another legislative issue of national importance. A good example of the veto as a disciplinary weapon upon an individual member of Congress was its use by President F. D. Roosevelt against Senator Pat McCarran of Nevada. McCarran had taken a leading role in opposing the President's Court Reorganization bill and other measures making up the administration's legislative program in 1937. Three times between 1937 and 1940 Senator McCarran was successful in piloting through Congress a measure, urged by constituent groups in his state, to extend the provisions of the Federal Stolen Property Act to cover the transportation of stolen livestock across state lines; three times his bill met with a presidential veto. The President, with what could only have been a tongue-in-cheek attitude, in his veto messages solemnly cited as the grounds for disapproval the inadvisability of extending federal authority over such matters of local police power concern.[23] On the whole, a President will find that the threat of veto, as is true with all elements of his constitutional power, must be used with caution and circumspection. A too truculent, uncompromising voicing of his objections in advance on a legislative proposal may be treated by legislators as a challenge and lead them to take a more recalcitrant stand than they would if the issue had not been thrust upon them in so stark a fashion.

THE EXECUTIVE VETO IN THE STATES

A veto power similar in broad outline to that of the President is now given to the governor in all the states except North Carolina.[24] It is a suspensive veto authority, subject to reversal by a special vote in the legislature; and in general its use has developed along lines similar to those already described in connection with the presidency. The states have displayed some ingenuity and individuality in this matter in that they have introduced a number of variations from the federal pattern. Their innovations provide a store of practical experimental knowledge about the feasibility of various ideas advanced from time to time for improvement of this familiar feature of the scheme of checks and balances.

[23] Eventually Roosevelt relented and gave his approval to a bill of this character in 1941. Cf. 55 *Stat.* 631.
[24] Despite the lack of a veto power, North Carolina governors have proved to be fairly effective legislative leaders. Cf. Coleman B. Ransone, Jr., *The Office of Governor in the United States* (University, Ala.: University of Alabama Press, 1956), pp. 213–214.

Viewed as a whole, state constitutional arrangements and practices with respect to the executive veto present differences from the federal model in five major categories: (1) the length of time allowed for executive consideration of bills; (2) opportunity to veto by inaction; (3) the legislative majority necessary to override a veto; (4) the veto of parts or items of a bill; and (5) opportunity for the executive formally to make suggestions for changes in measures to eliminate his objections.

TIME FOR CONSIDERATION

On the matter of time for executive consideration, state constitutions provide periods ranging from three days to 15 days, if the legislature is still in session, as compared with the 10 days granted the President. Older state constitutional documents tend to set the shorter time periods of three, five, six, or seven days, while the more recently adopted ones are more likely to specify 10 or even 15 days. Of even greater significance in view of the fact that a large part of the major legislation is passed near the close of a session are clauses found in the constitutions of approximately half the states giving the governor an extra period of time, usually 15, 20, or 30 days, for decisions on the disposition of the mass of measures reaching his desk at that time. New Jersey's constitution of 1947 and Hawaii's constitution, adopted in 1959, provide a postsession period of 45 days for gubernatorial consideration.

The trend in state constitutional revisions is clearly in the direction of giving the executive more time for deliberation on legislation. This implies, of course, that he is expected to make a decision on the fate of a bill in the light of considerations of public policy and not merely its constitutional or technical aspects. It signifies that he is expected to operate as a "third house," as it were, in the legislative process. It assumes that he should have ample opportunity to consult with interested groups and individuals as well as with members of his administrative corps and affected local governmental representatives before he acts. At the national level the constricting effect of the time limit has been ameliorated to some extent, as has been pointed out, by liberalized interpretations of the existing constitutional phraseology. Confronted by a similar problem with the governor's veto, some of the states have dealt with it frankly by changing the constitutional ground rules.

THE POCKET VETO

On the other hand, the pocket veto has not found favor generally with the states. State constitutions follow the federal rule in declaring that failure of the executive to approve a bill within the regular time limit while the legislature is in session causes it to become law without his signature; but only about one third, mostly in states with older constitutions, specify that his failure to act upon a bill following the close of a legislative session shall cause it to die without recourse. The more common rule is that he must either sign all such bills or return them unsigned to the legislature with reasons given for his failure to approve them, thus giving the legislature an opportunity to pass them over his veto. Furthermore, in the states that permit a veto by inaction following adjournment of the legislature, in about half of them unsigned bills are returned with a memorandum of disapproval (which has recently become the practice at the national level). Requiring the executive to take positive action if he wishes to exert his veto authority reflects the more modern view of the true character of this executive power of disapproval. If the executive is to be recognized as an active participant in the legislative process he should be required to take a positive stand on all proposed legislation; and executive disapproval in every case should be subject to an overriding vote in the legislature. To make the veto, in effect, an absolute veto on part of the legislative product is not consistent with the basic theory of a suspensive veto as an element in the legislative process.

VOTE NECESSARY TO OVERRIDE A VETO

The key element in the executive veto power is the rule governing enactment of a vetoed bill on reconsideration by the legislature. When the older states first began the process of incorporating veto provisions into their constitutions, some of them were unwilling to follow the national model all the way on this point. The legislature in some states was authorized to override a veto by a simple majority vote in each house, or by a majority of all the members elected thereto, rather than by a two-thirds majority. A pronounced trend toward substitution of stronger provisions for these veto arrangements eventually developed in the states. The rule that a simple majority vote may override a veto has been abandoned everywhere, and less than a half dozen states retain the rule that a majority of the members elected in each house may do so. A two-thirds or a three-fifths majority is now the general requirement; furthermore, in a number of states with such requirements, either by specific constitutional language or by accepted practice this majority must be determined on the basis of the entire membership in each house, rather than on the number actually participating in the voting. Alaska's recently adopted constitution broke new ground by specifying a three-fourths legislative majority to override an executive veto of a revenue or an appropriation bill. The trend in state constitutional practice is clearly toward buttressing the governor's veto power even more strongly than the President's by making reversals more difficult on legislative reconsideration.

THE ITEM VETO

The most significant innovations by the states connected with the executive veto are the "item" veto and the "conditional" or "amendatory" veto. These innovations are intended to strengthen the governor's hand in controlling legislative extravagance in public expenditures; to combat use by the legislature of "riders" to compel executive acceptance of items objectionable to him through their inclusion in an otherwise unobjectionable and necessary measure; and to facilitate the elimination or revision of some parts of a bill found unsatisfactory by the governor so as to avert a veto of the whole measure.

A grant of authority to the executive to veto individual items in appropriation bills was first included in the temporary plan of government drawn up in 1861 for the southern Confederacy. After the Civil War it was included in the 1865 revision of the Georgia constitution; it quickly found favor among the states, and by 1960 it was included in some form in the constitutions of 41 states. In two of these, Washington and South Carolina, the item veto may be used against parts of any type of measure; in Oregon it may be used against the clause of any bill giving it immediate effect. In all the others its use is limited to items in appropriation bills. A few of these states, including Massachusetts, Pennsylvania, California, Tennessee, Hawaii, and Alaska, grant the governor the power of "partial item veto," i.e., authority to reduce by a veto a part of an appropriation for a particular purpose, as well as the power to veto separately the item altogether.

Touted as a device by which the executive may impose a check upon wasteful, "pork barrel" expenditures of public funds by legislators under local political pressures, the item veto idea has achieved a degree of support greater than its results probably warrant. Since 1873, when President Grant urged submission of a constitutional amendment granting an item veto authority to the President, it has been regularly urged upon Congress by Presidents, but Congress has failed to respond.[25] In actual practice the item veto authority over appropriations is rarely used with vigor by governors.[26] One reason for this is that legislatures have shown ingenuity in manipulating the

---

[25] See the remarks of Senator Keating of New York in connection with his introduction of an amendment proposal of this character in 1961. According to his statement, every President since Grant has urged adoption of such an amendment. President Eisenhower repeatedly endorsed the idea strongly, calling it "one of the most important corrections that could be made in our annual expenditure program, because it would save tax dollars." *Congressional Record,* 87th Congress, 1st Session, p. 9184.

[26] Cf. Prescott, *op. cit.,* pp. 105–108.

language of items in appropriation measures so as to consolidate objectionable and unobjectionable matter into the same clause.

The item veto, particularly where it may be used to reduce as well as to strike out appropriations for specific purposes, also serves as an invitation to legislators to vote appropriations for particular purposes in excess of projected revenues in the expectation that the executive will have to bear the political onus of disallowing them. Many fiscal administration authorities believe that the objectives sought by the item veto can be achieved more directly by adoption of a strong executive budget system under which a special majority vote in the legislative body is required to introduce items not recommended or to vote sums for particular purposes larger than those recommended in the executive's budget plan; by more extensive use of lump sum appropriations along with a grant of authority to the executive to withhold funds not found to be needed;[27] and by strict adherence by legislative bodies to a self-denying rule by which nongermane substantive legislation is excluded from appropriations bills.

THE AMENDATORY VETO

The "amendatory" or "conditional" veto, now provided for in the constitutions of four states—Alabama, Virginia, Massachusetts, and New Jersey—embodies the newest idea in state practice designed to meet the problem of resolving differences of views between the executive and the legislature on particular parts of a measure. The mechanics of the system differ somewhat in these states, but the central idea in all is that, if the governor finds certain sections or clauses of an otherwise acceptable measure to be unsatisfactory, he may return the bill to the legislature with suggested specific changes or amendments he wants incorporated. The legislature must first consider the question of accepting these changes before attempting to pass the bill over his veto or returning it to him for final consideration.[28]

[27] In 1938 the House of Representatives included an amendment in the Independent Offices Appropriations bill which would have authorized the President to eliminate or reduce specific items in appropriations bills, provided that his orders to this end would become effective unless disallowed by a concurrent resolution of the two houses within a stipulated time. In the Senate the amendment was deleted on the alleged ground of constitutional doubts. A similar proposal met the same fate in 1942. Corwin, *op. cit.*, p. 284. At various times after World War II Presidents Truman and Eisenhower informed Congress that military defense appropriations voted by Congress for particular items not requested in the executive budget would be "impounded" and not spent. This can be done when an appropriation bill is so worded as to constitute an authorization to spend up to a specified amount for a particular purpose, rather than a directive to spend a specified sum.

[28] Cf. Prescott, *op. cit.*, p. 105. In a few other states governors have employed the amendatory veto idea informally by returning a technically defective measure for legislative correction, rather than subjecting it to a veto necessitating introduc-

Studies made of the operation of the amendatory veto system reveal that a high proportion of the gubernatorial recommendations for changes have been accepted. In Alabama, for example, only seven out of 235 changes in the language of bills recommended by the governor were rejected by the legislature during the first 45 years of use of the plan. In Virginia also the governor's recommendations are almost invariably accepted. In Massachusetts and New Jersey the proportion of rejections has been somewhat higher, partly because amendments suggested by governors in those states have tended more frequently to deal with substantively important matters.[29]

Because the amendatory veto system can be extended to revenue and appropriation measures as well as to ordinary bills, it offers more than the item veto does as a means of reconciling differences between executive and legislative viewpoints. It seems to be one of the most promising avenues for revision of the veto system as an element in the presidential system of government. Legislative bodies, recognizing the potentialities of the amendatory veto as a weapon by which the executive can counter the use of "riders" and put legislators in the uncomfortable position of having to go on record on controversial issues, have not yet displayed any enthusiasm for such a plan by proposing consitutional amendments embodying it.

EXTENT OF USE

The extent of actual use of their veto authority by governors varies considerably from state to state. In some of them, the tradition is to treat the veto as a "gun behind the door," to be used very infrequently. In some legislative sessions in such states no bills whatever are disapproved by the governor. In other states it is not uncommon to have 10 to 25 percent, or even more, of all bills subjected to the veto. The average percentage of bills vetoed among all those passed in all states during a year appears to range between 5 and 7 percent, with the median percentage being 2 or 3 percent.[30] In New York, as the following table shows, the proportion of vetoed bills always runs relatively high, with changes in the political party situation in the legislature and the governship apparently making no great difference in the proportion of bills vetoed. New Jersey, Pennsylvania, and California

---

tion of a new bill which would have to go through the entire legislative process. Having become familiar with this procedure while governor of New York, President F. D. Roosevelt once employed it on a bill sent to him by Congress. Cf. Bennett M. Rich, *State Constitutions: The Governor* (New York: National Municipal League, State Constitutional Studies Project, No. 3, 1960), p. 22.

[29] Rich, *op. cit.*
[30] Prescott, *op. cit.*, p. 191.

TABLE 4. *Gubernatorial Vetoes in New York*
in Selected Years

Year	Governor	Total Vetoes	Percent of All Passed Bills
1913	Sulzer (D)	378	32.2
1928	Smith (D)	180	17.0
1931	Roosevelt (D)	343	31.0
1937	Lehman (D)	272	22.6
1947	Dewey (R)	329	26.4
1951	Dewey (R)	426	33.7
1965	Rockefeller (R)	567	34.5

SOURCE: Prescott, "The Executive Veto in American States," *The Western Political Quarterly,* Vol. III (March, 1950); Samuel R. Solomon, "The Governor as Legislator," *National Municipal Review,* Vol. XL (November, 1951), pp. 515–520; *The New York Times,* April 15, 1951, and July 25, 1965; and the *New York Legislative Manual* (1928), p. 637.

are other states in which the percentage of vetoed bills tends to run higher than the national average.

As with presidential vetoes, comparatively few gubernatorial vetoes are overridden. In 1947, for example, only 22 bills out of a total of 1253 vetoed in all the states (1.6 percent) were overridden.[31] Even bills which have passed the legislature by unanimous or near-unanimous vote rarely are passed over the governor's veto. The conclusion seems warranted that the special majority requirement for repassage is not so much a deterrent as is the fact that so many vetoes come after the legislature has completed its work for the session. Even though the governor may be required to return all vetoed measures to the legislature for action at its next session, or in a resumed session following a recess, the lapse of time between the veto and the opportunity for reconsideration seems to kill legislative interest in the fate of such bills.

THE POLITICS OF LEGISLATIVE LEADERSHIP BY THE EXECUTIVE

Assumption of a leadership role in legislative matters by the chief executive has resulted from a number of factors: popular election of the chief executive, the rise of parties and of party government, in-

[31] Prescott, *op. cit.,* p. 103. In New York the governor's veto has acquired an almost absolute character in that since 1927 more than 90 percent of governors' vetoes have been of the postsession variety which the legislature has no opportunity to override. Samuel R. Solomon, "The Governor as Legislator," *National Municipal Review,* Vol. XL (November, 1951), pp. 515–517.

creased activity of organized interest groups in American politics, the headlessness of the separated legislative branch, and the extension of governmental functions into new areas of the economy with a consequent increasing dependence upon bureaucratic sources for the origination of public policy proposals. Responding to these influences, American national and state chief executives have extended the use of the constitutional devices at their disposal to supply needed leadership and direction to the legislative organs of government. Whether they have actively sought this wider responsibility or not, it has been thrust upon them; and it demands an increasingly large part of their time and energy.

A politically-minded President or governor does not limit his efforts in the field of legislation to use of his formal constitutional powers. These provide merely a broad legitimizing base for his activities in this area. He makes his influence felt in other more quiet, informal, subtle ways than those suggested by the phraseology of the fundamental law. The value of informal techniques in persuading legislators to accept their points of view has by no means been a recent discovery by chief executives. More than a century ago, Justice Story, commenting on the undesirability of the usage excluding department heads from open participation in legislative deliberations, lamented:

> The Executive is compelled to resort to secret and unseen influences, to private interviews, and private arrangements, to accomplish its own appropriate purposes, instead of proposing and sustaining its own duties and measures by a bold and manly appeal to the nation in the face of its representatives.[32]

While the "stiff-bosomed, frock-coated approach to politics"[33] suggested by this comment still has a degree of popular support, and in some states there have even been attempts to crystallize it into a constitutional rule governing executive behavior.[34] the facts of political life dictate that a chief executive, if he is to have any hope of even partial success in directing legislative action, must go beyond the open, straightforward means of influencing legislation outlined by the phraseology of a constitution. He must utilize all the instruments of political persuasion and indirect pressure available to him. If his methods sometimes appear to idealists too suggestive of a hard-eyed ruthlessness bordering on the unethical, if not actually the illegal, it should be remembered that politics is a game in which the stakes are high. Those who participate must be prepared to take a realistic

[32] Joseph Story, *Commentaries on the Constitution*, 1st ed., 1833, Sec. 866, quoted in E. P. Herring, *Presidential Leadership* (New York: Holt, Rinehart and Winston, 1940), p. 46.

[33] Herring, *op. cit.*, p. 46.

[34] Cf. the following language from Art. IV, Sec. 11, of the constitution of South Dakota:

view of human nature and personal motivations and govern themselves accordingly.

Writing a few years before he became President and no doubt with the examples offered by the current President, Theodore Roosevelt, in his mind, Woodrow Wilson declared:

> There are illegitimate means by which the President may influence the action of Congress. He may bargain with members, not only with regard to appointments, but also with regard to legislative measures. He may use local patronage to assist members to get or retain their seats. He may interpose his powerful influence, in one covert way or another, in contests for places in the Senate. He may also overbear Congress by arbitrary acts which ignore the laws or virtually over-ride them. He may even substitute his own orders for acts of Congress which he wants but cannot get. Such things are not only deeply immoral, they are destructive of the fundamental understandings of constitutional government, and therefore, of constitutional government itself. . . . But the personal force of the President is perfectly constitutional to any extent to which he chooses to exercise it . . .[35]

But it was the same Woodrow Wilson who as President found it expedient to withhold the loaves and fishes of federal patronage from his fellow partisans in Congress pending action by them on certain key measures of his legislative program during the special session he assembled soon after taking office. And it was he who, having failed to secure congressional authorization for arming American merchant vessels for protection against German U-boats in 1917 before the United States entered World War I, took what his earlier statement had seemingly condemned as an "immoral" course—issuing an executive directive to carry this policy into effect.

> Any governor of this state who . . . gives, or offers, or promises his official influence in consideration that any member of the legislature shall give his official vote or influence on any particular side of any question or matter upon which he may be required to act in his official capacity, or who menaces any member by the threatened use of his veto power, or who offers or promises any member that he, the said governor, will appoint any particular person or persons to any office created or hereafter to be created, in consideration that any member shall give his official vote or influence on any matter pending . . . or who threatens any member that he, the said governor, will remove any person from any office with intent to in any manner influence the official action of said member, shall be punished in the manner now, or that may be hereafter provided by law, and upon conviction thereon shall forfeit all right to hold or exercise any office of trust or honor in this state.

Similar clauses are found in the constitutions of North Dakota and Wyoming.

[35] Woodrow Wilson, *Constitutional Government in the United States* (New York: Columbia University Press, 1908), p. 71.

INFORMAL METHODS OF LEGISLATIVE LEADERSHIP

The informal methods of legislative control employed by chief
executives fall for the most part under the headings of the "four p's":
public relations, party leadership, personal persuasion, and patronage. "Public relations" in its broad aspect has reference to all the
avenues and arts through which a President or governor maintains
contact with the general public (or at least with the well-organized
interest groups which carry political weight) and helps to inform the
public on issues of the day, thereby molding and mobilizing the great
forces of public opinion. The modes through which this contact with
the public is established and maintained—through personal appearances, office interviews with prominent citizens, letters, messages to
the legislature, radio and television "reports to the people" and "fire-
side chats," press releases and press conferences—have varied over the
years as new communications media have appeared,[36] but the essential purpose remains the same. If the chief executive can show
tangible proof in the form of telegrams, letters, and newspaper comment that he has widespread public support for his legislative measures,
the individual legislator will hesitate before risking his political life
by flying in the face of public opinion. Creating a favorable public
image of his policies is the greatest challenge a chief executive faces in
securing endorsement of his program from a legislative body. As
President Truman expressed it:

> The biggest problem facing any President is to sell the American
> people on a policy. They have to be led forward. It is not merely a
> matter of keeping your ear to the ground to find out what the American
> people are saying and then trying to please them.
>   You can hear one opinion on Grand Street and another on Balti-
> more Street. The President of the United States has to mold that opinion
> and lead it forward. That's the biggest challenge every President faces,
> and one which he cannot escape.[37]

The effectiveness of appeals for legislative support of his program
in his role as party leader, as has already been pointed out, depends
upon the circumstances of a given situation. Highly disciplined legislative party organizations, responding without demur to every appeal

---

[36] The best comprehensive study of presidential public relations covering all
Presidents down to Truman is James E. Pollard's *The Presidents and the Press*
(New York: The Macmillan Company, 1947). For other studies dealing particularly
with the press conference see Elmer E. Cornwell, Jr., "The Presidential Press Conference: A Study in Institutionalization," *Midwest Journal of Political Science,* Vol.
IV (November, 1960), pp. 370–389; and John Herling, "World's No. 1 Quiz Program," *The New York Times Magazine,* June 8, 1957.

[37] Interview as reported by Drew Pearson, *Detroit Free Press,* January 8, 1954.

for support from the chief executive in his capacity of ex officio chief of party, are not characteristic of American executive-legislative political relationships. Yet party ties and the resulting influence upon legislative behavior that can be generated by executive appeals for party loyalty do count for something. Unless there are strong constituency interests impelling him to do otherwise, a legislator who is a member of the same party as the chief executive will usually resolve doubts and minor reservations about a given measure in favor of going along with the administration's program.

Keeping the channels of communication open for personal contact with individual members of the legislative branch, particularly with those who occupy key positions in the legislative hierarchy, is a must for a chief executive. His accessibility for face-to-face interchange of views facilitates the search for common ground and mutual understanding, the planning of legislative strategy, and, on occasion, the soothing of ruffled feelings. Assignment of executive staff personnel to legislative liaison duties exclusively, a notable development in recent administrations, is an indication of the importance attached by Presidents to the maintenance of a readily available communications system between the executive office and members of Congress, but the top job of maintaining cordial relations with individual members of Congress cannot be delegated to others—it must remain with the President himself.

Periodic meetings at the White House between congressional party leaders and the President became so frequent and regular during the Truman and Eisenhower administrations as to suggest that a new institution, a "legislative cabinet" of sorts, is in process of development. During Theodore Roosevelt's administration, evening conferences in the President's study with Speaker Joe Cannon were a frequent occurrence. Wilson relied more upon contacts with the chairmen of committees that had under consideration legislation in which he was vitally interested. Coolidge introduced the practice of having a rotation of congressional guests for breakfast in the White House, but these were primarily social meetings rather than conferences on legislative matters. With the rise to importance of the majority and minority Floor Leaders in the two houses since World War I, along with an increasing influence of the Vice President as a policy adviser, the emphasis has tended to shift to conferences involving the "Big Four"—the Speaker of the House, the Vice President or the President pro tem of the Senate, and the majority Floor Leaders of the two houses. Control of both houses by the opposition party during the last six years of the Eisenhower administration brought about an awkward political situation and led to infrequent assembly of this particular group of legislative leaders. However, consultations by President Eisenhower with his own party's Floor Leaders and other important figures in the hierarchy of his own congressional party organization occurred on a regular basis.

The experience in the Eisenhower administration, to say nothing of the first two years of Truman's administration when he was likewise confronted by a Congress controlled in both houses by the opposition party, would suggest that it might be a wiser course to keep the composition of the President's "legislative cabinet" in a fluid state. The President should be allowed the freedom to choose the legislative leaders with whom he wishes to consult in the light of the particular situation before him. Nor has Congress, for that matter, shown any enthusiasm for proposals looking toward the establishment of some type of legislative council or legislative cabinet with a predetermined membership through which legislators' contacts with the executive would be channelled.

The fourth "p"—patronage—is the chief executive's stock in trade for influencing the individual legislator's vote. A voice in the selection of an appointee to office, consideration for the claims of his state or district in the allocation of public works projects or government contracts, a promise of special attention to the claim or suit of a legislator's constituent, exertion of administrative discretionary authority in a matter of concern to the legislator or his constituents —these are types of favors the chief executive may be in a position to grant in exchange for an individual legislator's vote. Distribution of the bounty of official favor by the executive in return for legislator's votes is not regarded with universal favor by the public; and such deals as may be made are not widely advertised. Moreover, the executive may find in patronage more woe than satisfaction. Long ago Louis XIV, appreciating this fact, sighed, "Every office I bestow creates for me ten enemies and one ingrate." The importance of patronage in influencing legislators' behavior can easily be exaggerated. But the executive soon finds that he must deal, to some extent at least, in the only common coin of the political market place or resign himself to more limited success for his legislative program than he would like.

EXECUTIVE LEADERSHIP AND REPRESENTATIVE GOVERNMENT

Participation by chief executives in the legislative process through full use of their constitutional powers, supplemented by informal or extralegal methods of applying pressure, has had a profound effect upon the character of American politics. Through the executive, political elements whose voice would otherwise count for little in policy matters are given representation. The President, operating as a representative-at-large for the whole nation, or a governor acting similarly in his state, brings to bear a political point of view on public issues not always adequately reflected in the legislature.

Because of the character of the individual state and district constituencies from which they are chosen, the members of Congress, collectively, tend to overrepresent the point of view of the essentially conservative, middle-class, rural, and small-town segments of American society. Even more so is this true of state legislatures because of apportionment schemes designed to underrepresent those parts of the population who reside in the larger cities and metropolitan areas. Elected by a procedure that gives all voters in a state an equal voice in his choice, a state governor will be inclined to respond more readily than the legislative branch does to the political demands of the urban elements in American society. In view of the manner of operation of the electoral vote system, the same can be said of the President. For these reasons Presidents and governors are more inclined than their legislative parties, as a rule, to promote legislation directed toward protecting the consumer interest rather than the producer interest, the wage earner rather than the employer, racial and nationality minority interests, and toward meeting the problems generated by an urbanized, industrialized economy generally. Thus the injection of a stronger influence from the executive side of government into the legislative policy-making process effects a balancing of interests which is healthy, fair, and sensible in an overall way. Viewpoints and significant political interests that would otherwise lack adequate representation in the decision-making processes often find their champion in the person of the chief executive.

All this is not to say that the executive always should be regarded as the advocate and defender of the general interest and general welfare and the legislative branch as reflecting only special, localized, short-view interests. The political elements holding the balance of power in state-wide elections do not enjoy a monopoly of political virtue. Given the two-party, statewide type of contest between rival candidates for the office of President or governor, it is the politically marginal voters, whatever their political inclinations, whose views the chief executive tends to reflect to a degree extending beyond their actual numbers and importance. In our democratic system of government the political process is essentially a struggle for power and preferment in which a great variety of organized interest groups play important roles. They have their respective citadels of power—in political parties, in the economic sphere, in the opinion-influencing media, in the legislative organizational hierarchy, and in the offices of chief executives. It would be unwise and unrealistic to assume that only those that can exert the greatest pressure upon the office of chief executive are necessarily those that should always be identified with the general welfare in all its aspects.

Association of chief executives, prone to respond to the pressures of key political elements in their larger constituencies, with legislators who in their individual capacities respond to various other combinations of key political elements in theirs necessitates the reaching of a consensus on public policy questions between the two branches of government. Normally the result at the present time is a chief executive pressing for a program of moderately progressive legislation to appeal to the people who recognize the problems of an urbanized, industrialized society in a shrunken world; and a legislative body, more reluctant to move and bound by an instinctive allegiance to the idea of maintaining the status quo, cherishing the ideals of a rural America, and preserving proved institutions and values. Out of the interchange between them there is likely to emerge something that more closely approaches the desideratum of promotion of the general welfare than would be the case if either side in the executive-legislative seesaw were made permanently and unchallengeably dominant.

12

CHIEF OF ADMINISTRATION (PART 1)

If there was any proposition upon which the Framers of the Constitution were in full agreement it was on the need for a national executive invested with a general "superintending" authority over day-to-day administration of the national government's operations. Experience under the Articles of Confederation had demonstrated that the Congress was unable to supply continuous direction and coordination of administrative agencies. Investment of the President with a constitutional responsibility to "take care that the laws shall be faithfully executed" was a provision agreed upon without controversy.

Yet it was by no means made clear by the language of the Constitution how far the Framers expected this duty of general supervision over administration to extend, or the degree to which it was to be subject to an overriding congressional control. To be sure, the generation that wrote and adopted the Constitution could have had no inkling of the vast size and complexity the administrative bureaucracy of the national government would come to have or the problems that would arise in directing and controlling it. In Washington's day a force of a few hundred civil servants was enough to carry on the administrative tasks of the national government. Now more than 2,500,000 civil officers and employees, to say nothing of about as many additional people in the armed forces, are needed. The national civil administrative establishment today employs almost as many people as there were in the total population of the country in 1789. The Department of Defense alone disposes of goods and services amounting to one twenty-fifth of the world's total product and about one tenth of the annual gross national product.

THE ADMINISTRATIVE FUNCTION: LEGISLATIVE
VS. EXECUTIVE CONTROL

Maintenance of effective control over this vast administrative bureaucracy presents American democracy with one of its most per-

sistent and serious challenges.[1] Constitutional arrangements are of
such a nature as to divide responsibility for control between the
legislative, executive, and judicial authorities. By the United States
Constitution the President's position as Chief of Administration is reinforced by a grant of broad appointive authority covering all the more
important categories of executive and judicial officers, but subject to
the advice and consent of the Senate. The opening clause of the executive article vesting the "executive power of the United States" in the
President is so phrased as to suggest an intent to place in his hands all
powers executive in character. It is followed by a clause imposing
on him a duty to "take care that the laws be faithfully executed."
Presumably this includes the powers for a general superintending
control over administrative agencies.

On the other hand, the enumeration of the specific subjects upon
which Congress may legislate, supplemented by a grant of authority
to "make all laws which shall be necessary and proper for carrying
into execution . . . powers vested by this Constitution in the government of the United States or in any officer or department thereof"
appears to be a clear reservation of authority to Congress to regulate
by law the manner in which the President should go about discharging duties placed in his hands by the Constitution. The stipulation
in the same article that no money may be withdrawn from the Treasury
except "in consequence of appropriations made by law" is a further
reinforcement of Congressional authority in the area of administration. Presumably Congress may pass laws to implement and, incidentally, to control and limit the President's discretion in carrying out his
functions as Chief of Administration.

The constitutional language concerning control over the administrative establishment and its operation is thus quite ambiguous.
Whether the Framers intended to invest the President with an independent authority beyond the range of congressional control or
intended him to function in this regard merely as the agent of Congress,
was, and remains, one of the enigmas of the Constitution. Do the laws
he must execute include congressional enactments that in his judgment
violate the oath required of him to "faithfully execute the office of
President of the United States" and to "preserve, protect and defend
the Constitution of the United States"? Do they include laws that in
his judgment invade his own constitutional prerogatives as chief
executive? The Constitution gives no answer to this riddle. Its arrange-

[1] On the general subject see Peter Woll, *American Bureaucracy* (New York:
W. W. Norton and Company, 1963); Charles S. Hyneman, *Bureaucracy in a Democracy* (New York: Harper & Row, 1950); George B. Galloway, *Congress: It Contemporary Role*, 3rd ed. (New York: New York University Press, 1961); and Joseph
P. Harris, *Congressional Control of Administration* (Washington: Brookings Institution, 1964).

ments seem rather to set the conditions for a never-ending tug-of-war between the President and Congress in the area of administration. It is not surprising that there has been a continuing necessity to work out understandings and adjustments between the two about their respective spheres of control over this phase of governmental operations.

The courts are called upon from time to time to resolve some of the controversies that arise in this sphere, but many of the issues of this kind are never referred to them. More commonly, accommodations are reached by the legislative and executive authorities themselves. The occasional bickerings over matters of administration and administrative policy that punctuate the relations between the two serve to emphasize that the making of adjustments between these two centers of political power is a continual process. Such adjustments, once achieved, tend to accumulate precedental weight as time passes, but they are not regarded as necessarily final in every instance. Like proverbial cats with nine lives, they return to disturb the harmony of presidential and congressional relations in administration after administration.

Under the separation of powers system the chief executive is commonly regarded as the head of the administrative organization. He is the "Chief of Administration" or "Chief Administrator." Broadly speaking, this is a proper characterization of his position. Except for the courts, a specialized branch of administration concerned with adjudication of disputes over application of the laws to concrete situations, most of the administrative agencies are placed in the executive branch. But their accountability to the chief executive and their subjection to his exclusive direction and control do not automatically follow from the mere fact that they are elements of the executive establishment. The chief executive's position as the head of the administrative organization is weakened and undermined in various ways. In most of the states various independently chosen department heads who function largely outside the range of his supervision are provided for, either by constitutional mandate or by statutory arrangement. Typically, a state constitution declares that the governor shall be invested with the "chief" executive authority, rather than "the" executive authority of the state, thereby implying that other independently chosen executive officers share the executive power with him. Furthermore, in all states the principle of decentralized administration is applied in some degree. Administration of many state laws and policies is entrusted in the first instance to locally chosen county, municipal, and special district officials over whom the governor's direct supervisory authority is usually quite minimal.

While these two characteristic features of the state administrative organization are not found in the national government, some of the elements comprising the national administrative system nevertheless occupy a semiautonomous status so far as control by the chief executive is concerned. This is in large part attributable to the sheer size and complexity of the administrative bureaucracy itself. It is physically impossible for one man to exercise continual day-to-day supervision of all elements of it. Some long-established national administrative agencies, of which the Army Corps of Engineers is an often-cited example,[2] have tended over the years to develop a way of life of their own and to acquire an immunity from executive control that is not spelled out in statutory terms. Having developed strong political ties with the clientele they serve and with powerful elements in Congress, they can mobilize these elements to successfully resist attempts from above to interfere with their established procedure and programs.

Congress has also resorted to setting up agencies outside the regular departmental scheme or organization with deliberate design to minimize presidential control over their operations. Beginning with the establishment of the three-member Civil Service Commission in 1883 to administer the provisions of the Pendleton Act, Congress inaugurated the practice of creating multiheaded, "independent" agencies headed by officials protected against executive influence by statutory limitations on his power of removal and by quite definite descriptions of their powers, procedures, and duties. Agencies of this kind now constitute an important part of the federal administrative scheme. Thus the administrative arrangements at the national level exhibit some of the features of independence from direct executive control that characterize administration at the state level.

The most significant limit upon the scope of the chief executive's role as Chief of Administration, however, is an insistence by legislative bodies upon keeping a share of the administrative powers in their own hands. By detailed statutory specifications as to organization, powers, procedures, and relationships of administrative agencies, the legislative branch places executive supervision of them under constraint. Indeed, the chief executive sometimes finds initiation of new statutes of this kind his most effective way of exerting an influence upon administrative subordinates. Legislative bodies themselves enforce accountability upon administrative agencies by such devices as the requiring of periodic reports, the use or threatened use of inquisitorial procedures, and simply public airing of complaints and criticisms. Reinforcing all these methods stands the legislature's power of the purse and beyond

2 Cf. Robert de Roos and Arthur A. Maass, "The Lobby That Can't Be Licked: Congress and the Army Engineers," *Harper's Magazine*, Vol. 199, No. 1191 (August, 1949), pp. 21–30.

that the power of life or death over the very existence of administrative agencies themselves.

Under these conditions it is clear that the headship of the chief executive over administration is a position that is shared with the legislative branch. While he stands closer to the administrative bureaucracy in the sense that it is an extension of the department over which he presides and that he bears a continuing responsibility to oversee its operations, he must recognize that administration is a phase of government that is also directed by and responsive to control from the legislative side of government as well. Here, as is the case with most of his own powers and duties, the chief executive finds that the essence of the separation of powers system is to be found in the "separateness" of the three branches in terms of their *personnel,* independence from one another in *tenure,* and in their characteristic *modes of action,* rather than in separateness of function. It is a system of *shared* powers rather than *separated* powers.

The justification for legislative involvement in the administrative processes of government is stated in terms of familiar *clichés.* Legislative intervention in administration tends to promote "democratic control" over government; it protects the public interest against the "evils of the bureaucratic spirit"; it is necessary to prevent "waste and extravagance in public expenditures"; it guarantees that there shall be "a government of laws and not of men." Defenders of executive independence from legislative interference in administration state their case in terms of such slogans as "promoting economy and efficiency in administration"; the need for "making power commensurate with responsibility"; the advantages in "flexibility" as opposed to "rigidity and legal formalism" in administrative organizaton and procedures; and the increasing necessity for reliance upon "administrative expertise" as opposed to "political meddling and favoritism" in carrying on the affairs of government under the conditions arising out of the complexities of modern society.

Whatever weight should be assigned to these respective claims, it should be noted that the entire governmental process may be viewed as consisting essentially of two basic elements—policy-making and the administration of policies. But "politics"—the determination of what policies government shall pursue—and "administration"—the execution of policies that have been set by the policy-makers—are inseparably intermingled. There is no sharp line defining where one leaves off and the other begins. While legislation involves heavy emphasis upon policy-making, and the administrative organs of government are primarily concerned with execution of policies rather than with determining what they shall be, there is participation in both phases of the governmental process by both branches. Especially in the higher levels of executive supervision and control of administration, policy-making is a major aspect of the operation. At the same time, legislators, responding to political pressures, continually concern themselves individually and collectively with specific details of purely adminis-trative operations that have little or nothing to do with policy in the broad sense of the term. As for the chief executive, as has been pointed out in preceding chapters, he has also become deeply involved in the process of legislation through which policies are determined. In-deed, one of the distinguishing marks of a strong President is his successful effort in shaping policy in this manner. But a strong execu-tive performs a major role in shaping policy through administration as well.

CREATING THE ADMINISTRATIVE ORGANIZATION

The first step in carrying out a governmental policy is the creation of an agency to administer it. The constitutional theory in both the nation and the states is that such administrative offices and establish-ments are to be brought into existence, normally, by legislative act rather than by executive order. The United States Constitution itself creates only the offices of President and Vice President in the executive branch and assigns to the latter only an ex officio function of a legisla-tive nature. The language of the "necessary and proper" clause indi-cates that beyond that point Congress may by statute elaborate upon the executive departmental substructure. The task of setting up an executive departmental scheme by law was perforce one of the first to occupy the attention of the First Congress in 1789. A Department of Foreign Affairs (the title of which was soon changed to the Department of State), a Treasury Department, and a Department of War, each headed by a secretary appointed by the President with the Senate's collaboration, along with a Post Office establishment and the office of Attorney General, were created.[3] Further changes and additions have been made by Congress from time to time as need has dictated. The same principle of reliance upon the legislature to give form to agencies of administration has been followed in the states, but direct provision in state constitutions for some of the major elements in the state administrative structure has served to limit somewhat the latitude of choice of the state legislatures.

[3] Cf. Leonard D. White, *The Federalists: A Study in Administrative History* (New York: The Macmillan Company, 1948), Chap. I; James Hart, *The American Presidency in Action, 1789* (New York: The Macmillan Company, 1948), Chap. VII.

CREATION OF OFFICES BY EXECUTIVE ACT

A relaxation of the principle of legislative creation in favor of giving the chief executive the initiative in shaping the administrative structure has marked the course of national governmental policy, particularly during the past three decades. At both levels of government initiation by the chief executive of legislative proposals looking toward the creation or reshaping of the administrative structure has always been regarded as an appropriate use of his prerogative to recommend measures for legislative consideration. Congress has also displayed a willingness to delegate authority to the President, either by implication or in specific terms, to determine administrative structural details in particular areas. For example, until 1855 Congress followed the practice of voting lump sum appropriations for maintaining American diplomatic and consular offices abroad, and leaving it to the President, subject to the confirmation power of the Senate, to designate the particular posts to be filled.[4] When Congress enacted the Lever Food and Fuel Control Act in 1917 it included language authorizing the President to "establish such agencies and to utilize such federal officers and employees as he may find necessary" to carry out the provisions of the law.[5] Similar broad grants of discretionary power over administrative arrangements were incorporated in the National Recovery Act of 1933, in the first Agricultural Adjustment Act of the same year, and in a great number of measures relating to the prosecution of World War II.

Presidents have also acted on their own authority from time to time to designate agents or establish agencies to assist them in carrying on their duties. The dispatching of "personal" emissaries abroad by the President to carry on highly confidential representational and information-gathering functions is a practice of long standing.[6] Presidential designation of eminent citizens to serve as members of special fact-finding and advisory boards likewise is a well-established practice. Presidents Washington, Jackson, Van Buren, and Tyler made use of such nonstatutory commissions, but not without some questioning by Congress of their authority to do so. When Theodore Roosevelt, whose enthusiasm for appointing volunteer unpaid civilian advisory commissions was practically unbounded, resorted to this device on an

[4]Joseph P. Harris, *The Advice and Consent of the Senate* (Berkeley: University of California Press, 1953), pp. 281 ff. Since 1855 Congress has designated the particular major diplomatic posts for which it makes appropriations, thereby giving inferential approval to their establishment.

[5] 40 *Stat.* 276, Act. of August 10, 1917.

[6] Harris, *The Advice and Consent of The Senate,* p. 284. On the general subject see Henry Wriston, *Executive Agents in American Foreign Relations* (Baltimore: Johns Hopkins Press, 1929).

unprecedented scale, he eventually so aroused the ire of Congress that it attached a rider to an appropriation act in 1909 undertaking to forbid further use of this technique because of its alleged unconstitutionality. Roosevelt signed the bill but announced his intention of ignoring the restrictive clause, maintaining with typical Rooseveltian asperity that Congress could not restrict the freedom of the President in seeking advice nor of interested citizens in giving such services to the government.[7] The Rooseveltian view has prevailed, and Presidents since his day have regularly made extensive use of their authority in this way.

Setting up agencies of this kind involves not so much executive creation of offices as delegation to trusted individuals of responsibility to widen the range of the President's vision and hearing. Sometimes this becomes a technique for delay and, eventually, evasion of a problem. A "study group" makes a report, it is duly noted, and then quietly shelved. A somewhat more official status was enjoyed by various nonstatutory offices, such as the War Industries Board and the Committee on Public Information established by President Wilson by executive order during World War I. Legally, they had advisory and recommendatory functions only, but they exercised real power because they had the prestige of presidential support. Similarly during World War II some of the war-spawned administrative agencies grouped under the heading of President Roosevelt's Office of Emergency Management had no direct statutory basis. They had authority as emanations of powers and functions vested in the President by law or by the Constitution and delegated by him.

ADMINISTRATIVE REORGANIZATION BY EXECUTIVE DIRECTIVE

Undoubtedly the most significant development in executive control over the administrative structure has been resort to the device of delegating power by statute to the President to reshape the administrative organization by executive directive, subject to a reservation of authority to Congress to reject such changes if it finds them objectionable. Legislation of this sort, which has been aptly described as a system of "legislation in reverse," reflects a recognition by Congress that the executive branch is better equipped than is Congress for initiating concrete changes in the administrative structure and that the need to effect such changes is a continuing one as the processes of government evolve with the times. It also carries with it implicitly a confession that congressmen have learned from experience that they cannot be counted

[7] Edward S. Corwin, *The President: Office and Powers,* 4th ed. (New York: New York University Press, 1957), pp. 71 and 360, n7.

on to resist the political pressures generated by established bureaucratic interests and their clienteles against proposed changes in their status when the issue has had to be faced in the first instance by Congress. It is politically more palatable to "pass the buck" to the executive to initiate such changes.

This new approach to the problem of keeping the administrative organization properly attuned to its tasks was an outgrowth of earlier, more limited, statutes dating from 1903 on under which Congress delegated authority to the President to effect changes by executive order in designated parts of the administration. During World War I, for example, President Wilson was authorized by the Overman Act of 1918 to reallocate functions among agencies concerned with prosecution of the war effort. In 1932, following a decade of fruitless attempts to achieve a comprehensive overhaul of the federal administrative structure by the usual route of congressional statute, Congress at the earnest request of President Hoover included in the Economy Act a provision authorizing the regrouping and consolidation of administrative agencies by executive order. Unlike the Overman Act, this statute provided that such presidential orders were to become effective within 60 days after presentation to Congress unless *disapproved* by a simple majority of either house within that period. President Hoover submitted a number of such executive orders late in 1932, but Congress rejected them all on the theory that the incoming Roosevelt administration should take the responsibility for making needed changes. On the day before Hoover left office, however, a grant of authority to the President to reorganize the administrative establishment by executive order was extended by Congress for a two-year period.

During the following two years eight major and 15 minor changes in administrative structure were initiated by President Roosevelt. Congress allowed them all to stand. The grant of power was allowed to lapse temporarily in 1935, but a new, feasible approach had been found for dealing with administrative reorganization. In 1939, following one of the major recommendations of President Roosevelt's Committee on Administrative Management in Government (the so-called "Brownlow Committee," a study group set up by presidential order in 1936 to survey national administrative organization and procedures) Congress passed a new Administrative Reorganization Act. This Act granted to the President the authority to initiate reorganization plans which would become effective within 60 days after presentation to Congress unless disapproved by a concurrent resolution passed within that time. The grant was again made effective for only a two-year period; but 21 specific administrative boards and commissions were exempted from its coverage. Except for relatively short periods of time since that date Presidents have, under varying conditions and restraints spelled out in similar statutes, enjoyed authority to initiate structural changes in the federal administrative establishment.

The most recent legislation on this subject had its origin in 1949. In 1947 Congress, with President Truman's enthusiastic approval, created a special 12-member Commission on Reorganization of the Executive Branch to make a comprehensive survey of the entire administrative scheme of the national government, which had become even more complex from assuming new functions during and after World War II. The President appointed former President Hoover to head the Commission. The Hoover Commission Report, presented in 1949, featured a recommendation that Congress confer authority permanently upon the President to carry out administrative reshufflings by the method prescribed in the 1939 Act, but with no exemption of any administrative agencies or departments.[8] Congress responded by passing the Administrative Reorganization Act of 1949, but the terms of the law fell somewhat short of the Commission's recommendations. A reorganizing authority was granted the President for four years, subject, of course, to possible renewal. Plans were to become effective within 60 days after submission to Congress unless disapproved within that time by a "constitutional" majority of *either* house (that is, by a majority vote based on the entire membership of the House or Senate), but no plan could create new functions of government. The 1949 Act went beyond the earlier ones, however, in that no agencies were exempted from coverage, and a reorganization plan could even go so far as to create a new department by regrouping existing agencies. It was also made clear that Congress retained the right to enact legislation in the ordinary way affecting the administrative organization. This Act was renewed for two-year periods in 1953, 1955, and 1957.

During the 10 years covered by this Act, as extended, Congress displayed increasing restiveness at the surrender of so much initiative to the President in areas many of its members thought were vital to congressional control of administrative policy. For one reason or another the House or the Senate rejected 12 of the 51 reorganizational plans submitted by President Truman and three of the 17 submitted by President Eisenhower under this arrangement. Each time the grant was extended during the Eisenhower administration, Congress firmly rejected presidential requests that it be made for an indefinite period and extended it instead for only two years at a stretch. In the 1957 renewal, moreover, the requirement for rejection of a presidential reorganization plan was lowered from a constitutional majority of one house to a simple majority, and efforts to exempt various agencies

---

[8] Commission on Organization of the Executive Branch of the Government (1949), *Concluding Report*, p. 8.

from its coverage were defeated only with some difficulty. Eventually, when renewal was proposed in 1959 it failed altogether in the Senate, and the grant of presidential authority was allowed to lapse.

In 1961, following a request from President Kennedy, presidential authority under the terms of the 1957 version of the law was again restored for a two-year period. Four of nine plans submitted by President Kennedy during 1961–1963 were rejected by Congress. One of those rejected, which would have created a new Cabinet-rank Department of Urban Affairs, was highly displeasing to some members of Congress. The President had put them in a difficult spot by submitting a reorganization plan in order to force a vote on this issue after regular bills proposing the same project had been quietly buried in committee in both Houses. A factor making for added political embarrassment for some members of Congress was the President's announced intention of placing Robert Weaver, the incumbent Director of the Federal Housing and Home Finance Agency, but also a Negro, in the post of Secretary of the new department.

In the 1963 act renewing the President's reorganizational authority for two more years[9] the House was careful not to allow itself to be caught in such a political trap again by including language specifically denying to the President authority to initiate plans proposing the creation of new departments of Cabinet rank. Accordingly, when President Lyndon B. Johnson in March, 1965, advanced a proposal to create a Department of Housing and Urban Development, he had to request that it be created by legislative act. A bill carrying out his recommendation was passed by Congress and signed into law by the President on September 9, 1965.

In the states the principle of legislative delegation of authority to the governor to initiate administrative structural reforms, with or without legislative review of such changes, has not yet been widely accepted, but significant beginnings have been made. A few of the states have followed the lead of Congress by adopting "little Hoover Commission" acts conferring a limited power of administrative reorganizational initiative upon the governor, subject to potential legislative veto, along the lines of the Administrative Reorganization Acts of the national government. In Michigan a revised state constitution adopted in 1963 broke new ground by giving constitutional status to the gover-

[9] Act of July 6, 1964, P.L. 88–351, 88th Congress, 2nd Session. Because this Act was not passed until a year after the 1961 two-year law expired, the President's reorganizational authority lapsed temporarily from June 1, 1963, to July 6, 1964. A bill extending the Reorganization Act for a three-and-one-half year period, through December, 31, 1968, was passed by Congress in 1965. Cf. *Congressional Record* (Daily, June 3, 1965), 89th Congress, 1st Session, pp. 11945–11950.

nor's power to effect reorganizational changes, subject to veto by con-current action of the two houses of the legislature.[10] Main reliance in the states has been on achieving administrative structural change by legislative act and in some cases by constitutional revision.

Inasmuch as state governors have usually taken very active roles in governmental reform movements of this character, they have gained credit for much of the progress the states have made during the past four or five decades. Successes in this line of endeavor have been a major factor in building up the reputations of many "strong" gover-nors, as in the cases of Governors Lowden of Illinois, Smith of New York, and Byrd of Virginia. The end result of state administrative reorganizations has usually been a strengthening of the position of the governor as the head of the state administrative system through the regrouping of agencies into a smaller, more manageable number of departments, extension of the governor's power of appointment of department heads, the creation of central managerial agencies for fiscal, property management and personnel administrative purposes, and enlargement of the governor's immediate office staff.

Although the trend at both national and state levels thus appears to be toward enlargement of the chief executive's powers and responsi-bilities in shaping the administrative establishment, the power to create, alter, and abolish administrative offices remains basically in the hands of the legislative branch. The conditions under which modern government must operate require that increased reliance be placed upon the executive to put into operation the recommendations of managerial experts in this sphere. Presidential reorganization plans, it should be noted, actually have their origin in studies and recommendations made by administrative management specialists in the Office of Management and Organization, one of the units of the Bureau of the Budget in the Executive Office of the President. As the functions of government reach into new areas the administrative bureaucracy necessarily grows in extent and complexity. With techno-logical changes constantly impinging on many fronts so as to affect administration, the need to keep it properly adjusted to the tasks before it becomes a matter of continuing concern. There must perforce be increased emphasis on flexibility. This flexibility can most satis-factorily be provided by allowing higher executive authority more latitude in adapting the administrative machinery to its task and responsibilities. Continuous study and audit of administrative organ-

---

[10] Constitution of Michigan, 1963, Art. V, Sec. 2. Michigan had been one of the few states which had earlier enacted a law of this general character. The 1963 version of the Model State Constitution incorporates the principle of assigning this kind of power to the governor. See *Model State Constitution* (1963), Art. V, Sec. 5.06 (Appendix D).

ization and procedures must be carried on and corrective action taken in the light of knowledge thus acquired. The executive's share of managerial responsibility in this phase of administration is therefore more likely to increase, and that of the legislative branch to diminish, rather than the contrary, in the future.

APPOINTMENTS

While it is the prevailing practice in the United States to regard creation of the administrative structure as a phase of administrative management resting basically in the hands of the legislative branch, the second step in establishing an "administration"—designating the individuals who shall man the posts thus provided for—is generally regarded as a managerial function properly belonging to the chief executive or his subordinates. Logically, if the chief executive is to be held accountable for administration of the laws he should have a controlling voice in the selection of those through whom he must act in carrying out this responsibility. By selection of key administrative personnel in sympathy with his general objectives, the chief executive exerts a powerful influence on governmental policy in every field. But as in other phases of administrative management, by no means has a complete, untrammelled authority of this kind been conferred upon him. His powers are hedged about with various types of limitations so that he is left short of full control over the selection of those with whom he must collaborate in the administration of public policies. The chief executive may be the captain of the Ship of State; but he must function with a crew that is not entirely of his own choosing.

Under the Articles of Confederation as well as in most of the Revolutionary War-time instruments of state government the power to appoint major administrative officers had been entrusted to the legislative branch. The Framers of the Constitution were well aware of the shortcomings of the system of legislative appointment—diffusion of responsibility, petty bickerings, delays, logrolling deals, and so on; nevertheless, they came to their ultimate conclusion to vest in the President a broad appointive authority only with evident reluctance. Not until the closing weeks of their deliberations was the decision made to place in the President's hands, rather than in the Senate's, the responsibility to appoint judges and diplomatic officers, and only when the final draft was being reviewed did they delete a clause reserving to Congress the power to appoint the chief financial officer of the national government.[11]

[11] *Supra,* Chap. 2, pp. 63, 65; see also Harris, *The Advice and Consent of the Senate,* Chap. II.

METHODS OF APPOINTMENT

The constitutional language governing the matter of the President's appointive authority, which remains unaltered to the present, reads as follows:

> He shall nominate, and by and with the advice and consent of the Senate, shall appoint ambassadors, other public ministers and consuls, judges of the Supreme Court, and all officers of the United States whose appointments are not herein otherwise provided for, and which shall be established by law; but the Congress may by law vest the appointment of such inferior officers, as they think proper in the President alone, in the courts of law, or in the heads of departments.
>
> The President shall have power to fill up all vacancies that may happen during the recess of the Senate, by granting commissions which shall expire at the end of their next session.[12]

During the ratification struggle this part of the plan came under particularly strong fire from the Constitution's critics. On the one hand it was assailed by those who feared that the broad appointive power delegated to the President would give rise to such abuses as favoritism, the creating of unnecessary offices, undue pressure on Congress, and the eventual establishment of a privileged elite. Others saw in these provisions the likelihood that the Senate would have too great a voice in the placement process. So strong were the criticisms that Hamilton felt it necessary to devote an entire number of *The Federalist* essays (Number 76) to a defense of this feature of the new Constitution.

The Constitution, it will be noted, specifies four different methods by which appointments to federal offices may be made: (1) by the President with the advice and consent of the Senate; (2) by the President alone; (3) by heads of departments; and (4) by courts of law. The first was presumably meant to be used in filling all offices of major importance in the executive and judicial department; for the other modes were to be applied, subject to direction by Congress, only to "inferior" posts. The courts have never attempted to define what constitutes an "inferior" office. Accordingly, the decision on what offices shall be deemed "presidential" offices—those to be filled by the President with the advice and consent of the Senate—has been left to Congress. Indeed, the filling of posts in the federal service has not been confined by Congress entirely to the four modes of selection outlined in Article II. Congress has conferred the power of selection of administrative personnel upon officers below the rank of department head in some cases; and it has reserved to itself or to its individual members the choosing of persons for particular posts making up the

---

[12] Art. II, Sec. 2.

staff of assistants whose duties are related to the operations of Congress itself and its committees. In these categories the individuals involved technically must be regarded as "employees" of the United States rather than officers, since "officers" of the United States can be designated only by one of the four procedures prescribed in Article II of the Constitution.

In designating the mode of appointment for filling particular offices Congress usually has adhered closely to the rule that if an office is of major importance, confirmation by the Senate must be given. A few positions of nationwide significance—the Director of the Bureau of the Budget is perhaps the most notable example—have been made appointive by the President alone. For the most part, however, the posts the President may fill without senatorial approval are those that are most intimately associated with the functioning of the President's office itself, or positions of an emergency or temporary character.

Furthermore, Congress from the beginning has displayed a propensity for extending the principle of senatorial confirmation to a wide range of positions actually of inferior rank. For the first hundred years or so after the adoption of the Constitution, postmasterships, district attorneyships, United States marshalships, and posts in the internal revenue and customs services made up the majority of minor positions to which this mode of appointment was applied. But with the extension of welfare, service, and regulatory functions of the national government during the past half century, it has been applied as well to hundreds of other positions in the central and field services of federal administrative agencies. Patronage considerations on the part of congressmen as well as an honest belief that congressional participation in the appointive process is necessary to maintain "democratic" control over the burgeoning federal bureaucracy have been the main factors accounting for this practice.

The President's appointive authority, in a nominal sense at least, now covers an astonishingly wide number of posts. As of 1952 the civil administrative positions filled by him with the advice and consent of the Senate numbered approximately 26,500, of which 21,000 were postmasterships. In addition to these there were some 98,000 commissioned officers in the armed forces whose appointments were made by the President with senatorial confirmation.[13] In the course of a year's time the President will submit 50,000 to 60,000 or more nominations for original appointments, reappointments and promotional appointments, both civil and military, to the Senate for confirmation. Military offices account for about 90 percent of the total. The vast majority are confirmed in routine fashion.

[13] Harris, *The Advice and Consent of the Senate*, p. 339.

In 1962, for example, the figures were as follows:

TABLE 5.   *Senate Action on Nominations, 1962*

Postmaster nominations	1,579
Civilian nominations other than postmasters	3,418
Total civilian	4,997
Army nominations	9,880
Air Force nominations	17,483
Navy nominations	16,006
Marine Corps nominations	3,713
Total military	47,082
Grand total, all nominations	52,079
Total withdrawn	8
Total unconfirmed at end of Senate session	291
Total confirmed	51,780

SOURCE: *Journal of Executive Proceedings of the U.S. Senate,* Vol. 104, 87th Congress, 2nd Session, Pt. II, p. 1.

But it is one thing for the President to have the nominal power of appointment to an office and another thing for him to have and to exercise a meaningful choice in the actual designation of the person appointed. In exercising the appointive authority a President finds his freedom of choice is limited in a variety of ways. In the highest offices the maintenance of party harmony, payment of political debts, and insuring proper geographical distribution of appointees are important limiting considerations. Individuals whom he would like to draw into the federal administrative services, particularly to higher level positions, often decline appointment for personal reasons or at most agree to serve only for a limited time because of the financial sacrifice involved. The continued harassment and exposure to partisan, sometimes unfair, criticism which public office entails deters many able individuals from accepting appointments.[14] Specific qualifications set by law for some types of positions further limit the chief executive's range of choice. Inclusion of a position in the classified civil service category, which has the effect of setting up standards of proved fitness and ability to discharge the duties of the post—a type of qualifying limitation Presidents generally have shown more eagerness than has Congress to extend to all except the very highest administrative posts —also serves to limit his choice.

The constitutional rule disqualifying Senators and Representatives

[14] For an interesting account of the impact of these considerations as they affect presidential selection of department heads see Richard F. Fenno, Jr., *The President's Cabinet* (Cambridge: Harvard University Press, 1959), Chap. 2.

from appointment during their elected terms to an office "which shall have been created, or the emoluments whereof shall have been increased during such time" has on occasion served as a barrier to a presidential selection. President Washington, for example, was embarrassed to discover that his nomination of William Paterson to a position on the Supreme Court had to be withdrawn because Paterson was ineligible because as a Senator he had participated in passing the legislation creating the post.[15] Later, after the expiration of Paterson's senatorial term, he was appointed to the Court. In 1909, when President Taft wished to appoint Senator Philander Knox to the post of Secretary of State, the salary of which office had recently been increased by Congress, it was necessary in order to make him eligible for Congress to pass an act specifically withholding the salary increase until the end of Knox's senatorial term. Again, in 1946, President Truman's desire to appoint Senator Warren Austin of Vermont as the first head of a United States mission to the United Nations was temporarily balked until expiration of the Senator's term made him eligible for the post created by the United Nations Participation Act of December 20, 1945.

SENATE CONFIRMATION AS A CHECK

In setting forth his defense of this feature of the new Constitution, Hamilton maintained that the Senate's role would be purely that of a censor or screening agent upon the President's nominees. The President would be free, he insisted, to nominate whomever he saw fit. There would be "no exertion of choice on the part of the Senate," he wrote; and "it could hardly happen that the majority of the Senate would feel any other complacency toward the object of an appointment than such as the appearance of merit might inspire, and the proofs of want of it destroy."[16] Developments have demonstrated that on this point Hamilton was not a good prophet. In actual practice the Senate's influence in the making of most appointments extends beyond mere concern to keep out the unfit. The degree of its involvement in the appointing process varies, depending upon the nature of the post being filled.

Broadly speaking, positions may be grouped into four categories with reference to the degree of senatorial influence in the selective process.

1. First, there are a number of positions so closely involved with the President's discharge of his constitutional duties that the Senate, recognizing this fact, gives him practically a free hand in appointments.

---

[15] Richardson, *Messages and Papers of the President,* Vol. I, p. 137.
[16] *The Federalist,* No. 66.

Even if the Senate is controlled by the opposition party it will very rarely refuse confirmation of the President's nominees to such posts. Only when there is a very serious doubt as to the loyalty, probity, or competence of the individual will the Senate question the choice. Departmental secretaryships and assistant secretaryships and high diplomatic posts are illustrative of this class of positions. No Cabinet post nomination was rejected until 1834, when the Senate failed to act on President Jackson's nomination of Roger B. Taney to the post of Secretary of the Treasury. Altogether only eight Cabinet nominations have been rejected by the Senate since 1789, and four came during the administration of one President, John Tyler, who had lost the support of his own Whig party leaders in the Senate soon after he took office in 1841. The most recent case was that of Lewis B. Strauss, whose nomination as Secretary of Commerce by President Eisenhower in 1959 was rejected 46–49 by the Senate. Strauss' somewhat tactless behavior before the Senate committee that held a hearing on his nomination and his connection with the Dixon-Yates contract incident while serving as Chairman of the Atomic Energy Commission had made him persona non grata with too many members of the Senate.

Senatorial rejections of presidential nominations to diplomatic posts have been somewhat more numerous. Particularly in the earlier period of the nation's history rejections were not uncommon, but more recently the Senate has respected more strictly the practice of letting the President have his own way in such appointments. A notable exception was F. D. Roosevelt's nomination in 1943 of Edward J. Flynn, who was chairman of the Democratic National Committee at the time, for the post of Minister to Australia and as personal representative of the President, with the rank of Ambassador, in the South Pacific area. Mounting Senate opposition to the nomination at the committee stage on the ground of Flynn's alleged lack of qualifications for the post and his Tammany Hall background caused the President to withdraw the nomination. Strong opposition was voiced in some quarters of the Senate to President Eisenhower's nomination of Charles Bohlen to be Ambassador to Russia in 1953 and of Mrs. Clare Boothe Luce, who had served from 1953 to 1957 as Ambassador to Italy, to the post of Ambassador to Brazil in 1959. Both nominations were confirmed, nevertheless. Mrs. Luce, however, immediately after her nomination had been confirmed by a vote of 79 to 11 made a cutting personal remark about Senator Wayne Morse of Oregon, who had led the fight against her confirmation on the ground that her earlier tour of duty had shown her to be lacking in tact and calmness of temperament. Her remark was interpreted by many as a vindication of the Senator's judgment, and her proffered resignation from the post was immediately accepted by the President.

2. A second category of positions from the standpoint of senatorial influence on appointments is made up of those wherein senatorial influence counts for something more, but is still a secondary factor. These are positions for which the President also takes the initiative in selecting a nominee, but the Senate feels freer to reject his choice.

The classes of positions falling under this heading are not rigidly defined, but this view of its role is most commonly taken by the Senate in connection with Supreme Court and Courts of Appeals appointments, members of major independent boards and commissions exercising important policy-making powers, and heads of some of the subordinate agencies of the regular departments in whose functioning important business, labor, agricultural, or other constituency interests are concerned. A notable illustration was the rejection of President Truman's renomination of Leland Olds as chairman of the Federal Power Commission in 1949. A powerful oil and gas lobby opposed to his views on federal regulation of interstate transmission of natural gas brought about his rejection.[17] While the number of rejections of nominations for such posts is not a large proportion of the total, the Senate does not regard a rejection as a serious encroachment upon presidential prerogative. Of the 124 persons who have been nominated for positions on the Supreme Court since 1789, 21 have failed to be confirmed by the Senate.[18] Most of these rejections came in the earlier years, there having been only one—that of Circuit Judge Parker, nominated by President Hoover in 1930—since 1900.

3. A third category includes those positions to which the usage of "senatorial courtesy" extends. These are mainly in the field services of departments or other administrative agencies and district court judgeships. The Senate will confirm a presidential nominee for such a post only if the person named is acceptable to the Senator or Senators of the President's political party within whose patronage jurisdiction the position lies. If the Senator immediately concerned opposes the nominee on personal grounds, he objects to confirmation, and the Senate supports him in his opposition. As for postmasterships, the established usage is to get clearance from the House member within whose district the post lies, if he is a member of the President's party. The system of senatorial courtesy thus imposes upon the President

[17] Cf. Harris, *The Advice and Consent of the Senate*, Chap. XI, for a full account.

[18] Two nominees for Supreme Court posts—Roger B. Taney in 1835 and Stanley Matthews in 1881—were refused confirmation by the Senate but were subsequently renominated and confirmed. A number of nominations to Supreme Court posts since 1900 have encountered considerable Senate opposition. Those in this category include Justice Louis D. Brandeis, nominated by President Wilson in 1916; Justice Harlan F. Stone, by Coolidge in 1925; Chief Justice Charles E. Hughes, by Hoover in 1930; and Justice Hugo Black in 1937 and Justice Felix Frankfurter in 1938, by Roosevelt. See Harris, *The Advice and Consent of the Senate*, pp. 302 ff.

the necessity of obtaining the consent of a particular member of the Senate or some other local party representative on a particular appointment. Knowing this, he will usually get the advice of that Senator or party representative in advance. The Senator involved cannot compel the President to nominate someone to whose selection the President is opposed, but he can confine the President's choice to some person on the Senator's approved list. In effect, the Senator immediately concerned becomes the appointive authority, subject to the President's willingness to place his stamp of approval on an individual who has the Senator's backing.

The custom of senatorial courtesy is one of long standing—it made its appearance early in Washington's first administration. Some three months after he had taken office, Washington sent to the Senate the nomination of one Benjamin Fishbourn for the post of naval officer of the Port of Savannah, Georgia. Fishbourn, who had served under Washington as a military officer, was personally known to him, and had highly commendatory recommendations from various prominent citizens, was apparently well qualified for the post; because the Senators from Georgia preferred another candidate, however, the Senate as a "courtesy" to them rejected Fishbourn's nomination. The President reluctantly withdrew the nomination and submitted another name. In an accompanying message he remarked somewhat acidly:

> Whatever may have been the reasons which induced your dissent, I am persuaded they were such as you deemed sufficient. Permit me to submit to your consideration whether on occasions where the propriety of nominations appear questionable to you it would not be expedient to communicate the circumstances to me, and thereby avail yourselves of the information which led me to make them, and which I would with pleasure lay before you.[19]

Nevertheless, his acquiescence in the Senate's action in this instance was a concession the Senate was not slow to capitalize on.

4. A fourth category of appointments to which senatorial confirmation applies includes positions in the "career" civil service and commissioned officers in the military establishment. For the vast majority of these positions the President's nominations are based upon recommendations brought forward by the personnel agencies of the units concerned. For such positions the President's nominations and the Senate's actions thereon are little more than formalities. Sometimes such nominations, particularly in the military services, are submitted and acted upon en bloc. Responsibility for making such appointments might well be placed in the hands of department heads or the President alone, subject to regulations to insure their being made on the basis of merit and proved fitness. The same can be said

19 Richardson, *op. cit.*, Vol. I, p. 58.

for most of the positions to which the rule of senatorial courtesy applies. Senatorial opposition to removal of the requirement of confirmation and a carefully nurtured popular belief that senatorial participation in the appointive process promotes "democratic" control operate as barriers to change.

The Fishbourn incident was significant not only in laying a foundation for the custom of senatorial courtesy but also in that it played a part in establishing the procedure by which the Senate goes about acting upon a nomination. On the day the Senate rejected the Fishbourn nomination a motion was introduced in the Senate expressing the opinion that "their advice and consent to the appointment of officers should be given in the presence of the President"; but the motion was not adopted. Instead, a committee was appointed to consult with the President concerning the "mode of communication to be pursued between him and the Senate in the formation of treaties, and making appointments to office." President Washington met with this committee on August 8, 1789, two days after he had sent the message submitting another name for the position for which he had originally named Fishbourn. Recording his views on the subject in his diary after having conferred with this committee, Washington indicated that he felt that nominations should be made by written message. As for being present to participate in the Senate's deliberations, he was of the opinion that it would be "no pleasing thing . . . for the President, on the one hand to be present and hear the propriety of his nominations questioned; nor for the Senate on the other hand to be under the smallest restraint from his presence from the fullest and freest inquiry into the Character of the Person nominated."[20]

Washington's view on the advisability of keeping the nominating and confirming steps in the appointive process distinctly separate has prevailed. A formal nomination is always made in writing. It is usually referred to the appropriate standing committee of the Senate for such inquiry as the committee thinks necessary. After this inquiry, which may involve interrogation of the person nominated as well as of other interested persons, the committee makes a recommendation for action to the full Senate. Once confirmation is agreed to and the appointment made by delivery of a commission to the appointee, the Senate's authority over the matter is exhausted. It cannot, by reconsideration of its confirming action and subsequently rejecting the nomination, invalidate an appointment already effected.[21]

[20] Harris, *The Advice and Consent of the Senate*, p. 39.
[21] *United States* v. *Smith*, 286 U.S. 6 (1932). The attempted "recall" of an appointment, which involved a nomination by President Hoover to the Federal Power Commission, was held by the Court in this case to have been in violation of the Senate's own rules, rather than a violation of constitutional limitations. The latter would appear to have been the more appropriate ground. Cf. Corwin, *op. cit.*, p. 77.

RECESS APPOINTMENTS

Ordinarily a rejection by the Senate or failure on its part to take affirmative action by the end of its session is treated by the President as final, and another nomination is made. The President is not without further recourse, however, as events during Jackson's first administration amply demonstrated. When the Senate failed to take any action on his nomination of one Samuel Gwin to the office of register of lands at Mount Salus, Mississippi, President Jackson promptly gave a recess appointment to Gwin and resubmitted his name for consideration at the next session of the Senate. That body again failed to act upon the nomination, whereupon the President notified the Senate he would "abstain from any further attempt" to fill this and other offices in Mississippi for which his nominees had not been confirmed.[22] Inasmuch as the Senate cannot compel the President to make a nomination to fill a vacant post, a President can thus at least adopt a "dog-in-the-manger" attitude and refuse to give an individual Senator the satisfaction of having a candidate of his own choosing appointed to a patronage position. Such stalemates over appointments have in recent years most commonly involved district court judgeships. Presidents Hoover, F. D. Roosevelt, Truman, and Eisenhower all engaged in political squabbles with individual Senators over such judicial appointments.[23]

The use of the recess appointment power by the President in the case of judicial appointments is particularly irritating to the Senate. The Senate's objection to this practice in the case of Supreme Court nominees is that, since the appointees in such cases may already have begun their service on the Court before their names can be submitted for confirmation, the Senate's freedom to inquire into their qualifications and views on pending constitutional issues is inhibited. The revival of this practice by President Eisenhower, after a period of some 100 years during which no recess appointments to the Supreme Court had been made, led eventually to the adoption in 1960 of a resolution by the Senate, sponsored by Senator Hart of Michigan, expressing its disapproval of the practice.[24] With regard to filling

[22] Richardson, *op. cit.*, Vol. II, pp. 635–636.

[23] For an account of the controversies of the first three mentioned Presidents with the Senate over judicial appointments see Harris, *The Advice and Consent of the Senate*, pp. 413ff.

[24] *Congressional Record*, 86th Congress, 2nd Session, p. 18145. The vote on the resolution was strongly partisan, 48 Democrats supporting it and 33 Republicans and 4 Democrats opposing. Recess appointments had been given by President Eisenhower to Chief Justice Warren in 1953, Justice Brennan in 1956, and Justice Stewart in 1958. In 1959–1960 President Eisenhower encountered considerable opposition in the Senate in the filling of a number of vacant and newly created posts in federal district courts. When the Senate failed to act on some of these nominations in its

Supreme Court posts which became vacant during his term of office, President Kennedy respected the wishes of the Senate.

In the states the practice of subjecting major appointments of the governor to confirmation by the upper house of the legislature has become widespread. The original New York plan of vesting this confirming power in the hands of a four-member "Council of Appointments" composed of state senators eventually fell into disfavor and has not survived. In some of the New England states that retain the executive council, a confirming authority for major gubernatorial appointments is vested in that body. In a few states both houses of the legislature must confirm certain appointments; or the power to appoint certain officers, usually those whose duties relate to financial affairs, is placed in the hands of the legislature itself. The significance of legislative confirmation as a check on the governor's freedom of choice varies with the office and with the political relationship that exists between the executive and legislative body.[25] Since a governor's appointive authority does not include any great number of locally significant posts, the practice of senatorial courtesy has not taken root in the states to any great extent. Moreover, since legislatures are not usually in session for as much of the time as Congress, the recess appointment power takes on a relatively greater significance at the state level. A device recently introduced in Michigan, designed to prevent rejection by inaction and to minimize instances of stalemate between the governor and the confirming body, is a provision that a gubernatorial nomination, if not rejected by the state senate within 60 days after submission, will be deemed confirmed.[26] It is a device that might well be adopted in federal as well as state practice.

Like the President, a governor finds his freedom to make appointments hedged about with various types of statutory limitations respecting the qualifications and eligibility status of appointees, to

---

1960 session, he extended recess appointments to a number of the unconfirmed nominees. Most of these nominations were subsequently withdrawn by President Kennedy in 1961, but a few of them were renewed and confirmed.

[25] For example, see the account of the difficulties of Democratic Governor John Reynolds of Wisconsin in getting his nominees confirmed by the Republican-controlled Senate, *The New York Times*, October 20, 1963, p. 54. Of 49 nominations made by Reynolds requiring confirmation, only 12 were confirmed during his first year in office. In Michigan in the period from 1955 through 1960, during which time the state senate and the governorship were under control of the Republicans and the Democrats, respectively, out of a total of 557 nominations, 11 were rejected outright and 174 were not acted upon at all. Cf. Albert L. Sturm, *Constitution-Making in Michigan, 1961–1962* (Ann Arbor: Institute of Public Administration, University of Michigan Governmental Studies No. 43, 1963), pp. 194–195, n 62.

[26] Constitution of Michigan, 1963, Art. V, Sec. 6. The Michigan constitution also specifies that an individual rejected by the senate for a post shall be ineligible for a recess appointment to the same post, thus redressing the balance in the other direction. *Ibid.*, Sec. 7.

say nothing of practical considerations arising out of the need for maintaining party harmony, the use of appointments for advancing his legislative program, and the difficulty of attracting into the public service persons of superior talent. Nevertheless, it is undoubtedly true that one of the most significant ways the office of governor has taken on increased political stature in recent decades has been through acquisition of a broadened appointive authority as state governments have expanded the areas of their operations.

REMOVALS

In supervision of administration the logical complement to the appointive authority is the power to make removals. In establishing and directing an administration it is as important to a chief executive to be able to remove subordinates who in his judgment fail to measure up to the requirements of their official duties or to reflect his policy goals as it is to be able to select them in the first place. Despite the close connection the removal authority thus has to administrative leadership, direction, and control, the Framers of the Constitution failed to include any definitive language on this subject. To be sure, removal by impeachment of all "civil officers of the United States," including the President himself, was authorized for "treason, bribery and other high crimes and misdemeanors"; but it was generally conceded that impeachment was an extraordinary remedy not suitable for enforcing accountability upon the President's subordinates. As a matter of fact, impeachment has been employed only once against a subordinate federal executive official, and then only after the officer involved had already resigned his post.[27] Obviously, a more expeditious method of effecting removals in the executive branch was required.

Events soon after adoption of the Constitution quickly precipitated a debate on the question of the nature and location of the removal power. In general, three theories were advanced on the point. One was the proposition suggested by Hamilton in a number of *The Federalist* papers that the removal power was to be implied from the power to appoint, at least as far as appointments made with the consent of the Senate were concerned. The approval of the Senate would accordingly be required for removals from such offices as well as for appointment.[28] During the First Congress, in connection with

[27] The officer in question was President Grant's Secretary of War, W. W. Belknap. *Supra*, p. 206.

[28] In No. 77 of *The Federalist* Hamilton had insisted: "The consent of that body [the Senate] would be necessary to displace as well as to appoint." Later Hamilton endorsed Madison's theory that the removal power was an inherent part of the executive power.

the enactment of bills establishing the Departments of Foreign Affairs (later State), Treasury, and War, two other views were brought forward. On the one hand there were those, of whom Madison was the chief spokesman in the House, who maintained that the power to remove subordinates was inherent in the grant of the executive power to the President along with the duty imposed upon him by the Constitution to "take care that the laws be faithfully executed." It followed, according to this view, that the power of removal need not be conferred upon the President by statute for him to be able to exercise it. On the other hand, the proposition was advanced by other members of the Jeffersonian faction in Congress more distrustful of executive prerogative that the power to *establish* offices subordinate to the President—an authority which devolved upon Congress by reason of the "necessary and proper" clause—carried with it the power to assign to whomever Congress deemed appropriate the power of removal— to the President, to the courts, or to itself—and upon whatever terms and conditions Congress might see fit to impose. A few of those who held this view even went so far as to maintain that the only permissible method of removal other than impeachment which Congress might prescribe was action by the courts.

The upshot of the debate in the House was the inclusion of language in the bills at hand implicitly recognizing the Madisonian view that the Constitution by implication places a removal authority in the hands of the President. This "Decision of 1789" was accepted by the Senate only by the margin of the deciding vote cast by Vice President Adams. President Washington and his successors thereafter proceeded to act on the assumption that the power to remove subordinate executive officers was theirs by virtue of constitutional grant. John Adams himself, as President, demonstrated the point. Having lost confidence in the personal loyalty of his Secretary of State, Timothy Pickering, he asked for his resignation, but Pickering refused to tender it. Adams thereupon summarily dismissed him, and the principle of enforcement of accountability of Cabinet officers to their chief through use of a summary power of dismissal was established.[29]

President Jackson was to carry the matter a step further. In his famous message of protest to the Senate following its adoption of a resolution of censure for his actions relative to removal of United States deposits from the Bank of the United States, he vigorously defended his removal of Secretary of the Treasury Duane for refusing to obey his orders. Jackson not only cited the "Decision of 1789" as having settled conclusively the point that "all executive officers are removable at the will of the President" but went on to maintain that

[29] Page Smith, *John Adams* (Garden City, N.Y.: Doubleday & Company, 2 vols., 1962), Vol. II, p. 1029.

this was an unqualified power, derived from the Constitution itself and hence beyond the reach of the legislative authority.[30]

Later events were to demonstrate that the Jacksonian view of the presidential power of removal was not to go unchallenged by Congress. This became an issue of crucial importance during the vendetta between President Andrew Johnson and Congress in 1867–1868. On March 2, 1867, a Tenure of Office Act was passed by Congress over the veto of the President. In his veto message Johnson maintained that the proposed act was unconstitutional, the issue having been foreclosed by the historic "Decision of 1789" as well as by the controversy of the Jackson era. Proceeding on the theory that the presidential removal power was subject to whatever restraints Congress might choose to impose, the 1867 statute provided that all executive officers appointed with the advice and consent of the Senate and whose terms of office were not otherwise specified should hold office until a successor was appointed and confirmed by the Senate. The act provided further that Cabinet officers were to serve for the duration of the term of the President who appointed them and for one month thereafter. During a recess of the Senate the President might remove such an official for crime, misconduct, or incapacity and fill the vacancy by an ad interim appointment, but he was obliged to report the removal to the Senate within 20 days after it reconvened. If the Senate refused to confirm the appointment of the ad interim successor, the office would revert to the prior incumbent. Acceptance of or holding office in violation of the statute was made a misdemeanor punishable by fine or imprisonment.

Later that year, after Congress had adjourned, President Johnson removed Secretary of War Stanton, whom he believed to be disloyal to his administration, and made an interim appointment of General U. S. Grant to the vacated post. Believing that his constitutional prerogatives were infringed by the 1867 statute, President Johnson hoped to bring about a situation that would afford a judicial test on the removal question. He had expected that if Grant was not confirmed in the post by the Senate, he would continue on in it long enough to require a judicial determination whether the misdemeanor penalty provided in the act should apply and thus bring about a pronouncement on the act's constitutionality. But Grant proved uncooperative. When the Senate refused confirmation he promptly resigned. Hoping still to bring the issue to the courts, Johnson then

---

[30] Richardson, *op. cit.*, Vol. III, pp. 80–81. On the origins of the "Decision of 1789" and its bearing on the use of the removal power by Jackson, see Leonard D. White, *The Federalists: A Study in Administrative History* (New York: The Macmillan Company, 1948), pp. 20–25, and, by the same author, *The Jacksonians: A Study in Administrative History, 1829–1861* (New York: The Macmillan Company, 1954), pp. 33–44.

summarily removed Stanton (who had reassumed the post). By pursuing this course he only succeeded in giving the House of Representatives the excuse it had been waiting for to vote impeachment charges against him on the ground that he had openly violated a statute which it was his duty to respect. The ensuing impeachment trial, while it failed to result in Johnson's removal, left unresolved so far as the courts were concerned the specific constitutional issue of the presidential power of removal.

Nearly 50 years later the Supreme Court made a ruling in the case of *Myers* v. *United States*[31] which to all intents and purposes vindicated the positions of Presidents Jackson and Johnson on the removal issue. This case raised the question of the validity of President Wilson's summary dismissal of one Myers from the position of postmaster at Portland, Oregon. By the terms of a rider attached to an appropriation bill in 1876 all first-, second-, and third-class postmasters were to be appointed and could be removed only by and with the advice and consent of the Senate. The act specified also that such officers were to hold office for a period of four years unless sooner removed or suspended "according to law."[32] On February 20, 1920, approximately a year and a half before Myers' four-year term expired, he was removed by order of the Postmaster General, acting by direction of the President. Inasmuch as the President did not simultaneously nominate a successor and thereby afford the Senate an opportunity to give its implied consent by confirming a successor, Myers maintained his removal was illegal under the 1876 statute. He sought without success an administrative review of his dismissal. At the expiration of the term for which he was appointed he then filed suit in the Court of Claims for the salary for the portion of his term cut off by his removal. Having been denied relief by that tribunal on the ground of undue delay in raising the question, he appealed to the Supreme Court.

The manner by which Myers' removal was effected undoubtedly was in conflict with the terms of the 1876 act. Facing up to the constitutional issue squarely, the Supreme Court in a long opinion by Chief Justice Taft, who had the support of five other members of the Court, held the 1876 act to be unconstitutional insofar as it sought to restrict the President's power to remove subordinates in the executive branch appointed by him with the advice and consent of the Senate. Conceding that Congress might establish any restraints it thinks appropriate on removals of "inferior" officers—that is, those appointed by department heads—the Chief Justice maintained that

[31] 272 U.S. 52 (1926).
[32] 19 *Stat.* 80, 81, Chap. 179. It should be noted that the Tenure of Office Act of 1867, which related to officers of Cabinet rank, was repealed in 1887.

the historic "Decision of 1789," together with long-continued practice thereafter until the episodes of the post-Civil War period, had settled the constitutional issue with regard to presidential appointees. Citing the expressed views of Presidents Jackson, Johnson, Wilson, and Coolidge on the point, and no doubt mindful of his own experiences while serving as President, the Chief Justice found any congressional restraint on the President's power to remove his own appointees to violate the separation of powers principle. The executive power vested in the President by the Constitution along with the duty to see that the laws are faithfully executed conferred upon him an authority which, as Jackson argued, could not be qualified by statute.

This sweeping pronouncement of the Court, all the more remarkable in that it came through an opinion by a Chief Justice whose views on presidential prerogative powers were fundamentally other than Jacksonian,[33] embraced a constitutional dogma on executive versus legislative authority over administration which the Court itself soon reacted against. In his opinion the Chief Justice had indicated that the terms of federal statutes creating various so-called "independent" administrative commissions might well be unconstitutional also insofar as they sought to limit the President's authority to remove the heads of such agencies. Nine years after the *Myers* decision the Supreme Court was given an opportunity to consider this phase of the general problem in the case of *Humphrey's Executor* v. *United States*.[34] This case arose in somewhat the same fashion as had *Myers,* but it concerned a different type of statutory restraint on the removal power. Dissatisfied with the public policy views of W. E. Humphrey, a member of the Federal Trade Commission, President F. D. Roosevelt, after unsuccessfully seeking his resignation, summarily removed him from office in October, 1933. Originally a Coolidge appointee Humphrey had been reappointed to his post for a seven-year term by President Hoover in 1931. The Federal Trade Commission Act of 1914, which had created the agency, provided that members of the Commission might be removed during their respective terms only for inefficiency, neglect of duty, or malfeasance. Humphrey died in 1934 soon after his removal, but his executor sued in the Court of Claims for the salary due him from the time of his dismissal until his death, contending that the removal, which was for political reasons, had been invalid under the 1914 law. The Court of Claims was uncertain whether the restrictive clause in the 1914 statute was unconstitutional and referred this question to the Supreme Court.

The Supreme Court found the clause to be constitutional. Re-

[33] Cf. William Howard Taft, *Our Chief Magistrate and His Powers* (New York: Columbia University Press, 1925), pp. 139–140. *Supra,* pp. 245–246.
[34] 295 U.S. 602 (1935).

canting from some, but not all, of the doctrine spelled out in the *Myers* ruling the Court held the restrictive provisions of the Trade Commission Act were valid in view of the special relationship Congress had intended the Commission to have with Congress and the courts in applying to concrete situations the policies embodied in the Act. The Commission was not a "purely executive" agency. Indeed, in this enthusiasm for the point, Justice Sutherland, who gave the Court's opinion, went so far as to assert that the Federal Trade Commission "occupies no place in the executive department at all" —a statement which was to give substance later to characterization of the independent administrative agencies as the "fourth branch of government" in the separation of powers scheme.

The ruling of the Court came at a crucial time when the judicial branch was getting set to strike down important parts of President Roosevelt's New Deal program. It was hailed by many anti-New Dealers as a salutary check upon the growth of a dangerous executive authority. Whatever the soundness of the Court's judgment from the political or constitutional standpoint, it had the effect of raising new doubts and problems regarding the boundaries between legislative and executive authority in this area of administration. The President was still conceded to have an inherent power of removal which Congress might not restrict if it amounted to interference with the performance of "executive" functions, but as to officers invested with quasi-legislative or quasi-judicial powers Congress might validly impose restraints. As to these officers the Court evidently meant to say the Jeffersonian view of the nature of the removal power was applicable, that is, it could be limited by law as Congress should see fit. But many higher executive officers perform *both* executive and quasi-legislative or quasi-judicial functions. Does the President have an unqualified power of removal over them?

Subsequent rulings of the courts have sought to answer this riddle by placing an emphasis on the President's *purpose* in using his removal power as the determinant of his freedom from statutory restraint in its exercise. This is the inference to be derived from the later cases of *Morgan* v. *TVA*,[35] *Wiener* v. *United States*,[36] and *Cole* v. *Young*.[37] The first of these cases involved the validity of President Roosevelt's removal of one of the three directors of the Tennessee Valley Authority for "contumacy" in refusing to cooperate with the President's investigation into the circumstances of a controversy between Morgan and another director over policy matters that was threatening to bring the operations of the agency to a standstill.

[35] 115 F. (2nd) 990 (1940); *cert. denied,* 312 U.S. 701 (1941).
[36] 357 U.S. 349 (1958).
[37] 351 U.S. 536 (1956).

The law establishing the TVA gave the President specifically the authority to remove a director only for misuse of powers for partisan reasons and carried a further stipulation that Congress itself might remove a director by concurrent action of the two houses. Presumably Congress intended the TVA to function as an independent, nonpartisan administrative agency, outside the normal range of the President's removal power. Nevertheless the United States Court of Appeals construed this language as not to imply a denial to the President of power to remove summarily a member of the TVA directorate as part of his general supervisory authority over executive agencies in such situations.

The *Wiener* and *Cole* cases were swings of the pendulum in the contrary direction. In the *Wiener* case the Supreme Court found that President Eisenhower had exceeded his constitutional authority when in 1953 he summarily removed Wiener for political reasons before the task for which Congress had created the post had been completed. Wiener had been appointed by President Truman to serve as a special War Claims Commissioner in the settlement of certain types of claims arising out of the conduct of the Japanese phase of World War II. Even though the 1948 statute creating the position made no provision whatever regarding the length of term or the manner of removing a Commissioner, the Court held that the quasi-judicial nature of a Commissioner's duties gave him an implied protection against executive interference in performing them. Even so, President Eisenhower had the last word in the matter. He had already abolished the Commission by executive order in 1954 under his reorganizational authority some time before the decision of the Supreme Court was rendered!

In *Cole* v. *Young* the Supreme Court ruled that the dismissal of Cole, an inspector for the Food and Drug Administration, in pursuance of the terms of President Eisenhower's Executive Order No. 10,450 setting up a removal procedure for dismissals on security grounds throughout the federal civil service, was invalid in view of other legislation by Congress regulating tenure and dismissal of war veteran civil service personnel. The President's security dismissal order was held to have exceeded the authority conferred upon him by the Summary Suspension Act passed by Congress in 1950[38] authorizing dismissals for security reasons, without regard to regular civil service procedures, of persons holding "sensitive" jobs in 11 designated agencies. The empowering statute was construed not to embrace the type of position held by Cole. The Court's majority, over the protest of three dissenting members, refused to inquire into the constitutional question whether the President, by inherent authority vested in his office, could set up a plan for effecting removals on security grounds

---

[38] 64 *Stat.* 476, 5 *U.S.C.A.*, Sec. 22–1.

independently of, or even in conflict with, legislation by Congress for this type of position. Its failure to do so unfortunately served to becloud still further the question of the relationship between the executive and legislative authorities in the matter of removals on security grounds, independently of prescribed civil service procedures.

Again, as was pointed out in connection with the chief executive's freedom to choose his subordinates, his use or nonuse of his authority to remove depends ordinarily upon considerations lying beyond the sole question of his possession of legal power, limited or otherwise, to act. Extralegal considerations, such as the maintenance of party harmony, of administrative morale, of good relations with Congress, or with a significantly powerful interest group, loom large in the overall picture. Weighing all the factors involved, the President may well conclude for reasons of political expediency that he must refrain from removing some particular incumbent whose efficiency or political views he has good reason to question. President Lincoln's patience in his relations with some of the politically powerful figures who made up his Cabinet, particularly Secretary of State Seward, Secretary of the Treasury Chase, and Secretary of War Stanton, was a feature of his administration. Intent upon maintaining unimpaired the coalition of varied interests of the North in support of his primary goal of preserving the Union, he tolerated a great deal of personal criticism and underhanded intrigue against himself by members of his own Cabinet. Even when he became aware that Chase was maneuvering to make himself the candidate of the Republican party for President in 1864, Lincoln allowed Chase to continue in his post because he did not wish to offend the political element his Secretary of the Treasury represented. After Lincoln was renominated he accepted Chase's resignation, but after keeping him and his followers dangling during the course of the 1864 election campaign, Lincoln eventually smoothed Chase's ruffled feelings by appointing him Chief Justice of the Supreme Court.

Sometimes pressure from Congress or from some powerful political faction may become so strong as to compel the President to make a removal which he personally does not feel impelled to make. He may be confronted with the hard choice of throwing to the wolves some unpopular members of his administrative corps in whom he still has confidence or sacrificing some important political objective. During World War II, for example, President Roosevelt was faced with the alternative of removing his Price Control Administrator, Leon Henderson, whose official actions had antagonized many segments of the public and the Congress, or failing to get an extension of economic control legislation from Congress. He chose the former course. On the other hand, President Coolidge ignored a Senate resolution declaring it to be "the sense of the Senate" that the President immediately request the resignation of Secretary of the Navy Denby, who had been found to have had a connection with the Teapot Dome oil lease scandals. "I do not propose to sacrifice an innocent man for my own welfare," was Coolidge's pithy comment. But eventually he accepted Denby's voluntary resignation. Similarly, President Truman stubbornly refused to be influenced by a Republican congressional caucus demand that he dismiss Secretary of State Dean Acheson in the interest of greater bipartisan support for his foreign policy.[39]

The legislative branch may not only exert pressure on the chief executive to remove a subordinate by refusing to grant funds for continuing an agency's operations but it may even go to the length of enacting a so-called "ripper" law which abolishes the agency in question, thus cutting the ground from under an undesirable incumbent. Congressional animus against Edgar L. Warren, the head of the Labor Mediation and Conciliation Service in the Department of Labor, for example, was a factor leading to the abolition of this unit and the creation of a new "independent" organ for discharging the same functions under the terms of the National Labor Relations (Taft-Hartley) Act of 1947. The Supreme Court has held, however, that Congress may not go so far as to compel the President to remove specifically named individuals by providing in an appropriation act that after a specified date no funds shall be available for payment of their salaries unless they are reappointed and reconfirmed. When Congress attempted to use this maneuver to bring about the discharge of three officers of the Department of the Interior in 1943 on grounds of suspected pro-Communist leanings, the legislation was held to violate the bill of attainder guarantee of the Constitution.[40]

Despite occasional checks by the courts upon legislative interference with personnel management, a chief executive quickly comes to realize that the lines demarking the constitutional and legal limits of his authority to fire subordinates do not necessarily define the practical limits on his power in this area. Here, as is true generally in his functioning as chief executive, considerations inherent in the political situation confronting him and his capacity to manipulate the levers of political influence set the more immediate limits. He must accommodate himself to the fact that at times political expediency dictates that he must tolerate a certain amount of foot-dragging and even covert sabotage of his policies by members of his own administrative team.

[39] Cf. Fenno, *op. cit.*, pp. 213–215.
[40] *United States* v. *Lovett, Watson and Dodd*, 328 U.S. 303 (1946).

13

CHIEF OF ADMINISTRATION (PART 2)

DIRECTION AND SUPERVISION

Creating the organs of administration and manning the posts established are necessary first steps in providing an "administration" to carry out laws and public policies. As has been noted, responsibility is shared in these matters by the legislative and executive branches of government. In an even more involved fashion, they share responsibility in directing the operations of the administrative machinery thus set up.

Although the general public does not fully realize it, a major share of the time, energy, and attention of members of Congress is devoted to activities that, properly speaking, are of an administrative managerial character. Defining the authority and prescribing procedures of administrative agencies, making funds available to them under terms and specifications deemed appropriate, examining required reports on their activities, employing the inquisitorial authority available to supplement such reports, and taking up the complaints, inquiries and requests of their constituents with the appropriate officials are activities to which members of Congress devote a major portion of their time. Recognizing that a heavy responsibility for administrative supervision rests in its hands, Congress in reorganizing its committee system through the Congressional Reorganization Act of 1946 followed the principle of setting up its standing committees to parallel the major administrative branches of the executive department. Moreover, it specifically charged each standing committee to "exercise continuous watchfulness of the execution by the administrative agencies concerned of all laws, the subject matter of which is within the jurisdiction of such committee."[1]

An officer in the middle ranges of the administrative hierarchy accordingly looks to Congress, and particularly to members of the standing committee having special charge over his department's affairs, as well as to his executive superiors, for his cues and directives on what he should do and how he should do it. Indeed, he is likely to find he has more frequent contacts with those members of Congress who have

[1] 60 *Stat.* 832; *U.S. Code* (1964), Title 2, Sec. 190d.

reason to interest themselves in the operations of his office than he has with the higher officialdom on the executive side of government. A congressional committee chairman having oversight of matters affecting a particular administrative agency may even come to regard it as being in his personal charge. When Georgia's Representative Carl Vinson was Chairman of the House Naval Affairs Committee he was in the habit of speaking possessively—and not wholly inaccurately— of "my Navy" and of characterizing particular Navy Secretaries as "the best (or worst) Secretary of the Navy I ever had."[2] The story, possibly apochryphal, is told that when Vinson was once sounded out by an emissary from President Truman on his availability for appointment to the post of Secretary of the Navy his reply was, "No, I am not interested. I prefer to run the Navy Department from here."

THE DUAL RESPONSIBILITY OF ADMINISTRATIVE SUBORDINATES

The President is charged by the Constitution with the responsibility to "see that the laws are faithfully executed." Obviously he cannot personally supervise the carrying out of every statute. He cannot even carry out personally the surprisingly large number of laws which name the President himself as responsible for performing the acts authorized or directed to be done. A survey made in 1946 revealed that there were approximately 1100 different sections of federal statutes imposing administrative tasks upon the President directly, of which some 800 were current and continuing ones. He must delegate some of the less important of these chores to subordinates so that he can devote his attention to more important questions of policy. Indeed, many of the duties and powers of higher executive officials in the federal administration actually are vested by law originally in the President and subdelegated by him.

Taking note of this situation, the Hoover Commission in its Report in 1949 recommended that Congress pass a general statute authorizing the President to subdelegate any functions vested in him by law and setting up the conditions under which this might be done. Such a statute, the McCormack Presidential Subdelegation Act, was passed in 1950. The story is told that Representative McCormack, then the House Democratic Floor Leader, was moved to initiate action on the bill when he visited President Truman's office one day and found the desk buried under an avalanche of documents, many of trivial consequence, with the President laboriously going through them. "Why don't you let somebody else handle some of that stuff?"

[2] Bertram M. Gross, *The Legislative Struggle* (New York: McGraw-Hill Book Company, 1953), p. 105, quoting Jim G. Lucas, "Vinson the Invincible," *Washington Daily News*, October 17, 1949.

he asked the President. "I can't," said Mr. Truman. "The laws say the President must do it, and I'm the President."

The general conditions spelled out in the Presidential Sub-delegation Act of 1950[3] to govern the matter are: (1) the powers and duties which may be subdelegated must have been assigned to the President by statute; (2) the officer to whom the delegation is made must be a "presidential" officer, i.e., one appointed with the advice and consent of the Senate; (3) the delegation must be made in writing and must be published in the *Federal Register*; (4) the President must continue to bear responsibility for the action taken by a subordinate under the statutory authority involved; and (5) the delegation cannot be made irrevocable. The McCormack Act also covers statutes passed by Congress which assign duties and functions directly to subordinates of the President, but specify that actions they authorize shall be "subject to the approval of the President." The President may subdelegate this kind of approval authority as well.

Since a presidential subordinate may be acting in the name of the President or in accordance with specific directives from him, he may on occasion find himself confronted by a dilemma. He may have to choose between administering a law as he understands it, i.e., conforming to his own view of the legislature's commands, or following his superior's directive on a given point. To refuse to follow the legislature's command may expose him or his agency to the array of sanctions available to that body, including "grilling" by a committee, the withholding of funds, redefinition of his powers and duties by statute, or even the abolition of his post. To refuse to follow the chief executive's directive, on the other hand, may result in a variety of disciplinary measures culminating in removal from office if his post is one lying within the range of the chief executive's removal power.

The classic illustration of the point is afforded by the episode in President Jackson's administration relative to the removal of United States government deposits from the Second United States Bank. Convinced that the Bank was a growing evil influence in American political affairs, the President was determined to curtail its power and privileges. He directed his Secretary of the Treasury, William Duane, to discontinue use of the Bank as a depository for government funds. Under the statute of establishing the Bank the Secretary was

3 64 *Stat.* 419, *U.S. Code* (1964), Title 3, Secs. 301–303. For discussion of this act, the presidential overload problem it was designed to meet, and legal questions involved, see Sidney Hyman, "To Ease the Burden of the Presidency," *The New York Times Magazine*, March 23, 1958; Glendon A. Schubert, Jr., "Judicial Review of the Subdelegation of Presidential Power," *Journal of Politics*, Vol. 12 (November, 1950), pp. 668–693; and *ibid.*, "The Presidential Subdelegation Act of 1950," Vol. 13 (November, 1951), pp. 647–674; and C. Dwight Waldo and William Pincus, "The Statutory Obligations of the President: Executive Necessity and Administrative Burden," *Public Administration Review*, Vol. VI (Autumn, 1946), pp. 339–347.

directed to use it for this purpose, though he could discontinue doing so, but only if he found certain conditions prevailing with regard to the Bank's fiscal status. Duane, after looking into the Bank's condition, concluded that none of the grounds spelled out in the statute existed and maintained he therefore had no legal authority to withdraw federal deposits. Jackson thereupon removed Duane and appointed his Attorney General, Roger B. Taney, to the post of Secretary of the Treasury. In his capacity at Attorney General Taney had already rendered an opinion to the President defending the President's authority to impose his will upon his subordinate in this matter. Taney promptly complied with the President's directive.

There was, as might have been expected, a great uproar from the friends of the Bank in Congress. Theretofore the Secretary of the Treasury, among all the heads of departments, had been regarded as uniquely responsible to Congresss because of the fiscal management functions peculiar to his office. Jackson's action cavalierly challenged this understanding. The President's critics in the Senate apparently would gladly have entertained an impeachment charge against him from the House, but none came forth. The Senate had to content itself with refusing even to consider confirmation of Taney's appointment to the Treasury post (he had been given a recess appointment), and with voting a "Resolution of Censure" condemning the President for "assuming upon himself authority and power not conferred by the Constitution and laws, but in derogation of both." Jackson's reply in the form of a "protest" addressed to the Senate was a spirited defense of his actions and, in effect, an appeal to the people for support of his position.[4] The withdrawal order was not rescinded.

Fortunately, such clashes between the chief executive and the legislature over matters of administrative policy are rarely carried to the point of head-on collision between the two. Recourse to the courts to resolve questions concerning the scope of authority of administrative officers and the procedures to be followed by them is ordinarily the final step, taken only if accommodation between the two branches is not reached by the more normal process of interplay of political pressure and influence. The chief executive may himself initiate legal action in the courts through appropriate agents to restrain an administrative officer from acting in a manner contrary to the chief executive's views

---

[4] Richardson, *Messages and Papers of the Presidents*, Vol. III, pp. 69ff. The Senate ordered that the President's protest message not be entered in its Journal. Expungement of the Resolution of Censure from the pages of the Senate's Journal as a symbol of the vindication of the President became an objective of Jackson's supporters in that body thereafter. This was finally achieved in January, 1837, near the close of Jackson's second administration. For a vivid account of Jackson's "War on the Bank" and the censure matter, see Marquis James, *The Life of Andrew Jackson* (Indianapolis: The Bobbs-Merrill Company, 1938), pp. 647ff.

of his duties under the law or to compel him to perform duties required by law, if more direct means of control are not available to him. The courts thus are made to serve as instruments for compelling administrative officers to conform to the limitations inherent in the "rule of law" or coercing them into the performance of their legal duties, as perceived by the chief executive. They serve as umpires, as it were, in the game of administration.

THE COURTS AND THE CHIEF EXECUTIVE

This is not to say that the courts are always the compliant tool of the President for effectuating his conception of his role as chief administrator. Nor on the other hand does it mean that judicial authority is always available to impose a check upon the chief executive himself when he strays beyond the boundaries of authority vested in him by the Constitution and the laws. As was pointed out by Hamilton, the courts are the "least dangerous" of the three branches of government, since they possess "no influence over either the sword or the purse."[5] In most matters they are dependent upon officers subject to the control of the chief executive to give effect to their decrees, orders, and judgments. Executive powers and duties are usually defined in broad terms, and the courts recognize that by their nature they are not readily susceptible to narrow, constrictive definition. Moreover, the chief executive is the head of a coordinate branch of government, on a plane of constitutional equality with the courts. The President takes a special oath to "preserve, protect and defend" the Constitution and to "faithfully execute" the office he holds, and governors are bound by similar oaths. Presumably a chief executive acts in conformity with these solemn obligations, as he understands them, no less than do judges with respect to their own obligations as guardians of the Constitution and the laws.

As President Jackson put it in defending his right and obligation to veto on grounds of its unconstitutionality a bill for rechartering the Bank of the United States, even though the Supreme Court had already declared that Congress had constitutional authority to charter such a Bank:

> The Congress, the Executive, and the Courts must each for itself be guided by its own opinion of the Constitution. Each public officer who takes an oath to support the Constitution swears that he will support it as he understands it, and not as it is undersood by others. It is as much the duty of the House of Representatives, of the Senate, and of the President to decide upon the constitutionality of any bill or resolution which may be presented to them for passage or approval as it is of the supreme judges when it may be brought before them for

[5] *The Federalist,* No. 78.

judicial decision. The opinion of the judges has no more authority over Congress than the opinion of Congress has over the judges, and on that point the President is independent of both. The authority of the Supreme Court must not, therefore, be permitted to control the Congress or the Executive when acting in their legislative capacities, but to have only such influence as the force of their reasoning may deserve.[6]

Jackson's remarks, of course, had reference to the functioning of the President in his "legislative capacity," but the point he made has relevance also to performance of his other duties as well. The fact is that the courts tend to give chief executives considerable latitude to interpret and define for themselves their constitutional and statutory powers in the administrative sphere, and they apply rather generously the doctrine of "political questions" when called upon to resolve issues involving the chief executive's authority in the sphere of administration.[7]

Indeed, so far as an incumbent President is concerned, it is very doubtful whether he is personally answerable to the process of any court, other than the Senate sitting as a court of impeachment, for any action taken by him in his capacity as chief executive.[8] President Jefferson set an early precedent. During the trial of Aaron Burr on treason charges before a United State circuit court presided over by Chief Justice Marshall, the court issued a subpoena *duces tecum* to the President directing him to appear as a witness and to bring with him certain papers deemed pertinent by Burr to his defense. Jefferson did not deign to make a direct answer to the court's order, and the original documents sought by Burr's attorney were never produced. Nothing further was done by the court.[9] No court has since attempted to use its subpoena power against a President, nor has any court presumed to issue a mandamus to a President in an attempt to compel him to perform a duty, ministerial or otherwise, required of him by law or by the Constitution.

The President, moreover, may not be made the respondent in an injunction proceeding designed to resolve the question of the constitutionality of a statute which it becomes his duty to execute. This was the import of the ruling by the Supreme Court in the Reconstruction

---

[6] Richardson, *op. cit.*, Vol. II, p. 582.

[7] For a comprehensive analysis of judicial pronouncements on the subject of presidential powers see Glendon A. Schubert, Jr., *The Presidency in the Courts* (Minneapolis: University of Minnesota Press, 1957).

[8] Certain statutes, however, authorize the bringing of suits under them "in the name of the President," which has the effect of making the President technically a litigant in cases. Schubert, *The Presidency in the Courts*, p. 321.

[9] *United States* v. *Burr*, 25 Fed. Cas. 55, No. 14,693 (1807). Jefferson did allow excerpts from certain documents to be furnished the court through a third party, it should be noted. Cf. Schubert, *The Presidency in the Courts*, pp. 319–320, 327–329.

era case of *Mississippi* v. *Johnson*.[10] In this instance the state of Mississippi, seeking to bring about a judicial declaration of the unconstitutionality of two Reconstruction acts, asked that President Andrew Johnson be enjoined from enforcing them. The laws in question had been passed over his veto, and he had already indicated his belief that they were in some respects unconstitutional. Caught in the cross fire between the President and Congress, the Court dismissed the suit, ruling that the President's duty to see that the laws are faithfully executed was in no sense "ministerial" but was "purely executive and political" and hence beyond judicial control through this type of proceeding.

Showing that he fully appreciated the political practicalities of the situation, Chief Justice Chase, speaking for the Court, stated:

> The Congress is the legislative department of the government; the President is the executive department. Neither can be restrained in its action by the judicial department; though the acts of both, when performed, are, in proper cases, subject to its cognizance. . . .
> Suppose the bill filed and the injunction prayed for allowed. If the President refuse obedience, it is without power to enforce its process. If, on the other hand, the President complies with the order of the court and refuses to execute the acts of Congress, is it not clear that a collision may occur between the executive and legislative departments of government? May not the House of Representatives impeach the President for such refusal? And in that case could this court interfere, in behalf of the President, thus endangered by compliance with its mandate, and restrain by injunction the Senate of the United States from sitting as a court of impeachment?

When an attempt was made subsequently to bring the same question before the Supreme Court through an injunction proceeding initiated by the State of Georgia against the Secretary of War, who was entrusted with immediate administrative responsibility to carry out the acts in question, the Court again sidestepped the issue, holding that the suit presented a political question and was merely an effort to obtain by indirection what the Court had refused to grant in *Mississippi* v. *Johnson*.[11] The recent Supreme Court rebuff to Governor Wallace of Alabama—when he sought to enjoin the Secretary of Defense, acting under presidential directive, from preparing to use military force to support enforcement of court orders directing desegregation of public facilities in Birmingham—was in line with these precedents.[12]

While the President in his capacity as chief executive and Chief of Administration is personally immune from judicial process, his acts, when performed, may be subject to judicial cognizance "in proper

[10] 4 Wallace 475 (1867).
[11] *Georgia* v. *Stanton*, 6 Wallace 50 (1868).
[12] *Alabama, By and Through Wallace* v. *United States and McNamara*, 373 U.S. 545 (1963).

cases," as indicated by Chief Justice Chase's opinion in *Mississippi* v. *Johnson*. Since he cannot personally perform all administrative duties falling upon his office he must act through his subordinates for the most part. They may be subjected to judicial control in some instances even when their actions are based upon a presidential directive. This proposition was first enunciated by way of dictum in Chief Justice Marshall's famous opinion in the case of *Marbury* v. *Madison*.[13] The Chief Justice drew a distinction between the "ministerial" duties imposed by law on a subordinate executive official and duties of a "political" nature vested in him by law or presidential directive. The Secretary of State could be mandamused by a court to compel performance of a legally imposed duty of the former sort (in this instance, delivery of a commission of office) even though a presidential directive ran to the contrary, said Marshall. On jurisdictional grounds the Court did not actually issue a mandamus in that instance. In a later case during President Jackson's administration, however, the Supreme Court did sustain a lower court order directing Postmaster General Kendall to pay in full a claim to one Stokes after Congress had passed a special act ordering payment.[14] The Postmaster General's declaration that he was acting under presidential order in refusing to pay the claim in full was held by the Court to be an insufficient defense.

Presidential orders that have the effect of conferring powers or duties upon subordinates beyond the bounds of law may likewise be questioned through judicial proceedings and disallowed as acts exceeding presidential authority. Here again, while the scope of the President's legal or constitutional authority may be the essential issue at stake, his power to act in a given way must be tested through a proceeding directed toward the subordinate rather than the President in person. The Supreme Court first asserted this principle in the case of *Little* v. *Barreme*[15] in 1804, with Chief Justice Marshall acting as the Court's spokesman. Instructions given by President John Adams to the captains of American naval vessels directing them to make seizures of vessels bound to intermediate ports as the ultimate step in enforcement of an act restricting commercial intercourse with France were, in the Court's judgment, not authorized by law and were held to be invalid. Since that time there have been approximately 40 cases, most of them involving Supreme Court rulings, in which courts have found presidential proclamations, administrative orders, or instructions to subordinates to be invalid on constitutional or statutory grounds.[16]

A state governor does not enjoy immunity from judicial process

13 1 Cranch 137, 166 (1803).
14 *Kendall* v. *United States,* 12 Peters 524 (1838).
15 2 Cranch 170 (1804).
16 Schubert, *The Presidency in the Courts,* pp. 361–366, lists 38 cases of this character in chronological order which had been decided down to 1957.

to the same degree that the President does. Under the principle of supremacy of federal law set forth in Article VI of the Constitution, a governor may be directly restrained by use of a federal court's injunctive powers when the purpose is to prevent denial of rights based on national laws, treaties, or the Constitution, or to remove obstructions to the lawful processes of the national government. His duty to enforce the laws of his state or to maintain his state's "sovereignty" must give way to a superior regime of federal law applied by the courts. Recent illustrative cases are *Sterling* v. *Constantin*,[17] wherein resort to martial law by Governor Sterling of Texas to enforce state legislation regulating oil production was held to be enjoinable by a federal court to prevent violation of constitutional rights founded in the Fourteenth Amendment; and *Cooper* v. *Aaron*,[18] upholding a federal court injunction against interference by various parties, including Governor Faubus of Arkansas, with the desegregation of a public high school in Little Rock in accordance with a federal court order. In the latter case the Supreme Court, speaking through Chief Justice Warren, declared:

> No state legislator or executive or judicial officer can war against the Constitution without violating his undertaking to support it. . . . A Governor who asserts a power to nullify a federal court order is similarly restrained. If he had such power, said Chief Justice Hughes [in *Sterling* v. *Constantin*] in 1932, also for a unanimous Court, "it is manifest that the fiat of a State Governor, and not the Constitution of the United States, would be the supreme law of the land. . . ."

As an individual subject to national laws, moreover, a state governor enjoys no immunity from federal criminal prosecution and the imposition of the sanctions of federal criminal statutes. These may have the effect of disqualifying him from holding office or force his resignation.[19] He may be made the defendant in a state court proceeding questioning his title to the office he occupies.[20] Depending upon the particular terms of his state's constitution and laws he may be enjoined or mandamused directly through the courts of his state in connection with the exercise of certain of his official powers and duties.[21] As in the case of the President, his authority to act in his capacity as chief administrator may also be questioned in court proceedings involving officers acting in his name or under his directives and instructions. A notable exception to the general rule of subjection of a governor to

17 287 U.S. 378 (1932).

18 358 U.S. 1 (1958). For other recent cases illustrating the general point, see *Wilson and Co.* v. *Freeman*, 179 F. Supp. 520 (1960); and *U.S.* v. *Phillips*, 33 F. Supp. 261 (1940).

19 See the instances noted, *supra*, pp. 167, 210.

20 *Supra*, pp. 166–168.

21 Cf. *Jenkins* v. *Knight*, 46 Calif. (2nd) 220, 293 P. (2nd) 6 (1956), and cases cited therein.

federal judicial control was the holding of the Supreme Court in the century-old case of *Kentucky* v. *Dennison*.[22] In that case, the rule of which is still observed, Chief Justice Taney maintained that by reason of a governor's position as the head of a state's government, a mandamus proceeding was not appropriate to compel him to perform the legal duty laid upon him by the Constitution and national statute to deliver up fugitives from justice on proper demand of the governor of another state. Refusals by governors to comply with such requests for one reason or another still occur occasionally. This has given rise to the erroneous notion that a governor has a legal "right" to use his discretion in complying with such requests. The Court's opinion makes clear that he has a constitutional *duty* to cooperate, but that no sanction can be employed by the Court to compel him to do so.

ACCESS TO INFORMATION

Highly pertinent to supervision of administrative officers is the matter of access to information in their hands. Full knowledge of the facts relative to an administrative officer's conduct of affairs in his charge is essential in making decisions on how he should function and in holding him to account for his acts of omission or commission. The President must be armed with adequate authority to compel compliance with his requests for information of this kind; he usually has such authority through specific statutory grants as well as by virtue of the general supervisory power and influence associated with his office. By such devices as imposing through statutes the duty upon administrative officials to render reports to it, making informal inquiries, adopting resolutions requesting specific information, or conducting formal hearings, Congress may likewise cause pertinent data to be placed before it.

The volume of information flowing upward to the higher echelons in the administrative hierarchy and from the administration to Congress and to the public is truly staggering. A compilation in 1960 revealed no less than 274 separate sections of federal statutes requiring the President himself or various agencies of administration to render reports to Congress on one subject or another.[23] These were supplemented by numerous others requiring that reports be made to higher administrative officers or that information be published. If needful, Congress may use a subpoena process under threat of possible punishment for contempt of Congress to compel production of testimony and papers, so long as the information demanded has relevance to a

[22] 24 Howard 66 (1861).
[23] *Federal Statutes on Availability of Information*, House Committee on Government Operations, 86th Congress, 2nd Session (1960), (Committee Print), pp. 1–71.

properly defined legislative purpose and the individual involved does not invoke his constitutional right not to incriminate himself.[24]

Here again there is the possibility of a clash of wills between the President and Congress, although it must be kept in mind that in the vast majority of instances executive compliance with congressional requests for information is the rule. Information desired by Congress may be of such a nature that, in the President's judgment, to reveal it would be "incompatible with the public interest" or would involve a violation of the separation of powers principle by permitting legislative intrusion into matters lying within the province of the executive alone. For example, the President may feel that instructions given in secrecy to his subordinates relating to diplomatic negotiations, military plans and movements, or espionage operations should not be aired publicly because of the adverse effect this might have on the conduct of foreign relations or on national security. He may feel that the information sought might, if revealed, seriously injure the reputations of innocent persons or impair the morale of civil servants by exposing them to unjustified political attacks and reprisals. Sources of information upon which administrative authorities have relied under a pledge of secrecy may be foreclosed if their identity is publicly revealed, with consequent adverse repercussions on the processes of law enforcement. Public revelation of conversations carried on in confidence between the President and his advisers might impair the free interchange of views that must exist between him and those upon whom he relies in making politically thorny decisions.

In some measure these problems may be met by the President's conveying the information desired to individual members of Congress— a committee chairman, the party leaders in Congress, or even all the members of a particular committee—under a gentleman's agreement pledge that the information will not be made public; even this may not be considered feasible, however, if a "leak" would be extremely embarrassing. There are, therefore, occasional flat refusals by the President to furnish the information demanded by Congress or one of its committees.

A precedent was set during Washington's administration, and there have been few Presidents since who have not had occasion to invoke the "public interest" or "executive privilege" as justification for refusals to comply with congressional requests. In 1792 when the House of Representatives was conducting its first full-fledged investigation—an inquiry into the circumstances surrounding the disastrous outcome of

[24] Leading cases on the scope of congressional power to employ compulsion to induce production of testimony include *McGrain* v. *Daugherty*, 273 U.S. 135 (1927); *Watkins* v. *U.S.*, 354 U.S. 178 (1957); and *Barenblatt* v. *U.S.*, 360 U.S. 109 (1959).

the expedition of General St. Clair against the Indian tribes in the Ohio country—the committee involved was authorized by the House to "call for such persons, papers and records as may be necessary to assist their inquiries." The committee therefore called upon the President to furnish it with all the official documents relating to the expedition. After lengthy consultation with his department heads, President Washington complied with the request by releasing the papers asked for, but he included with the letter of transmittal a statement warning that the President in the future would deem it his duty to refuse to surrender papers when disclosure "would be injurious to the public."

Four years later he felt that a situation had arisen justifying application of this rule. The House of Representatives, some of whose members were reluctant to vote the funds needed to carry out the terms of the unpopular Jay Treaty with England, passed a resolution calling upon the President to submit a copy of the diplomatic instructions by which Jay had been guided in conducting the negotiations, along with any other documents relating to the treaty negotiations. President Washington promptly declined to furnish the requested information. To do so, he declared, would be "impolitic," for this might have "a pernicious influence on future negotiations, or produce immediate inconveniences, perhaps danger and mischief, in relation to the other Powers."[25] He went on to give the House a polite lecture on its proper role in connection with the treaty-making process, drawing on his own personal knowledge of the deliberations by the Constitutional Convention of 1787 on this subject.

Since that time the claim of executive privilege has been extended by succeeding Presidents to cover a great variety of other matters involving the President and those under his direction.[26] President Jack-

[25] Richardson, *op. cit.*, I, p. 194.

[26] A resume of instances of refusal by the Presidents from Washington to Truman to furnish information requested by the houses of Congress or their committees and a defense of this practice on constitutional and legal grounds is given in "The Power of the President to Withhold Information from Congress," a memorandum prepared by Attorney General Rogers and published by the Subcommittee on Constitutional Rights of the Senate Judiciary Committee, 85th Congress, 2nd Session (1958), (Committee Print). Essentially the same material is presented in Exhibit XVII, a memorandum from Attorney General Rogers, entitled "Is a Congressional Committee Entitled to Demand and Receive Information and Papers From the President and the Heads of Departments, Which They Deem Confidential, in the Public Interest," printed in *Availability of Information from Federal Departments and Agencies*, Part 12, Hearings before a Subcommittee of the House Government Operations Committee, 84th Congress, 2nd Session (June 20 and 22, 1956), pp. 2891–2945. Exhibit XXI, a House Government Operations Committee Print found in the same document, pp. 2997–3028, is a study by the staff of the Committee entitled "The Right of Congress to Obtain Information from the Executive and from Other Agencies of the Federal Government," which offers a rebuttal to the Attorney General's contentions.

son, for example, indignantly rejected a Senate demand that he furnish it a copy of a paper he had read in a Cabinet meeting on the subject of removal of deposits from the Bank of the United States. President Polk gave a new dimension to the privilege when he refused to comply with a House request to supply a list of payments made in secrecy, but with presidential approval, by Secretary of State Webster during the *preceding* Tyler administration. Presidents Fillmore, Buchanan, Lincoln, Grant, and Cleveland all had occasion to refuse congressional requests for information.

Theodore Roosevelt, as one might expect, battled with Congress over this type of issue. When the Senate passed a resolution calling upon his Attorney General to inform it whether or not antitrust law proceedings had been begun against the United States Steel Corporation, and if not, why not, Roosevelt replied that he had been advised by his legal officer that there were insufficient grounds for proceeding against the Corporation. Unsatisfied with this reply the Senate then sought to obtain the desired information from Herbert Knox Smith, head of the Bureau of Corporations in the Department of Commerce. Smith reported the matter to the President, who then ordered Smith to turn all the pertinent documents over to him. When this had been accomplished Roosevelt informed the Senate:

> I have those papers in my possession, and last night I informed Senator Clark of the Judiciary Committee what I had done. I told him also that the Senate should not have those papers and that Herbert Knox Smith had turned them over to me. The only way the Senate or the committee can get those papers now is through my impeachment. . . . Some of these facts which they want . . . were given to the Government under the seal of secrecy and cannot be divulged, and I will see to it that the word of this government to the individual is kept sacred.[27]

A resolution was subsequently introduced in the Senate declaring that "every public document, paper, or record or copy thereof" in the files of any department "is subject to the call or inspection of the Senate for its use in the exercise of its constitutional powers and jurisdiction," but after an acrimonious debate the Senate failed to bring the resolution to a vote.

In the period since World War II there have been many tiffs between the President and Congress over the exercise of executive privilege and alleged "management of the news" by executive officials. The conditions of the Cold War have induced officials concerned with defense matters and foreign affairs—in some cases, no doubt, unjustifiably—to continue wartime secrecy practices on grounds of national security. Moreover, statutory directives authorize and require maintenance of secrecy about many such matters and make disclosure to

[27] Attorney General Rogers, Exhibit XVII, *supra*, p. 2904.

an unauthorized person a crime. Both Presidents Truman and Eisenhower thought it necessary to impose a "freeze" on release of raw-file FBI data on governmental employees subject to loyalty check, much to the discomfiture of House and Senate investigative committees intent on exposing and routing out alleged Communist sympathizers and subversives. Both had occasion to refuse to allow their subordinates to reveal to congressional committees the substance of confidential exchanges between themselves and their subordinates on matters within this area of the chief executive's responsibility.

Some members of Congress have writhed in frustration at this unwillingness by the President to reveal what, as they see it, the public and Congress have a right to know. They have sought by various means to impose their will upon the President, but up to now no congressional challenge has been carried so far as to produce a definitive judicial pronouncement on the constitutional issue. In 1948 Congress passed a bill proposing to amend the Atomic Energy Act so as to authorize the Senate members of the Joint Congressional Committee on Atomic Energy to direct the FBI to conduct investigations and compile files on nominees for appointment to the Atomic Energy Commission and make the data available to the Senate when it considers the President's nominations. President Truman vetoed this measure on the ground that it would constitute an "unwarranted encroachment of the legislative upon the executive branch." His veto was sustained by the narrow margin of 47 to 29 in the Senate.[28]

Meanwhile, an even more formidable assault was launched in the House on the fortress of executive privilege. Secretary of Commerce W. Averell Harriman, acting on presidential order, had refused to produce under subpoena the FBI file of a departmental officer under fire from the House Un-American Activities Committee. Only a week before the President's narrow victory in the Senate on the AEC amendatory bill, the House passed by an almost purely partisan vote, 219 to 152, a bill sponsored by Representative Hoffman of Michigan. It would have directed all executive departments and heads thereof, exempting only the President himself, to make available to congressional committees information thought necessary "to enable them to properly perform the duties delegated to them by the Congress." Refusal by any federal officer to comply with a demand would have been made punishable by a fine of up to $1000 and/or one year of imprisonment. President Truman in a press conference stated flatly he would veto the bill if it ever got to him. He was spared that task, since the Senate failed to act on the measure.

Eventually, in 1958, a bill was passed by Congress and signed by

[28] *Congressional Record*, 80th Congress, 2nd Session (1948), pp. 5895, 6191, 6247ff.

President Eisenhower that had relevance to the subject of availability of information, but it was relatively innocuous and did not constitute a direct challenge to the principle of executive privilege. The Availability of Information Act,[29] as it was termed, merely had the effect of denying that any implication of statutory support for witholding information was to be drawn from an early "housekeeping" statute enacted in 1789 imposing custodial duties over governmental documents on certain administrative officers. In signing the measure President Eisenhower was careful to issue a clarifying statement pointing out that he had given his approval to it with the understanding that it in no way would affect the President's constitutional privilege to withhold information whose release he considered not compatible with the public interest. He likewise reserved his constitutional right to withhold information when he signed the Mutual Security Act of 1959, which with subsequently adopted appropriation acts contained clauses directing the cutting off of funds for foreign military aid unless certain information was supplied to congressional committees on demand. Subsequently his Attorney General rendered an opinion construing this legislation so as not to require him to release information thought incompatible with the public interest.[30]

One of the most significant of the incidents in the post-World War II period in the tug-of-war between Presidents and Congress over access to information occurred in 1953. Immediately upon assumption of office following the political overturn produced by the 1952 election, important figures in Congress and in the new administration busied themselves with investigations designed to bear out 1952 campaign charges that the preceding Truman administration had been "soft on Communism." Following the publication of a charge by Attorney General Brownell that President Truman, in appointing one Harry Dexter White as Director of the International Monetary Fund in 1946, had appointed and kept in office for 14 months a person "known at the time to have been regarded by the FBI as a Russian spy," Chairman Harold Velde of the House Un-American Activities Committee issued subpoenas to former President Truman, Governor James Byrnes of South Carolina, and Supreme Court Justice Tom Clark, to further an investigation into the circumstances of the appointment. Byrnes had been Secretary of State when the appointment of White was made, and Clark had been Truman's Attorney General at the time.

Issuance of these subpoenas fell like a bombshell on official Washington. Representative Walter, ranking Democratic member of the

[29] 72 *Stat.* 547; *U.S. Code* (1964), Title 5, Sec. 22. See Chap. 11, p. 359.
[30] — *Ops. Attys. Gen.* — (December 19, 1960). The opinion is presented in full in *House Report No. 818,* Committee on Governmental Operations, 87th Congress, 1st Session (1961).

Committee, assailed Chairman Velde for his unilateral decision to issue the subpoenas, terming it the "most incredible, insulting, un-American thing that I've encountered in my 21 years in Congress."[31] President Eisenhower in a press conference gently chided Velde, saying he "personally" would not have issued a subpoena to the former President, whose patriotism he did not question. Justice Clark refused to respond to the subpoena on the ground that the House lacked power to compel a Supreme Court Justice to testify before one of its committees. Governor Byrnes likewise refused to acknowledge the power of the Committee to compel his attendance in Washington. He contended it might interfere with his carrying on his duties as a state governor, but he indicated his willingness to supply what information he could by affidavit, and later did so.[32]

Ex-President Truman accepted service of the subpoena and at first gave every indication that he welcomed the opportunity to appear before the Committee and clear himself of the Attorney General's charges. On soberer second thought, he changed his mind. He issued instead a blistering public statement in which he stated that, although he would personally like to appear, he felt it was his "duty to the people of the United States" to decline to comply with the subpoena. Citing numerous precedents in support of his position, he concluded that the ground upon which earlier presidential refusals to supply information were based—the necessity for maintaining the independence of the executive branch under the system of separation of powers—were equally applicable to a President after his term of office has expired when the purpose of an inquiry is to examine into his official acts as President. A President in office, knowing that his acts might thus be subjected to congressional scrutiny after he left office, he maintained, could be intimidated in the performance of his constitutional duties.[33] Former President Truman's action in this instance had the effect of reinforcing the precedent set by President Polk in refusing to release confidential information in his possession involving the prior Tyler administration.

[31] *The New York Times*, November 11, 1953, p. 1.
[32] *Ibid.* In his statement, Governor Byrnes declared:

> I cannot, by appearing in response to this summons, admit your right to command a Governor to leave his state and remain in the city of Washington until granted leave by your committee to return. . . .
> A Governor must be the sole judge of when he can leave his state and he must be free to return to it without permission of a committee of the Congress.

Governor Byrnes' position does not appear to be altogether sound in the light of Supreme Court pronouncements on the obligation of a governor to comply with the constitutional commands of an agency of the national government operating within its proper sphere, but he was not without a precedent in adopting the view he advanced. In 1951 Governor Fuller Warren of Florida had refused on similar grounds to respond to a subpoena issued by the Senate Crime Investigating Committee after he had previously failed to respond to the Committee's repeated invitations to testify. The Senate Committee did not press the matter further.

[33] *The New York Times*, November 13, 1953, pp. 1, 4.

No further effort was made by the House committee to press the issue.

What the attitude of the courts might be on this constitutional question, if it were pressed upon them for resolution, is a matter of conjecture. In a recent case the Supreme Court's majority opinion clearly intimated that there is a subject matter field belonging exclusively to the President into which Congress may not intrude through use of its investigatory authority.[34] There are members of Congress, however, who contend that the existence of a constitutionally based executive privilege to withhold information from Congress is a "myth," and who urge that a judicial test on the point would establish their contention. Others more realistically point out that in certain areas of presidential operations, particularly where the conduct of diplomatic relations, military matters, and national security are involved, a persuasive argument can be made for recognition of the President's constitutional right to exercise discretion. Reports of the House Committee on Government Operations and hearings conducted by its Subcommittee on Government Information (the so-called "Moss Committee" presided over by Representative John E. Moss of California) over the past decade provide a vast mine of information and opinion on this controversial subject.[35]

It is significant to note that presidential refusals to supply information to Congress are usually accepted in good faith by Congress and its committees. There is significance also in the fact that Congress has never seen fit to carry a fight over this issue to the point of forcing a judicial pronouncement. The question where the constitutional dividing line should be drawn between the "right" of Congress, on the

[34] In *Barenblatt* v. *United States*, 360 U.S. 109 (1959), Justice Harlan's majority opinion stated (at pp. 111–112):

> Broad as it is, the [investigatory] power [of Congress] is not, however, without limitations. Since Congress may only investigate into those areas in which it may potentially legislate or appropriate, it cannot inquire into matters which are within the exclusive province of one or the other branches of the Government. Lacking the judicial power given to the Judiciary, it cannot inquire into matters that are exclusively the concern of the Judiciary. Neither can it supplant the Executive in what exclusively belongs to the Executive.

[35] *Availability of Information from Federal Departments and Agencies: Index and Bibliography*, House Committee on Government Operations, 88th Congress, 2nd Session (1964), (Committee Print), p. 94, provides a complete index on the inquires of that Committee into the question, along with an exhaustive bibliography. Among items relating specifically to the matter of executive privilege, see the Symposium on "Executive Privilege: The Public's Right to Know and Public Interest," *Federal Bar Journal*, Vol 19 (January, 1959); Senator Thomas Hennings, "Constitutional Law: The People's Right to Know," *American Bar Association Journal*, Vol. 45 (July, 1959); Bernard Schwartz, "Executive Privilege and Congressional Investigatory Power," *California Law Review*, Vol. 44 (March, 1959); Joseph W. Bishop, "The Executive's Right to Privacy: An Unresolved Constitutional Question," *Yale Law Journal*, Vol. 66 (February, 1957); Francis E. Rourke, "Administrative Secrecy: A Congressional Dilemma," *American Political Science Review*, Vol. 54 (September, 1960); and Clark Mollenhoff, *Washington Cover-up*, (Garden City, N.Y.: Doubleday & Company, 1963).

one hand, to be informed and to use compulsory process to enforce that right, and on the other hand, the prerogative of the chief executive to function independently as the head of a coordinate branch of government is a perplexing one under the system of separation of powers. The problem, it might be noted, has appeared also at the state level; and state courts, where they have spoken, have by no means provided definitive answers to this puzzle. As with many other types of issues involving constitutional relations between the executive and legislative branches, there is a twilight zone wherein political pressures, personalities, and influence, rather than legalistic formulas and pronouncements must supply the answers on what the working relationship shall be.

DELEGATION OF "LEGISLATIVE" POWERS TO THE CHIEF EXECUTIVE

In providing for the execution of laws Congress and state legislative bodies frequently find it expedient to vest in the chief executive or his subordinates some discretionary authority in implementing the policies embodied in particular legislative acts. Sometimes the discretion consists in placing responsibility upon the executive to make a judgment that certain conditions spelled out in an act have arisen so as to cause its provisions to come into effect, or to cause them to be suspended in whole or in part. Again, the legislative body, unable for practical reasons to include all the details that must be supplied in implementing a general policy provided in an act, authorizes the executive to supplement the provisions of a statute by appropriate directives, regulations, and orders which become effective parts of the law in question. Quite often both these "contingent" and "supplementary" types of delegated authority are found in the same statute.

Moreover, the very process of supervising administration of the laws inevitably entails some discretion on the part of the executive charged with carrying them into execution. Before an administrator can begin the process of giving effect to a statute, he must make initial decisions on its scope and meaning. Federal and state statute books are loaded with laws of a regulatory or punitive character. It is too much to expect that all can or should be enforced with equal vigor. Often a chief executive as a matter of course will have been elected on a platform pledging to give special attention to the enforcement of laws in a particular sphere—the antitrust laws, liquor traffic laws, traffic safety laws, or laws relating to subversive activities, for example. A pledge of this kind implies a degree of selectivity or a kind of priority ranking among the laws which it becomes his constitutional duty to "faithfully execute."

In all these kinds of situations, the chief executive becomes, in effect, a lawmaker of sorts. In the first type of situation mentioned the chief executive becomes a lawmaker in that his conclusion that the contingency described in the legislative act has arisen has the effect of putting a particular policy into operation—or suspending its operation. When the contingency specified in a statute is an emergency brought about by war, economic crisis, a natural disaster, a threat to the public security and order, or some other vaguely described unusual situation which is the chief executive's responsibility to proclaim, the element of discretion vested in him to call certain statutory rules and policies into play is so broad as to approach very closely lawmaking itself. This is especially so if the measures the executive can put into effect are outlined only in very general terms by statute and he must supply substantive supplementary details by directive.

Both contingent and supplementary delegations of power to the executive by statute give rise to constitutional issues of consequence. They may raise, of course, questions concerning possible invasion of the constitutionally guaranteed rights of individuals affected by the measures he adopts. But this is not all. It is axiomatic in a government of delegated, separated powers that only the legislative branch is invested by the Constitution with *legislative* power and that it cannot redelegate to the executive legislative functions allocated to it. Hence the question also has to be faced whether delegation to the executive of authority to apply or to suspend the operation of a given statute or to promulgate supplementary rules having the force of law amounts to an unconstitutional delegation of lawmaking authority to the executive by legislative act. Beyond this lies the further question whether such statutes, even if constitutionally valid, are politically sound. On the one hand there is the wisdom conveyed in the hoary maxim that only a "government of laws and not of men" is compatible with the ideal of limited, representative government and the maintenance of liberty. On the other, there is the practical, commonsense view that considerable flexibility in executive and administrative action in adjusting governmental policies to meet rapidly changing, complex situations is a must in this day and age.

By and large, the courts of the nation and of the states as well have viewed with a tolerant eye legislation granting broad discretionary power to executive agencies. Relatively early in the nation's history federal courts were called upon to pass on the validity of certain acts of Congress granting a contingent "quasi-legislative" power to the President in a matter of great interest to the country. In an effort to avoid involvement of the United States in the Napoleonic Wars which flared intermittently between France and England during his two administrations, President Jefferson asked for and obtained adoption of an Embargo Act in 1807 under which American commercial intercourse with both these countries was suspended. His object was to bring pressure upon those nations to desist from what the United States maintained was unlawful interference with American shipping. The Embargo Act proved highly unpopular with American shipping interests as well as ineffective in achieving the ends desired. On March 1, 1809, immediately before Madison's inauguration as President, the Embargo Act was superseded by another statute which authorized the President to suspend its operations against either of the belligerents which should give assurance that it would respect the United States government's claims of immunity from seizure for its vessels and their cargoes.

On the mistaken assumption that Great Britain had given such assurance, President Madison issued a proclamation on April 19, 1809, suspending the embargo on trade with that country. Later, having learned that his action was based on erroneous information, he issued another proclamation declaring the original Embargo Act, along with its supplementary enforcing statutes, to have been revived against Great Britain. Lower federal courts held his second proclamation restoring the embargo to be invalid, since there was at the time no specific authorization by law for him to restore it once he had suspended it. The Congress soon rectified this omission by a legislative act passed on May 1, 1810. It authorized the President to invoke the embargo against one of the countries if he found the other had taken proper steps to discontinue the policies which the United States found objectionable. Believing (again mistakenly, as it turned out) that France had taken these steps, Madison suspended the embargo against France and restored it against Great Britain. The Supreme Court found in an ensuing case that the Act of May 1, 1810, which the President had relied upon as a basis for his action, was within the competence of Congress. The 1810 Act did not unconstitutionally delegate legislative power to the President, declared the Court. It could see "no sufficient reason why the legislature should not exercise its discretion in reviving the act of 1809, either expressly or conditionally as its judgment should direct."[36]

These early congressional experiments looking toward flexibility in the application of policies embodied in statutes were only a modest beginning for what eventually has meant vesting vast powers in the chief executive or in specifically designated officers in the executive branch to give definitive form and substance to broadly defined legislative policies. So far as the President is concerned, delegations of quasi-legislative authority in this manner have been most extensive and spectacular in the areas of administrative organization, fiscal and

[36] *United States* v. *The Brig Aurora,* 7 Cranch 382 (1813).

personnel management, military affairs, foreign political and economic policy, internal security, and national economic matters. Whether it likes it or not, Congress has been compelled by circumstances to invest the President (or particular agencies found in the administrative branch) with an increasing measure of authority to make final major policy determinations affecting the national interest and welfare.[37] Congress is too overloaded with work for it to retain the responsibility for making the myriad day-to-day decisions required in the administration of policies.

In dealing with the question of the constitutionality of such legislation the courts have insisted that the Constitution requires only that grants of quasi-legislative authority to the chief executive or to other agencies of administration be "canalized" to hold them within prescribed bounds. Appropriate standards, procedures, and policy objectives must be set forth to guide the executive in exercising the discretionary powers vested in him by law. When these are provided, in the view of the courts the executive acts not as a lawmaker when he administers such statutes but as an agent to effectuate Congress' will. For example, Congress in the Fordney-McCumber Tariff Act of 1922 incorporated a so-called "flexible tariff" formula under which the President, upon recommendation from the United States Tariff Commission, was authorized to alter by proclamation the tariff rates on particular items by as much as 50 percent from the statutory rates provided in the Act. Such action was authorized if it was found necessary in order to equalize competitive advantages between American and foreign producers. The Supreme Court held that Congress had not delegated its lawmaking authority to the President, even though his action had the effect of altering tariff duties fixed by law. Congress had merely made him its agent "to ascertain and declare the event upon which its expressed will was to take effect."[38]

During the nation's history the Supreme Court has found congressional grants of quasi-legislative power to the President to have transcended constitutional limits on only two occasions. Both cases involved provisions of the National Recovery Act of 1933. In *Schechter Poultry Corp.* v. *United States*[39] the Court ruled that provisions in the Act authorizing the President to approve and enforce as law individ-

---

[37] See J. Malcolm Smith and Cornelius P. Cotter, *Powers of the President during Crisis* (Washington: Public Affairs Press, 1960); and Robert S. Rankin and Winfred R. Dallmayr, *Freedom and Emergency Powers in the Cold War* (New York: Appleton Century-Crofts, 1964) for general reviews and comments on such legislation.

[38] *Hampton and Co.* v. *U.S.*, 276 U.S. 394, 411 (1928). In reaching this conclusion, Chief Justice Taft's opinion relied heavily upon an earlier decision of the Court, *Field* v. *Clark*, 143 U.S. 644 (1891), wherein a grant of power by Congress to the President to apply a higher schedule of tariff rates to imports from countries failing to make reciprocal tariff concessions on American goods had been held valid.

[39] 295 U.S. 495 (1935).

ually tailored self-regulatory "codes of fair competition" for various industries having substantial impact upon the economic life of the nation violated the separation of powers principle. The Act's lack of sufficiently clearly stated standards to govern the content of the codes rendered it defective as an attempt to delegate legislative power unconstitutionally to the President. In the other case, *Panama Refining Co.* v. *Ryan*,[40] the Court declared unconstitutional on the same ground another section of the same Act which granted the President authority to prohibit interstate transportation of "hot oil," i.e., petroleum produced in violation of state-fixed production quotas. Again, in the Court's view, there was no sufficiently clear statement of conditions or standards set forth in the Act to guide the President in making a decision on whether the authorized policy of restraint should be applied or not.

These cases stand out as exceptions to the general rule. Delegations of quasi-legislative powers of vast proportions to the President or to specifically named executive officers operating under his direction were thereafter sustained by the Court without serious demur.[41] Indeed, during the controversy over the New Deal's legitimacy, the Court noted that the policy-making powers vested in the President by the Constitution in the field of foreign affairs and the powers of Congress to legislate in that area were so intermingled that the separation of powers principle raises no substantial barrier to grants of powers of a legislative character to him by statute.[42] In one of his many notable dissents, Justice Oliver Wendell Holmes in the 1928 case of *Springer* v. *Philippine Islands*[43] stated what has come to be the Court's modern view of this problem:

> The great ordinances of the Constitution do not establish and divide fields of black and white. Even the more specific of them are found to terminate in a penumbra shading gradually from one extreme to the other. . . .
>
> It does not seem to need argument to show that however we may

40 293 U.S. 388 (1935).

41 Illustrative cases include *United States* v. *Rock Royal Cooperative*, 307 U.S. 533 (1939), upholding a grant of authority to the Secretary of Agriculture to set the prices for various agricultural commodities under marketing agreements authorized by the Agricultural Marketing Agreement Act of 1937; *Opp Cotton Mills* v. *Wage and Hour Administrator*, 312 U.S. 126 (1941), sustaining the authority of the Wage and Hour Administrator to formulate rules for administration of the Fair Labor Standards Act of 1938 and make temporary exceptions to the application of the minimum wage standard provided in the Act in the case of certain industries; *Yakus* v. *United States*, 321 U.S. 414 (1944), upholding the grant of authority to the Price Control Administration by the Emergency Price Control Act of 1942 to establish price ceilings on goods and services; and *Woods* v. *Miller*, 333 U.S. 138 (1948), sustaining the continuance of administratively determined wartime price ceilings on rents after cessation of actual hostilities.

42 *U.S.* v. *Curtis-Wright Export Corporation*, 299 U.S. 304 (1936), at pp. 319–320.

43 277 U.S. 189, 209–211 (1928).

disguise it by veiling words we do not and cannot carry out the distinction between legislative and executive action with mathematical precision and divide the branches into watertight compartments, were it ever so desirable to do so, which I am far from believing that it is, or that the Constitution requires.

The more effective limitations that can be brought to bear on presidential authority to promulgate rules, proclamations, and orders that have the force of law are those established by Congress itself rather than those proclaimed by the courts acting as arbiters of the boundaries between executive and legislative powers. For the most part those who argue for a greater involvement of Congress in controlling the actions of the President and the administration stress this point. Other students of the problem have suggested that relief from too much concentration of authority in the executive branch should come through a more rigid insistence by the courts upon respect for the separation of powers principle.[44] Congress has shown an increasing awareness of the facts of political life by employing a variety of limiting devices when making grants of quasi-legislative powers to executive agents, including the President.

In the first place, Congress attempts to define with as much particularity as circumstances permit the nature of the authority it confers on the President and the conditions governing its exercise. It normally seeks to avoid giving such legislation a blank check character; indeed, it must do so in most areas if its actions are to escape judicial condemnation as violating the constitutional dogma that legislative power, per se, may not be delegated to the executive. Secondly, Congress usually places a time limit on such grants. The time limit may be stated in terms of a specific date or period of time named in the delegating statute, or in terms of the occurrence of a particular event. This device was widely employed in grants of emergency powers to President Roosevelt before and during World War II. Authority granted by many of these statutes was to terminate upon the cessation of war or within a stated time thereafter, or upon the issuance of a proclamation by the President that the emergency had ceased to exist, or within a stated period after the President issued a proclamation that hostilities had ceased[45] Termination provisions of this kind have

[44] This is one of the main themes expounded in the late New Jersey Supreme Court Justice Arthur T. Vanderbilt's *The Doctrine of Separation of Powers and Its Present-Day Significance* (Lincoln: University of Nebraska Press, 1953).

[45] Cf. *Report to the President by the Attorney General Concerning the Limitation, Suspension, or Termination of Emergency, National Defense and War Legislation*, made by Attorney General Clark to President Truman on September 1, 1945, 40 *Ops. Attys. Gen.* 421; House Document No. 282, 79th Congress, 1st Session. This 97-page report summarizes the termination provisions of the principal wartime statutes then in effect. President Truman issued a proclamation declaring "hostilities" were to be deemed as having terminated as of December 31, 1946. *Code of Federal Regula-*

the effect of causing the grant of authority to expire in the normal course of events, even though no repealing statute is enacted by Congress. The unwillingness of Congress to eliminate the time-limit clause from the grant of authority to the President to initiate changes in the administrative structure under the formula prescribed by the Administrative Reorganization Act of 1949, despite repeated requests from all the Presidents since that time, is indicative of the jealous regard Congress entertains for its right to review such grants of power from time to time with a view to permitting them to lapse, if this is thought advisable.

A third type of safeguard Congress has used with increasing frequency in recent years has been a clause in such acts reserving to Congress the right to terminate their effectiveness by its adoption of a concurrent resolution stating that the conditions giving rise to the grant of authority no longer exist. This has the effect of making it possible for Congress, in effect, to repeal the authorizing statute without having to run the gauntlet of a presidential veto. The constitutional validity of this device was questioned by President Roosevelt when it was included in the termination provisions of the Lend-Lease Act of 1941, although for reasons of political strategy he did not make his objections public when he signed the bill.[46] The constitutional question involved has never been tested in the courts. The practical view of the matter would appear to be that if Congress can declare that a grant of power to the President to act in a specified way shall

---

tions 1943–1948, Proc. No. 2714. His proclamation had the effect of terminating the effectiveness of a large number of statutes which were by their terms effective during a "state of hostilities" or for a specified period of time thereafter.

[46] The Lend-Lease Act of March 11, 1941, 55 *Stat*, 31, provided that its effectiveness was to terminate on June 31, 1946, or after passage of a concurrent resolution by the two houses before that date declaring that the powers conferred by it were no longer necessary to promote the defense of the United States. Believing that this provision was a subterfuge to enable Congress to repeal the statute without subjecting its action to a possible veto, President Roosevelt instructed Attorney General Jackson to prepare a memorandum explaining that the President had signed the bill despite this "clearly unconstitutional provision" only because the emergency was so great he felt he had no choice. A memorandum to this effect was prepared and the President signed it. He asked that it be put in the Department of Justice files to be released at some future time. It was revealed by the then Justice Jackson in 1953. The memorandum, it might be noted, reversed the usual process in that it was, in effect, a presidential legal opinion given to the Department of Justice. See Robert H. Jackson, "A Presidential Legal Opinion," *Harvard Law Review*, Vol. 66 (June, 1953), pp. 1353–1361.

On the general subject of the use of the concurrent resolution as a checking device on the President and other administrative officers see Robert W. Ginnane, "The Control of Federal Administration by Congressional Resolutions and Committees," *Harvard Law Review*, Vol. 66 (February, 1953), pp. 569–611; Cornelius P. Cotter and J. Malcolm Smith, "Administrative Accountability to Congress: The Concurrent Resolution," *The Western Political Quarterly*, Vol. IX (December, 1956), pp. 955–966; Smith and Cotter, *op. cit.*, Chap. VIII.

be contingent upon the existence of certain conditions to be ascertained by the President, there is a certain logic in its specifying that adoption of a concurrent resolution by the two houses of Congress that the circumstances no longer obtain shall be one of the conditions by which termination shall be governed.[47]

A fourth type of safeguard takes the form of a clause in a delegating statute stating that action taken under it shall be subject to review and possible disallowance by the legislative body or its designated agent. This type of control is illustrated in the Administrative Reorganization Act of 1949. Under it an executive plan for a change in administrative structure must be presented to Congress before it can go into effect. Either house may kill the plan by adopting a resolution of disapproval within a 60-day period. Another variety of this type of restrictive device is illustrated by a provision found in the Real Property Transactions Act of 1951. It states that the Secretaries of the Army, Navy, or Air Force or the Director of the Civil Defense Administration must first "come into agreement with" the House and Senate Armed Services Committees before any acquisition, lease, or transfer of real estate for a military purpose may be consummated if its value is $25,000 or more.[48] The Public Buildings Act of 1959 and later a Watershed Protection and Flood Protection Act signed by President Eisenhower contained similar clauses subjecting certain kinds of administrative actions to prior approval of the appropriate congressional committees. Both Presidents Eisenhower and Truman had used the veto against other bills containing such clauses on the ground that provisions of this kind were unwise and possibly unconstitutional. Again in 1964 President Lyondon B. Johnson signed the Water Resources Act of that year with this type of clause included, but he also registered a strong protest against such an invasion of executive responsibility.

Eventually, President Johnson felt compelled to challenge Congress on the issue. Following the disastrous floods of late 1964 in the Pacific Northwest, Congress passed a special relief bill for the area.

[47] Edward S. Corwin, *The President: Office and Powers*, 4th ed. (New York: New York University Press, 1957), pp. 129ff., discusses this question and comes to the conclusion that the concurrent resolution device for terminating legislative grants of authority is not only valid constitutionally, but sound and defensible from the policy point of view as well. Other constitutional law authorities question this conclusion.

[48] *U.S. Code*, Title 10, (1964) Sec. 2662. A clause requiring the Secretary of the Air Force to "come into agreement with" the House and Senate Appropriations Committees before acquiring land for guided-missile proving grounds was included in a 1949 act. Cf. 63 *Stat.* I, 66. The 1955 Defense Department Appropriation Act required the Secretary of Defense to secure the prior approval of the House and Senate Appropriations Committees before turning over any departmental function to private industry. Following a strong protest by President Eisenhower when he signed the bill, Congress eliminated this clause in the following year's appropriation act.

A section of the bill declared that the Committees of Public Works of the two Houses of Congress must approve by resolution release of funds to accomplish certain purposes of the act as administered by the President, acting through the Office of Emergency Planning. Johnson returned the bill with a stinging veto, saying that while he approved its general objectives, he could not sign it with such a stipulation included. His veto message went on:

> . . . This device requires an executive official to obtain the approval of a committee or other unit of Congress before taking an executive action. It is not only an undesirable and improper encroachment by the Congress and its committees into the area of executive responsibilities— it also leads to inefficient administration. The executive branch is given, by the Constitution, the responsibility to implement all laws—a specific and exclusive responsibility which cannot properly be shared with a committee of Congress.
>
> The proper separation of powers and division of responsibilities between Congress and the executive branch is a matter of continuing concern to me. I must oppose the tendency to use any device to involve congressional committees in the administration of programs and the implementation of laws. I have spoken out against this before. . . .[49]

This verbal spanking had its desired effect. Promptly, though with some grumbling, Congress passed a new bill with the objectionable clause deleted.[50] Meanwhile, the House returned to the attack when it agreed to a proposal of its Armed Services Committee to include in a Military Construction Authorization bill a clause requiring the Secretary of Defense, before "closing, substantially reducing, or consolidating any military camp, post, station, installation, or facility" in the United States or Puerto Rico to report his intention to the Armed Services Committees of the two Houses of Congress. It provided further that if either of these Committees should disapprove the proposed action within 30 days and that if the House or Senate body of which it is a part did not disavow its Committee's recommendation within 40 days thereafter, the proposed action could not be taken. Pro-administration members of the Senate were successful in getting a milder version substituted for this provision in the bill as finally passed. It required the Secretary of Defense to give advance notice to Congress of his intention to close down or consolidate such bases or facilities, and his orders to effect such changes were to lie before Congress for 120 session days before they could be consummated. President Johnson found this technique of delay, designed to give Congress an opportunity to overrule a closing order, to be objectionable, and he returned the bill to Congress with another blistering

    [49] *Congressional Record* (Daily, June 7, 1965), 89th Congress, 1st Session, p. 12216.
    [50] *Ibid,* (June 15, 1965), pp. 13206–13212; P.L. 89–41.

veto. The House did not attempt to repass the bill over the veto, but instead passed a new bill on the same subject with a clause requiring only 30 days' notice of a closing. It was understood that this would be acceptable to the President.[51]

These recent joustings between President and Congress on the matter of the control of administrative decisions heavily freighted with policy implications reflect a fundamental problem posed by the separation of powers system. Enlargement by legislative grant of the chief executive's sphere of policy-making—or, what amounts to the same thing, that of those serving under him—constitutes one of the seemingly irresistible trends in American government. It is apparent at both national and state levels. It accounts for the appearance on the American scene of what has been aptly termed the "administrative state." To some observers this trend provides one of the proofs of the continuing strength and vitality of our institutions of government. It demonstrates, they say, that the more or less artificial gulf created by the separation of powers system can be bridged and that the manner of the government's functioning can be adapted in a practical way to meet new challenges. Others, alarmed by the concentration of policy-making authority in the hands of the chief executive and the executive branch generally, cry out in alarm and call for resistance to the trend. They plead for a return to the ideals of "constitutional democracy," for reassertion by the legislative branch of its "rightful and proper place" in the governmental process, and they raise the specters of "executive dictatorship" and "government by an irresponsible bureaucracy." Their exhortations are likely to be in vain. The tide can be commanded to stand still, but it will not.

The more realistic approaches to the problem appear to lie in exploring and devising practical ways by which the legislative branch can hold the executive and his administrative subordinates to account in their exercise of quasi-legislative authority; this would be more feasible than trying to retain in the legislature's own hands the responsibility for making the necessary day-to-day decisions and adjustments in applying broadly defined governmental policies to concrete situations. The volume of administratively formulated rules, orders, contracts, agreements, etc., involving policy decisions of some magnitude, is great; also, the need for expedition in dealing with situations that give rise to many of them imposes practical limits on use of the prior-agreement-by-congressional-committee device. Furthermore, a

[51] Cf. *Congressional Record* (Daily, August 23 and September 7, 1965), 89th Congress, 1st Session, pp. 20458, 22134. The controversy had been triggered by Secretary of Defense McNamara's announcement on November 19, 1964, that some 95 military bases and shipyards were to be closed down or sonsolidated with others for reasons of economy and efficiency.

prime motive in the use of the device appears to be the desire of individual members of Congress to assure themselves control over "pork-barrel" expenditures in their states or districts, at the expense of executive discretion. In any case, the practice of vesting in an *agent* of Congress—a particular committee or a combination of two of them, a committee chairman, or some other nonexecutive body—the authority to withhold consent to a particular kind of action by an administrative officer is not the same thing as retaining control in the hands of *Congress*. If carried far enough, this system could result in making individual members of Congress, largely indebted to the seniority system for their positions of power, the actual heads of administrative departments and bureaus. The position of the chief executive as the independently elective, responsible head of the administrative branch could be seriously undermined.

The future of democratic government cannot be assured by paralyzing the governmental process. Modern conditions demand that government undertake a continually widening, more complicated range of tasks. If these tasks are to be efficiently performed, the administrative-executive side of government must be given an enlarged capacity to devise and put into effect measures calculated to implement the policy goals set by the legislative branch. In spite of grumblings and fears, this is a price that has to be paid if government is to grapple successfully with the complex problems of our time.

THE CHIEF EXECUTIVE'S STAFF

From the beginning, American governmental practice has recognized the chief executive's need for a corps of assistants to whom he can turn for information and advice. The presidential system requires that great, far-ranging responsibilities be concentrated in his hands, but he must have the necessary information and counsel in discharging them. This was an unmistakable lesson drawn from English governmental practice as well as from colonial experience. Variously composed executive councils or "bodies of assistants" to the governor were found in the colonial governments; in one form or another this feature was carried over into all the early state governmental plans. Members of the Constitutional Convention assumed from the start that some kind of conciliar body would be set up to advise with and, possibly, to control the President in his performance of his constitutional duties. In the end, as has been noted in Chapter 2, the idea of a separate executive council was abandoned by the Convention in favor of a plan giving the Senate an executive conciliar role limited to the areas of treaty-making and appointments. The idea that the

President might make use of subordinate executive officials in an advisory capacity was not totally lost from sight, however, for he was authorized in Article II, Section 2, of the Constitution to "require the opinion in writing, of the principal officer in each of the executive departments, upon any subject relating to the duties of their respective offices."

Developments in Washington's first administration soon gave a distinctive turn to these constitutional arrangements. Understandings and accommodations regarding the particular manner in which the Senate was to function in giving advice and consent in the President's exercise of appointive authority have been noted in Chapter 12. After attempting to make use of the Senate as a consultative council in the preliminary stages of treaty-making, President Washington soon found the Senate unsatisfactory for this purpose and discontinued his early practice of appearing before it in person to obtain its advice on instructions to be given negotiating agents. During the crisis over relations with France in 1793, moreover, he was rebuffed by the Supreme Court when he sought to use that agency as a source of legal advice. Given these circumstances, it is readily apparent why Washington should have turned in increasing measure to the "principal officers" in the executive departments for advice on weighty matters of general policy. In so doing he laid the foundation for that familiar feature of the executive side of the national government, the President's Cabinet.

THE CABINET

The first attempt to give status to the President's department heads meeting as a group appears to have been in 1791, when in anticipation of his impending absences from the seat of government on a tour of the South, Washington authorized the Secretaries of State, Treasury, and War, along with Vice President Adams and Chief Justice Jay, to consult together on any matters of general concern that might require their attention.[52] This conception of a council of state failed to develop, but in 1792, meetings of the President with his department heads, with Attorney General Randolph added, became more frequent. The Vice President and the Chief Justice did not become participants in these meetings. In 1793, during the buildup of the French crisis, meetings of the President with his four subordinate

[52] The rise of the Cabinet as a consultative body to the President and its role in the operation of the presidency have been dealt with in a number of excellent studies, the most recent of which is Richard F. Fenno, *The President's Cabinet* (Cambridge: Harvard University Press, 1959). See also Mary Hinsdale, *A History of the President's Cabinet* (Ann Arbor: George Wahr, 1911); and Henry B. Learned, *The President's Cabinet* (New Haven: Yale University Press, 1912).

officers were held "almost every day," according to Secretary of State Jefferson's account.[53] It was at that time that public reference was first made, by Madison, to the group as the "President's Cabinet." Within a decade the term was a matter of common usage. Thereafter the President's practice of assembling the heads of the principal departments on a more or less regular, formalized basis to consult with him on matters he might wish to lay before them became an established feature of national executive procedure.

As the departmental structure of the national government expanded from time to time, heads of new departments were added to the Cabinet. Although Justice was not accorded status as a department until 1870, the Attorney General was a regular member from the beginning. By Lincoln's time the Cabinet included seven members— the Secretaries of State, Treasury, War, Navy, and Interior, the Attorney General, and the Postmaster General. The Secretary of Agriculture was added in 1889, Commerce in 1903, and Labor in 1913. With the passage of the National Security Act of 1947 consolidating the armed services into a single defense establishment, the Secretary of Defense became a member and the Secretaries of War and the Navy were dropped. The Secretary of the newly created Department of Health, Education and Welfare was added in 1953, restoring the number of regular "Cabinet-rank" department head members to 10. Creation of a Department of Housing and Urban Development in 1965 added another.

These 11 do not comprise the entire Cabinet as now constituted, it should be noted. President Harding in 1921 invited his Vice President, Calvin Coolidge, to attend Cabinet meetings, thus reviving a practice that had fallen into disuse early in Washington's administration.[54] This practice is now the rule. It has the obvious advantage not only of associating with the Cabinet an official who has direct contact with one of the branches of Congress, but more importantly, of giving the Vice President an opportunity to meet with the President's top administrative personnel and gain firsthand knowledge of some of the problems of general policy discussed in Cabinet meetings. If the Vice President is suddenly called upon to assume the office of President, his familiarlity with some of the matters of executive concern cannot but help to make the sudden transition somewhat less

[53] Fenno, *op. cit.*, p. 17, quoting Jefferson, *Writings*, Vol. VI, p. 250.

[54] Vice President Jefferson was invited by President Adams to participate in Cabinet discussions, but Jefferson declined, having no "wish to see the scenes of 1793 revived as to myself, and to descend daily into the arena like a gladiator, to suffer martyrdom in every conflict." See his letter to Madison of January 22, 1797, in Bernard Mayo, *Jefferson Himself* (Boston: Houghton Mifflin Company, 1942), p. 200. During the 1908 presidential campaign William J. Bryan pledged himself, if elected, to invite his vice presidential running mate, John W. Kern, to attend Cabinet meetings. Cf. Paola H. Colleta, *William Jennings Bryan: Political Evangelist, 1860–1908* (Lincoln: University of Nebraska Press, 1964), p. 412.

of a shock to himself and the nation. Beginning with President F. D. Roosevelt's administration other officials of non-Cabinet rank have also been invited to sit in regularly on Cabinet meetings. The officers thus invited have varied from administration to administration, but among them at one time or another have been the Director of the Budget, the Director of the Office of Emergency Planning (formerly Office of Defense Mobilization), Chairman of the Board of Economic Advisers, the U. S. Permanent Representative to the UN, the Chairman of the Civil Service Commission, and various members of the President's Executive Office staff.

Resting as it does upon usage and executive convenience, rather than upon a statutory foundation, the Cabinet's role in the operation of the presidency has varied with individual Presidents and with the membership of the group at any particular time. Some Presidents have made extensive use of their Cabinets in arriving at weighty decisions; others, of whom Jackson, Wilson, and F. D. Roosevelt are notable examples, have preferred to rely in great measure on other sources for advice. Inasmuch as formal minutes of Cabinet meetings are not kept, most of the information available concerning actual proceedings is to be found in memoirs, diaries, and notes left by individual participants and made public long after the events recounted have taken place. During President Eisenhower's administration, in an attempt to give the public an inside look at what transpires in a typical Cabinet meeting, the President permitted a meeting to be televised. It was interesting enough to the average citizen and no doubt gave him an impression of being admitted to the high secret councils of the nation. Actually, it was little more than a staging of a public report by Secretary of State John Foster Dulles on the world situation following his return from one of his frequent journeys abroad, with the President and the other members of the Cabinet serving as background.

In earlier administrations Cabinet meetings were held at irregular intervals, depending upon the President's desires and the political situation of the moment. Beginning with President Polk, who was something of a stickler for formal procedure and complete devotion to public duty, meetings began to be held at regular intervals, most commonly twice a week on Tuesdays and Fridays. Since Wilson's administration Presidents have usually set aside only one day per week for regular meetings. In time of great emergency this regular procedure may be altered either in favor of specially called meetings, or more commonly, postponements of regular meetings to suit the President's convenience.

The President, of course, presides, but on occasion when he cannot be present he may delegate the function of presiding to the Vice President or to the Secretary of State. For example, when Wilson was attending the Paris Peace Conference, Vice President Marshall with his knowledge and approval presided over several routine meetings. Vice President Nixon likewise chaired several meetings of President Eisenhower's Cabinet during the latter's illnesses and absences from Washington. Wilson's Secretary of State, Robert Lansing, without Wilson's knowledge and approval presumed to call a Cabinet meeting during the time of Wilson's disabling illness in 1919, but the President interpreted his action as part of a scheme to bring about his own ouster from the presidency and forthwith called for and obtained Lansing's resignation.

Traditionally the agenda of Cabinet meetings consists of matters laid before the members by the President himself. Individual members may be given the opportunity to make reports of general interest concerning their respective fields or to bring up matters for general discussion, so far as time permits. There is a natural reluctance on the part of department heads to lay before the group matters they consider to be of concern only to their own departments. They prefer to take up such questions with the President on a direct, individual basis, and this is no doubt as it should be. As an administrative device the Cabinet, having no secretariat of its own, does not lend itself to use as an agency for study and development of new policy programs and plans, and its usefulness as a coordinating instrument over administration is very limited. Interdepartmental feuds, jealousies, and conflicts are better dealt with outside the Cabinet council; their airing before the whole group may merely serve to exacerbate them.

At the outset of President Eisenhower's administration, he took what was hailed by some observers at the time as a significant step in the direction of raising the Cabinet to a new level of prestige as a "general staff" for the Presidency. He assigned to one of his own Executive Office staff the function of serving as "Secretary to the Cabinet." This officer was directed to prepare an agenda beforehand for each Cabinet session by consulting with the President, with his Special Assistant, Sherman Adams, and with the other regular members of the Cabinet. The Secretary sat in on Cabinet meetings, took rough notes on the proceedings, and was instructed to keep the President informed about the "carry through" on determinations reached. The long-range impact of this move toward establishing a Cabinet secretariat and attempting to make Cabinet meetings more productive in terms of policy-planning remains inconclusive.[55]

Evaluation of the influence of the Cabinet upon the institution of the presidency and on the administrations of particular Presidents is a complex undertaking, and the conclusion reached is likely to be a

[55] Fenno, *op. cit.*, pp. 103–113 reviews in some detail the Eisenhower administration's experiment in this connection.

somewhat subjective one. It is certain that some Presidents have improved their performance by availing themselves of the collective counsel of a group of individuals chosen for their political judgment and connections as well as for their administrative competence. Some of the earlier Presidents—notably Washington and Jefferson—were in the habit of putting particular issues to a vote of their Cabinets and abiding by the result. Jefferson declared his own policy to have been

> . . . in the gravest cases of calling them together, discussing the question maturely and finally taking the vote, on which the President counts himself as one. So that in all important cases the executive is in fact a directory.[56]

This practice has not been typical of later Presidents. Votes or polls of opinion sometimes are taken, as the President may desire, but the President does not necessarily feel obligated to accept the majority judgment of his Cabinet on a given point. As a classic story has it, after Lincoln had put a question to his Cabinet he announced the result, "Seven Ayes, one Nay. The Nays have it"—the "Nay," of course, being his own. Rather than functioning as a collegial "directory" today the Cabinet discharges its primary function in serving as a sounding board for the testing of ideas on such matters as the President may wish to refer to it, as an interdepartmental news exchange, and as a point of personal contact for the President with his top subordinates for informing them about policies he is in the process of formulating or has already decided upon. For this reason he will have selected these top administrative aides, or at least a considerable number of them, not solely from the point of view of their expertise as administrators in their respective fields, but also for their capacity to serve as representatives of important sectional, political, and economic groups of the general public with which he desires to maintain channels of communication in his policy-making operations.

Even so, the likelihood that the Cabinet as an institutionalized advisory council will play an increasingly important role in the operation of the presidency in the future does not appear great. Several factors weigh heavily against this happening. One is the fact that as the departments have grown and supervision of their operations has become more burdensome, the heads have less opportunity to concern themselves with questions of general policy outside their own spheres of interest. Another factor is the steady enlargement of the Cabinet group itself, as outlined above. This creates a condition which tends to induce the President to rely more heavily upon one or more individuals in the group for general advice, rather than upon

56 Jefferson, *Writings*, Vol. IX, p. 273.

all equally. Hamilton in the later stages of Washington's administration acquired such an ascendancy in the President's counsels, while Secretary of State Madison and Secretary of the Treasury Gallatin were Jefferson's right-hand men. President Eisenhower's "strong men" among his Cabinet entourage were Secretary of State Dulles and Secretary of the Treasury Humphrey during the greater part of his two administrations. President Kennedy placed heavy reliance upon the advice of his brother, his Attorney General, on matters of politics and general policy.

Other Presidents, emulating President Jackson's practice of consulting with his so-called "Kitchen Cabinet," have turned for advice to lower echelon officials in the various departments. President F. D. Roosevelt's "brain trust" of the early New Deal period was such a collection of young minds given easy access to the President's ear. Sometimes a major source of advice will be found outside the regular officialdom of Washington, as was the case with President Wilson's Colonel House.[57] Increased use of special fact-finding commissions, boards of inquiry, and White House conferences provide the President with ideas and information independently of the department heads themselves. Creation of the National Security Council has given the President an official "inner Cabinet" for advice and information on matters involving national security and defense of our interests abroad. Most important of all, the enlargement of his own immediate staff has provided the mid-twentieth-century President with a corps of assistants whose functions to a considerable degree supplement and to a certain degree supplant those traditionally associated with the Cabinet.

THE EXECUTIVE OFFICE OF THE PRESIDENT

No visible feature more clearly demonstrates the tremendous accretion of presidential powers, influence, and responsibilities than does the spectacular growth in recent years of staff personnel and agencies attached to the President's office. During the first century or so of the Republic, Presidents managed to get their work done with the aid of a half dozen or so secretaries, clerks, and aides, some of whom were borrowed from the regular departments. As late as Grant's time the President's office staff consisted of six people, maintained on a budget of $13,800. By the end of the nineteenth century a gradual enlargement of presidential office staff had become noticeable. McKinley's immediate staff numbered 27, carried on a budget of $44,340.

---

[57] Louis W. Koenig's *The Invisible Presidency* (New York: Holt, Rinehart and Winston, 1960) presents studies of individuals, some of whom occupied official posts and others who did not, who played important roles in various presidential administrations.

By Coolidge's time there were 46 people, and a budget charge of $93,500.

A sudden and dramatic change came during the administration of F. D. Roosevelt. The Report of the President's Committee on Administrative Management (the "Brownlow Committee") in 1937 featured a series of recommendations looking toward enlargement of the President's office staff. In a widely publicized passage it declared:

> The President needs help. His immediate staff assistance is entirely inadequate. He should be given a small number of executive assistants who would be his direct aides in dealing with the managerial agencies and administrative departments of government. These assistants would be in addition to his present aides who deal with the public, with the Congress, and with the press and radio. . . . They would remain in the background, issue no orders, make no decisions, emit no public statements. Men for these positions should be carefully chosen by the President from within and without the Government. . . . They should be possessed of high competence, great physical vigor, and a passion for anonymity. They should be installed in the White House itself, directly accessible to the President.[58]

Congress saw fit to follow through on this recommendation. As previously noted, it also adopted another recommendation of the Committee, vesting in the President authority to initiate plans for reorganizing the administrative structure, subject to congressional veto. Significantly, the first reorganization plan initiated by Roosevelt under this authorization was one creating a revamped "Executive Office of the President" as the central organ for providing the President directly with the aid needed in performance of his official duties. The units placed in the Executive Office of the President by the 1939 order have changed somewhat, and the personnel involved has risen from 800 or so in 1939 to almost twice that number.

The units now making up the Executive Office of the President include the following:

> 1. *The White House Office.* This is the veritable "nerve center" of the national executive establishment. It includes the President's office staff, along with a number of assistants and deputy assistants for handling the great volume of business that descends upon the President's desk. It is housed in the Executive Office wing of the White House. Major figures include the Special Counsel to the President, a Press Secretary, a number of Special Assistants for designated tasks, and aides representing the various military services.
>
> 2. *The Bureau of the Budget.* This agency, created originally by the Budget and Accounting Act of 1921, with a total personnel numbering 600 or more is the largest single unit in the Executive Office of the President. Loosely attached at the beginning to the Treasury De-

[58] *Report of the President's Committee on Administrative Management,* 1937, p. 5.

partment, it was transferred to the Executive Office by President Roosevelt's reorganization plan in 1939. Presided over by a Director chosen by the President alone, its five divisions carry out activities that give meaning and substance to the President's function as general manager and controller of the operations of the national government's administrative machinery. Within the Bureau, the Office of Budget Review carries out the job of assembling the budget estimates and recommendations that are submitted by the President to Congress each year for implementation through appropriational authority. The Office of Financial Management maintains liaison with the Treasury Department, the operating departments, and the General Accounting Office in connection with the actual administration of the fiscal programs thus authorized by Congress. The Bureau's Office of Legislative Reference, as previously described in Chapter 10, conducts an audit or overall review of legislative proposals emanating from the executive branch, looks into their implications from the standpoint of their expected impact upon federal expenditures, and assists the President in the exercise of his approval or veto authority on measures passed by Congress by assembling and digesting views of the appropriate administrative agencies. The Office of Management and Organization conducts management studies with a view to improving administrative organization and practice and formulates proposals for changes therein to be effected by executive orders or reorganizational plans. The Office of Statistical Standards conducts studies looking toward improvement and better coordination of the government's various statistical services.

3. *The National Security Council.* Created originally by the National Security Act of 1947, this body is intended to function as the President's "inner Cabinet" on national security and military matters. Its members, by law, now include the President, the Vice President, the Secretary of State, the Secretary of Defense, and the Director of the Office of Emergency Planning. Under it, but not a part of the Council's organizational scheme itself, is the Central Intelligence Agency, which is responsible for gathering, collating and digesting information from abroad bearing upon this nation's security interests.

4. *The Council of Economic Advisers.* This agency, headed by three members appointed by the President with the advice and consent of the Senate, was created by the Economic Planning ("Full Employment") Act of 1946. The Council, with a supporting staff, is charged with the function of carrying on studies of economic trends and developments with a view to assisting the President in the formulation of economic programs for consideration by Congress or by other appropriate agencies of administration. The President transmits to Congress at least once each year a report, accompanied by a message, based on the Council's major findings and recommendations.

5. *The Office of Emergency Planning.* Developed out of experiences and programs connected with the prosecution of World War II and the preceding defense and preparedness programs of the late 1930s, this agency is the successor to the National Security Resources Board established by the National Security Act of 1947. It is charged with the responsibility of developing policies and programs generally for dealing with wartime emergencies in the event the nation should find itself engaged in all-out war. It administers programs for the stock-

piling of strategic materials, carries on in cooperation with the states and localities a program of civilian defense organization and planning, and keeps in readiness plans for mobilization of the nation's human and material resources in preparation for emergencies. Its Director participates as one of the regular members of the National Security Council to facilitate coordination of military defense policies and programs with plans and policies developed by its staff.

6. *The National Aeronautics and Space Council.* This body, made up of the Vice President, the Secretary of State, the Secretary of Defense, the Administrator of the National Aeronautics and Space Administration, and the Chairman of the Atomic Energy Commission, was established by the Aeronautics and Space Act of 1958. The Vice President serves as its Chairman. The function of this agency, as its title suggests, is to advise and assist in the development of plans and programs in the area of aeronautics and space exploration and to coordinate activities of the various departments concerned.

7. *The Office of Science and Technology.* Created by President Kennedy's Reorganization Plan No. 2 in 1962, this agency, functioning under a Director appointed by the President with the consent of the Senate, assists the President in coordinating federal governmental activities in science and technology, with particular reference to their relationship to national security and foreign policy. It administers various research programs, including those of the National Science Foundation.

This brief catalogue of the units now comprising the Executive Office of the President provides only an outside view or indication of the President's manifold duties as Chief of Administration. It serves to make clear, however, that the modern presidency stands at the center of a vast administrative apparatus which reaches into every phase of the nation's security, welfare, and hopes for the future. It demonstrates that the President has also become the nation's chief policy planner. As President F. D. Roosevelt observed shortly before assuming office, the Presidency is "not merely an administrative office" but a post for supplying the nation with moral and political leadership. The Executive Office of the President reflects that point. It is more than a corps of assistants to help him in his job of seeing that the laws are faithfully executed and serving as the manager of an aggregation of administrative departments. Rather it is a mechanism for providing him with advice, information, and ideas as well throughout the range of his constitutional duties. It helps him to give the leadership and direction the nation expects of him. At the great moments of decision every President must face in the discharge of all his chiefship roles—Chief Legislator, Chief Diplomat, Commander-in-Chief, and so on—it renders vital aid. In short, it enables him to be "the President" and all that is now implied by that term.[59]

[59] The post-World War II years have brought forth a great many studies of the Executive Office of the President as well as numerous excellent case studies in depth of the decision-making process in the White House. Among those that might be

This complex of agencies making up the Executive Office of the President, it should be noted, has for the most part come into existence relatively recently. It reflects a new character, a new dimension of the presidency. At the state level similar developments have been taking place to provide the governor, particularly in the large, populous states, with an amplified staff to assist him in discharging his functions of overall administrative management and planning.[60] The effect generally is to cause the office of chief executive in its actual operations to reflect the functioning of many minds. A central corps of aides participates actively in carrying on the work of the President and governor. They give to the office of chief executive a momentum and continuity extending beyond the person who stands in the public view as the chief executive. They provide it with a stability enabling it to surmount the vicissitudes of change in person and outlook of the individual who suddenly comes to occupy the topmost post, as did Truman in 1945 and Johnson in 1963. They help to give the office an institutionalized character.

Yet there is a word of caution to be sounded. One man still stands at the center of action. In the eyes of the nation or of the state, *he* must assume the ultimate responsibility for the decisions made. The staff system should not become his excuse for evading his own responsibility for the results. Looking back on his own experiences in the office of President, and no doubt mindful of developments during the succeeding Eisenhower administration in which the staff system

mentioned are Edwin H. Hobbs, *Behind the President* (Washington: Public Affairs Press, 1954); Richard E. Neustadt, *Presidential Power* (New York: John Wiley and Sons, 1960); Theodore C. Sorensen, *Decision-Making in the White House* (New York: Columbia University Press, 1963); J. C. Heinlein, *Presidential Staff and National Security Policy* (Occasional Papers No. 2, Center for the Study of U. S. Foreign Policy, Department of Political Science, University of Cincinnati, 1963); George Graham, "The Presidency and the Executive Office of the President," *Journal of Politics,* Vol. XII (November, 1950); and Clinton Rossiter, "The Constitutional Significance of the Executive Office of the President," *American Political Science Review,* Vol. XLIII (December, 1949). Case studies of decisional crises in recent administrations include Grant McConnell, *Steel and the Presidency—1962* (New York: W. W. Norton & Company, 1963); Louis W. Koenig, "Kennedy and Steel: The Great Price Dispute," in Alan F. Westin, ed., *The Centers of Power* (New York: Harcourt Brace & World, 1964); David L. Larson, ed., *The Cuban Crisis of 1962* (Boston: Houghton Mifflin Company, 1963); and John W. Spanier, *The Truman-MacArthur Controversy and the Korean War* (Cambridge: Belknap Press, Harvard University, 1959). Richard Morris, *Great Presidential Decisions* (Greenwich, Conn.: Fawcett Publications, 1960), is a collection of 34 state papers embodying major policy decisions of various Presidents from Washington to Eisenhower.

[60] Chap. 10 in Coleman B. Ransone, Jr.'s *The Office of Governor in the United States* (University, Ala.: University of Alabama Press, 1956) presents a detailed analysis of developments in the states with reference to providing the governor's office with staff personnel. As of 1951 he found the number of such aides to range from a minimum of three in a number of the less populous states to 43 in New York, 42 in California, and 21 in Michigan. *Ibid.,* p. 344.

in the presidency reached its apogee under a President thoroughly imbued with a belief in its purported virtues on the basis of his military background, former President Truman observed:

> The President must make his own decisions. He cannot pass the buck up or down. Therefore, he must keep in close touch with the men who run the government at his direction. A layer of Presidential aides has been placed between the President and his appointed officials. Mostly, these aides get in one another's way. They tend to insulate the President. The President needs breathing space. The smaller the staff around him, the better. Information is what he needs. When he has the right information, he is in a position to make the right decisions —and he, and only he, must make them.[61]

In short, only the President can be the President, however much the office may become institutionalized.

[61] Harry S Truman, *Mr. Citizen* (New York: Popular Library, 1961), p. 179.

14

CONSERVATOR-IN-CHIEF OF THE

PUBLIC ORDER AND SAFETY

Constitutional, statutory, and political powers associated with the offices of President and state governor impose on these public figures a major role in discharging a function central to the very purpose of government itself—maintaining the public peace, order, and security. Chief executives not only symbolize but they actually wield the ultimate force that resides in organized government. They hold controls over mechanisms by which sanctions may be applied to compel obedience to the government's mandates from elements that would challenge its authority, obstruct its processes, and substitute illegal force for a regime of ordered, legitimate rule. They are in a position to initiate appropriate action to meet crises threatening the well-being of society, whether arising from man-made disturbances or from natural disasters. In so doing they perform a function as old and elemental as government itself.

This aspect of the chief executive's office is often referred to as the "executive" or "chief of law enforcement" function. But as has been pointed out before, "executive" duties and responsibilities embrace everything that a chief executive is expected to do. In the functional sense each of his chiefship roles is executive in nature. For this reason the term "Conservator-in-Chief of the Public Order and Safety" has been adopted for the particular aspects of his office to be dealt with here, as distinguished from his other powers, duties and responsibilities.

As with all his other chiefships, this one cannot be completely detached from the others. It is related to all of them in some degree. In the most immediate sense it is an extension of his function as Chief of Administration; for normally the ordinary processes of law enforcement through the civil administrative authorities, with assistance from the courts, suffice to insure domestic peace, tranquillity, and respect for the rule of law. But on occasion there arise conditions requiring extraordinary measures to attain these goals. The chief executive is the ultimate resource that is called upon to supply them. This may involve use of his powers as Commander-in-Chief of the military forces. His function as Conservator-in-Chief of the Public Order and Safety also derives support from his roles as Chief of State and popular spokesman, Chief Legislator, Chief of External Relations, and from his extraconstitutional position as Party Chief. In a sense the role of Conservator-in-Chief of the Public Order and Safety constitutes the very essence of the office of chief executive. It presents him with challenges demanding the utmost in cool judgment, patience, understanding, moral courage, and selfless devotion to the public weal. Many of the "strong" Presidents and governors have achieved or strengthened their ratings as such by successfully discharging this often trying phase of their official duties.

CONSTITUTIONAL FOUNDATIONS OF THE ROLE

As noted in Chapter 2, a generally felt need for a central executive authority to compel respect for the national government and to supplement state resources in maintaining public order was one of the prime motivating forces leading to the creation of the office of President. The members of the Convention of 1787 were for the most part men of substance who in their enlightened conservatism placed a high value upon the rights of personal security and property. The lessons of the times had taught them that unlicensed liberty and weak government could be as inimical to the good life as could tyrannical government. Four years before the Convention met the Confederation Congress had been subjected to the humiliation of being forced to flee from Philadelphia by a band of 80 mutinous and drunken soldiers of the Continental Army clamoring for their back pay.[1] An appeal by Congress for protection to the executive authority of Pennsylvania had been fruitless, the president of the Commonwealth being reluctant to summon the state militia for fear they might side with the rioters. In 1786 an uprising against state authority in Massachusetts by debtor elements led by Daniel Shays had been suppressed with some difficulty and bloodshed only after Governor Bowdoin had called into service an army of 4400 militiamen.[2] Indian troubles on the frontiers were a constant threat, while the dangers of internal subversion and interstate armed conflict were potentially serious.

These circumstances help to explain why the Framers of the Constitution decided with relatively little dissent upon the incorporation of clauses in the fundamental law laying a strong foundation for assumption of the role of Conservator-in-Chief of the Public Order

[1] For an account of the affair see John Fiske, *The Critical Period of American History* (Boston: Houghton Mifflin Company, 1902), pp. 133ff.

[2] *Ibid.*, pp. 210ff.

and Safety by the President. The language of Article II vesting in him the "executive power of the United States" and imposing upon him the duty to see that national laws are faithfully executed has been looked upon by strong-minded Presidents as providing them with a reservoir of power to act in the public interest in the face of emergencies. By Article I, Section 8, Congress was empowered to pass laws providing for "calling forth the militia to execute the laws of the Union, suppress insurrections and repel invasions"; and by Article II the President was made "Commander-in-Chief of the Army and Navy of the United States and of the militia of the several states when called into the actual service of the United States." The last clause of Article IV, Section 4, obligated the United States to "guarantee to every state in this Union a republican form of government," "to protect each of them against invasion," and "upon application of the legislature or of the executive (when the legislature cannot be convened) against domestic violence"—presumably by use of military force, if necessary.

A clause in Article II vesting in the President power "to grant reprieves and pardons for all offenses against the United States" was also perceived by the Framers as a valuable adjunct to his functioning as the protector of the public order and safety. Armed with constitutional authority, independent of congressional grant, to extend clemency to those who might combine and through illegal acts seek to obstruct the national government's operations, the President would have available an effective bargaining weapon. In exchange for a promise of pardon in advance he might induce them to desist from their unlawful course and lay down their arms. As Hamilton put it, "the principal argument for reposing the power of pardoning in this case [i.e., violent resistance against the government of the United States] to the Chief Magistrate is this: in seasons of insurrection or rebellion there are often critical moments when a well-timed offer of pardon to the insurgents or rebels may restore the tranquillity of the commonwealth; and which, if suffered to pass unimproved, it may never be possible afterwards to recall."[3] National experience, particularly during the Civil War period, demonstrated the soundness of this view.[4]

These constitutional foundations, along with later implementing legislation, do not define the uttermost limits of the Conservator-in-Chief role, as conceived and acted upon by some of the most energetic, bold-minded Presidents. Some of them have claimed executive "prerogative authority" to take necessary and proper action to protect the public interst in emergency situations even in the absence of express statutory authorization. This latitudinarian view of executive respon-

---

[3] *The Federalist*, No. 74.
[4] Cf. Jonathan T. Dorris, *Pardon and Amnesty under Lincoln and Johnson* (Chapel Hill: University of North Carolina Press, 1953).

sibility and power has a respectable ancestry in Anglo-American political thinking. John Locke, whose *Two Treatises of Civil Government* was a lexicon of political principles to the Framers of the Constitution, had written:

> Where the legislative and executive power are in distinct hands, as they are in all moderated monarchies and well-framed governments, there the good of society requires that several things should be left to the discretion of him that has the executive power. For the legislature not being able to foresee and provide by law for all that may be useful to the community, the executor of the laws, having the power in his hands, has by the common law of Nature a right to make use of it for the good of society, in many cases where the municipal law has given no direction, till the legislative can be conveniently assembled to provide for it; nay, many things there are which the law can by no means provide for, and those must necessarily be left to the discretion of him that has the executive power in his hands, to be ordered by him as the public good and advantage shall require; nay, it is fit that the laws themselves should in some cases give way to the executive power, or rather to this fundamental law of Nature and government—viz., that as much as may be all the members of the society are to be preserved.[5]

Three quarters of a century later, William Blackstone in his *Commentaries on the Laws of England,* a treatise with which most of the lawyer members of the Convention were familiar, had echoed these views.[6]

Locke and Blackstone, of course, were writing on the nature of royal authority in Great Britain, a limited monarchy, and they were both advocates fundamentally of the principle of parliamentary supremacy. Nevertheless, their views provide a plausible basis for the contention that executive power, by its very nature, carries with it an implied authority to act in the public interest in emergency situations when the legislative branch cannot provide a specific directive beforehand. As was pointed out in Chapter 1, the thought that the executive must be expected on occasion to take the initiative in dealing with certain types of emergencies had not been entirely lost sight of in the early state constitutional plans.[7] Developments during the administrations of the first three Presidents were soon to demonstrate that the vesting of executive power in the chief executive officer of the national government carried with it far-reaching implications regarding his responsibility to take the initiative in meeting crises arising in the domestic sphere as well as in foreign relations.

President Lincoln provided the nation with perhaps its most striking application of the Lockean concept of "prerogative power." Faced

[5] Chap. 14, "On Prerogative" (New York: E. P. Dutton & Co., Everyman's Library No. 751).

[6] Cf. Book I, Chap. VII, "The King's Prerogative."

[7] *Supra,* pp. 20, 27.

with armed resistance to the government by secessionist regimes in some of the southern states, he took measures lying wholly beyond his statutory powers. Theodore Roosevelt endorsed similar views on the nature of the chief executive's role. Seeking to justify acts he had taken as President that had no basis in law, particularly in connection with his intervention in labor-management disputes, he set forth in his *Autobiography* his often-quoted "stewardship theory" of the Presidency— that "it was not only the [President's] right but his duty to do anything that the needs of the Nation demand unless such action was forbidden by the Constitution or the laws." President Franklin Roosevelt in his First Inaugural Address declared that if the particular measures he would soon ask Congress to enact or those which Congress itself might originate did not suffice to bring order out of the threatened economic and social chaos of the Great Depression, he would ask Congress "for the one remaining instrument to meet the crisis—broad Executive power to wage a war against the emergency great as the power that would be given to me if we were in fact invaded by a foreign foe."[8] His first important official act as President was to issue a proclamation ordering the closing of all the banks and stock exchanges in the country and prohibiting gold and silver exports as well as foreign exchange transactions. Inasmuch as the statutory authorization upon which his "bank holiday" directive rested was generally recognized as flimsy, as soon as he assembled Congress in special session five days later he asked for and immediately received congressional approval and validation of this action.

A still bolder claim of inherent executive prerogative was made in Roosevelt's message to Congress on September 7, 1942, asking for a stronger wartime price and wage control law. In it he declared:

> I ask the Congress to take this action by the first of October. Inaction on your part by that date will leave me with an inescapable responsibility to the people of this country to see to it that the war effort is no longer imperiled by threat of economic chaos.
>
> In the event that the Congress should fail to act, and act adequately, I shall accept the responsibility, and I will act. . . .
>
> The President has the powers, under the Constitution and under Congressional acts, to take measures necessary to avert a disaster which would interfere with the winning of the war. . . .
>
> The American people can be sure that I will use my powers with a full sense of my responsibility to the Constitution and to my country. The American people can also be sure that I shall not hesitate to use every power vested in me to accomplish the defeat of our enemies in any part of the world where our own safety demands such defeat.
>
> When the war is won, the powers under which I act automatically revert to the people—to whom they belong.[9]

[8] *Congressional Record,* 73rd Congress, Special Session of the Senate, (1933), p. 6.
[9] *Congressional Record,* 77th Congress, 2nd Session (1942), p. 7044.

Prompt response by Congress granting the requested powers averted the need for his carrying out this threat to resort to unsupported executive prerogative. Roosevelt may well have had reason to believe that he would not be compelled to put his claim to the test because he knew public opinion was behind him.[10] The incident stands as a high bench mark to which some later President, relying on his inherent executive authority and his powers as Commander-in-Chief and the implications derived therefrom, may point in laying claim to a right to act in the public interest as he perceives it, whether or not the laws directly sanction his right to so act.

Instances of state governors acting in a similar high-handed manner are not lacking. In Illinois when the Democratic majority in the state legislature was readying a number of bills designed to obstruct the nation's war effort during the Civil War, Governor Richard Yates "prorogued" the session by threat of military force and ordered the legislators home. Faced with a similar situation in Indiana, Governor Oliver P. Morton induced the Republican members to absent themselves, thereby preventing a quorum from assembling. Thereafter he governed the state for a time as a kind of dictator, financing state operations by personal loans and by a grant of $250,000 from the United States War Department.[11]

EXTRAORDINARY MEASURES IN FEDERAL LAW ENFORCEMENT

Events soon demonstrated the wisdom of the Constitution's Framers in legitimizing the use of extraordinary measures by the nation's chief executive to uphold the authority of the new national government and enforce its mandates. Each of the first three Presidents was confronted by challenges of this kind. Elements in the citizenry, appealing to the still-fresh Revolutionary War-time spirit of resistance to anything that smacked of "tyranny," opposed with violence a number of measures of the national government which to them seemed no less destructive of their liberties than those of the British government that had brought on the Revolutionary War. Ironically enough, the measures to which they objected were of the very same genre that had aroused the colonists to rebellion—tax levies and laws interfering with their foreign trade. The firmness displayed by the Presidents concerned

[10] Cf. John P. Roche, "Executive Power and Domestic Emergency: The Quest for Prerogative," *Western Political Quarterly,* Vol. V, (December, 1952), pp. 592–618.

[11] See Carl Sandburg, *Abraham Lincoln: The War Years* (New York: Harcourt, Brace & World, 4 vols., 1939), Vol. II, p. 157; and Bruce Catton, *The Glory Road* (New York: Pocket Books, 1964), pp. 118–133.

was instrumental not only in strengthening popular respect for the new central government but also in setting patterns and teaching lessons for their successors to follow.[12]

THE WHISKY REBELLION

In 1791, as part of Secretary of the Treasury Hamilton's revenue-raising program for the new government, Congress levied an excise tax of 60 cents per gallon of capacity upon whisky distilleries. The measure was bitterly opposed by residents of the western regions of Pennsylvania, Virginia, and the Carolinas. It not only bore heavily upon one of the major marketable products of these regions, but it was being imposed by a government which in the eyes of the back-country people was giving little attention to their pressing public needs. In 1792, with a view to enabling the President to deal by force, if necessary, with the rising tide of violent resistance to the revenue act, Congress passed a statute authorizing him to call state militias into national service to aid in the execution of the laws of the Union. The act referred only to the state militias because the standing army of the United States at the time consisted only of a few hundred men stationed at frontier posts. The 1792 law contained a stipulation that as a condition precedent to use of armed force, the President must first be formally notified by a federal district court that execution of the laws of the United States was being opposed and obstructed "by combinations too powerful to be suppressed by the ordinary course of judicial proceedings or by the powers vested in the marshal of the the district."[13] Furthermore, the President was directed, before he actually resorted to force, to issue a proclamation warning the obstructing element of the lawlessness of their course and giving notice that military measures would be undertaken if they did not desist.

In 1792 President Washington issued such a proclamation, and for a time it appeared that his effort to resolve the matter through negotiation and patient persuasion might prove successful. His attempts at a pacific solution eventually failed, however, and by 1794 the situation had become so serious in western Pennsylvania that he resolved upon sterner tactics. A second proclamation was issued, and when it failed to produce the desired results he issued a call to the governors

[12] On the general subject see Bennett M. Rich, *The President and Civil Disorders* (Washington: Brookings Institution, 1941); Edward S. Corwin, *The President: Office and Powers*, 4th ed. (New York: New York University Press, 1957), pp. 130ff; and Robert S. Rankin and Winfried R. Dallmayr, *Freedom and Emergency Powers in the Cold War* (New York: Appleton-Century-Crofts, 1964). Senate Document 263, 67th Congress, 2nd Session (1922), *Federal Aid in Domestic Disturbances*, prepared by Frederick T. Wilson, surveys compendiously all instances of the use of federal troops in domestic disturbances from 1787 to 1922

[13] Act of May 2, 1792, 1 *Stat.* 264.

of the states of Pennsylvania, Maryland, Virginia, and New Jersey for militia contingents totalling some 13,000 men. The troops were assembled at Carlisle, in central Pennsylvania, and organized into an army. Governor Henry Lee of Virginia was placed in overall command, with Governors Thomas Mifflin of Pennsylvania and Richard Howell of New Jersey as the next officers in rank.

President Washington, who in the meantime had issued still a third proclamation, joined the forces at Carlisle, assisted in their organization, and accompanied the troops for part of their advance toward the major centers of opposition in the western part of the state. His presence with the army as it moved through the Pennsylvania towns helped to generate support for his policy among the populace and also with the militiamen, many of whom had been highly unenthusiastic about the enterprise at the beginning. The show of strength proved effective. As the armed forces approached, the opposition melted away, and a number of the ringleaders were taken into custody. Washington authorized the issuance of pardons for all who had taken up arms except for those against whom indictments were brought by federal grand juries in the area. A small number of the leaders were tried on a charge of treason for having "levied war" against the United States, and two of them were convicted and sentenced to be hanged. The President eventually pardoned both of them when he learned, through petitions on their behalf, that one was "a little short of an idiot" and the other "a miserable fellow in the hindmost train of the rebellion," as Hamilton put it. Thus ended the first trial of strength of the new government in the domestic sphere. The machinery had worked, ponderously but effectively, and a lesson in self-government had been impressed on the American people.

THE FRIES REBELLION

The challenge that confronted President John Adams in 1799 was far less formidable than the one Washington had had to deal with, but in some respects it paralleled the Whisky Rebellion. As in the earlier case, it was an insurrection against collection of a federal tax. The tax involved was the first and one of the few instances of use by Congress of its authority to levy a direct tax upon lands and dwellings under the apportionment formula set forth in the Constitution for this type of levy. Again the resistance took place in Pennsylvania, this time in the eastern part of the state. Federal assessors carrying out their duties under the act were assailed by a mob of hostile German-American farmers. When a number of the defiant property-owners were taken into custody by a federal marshal and his posse who accompanied one of the assessors, another armed mob of about 100 men led by one

Jacob Fries descended on the marshal and forced him to release the prisoners.

The statute authorizing the use of militia forces to execute the national laws had in the meantime been revised by Congress in 1795 so as to dispense with the requirement of a formal judicial notice to the President certifying the necessity of the use of military force. Nevertheless such notification was given to President Adams. Without making a thorough independent investigation of the situation for himself, as Washington had done, President Adams promptly responded by issuing the required proclamation and immediately thereafter called upon Governor Mifflin of Pennsylvania for a contingent of militia to be placed at the disposal of the government. At the same time the President issued orders to include several companies of regular United States army troops then stationed in New York and New Jersey, along with a volunteer cavalry company, as a complement to the state militia force. This was a use of federal military forces not yet covered by statute, it should be noted.

There was no show of resistance whatever to the troops when they arrived at the scene of the disturbances. According to one contemporary account, the only casualty of the insurrection was a bull, shot by a militiaman when it evinced too great an interest in the contents of a forage wagon. Fries was apprehended while peacefully pursuing his calling as an auctioneer, along with several other participants in the mob action. He and two others were subsequently indicted on a charge of treason, found guilty, and sentenced to be hanged. After long consideration of the matter, President Adams concluded that Fries and his two companions were not so much the instigators of the insurrection as they were the dupes of unscrupulous anti-Federalist political agitators, who in the President's judgment were the real culprits. Furthermore, he was dubious whether the definition of the crime of treason—"levying war against the United States"—could be stretched so far as to include the type of offense the men had been found guilty of committing. Against the unanimous advice of his Cabinet and to the dismay of many ardent Federalists, he finally decided to pardon the condemned men. At the same time he issued a general pardon for all who had been involved in the affair. The incident was something of a tempest in a teapot; yet it was one more demonstration that the nation's chief executive was not lacking in resources to overcome defiance of national governmental authority.

THE EMBARGO TROUBLES

Elevated to the presidency in 1801 on a wave of resentment against his Federalist predecessor for strong measures against those who opposed his policies, President Jefferson by a turn of fate eventually found himself in the same position of having to resort to extraordinary procedures in enforcing laws highly resented by large segments of the populace. His difficulties sprang from the Embargo Act of 1807, through which the government sought to bring economic pressure upon England and France by interdicting American trade with those countries and their European dependencies. The act caused considerable economic distress to American commercial interests, particularly in New England, and smuggling on an extensive scale across the American-Canadian border soon developed. Ordinary law enforcement procedures proved ineffective.

By an act passed in 1807 Congress had authorized the President to make use of the land and naval forces of the United States as well as state militia forces to suppress insurrections or to enforce the laws of the United States, and the next year the existing legislation on the use of state militia forces for these purposes was broadened to cover all cases whenever, in his judgment, "the exigencies of the United States require it."[14] Jefferson was reluctant to employ military force on a broad scale to enforce the Embargo Act. Moreover, the nature of obstruction to its enforcement—clandestine, small-scale operations for profit—made the use of large bodies of troops impractical. He therefore sought to devise procedures by which the Secretary of the Treasury and local federal collectors of the revenue might cooperate with federal marshals and the governors of the states involved to bring to bear available manpower resources, including military contingents, in suppressing smuggling.

When the collector for the Vermont district informed the President that enforcement of the Act would be impossible without the aid of the military, Jefferson devised a complicated system to meet the emergency. The Secretary of the Treasury was empowered to instruct the collector to arm and equip such vessels on Lake Champlain as he might deem necessary and to engage "volunteers" to assist him in carrying out his duties. If this proved inadequate, the Secretary of State was authorized to request the local United States marshal to raise a *posse comitatus* from the vicinity to assist the collector. If this failed to achieve the desired results, the governor of the state was requested to call out the state militia on the authority of the President, following the release of a presidential proclamation put in his hands, and place them at the disposal of the federal authorities in the area. In New York the President followed a different plan. It was simply one of inviting the governor of the state to assume responsibility for deciding when the state militia should be called into the federal service on the

14 Act of March 3, 1807, 2 *Stat.* 443; Act of March 30, 1808, 2 *Stat.* 478.

President's authority. Shortly before Jefferson's term of office expired in 1809, Congress, at his request, passed new enforcement legislation relative to the Embargo Act which in effect regularized this procedure by authorizing the use of both land and naval forces of the United States as well as state milita forces under the direction of local collectors of the revenue. President Jefferson had prepared a general directive to the governors of all the states designed to effectuate this mode of action when Congress a month later made an abrupt change of front. In response to general popular dissatisfaction it repealed the Embargo Act and this special enforcement provision and substituted a more flexible policy of trade restriction.

The first three Presidents' contributions toward establishing procedures for dealing with crises in federal law enforcement were considerable. Washington's patience, his attempts to find means of resolving his difficulties by measures short of actual use of military force, and his carefulness in apprising himself fully of the facts before he acted set a good example for his successors. Both he and Adams tempered justice with mercy by a judicious use of the pardoning power, thereby helping to allay resentment against their strong measures. President Adams' use of federal troops without explicit legislative sanction laid the foundation for later presidential claims that this was a matter of executive discretion lying within the range of the executive's constitutional prerogative. President Fillmore, for example, was to advance this point in 1851 in connection with his troubles in enforcing the Fugitive Slave Law. He observed that it was doubtful whether Congress had any constitutional power to control the President's discretion in using federal forces for law enforcement purposes, since by the Constitution the Army and Navy are placed under his command.[15] His request that Congress repeal the provision in the 1795 act requiring issuance of a proclamation calling upon resisters to desist before a President might use federal military force was not regarded with favor by Congress, however, and it remains on the statute books as a procedural requirement in connection with employment of military force to execute federal laws.[16] In actual practice it has not always been observed.[17]

Jefferson's idea of directing that any federal forces or state militia called into national service be treated as a *posse comitatus* under the

[15] See his message of February 10, 1851, responding to a request from the Senate for information regarding his actions in dealing with violence in Boston resulting in the freeing of an alleged fugitive slave from federal authority. Richardson, *Messages and Papers of the Presidents*, Vol. V, pp. 101–106.

[16] See *U. S. Code* (1964), Title 10, Chap. 15, Sec. 334. Fillmore's contention was that the proclamation requirement impeded law enforcement efforts in that it caused delay, placed offenders on notice, and consequently made apprehension of them more difficult.

[17] Cf. Rich, *op. cit.*, pp. 201ff., for specific instances.

direction of federal marshals was applied in practice by Presidents Pierce and Buchanan in dealing with troubles in Kansas during the 1850s and by President Grant in the South during the Reconstruction era. By legislation still in effect Congress in 1878 put an end to this practice by specifying that troops of the United States shall not be used as a *posse comitatus* "except in such cases and under such circumstances as such employment of said force may be expressly authorized by the Constitution or by act of Congress."[18] The effect of this law is to require that military or naval forces used in carrying out federal law enforcement functions be normally considered subject to the control of the President only through military channels of command. They may and usually do cooperate with the federal and state civil authorities on the spot, but cannot be made subject to their direct orders unless Congress so stipulates.

STATE INTERPOSITION, NULLIFICATION AND SECESSION

The most serious internal challenges to the national government's authority Presidents have had to meet have been those supported by state governments themselves. Controversy over the nature of the Union and the relationship of the states to the national government is as old as the nation itself. It has revolved around such questions as whether the Constitution is a compact formed by sovereign states which they may individually repudiate or is an instrument adopted by the people of the whole nation for their governance; where ultimate authority to decide questions concerning the allocation of powers as between the national government and the states is located; and whether the national government has the capacity to coerce a recalcitrant state. For all practical purposes these issues have been settled by general acceptance of the supremacy of the Constitution, the paramountcy of the national government within its appropriate sphere of authority, recognition of the United States Supreme Court as the ultimate arbiter of conflicts involving national and state powers under the Constitution, and by the outcome of the Civil War. Still the controversy goes on. Recent attempts to resurrect the long-dormant doctrine of state "interposition" and violent reaction by some southern state legislatures and executive officials to enforcement of the Constitution's mandates against racial discrimination as expounded by the Supreme Court show that belief in the right of states to oppose presidential acts designed to carry out national laws and decrees of the federal courts is by no means dead.

[18] *U.S. Code* (1964), Title 18, Sec. 1385. This legislation was designed to repudiate tactics that had been used by federal authorities during the Reconstruction period in the South and in recent strike disorders.

The theory that state governments might officially "interpose" their authority against that of the United States and resist what they think are unconstitutional encroachments upon their rights and those of their people was first given concrete expression in 1798. Firmly convinced that the Alien and Sedition Laws enacted by the Federalist-dominated Congress violated individual rights secured by the Constitution, the legislatures of Virginia and Kentucky, with the support and encouragement of Vice President Jefferson and James Madison, adopted resolutions declaring the acts to be void. The resolutions also defended the right of states to make such determinations. The Kentucky legislature's resolution sounded a warning that acts such as these might tend to "drive the states into revolution and bloodshed." The crisis subsided when the Jeffersonian party was placed in control of the nation's affairs following the 1800 election. The obnoxious laws were terminated and persons who had been convicted under them were pardoned by President Jefferson, but a seed had been planted that was destined to bear bitter fruit.

Madison himself as President was confronted by state challenges to the federal government's authority on two occasions. In 1809, following a United States district court judgment for a claimant, one Gideon Olmstead, against the Commonwealth of Pennsylvania in a long-pending case originating out of a Revolutionary War-time prize capture, that state's legislature passed an act authorizing and directing the governor to resist execution of the court's writ, even to the extent of employing troops, if necessary. The governor directed his adjutant general to carry out this mandate. Olmstead, appealing the issue to the United States Supreme Court, obtained a writ of mandamus to the United States district court judge involved directing him to effectuate the judgment in the face of the state's opposition.[19] Chief Justice Marshall in his opinion in the case left no doubt where he stood on the question of state interposition and nullification. He declared:

> If the legislatures of the several states may, at will, annul the judgments of the courts of the United States, and destroy the rights acquired under those judgments, the Constitution itself becomes a solemn mockery; and the Nation is deprived of the means of enforcing its laws by the instrumentality of its own tribunals.

For a time a clash between federal and state forces appeared inevitable; eventually Pennsylvania yielded, however, when the legislatures of 11 of the other 16 states, to which her legislature had appealed for support, refused to take up her cause. State officials who under the governor's orders had forcibly resisted carrying out the federal court's

[19] *United States* v. *Peters,* 5 Cranch 115 (1809). For a full account of the affair see Charles Grove Haines, *The Role of the Supreme Court in American Government and Politics, 1789–1835* (Berkeley: University of California Press, 1944), pp. 270–279.

judgment were subsequently tried and convicted of unlawful obstruction of the national government's processes, but all involved in the affair were ultimately pardoned by President Madison.

Madison's other challenge came from Massachusetts, with the backing of other New England states. Soon after the onset of the War of 1812 Madison issued calls upon the New England states and New York to furnish militia forces for national service against British and Canadian forces threatening to invade the country along its northern borders. Judging for himself that the threat of invasion was not imminent, Governor Caleb Strong of Massachusetts, citing in support of his action an advisory opinion of the Massachusetts Supreme Court,[20] refused to respond to the call. The President could do little about it. Twelve years after the War of 1812 had ended, the United States Supreme Court definitively settled the point at stake through another case, *Martin* v. *Mott*,[21] which originated in New York. This case arose out of an attempt by Mott, a militiaman, to recover property seized by federal authorities in satisfaction of a fine levied upon him by a court-martial for failure to report for duty when his company was called into federal service during the War of 1812. Justice Story, in his opinion for the Court, declared that "the authority to decide whether the exigency [requiring use of the state militia by the national government as provided by the laws of Congress] has arisen, belongs exclusively to the President, and . . . his decision is conclusive upon all other persons." This sweeping statement still stands as the law of the land on the power of Congress to vest in the President final judgment in this kind of situation.

In 1832 the South Carolina Nullification crisis brought the question of state versus nation into even sharper focus. Indignant at the enactment of tariff acts in 1828 and 1832 which in its judgment transcended powers vested in Congress, the South Carolina legislature authorized the assembling of a convention of the people of the state to consider the matter. By a large majority the convention adopted an "ordinance of nullification." It declared the obnoxious tariff laws void and recommended to the legislature that it take appropriate steps to prevent their enforcement within the state after February 1, 1833. It also invited other states to join South Carolina in its course of defiance. The South Carolina legislature promptly passed a series of measures in conformity with the convention's recommendations, including one empowering the governor to raise 10,000 State Guard troops, if needed, to resist infringement upon the state's "sovereign" rights.

Keeping in touch with elements in the state that were opposed to nullification, President Jackson responded to these developments

---

20 *Opinion in re Governor's Control over State Militia,* 8 Mass. Repts. 549 (1812).
21 12 Wheaton 19 (1827).

with a 9000-word proclamation. In this remarkable document, generally regarded as his most important presidential state paper, he condemned the doctrine of nullification and the course of conduct of the South Carolina authorities as "subversive of the Constitution," pointed to his inescapable duty to enforce the laws of the United States, and warned that military force would be used, if necessary, to maintain the integrity of the national government's processes.[22] At the same time he quietly issued directives for strengthening United States military and naval forces in the area and readied plans for calling into federal service a large complement of state militia troops. He wisely kept open the channels of communication with the South Carolina nullification leaders, however. When they received no assurances of support from other states and an understanding was reached that there would be a downward revision of the tariff rates, these leaders at an informal meeting of the convention in Charleston effected a suspension of the nullification ordinance. It was eventually rescinded when Congress passed the promised revised tariff legislation.[23]

The 1832 nullification controversy was only a prologue for the crisis that erupted into the Civil War some 30 years later. As soon as the 1860 election results made it apparent that Lincoln would become the next President, southern states, led by South Carolina, on December 17, 1860, assembled conventions to consider the question of seceding from the Union. By the time Lincoln took the oath of office on March 4, 1861, seven states had adopted ordinances of secession declaring the authority of the United States government to be at an end within their boundaries. Four other states eventually followed suit.

Within the seceded states United States customs houses, forts, arsenals, and post offices were taken over by the insurgent governments. Lincoln' reaction was to regard these actions as challenges which he in his capacity as the chief executive of the nation had the primary responsibility to meet. Eager to find a way short of war out of the crisis, but determined at all costs to preserve the Constitution and the Union, he temporized, negotiated, and attempted to placate the rebellious states for the first six weeks of his term. His efforts came to nought with the firing on Fort Sumter by South Carolina troops on April 12. His response in meeting this armed resistance was built on the foundations laid by his predecessors, but in many respects he went much farther than any President before had dared to go.

Lincoln's first response was to issue on April 15 a triple-purpose proclamation. It consisted of a warning to the insurgents to cease and

[22] Richardson, *op. cit.*, Vol. II, pp. 640–656.

[23] For a more complete account of the South Carolina Nullification controversy see Alfred H. Kelly and Winfred A. Harbison, *The American Constitution: Its Origins and Development* (New York: W. W. Norton & Company, 3rd. ed., 1963), pp. 304–316.

desist from their unlawful course within 20 days; a call to the governors of the states to supply 75,000 militia troops for federal service to assist in quelling the insurrection; and a call to Congress to meet in extraordinary session on July 4, some 10 weeks later. These were all matters, of course, clearly within his authority under existing law as well as in line with precedent. But before Congress convened he took further steps. On April 19 and 27 he issued proclamations putting into force a naval blockade of the ports of the seceded states "in pursuance of the laws of the United States and of the law of nations in such cases provided." This was followed by another proclamation on May 3 enlarging the regular Army by some 23,000 men and the Navy by 18,000 and authorizing the enlistment of 40,000 volunteers to augment these regular forces. In a series of orders he directed General Winfield Scott, commanding general of the Army, to employ "prompt and efficient means," including suspension of the writ of habeas corpus as to persons arrested by the military in designated areas, with a view to protecting the line of communications by rail and telegraph between Washington, Philadelphia, and New York. Another order required all officers of the armed forces to reaffirm by oath their loyalty to the United States. This, in effect, accomplished a purge of officers whose reliability was questionable. Still another order provided for the release of some $2,000,000 in unappropriated government funds to designated persons to be used in financing the mobilization effort.

Some of these actions, Lincoln conceded in his special message to Congress when it eventually assembled, "whether strictly legal or not, were ventured upon under what appeared to be a popular demand and a public necessity, trusting then, as now that Congress would readily ratify them."[24] Most of the members of Congress from the seceding states had quit their seats or voluntarily absented themselves, and the necessary legitimizing legislation was promptly passed, putting the nation on a war footing. Two years later the Supreme Court placed the stamp of legality of these proceedings when it ruled that the President's blockade proclamation, together with subsequent supporting legislation by Congress, had the effect of recognizing a state of war and thus brought into play international law governing the conduct of war between belligerents.[25]

In justifying his course to the Congress and to the nation, Lincoln maintained he was invoking the "war power" granted by the Constitution to the United States government. This concept, upon which he was to rely as justification for other measures he subsequently took on his own authority during the course of the war, involved an extremely broad view of executive power and responsibility. In his view

[24] Richardson, *op. cit.*, Vol. VI, p. 24.
[25] *The Prize Cases,* 2 Black 635 (1863).

the chief executive's "war power" drew sustenance not only from statutes but also directly from the Constitution, particularly from the faithful execution of the laws clause, the President's special oath of office obligating him to "preserve, protect and defend" the Constitution, and from his powers as Commander-in-Chief of the armed forces. From time to time during the next four years he invited congressional support, either before or after the fact, for various steps he undertook with the intent of preserving the integrity of the national government and restoring the tranquillity to the Union. In essence his conception was that, as President, his duty under the Constitution and the laws gave him a choice of means so long as they were appropriate and necessary to meet the exigencies of the situation confronting him, with or without the express sanction of Congress. A domestic crisis of unprecedented dimensions had made him a wartime President. Fuller consideration of this aspect of the office of President will be undertaken in connection with his Commander-in-Chief role, discussed in Chapter 16.

RECENT FEDERAL LAW ENFORCEMENT PROBLEMS

Few Presidents have not been confronted by internal security and law enforcement crises requiring extraordinary measures. During the first century of the nation's history, Indian troubles, the Mormon troubles, lawlessness in frontier areas, border incidents, and opposition to enforcement of the Fugitive Slave Law of 1850, along with the difficulties already described, were the major causes. In recent times federal law enforcement problems that have caused the greatest presidential concern have been those resulting from the Eighteenth (Prohibition) Amendment and the disorders following attempts to implement the Supreme Court's 1954 ruling in the school desegregation cases and subsequent ones holding state segregation practices void under the Fourteenth Amendment.

CURRENT LEGISLATION ON USE OF MILITARY FORCE

Before turning to a review of these developments the nature of current federal statutory provisions concerning the use of troops in law enforcement should be noted. The law on this subject was restated by Congress in 1956. It is now found in Title 10, Sections 331–334, of the *United States Code*. Section 331, which goes back to the 1792, 1795, and 1807 acts of Congress, authorizes the President, upon request of a state's legislature or of its governor if its legislature cannot be convened, to call into the federal service state militia (National Guard) forces in the number requested and use them, as well as United States armed forces, to suppress an insurrection against a state. Section 332, whose antecedents are the same acts of Congress, reads as follows:

> Whenever the President considers that unlawful obstructions, combinations, or assemblages, or rebellion against the authority of the United States make it impractical to enforce the laws of the United States in any State or Territory by the ordinary course of judicial proceedings, he may call into Federal service such of the militia of any State, and use such of the armed forces, as he considers necessary to enforce those laws or to suppress the rebellion.

Section 333 was originally enacted as a part of the Civil Rights Act of 1871, designed to secure to individuals rights protected by the Fourteenth Amendment. It overlaps in some degree the provisions of Section 332. It reads:

> The President, by using the militia or the armed forces, or both, or by any other means, shall take such measures as he considers necessary to suppress, in a State, any insurrection, domestic violence, unlawful combination, or conspiracy, if it—
> 1. So hinders the execution of the laws of that State, and of the United States within the State, that any part or class of its people is deprived of a right, privilege or immunity, or protection named in the Constitution and secured by law, and the constituted authorities of that State are unable, fail or refuse to protect that right, privilege, or immunity, or give that protection; or
> 2. Opposes or obstructs the execution of the laws of the United States or impedes the course of justice under those laws.
> In any situation covered by clause 1, the State shall be considered to have denied the equal protection of the laws secured by the Constitution.

It should be noted that this section goes farther than Section 332 in that it authorizes the President not only to use military force but "any other means" as well to accomplish the objectives of the statute. It also permits federal intervention if a state defaults in its duty to maintain and protect equally the constitutional and legal rights, privileges, and immunities of all individuals. Section 334, as already noted, restates the requirement of issuance of a proclamation by the President before resorting to use of military force under these sections.

Until 1957 a further authorization of the use of military force to secure the civil rights of individuals was included in Title 42, Section 1993, of the *United States Code*. This provision grew out of legislation by Congress in 1866 and 1870 designed to protect Negro civil and political rights in the South. This law, which had never been invoked by a President since Reconstruction days, made it "lawful" for him or "any such person as he may empower for that purpose" to employ the land or naval forces of the United States or state militia forces to "aid in the execution of judicial process usual under any preceding provisions" of the statutes of which it was a part. When the Civil Rights Act of 1957 was passed, creating the Civil Rights Commission and empowering it to make investigations into alleged discriminatory practices in suffrage and election law administration, this section of the *Code* was repealed as a gesture of appeasement to southern opponents of the bill.[26]

Some authorities have raised the point that this repealing action has deprived the President of power to use troops to enforce federal court orders in desegregation matters. Their contention is two-pronged: that this authority is dependent exclusively upon congressional sanction; and that his statutory authority to do so is limited to enforcement of the "laws," i.e., particular statutory enactments, and there are no federal statutes requiring school desegregation. It would appear, however, that the language of Section 333 of Title 10, noted above, is broad enough to sustain use of troops to enforce court orders arising directly out of the Fourteenth Amendment's provisions. By its own terms the Constitution is a part of the "supreme law of the land." Section 333 authorizes the use of troops to deal with obstructions to the "course of justice" under the laws of the United States. The Supreme Court has declared that in connection with maintaining the safety of person of its officers "there is a peace of the United States" justifying necessary protective measures involving force; and in this connection it has adopted a broad view of what an act done "in pursuance of a law of the United States" may involve.[27] Both President Eisenhower and President Kennedy were acting under the authorization of Section 333 when they used troops to enforce judicial orders directing desegregation of public educational facilities in Arkansas, Mississippi, and Alabama, and the federal courts have found no legal infirmity in their power to do so. In any event adoption of the Civil Rights Act of 1964 has provided a specific statutory base for use of the procedures provided by Section 333 in dealing with certain racial discrimination matters, if normal enforcement procedures prove ineffective.

---

[26] Act of September 9, 1957, 71 *Stat.* 634.

[27] *In re Neagle*, 135 U.S. 1 (1890). In this case the Supreme Court held that a United States deputy marshal who had killed a man while assigned by order of his superiors to act as a bodyguard to a United States Supreme Court Justice was acting "in pursuance of a law of the United States." For a more extended discussion of the legal question involved in the President's use of troops to enforce federal court orders see Rankin and Dallmayr, *op. cit.*, pp. 213–226, and other authorities cited therein.

THE EIGHTEENTH AMENDMENT

Section 2 of the Eighteenth Amendment, adopted in 1919, declared that Congress and the several states were to have "concurrent" power to carry out the prohibitory clause of the first section forbidding the manufacture, sale, transportation, importation, or exportation of intoxicating liquors for beverage purposes. Congress promptly discharged its responsibility by enacting the National Prohibition (Volstead) Act[28] to accomplish the objective of the Amendment, but some of the states were laggards. Maryland never enacted a prohibitory statute, New York repealed its enforcement law in 1923, and eventually four others did likewise. Still others grew lax in their enforcement endeavors, thus shifting the burden of responsibility entirely to the national government's shoulders. The national government found itself confronted by an increasingly vexatious law enforcement problem as popular hostility to the Amendment grew and scandals multiplied. Repeal of the Amendment became a clear-cut issue between the major party candidates in the 1932 presidential election. When F. D. Roosevelt was elected on a platform pledging repeal, Congress lost no time in submitting a repealing Amendment to the states, which was soon ratified and made effective in 1933.

During the 14-year period the "noble experiment" was under way, several law enforcement developments involving unusual presidential action occurred. In 1923 President Coolidge, under increasing pressure from the prohibitionist element to take more vigorous steps to stem the flow of illegal liquor from rumrunners operating a profitable smuggling business along the coasts, requested an advisory opinion from his Attorney General on whether he had authority to use the Navy to supplement the efforts of Treasury Department officers trying to cope with the smugglers. He was advised by Attorney General Daugherty that he lacked authority to do so, since there existed no emergency situation of the kind specified by law providing for use of such forces.[29] Subsequent efforts in Congress to obtain passage of legislation authorizing use of naval contingents for this purpose were unsuccessful.

The smuggling problem also produced presidential action on another front. Treasury Department enforcement agents in our ports, expanding the area of their operations beyond the traditional three-mile limit, boarded foreign vessels suspected of being engaged in liquor smuggling, thereby giving rise to protests of violation of rights under

[28] Act of October 28, 1919, 41 *Stat.* 305. The statute was passed over President Wilson's veto. He had objected to parts of the bill continuing in effect the system of wartime prohibition until the date the Eighteenth Amendment was to come into effect, January 17, 1920.

[29] 33 *Ops. Attys. Gen.* 562 (1923).

international law from the countries under whose flags the vessels were registered. Meanwhile the Supreme Court, construing the Eighteenth Amendment and its enforcing act literally, held that ship liquor stores on foreign liners touching at our ports fell under the ban of our laws.[30] These international embarrassments were eventually resolved by the negotiation of a series of treaties with most of the foreign countries concerned. They stipulated that, in exchange for a concession by the United States permitting foreign ships entering our ports to bring in their regular liquor stores provided they were kept under seal while in American waters, United States law enforcement agents were to be conceded the right to board foreign vessels as soon as they came within one hour's sailing distance of our shores.[31]

On still another front, President Coolidge's attempt to unite federal and state liquor law enforcement agencies under a single command met with failure. On May 8, 1926, he issued an executive order authorizing the appointment of state, county, and municipal law enforcement officers by the Secretary of the Treasury and the Attorney General as members of the prohibition enforcement staffs of their respective departments. The purpose was to facilitate cooperation between federal and local agencies, and, one may suspect, to shift some of the financial and political burden of enforcing an unpopular law to the states. The order was greeted by a violent protest in the Senate, where it was assailed by some members as an attempt to convert state and local officials into a federal police force.[32] The controversy subsided after it turned out that the federal authorities were making no attempt to carry the order into effect.

DESEGREGATION OF SCHOOLS AND OTHER PUBLIC FACILITIES

State attitudes of indifference toward their implied constitutional obligation to assume a share of the responsibility for enforcement of the Eighteenth Amendment were a factor hastening the demise of that experiment in social reform. At no time, however, did a state or its officials assume a pose of actual hostility to the federal government's

[30] *Cunard Steamship Co.* v. *United States,* 262 U.S. 100 (1923).

[31] The first of the treaties, which became the model for others, was with Great Britain. Cf. 43 *Stat.* 176 (1924). On the general subject see Robert L. Jones, *The Eighteenth Amendment and Our Foreign Relations* (New York: Thomas Y. Crowell Company, 1933).

[32] Cf. *Congressional Record,* 69th Congress, 2nd Session (1962), pp. 9923, 9944, 9989. A presidential order authorizing such appointments was deemed necessary in view of the executive order of President Grant in 1873 forbidding "dual officeholding" by federal executive officers, *Supra,* p. 162, note 10. For a fuller discussion of the problems of Presidents Harding, Coolidge, and Hoover in connection with enforcement of the Volstead Act, see Carl Brent Swisher, *American Constitutional Development* (Boston: Houghton Mifflin Company, 2nd ed., 1954), pp. 703–715.

efforts to enforce prohibition. On the other hand, there has been active opposition by state authorities in the South to compliance with federal court rulings on racial desegregation of schools and public facilities. Incidents reminiscent of pre-Civil War challenges to federal authority have occurred, and federal troops have had to be used on several occasions. In January, 1956, the state legislature of Alabama, invoking the long-discredited doctrines of state interposition and nullification, adopted a resolution declaring the 1954–1955 school segregation rulings of the Supreme Court to be null and void. Subsequently the legislatures of Virginia, Mississippi, Georgia, South Carolina, Tennessee, and Florida followed suit. A variety of laws were enacted in these and other southern states designed to impede, oppose, or evade the carrying out of the Supreme Court's rulings.[33]

The first crisis requiring intervention by the President occurred in Little Rock, Arkansas, in September, 1957. The situation was a complicated one, involving a series of opposing national and state court rulings on implementation of a desegregation plan for Little Rock schools. A gradual desegregation program formulated by the local school authorities had received approval from federal district court and the Court of Appeals in the area as being in accord with the Supreme Court's 1954–1955 decisions. A white parent then succeeded in obtaining a state court injunction against the school board's proceeding with its plan. On the day before the schools were to open, Governor Orval Faubus, declaring that there was an "emergency" because of anticipated mob violence, called out the Arkansas National Guard to maintain "law and order." His instructions to the commanding officer of the troops directed them to prevent Negro children from enrolling in previously white schools and white children from enrolling in previously all-Negro schools.

The governor's action clearly amounted to interference with effectuation of the federal court order. A suit was immediately begun in the Eastern Arkansas Federal District Court to enjoin him and any others from such interference. The injunction was granted and was ultimately upheld by higher federal courts.[34] After this injunction had been issued Governor Faubus withdrew the National Guardsmen from Little Rock—an action the injunction did not require him to take— indirectly inviting the defiant antisegregationists to take over. The frightened school authorities requested the district court to de-

[33] For detailed accounts of southern efforts to frustrate enforcement of court-ordered policies of desegregation see Rankin and Dallmayr, *op. cit.*, Chap. 4; and Richard Longaker, *The Presidency and Individual Liberties* (Ithaca: Cornell University Press, 1961), pp. 152ff.

[34] *Aaron* v. *Cooper*, 156 F. Supp. 220 (1957); *Faubus* v. *United States*, 254 F. 2nd (1958), *cert. denied*, 358 U.S. 829 (1958).

lay execution of its desegregation order, but it would not do so. The disorders grew in intensity. On September 23 President Eisenhower issued a proclamation as required by law directing that obstructions to the course of justice cease, and he followed this the next day by ordering contingents of the 101st Airborne Division to Little Rock. At the same time he authorized the Secretary of Defense to call in to federal service the Arkansas National Guard. This was done, having the effect of depriving the governor of an organized military force with which to oppose the national government's measures. Order was eventually restored, and desegregation of Central High School, the focal point of the disturbances, was carried out under military protection for the rest of the year.[35]

The Little Rock incident proved to be instructive for President Kennedy, who was later faced with similar crises in enforcing federal court desegragation orders in Mississippi and Alabama. One valuable lesson learned was the maneuver of calling into national service local National Guardsmen, on whom a governor might seek to rely as a force to resist federal authority. Another was the advisability of the President's making clear in public statements and appeals to the state authorities, as President Eisenhower had done, that primary responsibility lies with local officials, including the governor, to maintain order in the face of threatened violence.

Another lesson gleaned from the Little Rock incident was the necessity of the President's leaving no room for doubt that the full power of the national government will be used, if necessary, to see that the mandates of its courts are respected—and making the necessary preparations to do so as a crisis develops. While President Eisenhower had acted firmly enough after the Little Rock situation had deteriorated to a point that left him with no choice but to use military force or permit the orders of federal courts to be flouted, his earlier course had not been one calculated to impress upon would-be challengers of federal authority that he would do so. During his tenure he steadfastly refused every opportunity to declare his personal commitment to the Supreme Court's pronouncements that segregation under state auspices was forbidden by the Fourteenth Amendment, and he had repeatedly disavowed the principle of use of federal military force in such matters. As late as July, 1957, he was quoted as saying

35 This was not the end of the struggle over school desegregation in Little Rock. In February, 1958, school officials filed a suit in the federal district court asking suspension of the integration plan until 1961, in view of the public opposition to it at the time. This petition was granted, but on appeal to the Court of Appeals this order was reversed, and the Supreme Court upheld the Court of Appeals on the point. *Cooper* v. *Aaron*, 358 U.S. 1 (1958). The schools remained closed during the 1958–1959 school year when Governor Faubus, acting under newly passed state legislation, issued a closing order. This legislation was held invalid by the Supreme Court in 1959. Cf. *Faubus* v. *Aaron*, 361 U.S. 197 (1959).

that troops would be used to compel school integration only "over my dead body."[36] The instruments of public persuasion and leadership for bringing about popular acceptance of school desegregation had remained largely unused in his hands.

Still another lesson derived from the Little Rock experience was the advisability of employing to the fullest extent practicable a supplemental force of deputy United States marshals, rather than troops in uniform, as agents of the national government. Troops should be alerted and stationed conveniently near so that they can be called upon if needed, but resort to the rule of the bayonet should be a last resource, used only when all other means have failed.

President Kennedy sought to apply these lessons in dealing with desegregation crises in Mississippi and Alabama, but he was unable to avoid having to resort to the use of military force or the immediate threat thereof on three occasions. The most serious of these challenges came in 1962. James Meredith, a Negro, had obtained a Court of Appeals order directing his admission to the University of Mississippi in September of that year. Governor Ross Barnett, citing the earlier "interposition" resolution of the state legislature, personally appeared on three separate occasions during registration week to refuse compliance with the court order presented by civilian officers of the Department of Justice. Lieutenant Governor Paul B. Johnson (who was subsequently elected governor of the state in 1963) likewise refused Meredith admission at another such confrontation.

President Kennedy eventually issued the required proclamation, dispatched a force of 300 deputy marshals to Oxford, Mississippi, nationalized the Mississippi National Guard, and arranged to have other troops on a standby basis at nearby Memphis. In the face of this show of determination, state authorities allowed Meredith to enter the University, but his presence touched off a riot on the campus that threatened to overwhelm the force of marshals who had been stationed there for his protection. Before the riot was quelled, troops had to be summoned from Memphis. Two nonparticipants in the rioting were killed, and some 35 deputy marshals and 20 members of the 3000-man military contingent at the scene were injured. Meredith remained at the University under protection of federal marshals and was graduated the following summer. Governor Barnett and Lieutenant Governor Johnson were cited on criminal contempt charges in the United States Court of Appeals, but the charges eventually were dismissed.[37] The use

[36] Longaker, *op. cit.*, pp. 153, 168, 214.

[37] The Court of Appeals found itself divided 4–4 on the question of whether the defendants were entitled to a jury trial on the contempt charge. On reference of the question to the United States Supreme Court, that body in a 5–4 ruling held that a jury trial was not required and remanded the case for further proceedings. *United States v. Barnett*, 376 U.S. 681 (1964). In a 4–3 ruling on May 5, 1965, the Court of Appeals dismissed the criminal contempt charges. *United States v. Barnett*, 346 F.

of federal marshals, augmented by local National Guard units called into federal service in the last two instances, proved sufficient to overcome resistance to federal court desegregation orders in Montgomery, Alabama, in 1961, and in Tuscaloosa and Birmingham in the same state in 1963.

CHIEF EXECUTIVES AND INDUSTRIAL DISPUTES

Maintenance of the public order and security in connection with industrial disputes is one of the new emergency power operations by American chief executives, both state and national. In any review of the history of American industrial relations, Presidents and governors must be accorded leading roles. In general it may be observed that governmental intervention in labor-management relations in this country has progressed through a series of phases, each characterized by a broader conception of the kinds of action required of government to protect the public interest. Each phase has involved initiative on the part of chief executives in one way or another.

Originally the government's role was viewed solely as that of a policeman. Its duty was thought to be merely the maintenance of order when disagreements between management and labor became violent. Since striking employes usually tried to make their resort to economic pressure effective by using force to prevent strikebreakers from taking over their jobs, this view of the government's role not infrequently put government itself into the business of strikebreaking. It simply employed its law enforcement agents, its courts, and the military against the strikers to prevent interference with "business as usual" and "the right to work." A second phase in governmental intervention was reached when public authorities assumed a responsi-

---

(2nd.) 99. The majority opinion based the dismissal on "the lapse of time since this Court ordered the criminal contempt proceedings to be instituted, and the changed circumstances and conditions" since that time. There was a strong dissent by Chief Judge Tuttle, supported by two other members of the Court. In his dissent the Chief Judge wrote (at p. 107):

> The serious threat Governor Barnett posed was to the constitutional relationship of the States to the National Government. A public wrong of such enormity carries with it a corresponding and unshirkable duty on the federal court to vindicate the rights of the Nation by bringing the alleged contemnor to trial. . . . There was more at issue, therefore, than an affront to this Court's dignity when Ross Barnett, as the head of the State of Mississippi, mobilized sheriffs, highway troopers, and local police officers *and by force of arms overcame United States marshals enforcing the law.*

For more complete accounts of the desegregation crisis at Oxford see Russell H. Barrett, *Integration at Ole Miss* (Chicago: Quadrangle Books, 1965), and Theodore C. Sorensen, *Kennedy* (New York: Harper & Row, 1965), pp. 483–488.

bility to conduct impartial inquiries into cases of industrial unrest, to provide machinery to facilitate peaceful settlement of disputes, and to adopt remedial legislation designed to remove the often legitimate grounds for labor discontent. Governmental intervention went a step further when it came to be recognized that the economic and social costs of strikes are too great to allow them to occur, if there is any feasible way to avoid them. This meant that, by use of pressure and persuasion supplemented by court injunctions against a strike or a lockout for a time, chief executives were expected to bring about a cooling off period during which intensive efforts could be made to get the disputants to evolve a peaceful solution. The ultimate phase of governmental intervention, most commonly associated with wartime emergencies but not necessarily limited to them, occurs when the government seizes privately owned plants or other facilities threatened by a shutdown and continues to operate them pending agreement by the contending parties; or it achieves the same end by imposing on the parties a legal obligation to resolve their differences by compulsory arbitration.

These various approaches in dealing with industrial disputes are not necessarily mutually exclusive; nor do they presuppose independent courses of action by state and national authorities. On the contrary, the field of labor-management disputes and preventive or corrective governmental action is one of the prime areas in which cooperative effort by national and state governments occurs. With the development of continually expanding bodies of law at both levels dealing with labor conditions and the settlement of labor disputes, the role of Presidents and governors has become increasingly one of supervising the administration of policies laid down in statutes. Nevertheless this remains one of the crucial areas in which chief executives have been forced to act on their own initiative from time to time, to display ingenuity and boldness in devising expedients, and on occasion to invoke a broad conception of executive prerogative to act in the public interest independently of the statutory law.[38]

Since the 1870s state governors have felt compelled from time to time to employ state militia forces to assist local law enforcement officers in maintaining order in strikebound areas. In more serious cases they have called upon the President for military aid. A climax of a sort was reached in 1877 during the course of a nationwide railway strike. Railroad managements had imposed a 10 percent cut in railway workers' wages, and an ensuing strike resulted in numerous outbreaks of violence in 14 states as managements continued to try to

[38] On the general subject see Clinton Rossiter, "The President and Labor Disputes," *Journal of Politics*, Vol. II (February, 1949); and Rankin and Dallmayr, *op. cit.*, Chap. 3.

operate the trains with nonunion employees. In a period of eight days during July, 1877, the governors of nine of these states requested military aid from President Hayes. He responded as best he could with the limited federal forces available. While he recognized that national governmental interests were involved and was prepared to declare a state of martial law in the areas most affected by disorders, he confined his activities to rendering aid as requested by the governors concerned.

These events were a prelude to those of President Cleveland's second term, when the national government acted on its own initiative in dealing with another strike affecting the railroads. In 1894 some 2500 employees of the Pullman Company in Chicago struck in protest against a 25 percent cut in wages, and railroad employees of the American Railway Union joined them by refusing to operate trains that included Pullman cars. Chicago became the focal point of the struggle, but railroad traffic throughout the country was more or less affected. Governor John P. Altgeld of Illinois, who was not unsympathetic with the strikers' goals, took no action immediately, but Cleveland, following the advice of his Attorney General, Richard Olney, determined to act on his own.

Declaring that national interests were involved, President Cleveland authorized the seeking of an injunction against violent interference with movement of mail cars, obstruction of interstate rail traffic, or destruction of government property. The United States district court for the Chicago area granted a sweeping injunction of this character. It was ignored by union officers directing the strike. A force of some 5000 deputy marshals, many of whom had previously been employed as "detectives" and "guards" by the railroad companies involved, was dispatched to the scene, along with a contingent of armed forces, to assist in the enforcement of the court order. Governor Altgeld protested these actions, insisting that state power was adequate to maintain order. Eventually he also sent state militia units into the Chicago area. At the height of the disturbances some 14,000 men were engaged in policing operations in Chicago—3000 local police, 4000 militiamen, 2000 federal troops, and 5000 deputy marshals—to say nothing of a large number of private guards employed by the companies.

Eugene Debs, the leader of the embattled railroad workers, continued to carry on strike activities in violation of the terms of the injunction. He and other union officials were cited for contempt, convicted, and given jail sentences by the United States district court. The Supreme Court of the United States sustained the convictions.[39]

---

[39] *In re Debs*, 38, 158 U.S. 564 (1895). The six-month jail sentence imposed on Debs was not served. It was commuted to the time he had actually spent in jail while his case was being heard.

Justice Brewer's opinion for the Court was notable not only for the broad view it advanced regarding the scope of the national government's authority to deal with such emergencies but also for its unqualified endorsement of what the President had done. In it he declared:

> The entire strength of the Nation may be used to enforce in any part of the land the full and free exercise of national powers and the security of all rights entrusted by the Constitution to its care. The strong arm of the national government may be put forth to brush away all obstructions to the freedom of interstate commerce or the transportation of the mails. If the emergency arises, the army of the Nation, and all its militia, are at the service of the Nation to compel obedience to its laws. . . .

While this was a statement given in support of a more or less one-sided policy of intervention by the national chief executive, since the President's actions had effectively broken the strike, it signalized a new era of involvement of the national government in major industrial disputes. The President and Congress could no longer sit idly by, permitting the seeds of economic warfare to grow into violence without taking some kind of preventive action. The national interest demanded a more positive role of them.

Four years after the Pullman Strike, Congress passed the Erdman Act of 1898, in which it sought to protect the right of railroad workers to organize into unions and provided machinery to facilitate voluntary arbitration of railway labor disputes. In 1902 when a strike in the anthracite coal industry threatened to bring about a state of national distress, President Theodore Roosevelt intervened personally. By dint of persuasion and pressure, including the leaking of hints that he was prepared to occupy the closed mines with troops and put them back into operation, he induced the operators to submit the issues to a presidentially selected arbitration commission. The next year at his urging Congress passed long-pending legislation creating a Department of Commerce and Labor, one important unit of which was a Mediation and Conciliation Service empowered to extend its good offices in bringing about peaceful settlement of industrial disputes. This agency, given independent status by the Taft-Hartley Act of 1947, has continued to function as the national government's frontline industrial peace-promoting unit.

From Theodore Roosevelt's administration to the present, presidential involvement in industrial disputes has taken a variety of forms. In the first place, Presidents have continued to respond from time to time to state requests for military assistance in maintaining order at the scenes of industrial strife. Since Theodore Roosevelt's time, however, they have displayed a greater degree of caution in responding to such requests than did Presidents Hayes, Harrison, Cleveland, and

McKinley. If Presidents have not been satisfied through independent investigation by their own emissaries that federal aid is actually needed, or if they have felt that the state authorities were in reality seeking to shift the political and financial burden of taking extraordinary measures to the national government's shoulders, they have delayed, given only limited aid, and sometimes even refused to respond to such calls. For example, when Governor Sparks of Nevada in 1907 requested federal troops to maintain order during a miners' strike in and around Goldfield, President Roosevelt after some delay supplied the requested forces, but he placed them under strict orders that they were there only to preserve order, not to break the strike. After he had sent a three-man investigating team to survey the situation and report, he notified the governor that the federal troops would be removed within a specified time limit, and that the state would thereafter have to assume the policing function with its own militia.[40] His ultimatum had the intended effect. State authorities took steps to assume the policing of the strike. It should be noted that the Supreme Court has from the beginning regarded the obligation of the President to respond to a state request for military aid as posing a "political" question which the President, not the courts, must decide.[41]

In the second place, Presidents and governors have usually taken the lead in championing legislation designed to eliminate causes of labor-management disputes, to promote their settlement by peaceful means, and to improve the economic status and job security of industrial workers generally. Among the many presidentially initiated acts of this nature that might be cited are a number associated with President Wilson: the Newlands Act of 1913, creating special mediation machinery for the railroad industry; the Clayton Antitrust Act of 1914, which sought to exempt labor unions from the constrictive effects of the antitrust laws; and the Adamson Act of 1916, under which Congress imposed by legislative decree new temporary wage and hour terms for railway labor pending study of the issues by a special commission and negotiation of a permanent settlement. President F. D. Roosevelt's administration brought into being the short-lived National Industrial Recovery Act of 1933, with its industrial codes eliminating various unfair labor practices and raising labor standards; the National

[40] Cf. Rich, *op. cit.,* pp. 125–135.

[41] Cf. *Luther* v. *Borden,* 7 Howard 1 (1849). This case arose out of the Dorr Rebellion in Rhode Island, discussed *supra,* p. 87. On four different occasions the governor of the state under the old regime in Rhode Island requested President Tyler to furnish military aid in subduing the "rebels," but for one reason or another the President failed to comply, although he made preliminary preparations for doing so at the last. This was the first instance of formal request by a state for implementation of the aid-to-the-states clause of the Constitution.

Labor Relations (Wagner) Act of 1935, guaranteering free collective bargaining rights to labor in industries affecting interstate commerce; the Railway Labor Disputes Act of 1934, which did the same for railway labor and established improved machinery for peaceful adjustment of railway disputes; and the Fair Labor Standards Act of 1938, setting up minimum wage and other types of work standards for workers in major industries.

The third avenue through which chief executives have acted has been use of their personal prestige and official influence, as well as procedures made available to them under the law, to postpone resort to economic force and thereby promote peaceful settlement of issues threatening to disrupt normal labor-management relations. The Labor-Management Relations (Taft-Hartley) Act of 1947 includes a section providing that if the President finds that an actual or threatened strike or lockout imperils the national health or safety, he can obtain a court injunction against the strike or lockout or its continuation for as long as 80 days during which special efforts are made to bring the issues to a negotiated conclusion.[42] Although President Truman had characterized this provision of the proposed Act as "ineffective," "unnecessary," and "discriminatory" in his message defending his veto of the bill, he nevertheless employed it on 10 occasions during his administration. President Eisenhower used it seven times, and President Kennedy six times. The emergency provisions of the Taft-Hartley Act have been applied in the coal mining, atomic energy, nonferrous metals, shipping, aviation, meat packing, locomotive, and telephone industries.[43] Intervention under this procedure has not always averted a threatened strike, it should be noted; nor has the existence of the procedure stood in the way of Presidents using their influence, some-

---

[42] 69 *Stat.* 155 (1947), *U.S. Code,* Title 29, *Secs.* 176–180. The first step the President takes in this kind of situation is the appointment of a special board of inquiry. Upon receiving a report from the board, the President may then authorize the Attorney General to seek a 60-day injunction against the strike or lockout. The court must issue such an injunction if it finds that the beginning or the continuance of a work stoppage will imperil the national health or safety. During this period mediation efforts are made by the Mediation and Conciliation Service. At the end of the 60 days, if the parties have not achieved agreement, the board is reconvened, makes a report to the President, and the injunction may be continued for another 20 days, during which time the National Labor Relations Board may conduct a poll of the employees involved on acceptance of the "last offer" of management for settlement. When the results of the poll have been certified to the Attorney General the injunction is automatically dissolved, whether or not the strike has been averted. The President then must submit the record of the entire proceedings to Congress, together with any recommendations for legislative action he may choose to offer.

[43] A résumé of the major instances of use of the emergency provisions of the Taft-Hartley Act and a critical evaluation thereof is given in Rankin and Dallmayr, *op. cit.,* pp. 115ff. See also Charles M. Rehmus, "The Operation of the National Emergency Provisions of the Labor Management Relations Act of 1947," *Yale Law*

times successfully, to induce voluntary postponements of strikes and ultimate resolution of differences by negotiation. Similar laws have been adopted in a number of states. A growing recognition of the principle that in major industries the government, representing the public interest, is always an interested third party has characterized labor-management relations in this country since the end of World War II.

The ultimate recourse of chief executives in preserving economic peace is governmental seizure of plants and facilities threatened with a shutdown because of labor-management strife. They are then continued in operation under governmental auspices to prevent interruption of production or services vital to the public. A number of states have experimented with laws imposing upon industries, particularly in the public utilities field, a system of compulsory arbitration, but this type of legislation has encountered considerable hostility in the courts as violating rights protected by the Fourteenth Amendment or as invading a field of control occupied by the United States government under its commerce and war powers.[44] (Governmental seizures of plants for the most part have been effected by the national government during wartime and have been justified by reference to wartime emergency legislation and the powers of the President as Commander-in-Chief; a fuller discussion of this aspect of the subject, therefore, follows in Chapter 16.)

Two recent episodes have illustrated dramatically the role of the President as an economic troubleshooter in labor-management difficulties, as well as demonstrating the great power and influence the President wields in his own right over the nation's economy. The first, which was a threat of a nationwide strike by railroad engineers

---

Journal, Vol. 62 (June, 1953), pp. 1047–1063. In *United Steelworkers of America* v. *United States,* 361 U.S. 39 (1959), the Supreme Court sustained the injunction provisions of the law against various contentions and held that a threatened steel industry strike came within its scope as threatening the national health and safety. In spite of the fact that President Eisenhower had invoked the cooling off procedures of the Taft-Hartley Act in this instance, a strike involving some 500,000 steelworkers eventually ensued and lasted for 116 days, idling an additional 350,000 workers in related industries.

[44] An early Kansas experiment in compulsory settlement of industrial disputes was cut down by the Supreme Court in three decisions. Cf. *Wolff Packing Co.* v. *Court of Industrial Relations,* 262 U.S. 522 (1923); *Dorchy* v. *Kansas,* 264 U.S. 286 (1924); and *Wolff Packing Co.* v. *Court of Industrial Relations,* 267 U.S. 552 (1925). A leading case on exclusion of state authority over the subject by reason of federal occupation of the field is *Amalgamated Association of Street, Electric Railway and Motor Coach Employees* v. *Wisconsin Employment Relations Board,* 340 U.S. 383 (1951). A review of state efforts seeking to impose industrial peace through mediation, compulsory arbitration, military intervention and seizure powers during the postwar period is given in Rankin and Dallmayr, *op. cit.,* pp. 164–187.

and firemen, involved three Presidents—Eisenhower, Kennedy, and Johnson—in a series of actions. Following protracted fruitless negotiations on numerous points of difference, leading railroad managements, over the strong protests of the unions concerned, announced in 1959 their intention to put into effect new work rules which would eliminate a considerable number of train crewmen's jobs. President Eisenhower intervened and obtained a postponement of introduction of the new rules, pending a study of the issues and recommendations for their settlement by a special 15-member presidential commission, which he appointed in November, 1960. It reported in February, 1962, after President Kennedy had assumed office. Some of its recommendations were accepted by the parties to the dispute, but major points of disagreement remained unsettled.

Efforts to reach a settlement through negotiation continued until July, 1962, when the railroads announced their intention to put into effect the recommended work rules changes not yet accepted by the unions. The unions sought and obtained temporary lower federal court injunctions against their doing so; on March 4, 1963, however, the Supreme Court ruled that except for the creation of an emergency board of inquiry as provided for under the Railway Labor Disputes Act of 1934, the parties had exhausted the remedies provided by law for resolving the issue of imposition of the new rules.[45] On April 3, 1963, President Kennedy appointed such a board. This postponed the threatened strike for 60 days, while mediation efforts continued. No agreement having been reached at the end of that time, President Kennedy twice obtained further voluntary short postponements of a showdown between the parties. At length, on July 22, 1963, when a strike tying up the nation's railroad system seemed imminent, he asked Congress for special legislation to deal with the emergency. Congress responded with the first peacetime compulsory arbitration law ever adopted by it.[46] The act froze established work rules on points still in dispute and prohibited a strike, pending the making of binding rulings by an arbitration board on the major remaining points of disagreement. A special seven-man board—three members to be appointed by the President and two by each of the parties—was set up. The board made its report on November 26, but there remained other issues which had not been resolved, and the unions were unhappy with some aspects of the board's award. President Johnson, who had in the meantime succeeded to the presidency, continued to press for a peaceful settlement. Finally, on April 22, 1964, he was able to an-

[45] *Locomotive Engineers* v. *Baltimore and Ohio Railroad Co.*, 372 U.S. 284 (1963).

[46] Joint Resolution of August 28, 1963, 77 *Stat.* 129.

nounce triumphantly that the disputants had been able to resolve all the points still at issue.[47] A dispute that had dragged on for nearly five years was finally resolved without resort to a disastrous strike.

The other episode, in which President Kennedy was the chief actor, occurred in 1962. With the assistance of his Secretary of Labor, Arthur Goldberg, formerly an attorney for the Steelworkers Union, President Kennedy had been successful in bringing about a negotiated wage settlement in March between the Steelworkers Union and the major steel producing companies. Under strong White House pressure the union had reluctantly agreed to a wage settlement far less than originally demanded on a plea from the President that the wage structure decided upon be noninflationary, i.e., that it not cause the steel industry to raise prices for its product on grounds of greatly increased costs, thereby setting off a spiral of rising prices.

Despite this implicit, though not explicit, understanding that the new contract terms would not trigger a rise in steel prices, on April 10, some 10 days after agreement on the new contract had been reached, the president of the United States Steel Corporation informed President Kennedy that his company was revising prices upward for its products generally by some 3.5 percent. President Kennedy was both astounded and furious. Treating the matter as a double cross on the part of United States Steel and other industry managements who were preparing to follow its lead, he immediately mobilized for action to induce the steel companies to rescind the price increase. Investigations were launched by the Justice Department to determine if there had been collusive price fixing in violation of the antitrust laws. The Secretary of Defense prepared to cancel government contracts with companies that went along with the price increase. Mutterings about enactment of a price ceiling law or legislation authorizing seizure of steel plants were heard in Congress and were not explicitly disavowed by the President. In a televised news conference he left no doubt in the public mind that he considered the price rise action to be seriously detrimental to the public interest. The issue had suddenly blossomed into a dramatic contest commanding nationwide attention.[48]

It subsided almost as quickly as it arose. When a number of other steel companies issued statements that they would not go along with the price increase, the ground began to collapse under the offending companies. Four days after it had given notice of the intended price boost, United States Steel issued a statement rescinding its

[47] *The New York Times,* April 23, 1964, pp. 1, 25.

[48] For detailed accounts of the episode see Grant McConnel, *Steel and the Presidency—1962* (New York: W. W. Norton & Company, 1963); Louis W. Koenig, "Kennedy and Steel: The Great Price Dispute," in Alan F. Westin, ed., *The Centers of Power* (New York: Harcourt, Brace & World, 1964); and Sorenson, *Kennedy,* pp. 443–459.

earlier action. Other companies that had followed its lead did like-wise. By utilizing the prestige and the ancillary powers of his office and by marshalling the forces of public opinion to his side, the President had scored a notable victory. In a thoroughly Rooseveltian manner he had interpreted his role as Conservator of the Public Peace and Safety to include protection of the economic stability of the nation. Wall Street and the business centers of the nation duly registered alarm at this display of raw power in the presidency,[49] but the reaction soon subsided as other problems and crises absorbed the attention of the President, the business community, and the nation.

THE CHIEF EXECUTIVE AND "EMERGENCY" GOVERNMENT

The incidents described so far in this chapter have for the most part involved a basic type of emergency situation that was of im-mediate concern to the Framers of the Constitution, namely, how to deal with internal challenges to the authority of government itself. As has been seen, the machinery they provided for handling this type of emergency has well withstood the tests of time. The nation has remained united; the writ of the government in Washington still runs throughout the length and breadth of the land—the rantings of some southern segregationist diehards to the contrary notwithstanding—and the nation has grown and prospered to a degree that makes its wealth and power the envy of the world.

But emergencies growing out of the social and world order of a kind the Framers could not foresee have also developed and tested the governmental machinery they devised. Beginning with a series of measures enacted by Congress during its famous "Hundred Days Ses-sion" to meet the threat of social and economic chaos in 1933, through the crisis of World War II, and on into the post-World War II nuclear and space age, "emergency" as a justification for undertaking unusual measures by government has become a commonplace. Through legis-lative grant or authorization chief executives at both the national and state levels have been invested with a vast arsenal of emergency powers under which they may take appropriate steps to relieve distress, main-tain economic stability, and protect the national security. To meet the challenges posed by the dynamic world and society of the modern age, chief executives in ever-increasing measure have had to be

[49] The Republican Party Platform of 1964 took note of the affair by "indicting" the Kennedy administration in these terms: "This administration has violently thrust federal power into the free market in such areas as steel prices, thus establishing precedents which in future years could critically wound free enterprise in the United States."

equipped with the tools of what might be termed "instant government."

The Constitution itself does not use the word "emergency," but
the Supreme Court has solemnly and repeatedly enunciated the proposition that while emergency does not create power it may call into
play hitherto unused granted powers[50]—a prime example, it might
be noted, of the Court's skill in making a distinction without a difference. The principle has become accepted that the legislative branch,
by making a finding for itself that a combination of unforeseeable
and unpredictable circumstances has developed or by delegating to
the chief executive the responsibility to make such a finding, can
legitimize measures calculated to preserve the public order, interest,
or security in the face of unexpected dislocating events or circumstances. The nature of the emergency that can bring these unusual
procedures into play has been spelled out in various kinds of phrases
—"war," "a state of hostilities," "danger to the public health or safety,"
and so on.

It is not the purpose here to examine at length the vast, complex
array of national and state legislative acts authorizing the employment
of unusual procedures by chief executives to meet unexpected contingencies, nor to deal with the constitutional issues presented by them.
They run the gamut from authorizations to extend loans, grants,
and other forms of material aid to people in areas of natural disasters
such as drought, flood, earthquakes, pests or disease, through measures
to preserve the economic health and equilibrium of the nation, to
the institution of what amounts practically to a form of "constitutional
dictatorship" in an all-out wartime emergency.[51] (These matters will

[50] In *Wilson* v. *New*, 243 U.S. 332 (1917), Chief Justice White in his opinion
sustaining the Adamson Act by which Congress temporarily set wage and hour terms
for railway employees because of an emergency situation, observed:

> . . . although an emergency may not call into life a power which has never
> lived, nevertheless emergency may afford a reason for the exertion of a living
> power already enjoyed.

In a similar vein Chief Justice Hughes declared in *Home Building and Loan
Association* v. *Blaisdell*, 290 U.S. 398 (1934) wherein the validity of a Minnesota mort-
gage moratorium law was upheld:

> Emergency does not create power. Emergency does not increase granted
> power or remove or diminish the restrictions imposed upon power granted or
> reserved . . .
> While emergency does not create power, emergency may furnish the occa-
> sion for the exercise of power. . . . The constitutional question presented in
> the light of an emergency is whether the power possessed embraces the particu-
> lar exercise of it in response to particular conditions. . . .

[51] For an analysis in detail of this type of legislation at the national level see
J. Malcolm Smith and Cornelius P. Cotter, *Powers of the President During Crises*
(Washington: Public Affairs Press, 1960). Rankin and Dallmayr, *op. cit.*, presents
analyses in depth of emergency executive powers in relation to nonmilitary defense,

be considered further in Chapter 16.) It suffices to say here that the vesting by legislative act of broad discretionary power in the President and in state governors to take extraordinary steps to meet the public needs in such situations has extended their Conservator-in-Chief role to limits undreamed of by the Constitution's Framers. Hamilton observed in one of his essays in *The Federalist* that "energy in the executive is a leading character in the definition of good government."[52] The principle he enunciated has been applied and exemplified in modern American government in manifold ways to an extent that would no doubt astound that staunch advocate of strong executive authority, were he here to view them.

---

labor disputes, and racial equality. Albert L. Sturm, "Emergencies and the President," *Journal of Politics,* Vol. II (February, 1949), pp. 121–144 is a good shorter treatment of the subject.

[52] *The Federalist,* No. 70.

15

MANAGER-IN-CHIEF

OF EXTERNAL RELATIONS

The men who wrote the Constitution felt that improvement in the system for handling the nation's foreign affairs was sorely needed. Truly enough, the nation had fought for and won its independence under a governmental plan in which the conduct of its foreign affairs was entrusted to the Congress of the United States, functioning through a Department of Foreign Affairs and a corps of diplomatic agents under its direction. Nevertheless, the necessity for a more solid foundation for management of external relations was one of the important considerations leading to the assembling of the Convention of 1787. Hamilton stated the case for reform in these terms:

> We may indeed with propriety be said to have reached almost the last stage of national humiliation. There is scarcely anything that can wound the pride or degrade the character of an independent nation which we do not experience. Are there engagements to the performance of which we are held by every tie respectable among men? These are the subjects of unblushing violation. Do we owe debts to foreigners and to our own citizens contracted in a time of imminent peril for the preservation of our political existence? These remain without any proper or satisfactory provision for their discharge. Have we valuable territories and important posts in the possession of a foreign power which, by express stipulations, ought long since to have been surrendered? These are still retained, to the prejudice of our interests, not less than of our rights. Are we in a condition to resent or repel the aggression? . . . Are we even in a position to remonstrate with dignity? The just imputations of our own faith, in respect to the same treaty, ought first be removed. . . . Is respectability in the eyes of foreign powers a safeguard against foreign encroachments? The imbecility of our government even forbids them to treat with us. Our ambassadors abroad are the mere pageants of mimic sovereignty. . . .[1]

Hamilton's strictures may have overstated the case somewhat, but improvements in the system for handling the nation's foreign relations were undoubtedly needed. For the first quarter of a century or so after adoption of the Constitution, foreign affairs and foreign

[1] *The Federalist*, No. 15.

policy issues dominated the American political scene. But with the downfall of Napoleon and the termination of the Napoleonic wars—a struggle into which the United States had eventually been drawn—the emphasis in American politics changed. Enunciation of the Monroe Doctrine in 1823, warning the European powers that any attempt to re-establish colonial regimes in the Americas would be regarded by the United States as an unfriendly act and pledging that this country would not become involved in the international affairs of Europe, marked the new era. For the next three quarters of a century the United States concentrated its attention upon internal political problems. Its international problems were largely confined to those growing out of westward expansion of the nation's territorial boundaries.

The year 1898 signaled the beginning of a change in this emphasis. In that year as a result of the Spanish-American War and the annexation of Hawaii the United States became a colonial power, with territories lying outside continental North America. Its growing commercial interests and the development of its economic and military strength brought the United States into the circle of the world's leading powers. Reluctant at first to assume all the responsibilities implicit in its position, the United States nevertheless found itself drawn into the vortex of World War I by these interests. With the end of the war and the Senate's refusal to approve unqualified participation in the League of Nations set up by the Versailles Treaty, the United States attempted to retreat again into its shell of isolationism. The retreat proved to be only partial and temporary. The outbreak of World War II, our eventual involvement in it, our assumption of a leading role in the formation of the United Nations organization, American leadership of the Western powers against the Communist bloc of nations in the Cold War era following the end of World War II, and the advent of the nuclear and space age have brought about a condition making impossible a policy of isolationism by the United States. Foreign policy issues and their repercussions upon our own domestic problems have again become dominant in American political life, and to a degree hitherto unknown.

As has been pointed out in Chapter 7, the effect of these developments upon the presidency has been profound. By reason of his constitutional position the President has a primary role both in the initiation and in the execution of policies in the foreign affairs field. While Congress is by no means excluded from a share in this power and responsibility, the very nature of foreign policy management places it in a position of greater dependency upon the leadership of the President than is the case with purely domestic matters. Decisions of the gravest importance to the security of the nation and to the peace of the world thrust themselves upon him. Realizing this, the people of the United States, and of the Western world as well, observe his performance in this phase of his official duties with the utmost concern. In a sense all the people of the free world are numbered among his constituents. During a time of great tension, as in the Hungarian revolt of 1956, the Suez crisis of the same year, or the Cuban crisis of 1962, the White House becomes the focal point for decision-making and action important to the very fate of mankind. It is not hard to understand why the peoples of the Western world follow our national nominating conventions and presidental election campaigns with as great a degree of interest as do the American people themselves. When President Kennedy on his visit to West Berlin in 1963 closed his speech of greeting to hundreds of thousands of the local citizens with the words, "Ich bin ein Berliner," the approving roar that followed signified appreciation of the fact that he was in a sense *their* President. His tragic death a few months later left millions of people throughout the world with a deep sense of personal loss.

THE CONSTITUTIONAL SETTING

The constitutional framework within which a President operates in discharging his responsibilities as Manager-in-Chief of External Relations is indeed a spacious one. Article II, Section 2, of the Constitution assigns to him the power "by and with the advice and consent of the Senate, to make treaties, providing two thirds of the Senators present concur"; to appoint ambassadors, public ministers, and consuls, subject to confirmation by the Senate; and makes him Commander-in-Chief of the nation's armed forces. Section 3 of the same article authorizes him to "receive" ambassadors and other public ministers of foreign powers. To the Congress are assigned a number of powers having more or less direct relevance to foreign policy matters—to lay and collect taxes; to borrow money on the credit of the United States; to authorize expenditures for the common defense and general welfare; to regulate commerce with foreign nations; to regulate the value of foreign coin; to define and punish piracies and felonies committed on the high seas and offenses against the law of nations; to declare war; to establish and maintain the nation's armed forces; and to make laws necessary and proper for carrying into execution those powers or those vested by the Constitution in the government of the United States or in any department or officer thereof.

The states are excluded from direct participation in the handling of foreign relations by clauses in Article I, Section 10, prohibiting them from entering into any "treaty, alliance or confederation"; from levying, without the consent of Congress, tonnage duties or duties on imports or exports, except for raising amounts sufficient to pay the costs of enforcing their inspection laws; from entering into any "agreement or compact" with another state or a foreign power without the consent of Congress; or from engaging in war, unless they are actually invaded or in such imminent danger as will not admit of delay. Topping off these provisions is the language of Article VI, obligating the states to accept treaties of the United States as well as the laws enacted by Congress pursuant to the Constitution as a part of the "supreme law of the land," overriding any conflicting provisions of their own laws or constitutions.

So far as the subject matters with which the United States government may deal are concerned, they are as broad and as varied as the exigencies arising out of the interdependence, mutual interests, and conflicts of this nation with the rest of the world. In the sphere of international affairs, its powers are inherent, plenary, and exclusive. They flow from membership of the United States in the international community of nations. The Supreme Court has declared that "the right and power of the United States in the [international] field are equal to the right and power of the other members of the international family."[2] Since its authority to act in this sphere is a necessary concomitant of nationality, its competence to enter into international agreements on matters of mutual concern and to carry those agreements into effect is not circumscribed by the Tenth Amendment, reserving to the states powers not delegated to the United States.[3] However, this is not an unlimited power. "No agreement with a foreign nation," the Supreme Court has asserted, "can confer power on the Congress,

---

[2] *United States* v. *Curtis-Wright Export Corporation*, 299 U.S. 304 (1934).
[3] Cf. *Hauenstein* v. *Lynham*, 100 U.S. 483 (1880); *Missouri* v. *Holland*, 252 U.S. 415 (1920); *Askura* v. *Seattle*, 265 U.S. 332 (1924); *United States* v. *Belmont*, 301 U.S. 324 (1937); and *United States* v. *Pink*, 315 U.S. 203 (1942). In the *Belmont* case, Justice Sutherland stated in the Court's majority opinion:

Plainly, the external powers of the United States are to be exercised without regard to state laws or policies. The supremacy of a treaty in this respect has been recognized from the beginning. . . . And while this rule in respect of treaties is established by the express language of clause 2, Art. VI, of the Constitution, the same rule would result in the case of all international compacts and agreements from the very fact that complete power over international affairs is in the national government and is not and cannot be subject to any curtailment or interference on the part of the several states. . . . In respect of all international negotiations and compacts, and in respect of our foreign relations generally, state lines disappear. As to such purposes the State of New York does not exist. Within the field of its powers, whatever the United States rightfully undertakes, it necessarily has warrant to consummate. And when judicial authority is invoked in aid of such consummation, state constitutions, state laws, and state policies are irrelevant to the inquiry and decision.

or on any other branch of the government, which is free from the restraints of the Constitution."[4]

Subject to this general caveat from the Court, the political organs of the national government may act upon all matters of import to the United States in its relations with other nations. The Supreme Court applies with a generous hand the doctrine of "political questions" in this sphere, under which the courts are held to be bound by the decisions of the political branches on certain questions.[5] The Constitution assigns particular roles to the President, to Congress, and to the Senate in the exercise of the national government's broad authority over foreign affairs. No one of these organs has the complete authority to formulate and direct the course of foreign policy; and no one of them can obligate and bind the others to exercise their respective constitutional powers in a particular way. The President has a primacy in making determinations in this sphere which sometimes leaves Congress at a serious disadvantage in trying to oppose or check his course by failing to cooperate; but in the long view the executive and legislative branches share responsibility in this area and must cooperate with one another to make effective policy.

Foreign affairs management is a field that highlights in the most extreme degree some of the difficulties inherent in the separation of powers system. Opportunities for the separate political organs of government to work at cross purposes arise from time to time, and the likelihood that the President, the Senate, and the House of Representatives may not see eye to eye on all issues is greater in foreign policy than it is in domestic matters.. The President may be in possession of information justifying his course of action which for reasons of state he cannot fully disclose to Congress or to the public. Organ-

[4] *Reid* v. *Covert*, 353 U.S. 1, 16, (1957); opinion by Justice Black. In this case the Court ruled that the Status of Forces Agreement between the United States and Great Britain could have no efficacy in authorizing trial by military courts-martial of American civilians stationed in Great Britain in pursuance of North Atlantic Treaty objectives. When such individuals are accused of having committed crimes against other Americans making up the defensive mission they are entitled to the various Bill of Rights guarantees such as a grand jury indictment, jury trial, etc., applicable to the trial of civilians in American civil courts.

[5] For example, the Court has held that the boundary line claimed by the political departments of the United States government under the terms of a treaty must be accepted as binding by the courts, *Foster and Elam* v. *Nielsen*, 2 Peters 253 (1829); in American law the de jure government of another country is the one recognized as such by the political departments, *Oetgen* v. *Central Leather Company*, 246 U.S. 297 (1918); whether a treaty with another country is regarded as still in force is governed by the view of the political branches on the point, *Charlton* v. *Kelly*, 229 U. S. 447 (1913). An important exception to the Court's general rule of according to the President a broad discretionary power in foreign affairs matters was its holding in *Valentine* v. *United States ex rel Neidecker*, 299 U.S. 5 (1936), wherein it ruled that the President, in the absence of express authorization by treaty or statute, lacks authority to extradite an American citizen wanted for trial in another country.

ized pressure group influences upon which he can rely in bringing Congress into line in support of his domestic policies are often lacking in foreign policy matters. There is no powerful lobby in Washington to speak for the peoples of the Congo or of Vietnam. Localized opposition to his measures carrying much weight with individual congressmen is at times an obstacle. The seniority system in allocating committee chairmanships important in foreign policy matters may put into places of power members of Congress totally unsympathetic with the President's views and programs.

There remains among the American people a considerable residue of enchantment with the nineteenth-century policy of isolation from Old World affairs. The public tends to be parochial in its view of the world, if not entirely apathetic and untouched by world events and problems. At the same time there is among Americans generally an idealistic fervor, an unquestioning faith in the "American way" as the salvation of all mankind, a trust in the unimpeachable purity of this nation's motives at all times in its dealings with other countries. Many Americans seem to entertain the naive belief that every country's government and people are as strongly committed to the promotion of democratic values as are our own. This is joined with a frontier-like readiness on the part of some elements of the population to endorse use of the "big stick" against any nation daring to challenge the interests of the United States. Complete annihilation or "unconditional surrender" of our enemies is demanded by the public, once the struggle is joined. More cognizant of the realities of the mid-twentieth-century world order, the President often finds it difficult to generate support for his policies in Congress, which tends to reflect in great measure these stereotypes of popular thinking.

The Constitution's built-in invitation to struggle between Presidents and Congress in the foreign policy field is by no means unique.[6] As has been shown in Chapter 12, this invitation runs through the entire range of governmental policy formulation and execution. However, the foreign policy field is one in which serious conflict and deadlock between the two policy-making branches can be most dangerous to the nation's best interests. For this reason there are those who preach the gospel of a bipartisan approach to foreign policy matters

[6] For a thoughtful analysis of the built-in features of the American system for controlling foreign policy which tend to generate differences in outlook between the President and Congress see Robert A. Dahl, *Congress and Foreign Policy* (New York: Harcourt, Brace & World, 1950). See also on this general point James A. Robinson, *Congress and Foreign Policy Making* (Homewood, Ill.: The Dorsey Press, 1962); Daniel S. Cheever and H. Field Haviland, Jr., *American Foreign Policy and the Separation of Powers* (Cambridge: Harvard University Press, 1952); and Marshall Knappen, *An Introduction to American Foreign Policy* (New York: Harper & Row, 1956), especially Chaps. 4 and 6.

—a noble and idealistic approach, to be sure, but one which, given the intensity of the partisan struggle in American politics and the fact that foreign policy issues are becoming more and more inter-twined inextricably with domestic issues, is very difficult if not im-possible to realize in practice. It is easy to understand why the sep-aration of powers system has been subjected in recent years to some of its most serious and penetrating criticism, and proposals for alter-ing the existing constitutional arrangements, usages, and practices have been advanced with the greatest urgency.

THE CONDUCT OF DIPLOMATIC RELATIONS

At no place does the Constitution assign to the President in specific terms the responsibility of serving as the instrument of com-munication with the governments of other powers, but usage, under-standing, and the practicalities of international diplomatic intercourse have combined to place in his hands that function. Exceedingly im-portant consequences flow from that circumstance. In his capacity as official spokesman for the United States in its international dealings the President may enunciate policies and initiate measures with respect to matters of international concern that go far toward com-mitting the United States toward a particular course of action. Con-gress may, of course, through legislation also declare the attitude and policy of the United States government on a wide variety of subjects having relevance to this nation's foreign affairs, and it becomes the President's responsibility as chief executive to give force and effect to such laws. Congress may also by formal or informal means express its views and opinions on matters in this sphere. Furthermore, in the long run, policies initiated by the President in the field of foreign affairs may be undercut or defeated by the refusal of Congress to supply financial and other types of implementing legislation to make them effective. Yet the point is clear that presidential initiative in this sphere is an inescapable result of his being in command of the channels of official communication.

How far the Framers of the Constitution expected and intended the President's functioning as the instrumentality of communication to encompass policy-making in the foreign relations field remains one of the puzzles of the constitutional plan. The Founding Fathers were familiar with Locke's tripartite categorization of governmental powers under which the legislative, executive, and "federative" functions of government were distinguished. As Locke defined it, the "federative" power involved the "power of war and peace, leagues and alliances, and all the transactions with all persons and communities without the commonwealth."[7] In his view this power and the "executive" or internal law enforcement function must be united in the same hands, for "though this federative power in the well or ill management of it be of great moment to the commonwealth, yet it is much less capable to be directed by antecedent, standing, positive laws than the executive, and so must necessarily be left to the prudence and wisdom of those whose hands it is in, to be managed for the public good." Montesquieu had drawn a similar distinction between the "executive [power] in respect to things dependent on the law of nations" and the "executive in regard to matters that depend on the civil law."[8] Yet the Framers deliberately parcelled out this "federative" executive power by explicitly assigning to Congress the right to declare war and by associating the Senate with the President in the making of treaties. They left unanswered the question where the ultimate directive responsibility should lie.

Events of the first presidential administration soon demonstrated that the President's role in foreign affairs management could not be confined to acting merely as an agent to carry out policies formulated by Congress or by the Senate. President Washington quickly came to realize the impracticability of appearing personally before the Senate to discuss with and secure advance clearance from that body on the form and content of instructions to commissioners dispatched to negotiate treaties. When in August, 1789, he made such an appearance, in company with his Secretary of War, General Knox, to discuss the instructions that should be given to commissioners assigned to negotiate a treaty with the Creek Indians, much to his annoyance the Senate insisted on referring his questions to a committee for study.[9] He returned a few days later to receive the Senate's reply, but this incident marked the early demise of efforts by the President to employ the Senate as an advisory council on the conduct of foreign affairs. Thereafter communications from him in writing, or informal contacts with individual members of the Senate, became the customary mode of consultation. This had the inevitable result of the President's assuming a larger degree of discretion in the instruction of American diplomatic agents.

Of even greater significance were the steps leading up to an important policy statement by Washington in connection with the French crisis of 1793. By the terms of a treaty of 1778 the United States had entered into a defensive alliance with France. Concerned with what our policy toward the new revolutionary regime in France should

[7] *Two Treatises of Civil Government,* Bk. II, Secs. 145–148.
[8] *Spirit of the Laws,* Bk. XI, Chap. 6.
[9] Cf. James Hart, *The American Presidency in Action, 1789* (New York: The Macmillan Company, 1948), pp. 86–97, for an interesting account of the affair.

be following the outbreak of war in 1793 between it and a coalition of European powers including Great Britain, President Washington viewed the situation with anxiety. At length, with the reluctant approval of his Secretary of State, Jefferson—who had urged him to assemble Congress in special session to consider the course this government should take—he issued a proclamation declaring the attitude the United States would assume toward the belligerents. It stated the intention of the United States to "adopt and pursue a conduct friendly and impartial" toward the belligerent powers and warned the citizens of the nation to avoid all acts and proceedings not in conformity with this policy of neutrality.[10] The next year Congress saw fit to assert itself by adopting a Neutrality Act embracing generally the outlines of the policy set forth in the President's proclamation, but the President had demonstrated the great potential residing in his office for taking the initiative in foreign policy matters.

The significance of Washington's bold assumption of a policy-making role was not overlooked by his contemporaries. It produced the first of a series of great debates which have been staged from time to time in the halls of Congress and in the public prints on the subject of the constitutional powers and functions of the President versus those of Congress generally in the management of the nation's foreign affairs. Secretary of the Treasury Hamilton chose the occasion of the President's issuance of the Neutrality Proclamation, which he had warmly supported in Cabinet discussions, to advocate in the public press a broad view of the President's constitutional responsibilities and authority in this area. Using the pseudonym of "Pacificus," he published in *The Gazette of the United States,* a Federalist newspaper which he had helped to establish in 1789, a series of articles setting forth the general proposition that the executive power clause of Article II of the Constitution vests in the President authority to perform all acts executive in character, subject only to the specific limitations found elsewhere in the Constitution.[11] As to the management of foreign relations, this meant, according to Hamilton, that the President might take appropriate steps to deal with any situation that develops, al-

[10] Richardson, *Messages and Papers of the Presidents,* Vol. I, p. 156. This proclamation was followed by another a month later warning the inhabitants of Kentucky against assembling and organizing armed forces for the purpose of "invading and plundering the territories of a nation at peace with the United States," i.e., Spain. The French Minister to the United States, Genêt, had been encouraging warlike activities against Spanish-held Louisiana. *Ibid.,* p. 157.

[11] For a more extended analysis of the "Pacificus-Helvidius" debate see Edward S. Corwin, *The President: Office and Powers,* 4th ed. (New York: New York University Press, 1957), pp. 178–181. In setting forth these views Hamilton was elaborating upon views he had expressed in No. 75—and had also been expressed by John Jay in No. 64—of *The Federalist.*

though he could not go so far as to obligate Congress to exercise its own constitutional powers in this sphere. In short, his point was that the President possessed a *concurrent* policy-making function with Congress in the foreign relations field.

Disturbed by these views, Secretary of State Jefferson urged Madison, then a member of the House, to refute these contentions and "cut him [Hamilton] to pieces" in the public press. Madison did so in an answering series of articles published under the pseudonym, "Helvidius." In his refutation Madison advanced the view that the basic power to determine foreign policy was lodged in Congress by virtue of its expressly acknowledged right to declare war and by reason of the Senate's participation in the treaty-making process. Except where stated otherwise in the Constitution the President's role in this sphere, he contended, was that of an agent or instrument of the legislative branch in which ultimate control resided. His discretion did not extend to determination of policy in such a way as to leave Congress with no choice but to follow his lead.

This notable exchange of viewpoints proved to be only the first of many that have been generated by the basic question. As new problems have arisen in foreign affairs it has been presented in a variety of forms and contexts. On the whole, the pragmatic answers that have been arrived at have tended to vindicate Hamilton's position. Congress is at a fundamental disadvantage in seeking to be the active, directing force in making foreign policy. The attitudes and probable actions of other nations are always factors that must be taken into account in directing this country's diplomatic moves. The President has superior means to evaluate those factors and to shape responses to them, at least in the immediate sense. The result has been that on occasion Congress has found itself confronted by a *fait accompli*. It must make the uncomfortable choice of having to trust the President's judgment and follow his lead or risk national embarrassment or even endanger the national interest and security. Delegation of power to the President by statute to react to the exigencies of the moment, it should be noted, has reached its highest levels in this sphere. Both Jefferson and Madison came to view the President's functions in managing foreign relations in a different light when they saw the problem from the vantage point of the presidency itself. Both asked for and received broad powers in controlling foreign trade policy. Jefferson swallowed his constitutional scruples and authorized negotiations that led to the purchase of all the Louisiana Territory when the opportunity presented itself, even though the Senate had approved negotiations for the purchase only of a lesser area. Madison dispatched commissioners to Europe to negotiate the terms of the Treaty of Ghent ending the War of 1812 without even having submitted their names to the Senate for approval or clearing their instructions with that body.

CONTROL OVER THE AGENTS OF COMMUNICATION

From the outset a special degree of presidential control over the selection of subordinates entrusted with carrying on American diplomatic intercourse has been recognized by Congress. In Chapter 12 reference has been made to the "Decision of 1789," wherein Congress tacitly conceded that the Secretary of Foreign Affairs (State) should be subject to the President's direction and summary removal authority because of his close relationship to the President's function of conducting foreign relations. Congress has also displayed a remarkable readiness to follow presidential initiative in the establishment of diplomatic and consular missions at places of his own choosing, recognizing that this is a phase of administration over which he should have a primary voice.

In earlier years the Senate aspired to a closer control over the designation of and instructions given American diplomatic agents than is now the customary practice. Nevertheless, the feeling that American diplomatic officers are in a particular sense representatives of the President himself and that he must therefore have a free hand in choosing, directing, and replacing them has always carried weight with the Senate. Furthermore, the employment of "personal agents," "unofficial" emissaries, and "observers" whose appointments need not be submitted to the Senate for confirmation has been a more or less regular practice since Washington inaugurated it during his first year as President. Early in the nation's history Congress saw fit to provide a legal underpinning for the President's monopoly over communications with foreign governments. In 1799 it enacted a law, popularly known as the "Logan Act" and still on the statute books in a slightly amended form, making it a crime for any person not a duly accredited agent of the President to enter into correspondence with a foreign government with a view to influencing that government's policies toward the United States.[12] No person has ever been convicted of

---

[12] Act of January 30, 1799, 1 *Stat.* 613; *U.S. Code* (1958), Title 18, Sec. 954. This act, entitled "An Act to Prevent Usurpation of Executive Functions," was passed at the request of President Adams when he learned that Dr. George Logan, a Philadelphia Quaker, equipped with letters of introduction from Vice President Jefferson, had sought and obtained an interview with the President of the French Directory. Logan was seeking to bring about a restoration of diplomatic relations between the United States and France following the rupture of friendly relations induced by the "XYZ Affair" in 1798. Cf. "Memorandum on the History and Scope of the Laws Prohibiting Correspondence with a Government," *Senate Document No. 696*, 64th Congress, 2nd Session (1917).

violating this statute, but the issue has been raised from time to time whether certain political figures, including members of Congress itself, may have overstepped the bounds set by it.[13]

Viewed from the other direction, the official channels of communication with foreign powers are subject to the President's control in another way. Before a foreign diplomatic chief of mission can enter upon his duties here as the official representative of his government he must be "received," that is, officially acknowledged as such by the American Chief of State. This is accomplished by a formal ceremony at which the diplomat presents his credentials and is greeted as his government's official representative. The Constitution imposes upon the President the function of "receiving foreign ambassadors and ministers," thus making this explicitly a matter of executive concern. In international practice, a consular officer must present his credentials to the foreign affairs ministry of the country to which he is assigned, whereupon he is issued a document known as an exequatur authorizing him to carry on the functions of a consul.

Here again important precedents tending to enhance the President's role as a policy-maker were set in Washington's administration. Following the overthrow of the monarchy in France and the establishment of a new republican regime there, the new government dispatched "Citizen" Genêt as its minister to this country. Realizing that the reception of Genêt would constitute recognition of the new regime as the government of France and possibly endanger our status as a neutral in the war which France was engaged in against other European powers, President Washington only with some reluctance decided to receive him as an accredited envoy. Having found considerable sympathy among the American public for his country's revolutionary cause, Genêt proceeded to engage in activities detrimental to our maintenance of friendly relations with both England and Spain. He encouraged inhabitants on the western frontier to organize a military expedition against Spanish Louisiana; appointed French consular agents with a view to setting up prize courts under them in American ports to condemn seized British and Spanish ships; undertook to outfit French privateers in American ports; and, in general, persisted in following a course at odds with the policy of neutrality that Washington had proclaimed. The President therefore found it necessary to request the French government to recall him. The request was

---

[13] Cf. Corwin, *op. cit.*, pp. 183–184; and Elmer Plischke, *The Conduct of American Diplomacy*, 2nd ed., (New York: D. Van Nostrand Company, 1961), pp. 100–102, for accounts of instances of alleged violation of the Logan Act. The question of its possible violation was raised in 1947 in connection with ex-Secretary of Commerce Wallace's tour of European capitals to drum up sentiment against President Truman's policies for containment of Communist aggressions.

acceded to,[14] but the French government, as is often the case in such matters, saved face by insisting that we recall the American Minister to France, Gouverneur Morris, on the ground that he was engaging in intrigues designed to bring about restoration of the old regime in that country. President Washington salvaged what he could out of the situation by sending Morris as his private agent to the British court in London to "converse with his Britannic Majesty as to certain measures affecting relations between the two countries."

RECOGNITION AND ITS IMPLICATIONS

The Genêt Affair is instructive in a number of ways as to the significance, from the policy-making point of view, of the President's control over the channels of communication with foreign states. As this incident shows, he may bring about the recall of a foreign diplomatic agent whose conduct has made him *persona non grata* to this country; or for a similar reason in reverse he may find it necessary to replace one of our diplomats abroad. In more extreme cases the President does not have to wait for the offending diplomat's home government to act, but may adopt the stronger measure of simply expelling him from this country. The official status of consular agents who engage in activities deemed improper and detrimental to this country's interests may likewise be terminated on presidential order by withdrawal of their exequaturs.

The President may even go so far as to sever normal diplomatic relations with a particular government altogether. Severance of diplomatic relations is a kind of strong protest against another nation's attitude on some matter or matters of importance in dispute. It indicates that disagreement has reached the point that no expectation is entertained that pending disagreements can be resolved by the normal processes of diplomatic negotiation. It may even be the prelude to war, as in 1917 when President Wilson's expulsion of the German Ambassador, Count von Bernstorff, and his simultaneous recall of our diplomatic staff from Berlin preceded by a matter of weeks our declaration of war on Germany. A milder form of protest against another country's attitude may be made through calling home the head of the American diplomatic mission there for "consultations" and "instructions," leaving the mission in charge of an officer of lower rank for an indefinite period of time. By these various techniques of manipulating the instruments through which diplomatic intercourse is carried on the President is able to bring pressure to bear in support of his policies.

14 It is of interest to note that Genêt did not actually leave the United States, although he was relieved of his ministerial post. He later married the daughter of Governor Clinon of New York and lived the rest of his life in this country.

Just as the President's control over the conduct of diplomatic relations encompasses authority to suspend or terminate normal contacts with a foreign government in his own right, it likewise extends to re-establishing them whenever he deems conditions propitious. It also includes the authority to determine whether such contacts shall be established in the first instance when a new regime in a foreign nation has come into power through revolution or some other extraordinary kind of event. The Supreme Court has expressed the opinion that the decision of the President in this kind of situation is a "political" question lying entirely within the competence of the political departments of the government.[15]

Recognition and establishment of diplomatic relations can become extremely significant for expressing an attitude in the conduct of foreign affairs. This is particularly true when the issue concerns recognizing the government of a new nation claiming to have acquired its independence from another of which it has hitherto been a part. Premature extension of recognition to the fledgling state may be regarded by the parent country as an unfriendly act amounting to intervention in its domestic affairs. For example, President Theodore Roosevelt's precipitate action in recognizing the independent status of Panama in 1903 only two days after it had declared its independence from Colombia following a revolt which the United States covertly helped to carry to a successful conclusion gave Colombia a legitimate grievance against this country. It was resolved only after years of negotiations. Eventually in 1921 the United States Senate approved with certain amendments a treaty with Colombia negotiated by Secretary of State Bryan in 1914 under which this government agreed to pay to Colombia $25,000,000 in reparations for loss of its Panamanian territory and in return Colombia belatedly recognized Panama's independence.[16]

15 *Oetjen* v. *Central Leather Company*, 246 U.S. 297 (1918). The case, which was a private suit to recover possession of a shipment of hides, raised the issue whether the United States had recognized as the de jure government of Mexico the government headed by General Carranza.

16 President Roosevelt's hasty recognition of the independence of Panama was, of course, only one step in his "Isthmian Diplomacy" through which the United States subsequently acquired by treaty with Panama the right to construct and operate the Panama Canal. He attempted to justify his course of action in connection with the Panama revolt in his annual message to Congress in 1903 and again in a special message on January 4, 1904. Several years later, after he had left office, he expressed what was his real view of the matter when he declared in a public address: "If I had followed traditional conservative methods I should have submitted a dignified state paper of probably two hundred pages to the Congress and the debate would be going on yet, but I took the Canal Zone and let Congress debate, and while the debate goes on the canal does also." See John H. Latané, *A History of American Foreign Policy* (Garden City, N. Y.: Doubleday & Company, 1927), Chap. XXII, for a full account of American diplomacy in connection with the Panama Canal question. Negotiations are now under way to revise the 1903 treaty with Panama by which the United States acquired control of the Canal Zone.

Depending upon the particular situation, policies of recognition or nonrecognition of foreign regimes which Presidents have initiated have given basic direction to American diplomacy from time to time. During the first two decades of the nineteenth century the question of extending recognition to the various Latin American states which had declared their independence from Spain loomed large in American foreign relations. After their independence had been recognized by the United States, a belief on our part that the Holy Alliance formed by Spain, Austria, and Russia had as one of its objectives the restoration of Spanish rule in Latin America led to the announcement of the Monroe Doctrine in 1823. Nonrecognition of the Communist government in Russia was a cardinal point of American foreign policy from 1917 until 1933, when President F. D. Roosevelt established diplomatic relations with the new regime. Current manifestations of the importance of recognition policy are seen in the refusal of the United States to establish diplomatic relations with Communist regimes in China, North Korea, North Vietnam, and East Germany and continuance of a diplomatic break effected by President Eisenhower in 1960 with the Castro government in Cuba. While these are policies that appear to have the strong support of Congress and the American people, it should be noted that they were all presidentially initiated and can be altered or modified only through presidential action.

Recognition of a foreign government may be extended through a variety of procedures, but all of them require participation by the President in some manner. Mere adoption of a resolution by Congress expressing its attitude has no binding effect internationally, although it may serve to give political support to the President's course of action if he chooses to follow the line indicated by Congress. For example, both houses of Congress had passed resolutions endorsing recognition of the independence of Texas from Mexico and recommending establishing diplomatic relations before President Jackson took steps to do so in 1837.

The normal manner of extending recognition is through exchange of diplomatic representatives by the governments concerned. This ordinarily involves affirmative action by Congress in providing funds for maintenance of a diplomatic establishment at the foreign capital, and the Senate must confirm the appointments of the top diplomatic officers assigned there. The latter step may actually become the means for checking the President's desires. In 1951 President Truman proposed a reversal of a long-standing American policy dating from 1868 against maintainence of formal diplomatic relations with the Vatican. He did so by nominating General Mark Clark to serve as our ambassador there. Strong public disapproval, particularly from among prominent Protestant leaders, was immediately voiced against the proposed change in the traditional American policy of noninvolvement with the Catholic Church in its temporal capacity. Responding to this feeling, the Senate delayed action on the nomination while the opposition forces prepared to marshal their political strength. Acknowledging the adverse state of public feeling on the issue, President Truman did not press the matter.[17] The issue was resurrected during the 1960 presidential campaign by opponents of Senator Kennedy, a Roman Catholic. To allay fears expressed by rabid anti-Catholics, he found it necessary to disavow any intention to establish diplomatic relations with the Vatican if he were elected President.

Another procedure the President may employ to extend recognition is use of the treaty-making machinery. Recognition may be extended by entering into a treaty with the government of the country which is being recognized, or recognition may be covered in a treaty entered into by the United States with a third power or powers. In either case the recognition becomes subject to senatorial scrutiny when the treaty is submitted to it for approval. In his capacity as the acknowledged spokesman for the United States government the President, if he chooses, may extend recognition to a new government by his own independent act through simply issuing a proclamation. This was the course pursued by Theodore Roosevelt in 1903 in recognizing the independent status of Panama. A proclamation was also the procedure employed by Wilson when in 1918 he recognized the "government-in-exile" of Czechoslovakia. He did this even before that government had acquired a territorial base in its homeland or its people had made good their claim to independence from the Austro-Hungarian Empire. President Truman likewise used a proclamation in recognizing the independent state of Israel in 1948.

"PERSONAL" PRESIDENTIAL DIPLOMACY

Normally, diplomatic communications between the United States and foreign governments are transmitted between our Department of State and the ministry of foreign affairs of the other government. It is understood, however, that our diplomatic representatives abroad or in the home offices of the Department of State speak and act in a special sense on behalf of the President. The Supreme Court has characterized him as the "sole organ" of official communication for

---

17 The nomination was submitted only a day or two before the Senate adjourned. By constitutional rule, it would have had to be resubmitted for the Senate to have acted upon it at its next session. Because of General Clark's military status the Congress would also have had to pass legislation making him eligible for the post without his having to give up permanently his status as a reserve officer.

the United States in its international dealings.[18] The President may also choose to express his views on foreign affairs by more indirect means than through use of these channels, realizing that foreign governments will take due notice of what he may say or do as being indicative of this country's attitude or probable response to a particular situation. The President employs various media for enunciating his views on these matters—messages to Congress, public addresses, newspaper and television interviews, White House and State Department press releases, etc. The famous Monroe Doctrine, for example, was first announced in a presidential message to Congress. President Truman unveiled his well-known "Point Four" program of extending technical and economic aid to underdeveloped countries in his 1949 Inaugural Address, which was devoted almost entirely to an outline of the foreign policies he expected to pursue. President Johnson has repeatedly sought through televised news conferences to make clear to the North Vietnam regime as well as Communist China and Russia this country's willingness to enter into negotiations for resolution of the conflict in South Vietnam.

A more subtle but nonetheless effective way of making known this country's foreign policy attitudes or proposals is through public statements made by Cabinet officers or other highly placed executive officials known to have had presidential clearance for the views they advance. For example, in 1947 Secretary of State Marshall announced in a Harvard University commencement address the President's intention to embark on a vast program of economic aid to assist European countries in reconstructing their war-devastated economies. A still more subtle technique of communication is the use of planned "leaks," hints, and rumors which are quickly seized upon by the press, the columnists, and Washington society. It therefore becomes a necessary part of the job of a foreign diplomatic representative to keep in touch with these sources of information, to try to separate the wheat from the chaff, and to make an intelligent report on the drift of presidential thinking on matters of concern to his home government.

By way of contrast to these techniques of indirect communication, engagement in direct negotiations by Presidents has become more frequent since Wilson's time. Presidents before Wilson, to be sure, had addressed themselves directly to the heads of other governments from time to time through exchange of notes, as well as through direct conversations on ceremonial visits by foreign heads of state to this country. President Jefferson, for example, carried on a personal correspondence with the Czar of Russia during the course of the Napol-

---

[18] Cf. *United States* v. *Curtis-Wright Export Corporation,* 299 U.S. 304, 320 (1936).

eonic Wars. Having served as the American minister to France and as Washington's Secretary of State, Jefferson was experienced in the ways of diplomacy. Wilson took over the handling of momentous diplomatic correspondence to a degree unknown before his time. A well-known Wilson scholar has described his methods in dealing with questions growing out of the Mexican and World War I crises in this fashion:

> [Wilson] wrote most of the important notes to foreign powers on his own typewriter, by-passed the State Department by using his own private agents, ignored his secretaries of state by conducting important negotiations behind their backs, and acted like a divine-right monarch in the general conduct of affairs.[19]

Wilson climaxed his contributions to the evolution of presidential practice in this connection by attending in person the Paris Peace Conference in 1918–1919 as the head of the United States delegation.

After that, engagement in direct "personal" diplomacy by the Presidents became even more common.[20] Since World War I every President except Harding has gone abroad on official visits or to attend various conferences and discussions with heads of other governments.[21] Visits of foreign chiefs of state to this country have likewise increased in number. Whereas up to the end of World War I there had been a total of only some 30 such visits, there have been more than 200 since 1939. Beginning with his famous Atlantic Charter conference with Prime Minister Churchill aboard a British war vessel in the North Atlantic, through wartime meetings with heads of various allied governments at Casablanca, Cairo, Teheran, and Yalta, to say nothing of other visits with Prime Minister Churchill at the White House, F. D. Roosevelt probably carried the practice of personal diplomacy to its greatest heights to date. During World War II he exchanged some 1750 personal messages with Churchill and some 300 with Premier Stalin. Symbolic of the new dispensation in the conduct of foreign relations was the so-called "hot line" agreement reached in 1963 by President Kennedy and Premier Khrushchev. By this it was agreed that at all times there would be kept open for instantaneous contact

[19] Arthur S. Link, "Wilson the Diplomatist," in *The Philosophy and Policies of Woodrow Wilson*, Earl Latham, ed. (Chicago: University of Chicago Press, 1958), p. 161.

[20] For an excellent analysis of presidential engagement in direct diplomacy see Elmer Plischke, *Summit Diplomacy: Personal Diplomacy of the President of the United States* (College Park, Md.: Bureau of Governmental Research, University of Maryland, 1958). See also the treatment of this subject by the same author in his *Conduct of American Diplomacy*, pp. 45–55.

[21] Plischke, *Summit Diplomacy*, p. 54. President Johnson announced soon after assuming office in November, 1963, that he would not make any trips abroad during the remainder of the term, since there was for the time being no Vice President to take over the office in the event a mishap should befall him.

a line of direct communication between the White House and the Kremlin, the object being to afford a means of immediate contact between the two heads of government in the event an international emergency should arise. It was hoped thereby to avoid the danger of possible misunderstanding and a consequent disastrous shattering of world peace.

Personal engagement by Presidents in the conduct of diplomatic relations has been both strongly criticized and warmly defended. With particular reference to his engagement in so-called "summit diplomacy," the pros and cons of the matter have been summarized by a close student of the subject.[22] On the side of advantages are: (1) opportunity to establish better understanding, more personal respect and esteem for each other by the participating heads of government; (2) opportunity to reach determinations speedily and directly; (3) promotion of broad agreements on principles, paving the way for settlement of definitive details later at lower diplomatic levels; (4) opportunity to resolve an impasse reached at the traditional level by suggestion of new formulas or broadening the scope of the issues to be resolved; and (5) through attracting wider public attention, improvement of the chances for generating an informed popular understanding of the issues and the necessity for reaching compromise agreements on them.

Disadvantages include: (1) the morale of the regular diplomatic staffs may be damaged through their being by-passed; (2) determinations may be reached too hastily, without full consideration of all the possible implications and consequences; (3) determinations reached may be regarded as final, rather than *ad referendum,* thus eliminating possible recourse to subsequent higher review and modification; (4) serious risks may be run if diplomacy is left in the hands of a dilettante, amateur negotiator, which the President may be; (5) the President may be inadequately informed on technical points because of insufficient professional staff; (6) the fishbowl atmosphere in which such negotiations are usually carried on may inhibit free give-and-take negotiations; (7) the President, being unable to commit the United States finally because of a possibly hostile or uncooperative Congress is at a disadvantage in dealing with a prime minister who can count on parliamentary support for his position; (8) summit meetings may give rise to false or premature hopes that pending issues will be resolved, with a consequent letdown if these hopes fail to be realized.

Regardless of what weight one assigns to these claims and counterclaims, it is safe to conclude that summit diplomacy will continue to be practiced by Presidents on a considerable scale. In large measure it is a product of world conditions in the mid-twentieth century. It

[22] *Ibid.,* pp. 119–125.

reflects the dynamic character of modern international politics and the relative ease and speed of transportation and communication today. If Thomas Jefferson could have flitted by jet to London in a few hours or talked by transatlantic telephone with Napoleon Bonaparte, no doubt he would have set some interesting precedents in summitry in his day. The people of the nation expect the President to pursue personally and actively the basic objectives of preserving world peace and promoting international harmony, consistent with maintaining national security. Congress itself recognized this point by provisions it included in the United Nations Participation Act of 1945 which set up the machinery for representation of the United States in that body. It specifies that the President himself may, if he so desires, act as the head of the United States delegation "at any meeting or session of any organ or agency of the United Nations."[23] Engagement in personal diplomacy by the President is a manifestation of the increased importance that both he and the public now assign to his role as Manager-in-Chief of Foreign Relations.

INTERNATIONAL AGREEMENTS

The end product of an important part of international diplomatic intercourse appears in the form of treaties, compacts, or other types of formal and informal agreements between nations. Such agreements may be likened to contracts which play so large a part in the operations of private business concerns. By creating reciprocal rights, duties, and obligations, international agreements serve to adjust current disputes or eliminate potential causes of friction. The Constitution mentions only one type of international agreement which the United States may enter into, that is, treaties. In setting up limitations on the agreement-making authority of the states, however, Section 10 of Article I makes use of the terms "treaties," "alliances," "confederations," "compacts," and "agreements" to designate various types of intergovernmental arrangements which the states might contemplate entering into. The question naturally has arisen whether the United States may employ agreement-making devices other than treaties to regulate its relationships with other nations.

TREATIES AND EXECUTIVE AGREEMENTS

In actual practice, treaties are only one type of agreement which the United States makes with other states in the international community. The term "treaty" has been construed broadly to include

[23] Act of December 20, 1945, 59 *Stat.* 619, Sec. 2(e).

agreements technically described as "conventions," "covenants," "protocols," "declarations," "pacts," or "charters." In addition, the United States is competent as a sovereign nation to make another kind of international commitment having objectives similar to those of a treaty, that is, "executive agreements." This term covers a wide variety of agreements and understandings that are reached by the executive authorities of the governments concerned in the course of administering international business.

In their most formal character, executive agreements are embodied in a document similar to a treaty, signed by the heads of government or on their behalf by their representatives and publicized in the same way as treaties. Sometimes an executive agreement is contracted through an exchange of identical notes by these heads of government outlining the terms of an understanding reached on a given matter, or by mutual endorsement of the minutes (procès-verbal) of a meeting at which an accord was reached. Beyond these more formal agreements there are numerous understandings and arrangements worked out at lower diplomatic levels in the course of resolving relatively minor questions. For example, the particular manner of enforcement of customs or immigration laws and regulations, agreements concerning the exchange of information by law enforcement authorities regarding the movements or activities of persons suspected of being engaged in illegal enterprises, or the procedures to be followed in applying navigation, quarantine, or other types of regulations to foreign vessels in American ports may become the subject matter of such informal, routine executive understandings. Executive agreements on routine matters of this kind are an inescapable and entirely normal aspect of the administration of laws in situations wherein the United States government and foreign governments have a mutual interest.

A capacity to enter into international agreements by the executive authority of the nation is therefore necessarily to be implied from the President's function as the official organ of communication with foreign governments, coupled with his responsibility to execute the laws and his duty to take appropriate steps to protect the rights of American citizens under international law when their activities bring them into contact with a foreign government or its agents. Furthermore, the President may be explicitly authorized by the terms of a treaty or a law of the United States to make executive agreements to effectuate their provisions in appropriate ways. In these cases executive agreements have a legal standing similar to the orders, proclamations, and directives he issues on the basis of delegated authority conveyed to him by statute in his capacity as Chief Administrator, as described in Chapter 13. A well-known example is the Reciprocal

Trade Agreements Act of 1934, which has been continued in effect with modifications from time to time since that date. By this Act the President is expressly authorized to make executive agreements providing for mutual concessions in tariffs or other forms of international trade restrictions. Such agreements have the effect of superseding the provisions of our own tariff laws that conflict with them.

Again, the President may enter into an executive agreement subject to an understanding that it shall become binding only upon adoption by Congress of approving and implementing legislation. In this case the executive agreement-making procedure is similar to that of treaty-making, except that affirmative action by a majority vote of both houses of Congress, rather than a two-thirds majority vote by the Senate, is necessary to give the agreement binding effect. Examples are: the annexation of Texas to the United States in 1845 by an executive agreement subject to adoption of a joint resolution of Congress carrying out its terms; the annexation of Hawaii in a similar manner in 1898; and the passage of the St. Lawrence Seaway Agreement Act of 1954, giving effect to an executive agreement under which the United States and Canada entered into an agreement for construction of navigation improvements and power development facilities on the St. Lawrence River. In all these instances the device of a congressionally sanctioned executive agreement was employed after failure had attended efforts to achieve the same results through use of the treaty-making procedure.

Much ink has been spilled and countless words spoken in the halls of Congress and elsewhere in debate on the question whether there is an essential difference, in terms of the subject matters that they may deal with, between a treaty and a congressionally approved executive agreement. In the light of actual practice, the nub of the matter seems simply to lie in the manner of their making, nothing more. Treaties are agreements that are entered into only with the concurrence of two-thirds of the Senate; executive agreements are binding international compacts entered into in some manner not involving such a concurring vote by the Senate.[24] In a Senate discussion of the question, Senator Guy Gillette of Iowa told an amusing story which, by

[24] An authority who takes this position on the question is Wallace McClure, *International Executive Agreements: Democratic Procedure under the Constitution of the United States* (New York: Columbia University Press, 1941). For a contrary view see Edwin M. Borchard, "Treaties and Executive Agreements," *American Political Science Review,* Vol. XL (August, 1946), pp. 729–739; and "Executive Agreements and Treaties: Shall the Executive Agreement Replace the Treaty?" *American Journal of International Law,* Vol. XXXVIII (October, 1944), pp. 637–643; Herbert Wright, "The Two-thirds Vote of the Senate in Treaty-Making," *ibid.,* pp. 643–650. Randall H. Nelson, *Recent Developments in the Law and Practice of the United States Respecting the Negotiation and Conclusion of International Agreements and Commentary on Proposed Changes* (MS., University of Michigan, 1955) is an excellent comprehensive review of the general subject.

analogy, illustrates the point very well. When he was a farm boy, he related, he asked a hired man how to tell the difference between a male and a female pigeon. The hired man replied, "You put corn in front of the pigeon. If he picks it up, it is a he. If she picks it up, it is a she."[25]

The Supreme Court has taken the position that some types of executive agreements, if not all of them, partake of the nature of treaties in that they form a part of the "supreme law of the land." Like treaties, they must be given an overriding effect if in conflict with state laws, particularly if they have behind them the direct or implied sanction of a regular treaty or an act of Congress.[26] The President in his capacity as chief executive and organ of communications with foreign powers therefore has a choice as to whether he shall employ the treaty-making procedure or some form of executive agreement-making procedure in arriving at an understanding with a foreign government on a particular matter. Statistical data bearing on the point indicate an increasing use of the formal executive agreement device as compared with treaties. Frequency of use by 50-year periods during the first 150 years after adoption of the Constitution has been as follows:

TABLE 6:   *Treaties and Executive Agreements, 1789–1939*

Years	Treaties	Executive Agreements
1789–1839	60	27
1839–1889	215	238
1889–1939	524	917
	799	1182

SOURCE: Wallace McClure, *International Executive Agreements: Democratic Procedure under the Constitution of the United States* (New York: Columbia University Press, 1941), pp. 3–4.

The trend toward increased use of the executive agreement has been sharply accelerated in recent years. In the period from 1940 to 1954 the United States entered into 139 treaties, but during the same time it

[25] *Congressional Record*, 83rd Congress, 2nd Session (1953), p. 1742; quoted in Nelson, *op. cit.*, p. 20.

[26] Cf. *B. Altman and Co.* v. *United States*, 224 U.S. 583 (1911); *United States* v. *Belmont*, 301 U. S. 330 (1937); *United States* v. *Pink*, 315 U.S. 203 (1942).

became a party to no less than 1948 formal executive agreement,[27] making the overall totals for the two types of agreements up to 1954, 938 and 3130, respectively.

THE TREATY-MAKING PROCESS

In actual practice treaty-making on behalf of the United States is a process normally involving five distinct steps. The first, the negotiation phase, lies within the President's discretion and control. Only he or his accredited representatives may participate in official conversations with other powers. The Senate or the House of Representatives may give him advice and support in advance by expressing views on whether negotiations should be undertaken and indicating the objectives this government should seek. For example, the Vandenberg Resolution passed by the Senate on June 11, 1948, calling on the President to negotiate regional security pacts within the range permitted by the United Nations Charter helped to pave the way for development of the NATO system of treaties and a later brood of regional security pacts in other areas of the world. The President also is free to consult with individual members of Congress in the course of treaty negotiations.

The second step is submission of the completed draft treaty to the Senate for its action. This, again, is a matter lying within the President's discretion. He is not obligated to submit a negotiated treaty to the Senate for consideration. He may withhold it altogether, or submit it to the Senate merely for its information without requesting action.

The third stage is the step wherein the Senate performs its major constitutional function of giving its "advice and consent." In popular parlance this is referred to as "ratification," but actually this is incorrect. Senatorial approval is only a necessary prelude to the ratification step. By a two-thirds majority vote of those present and voting, the Senate may approve a treaty unconditionally; it may reject it outright by failing to give it such approval; it may fail to take any action at all; or it may approve the treaty with clarifying or qualifying interpretations in advance (reservations) or with suggested textual changes or deletions (amendments). In the last-mentioned case it then be-

---

[27] Plischke, *The Conduct of American Diplomacy*, p. 424. It should be noted that there is some difficulty in determining just what constitutes an "executive agreement." If all kinds of informal agreements and understandings reached at the administrative level are included, the number may reach several thousand each year. The figures given above are based on treaties and executive agreements published in the *United States Statutes at Large* from 1940 to 1950 and in *United States Treaties and Other International Agreements* (TIAS) since 1950.

comes necessary for the President to obtain acceptance of the reservations or amendments by the other nation or nations concerned before proceeding further. Insistence by a substantial number of Senators upon inclusion of a number of reservations unacceptable to President Wilson resulted in the failure of the Versailles Treaty of 1919 to win Senate approval and thus kept the United States from becoming a member of the League of Nations.[28]

The fourth step is the exchange of ratifications with the other contracting power or powers. This consists of a formal exchange of duly signed and sealed copies of the instrument of agreement, which causes the treaty to become an internationally binding contract. Here again the President may proceed or not as he deems proper; but, of course, the ratification step normally follows if the treaty has been given clearance by the Senate. The fifth and final step, promulgation, is an official proclaiming of the treaty, having the effect of incorporating it into the body of the supreme law of this country. By the terms of the United Nations Charter the United States is required to deposit a copy of any treaty with that organization for subsequent publication in its *Treaties and Other International Acts* series. This series also includes important executive agreements that have been made by participating nations.

The significance of the Senate's participation in the making of treaties is indicated in the following tabulation[29] covering all treaties negotiated during the period from 1789 to 1944. These figures are somewhat misleading in that they show only a small number of treaties actually rejected. The first treaty ever to be rejected by the

---

[28] Whether the major share of the blame for this outcome should be placed on the Senate, or on President Wilson, or on fate (Wilson suffered an incapacitating physical breakdown just as the League issue was approaching its climax in the Senate) is a matter of debate among historians. For detailed studies of the League of Nations treaty fight, see Thomas A. Bailey, *Woodrow Wilson and the Lost Peace* (New York: The Macmillan Company, 1944), and Denna F. Fleming, *The United States and the League of Nations, 1918–1920* (New York and London: G. P. Putnam's Sons, 1932).

[29] Cf. Plischke, *The Conduct of American Diplomacy*, p. 393. A later unofficial compilation, published in *The New York Times* for August 25, 1963, when the Nuclear Test Ban Treaty was submitted to the Senate by President Kennedy, gave the following figures up to that date:

Treaties approved unconditionally	944	69 percent
Approved with amendments and reservations	252	18.4 percent
No action or withdrawn	118	8.6 percent
Rejected	15	1.1 percent
Pending	29	2.1 percent
Total number submitted, 1789–1963	1368	99.2 percent

The discrepancy in the subtotals as compared with the overall total of 1368 would be accounted for by 10 treaties, involving approximately .7 percent of the total, which were submitted with no action requested.

TABLE 7. *Senate Action on Treaties, 1789–1944*

	Number	Percent
Approved unconditionally	753	72
Approved with amendments or reservations	167	16
No final action	90	8.5
Rejected by roll-call vote	14	1.3
Withdrawn by President	14	1.3
Submitted only for information; no action requested	8	.8
Total number submitted	1046	100.0

Senate was a pact with Colombia concerning suppression of the slave trade. It was rejected by a vote of 40–0 in 1825. Inclusion of the treaties that the Senate pigeonholed or failed for some reason to take final action on and those to which it insisted upon adding amendments unacceptable to the President or to other powers must also be taken into account in measuring the effect of the Senate's right to say "No." Moreover, some of the treaties rejected, choked to death by inaction, or given only conditional approval and consequently not put into effect, have been of major importance. They include, in addition to the treaties for the annexation of Texas and Hawaii mentioned above: a similar treaty for the annexation of Santo Domingo negotiated in President Grant's administration; a number of arbitration treaties negotiated in the Roosevelt, Taft, and Wilson administrations; the Versailles Treaty and League Covenant; and the protocol that would have made the United States an adherent of the pre-World War II World Court system.

Depending on the nature of the subject dealt with, a treaty may or may not be self-executing; that is to say, it may or may not require implementing legislation to give it concrete effect as domestic law. For example, an extradition treaty becomes immediately enforceable as supreme law through executive and judicial action, but the Migratory Bird Treaty of 1916 under which the United States and Canada undertook to adopt and enforce regulations to protect migratory birds in which both countries have an interest required implementing legislation by Congress. In some cases because of the allocation of powers over some governmental functions to the states in our federal system actual implementation of treaty obligations becomes a responsibility of the states. For example, when the United States undertakes to extend protection to the lives and property of a foreign nation's citizens living in the United States, initial responsibility for carrying out this guarantee rests with the states. Again, treaties or sections thereof may be classified as executed or executory in form. In the former case, performance of the action agreed upon exhausts the treaty's force. An illustration would be the treaty of cession between the United States and Denmark in 1917 under which the United States acquired sovereign rights over the territory of the Virgin Islands upon payment of $25,000,000 to Denmark. An executory treaty or treaty provision, on the other hand, involves creation of a continuing obligation or right on the part of the contracting states. Commercial treaties setting up terms under which trade relations between citizens of the respective countries may be carried on and the protections of the law afforded them illustrate this type of agreement.

PROPOSALS FOR CHANGE IN AGREEMENT-MAKING PROCEDURES

Since World War I there has been considerable agitation from time to time for a constitutional amendment changing the procedures by which the United States may enter into international agreements. Following the defeat of the Versailles Treaty in the Senate, and again after the United States became a belligerent in World War II, attention was directed mainly toward altering the Senate's role in the treaty-making process.[30] Various proposals were advanced. One was that the two-thirds vote requirement for approval of a treaty by the Senate be lowered to a simple majority of those voting, or to a "constitutional" majority, i.e., a majority of the Senate's membership. Another was that concurrent majorities in the two houses of Congress should govern the result, thus giving the House equal status with the Senate in approving treaties.[31] Another milder proposal, which would have required merely affirmative action by the Senate itself to adopt, was that it change its rules of procedure so that a treaty could not be killed by mere inaction or a filibuster by a small minority. Another suggestion of this type was that the Senate adopt a rule requiring that there be a formal, roll-call vote in every instance of final Senate action on a treaty.

The movement to restrict the treaty veto powers of the Senate by one or another of these means gathered force as World War II

[30] Indicative of interest in the subject at that time were a number of studies of the Senate's performance in connection with treaty-making. Cf. Royden J. Dangerfield, Jr., *In Defense of the Senate: A Study in Treaty-making* (Norman: University of Oklahoma Press, 1933); Denna F. Fleming, *The Treaty Veto of the American Senate* (New York: G. P. Putnam's Sons, 1930); W. Stull Holt, *Treaties Defeated by the Senate* (Baltimore: Johns Hopkins Press, 1933); and Kenneth Colegrove, *The American Senate and World Peace* (New York: Vanguard Press, 1944).

[31] It might be noted that James Madison and James Wilson had contended strenuously for inclusion of a provision of this kind in the original Constitution, but the small-state—independent executive coalition had defeated their efforts. Cf. Chap. 2, pp. 63–64.

approached its end. Fears were felt that a repetition of the events of 1919 might occur when the issues of the peace settlement would come before the Senate again in the form of treaties. In 1945 the House of Representatives by a vote of 288 to 88 passed a constitutional amendment proposal (the Bloom-Sumners Amendment) long championed by Representative Sol Bloom, Chairman of the House Foreign Affairs Committee, and other members of the House. It would have required that treaties be approved by a constitutional majority vote in both the House and Senate.[32] The proposal had strong popular support as well as backing by some members of the Senate;[33] the Senate leadership received the proposal coldly, however, and it failed to come to a vote in that body.

In the post-World War II period criticism of the two-thirds rule for approval of treaties has become somewhat muted. A number of factors have contributed to this. The Senate generally has displayed a far more cooperative attitude in dealing with treaties submitted to it by Presidents since 1945. A bipartisan approach to foreign affairs issues has been displayed by most of the Senate's members, and it has not stood in the way of United States participation in various world organizations including the United Nations, regional alliances, and other programs having as their object the promotion of world peace and international cooperation. Presidents Roosevelt, Truman, and Eisenhower, mindful of criticisms of President Wilson's failure to associate leading members of the Senate with himself in the negotiations of the Versailles Treaty, helped to contribute to this good record by frequent use of Senate and House members as "special advisers" on United States negotiating teams and delegations attending international conferences.[34] A more extensive

[32] *Congressional Record,* 79th Congress, 1st Session (1945), p. 4367. *House Report* No. 139, which accompanied the amendment proposal as reported from the House Judiciary Committee, presented a very persuasive defense of it on both theoretical and practical grounds. The amendment proposal was originally introduced by Representative Sumners of Texas, Chairman of the House Judiciary Committee.

[33] Cf. Senator Claude Pepper, "Peace Despite the Filibusterers," *The New York Times Magazine,* June 25, 1944. Public opinion polls conducted during the time an amendment of this kind was under serious discussion showed that approximately 60 percent of the people favored the change, and only 25 percent or less favored retaining the existing arrangement. See the Institute of Public Opinion (Gallup) poll results as reported in *The Detroit News,* January 7, 1945.

[34] The practice of naming congressmen as members of negotiating teams in the formulation of treaties was introduced by President McKinley in 1898 when he appointed three members of the Senate Foreign Relations Committee to serve on the delegation to negotiate the Treaty of Paris ending the Spanish-American War. Some members of Congress object to this practice. They contend that it violates the constitutional rule against a member of Congress holding any other "office" while serving in Congress, and that it tends to commit Congress in advance to support any agreement that might be negotiated. For a discussion of this practice see Plischke, *The Conduct of American Diplomacy,* pp. 404–409.

use of the congressionally approved executive agreement device in recent years, moreover, has served as a warning to the Senate that there are ways by which its one-third-plus-one-member veto over treaties can be bypassed, if necessary.

During the first part of the decade of the 1950s a movement of an entirely different sort gathered support. It had as its objective the adoption of a constitutional amendment designed to limit the agreement-making power of the national government. A proposal of this kind, which was first introduced and championed by Senator John Bricker of Ohio, in its original 1951 version was aimed only at restricting the President's executive agreement-making authority by making it wholly dependent upon congressional authorization and control and subjecting it explicitly to all limitations of the Constitution. Increased use of the exeecutive agreement-making process to implement United Nations programs and regional military assistance pacts had aroused fears in some quarters that the President was taking matters of major concern out of the hands of Congress.

In later versions the Bricker Amendment took a broader character. In 1953 the Senate Judiciary Committee reported out a revised version of it which contained three major clauses: (1) a statement that a treaty provision in conflict with any part of the Constitution must be regarded as void; (2) a statement declaring that no treaty could become enforceable as internal law except through legislation "which would be valid in the absence of a treaty"; and (3) a declaration that Congress should have power to "regulate" all executive agreements with foreign powers, and that all such agreements were to be subject to the same constitutional limitations as to subject matters as are treaties. The second and third clauses were particularly significant. They would have denied self-executing force to all treaties and executive agreements and subjected the President's authority to enter into the latter to congressional control. Subsequent implementing statutes by Congress, and by state legislatures in some instances where such affirmative action is currently not thought necessary, would have been required to make treaties and executive agrements judicially enforcable as elements of the supreme law of the land.

Senate debate on the proposal in 1954 led to the substition of a milder version advanced by Senator Walter George of Georgia. The George substitute would merely have retained the language requiring that all treaties and executive agreements be subject to the limitations of the Constitution and denying self-executing force to executive agreements. In this milder form the Bricker Amendment failed of passage by the necessary two-thirds majority in the Senate by the margin of only one vote, 60 to 31, on February 26, 1954.[35]

[35] *Congressional Record,* 83rd Congress, 2nd Session (1954), p. 2374. There was a voluminous literature on the Bricker Amendment at the time it was before the

Thereafter agitation for adoption of a constitutional amendment of the character advocated by Senator Bricker gradually subsided. The proposal, which had never mustered a substantial degree of popular support or attention, dropped from view when Senator Bricker himself was defeated for re-election in 1958.

Currently interest in the question of a constitutional amendment changing existing arrangements for making international agreements is at a low ebb, both on the part of Congress and of the public. A number of factors account for this. The neo-isolationist type of thinking, from which the Bricker Amendment forces drew much strength during and following the Korean War of 1950–1953, is no longer so potent. There has come to be a general acceptance of the idea that the United States must play an active role befitting the great power it is in the modern world of international power politics. Its capacity to enter into international commitments to further its policies and interests should not be hampered by the kinds of restrictions the Bricker Amendment sought to impose. The Supreme Court has made clear in its 1957 ruling in *Reid* v. *Covert*[36] that treaties and executive agreements may not violate fundamental individual rights guaranteed by the Constitution, thus giving the *coup de grâce* to the contention based upon certain unguarded statements in earlier judicial opinions which implied that a treaty may violate provisions of the Constitution. Furthermore, the Court in a long series of rulings beginning with the *School Segregation* cases of 1954[37] has held that the Fourteenth Amendment establishes prohibitions upon state discrimination against minorities and affords a basis for positive federal governmental action to this end. A fear entertained by states' rights elements that the treaty or executive agreement-making power of the national government might be used to provide a basis for federal enforcing legislation in this sphere had helped to generate support for the Bricker Amendment from anti-civil rights elements in Congress.

Finally, courses of action pursued by Presidents Eisenhower, Kennedy, and Johnson during recent international crises have tended to allay fears that the President may go too far on his own independent authority. All three Presidents have consulted closely with congressional leaders, and, when feasible, have secured advance commit-

---

Senate. Representative articles include Hardy C. Dillard, "The Treaty-making Controversy: Substance and Shadow," *Virginia Quarterly Review,* Vol. XX (Spring, 1954), pp. 178–191; Arthur H. Dean, "The Bricker Amendment and Authority over Foreign Affairs," *Foreign Affairs,* Vol. XXXII (October, 1953), pp. 1–19; George A. Finch, "The Need to Restrain the Treaty-making Power of the United States Within Constitutional Limits," *American Journal of International Law,* Vol. XLVIII (January, 1954), pp. 57–82; and John B. Whitton and J. Edward Fowler, "Bricker Amendment—Fallacies and Dangers," *ibid.,* pp. 23–56. Nelson, *op. cit.,* Chap. XI is an excellent comprehensive treatment of the general subject.

[36] 353 U.S. 1 (1957).
[37] 347 U.S. 483 (1954).

ments from Congress in connection with possible resort to military force in critical situations. On the other hand, their increased use of the congressionally approved executive agreement to implement policies in this sphere has shown that present constitutional arrangements permit an agreement-making procedure that conforms to the ideas of those who believe the House, as the more popular branch of Congress, should share power and responsibility equally with the Senate in this regard. Presidential initiative in using the presently available alternative methods of entering into international compacts should, and no doubt will, be retained. Meanwhile, the congressionally approved executive agreement type of international compact will no doubt continue to be employed over a widening area of subject matters heretofore dealt with only through use of the treaty-making machinery. It is possible, though not probable, that in time the traditional treaty-making procedure may be completely eclipsed by the congressionally approved executive agreement device.

PRESIDENTIAL USE OF MILITARY FORCE

In the conduct of international relations undoubtedly the most crucial decision a President is called upon to make is whether a situation justifies the use of military force, or the threat thereof. When shall pursuit of the nation's rights and interests through peaceful negotiations be supplemented, or even entirely supplanted, by more forceful, warlike measures? When shall there be an outright appeal to the arbitrament of war itself?

The architects of the Constitution were keenly aware of these practical questions, and they sought to provide a safeguard against too rash action on the chief executive's part by reserving to Congress the authority to "declare war." But at the same time they invested the President with command of the armed forces, and, as has been seen, they placed the conduct of foreign relations under his immediate direction. Military might in being is a trump card in the deadly serious game of international diplomacy. The President's authority as Commander-in-Chief of this nation's armed forces certainly includes the power to control their placement and movements. But in a critical diplomatic situation even the deployment of an armed striking force near the scene of potential trouble conveys a strong message to an adversary. If hostile acts occur, the President's power of military command undoubtedly includes the authority to order these forces to defend themselves or to carry out reprisals against an adversary.

The carefully devised scheme of the Founding Fathers to keep in the hands of Congress the ultimate decision whether the United States shall resort to war has proved in practice to be somewhat unrealistic. The war-making power cannot be excised and separated from the general authority to conduct the nation's foreign affairs. Congress has actually "declared" wars only on five occasions during the nation's history—in 1812 against Great Britain, in 1846 against Mexico, in 1898 against Spain, in 1917 against Germany and her allies, and in 1941 against Japan, Germany, and Italy. Yet the United States has been involved in military hostilities on numerous other occasions. In only two of these declared wars—the War of 1812 and the Spanish-American War—can it be said that Congress had the leading role in making the decision to resort to arms. In the other three instances the declarations of war were made at the request of the President after the situation had deteriorated to a point that left Congress little or no choice.

In fact, war-declaring resolutions by Congress have usually been worded in terms of recognizing that a state of war existed by reason of the acts of other nations which have left this country with no option but to reply with armed resistance. For example, after dispatching armed forces under General Taylor into territory in dispute between the United States and Mexico where they were attacked by Mexican troops, President Polk in 1846 sent a message to Congress asserting that "Mexico has passed the boundary of the United States, has invaded our territory and shed American blood upon the American soil." He then went on to say that inasmuch as war "exists by the act of Mexico herself," Congress should "recognize" the existence of war and take prompt measures to enable the President to prosecute it "with vigor."[38] American involvement in World War II was preceded by a series of diplomatic moves and the assumption of an attitude of more-than-benevolent neutrality toward Great Britain and her Western allies, supported in large measure by Congress through legislation, that pointed inevitably toward this country's eventual active participation as a belligerent.[39] The Japanese air attack

[38] Richardson, *op. cit.*, Vol. IV, pp. 442–443.

[39] For a review of events involving actions of the President and Congress in the period from the invasion of Poland to the attack on Pearl Harbor, see Louis W. Koenig, *The Presidency and the Crisis* (New York: King's Crown Press, 1944). The question whether President Roosevelt's diplomacy prior to Pearl Harbor was deliberately designed to goad the Axis powers into committing aggressions against the United States which would sooner or later force this country into World War II became a lively subject of debate among historians during and after the War. See Charles A. Beard, *President Roosevelt and the Coming of the War* (New York: Yale University Press, 1941); William Henry Chamberlin, *America's Second Crusade* (Chicago: Henry Regnery Company, 1950); Forrest Davis and Ernest K. Lindley, *How War Came* (New York: Simon and Schuster, 1942); Herbert Feis, *The Road to Pearl Harbor* (Princeton: Princeton University Press, 1950); and Charles C. Tansill, *Backdoor to War: The Roosevelt Foreign Policy* (Chicago: Henry Regnery Company, 1952).

on Pearl Harbor on December 7, 1941, left Congress and the President with no option but to recognize an already existing state of war. Indeed, it may well be argued that declarations of war in the traditional sense of the term have become outmoded under the conditions of modern warfare. Given the weaponry now available to major powers, the element of surprise is so important to an aggressor nation that it cannot be expected to put a potential opponent on notice to prepare to meet an attack, which a declaration of war before actual hostilities occur affords. "Undeclared" wars or wars declared after the fact appear to be the order of the day.

Two major wars which this nation has fought—the Civil War and the Korean "police action" of 1950–1953—were not declared wars in the formal sense. In addition to these conflicts the nation has engaged in military "defensive actions," "punitive" expeditions, Indian "wars," more or less "peaceful" blockades, "temporary" military occupations, and the like, on more than 150 occasions.[40] President Johnson's ordering of defensive naval and air reprisals in the Tonkin Gulf region on August 4, 1964, against the naval forces of North Vietnam, his decision in February, 1965, to begin retaliatory bombing of North Vietnamese military installations and supply lines, and his dispatching of United States military forces to the Dominican Republic in late April of the same year to protect American lives and property and assist in restoring order following outbreak of a revolution—all are merely among the most recent in a long series of incidents illustrating the point that the President, rather than Congress, must sometimes make the immediate decision in certain kinds of situations whether the armed forces of the United States shall engage in warlike activities.

This is not to say that the President need feel no obligation to keep Congress informed about a critical international situation or to seek its cooperation in support of a mutually acceptable course. Within practicable limits this is what Presidents have usually sought to do. For Congress to indicate openly and forthrightly its readiness to go along with a policy of firmness even at the risk of involving the nation in military action adds strength to the President's diplomatic position by making it clear that he speaks for a united nation. It also gives him the assurance that if resolution of a critical dispute without resort to warlike measures proves impossible, he can count upon congressional support in mustering the necessary financial, material, and manpower resources.

Numerous instances can be cited to illustrate the President's willingness to obtain congressional approval in advance for employ-

[40] *House Report No. 127*, 82nd Congress, 1st Session (1951), pp. 55-62, lists some 150 incidents of this kind which had occurred before 1945.

ment of military force "short of war" in critical situations. President Adams had the approval of Congress in conducting an undeclared naval war against France in 1798 in which a number of pitched battles between American and French war vessels occurred and some 80 French vessels were seized by our navy or by American privateers. In 1914 President Wilson felt it advisable to obtain approval of Congress in advance for his ordering naval and marine forces to seize control of the port of Tampico, Mexico, to enforce a demand for an apology from General Huerta's government for having imprisoned a number of American sailors enjoying shore leave in that city. Congress promptly responded by passing a joint resolution declaring that "the President is justified in the employment of the armed forces of the United States to enforce his demand for unequivocal amends for certain affronts and indignities committed against United States."[41] The port was occupied at the cost of 18 American lives and remained in American hands for six months. Again, in 1916 President Wilson obtained congressional approval for dispatching a military expedition of 15,000 men under General Pershing into Mexico in a vain attempt to capture the Mexican revolutionary leader Pancho Villa, whose "bandit" troops had made a raid across the American border into New Mexico, killing a number of Americans and destroying property. The troops remained in Mexico for nine months, but failed to capture Villa. In 1917, however, when the Senate was prevented by filibuster from passing a resolution authorizing the arming of American merchant vessels to enable them to resist German submarines, President Wilson proceeded to give the necessary orders on his own authority.

In the post-World War II period, advance approval from Congress for resort to military measures has been sought and obtained by the President on a number of occasions. President Truman did not ask for explicit approval from Congress when, in response to a recommendation of the United Nations Security Council, he committed American land, naval, and air forces to assist South Korea in repelling North Korean forces which had suddenly invaded it; but the prompt response of Congress in passing necessary implementing legislation to put the nation on a war footing was indicative of nearly unanimous support of his policy.[42] In 1955, President Eisenhower went to Congress

41 Joint Resolution of April 22, 1914, 38 *Stat.* 770.

42 In view of later criticisms of President Truman for his unilateral decision to commit American military forces in aid of South Korea, it is interesting to note comments made at the time by prominent Republican members of Congress. Senator Knowland, Republican Minority Leader in the Senate, said: "I am not one of those who dispute the powers of the President of the United States to take the necessary police action. I believe that he has been authorized to do it under the terms of

and asked for passage of a resolution giving him authority to make full use of American military strength, if necessary, to repel a threatened Chinese Communist assault against the Chinese Nationalist stronghold of Formosa and its island territories just off the Chinese coast. The authorizing Formosa Resolution, amounting to a blank check underwriting any military action he might take in that area, was promptly passed by an overwhelming vote in both houses of Congress.[43] A similar though somewhat more guarded resolution of support for use of military force in the Middle East was voted by Congress in 1957 when an uprising in Lebanon thought to have been inspired by Communist agents with Russian support occurred and the President had ordered an American military force to land and assist the established government.[44] Congressional support in advance was also voiced by resolution in 1962 in connection with President Kennedy's naval quarantine of Cuba to check a Russian-assisted build-up of nuclear missile capabilities there, even though the President had not requested congressional action.[45]

The North Vietnam reprisal action ordered by President Johnson in 1964 was followed immediately by a request from him for congressional support, which was immediately given. The supporting resolution, passed by a 416–0 vote in the House and an 88–2 vote in the Senate, was practically a delegation to the President of authority to

---

our obligations to the United Nations Charter. I believe he has authority to do it under his constitutional powers as Commander-in-Chief of the armed forces of the United States." *Congressional Record,* 81st Congress, 2nd Session (1950), p. 9540.

Senator Bridges of New Hampshire observed: "I am willing to follow the leadership of the President, the Secretary of State, and their military advisers in taking all measures that are necessary to aid the authorities and people of Korea in repelling and pushing back the Communist threat." *Ibid.,* p. 9156.

Representative Hugh Scott of Pennsylvania declared: "Personally, although I have heard opinions to the contrary, I agree with the President in the action which he took without waiting to secure congressional sanction. I do not think that time would have permitted congressional procedure to be used. I have in mind the fact that the President proceeded in accordance with the provisions under which the United Nations was established, and engaged in an action to repel an aggressor as one nation acting in concert with other nations, as agents and representatives of the United Nations." *Ibid.,* p. 9960.

[43] Resolution of January 29, 1955, 69 *Stat.* 7. The resolution passed the House by a 410–3 vote; the Senate by a vote of 85–3.

[44] Joint Resolution of March 9, 1957, 71 *Stat.* 5.

[45] Cf. Joint Resolution of October 3, 1962, 76 *Stat.* 697. The resolution was passed before the Cuban crisis had reached a climax, which came after Congress had adjourned. The resolution declared that the United States was "determined":

1. to prevent by whatever means may be necessary, including the use of arms, the Marxist-Leninist regime in Cuba from extending, by force or the threat of force, its aggressive or subversive activities to any part of this hemisphere;

2. to prevent in Cuba the creation or use of an externally supported military capability endangering the security of the United States; and

3. to work with the Organization of American States and with freedom-loving Cubans to support the aspirations of the Cuban people for self-determination.

make war, if he determined that conditions necessitated it.[46] Section 1 expressed congressional "approval and support" for the President in his determination, as Commander-in-Chief, to "take all necessary measures to repel any armed attack against the forces of the United States and to prevent further aggression" against them. Section 2 declared that the United States was "prepared, as the President shall determine, to take all necessary steps, including the use of armed force," to assist any signatory power to the Southeast Asia Collective Defense Treaty to defend its freedom. Employing language also found in the Middle East Resolution, the North Vietnam Resolution stated that it should continue in force until "the President shall determine that the peace and security of the area is reasonably assured," provided that Congress might itself terminate its effect earlier by adopting a concurrent resolution so stating.

A few members of Congress have deplored this tendency on the part of Presidents to come to them for resolutions underwriting what they regard as adventures in international "brinkmanship." On the one hand it is contended that the President already has the constitutional authority to proceed as he sees fit in making use of the military forces under his command to defend American rights and interests. Critics have condemned them as "conditional declarations of war." Another complaint is that the request usually comes after steps have been taken that have already committed the United States to a course which leaves Congress no choice but to endorse what the President has done. As Representative Henry Reuss of Wisconsin observed in connection with the North Vietnam Resolution, he was reminded of the story about a bartender and the proprietor of a saloon. The bartender calls the proprietor on the intercom to ask, "Is Casey good for a drink on credit?" The proprietor asks, "Has he had it?" Answer: "He has." Reply: "He is."[47]

It may be surmised that one reason for the reluctance of members of Congress to vote for such advance endorsements of a President's policy is that it tends to put them in an awkward position when the opportunity arises later to make political capital out of second-guessing the President. When a war or quasi-war develops and popular opinion swings against the President's course which has brought about hostilities, members of Congress like to be able to join in the chorus of criticism.[48] The War of 1812, which had actually been forced upon

---

[46] Joint Resolution of August 10, 1964; Public Law 88–408.

[47] *Congressional Record*, 88th Congress, 2nd Session, (August 7, 1964), p. 17967.

[48] Cf. Richard H. Rovere, *The Eisenhower Years* (New York: Farrar, Straus & Cudahy, 1956), pp. 251–252, commenting relative to the passage of the Formosa Resolution:

> It is ironic that the President's surrender of executive power in this case is one that Congress, normally eager for whatever it can get, would just as soon

President Madison by the "War Hawk" element in Congress, became "Mr. Madison's War" before it ended. The Mexican War, unpopular from the beginning in the northeastern section of the country, became "Polk's War." The Korean War was derisively referred to by some before it was over as "Mr. Truman's War," and so on.

LEGISLATIVE-EXECUTIVE COORDINATION

For better or for worse, by our constitutional system Congress and the President are joined together as partners in the management of the nation's foreign relations. The system has worked reasonably well, given the various handicaps under which it has had to operate: a federally organized system of government with its complications; a Congress with a dispersed system of internal leadership; a nation of people whose history, until recently, had not been calculated to school them in understanding the complex, seemingly intractable problems generated by interactions of the conflicting power systems in the modern community of nations; a commitment to the idea that this nation's foreign policy should be formulated and executed in a democratically responsible manner; and a belief that this nation's foreign policy should advance the cause of "democracy" in all nations, whether they are capable of practicing it or not. The President's share of the power and responsibility in this field has contributed toward assuring the "secrecy" and "despatch" which, as Jay pointed out in Number 64 of *The Federalist,* are essential to the conduct of negotiations. His command of the armed forces has enabled him to supply the necessary element of energy and force in maintaining the nation's rights and interests vis-à-vis other nations. His position as Chief of State has given him the role of national spokesman, leader, and educator of the people in the realm of foreign policy.

But the broad legislative authority conceded to Congress in this sphere, reinforced by its control of the purse, has permitted Congress to retain an effective share of authority in this area. Through the various controls available to it Congress is able to bring to bear points

---

not have received. For although the President seemed to be taking Congress into partnership in the making of foreign policy, the really important thing he was after was its approval of a particular piece of military strategy. . . . While Congress has always treasured its right to conduct post-mortems over military decisions and to raise general hell over military blunders, it has never revealed any wish to be an accessory before the fact. It has—since the Civil War at any rate—been altogether content to have the chain of military command come to an end at the White House, and there is no doubt that if there had been any quiet and passably ethical way of rejecting the President's generous offer to a share in the determination of strategy in the Formosa Strait, and the East China Sea, Congress would have made a grab for it.

of view on foreign policy issues not always reflected on the executive side of government. Consultation and close collaboration between the President, the higher officials in the Department of State, and other executive agencies having a hand in foreign affairs policy matters on the one hand, and Congress and its leadership on the other, are both necessary and desirable. Mechanisms, procedures, and usages directed to this end have been developed; but the problem of insuring proper executive-legislative coordination in this sphere is far from being solved.[49] In times of grave crisis or when legislation of vital importance in the nation's foreign relations is under consideration, meetings of the President and members of his staff with the congressional leaders concerned have become a more or less regular feature of Presidential-congressional relations since World War II.

It has been suggested that this practice be "institutionalized" by creating through legislation a "Council on Foreign Affairs," or a "Foreign Relations Cabinet." Such a body, it is suggested, might be composed of selected members of the executive departmental organization, including the Secretaries of State and Defense, or their representatives, along with the chairmen and ranking members of the Senate Foreign Relations and Armed Services Committees and their counterparts from the House of Representatives. This would be a formally recognized advisory body which the President would be expected to assemble and consult in connection with any major policy decisions he might be required to make affecting the nation's foreign relations.

It is unlikely that such a body will be created on a formal basis; in any case, it would be undesirable. For one thing, there is nothing now to prevent the President from seeking the advice and opinion of these particular officials, singly or collectively. On occasion they or a similarly composed group are brought together at his request at the White House for conferences and "briefings." The makeup of the group of executive officials and legislative leaders with whom the President may wish to consult should be kept fluid. Depending on the nature of the question under consideration, he may wish to vary his selection of those whom he consults in order to smooth out differences of approach and bring about coordination of effort. For example, cooperation from the chairman of a subcommittee of the House or Senate Appropriations Committee on a particular foreign aid program may be more important than support from the committee leaders named above. Again, an issue of foreign economic policy may concern some particular industry in the United States, such as meat, petroleum, or commercial fishing, for which other executive departments and com-

[49] For an illuminating analysis of the problem see Daniel S. Cheever and H. Field Haviland, Jr., *American Foreign Policy and the Separation of Powers* (Cambridge: Harvard University Press, 1952).

mittes of Congress speak. It should be noted that by the use of House or Senate resolutions or concurrent resolutions the two houses may express their views on foreign policy matters, independently of the President. Though not binding as law, such expressions of views carry much political weight, and a President is well advised to pay heed to them.

It should be kept in mind that the problem of obtaining coordination between the executive and legislative branches of government is not confined to foreign affairs. It runs throughout the entire range of policy-making. Moreover, foreign policy issues often have domestic connotations and impacts. If new institutional arrangements of a far-reaching, fundamental character are to be established to meet the problem of divided responsibility and authority posed by the separation of powers system, they should be directed at resolving it throughout the range of governmental operations. Until and unless this is done, reliance must continue to be placed on *ad hoc* procedures, understandings, usages, and established practices for effecting coordination of outlook and effort among leadership elements of the two policy-making branches of government.

GOVERNORS AND THE EXTERNAL RELATIONS OF STATES

As has been already pointed out, the states are excluded by constitutional rule from direct participation in the management of foreign affairs. For all practical purposes, this field is a monopoly of the national government. Furthermore, by creating a national government operating directly upon the people and invested with authority to legislate on most matters of general concern, the Constitution has removed from the range of state authority a major share of domestic political matters affecting more than one state. Consequently the states in their relations with one another have no need to resort on any large scale to the methods employed by the national government in handling the nation's foreign relations. The Constitution sets forth a number of basic principles and rules by which the relations of the states with the national government and with one another shall be governed, thus disposing of many of the issues that might be expected to arise in the areas of interstate and state-federal relations. The three departments of the national government maintain direct relations for the most part with their counterparts at the state and local levels, making it unnecessary for the chief executive to serve as the exclusive channel of communication between the two sets of governments in the federal system.

Nevertheless, in managing the external relations of the governments they head, state governors perform a number of functions that parallel those of the President in his management of the nation's foreign affairs. The governor is the official organ of communication between his state and the national government with respect to a number of matters of mutual concern. For example, he is the avenue of communication in connection with state action upon federal constitutional amendments submitted by Congress; he certifies officially the election results from his state for national officers; he is the official agent of his state in requesting federal military assistance when the legislature is not in session; and he may make temporary appointments to fill vacancies in Senate representation from his state. State participation in some types of federal-state cooperative programs has been made contingent upon approval and action by the governor. He is the official representative of his state's government during visits to his state by national and foreign dignitaries. State governors have even developed an interest in recent years in paying visits to foreign nations in a semiofficial capacity. In 1959 a group of 10 governors made a widely publicized goodwill visit to Russia; in 1960 a group of 28 made a tour of Latin America in the interest of generating friendlier relations.[50] Again in 1965 a group of 10 governors made a goodwill tour of the Far East.

In the sphere of interstate relations the Constitution makes the governor the official organ of his government for requesting cooperation from another state in rendering up fugitives from justice and in determining whether such requests shall be honored. By initiating and sponsoring appropriate administrative and legislative measures governors have an important role in carrying forward cooperative programs in the area of interstate and federal-state relations. They frequently have taken the lead in promoting the resolution of interstate problems through use of the interstate compact device. For example, during his tenure as governor of New York, F. D. Roosevelt, in collaboration with Governor Gifford Pinchot of Pennsylvania, took the lead in assembling an Eastern Interstate Conference on Labor Compacts, through which it was hoped the states of that region could reach agreement on setting up standards in the area of labor matters. This was a field from which at that time the national government was largely excluded by reason of the Supreme Court's narrow view of federal powers over the subject. The effort was not generally a success owing to the unwillingness of the legislatures of the states involved to implement the agreements reached; but the move stimulated action by the states generally toward greater use of the interstate compact. This device has been used increasingly to deal with conserva-

50 W. Brooke Graves, *American Intergovernmental Relations* (New York: Charles Scribner's Sons, 1964), p. 397.

tion and river basin development and water use problems, law enforcement, and other matters of mutual concern.[51]

It is through the political influence they can bring to bear upon the policies of the national government that governors have the most effective control over matters of concern to their states where an outside government is concerned. From the beginning Presidents have recognized the desirability of cultivating the support of governors in advancing their national programs and policies. Seeking state cooperation in making his Embargo Act policy work, Thomas Jefferson in 1807 wrote the governor of Massachusetts, expressing a desire for "a more intimate correspondence between the executives of the several states, and that of the Union."[52] Lincoln maintained close liaison with the "loyal" governors of the northern states during the Civil War, and his success in enlisting their cooperation was in no small measure responsible for the vigor with which the war for preservation of the Union was prosecuted.[53] On the other hand, when open resistance to alleged unconstitutional encroachments by the federal government into matters reserved to the states has occurred, governors have usually been found in the front ranks of the objectors and obstructors.

In 1907 President Theodore Roosevelt took what proved to be a significant step when he invited the governors of the states to attend a White House conference designed to enlist their support in promoting his conservation programs. The idea caught the fancy of the governors, who proceeded to set up an annual Governors' Conference to discuss matters of mutual concern on a regular basis. The Governors' Conference, along with regional gatherings of state chief executives, has become a vehicle for concerted expression of views on many matters of common state interest.

Besides serving as an important arena in presidential election years for preliminary skirmishing among aspirants for party nominations, the Conferences in recent years have tended to become vehicles for the expression of views of governors on questions of national policy, both foreign and domestic, rather than on purely interstate matters.[54]

---

[51] *Ibid.*, p. 597. On the general subject of interstate compacts and their use see Frederick L. Zimmermann and Mitchell Wendell, *The Interstate Compact Since 1925* (Chicago: Council of State Governments, 1951); Vincent V. Thursby, *Interstate Cooperation: A Study of the Interstate Compact* (Washington: Public Affairs Press, 1953); and Richard H. Leach and Reddig S. Sugg, Jr., *The Administration of Interstate Compacts* (Baton Rouge: Louisiana State University Press, 1959).

[52] Graves, *op. cit.*, p. 585.

[53] Cf. William Hesseltine, *Lincoln and the War Governors* (New York: Alfred A. Knopf, 1948).

[54] Glen T. Brooks, *When Governors Convene: The Governors' Conference and National Politics* (Baltimore: Johns Hopkins Press, 1961), is a comprehensive study of the Governors' Conference and its political significance. According to national news dispatches of September 1, 1965, a Washington office had been set up by the Republican Governors' Association, consisting of the 17 current Republican gov-

Their activity in national political affairs is attested by the fact that in the period from 1943 to 1959, 148 governors presented testimony before congressional committees, making a total number of 781 appearances.[55] Representing political power of very considerable weight in their respective states, when they speak with a united voice it behooves Congress and the President to pay heed. State executives championing state's rights in the federal community of states play a role similar to that of the heads of government in the international community of nations. The latter are expected to maintain the sovereign rights of their respective countries against the forces of world government as represented by the United Nations and its allied agencies. Governors similarly see themselves as spokesmen for state sovereignty as against encroachments by the federal government. Like the President, governors are key figures in the promotion of harmony and cooperation, or, as the case may be, of particularism and discord in the larger political community of which their governments are an inseparable part.

---

ernors. This organization was formed in 1963 at the annual Governors' Conference in Miami. Its object is to maintain contact with the headquarters of the Republican National Committee and with Republican members of Congress. Cf. *The Ann Arbor News*, September 1, 1965, p. 1.

[55] Brooks, *op. cit.*, p. 54.

16

COMMANDER-IN-CHIEF

The decision of the Framers of the Constitution to associate the function of Commander-in-Chief of the nation's military forces with the office of President was reached with comparatively little controversy. The teachings of history pointed clearly in that direction. The exploits of Great Britain's "Warrior Kings" and those of other countries were familiar. Closer at hand they could point to the colonial governors who had performed as military commanders in the field against the Indians and rival colonial powers. Some of the Revolutionary War-time state governors, all of whom had succeeded to this function in the early state governmental plans, served actively as military leaders when the course of the struggle had made their states the scene of military operations. Above all, the unspoken thought that the post of President would be filled in the first instance by George Washington made easy and logical the assumption that the overall power of military command should be associated with it. In a sense, what the Framers conceived they were doing was reviving and revamping the post of commander-in-chief of the Continental armies Washington had occupied during the Revolutionary War, making it permanent, and adding to it a number of civil functions. So general was the feeling on this aspect of the presidential office that Hamilton felt it necessary in *The Federalist* to devote only one brief paragraph to defense of it. It was a provision "the propriety of [which] is so evident in itself, and . . . at the same time, so consonant to the precedents of the State constitutions in general" that he felt "little need be said to explain or enforce it."[1]

This is not to say that the men who wrote the Constitution were unconcerned about military matters. On the contrary, they were very defense- and security-minded men, as evidenced by the numerous provisions having reference to military affairs and warmaking elsewhere in the Constitution. Approximately half the clauses in Article I, Section 8, outlining the delegated powers of Congress have to do with military matters and the conduct of war. Section 10 of the same Article lays down general principles with regard to military functions and activities of the states. Amendments II and III in the Bill of Rights

[1] *The Federalist*, No. 74.

added to these original provisions by recognizing the right of potential members of the militia to "keep and bear arms" and limiting governmental authority in the matter of quartering troops on civilians.

Taking the Constitution as a whole, the theories and principles which the designers of the governmental plan sought to apply were clear enough. First, they accepted without question the principle that immediate control over the nation's military forces should be in the hands of the President. He was Commander-in-Chief not only of the army and navy of the United States, but also of the militia of the several states "when called into the actual service of the United States." In the second place, it was a truism with them that the military should be subordinated to the civilian arm of government. This was achieved not only by conferring the power of supreme command on the President, who would perforce be a civilian, but also by delegating to Congress fundamental powers in the sphere of military affairs. National forces could be brought into being only at its behest. Appropriations for their support could be made by Congress for no longer a term than two years, thus necessitating review of money grants for maintaining military forces at relatively short intervals. Congress was expressly empowered to "make rules for the government and regulation" of these armed forces. It was also authorized to provide for the calling of state militia forces into the service of the national government to execute the laws of the Union, suppress insurrections, and repel invasions as well as to establish rules for organizing, arming, and disciplining them and for governing them when called into national service. To Congress was reserved the power to declare war, to grant letters of marque and reprisal, and to make rules for captures on land and sea. By these various means the Founders sought to obviate what they had listed in the Declaration of Independence as one of their major grievances against King George III—his "affecting to render the military independent and superior to the civil power."

A third principle evident in the constitutional arrangements was an intent to leave in the hands of the states a large share of responsibility for providing the military strength necessary to maintain domestic peace and national security. At the same time it was made clear that the military role of the states should be subordinate to that of the national government. They could not maintain troops or ships of war in time of peace except with the consent of Congress, nor make war unless actually invaded. Their militia forces, subject to call into national service, were to be controlled by Congress in organization, arming, and disciplining, insofar as Congress might think it proper to exercise its authority in this respect. They might supplement their own military forces only by calling on the national government for aid. Implicit in all these arrangements, but not explicitly stated, was the idea that both the national and state governments should place primary reliance on the part-time citizen soldier rather than on a permanent, professional military caste.[2] The idea of a standing army manned by a professional officer class was still anathema to a people who had been goaded into revolt because George III, among his other transgressions, had "kept among us, in times of peace, standing armies without the consent of our legislatures," as the Declaration had put it. However, over the years there has been a gradual change since the Civil War in the direction of placing primary reliance for defense on a professionalized, permanent national military establishment. The effect has been to add immeasurably to the President's role as Commander-in-Chief of the nation's armed forces.

Where military affairs are concerned, as in so many other matters, the Constitution's language is far from clear and explicit on the great question of the division of authority between the executive and the legislative branches. To be sure, there is an unusually detailed specification of the matters affecting the military establishment on which Congress may legislate. But opposed to these provisions is the statement that the President shall be the Commander-in-Chief of the nation's armed forces. The language employed is unique among the clauses outlining the powers and duties of the President in that it confers an *office* rather than merely a *function* upon him.[3] By this clause a military office is joined to the chief executive's functions in the civil realm. The implication is that whatever powers and duties are necessarily associated with the exercise of supreme military command belong to the President by constitutional prescription and cannot be constitutionally diminished or controlled by statute.

As is the case with the executive power clause, the content of the commander-in-chief clause has been shaped in considerable degree by Presidents themselves. Hamilton, it is true, had described the President's role as amounting to "nothing more than the supreme command and direction of the military forces, as first general and admiral of the Confederacy."[4] On one occasion the Supreme Court declared that the President's duty and powers as Commander-in-Chief were "purely military."[5] But these narrow views of the President's role have given way to a much broader one. Ever since the Civil War, when President Lincoln cited the commander-in-chief clause as the constitutional source of his authority to undertake a wide variety of acts going beyond purely military matters into the area of political affairs,

---

[2] Dorothy Burne Goebel and Julius Goebel, Jr., *Generals in the White House* (Garden City, N.Y.: Doubleday & Company, 1952), p. 9.

[3] Cf. Samuel P. Huntington, *The Soldier and the State* (New York: Random House, Vintage Books, 1964), p. 178.

[4] *The Federalist,* No. 69.

[5] *Fleming v. Page,* 9 Howard 603, 615 (1850).

the concept of the reach of this constitutional language has been subjected to a continual stretching process. Today its significance as the basis for assertion of presidential prerogative power is as great as, if not greater than, any other clause in the Constitution.

THE CHIEF EXECUTIVE AS A MILITARY COMMANDER

To the men who wrote the Constitution the commander-in-chief clause undoubtedly was meant to confer authority on the President to take over active command of forces in the field, if he should so choose. That they contemplated this was indicated by their failure to qualify this right in any manner. The New Jersey Plan, which proposed a plural executive body, had contained a clause placing in the Executive the authority to "direct all military operations"; but it had gone on explicitly to forbid "any of the persons composing the Federal Executive . . . on any occasion [to] take command of any troops, so as personally to conduct any enterprise, as General, or in any other capacity." Hamilton's plan also failed to designate the President as the commander-in-chief of the armed forces, proposing instead to vest in him only the power of "direction of war when authorized or begun." Coupled with the fact that some of the state constitutions stipulated that a governor in his capacity as commander-in-chief or "captain-general" of the state's militia forces could take over direct command of them in the field only with the approval of the legislature or of his council, it is apparent that the omission of any restrictive language on this point was significant.

Although they could have chosen to do so, Presidents have not taken on this responsibility. The Napoleonic concept of the warrior-statesman has not taken root in the United States. State governors, who in earlier years of the nation's history in many instances did place themselves at the head of militia forces in the field, have likewise chosen in more recent times to confine their military leadership role to its less martial aspects. The constitutions of Alabama, Maryland, and Kentucky, it might be noted, still require that the legislature give its approval to the governor's taking personal command of the state milita; while Vermont's requires that such consent be given by the state senate.

Probably the nearest approach to a President's assuming command of military forces in action occurred in 1794, when Washington took part personally in organizing into an army the militia forces assembled in Pennsylvania to put down the Whisky Insurrection. He did not actually lead the troops on their expedition into the western part of the state, however, but placed them under the command of the governors of the respective states from which they had been called.[6] During the French crisis of 1798, President Adams, who had had no military experience, nominated retired President Washington to the post of "Lieutenant General and Commander-in-Chief of all the armies raised or to be raised in the United States." The Senate confirmed the appointment and Washington reluctantly accepted the assignment. The crisis failed to develop into a full-scale war. This left unsettled the question whether a President might, as Adams apparently proposed to do, delegate to a military officer the entire commander-in-chief power itself. Later, Lincoln was to appoint General Grant to the post of "Lieutenant General of the Armies of the United States" and to place under his immediate direction all the land forces of the Union, but he stopped short of delegating to Grant the commander-in-chief function itself. For him to have done so would have meant the surrender of one of the most important elements of the presidential office itself, as Lincoln conceived it.

The manner and extent to which Presidents confronted by wartime or warlike situations have involved themselves in decision-making affecting military operations provides one of the most fascinating chapters in any account of the evolution of the presidency.[7] In general it may be said that while Presidents have left to officers in the field the actual tactical and local strategic decisions in the use of troops and ships, they have insisted on keeping in their own hands the responsibility for making ultimate decisions on grand strategy, the definition of objectives, and questions of a political nature. A President must concern himself not only with the immediate task of defeating enemy forces but also with problems arising on the home front. He must also be looking ahead to the state of affairs that will be brought about by a military victory, a stalemate, or a defeat, and be prepared to take the appropriate steps demanded by the situation. War-making is far too complex and serious a business to be left solely to the discretion of the generals and admirals engaged in the actual fighting, as French Premier Georges Clemenceau once observed.

Typical of the role a President may fill as Commander-in-Chief in the conduct of war operations was that of President Polk during the

[6] See Chap. 14, p. 453. President Jackson was said by Martin Van Buren to have "yearned" to place himself at the head of the troops he was prepared to raise to suppress the "tariff insurrection" in South Carolina in 1832. Marquis James, *The Life of Andrew Jackson* (Indianapolis: The Bobbs–Merrill Company, 1938), p. 619.

[7] For very interesting reviews and evaluations of the performances of the eight Presidents who have had to conduct wars of major significance see the symposium by Ernest R. May, ed., *The Ultimate Decision: The President as Commander-in-Chief* (New York: George Braziller, 1960). Different authors evaluate the administrations of Presidents Madison, Polk, Lincoln, McKinley, Wilson, F. D. Roosevelt, Truman, and Eisenhower.

Mexican War. He assumed responsibility for the decisions on overall strategy—an overland invasion of Mexico from Texas under General Taylor, a seaborne invasion under General Scott aimed directly at capturing the Mexican capital, and occupation of the California area by American military and naval forces. Yet he found himself balked by Congress in his desire to have direction of all military operations placed in the hands of one commanding general. When he proposed to revive the rank of lieutenant general last held by Washington, which he intended to fill by appointing Senator Thomas Hart Benton, in whom he had complete confidence, Congress refused to cooperate. He was forced to conduct the main campaigns of the war through politically ambitious generals with whom his relations were not good.[8]

At the outset of the Civil War, President Lincoln, after consultations with General Scott, settled upon the so-called "Anaconda Plan" of gradual envelopment of the South by probing land offensives at various points along the northern and western borders of the Confederacy, coupled with a naval blockade of southern ports. Although challenged and harassed in his conduct of the war from time to time by strident voices in the northern press and by the special Joint Committee on the Conduct of the War set up by Congress, he adhered to this basic strategy and saw it vindicated by the results. During the first three years of the war Lincoln presumed to give direct orders to generals in the field regarding their military movements, for which he has been criticized by some military historians. But his directives were couched in terms that left discretion in the hands of the field generals concerned, and their failures were probably as much attributable to inferior generalship on their part as to the meddling of the President in purely military matters.[9] In the end, after he had found in Grant a man whose judgment, boldness, and energy he could trust, he was willing enough to assign to him responsibility for the purely military decisions.

Among the other war Presidents—McKinley, Wilson, F. D. Roosevelt, Truman, and Eisenhower—Roosevelt stands out as having involved himself most deeply in the making of strategic decisions in the prosecution of the military phases of war. In consultation with Prime Minister Churchill and other allied heads of government, it was he who was ultimately responsible for the decision to concentrate American

---

[8] Cf. Leonard D. White, "Polk (1845–1848)," Chap. III in May, ed., *op. cit.* Polk complained in his *Diary:* "I am held responsible for the conduct of the War, and yet Congress refused to give me a commander in whom I have confidence, and I am compelled to employ the officers whom the law has provided, however unfit they may be." Arthur Bernon Tourtellot, *The Presidents on the Presidency* (Garden City, N.Y.: Doubleday & Company, 1964), p. 323.

[9] Cf. T. Harry Williams, "Lincoln (1861–1865)," Chap. IV in May, ed., *op. cit.,* pp. 83ff.

strength at the outset in the European theater of action, while fighting what was essentially a holding action in the South Pacific against Japanese forces. The plan for an invasion of North Africa followed by an assault on Sicily and the Italian peninsula was a part of the general strategy he helped to originate, as was the character of the final cross-channel assault on the German positions in France. His decision to pour huge sums into development of the atomic bomb proved to be one of the epoch-making events in history. It was the best kept military secret of World War II.

By way of contrast, President Wilson was inclined to avoid so far as possible the making of purely military strategic and tactical decisions. He preferred to confine his functioning as Commander-in-Chief to the home front and to phases of the war having obvious political implications and overtones. Declaring that he felt he had "no choice . . . but to follow experts in a war of experts,"[10] after having named General Pershing as commanding general of the American Expeditionary Forces overseas and having placed Admiral Sims in charge of American fleet operations in the Atlantic, he adopted the policy of trusting to their judgments and recommendations on matters of military organization, strategy, and tactics so far as possible. He eschewed the idea of regarding himself as a military leader and expert so far that he was deeply disturbed when an artist presumed to make an etching of him dressed in a military uniform. He wrote the artist a scolding letter, reminding him that putting the President in uniform "violates a very fundamental principle of our institutions, namely that the military power is subordinate to the civil."

President Truman's most fateful decisions as a wartime Commander-in-Chief undoubtedly were his approval of the use of the atomic bomb to hasten Japanese surrender in 1945; his directive of January 31, 1950, ordering the Atomic Energy Commission to proceed with plans for developing the hydrogen bomb; and his removal of General MacArthur as Supreme Commander of the Allied Forces in Korea in 1951 when it became apparent that the General was following a course at odds with the more limited objectives to which President Truman and the cooperating United Nations powers were committed. His penchant for naming men with professional military backgrounds to high political posts was a feature of his conduct of the presidential office. His naming of General George C. Marshall as Secretary of State in 1947 and later as Secretary of Defense, along with appointment of a number of other career officers of the Army and Navy to high diplomatic posts,[11] was obviously indicative of his belief

[10] Ernest R. May, "Wilson (1917–1918)," Chap. VI in May, ed., *op. cit.*, p. 116.
[11] Cf. Huntington, *op. cit.*, p. 360, for a list of such appointments.

that the political and military problems of the Cold War era had become inextricably intermingled.

The importance of the President's commander-in-chief function raises the question of the qualifications, from the standpoint of military experience, of the individuals who have been chosen to this high office. Few could cite a happy blend of roles as soldier and statesman in their earlier careers, as could Washington; but collectively the amount of military experience possessed has been astonishingly great. Twenty-one of the 35 men who have filled the office have had some actual wartime military experience. Ten have been generals, of whom six— Washington, Jackson, William H. Harrison, Taylor, Grant, and Eisenhower—were of major rank. Two—Grant and Eisenhower—were West Point graduates. If he holds a commission as an officer in the armed services, however, a successful candidate for the presidency must perforce surrender it upon becoming President. The presidency is the only office he may hold. The question whether the President by reason of his role as the Commander-in-Chief of the armed forces, in wartime at least, is actually a member of the armed forces has never been answered conclusively.[12]

The list of major party candidates for the presidency who failed to win election also includes a number of men whose advancement was attributable to fame won in military service. In this category were Generals Winfield Scott (1852), George B. McClellan (1864), and Win-

[12] The decision to establish a special military commission for the trial of the assassins of President Lincoln was based in part on the theory that his murder was a military crime, committed against the Commander-in-Chief while in actual service. Cf. Clinton Rossiter, *The Supreme Court and the Commander-in-Chief* (Ithaca: Cornell University Press, 1951), p. 110. The question was also raised whether President F. D. Roosevelt was, by virtue of his status as Commander-in-Chief at the time of his death, a member of the armed forces. Under the terms of national revenue laws certain rebates on inheritance tax liabilities were required to be granted if he had died "while in active service as a member of the military or naval forces of the United States." The Roosevelt heirs waived all claims on this account, but the administrators of the estate asked for and received a ruling from the surrogate for Dutchess County on the point. He ruled that the President was not a member of the armed services, within the purview of the revenue laws, at the time of his death. He observed that the question of the President's status as a military man was "unique," and intensive research had disclosed no precedent to serve as a basis for its solution. *The New York Times,* May 26, 1950, and July 26, 1950.

During his term of office, President Truman was charged the regular day rates for time he spent as a patient in Walter Reed Hospital instead of the reduced rate for military personnel on active duty, but President Eisenhower was charged the reduced rate at another Army hospital during his illnesses while serving as President. He had resigned his commission as General of the Army upon becoming an active candidate for the presidency. This differentiation in treatment of the presidents involved led one observer to remark jocularly that the conclusion seems justified that Republican Presidents are members of the armed services while Democratic ones are not. Cf. C. H. Pritchett, *The American Constitution* (New York: McGraw Hill Book Company, 1959), p. 349n.

field S. Hancock (1880). Former General Lewis Cass (1848) and Senator
John C. Frémont (1856) owed some of their favor in the public eye to
earlier careers in military service. Higher naval officers, probably reflecting the more narrowly professional character of their service and
their tendency to live in a world apart from civilian society, have not
been prominent among those advanced for the presidency. Only one,
Admiral George Dewey of Spanish-American War fame, ever presented
himself as a candidate. Announcing his availability for the presidency
in 1900, he simultaneously killed any chances of being seriously considered with his incredibly naive statements about his view of the
office. Explaining why he was making himself available, after having
earlier declared he had no interest in seeking the presidency, he said:
"Since studying this subject I am convinced that the office of the
President is not such a difficult one to fill, his duties being mainly to
execute the laws of Congress as faithfully as I have always executed
the orders of my superiors."[13]

It is one of the paradoxes of American political life that in a nation
committed to the idea of subordination of the military to the civilian
side of government, the "war hero" type of candidate has had such
remarkable success in seeking the highest political office in the land.
But as has been pointed out,[14] it has been the "citizen soldier" war
hero rather than the professional officer type who has been so favored
in most instances. Not all military heroes who might well have parlayed
their fame into a successful candidacy for President have chosen to do
so. When General William T. Sherman learned that some Democrats
were seeking to launch a boom for him as their candidate in 1864, he
wrote General Halleck: "Some fool seems to have used my name. If
forced to choose between the penitentiary and the White House for
four years . . . I would say the penitentiary, thank you."[15] Later he
scotched a movement to make him the Republican nominee in 1884
with what has become the classic language of flat refusal: "I will not
accept if nominated and will not serve if elected."[16] General Eisen-

---

[13] *The New York Times*, April 5, 1900. The Admiral went on to say: "[Since
returning from Manila] I have discovered that the position of Admiral is not the
highest in the United States. The highest position in the United States is that of
President, and if the American people want me to act as President, how can I
refuse?" Queried as to which party's nomination he would seek, he said he had not
decided on that, and indicated he might run as an "independent." Asked what
policies he would advocate, he answered: "It is not my idea that the President
should dictate to Congress; . . . I remember the denunciation which once followed
the announcement by a President of the United States of 'my policy.' "

[14] Huntington, *op. cit.*, pp. 158ff. See also on this aspect of the presidency
Sidney Hyman, *The American President* (Harper & Row, 1954), pp. 210–217; and
Goebel and Goebel, *op. cit.*, Chaps. I and II.

[15] Lloyd Lewis, *Fighting Prophet* (New York: Harcourt, Brace & World, 1932),
p. 411.

[16] *Ibid.*, p. 631.

hower, in a letter to a New Hampshire newspaper editor asking that his name not be entered in the 1948 presidential primary in that state, gave a well-reasoned statement why professional soldiers should not allow themselves to become involved in presidential politics.[17] Nevertheless, in the light of the actual record, a President can hardly be blamed if he allows political considerations to play a part in his decisions about whom to assign to high-level military positions when a war is on. He may well be choosing a future President.

THE PRESIDENT, CONGRESS AND THE "WAR POWER"

In no respect have the American constitutional principles of separation of powers, federal division of powers, and limited government been subjected to greater strain than in connection with the conduct of war. Wartime exigencies have necessitated continual reevaluation and redefinition of these principles in their application to the situation of the moment. Traditional modes of action have had to give way to the demands of national survival itself. Total war and constitutional government as usual are incompatible bedfellows. So far as the presidency is concerned, the commander-in-chief clause, reinforced as it may be by congressional delegation of authority, becomes a vast reservoir of prescriptive power to act as the public needs require in dealing with the emergencies generated by war. As President Lincoln put it in his simple but effective way: "As commander-in-chief of the army and navy, in time of war I suppose I have a right to take any measure which may best subdue the enemy."[18]

The Supreme Court, which has perforce been called upon to wrestle with this constitutional problem from time to time, has equivocated, evaded, advanced, retreated, and spoken with a divided voice. Those who would place reliance upon it to enforce constitutional limitations can find comfort in some of its ringing pronouncements in defense of liberty, law, and the constitutional proprieties. They can quote Justice Davis' rhetoric in *Ex parte Milligan:*

> The Constitution of the United States is a law for rulers and people, equally in war and in peace, and covers with the shield of its protection all classes of men, at all times, and under all circumstances.

[17] Cf. Dwight D. Eisenhower, *Mandate for Change, 1953–1956* (Garden City, N.Y.: Doubleday & Company, 1963), p. 7. For a view of General Eisenhower's rise to the presidency as having been brought about by designing politicians who sought to capitalize on his great popularity, see Marquis W. Childs, *Eisenhower: Captive Hero* (New York: Harcourt, Brace & World, 1958).

[18] Tourtellot, *op. cit.*, p. 328, quoting John G. Nicolay and John Hay, eds., *Complete Works of Abraham Lincoln* (New York: F. D. Tandy Company, 12 vols., 1905), Vol. VIII, p. 31.

No doctrine involving more pernicious consequences was ever invented by the wit of man than that any of its provisions can be suspended during any of the great exigencies of government.[19]

Or they may cite Justice Miller's forthright declaration in *United States* v. *Lee:*

No man in this country is so high he is above the law. No officer of the law may set that law at defiance with impunity. All the officers of the government, from the highest to the lowest, are creatures of the law, and are bound to obey it.[20]

Yet when the record is looked at in its entirety, one is forced to conclude that the Court recognizes, as Chief Justice Hughes once said, that we have a "fighting Constitution," one that permits to be done what is necessary to be done to preserve the nation. In dealing with the question of the nature of the President's powers as Commander-in-Chief, as Professor Rossiter has pointed out in his excellent analysis of the matter,[21] the Court has usually chosen to speak in guarded terms. Its pronouncements have tended to be general, and it has refrained from attempting to define the boundaries of presidential power with finality and precision. Whenever the President's authority as Commander-in-Chief has been challenged, the Court has chosen to approve his actions, if at all possible, on some ground other than an outright recognition of prerogative power derived from his position as head of the nation's military forces. It has refused to draw a clear line between the powers of Congress and those of the President in this sphere. It has vacillated in its estimate of its own right to intervene and check an improper exercise of power by Congress or the President where the national security is gravely at stake. At the height of public danger it has generally refrained from interfering, taking refuge in evasions on technical grounds or in resort to the doctrine of political questions. Its most forthright pronouncements upholding constitutional limitations have usually come after the emergency has passed, when it is safe to indulge its proclivity for maintaining the constitutional niceties. In short, the Court has chosen to be realistic and practical, rather than unyielding and doctrinaire, in its exegesis of the law of the Constitution in this area of governmental action.

It follows that the war powers of the President in his role as Commander-in-Chief have been traced for the most part through the initiative of the Presidents themselves, supported in great measure by affirmative action, before or after the fact, by Congress. One must turn to the detailed studies of the record of each of the war Presidents to discover the actual dimensions of this phase of his official powers

19 4 Wallace 2, 120 (1866).
20 106 U.S. 196, 220 (1882).
21 Cf. Rossiter, *The Supreme Court and the Commander-in-Chief*, pp. 2-10.

and duties.[22] What one President has done sets a precedent for others to follow. In this area of constitutional development there has been a great deal of "playing by ear," both by Presidents and by Congress. Their assessment of what is necessary and practicable, taking into account the state of public opinion and the nature of the exigency to be dealt with, has been the major factor giving shape and content to the constitutional proprieties in this sphere.

INITIATION AND TERMINATION OF HOSTILITIES

The relationship between the war-declaring power of Congress and the President's authority to engage military forces in hostile actions against another nation has been discussed in Chapter 15 and need not be further examined at this point.[23] So far as the termination of hostilities is concerned, a similar relationship exists. That is to say, the President in his capacity as Commander-in-Chief can order a cessation of actual fighting, but some form of action by Congress is required to end a state of war once it has been declared by that body. Armistice agreements entered into by the President in his capacity as chief executive and Commander-in-Chief brought to a close actual military operations at the end of the Mexican War, the Spanish-American War, World War I, and World War II. The conditions laid down foreshadowed the terms of peace eventually made.

If war has been declared by Congress, restoration of a state of peace depends upon some affirmative action by Congress terminating the legal state of war. This is normally effected through Senate consent to ratification of a treaty defining the conditions under which peaceful relations are to be restored. The treaty as a later expression of the will of this government is considered to have superseded the joint resolution declaring war. Thus the Treaty of Guadalupe-Hidalgo terminated the state of war with Mexico in 1848; the Treaty of Paris in 1899 the war with Spain; and the Japanese Peace Treaty of 1952 the Pacific phase of World War II.

[22] In addition to the works by May and Rossiter cited in notes 7 and 12 above, see James G. Randall, *Constitutional Problems under Lincoln*, rev. ed. (Urbana: University of Illinois Press, 1951); C. A. Berdahl, *War Powers of the Executive in the United States* (Urbana: University of Illinois Press, 1922); Howard White, *Executive Influence in Determining Military Policy in the United States* (Urbana: University of Illinois Press, 1925); E. S. Corwin, *Total War and the Constitution* (New York: Alfred A. Knopf, 1947); Clinton Rossiter, *Constitutional Dictatorship* (Princeton: Princeton University Press, 1948); and Charles Fairman, *The Law of Martial Rule*, 2nd ed. (Chicago: Callaghan and Company, 1943).

[23] For fuller discussion of this aspect of the President's authority see Berdahl, *op. cit.*, Chap. 4; Rossiter, *The Supreme Court and the Commander-in-Chief*, pp. 65–77; and C. C. Tansill, "War Powers of the President of the United States with Special Reference to the Beginning of Hostilities," *Political Science Quarterly*, Vol. 45 (March, 1930), pp. 1–55.

Although the treaty procedure was undoubtedly intended by the Constitution's Framers to be the normal method of terminating a state of war, other methods of achieving this purpose have at times been employed. Because of the Senate's refusal to agree to the Versailles Treaty following World War I, Congress later adopted the course of repealing the declaration of war against Germany and Austria-Hungary by adoption of a joint resolution so stating in 1921.[24] The same method was used to terminate the German phase of World War II in 1951.[25] Proclamations issued by President Andrew Johnson were held by the Supreme Court to have terminated the invocation of the laws of war by President Lincoln against the South during the Civil War.[26]

In this connection an interesting aspect of the recent congressional resolutions expressing approval of the use of American military forces by the President in various critical areas of the world should be noted. These resolutions, which are in a sense conditional declarations of defensive war, raise a number of constitutional issues. If the President undertakes defensive military measures resulting in hostilities, is the United States at war in the legal sense? To what extent, if at all, do they invest the President with an authority to adopt warlike measures going beyond what he already may undertake in his capacity as chief executive and Commander-in-Chief of the armed forces? How should such congressional underwritings of his war-making power be terminated? The answers to these questions are by no means clear. The Formosa Resolution, it should be observed, left to the President the responsibility of terminating it by making a finding that the conditions giving rise to it no longer exist. The Middle East and North Vietnam Resolutions contained similar language, but they also included provisos stating that Congress may declare by concurrent resolution that conditions justifying his taking the actions described therein no longer exist. They thus illustrate the more sophisticated view of the means Congress may use to make easier the cancellation of advance approvals or delegations of authority to the President, as discussed in Chapter 13. Cancellation of a resolution's effect by this means would

24 Joint Resolution July 2, 1921, 42 *Stat.* 105. The Supreme Court in *Commercial Trust Co.* v. *Miller*, 262 U.S. 51 (1923) and *Swiss Insurance Co.* v. *Miller*, 267 U.S. 42 (1925) took notice of the Resolution as marking the end of the state of war.

25 Joint Resolution of October 19, 1951, 65 *Stat.* 451. President Truman by proclamation declared an end to the state of hostilities of World War II as of December 31, 1946.

26 Cf. Proclamation of April 2, 1866, Richardson, *Messages and Papers of the Presidents*, Vol. VI, p. 429; Proclamation of August 20, 1866, *ibid.*, p. 434. The first of these declared the war to have terminated in all parts of the South except Texas; the latter as to Texas. See *The Protector*, 12 Wallace 700 (1871), as to the Court's recognition of the effectiveness of these proclamations in fixing the date of the termination of a state of war.

undoubtedly exert strong political pressure on the President to alter his policies accordingly.

DISPOSITION AND USE OF MILITARY FORCES

Clauses in the Constitution placing in the hands of Congress the power to raise and support military forces, read in conjunction with the "necessary and proper" clause, provide a plausible basis for the contention that Congress may determine the uses to which such armed forces may be put as well as the places where they may be stationed. Opposed to this contention is the proposition that, at the barest minimum, the President's constitutionally recognized power of overall command includes the authority to determine the placement of troops and ships and to direct their operations as military units. Here again one is confronted by a constitutional enigma. Accommodations have had to be reached between Presidents and their Congresses on the point. Speaking very generally, it may be said that the Congress makes provision for the raising of armed forces, while the President as chief executive supervises the administration of the laws providing for their being brought into existence and as Commander-in-Chief directs their employment in the service of the United States.

Nevertheless, Congress has from time to time insisted upon its right to direct and control their use. In connection with the use of troops in enforcing national laws and suppressing insurrection, Congress early asserted its authority.[27] Presidents have generally complied with the limitations thus established by statute. In connection with using military forces to combat foreign powers Congress has left to the President a far wider discretion, but even in this sphere it has at times asserted its authority to limit presidential discretion. When the first peacetime draft law was enacted by Congress in 1940, it sought to restrict the use to which troops so raised could be put by including a proviso that they could not be employed outside the "Western Hemisphere."[28] President Roosevelt respected this limitation, but when he decided to station some of these forces in Iceland to facilitate American convoy operations in cooperation with the British, he had to stretch a point. (He was able to cite certain geographical authorities who held to the view that Iceland should be considered as lying within the Western Hemisphere, even though it lies east of the 30th meridian of longitude.) With the entrance of the United States into World War II as a belligerent, the restriction was, of course, eliminated.

Another illustration of efforts by Congress to retain a voice in the

[27] See Chap. 14, pp. 452, 454–456, 462–464.
[28] Act of September 16, 1940, 54 *Stat.* 885, Sec. 3 (e).

uses to which American military might may be put is afforded by the United Nations Participation Act of 1945. Section 43 of the United Nations Charter contemplates the establishment of an international police force made up of contingents supplied by member nations for the purpose of maintaining international peace and security. Section 6 of the Participation Act authorizes the President to negotiate an agreement or agreements with the Security Council, *subject to the approval of the Congress by appropriate act or joint resolution,* providing for the numbers and types of armed forces to be made available by the United States.[29] A proviso makes clear that the Participation Act itself is not to be construed as an approval of any such agreement. While the failure of the major powers to agree upon plans for implementing this United Nations international police force idea as originally contemplated has obviated application of this part of the Act in practice, this legislation stands as a reminder that Congress may insist upon exercising control over use of American military forces as a part of any internationally directed peacekeeping and policing organization.

The issue of the power of Congress versus that of the President over the dispatching of troops abroad on defensive or peacekeeping missions is one that simply will not down easily. It has appeared and reappeared in one form or another repeatedly. It was this issue, more than any other, that brought about defeat of the League of Nations Covenant as a part of the Versailles Treaty in the Senate in 1919–1920. The web of regional alliances directed against potential Communist aggression in which the United States has become involved since the end of World War II has brought the issue to the fore in an insistent fashion.

The North Atlantic Treaty of 1949, for example, provides in Article 5 that the participating nations agree that "an armed attack against one of them shall be considered an attack against them all"; and if such an attack occurs each "will assist the party or parties so attacked by taking forthwith, individually and in concert with the other parties, such action as it deems necessary, including the use of armed force, to restore and maintain the security of the North Atlantic Treaty area." In December, 1950, President Truman, fearing that Russia might take advantage of American involvement in Korea to launch an attack against our Western European allies, undertook to strengthen NATO military complements by dispatching four additional American divi-

---

[29] Act of December 20, 1945, 59 *Stat.* 619 (emphasis added). Section 5 of the Act authorizes the President to cooperate in carrying out economic sanctions imposed by the Security Council against an offending power, but does not require congressional approval of the trade restrictions he sets up for this purpose. The section goes on to provide for penalties up to a $10,000 fine and/or 10 years' imprisonment for violation of the regulations thus established by presidential order.

sions to various stations in that area. With the approval of the NATO countries he also called General Eisenhower back into active service and placed him in supreme command of NATO forces. These moves, coming on the heels of his action six months before in committing American land, sea, and air forces to the United Nations effort to throw back the North Korean invaders—a step which he had taken following a recommendation of the UN Security Council without consulting Congress or obtaining its express approval in advance— precipitated what came to be referred to as the "Great Debate" in Congress during the months of January, February, and March of 1951.

The debate developed following introduction of a Senate resolution by Senator Wherry of Nebraska, expressing the sense of the Senate that no ground forces of the United States be assigned to duty in the European area for purposes of strengthening NATO defenses "pending the formulation of a policy with respect thereto by Congress." A House joint resolution of similar import was introduced by Representative Coudert of New York. The latter resolution went much further than the Wherry Resolution in that it would have declared it to be the sense of Congress that no additional forces be sent or maintained outside the United States, its territories or possessions, without the prior authorization of Congress. Reinforcing this view, another section of the Coudert Resolution would have denied use of any current or future appropriations for the purpose of maintaining such forces without prior approval of Congress. Since the Coudert Resolution, being a joint resolution, would have had the force of law if passed, it would thus have effectively tied the hands of the President and made Congress the decision-making authority on when, where, and what types of military missions should be dispatched abroad.

Neither of these resolutions was passed, but the Senate passed a substitute brought forward by Senators Russell and Connally, chairmen of the Senate Armed Services and Foreign Relations Committees, respectively, which had the administration's approval. Adopted by the Senate both in the form of a Senate resolution and as a concurrent resolution (which the House failed to act upon), it expressed approval of the assignment of General Eisenhower to the post of Supreme Commander of NATO forces and the dispatching of the four additional divisions to Europe. It went on to express the view that the President should consult with the Senate Foreign Relations and Armed Services Committees and their counterparts in the House before making any further troop commitments of this kind. It also advised the President that he should keep Congress informed on developments with respect to the efforts of other NATO powers to build up their armed strength, and advanced various suggestions to further endeavors in this regard.

While the "Great Debate" of 1951 did not result in a direct congressional challenge to the President's authority to make such dispositions of United States military forces as he deems to be in the best interest of American security, it nevertheless had important results and repercussions. For one thing, it brought about a thorough airing of the constitutional and foreign policy issues involved and thus contributed to a better understanding of them in Congress and among the citizens. An indirect result may well have been the placing of General Eisenhower, rather than Senator Robert A. Taft of Ohio, in the presidency in 1953. Senator Taft had been one of 13 senators who had voted against approval of the North Atlantic Treaty in 1949. The negative attitude displayed by him toward the underlying idea of NATO and his rigid insistence that Congress, rather than the President, should be responsible for making the ultimate decisions on how military forces of the United States should be deployed and used under NATO were decisive factors in causing General Eisenhower to revise his thinking about his own availability for the Republican nomination in 1952.[30] Another of its long-range effects has undoubtedly been to induce Presidents since that time to collaborate more closely with Congress in their handling of international crises and to obtain congressional concurrence in the use of force when that has seemed necessary. The Formosa, Middle East, and North Vietnam Resolutions[31] are tangible evidence that the Presidents concerned have learned this lesson well.

ACQUISITION AND GOVERNMENT OF CONQUERED TERRITORY

Military operations abroad have sometimes resulted in bringing under American control portions of the territory of foreign countries. When this occurs the President's position as Commander-in-Chief permits him to take whatever measures he thinks necessary to insure and well-being of the American occupying forces and of the people of the occupied area. This may involve taking over entirely the government of the area under military control. During and after the Mexican War, the Spanish-American War, World War I, and World War II, in particular, the United States found itself confronted by this kind of

[30] During the early stages of the debate, according to General Eisenhower, a senator whom he does not identify came to his office secretly and endeavored to enlist his aid in the cause of trying to rebuke President Truman for his actions. He goes on to say: "I was resentful toward those who seemed to me to be playing politics in matters I thought vital to America and the Free World. . . . I finally concluded that it might be more effective to keep some aura of mystery around my future personal plans. For the moment I decided to remain silent, not to declare myself out as a potential political factor, and went off to Europe." Cf. his *Mandate for Change, 1953–1956*, p. 14. For his account of the steps leading up to his actual decision to declare himself available as a candidate see *ibid.*, pp. 16ff.

[31] Chap. 15, pp. 515–517.

situation. The Supreme Court has conceded that the President's authority as Commander-in-Chief to adopt and carry out measures he deems necessary and expedient in an occupied region becomes practically absolute, subject only to the vaguely defined international "laws of war." He may legislate by decree, establish forms of government which may or may not take into account previously established governmental institutions in the area, supervise the administration of justice, impose taxes, requisition property, etc., all without interference by Congress.[32]

The President's authority to provide for the government of occupied territory stops short of power to annex it to the United States permanently, however. Permanent acquisition of new territory is a step that requires participation by Congress in some manner.[33] This is normally achieved through approval of a treaty of cession, a treaty defining the conditions for restoration of peace, or adoption of legislation by Congress governing the point. After new territory has come into possession of the United States, Congress may permit military government to continue to exist indefinitely in some form therein pending establishment by law of a regime of civil government under the power delegated to Congress by Article IV of the Constitution to "make all needful rules and regulations respecting the territory or other property belonging to the United States."

Speaking of the relationship between congressional and presiden-

[32] Cf. Rossiter, *The Supreme Court and the Commander-in-Chief*, pp. 120–125 and cases cited. See also Glendon A. Schubert, *The Presidency in the Courts* (Minneapolis: University of Minnesota Press, 1957), pp. 191–199, and Charles Fairman, "Some Observations on Military Occupation," *Minnesota Law Review*, Vol. 32 (March, 1948), pp. 319–348.

[33] *Fleming* v. *Page*, 9 Howard 603 (1850); *Jones* v. *United States*, 137 U.S. 202 (1890). In *American Insurance Co.* v. *Canter*, 1 Peters 511 (1828), Chief Justice Marshall had declared for the Court that the United States government possesses authority under the Constitution to acquire new territory by virtue of its power to make war and to enter into treaties. This question had given President Jefferson, with his views on strict construction of the Constitution, same qualms when he negotiated the Louisiana Purchase Treaty in 1803. On the general point see Lawson Reno, "The Power of the President to Acquire and Govern Territory," *George Washington Law Review*, Vol. 9 (January, 1941), pp. 251–285.

The well-known "destroyer deal" of 1940, in which President Roosevelt entered into an executive agreement with Great Britain providing that in return for some 50 obsolescent destroyers and patrol vessels the United States should acquire 99-year leases on a number of sites for military bases on British possessions in the western Atlantic, did not result in a transfer of sovereignty over the sites. Edward S. Corwin, in *The President: Office and Powers 1787–1957*, 4th ed. (New York: New York University Press, 1957), p. 238, criticizes Attorney General Jackson's opinion upholding the legality of the President's action as unsound on the ground that he construed the power of the President to "dispose" the armed forces into a power to "dispose of" them. The Attorney General's opinion actually sought to justify the President's action on the basis of statutes which authorized him to "dispose of" obsolete military equipment. Cf. 39 *Ops. Atty. Gen.* 484, 489 (1940). In any event, subsequent authorizations of appropriations by Congress to set up the bases had the effect of impliedly ratifying the President's agreement.

tial power in providing a government for recently acquired territory, the Supreme Court declared in *Santiago* v. *Nogueras:*

> The civil government of the United States cannot extend immediately and of its own force over conquered and ceded territory. Theoretically, Congress might prepare and enact a scheme of civil government to take effect immediately upon the cession, but, practically, there always have been delays and always will be. Time is required for a study of the situation and for maturing and enacting of an adequate scheme of civil government. In the meantime, pending the action of Congress, there is no civil power under our system of government, not even that of the President as civil executive, which can take the place of the government which has ceased to exist by the cession. . . . Is it possible that, under such circumstances, there must be an interregnum? We think clearly not. The authority to govern such ceded territory is found in the laws applicable to conquest and cession. That authority is the military power, under the control of the President as Commander-in-Chief.[34]

The situation brought about by the Civil War, as areas formerly under control of the Confederate government fell under the sway of Union military forces, was unprecedented and gave rise to a host of constitutional and political problems. Acting on the theory that the southern states had never actually ceased to be members of the Union, Presidents Lincoln and Johnson proceeded to set up temporary military governments for the reoccupied areas under their powers as Commander-in-Chief. Subsequently they took appropriate steps to permit the loyal elements in the population to re-establish civil rule through state and local governments based upon revised state constitutions. The Radical Republican element in Congress viewed the matter in a different light. Adopting the theory that the states that had attempted to secede had committed "state suicide" or at any rate had forfeited their right to be treated as states under the Constitution, they likened them to "conquered provinces." After the war they insisted on enacting legislation over President Johnson's veto setting up a form of military government over the ex-Confederate states. As new civil governments were ultimately organized in each state in accordance with the conditions laid down by Congress, military government was to be terminated and the states were to be restored to full status as members of the Union.

At no time during the war or later did the Supreme Court question the legality of the provisional military governments established under presidential auspices in the South. It was able, through one means or another, to avoid having to come to grips with the question of whether the military government regimes set up under the terms of Congress' Reconstruction policies were constitutional. In the well-

[34] 214 U.S. 260, 265 (1909).

known case of *Texas* v. *White*[35] it discountenanced by implication the "conquered provinces" and "state suicide" theories advanced in support of congressional policy by holding that Texas, despite its ordinance of secession which in the Court's view was unconstitutional, had never ceased to be a member of the Union. The Court went on to place its stamp of approval on the measures taken by the President on his own authority to establish provisional governments pending action by Congress; but it did not go into the question of the legality of the governments subsequently organized under the terms of congressional Reconstruction policy. It intimated, however, that they might be considered legitimate under the constitutional provision giving to the national government the responsibility of assuring to each state a "republican form of government."

GOVERNMENT OF THE ARMED FORCES

The Constitution specifically delegates to Congress the authority to pass laws for the "government of the land and naval forces" and of "such part of [the state militia] as may be employed in the service of the United States." An elaborate body of law has been built up over the years by Congress in pursuance of this authorization. But as is the case in the area of civil government generally, it has been necessary for Congress to delegate to the President in his capacity as Commander-in-Chief a broad subsidiary authority to supplement the military code with regulations of his own. The fact that the President is named as the Commander-in-Chief by the Constitution, moreover, implies that he has an authority in his own right to promulgate regulations for the armed services, at least insofar as they do not conflict with congressionally established rules.

During the Civil War President Lincoln ordered into effect a comprehensive body of regulations prepared by General Lieber in the Adjutant General's office which became the basis upon which military regulations thereafter were elaborated and revised. As Commander-in-Chief the President becomes the ultimate administrative authority in supervising the enforcement of the code of military regulations thus formulated in collaboration with Congress. For example, the military code now provides that a sentence of death or any sentence involving a general or flag officer pursuant to a court-martial must be approved by the President before it can be carried into execution. His power to grant clemency in cases of offenses against the code as found through

---

[35] 7 Wallace 700 (1869). For other cases upholding the President's authority to set up temporary governments in the southern states following occupation by Union forces see *The Grapeshot,* 9 Wallace 129 (1869) and *Mechanics Bank* v. *Union Bank,* 22 Wallace 276 (1874).

court-martial procedures is covered by his constitutional authority to pardon offenses against the United States generally, as well as by his functions as Commander-in-Chief.[36]

MILITARY POWER AND INDIVIDUAL RIGHTS

Exercise of the war power exposes the American system of constitutionally guaranteed individual rights to perhaps its severest tests. Resort to military measures represents the ultimate in appeal to force. It is an exertion of the right of self-preservation by society itself. The law of necessity is its measure. Judicial pronouncements on the extent to which the constitutional guarantees of individual rights operate as a check upon the military have usually concerned actions having their basis originally in legislation. They have thus more commonly raised the issue of the scope of the war power as employed by the political branches of government acting in concert, rather than the question of the scope of the chief executive's authority alone in his capacity as Commander-in-Chief. Nevertheless, they have contributed in some degree to delineation of the contours of the chief executive's role when he relies upon the commander-in-chief clause as the source of his authority.

SUSPENSION OF THE WRIT OF HABEAS CORPUS

Among the rights and guarantees of individuals spelled out in the Constitution as against the national government, only two are recognized as suspendable or inapplicable under certain circumstances. Article 1, Section 9, declares that the privilege of the writ of habeas corpus—the right to invoke judicial examination into the legality of one's detention by officers of the government—may not be suspended "unless in cases of rebellion or invasion the public safety may require it." Amendment V in the Bill of Rights specifically exempts "cases arising in the land or naval forces, or in the militia when in actual service in time of war or public danger" from its guarantee that all prosecutions for capital or otherwise infamous crimes must be initiated by a grand jury indictment. Both have relevance to governmental actions involving the military. The one permits arrests and detentions of civilians by the military in time of public danger without interference by the civil courts; the other implies that a system for administration of justice distinct from that provided for civilians may be set

---

[36] For an analysis of Supreme Court cases bearing upon the President's powers in these respects, see Rossiter, *The Supreme Court and the Commander-in-Chief* pp. 102–109; and Corwin, *op. cit.*, pp. 260–261.

up to cover persons in military service. These exceptions are further interrelated in that when the civil processes of government are superseded by a regime of martial law, administration of justice for civilians may be placed in the hands of military courts or commissions operating independently of the regular system of courts.

So far as the writ of habeas corpus guarantee is concerned, the Constitution is notably silent on where the responsibility lies—with Congress, the President, or the courts—to determine when and where an exigency has arisen justifying its suspension. The placement of the clause itself in the Constitution in the section immediately following one that lists most of the delegated powers of Congress suggests that it is directed toward the Congress, rather than the other branches of government. This would imply that it was intended that Congress, rather than the President, should declare when circumstances have arisen warranting suspension of the privilege. Answers given to this question during the course of the Civil War, however, went far toward demonstrating that the President on his own authority as chief executive and Commander-in-Chief shares power with Congress in this regard.

Immediately after the outbreak of hostilities President Lincoln assumed the responsibility of authorizing General Scott, the commanding general of the Army, personally, or through any officer under him, to suspend the writ at any point on or in the vicinity of any military line between Philadelphia and Washington. Later this authorization was extended to cover the line between New York and Washington.[37] A Maryland secessionist sympathizer, John Merryman, who had made himself a danger to the Union cause by attempting to arouse the citizenry in Baltimore to violent resistance against the moving of Union forces through the city, was apprehended by the military and placed in custody at Fort McHenry. Merryman immediately appealed to Chief Justice Taney, who as a member of the Supreme Court was empowered by law to entertain a petition for a writ of habeas corpus, for a hearing on the propriety of his detention. The Chief Justice issued the writ, but the officer to whom it was directed, citing the President's order, refused to produce the prisoner for a hearing. Taney thereupon delivered an opinion holding the President's action authorizing the suspension of the writ to be void on the ground that only Congress could suspend it.[38] The President ignored the ruling. After a time Merryman was turned over to the civil authorities and indicted for treason, but he was eventually released.

When Congress assembled on July 4 soon after this incident, President Lincoln in his message to it defended the course he had fol-

[37] Richardson, *Messages and Papers of the Presidents*, Vol. VI, pp. 18, 19.
[38] *Ex parte Merryman*, 17 Fed. Cases 144 (1861), No. 9487.

lowed. Posing the query, "Are all the laws *but one* to go unexecuted, and the Government itself go to pieces lest that one be violated?", he went on to say:

> Now it is insisted that Congress, and not the Executive, is vested with this power [to suspend the writ]; but the Constitution itself is silent as to which or who is to exercise the power; and as the provision was plainly made for a dangerous emergency, it cannot be believed the framers of the instrument intended that in every case the danger should run its course until Congress could be called together, the very assembling of which might be prevented, as was intended in this case, by the rebellion.
>
> . . . Whether there shall be any legislation on the subject, and, if any, what, is submitted entirely to the better judgment of Congress.[39]

The next day Attorney General Bates delivered an opinion holding that, in his view, the President shared with Congress the power to suspend the writ. His argument followed generally the line of the necessities of the case, as outlined in Lincoln's message.[40] Congress did nothing on the matter immediately; but eventually in 1863 it passed an act authorizing the suspension of the writ in all cases and areas where the public safety might require it. Several months before Congress acted President Lincoln had already issued a comprehensive proclamation on the subject declaring the writ to be suspended as to "all rebels and insurgents, their aiders and abettors, within the United States, and all persons discouraging volunteer enlistments, resisting militia drafts, or guilty of any disloyal practice affording aid and comfort to rebels against the authority of the United States."[41] After Congress had passed the Habeas Corpus Act of 1863 he issued a second proclamation of the same import, citing the Act as the basis of his authority to do so.[42]

The question whether the President might on his own authority suspend the writ was never faced and definitively answered by the Supreme Court as a whole during the Civil War. Numerous military arrests and detentions of civilians, including various members of the Maryland state legislature and officials of the city of Baltimore, were made during the course of the war. They were held in prison, with no attempt being made to charge them and bring them to trial. When the House of Representatives adopted a resolution requesting information as to the grounds upon which the police commissioners of Baltimore were being held, President Lincoln refused to comply. His refusal

[39] Richardson, *op. cit.*, Vol. VI, p. 25.

[40] 10 *Ops. Attys. Gen.* 74 (1861). Bates neatly turned the tables on Chief Justice Taney by citing him as Attorney General for support on the proposition that each of the three departments of government is obligated, where its own powers are concerned, to apply the view of the Constitution it believes proper.

[41] Richardson, *op. cit.*, Vol. VI, p. 98. Proclamation of September 24, 1862.

[42] *Ibid.*, p. 170. Proclamation of September 15, 1863.

was couched in the usual terminology—that it would be "incompatible with the public interest" for him to do so. A number of lower federal and state court rulings on the point were made, some of which challenged the President's right to act independently of Congress, but none of the adverse rulings was appealed by the Department of Justice to the Supreme Court. Subsequent pronouncements by the Court on the question of suspension of the writ of habeas corpus came in cases involving the broader issue of subjection of civilians to martial law and their trial by military courts. Consequently they did not directly pose the question of whether Congress or the President was invested with the power to determine when it might be suspended.

TRIAL OF CIVILIANS BY MILITARY COURTS

Suspension of the writ of habeas corpus merely makes possible military arrests and detentions without interference by the regular courts. A more serious question of possible violation of constitutional guarantees of individual rights arises when civilians are subjected to trial before military tribunals, rather than before the regular courts, without proper regard for all the procedural guarantees spelled out in the Constitution. Again it was the Civil War that provided the most noteworthy controversies on this point. In his proclamation of September 24, 1862, in which President Lincoln suspended the privilege of the writ of habeas corpus throughout the North with respect to individuals interfering with the war effort, he also declared that such offenders "shall be subject to martial law and liable to trial and punishment by courts-martial or military commissions." In American practice this was an unprecedented extension of the principle of subjecting civilians to military justice. It meant that such offenders, whether or not their acts occurred in the immediate vicinity of military action, and whether or not the regular courts were open and available to hear their cases, were made liable for trial and punishment in a judicial forum differing in material respects from that prescribed by the Constitution.

The first opportunity the Supreme Court had to rule on the constitutionality of this procedure came about when former Representative Clement C. Vallandigham of Ohio, a "Peace Democrat" who had been outspoken in his opposition to the war and to measures for its prosecution, was tried before a military commission. He was sentenced to be imprisoned for the duration of the war. He sought a review of his conviction through a writ of certiorari directed to the Supreme Court. Taking refuge in the technical point that its appellate jurisdiction under this mode of appeal did not extend to review of the judgment of a military commission, since the commission was not a "court" within the meaning of the constitutional language and statutes defining its appellate jurisdiction, the Court held that it had no jurisdiction over the case.[43] President Lincoln, who was somewhat embarrassed by the affair, in a semi-humorous gesture had already commuted Vallandigham's sentence to banishment behind the Confederate lines, and the "traitor" had been turned over to Confederate authorities under a flag of truce.[44] Soon afterwards Vallandigham made his way to Canada. While still in exile there, he was nominated in 1864 as the Democratic party's candidate for governor of Ohio. He failed to win election, although he made a respectable showing of political support.

A different result followed the second attempt to bring before the Supreme Court the matter of the validity of military trials of civilians. Lambdin P. Milligan, an Indiana citizen who had actively collaborated with Confederate military authorities in planning and executing a raid across the Ohio River during the late stages of the war, was arrested by the military in October, 1864, and put on trial before a military commission. He was found guilty by it on May 9, 1865, and sentenced to be hanged. The sentence was approved by President Johnson. Taking cognizance of the fact that the regular federal courts in Indiana were open and citing provisions in the Habeas Corpus Act of 1863 which authorized United States circuit and district courts to intervene in cases of military arrests under certain circumstances, Milligan's attorneys sought a review of his case through a writ of habeas corpus before the appropriate United States circuit court. That body was evenly divided on whether it should entertain the petition for the writ in view of the President's suspension order, and on how it should dispose of the case if the writ were granted. The issue came on to the Supreme Court for determination.

In 1866, about a year after the fighting phase of the Civil War had ended, the Court held unanimously that under the circumstances the writ should be issued, and that upon a return to it, Milligan should be released from military custody. His subjection to trial before a military commission, said the Court, violated the guarantees of trial before a civil court and the attendant procedural rights for the protection of the accused spelled out in Amendments V and VI of the Constitution.[45] The opinion for the Court, given by Justice Davis, a Union Democrat appointed to the bench by President Lincoln and a close personal friend of his, spared nothing in its condemnation of the idea that the President possesses power in his own right to institute military commissions for trial of civilians in areas where the regular courts are open

---

[43] *Ex parte Vallandigham,* 1 Wallace 243 (1864).

[44] For a full account of the incident see Carl Sandburg, *Abraham Lincoln: The War Years* (New York: Harcourt, Brace & World, 4 vols., 1939), Vol. II, pp. 161–165.

[45] *Ex parte Milligan,* 4 Wallace 2 (1866). Before the Supreme Court made its ruling Milligan's sentence had been commuted by President Johnson to life imprisonment.

and functioning. On the question whether in any circumstances this might be done if authorized by Congress, the Court was divided. Four of its members, including Chief Justice Chase, were unwilling to go so far as to hold that Congress could not authorize suspension of the writ under certain conditions even though the regular courts were open.

The importance of this case in setting a limit on the President's authority, unilaterally, to substitute military trials of civilians for proceedings in the regular courts is undoubtedly very great. It stands as a monument dedicated to the proposition that the presidential war power is not unlimited and that under the American system of government the military is subordinate to the civil authority. Its psychological and political impact has been profound. During World War I, when Assistant Attorney General Charles Warren advanced the idea that Congress should enact legislation subjecting to summary military trial persons charged with a variety of offenses involving attempted interference with the war effort, President Wilson announced his unalterable opposition to such legislation. He condemned it as "unconstitutional," "unnecessary," and "inconsistent with the spirit and practice of America."[46] The bill embodying the idea was withdrawn from consideration in Congress.

While the Milligan case is an important landmark in the evolution of constitutional principles relevant to presidential power, the practical aspects of the matter should not be overlooked. It was a pronouncement that came *after* the emergency was over. In some respects the majority opinion undoubtedly went too far in attempting to draw the line defining the limits of the war powers of the President and Congress in dealing with the kind of internal security situation presented by war. As a footnote to it, it should be pointed out that the assassins of President Lincoln were ordered to be tried before a special military commission. After the sentence condemning four of them to death was pronounced, President Johnson by specific order suspended the writ of habeas corpus as to the one woman defendant involved, thereby scotching a last-minute move to bring about a review of her case before a civil court. The state of public opinion at the time would hardly have countenanced judicial interference with the conclusions of the military commission, whatever the legal proprieties may have been. For that reason it is well to bear in mind that what was done *during* the conflict when tension was high may be a safer guide to what may occur in the future than what the Court said in calmer times when public opinion against would-be saboteurs of the nation's war measures was not running so high.

Since the Civil War the Supreme Court has made other rulings

[46] *The New York Times*, April 23, 1918. The incident is fully discussed in Carl B. Swisher *American Constitutional Development* (Boston: Houghton Mifflin Company, 2nd ed., 1954), pp. 615–619.

extending to civilians the constitutional protections of trial before the regular courts, rather than permitting them to be tried by courts-martial. In 1915 the Court held unconstitutional a provision of the 1950 Uniform Code of Military Justice that extended the jurisdiction of courts-martial to cover more serious criminal offenses committed by persons while in military service, *after* they had been honorably discharged therefrom and had assumed civilian status.[47] The Uniform Code also made subject to trial by court-martial "all persons serving with, employed by, or accompanying the armed forces without the continental limits of the United States." In a series of cases arising under this provision, as implemented through various Status of Forces agreements negotiated by the President with foreign countries in which American forces were stationed after World War II, the Court held it to be invalid as applied to civilian dependents and employees accused of committing offenses against other Americans. They were entitled to be tried in a regular court, with due respect being given to the procedural protections afforded by the Constitution to persons accused of crimes.[48] Inasmuch as these cases involved implementation of laws enacted by Congress, they were not so much rebukes to the exercise of military powers by the President as they were limitations upon the authority of Congress to legislate to this effect.

So far as enemy aliens and members of the armed forces of enemy powers are concerned, the Supreme Court has shown less concern about their subjection to military trial and punishment. Enemy aliens who penetrate our lines in an effort to commit sabotage may be tried and condemned to death by a special military commission set up by presidential order, as may also captured members of enemy armed forces accused of war crimes.[49] So long as the Court is satisfied that the military commissions set up to try them have jurisdiction under the laws of war, the Court will not inquire into the conformity of their proceedings to the requirements of due process of law. It likewise has

[47] *United States ex rel Toth* v. *Quarles,* 350 U.S. 11 (1955). The case arose when Army authorities sought to have Toth, who had been honorably discharged, returned to Korea to stand trial before a court-martial on a charge of murder committed while he was in the service. In an earlier case, *United States ex rel Hirschberg* v. *Cooke,* 336 U.S. 210 (1949), the Court had ruled that an enlisted Navy serviceman who had been honorably discharged with the expiration of his enlistment and who had then re-enlisted immediately could not be subjected to a court-martial trial for an offense that had occurred during his first enlistment. The honorable discharge and his assumption of civilian status for a time, however short, had the effect of barring his trial for the earlier offense by a court-martial.

[48] *Reid* v. *Covert* and *Kinsella* v. *Kreuger* 354 U.S. 1 (1957); *Kinsella* v. *United States ex rel Singleton,* 361 U.S. 234 (1960); *Grisham* v. *Hagan,* 361 U.S. 278 (1960) and companion cases.

[49] *Ex parte Quirin* (The Nazi Saboteurs' Cases), 317 U.S. 1 (1942); *In re Yamashita,* 327 U.S. 1 (1946); *Homma* v. *Patterson,* 327 U.S. 759 (1946); *Hirota* v. *McArthur,* 335 U.S. 876 (1948); *Milch* v. *United States,* 332 U.S. 789 (1947).

refused to look into the procedures employed by such military courts in the trial of enemy aliens for crimes committed outside the United States against the military security of this nation.[50] In short, in time of war the Constitution does not follow the flag abroad as to such persons, even though our military power may be exerted there.

MARTIAL LAW

The ultimate stage in displacement of civil government by military rule is reached when a state of "martial law" is proclaimed by the chief executive. Such displacement may be absolute, or it may be limited. For example, the subjection of certain types of offenders to military arrests and subsequent trial and punishment by military commissions in accordance with President Lincoln's proclamation of September 24, 1862, as described above, constituted a form of limited martial law. Later, on July 5, 1864, he issued a more far-reaching proclamation putting the entire State of Kentucky under martial law;[51] but even in this case the condition resulting was something less than one of total, or absolute, martial law. The regime of martial law, as stated by the terms of the proclamation, was not to be deemed an interference with the holding of lawful elections, or with the proceedings of the constitutional legislature of Kentucky, or with the administration of justice in any proceedings which did not affect the military operations or the functioning of the constituted authorities of the United States government. Lincoln's invocation of the laws of war in connection with his efforts to subdue the rebellion in the southern states by a blockade, which the Supreme Court held to be legal in the *Prize* cases,[52] could be regarded as having the effect of placing under a state of total martial law those areas of the country under domination of the insurgents. As these areas were occupied by Union forces they could accordingly be regarded as temporarily subject to control by the military for all governmental purposes.

The place that martial law occupies in the American scheme of government is a problem that has given the courts much difficulty. On the one hand the theory has been advanced that martial law is unknown to the common law. Under the Constitution no such thing as martial law is or can be recognized, it is contended, since that term is not mentioned therein. It is simply a regime of no law, based on naked force. On the other hand the idea is suggested that martial law is implicitly recognized by the very existence of an organized government.

---

[50] *Johnson* v. *Eisentrager,* 339 U.S. 763 (1950).
[51] Richardson, *op. cit.,* Vol. VI, p. 219. The proclamation was rescinded by President Johnson on October 12, 1865, *ibid.,* p. 331.
[52] 2 Black 635 (1863).

Martial law rests ultimately on the will of the constituted governmental authorities, according to this view. It is an extreme measure put into execution by the chief executive in his capacity as Commander-in-Chief. The will and purposes of the state are carried out temporarily by lawful military force, rather than through normal channels. It is abnormal but none the less legitimate government.

The Supreme Court first encountered this question in the case of *Luther* v. *Borden*,[53] growing out of the Dorr Rebellion in Rhode Island. The immediate issue was whether Borden, a member of the state militia, was liable for damages through a trespass suit brought by a citizen whose house was forcibly entered by the militiaman. Borden set up in his defense that he was acting under orders of his superiors as a member of the militia following a proclamation of martial law. Chief Justice Taney, speaking for the Court, upheld Borden's contention. The court found that the lawfully recognized state authorities had not violated any rights protected by the Constitution in declaring what amounted to a "state of war" and therefore could resort to the "rights and usages of war." An appeal to military force to vindicate the authority of a lawfully constituted government was itself lawful, provided "no more force . . . [is] used than is necessary to accomplish the object." In other words, martial law is no less law because it is justified by the necessities of the situation.

Several questions are implicit in this earliest pronouncement by the Court on the subject of martial law. Who is competent to declare martial law? What limits, if any, are there on the discretion of the agency entrusted with this responsibility with regard to when and in what measure a regime of martial rule shall supplant the regular processes of government? How is a regime of martial law to be distinguished from other extraordinary measures in law enforcement which may involve use of military force? Answers given by the courts have helped in some measure to clarify these points, but this remains one of the areas involving the executive authorities of the nation and the states directly wherein the paths of the law are marked only dimly, if at all.

Who may declare martial law? The presumption is that unless otherwise provided this is an executive function growing out of the chief executive's responsibility to execute the laws, coupled with his powers as Commander-in-Chief of the armed forces. Some state constitutions deal explicitly with this matter either by recognizing this as being within the governor's responsibility or by authorzing or directing the legislature to enact implementing legislation on the subject. Martial law in the sense of unrestricted military power over civilians and their

[53] 7 Howard 1 (1849).

property is forbidden altogether in a few states. Other state constitutions reserve to the legislature itself the exclusive power to determine whether resort to martial law is necessary or limit punishments under it to persons in active military service. Practically all
declarations of martial law since the Civil War—and there have been
many—have been made by governors of states in which civil disturbances or natural disasters have required extraordinary measures to
preserve law and order.[54]

Since the Civil War era there have been no proclamations of martial law by Presidents directly on behalf of the national government,
although President Hayes very seriously considered issuing such a
proclamation during the railroad strike crisis of 1877. There have been
conditions of limited martial law established with the explicit or implied approval of the President by officers in the field, however. It is interesting to note that one of the first, if not the first, instances of
establishment of martial law by an agent of the national government
occurred through act of a commanding general in the field. This was
in 1814, when, just before the Battle of New Orleans in which he was
to win immortal glory as a war hero, General Andrew Jackson proclaimed martial law in that city. His authority to do so was questioned
in the federal district court in that area, and when Jackson ignored
a writ of habeas corpus issued on behalf of a citizen being held for
trial by court-martial for violating regulations established by his orders,
the court fined the General $1000 and costs for contempt.[55] (He paid
the fine, but 30 years later Congress reimbursed him for the amount
of the fine, plus accrued interest. The aged ex-President, who was in
financial straits at the time, accepted the grant gratefully.)

There have been other instances of declarations of limited martial
law by federal military commanders in the field. For example, Briga-
dier General H. C. Merriam, in command of federal troops dispatched
to Idaho in 1899 during the Coeur d'Alene labor troubles, took it
upon himself to declare a state of limited martial law. President
McKinley approved his order.[56] General Leonard Wood on two occasions in 1919 on his own authority declared a state of limited martial
law—once while in command of federal troops at Omaha, Nebraska,
during a race riot and the other time at Gary, Indiana, during a strike.[57]

On the second question mentioned above, the courts have spoken

[54] A review of several recent incidents involving the use of state militia in
connection with labor disputes is given in Robert S. Rankin and Winfried R. Dallmayr, *Freedom and Emergency Power in the Cold War* (New York: Appleton-
Century-Crofts, 1964), pp. 172–187.

[55] For an account of the affair see James, *op. cit.*, pp. 211, 260, 262, 760.

[56] Bennett M. Rich, *The Presidents and Civil Disorders* (Washington: The
Brookings Institution, 1941), pp. 114, 119.

[57] *Ibid.*, p. 210.

on occasion, but the very nature of the problem—drawing a conclusion on whether the degree of military force employed is justified by the facts of the situation—makes judicial second-guessing of chief executives who have had to take immediate responsibility a dubious kind of adventuring. It should be noted that in most of the instances in which courts have overruled the judgment of Presidents or governors on the necessity of the military measures they had taken, the rulings came after the emergency had passed and it was safe to indulge in the luxury of making hindsight evaluations. This was certainly true in the *Milligan* case, when the Supreme Court found that the particular kind of martial law procedure involved violated constitutional limitations. A similar observation may be made concerning the *Hawaiian Martial Law* cases[58] of World War II. In these cases the Court held that the organic act setting up the Hawaiian Territorial Government which authorized the governor of the Territory, subject to the approval of the President, to declare martial law in the event of actual or threaened rebellion or invasion, was not intended to authorize supplanting the regular civil courts by military tribunals when the former were actually open and functioning. A regime of total martial law had been proclaimed by the territorial governor immediately after Pearl Harbor, and it had been retained in somewhat relaxed degree throughout the war. A strong dissent was registered by Justices Frankfurter and Burton to the Court's setting a precedent which might deter chief executives in the future from taking the measures they deem necessary to meet an emergency in the light of the circumstances as they evaluate them at the time. They insisted that conditions in 1946 when the Court rendered its decision should not be the Court's criterion for judgment on the situation as it existed in Hawaii in 1942 and 1943.

Pronouncements by the Supreme Court in cases raising the issue of judicial review of resort to martial law by state governors also reveal a stiffening of the Court's attitude in more recent years from the hands-off approach implicit in the 1849 *Luther* v. *Borden* ruling. In *Moyer* v. *Peabody*,[59] a case decided in 1909, the Court took the position that no constitutional limitations were violated when the governor of Colorado instituted martial law during the course of a strike and then ordered the arrest and detention of one of the strike leaders pending the restoration of order. Justice Holmes, giving the opinion of the Court, declared:

> So long as such arrests are made in good faith and in the honest belief that they are needed in order to head the insurrection off, the Governor is the final judge and cannot be subjected to an action after he is out of office on the ground that he had not reasonable ground for

58 *Duncan* v. *Kahanamoku* and *White* v. *Steer*, 327 U.S. 304 (1946).
59 212 U.S. 78 (1909).

his belief. . . . When it comes to a decision by the head of the State upon a matter involving its life, the ordinary rights of individuals must yield to what he deems the necessities of the moment. Public danger warrants the substitution of executive process for judicial process.

But in the later 1932 case of *Sterling* v. *Constantin*,[60] the Court affirmed a ruling of a three-judge federal district court granting an injunction against continuance of a state of martial law proclaimed by Governor Ross Sterling in the East Texas oil fields. There was no actual state of riot or lawlessness in the area, the Court concluded. The governor's purpose in resorting to martial law was actually to shut down oil production pending settlement of a controversy about the state's economic regulatory policy. The governor's action was held to violate property rights protected by the Fourteenth Amendment. This case, along with the later *Hawaiian Martial Law* cases, reinforces the Court's holding in the *Milligan* case that judgments of chief executives in establishing martial law will not necessarily be regarded as "political" questions lying entirely outside the purview of judicial examination.

A third question presented by resort to military force in maintaining public order is whether there results, in fact, a state of martial law, "unlimited," "qualified," "partial," or otherwise. Mere use of troops as an adjunct to the regular civil police authority in an area does not, per se, create a state of martial law. They may be used simply as an auxiliary police force, supplementing the regular civil law enforcement authorities in an area. With the development in recent decades of an ever-expanding body of legislation conferring power upon chief executives at both the national and state levels to take extraordinary steps during a state of "emergency," "limited emergency," "hostilities," "war," or some other kind of unusual situation, the distinction between measures based upon martial law and those regarded as statutorily authorized emergency actions has become blurred. The use of troops in maintaining order, whether martial law has been declared or not, frequently necessitates emergency regulations on such matters as curfews, the closing of places of amusement, restriction of popular assemblies, surrender of arms, and similar measures related to the public order.

An illustration of what may be done through the military, short of declaring a state of martial law, is afforded by the Japanese evacuation program of World War II. On February 19, 1942, President Roosevelt, in response to a great deal of pressure from military, congressional, and other sources, issued Executive Order No. 9066.

---

[60] 287 U.S. 378 (1932). The events leading up to the ruling are described in detail in Warner E. Mills, Jr., *Martial Law in East Texas*, Inter-University Cases Program, No. 53 (University, Ala.: University of Alabama Press, 1951).

It authorized the Secretary of War and military commanders whom the former might designate to establish "military areas" from which any persons deemed dangerous were to be excluded, expelled, or restricted, in order to prevent espionage and sabotage. The order was actually aimed at persons of Japanese descent, largely congregated in the Pacific Coast states. Congress gave approval to the order by legislation passed on March 21, 1942, and provided criminal punishments in the regular courts for violations of regulations thus established. There followed the deplorable Japanese evacuation and relocation operation in which some 112,000 persons, of whom some 70,000 were American citizens, were removed from the Pacific Coast states. Those found to be loyal were ultimately resettled at various points in the interior. The operation was carried out under supervision of the military, for the ostensible protection of our military security. There was no effective interference by the courts.[61] Yet this extraordinary action did not rest upon an establishment of martial law.

In the event of involvement of the United States in all-out war in the future, in view of the complex body of national and state civil defense and war mobilization legislation now on the statute books and the precedents already at hand, extraordinary action taken would no doubt amount to the establishment of a military police state— though it might be called by some other name.[62]

SEIZURES OF PROPERTY

The emergency of war inevitably results in more or less extensive infringements upon private property rights. Under long-established international usages, the property of the enemy becomes subject to confiscation under certain circumstances. This right of seizure extends to the property of enemy aliens located within the territorial boundaries of the nation at war. Trade by neutrals with an enemy power

---

[61] In *Hirabayashi* v. *United States*, 320 U.S. 81 (1943), the Supreme Court upheld the validity of a curfew regulation set up for Japanese-Americans by the military in the earlier stage of the evacuation program. In *Korematsu* v. *United States*, 323 U.S. 214 (1944) it sustained the conviction of a Japanese-American citizen for violation of the evacuation regulations. Justice Black, who has since achieved fame as the Court's leading defender of civil liberties, gave the majority opinion for the Court. In *Ex parte Endo*, 323 U.S. 283 (1944), decided at the same time as the *Korematsu* case, the Court ruled that a Japanese-American citizen who had been found to be loyal could not be held indefinitely under detention and was entitled to be released by the War Relocation Authority charged with the administration of this phase of the program. For a discussion of this episode in the history of American civil liberties see Rossiter, *The Supreme Court and the Commander-in-Chief*, pp. 40–54; Schubert, *op. cit.*, pp. 210–220; and Morton Grodzins, *Americans Betrayed* (Chicago: University of Chicago Press, 1949).

[62] Cf. Rankin and Dallmayr, *op. cit.*, Chap. 2; and Schubert, *op. cit.*, Chaps. 6, 7 and 8 for detailed discussion of the impact of war emergencies upon presidential powers over home-front affairs generally.

may be interdicted and property thus seized confiscated under certain conditions. Neutral property within the jurisdiction of the warring nation may be requisitioned, with proper remuneration being made, if it is vital to prosecution of the war. The Constitution recognizes that property of American citizens may be taken for public use if required, subject to the rule that just compensation be rendered. Restraints upon private enterprise not usual in peacetime may be instituted, having the effect of limiting rights of property to a degree that materially affects its value.

Generally speaking, Congress through its expressly delegated authority to "make rules concerning captures on land and sea" and its implied powers to legislate for the waging of war has sought to regulate the manner and extent to which private property shall be dealt with during a war emergency. Since the Civil War a long succession of statutes has been passed authorizing the President to make seizures of private property in specified types of situations. For example, in 1916, before our entry into World War I, Congress passed legislation authorizing the President in time of war to seize any system of transportation deemed vital to prosecution of war. Under this authorization the nation's railroads were placed under governmental control by executive order in 1917 and remained in this status until 1920, when they were returned to private operation. Similar legislation was passed in 1918 authorizing the President to take over any telegraph or telephone system. Telegraph and telephone systems were placed under governmental operation by presidential order immediately and eventually cable lines were included. During World War II the War Labor Disputes Act of 1943 permitted governmental seizure and operation of any essential industrial facility threatened with closing because of an industrial dispute. During the course of the war a number of seizures of industrial plants to avert closures because of labor-management disputes were effected under this statute. This legislation expired by its terms upon the issuance of President Truman's proclamation declaring an end to hostilities on December 31, 1946; in the Selective Service Act of 1948 and the Defense Production Act of 1950, however, statutory authorization was made for presidential seizure of facilities if they are vital to carrying on war production and the owners refuse to permit them to be used for that purpose.

In the great majority of instances where seizures of private property have been made by the President, he has acted on the basis of statutory authorizations of this kind. Generally speaking, the courts have been quite zealous in denying to the President power to seize private property, except in pursuance of laws passed by Congress. The first rebuff administered by the Supreme Court to a President was of this character. In the early case of *Little* v. *Barreme*,[63] the Court held that

---

[63] 2 Cranch 170 (1804).

seizure of an American vessel en route between two West Indian ports by an American naval ship was not covered by the Non-Intercourse Act of 1799 authorizing the interdiction of trade with France during the "quasi-war" with that country. In an ensuing private suit the captain of the naval ship set up in his defense that he was acting in accordance with presidential orders in making the seizure. The Court disallowed this defense in the light of the fact that Congress had legislated on the matter and had not authorized seizure under the particular circumstances of the case. Similarly, the strong language used by Justice Miller for the Supreme Court in condemning confiscation of Robert E. Lee's estate during the Civil War pointed out that United States government authorities were seeking to justify their possession of the property solely on the basis of a presidential order. Justice Miller's indignant rejection of this contention was based on the Court's finding that the seizure had been originally effected in a manner other than the one provided by act of Congress for the confiscation of property of persons in rebellion against the United States.[64]

The most recent rebuke administered to a President by the Supreme Court connected with the seizure of private property, the widely noted *Steel Seizure* case of 1952,[65] falls into this same general pattern. Following the breakdown of negotiations between the Steel Workers Union and the Youngstown Sheet and Tube Company, a strike was threatened. After having induced a postponement of the strike for four months, during which time the Wage Stabilization Board made recommendations for terms of settlement which the Company found unsatisfactory, President Truman ordered Secretary of Commerce Sawyer to take possession of the plant to insure the continued production of steel. Steel production was thought to be vital to prosecution of the Korean War, which was still in progress. In disallowing the seizure, Justice Black's majority opinion for the Court applied the simple formula that the seizure was not effected under sanction of Congress and therefore was invalid. The Defense Production Act of 1950 and the Selective Service Act of 1948 had no bearing on the matter. The President, moreover, had failed to make use of the cooling off procedures available under the Taft-Hartley Act, under which he might have obtained further postponement of the strike for 80 days by court injunction. When the Taft-Hartley Act was under consideration in Congress, a clause authorizing the President to effect seizures as a means of preventing plant shutdowns had been proposed, but Congress had failed to include such authorization in the Act as finally passed. All

[64] *United States* v. *Lee*, 106 U.S. 196 (1882). The property involved was later purchased from the Lee heirs by the United States government and now is the site of Arlington Cemetery and Fort Myers.

[65] *Youngstown Sheet and Tube Co.* v. *Sawyer*, 343 U.S. 579 (1952).

this being so, Justice Black went on to say, the President by his action had assumed authority to "legislate" by making the seizure, in contravention of the principle that all legislative power is vested by the Constitution in Congress.

The Court's majority opinion approach to the question of the constitutional limits upon the President's authority as chief executive and Commander-in-Chief during a national emergency has been widely criticized as being unduly rigid and unrealistic.[66] There were three dissenters to the ruling, including the Chief Justice, who wrote a vigorous opinion. In view of the fact that all five of the Justices who joined in the majority ruling wrote concurring opinions, and that at least three of them were careful to qualify their positions so as to indicate that they did not intend to hold that the President's seizure power in all instances must depend upon congressional grant, the case has less precedental authority as a denial of inherent presidential prerogative than might be supposed. Justice Jackson's concurring opinion, in which he pointed out that in some respects the President's powers in an emergency may depend upon congressional grant, that in others they may be exercised independently of congressional authorization, and in still others even in defiance of the law as expressed by Congress, is a more realistic analysis of the actual situation.

There have been a number of precedents tending to support this view. During the Civil War Lincoln effected seizures of telegraph lines on several occasions without express authorization by Congress. His Emancipation Proclamation, which went beyond existing congressional legislation and which he regarded as an exercise of his powers as Commander-in-Chief, had the effect of divesting all individuals still in rebellion against the United States as of January 1, 1863, of their property right in slaves. Without clear legislative authority to go on, President Wilson issued an executive order taking possession of a wireless station (at Siasconset, Massachusetts) that had refused to comply with naval censorship regulations. His action was supported by his Attorney General, who stressed the President's inherent authority in the conduct of foreign relations and his powers as Commander-in-Chief.[67] During the pre-World War II rearmament period President Roosevelt effected seizures of certain industries to avert stoppages by strikes, although his statutory authority to do so was highly question-

[66] Cf. E. S. Corwin, "The Steel Seizure Case: A Judicial Brick Without Straw," *Columbia Law Review*, Vol. 53 (January, 1953), pp. 53–56; John P. Roche, "Executive Power and Domestic Emergency: The Quest for Prerogative," *Western Political Quarterly*, Vol. 5 (December, 1952), pp. 592–618; and Glendon P. Schubert, Jr., "The Steel Case: Presidential Responsibility and Judicial Irresponsibility," *ibid.*, Vol. 6 (March, 1953), pp. 61–77.

[67] 30 *Ops. Atty. Gen.* 291 (1914).

able at the time.[68] The lessons of history are that Congress, by defaulting in its duty to equip the President with adequate authority by statutory grant to deal with wartime or other emergencies, cannot expect in every situation to foreclose him from taking this kind of step. If it is inescapably necessary to protect the public interest and security for the President to act he will be expected to do so, whether or not Congress has given advance clearance and authorization.

TOTAL WAR AND ITS IMPLICATIONS WITH REGARD TO THE COMMANDER-IN-CHIEF ROLE

The challenge posed by conditions of the mid-twentieth century to the traditional concepts of limited, "constitutional" government in the United States is extremely formidable. The instruments of modern warfare, based upon constantly expanding technological knowledge, are so terrifying as to be beyond the comprehension of the average person. All-out, total war today has become war by all the people. The distinction between those engaged in the active fighting and those who are noncombatants behind the front lines has disappeared for all practical purposes. The whole nation becomes a theater of war, and all are exposed to the danger of annihilation by the striking power of a potential enemy. As Commander-in-Chief the President must lead all the people, not merely those in the armed services.

Thus it is fatuous to assume that in the event of all-out war there could continue to be anything like government as usual. The nation would become a gigantic military camp. Traditional modes of governmental procedure and practice would have to give way temporarily, if not indefinitely, to a regime of practically absolute rule through executive and military authorities. What might be termed a "constitutional dictatorship" of unprecedented proportions would emerge. It would be "constitutional" in the sense that—as far as we can foresee—its inception would be orderly and in accordance with the processes of law, but governmental authority would be centered in the executive branch to a degree that would reduce the other branches to insignificance.

Two fundamental problems are raised by the threat of all-out war under present conditions. One is how to insure that necessary political

---

[68] One of the most spectacular of these seizures was the occupation of the North American Aviation plant at Los Angeles by federal troops in 1941. The plant was restored to operation by the Company within a few days, after disorders resulting from a labor dispute were quelled. Cf. Rich, *op. cit.*, Chap. XI. On the question of the President's authority to make seizures of plants essential to war production without express congressional authorization see *United States* v. *Peewee Coal Co.*, 341 U.S. 114 (1951).

decisions that run the risk of precipitating a nuclear holocaust remain in the hands of politically responsible authorities. The second is how we may assure ourselves that the decisions that have to be made in keeping our military might in a state of readiness for any challenge are made with an intelligence that comprehends all the political, social, and economic factors involved, as well as purely military considerations. This two-fold problem is undoubtedly the most crucial one facing American statesmanship in today's world. Is the presidency properly organized and equipped to meet the dual challenge?

Facets of this great underlying problem of modern American government have been brought out during the presidential campaigns of the 1950s and 1960s. Was Senator Goldwater correct in his charge that the Johnson administration was neglecting an important area of military defense by failing to plan and provide more adequately for a nuclear striking force in the form of manned bombers? Was he right in insisting that discretionary authority to use "conventional" atomic weapons be vested in field commanders under certain circumstances, rather than continuing the policy of requiring that only on direct orders of the President should such weapons be actually used? Have we achieved through the present Joint Chiefs of Staff organization and the National Security Council the most satisfactory system for coordination of decision-making to insure responsible political control over policy matters where political considerations merge with those of a purely military and strategic character? What are the strengths and weaknesses of the "military mind"? Have we too long and too much trusted, or distrusted as the case may be, the judgments of professional military men on matters affecting the military security of the nation? Have we allowed decisions in this area to be influenced too often by political considerations in the less savory sense of that term?

It is not the purpose here to offer answers to these very critical and complex problems of present-day public policy.[69] The object in raising them is merely to show that the President, by virtue of his position in the governmental scheme, has become the center around which such issues as these revolve—issues that concern the very survival of the nation and the political society to which it has given rise. To date the presidency has shown itself to be flexible, adaptable, and efficacious in discharging the various roles that have been thrust upon this remarkable part of our institutions of government. It can only be confidently predicted that in the future the President and the presidency will have even more critical importance in shaping the destiny of the nation.

[69] For a consideration of some of these questions see Huntington, *op. cit.*, and the extensive body of literature therein cited. See also Harry H. Ransom, *Can American Democracy Survive the Cold War?* (Garden City, N.Y.: Doubleday and Company, Anchor Books, 1964).

 PART FOUR

EPILOGUE

17

THE PRESIDENTIAL SYSTEM

IN PERSPECTIVE

In the presidential type of executive American political pragmatism has given the world one of the basic forms of representative, democratic governmental organization. Through 175 years it has withstood shocks, strains, and pressures while differently structured governments based upon democratic principles have foundered elsewhere. Tentative, experimental executive systems devised by the states in the crucible of the Revolutionary War were perfected in the plan of balanced powers that came from the hands of the Constitution's Framers in 1787. With only minimal change in the original constitutional arrangements the plan of the Founders has evolved into a workable scheme of government for a nation that has become the chief bulwark of representative democracy in the world.

Drawn as by a giant magnet to the improved plan set forth by the Founders, the states have reshaped their own separate plans of government in the image of the national model. In every one of the 50 states a scheme of governmental organization embodying the basic features of the presidential system has been put into operation. The prosperity, strength, and political stability of the nation testify to the soundness of its governmental institutions. Suggestions that drastic changes affecting the character and status of the chief executiveship as now constituted in national and state governments, understandably enough, fall on deaf ears. In the estimation of the American public, the merits of the presidential system have been demonstrated beyond question. Proposals looking toward fundamental change meet a cool reception. They are dismissed by the public as impractical theorizings.

Yet it must also be acknowledged that from the beginning there has been an underlying uneasiness in this country about the executive side of government. If, as the old adage has it, "eternal vigilance is the price of liberty" the feeling appears to be that such vigilance is particularly in order where the chief executive and his works are concerned. A steady trend toward concentration of greater power and influence in this element of the governmental system has been a cause of concern to many, from the earliest times to the present.

As the preceding pages have demonstrated, it cannot be denied that there has been a more or less steady aggrandizement of the chief executive's role at the expense of the legislative and judicial branches. Local autonomy has had to give way to a wider authority in state governments over matters heretofore of local concern. State autonomy in turn has been encroached upon by the national government in many respects, so that the lines demarking the respective spheres of authority and function of the states and the national government in the federal scheme have been largely obliterated. Problems heretofore regarded as matters solely of internal concern to the nation have become subjects for treatment through international agreements, which only the national government may make. Government has assumed a vast range of new functions generally growing out of the interdependent society produced by modern science and technology. Increased reliance upon the executive side of government to supply the necessary leadership, energy, and coordination of public effort in meeting these new responsibilities has come to be recognized as an imperative. It would be strange if these developments had not been accompanied by a drumfire of criticism from the Cassandras of every period, warning of the dangers in an increasingly powerful, more prestigious one-man executive.

CRITICS AND REFORMERS

As has been noted in Chapter 2, the Constitution was launched on a sea of doubt and anxiety. Not least among its innovations that gave rise to misgivings were the arrangements for the presidency itself. Typical of the skeptical attitude of some of the Framers on this point was Franklin's pessimistic comment in reply to a question from his landlady after the Convention had completed its work. "Well, Mr. Franklin, what have you given us, a republic or a monarchy?" she asked. "A republic—if you can keep it," was his none too reassuring reply. After the new plan was put into operation the virulence of the attacks upon Washington and Adams from the Jeffersonian Republican press for their alleged monarchist attitudes and practices continued to keep this feeling of distrust alive.

The anti-executive chorus reached a veritable crescendo during the administration of Andrew Jackson. Swept into office on a wave of popular protest against the "political establishment" of that day, Jackson proceeded to build the presidency into a fearsome instrument of political power. Critics in his time were unsparing in their warnings of the dire consequences to come. "I look upon Jackson," wrote Chancellor Kent in 1834, "as a detestable, ignorant, reckless, vain and malignant tyrant. . . . This elective monarchy frightens me. The experiment, with its foundation laid on universal suffrage and our unfettered press, is of too violent a nature for our excitable people." "The President," Webster charged in the Senate, "carries on the government; all the rest are sub-contractors. . . . A Briareus sits in the centre of our system, and with his hundred hands touches everything, controls everything." "We are in the midst of a revolution," warned Henry Clay, "hitherto bloodless, but tending rapidly towards a total change of the pure republican character of the Government, and to the concentration of all power in the hands of one man."[1]

Whig reaction to the Jacksonian concept of an independent chief executive functioning as the tribune of the people failed to produce any changes in the original constitutional arrangements, but numerous constitutional amendment proposals were launched in Congress during the 1830s and 1840s—without success, of course—to cut back the presidential veto authority and to subject the occupants of the office to a one-term limit. The next round of strong assaults on executive pretensions came during and after the Lincoln "dictatorship" of the Civil War period. In the bitter struggle that ensued between President Johnson and Congress over Reconstruction policies, the presidency suffered a temporary setback at the hands of Congress. Legislation passed over the executive's veto seriously encroached upon the President's constitutional authority to control his own subordinates; his powers as Commander-in-Chief were in effect transferred to the Secretary of War; and for the first and only time, the bludgeon of impeachment was aimed at the head of a President. The institution of the presidency as it had come to be understood was subjected to its greatest challenge in American history.

Yet it survived the assaults upon it. Its original position in the constitutional scheme remained unimpaired. In time its independence of Congress was re-established and the trend toward enhancement of presidential power and prestige was resumed. Theodore Roosevelt's assertion of his stewardship theory of the presidency—an amalgam of the Jacksonian concept of the tribunative function of the office and of a broad Lincolnian view of presidential prerogative power—marked unmistakably the beginning of a new era in the history of the presidency. Although Roosevelt's application of his theory in practice was discreetly tempered by recognition of the limitations imposed by practical political considerations, he set in motion evolutionary changes which were built upon and extended by his successors. Woodrow Wilson with his efforts to give a prime ministership cast to the presidential role and F. D. Roosevelt with his successes in making the presidency the prime center of action and decision-making on broad issues of public

[1] Quotations in Edward S. Corwin, *The President: Office and Powers*, 4th ed. (New York: New York University Press, 1957), pp. 21–22.

policy carried presidential influence and pretensions to new heights.

As the power, influence, and responsibilities of the office have continued to expand, the voices of the critics, the viewers with alarm, and the prescribers of remedial measures have continued to be heard. In recent decades the pages of the *Congressional Record,* the press, the scholarly journals and prints have been filled with comment of this kind. Repeatedly the issue whether the "strong" presidency should be curbed has been posed in recent presidential campaigns. With the exception of the elections of 1920 and 1952, the verdict of the people has been an endorsement of the idea of strong presidential leadership and initiative in policy-making. This was particularly evident in the elections of 1936, 1948, 1960, and 1964. Putting the issue squarely before the electorate in 1964, Senator Goldwater asserted:

> . . . We hear praise of a power-wielding, arm-twisting President who "gets his program through Congress" by knowing the use of power.
>
> Throughout the course of history, there have been many other such wielders of power. There have even been dictators who regularly held plebiscites, in which their dictatorships were approved by an Ivory-soap-like percentage of the electorate. But their countries were not free, nor can any country remain free under such despotic power.
>
> Some of the current worship of powerful executives may come from those who admire strength and accomplishment of any sort. Others hail the display of Presidential strength . . . simply because they approve of the *result* reached by the use of power. This is nothing less than the totalitarian philosophy that the end justifies the means—or, put in culinary terms, that you have to break some eggs to make an omelet. If ever there was a philosophy of government totally at war with that of the Founding Fathers, it is this one.
>
> To a constitutionalist, it is at least as important that the use of power be legitimate as that it be beneficial.[2]

This charge of presidential usurpation of power has been reiterated time and time again in the United States. Yet so far as concrete change involving revision of the Constitution's language is concerned, the only result to date has been the adoption of the Twenty-second Amendment in 1951, restricting a President to not more than two full terms of office. In reality a posthumous slap at Franklin D. Roosevelt for having successfully challenged the long-established two-term tradition, it is a measure unlikely to have much of an impact in resolving the problem at which it is ostensibly directed. By introducing an inflexible rule of forced rotation in office, it may merely help to induce a false sense of security while failing to come to grips with the problem it seeks to resolve.

As one surveys the critical scholarly literature dealing with the

2 Barry Goldwater, "My Case for the Republican Party, 1964," *Saturday Review,* October 17, 1964, pp. 21ff; an address given before the American Political Science Association in Chicago on September 11, 1964.

executive under the system of separation of powers, certain patterns of thinking emerge. There is a wide range of views as to what the essential nature of the problem concerning it really is and, therefore, what should be done about it. The danger in entrusting to one man the frightening power and responsibility that have come to be associated with the office is one theme continually reiterated. An elective process that places a premium on the arts of demagoguery, these critics maintain, adds to the danger. The job has simply become too big for one man to fill. The prime remedy proposed by those who assess the problem in these terms is to place this power "in commission," that is, to vest it in a plural organ of some kind.

More recently, critics who belong to this school of thinking, familiar with the principles of parliamentary government along the lines of the British model, have proposed to meet the issue by introducing into American practice in more or less modified form various elements of the parliamentary scheme of government. This, they maintain, will not only resolve the problem of overdependence upon one individual for supplying necessary leadership and coordination in the governmental process, but the changes made can be adapted to American traditions and practices so as to preserve some of the more desirable features of the separation of powers system. By insuring closer coordination of effort as between the legislative and executive organs or government, it is urged, changes of this kind will at the same time eliminate or greatly minimize one of the fundamental weaknesses in the presidential system, namely, the possibility of frustrating deadlocks and functioning at cross-purposes as between the two political branches. The constitutional amendment proposal introduced by Senator Fulbright in 1947, discussed in Chapter 5, is an example of proposals of this type. Under this system, a vote expressing lack of confidence in the President by Congress, or a failure on its part to give him support on an issue he regarded as crucial, would bring about the President's resignation, dissolution of Congress, and new elections, as is the case in a parliamentary system of government.

Another school of reformists sees the problem solely in terms of inadequacy of the presidential system in providing the legislative branch with effective, responsible leadership. They perceive the major need to be one of redefining the political relationship between the executive and legislative branches. Without necessarily changing the one-man character of the office or redefining its constitutional functions, they would adapt to the American political system certain features of parliamentary government calculated to induce closer interaction between the two policy-making organs. The chief executive should be provided with means to function more effectively and responsibly as the leader of his party element in the legislative branch. This might be furthered, it is suggested, if he and his major administrative aides were given access to the legislative floor, with opportunity to introduce bills, participate in debates, and reply to questioning from the opposition party. More reliance should be placed upon a well-disciplined opposition party to hold the chief executive and his party's administration of affairs to account, and less reliance should be placed upon the traditional mechanisms of the checks and balances system. Instruments of party government and practice, both within and outside the legislative branch, should be reshaped so as to convert political parties into more useful and reliable adjuncts to the governing process. The chief executive should be equipped with a stronger party leadership authority as a part of this recasting of party machinery, it is contended.

Finally, there are those who maintain that the remedies for the problem of an overextended, irresponsible executive authority are already at hand. All that is needed is to put them into more effective operation. As those who assess the problem in these terms see it, as exemplified in the statement of Senator Goldwater quoted above, there should be a return to the constitutional fundamentals that have been disregarded or twisted from their original intent and purpose. Critics belonging to this school would have the legislative branch simply reassert its political independence from the executive, reassume its proper role as the primary organ for policy-making, involve itself more actively in overseeing administration, and see to it that the executive is kept in his proper place. The executive should be converted from a maker of the law into a servant of the law. A more diligent, unyielding policing by the courts of the constitutional boundaries demarking the respective spheres of authority and function of the legislative and executive organs and of the nation versus the states would become, as a matter of course, a necessary complement to this program of rescuing the nation from the dangers of dictatorial, irresponsible executive power.[3]

So far as those who see salvation in some sort of plural executive are concerned, it should be noted that the idea that there is safety in numbers is as old as the Constitution itself. As pointed out in Chapter 2, the fundamental issue of a single versus a plural form of executive

---

[3] Paradoxically, however, Senator Goldwater has apparently lost faith in the efficacy of the Supreme Court as the guardian of the constitutional verities. Further on in his statement blueprinting what he thinks the country needs, he charges today's Supreme Court with being the "least faithful [of all the three branches of government] to the constitutional tradition of limited government and to the principle of legitimacy in the exercise of power." *Ibid.*, p. 23.

For a scholarly plea that the Supreme Court rise in its majesty and, by a rigid insistence on maintaining proper respect for the principle of separation of powers, put the executive branch in its proper constitutional place, see the late Justice A. T. Vanderbilt's *The Separation of Powers and Its Present-Day Significance* (Lincoln: University of Nebraska Press, 1953).

was thoroughly considered in the Convention of 1787. Its conclusion that the single executive should be preferred was reached in the light of immediate, practical experience with various versions of the plural type of executive then in existence in some of the states. Some members of the Convention continued to urge reconsideration of this decision to the bitter end. During the course of its proceedings, Randolph of Virginia repeatedly sought in vain to substitute a three-man executive system for the one-man presidency as finally incorporated in the constitutional plan. The states that had had experience with the plural executive form abandoned it soon after the Constitution was adopted, and the idea for all practical purposes has fallen into disuse at the state level. The nearest remaining approaches to it are found in three New England states that have retained the elective executive council as an organ for sharing in the exercise of some of the governor's administrative powers, particularly the appointive authority. In a few others—Florida and North Carolina are notable examples—the governor and the other major elective executive officials together form a council or "cabinet" in which certain general administrative functions are vested. Providing for a number of other independently elected officers to handle specific phases of state administration—a very widespread practice at the state level since the Jacksonian era—does not exemplify the plural executive idea in its true form. It fragments the administrative structure and curtails the governor's authority as chief administrator, but it leaves in his hands alone the other chief executive functions usually associated with the presidential system.

Advocates of the plural executive idea for national purposes have proved to be a hardy lot. Twenty years after the Constitution went into operation Augustus B. Woodward, who played an important role in early Michigan affairs as Chief Justice of its Territorial Court, produced an essay in which he advocated conversion of the one-man presidency into a five-man executive organ. According to his plan, one man would be elected to the executive council each year for a five-year term. The senior man on the council would serve as its presiding officer during his fifth year of incumbency, but his special duties would only be of a ceremonial nature.[4] The similarity of his plan to that eventually incorporated in the Swiss Constitution of 1848 is striking.[5] At the height of the slavery controversy a number of amendment proposals were introduced in Congress which would have provided for two or three Presidents, chosen on a sectional basis and serving as coequals in power. A similar proposal for a three-man presidency was offered by

[4] Augustus B. Woodward, *Considerations on the Executive Government of the United States* (Flatbush, N.Y.: I. Riley, 1809).

[5] Cf. Charles F. Strong, *Modern Political Constitutions*, 3rd ed. (London: Sidgwick and Jackson, 1949), pp. 246–247.

Representative Milton I. Southard of Ohio in 1878 following the Hayes-Tilden electoral dispute.[6] These suggestions failed to attract any support.

In 1884, after having witnessed close at hand the people's choice of a politically naive and inept war hero, General Grant, as President, and with subversion of the French Republic by Napoleon III to draw upon for instruction, William B. Lockwood published a notable critical essay entitled *The Abolition of the Presidency*. In it he developed at length the thesis that the people are too prone to be misled by glamor and hero worship and too lacking in sound political judgment to be entrusted with the responsibility of choosing a chief executive whose powers had become so great that he could lead the country to disaster. The solution he proposed was the simple one of setting up a multimember executive council in whose collective hands the powers and functions of the presidency would be vested.[7]

Among the more recent studies proposing basic reform of the presidential system in the direction of converting it into something more like the British parliamentary plan of government are those of William Y. Elliott,[8] Henry Hazlitt,[9] Thomas K. Finletter,[10] Rexford G. Tugwell,[11] C. Perry Patterson,[12] and Herman Finer.[13] Professor Tugwell concludes a very perceptive study of the growth of presidential powers and functions with the comment that what should be done to deal with the problem of a one-man presidency, on which he maintains an impossible burden of responsibility has come to rest, would require the space of another book. However, he goes on to make clear his belief that it will be necessary to go back and rethink the basic issue of a single versus a plural executive and that when the problem has been fully analyzed in the light of modern conditions, the conclusion might well be justified that the responsibilities of the office should be placed "in commission" in some way or another.[14]

Professor Finer, on the other hand, has no doubts whatever about what should be done. To him it is no longer reasonable to think that

[6] Cf. Ames, *Proposed Amendments*, pp. 69–70.

[7] Cf. Corwin, *op. cit.*, pp. 25–26.

[8] Elliott, *The Need for Constitutional Reform: A Program for National Security* (New York: McGraw-Hill Book Company, 1935).

[9] Hazlitt, *A New Constitution Now* (New York: McGraw-Hill Book Company, 1942).

[10] Finletter, *Can Representative Government do the Job?* (New York: Reynal & Hitchcock, 1945).

[11] Tugwell, *The Enlargement of the Presidency* (Garden City, N.Y.: Doubleday & Company, 1960).

[12] Patterson, *Presidential Government in the United States: The Unwritten Constitution* (Chapel Hill: University of North Carolina Press, 1947).

[13] Finer, *The Presidency: Crisis and Regeneration* (Chicago: University of Chicago Press, 1960).

[14] Tugwell, *op. cit.*, pp. 494–495.

the enormous burden of responsibility that the President bears can safely be rested in the hands of one man. The "gamble" involved in the "floating crap game" methods by which we nominate and elect a President is too great, he avers. The "indispensable solution" he recommends is that the presidency as now constituted be replaced by a President and 11 Vice Presidents, elected together for a four-year term as a kind of ministry through which executive functions of government would be discharged. The President would preside over the group, assign them to their respective jobs, dismiss any of them if he so wished, and appoint others in their place. Only individuals who had served for at least one term in Congress would be eligible for the presidency or a vice presidency. Upon election the President and his cabinet of Vice Presidents would have full membership rights in the House of Representatives. The terms of members of Congress would be four years for both Representatives and Senators, and they would all be chosen at the same time the President-Cabinet group was elected by the people at large. With the concurrence of a majority of his Cabinet of Vice Presidents, however, the President could bring about the resignation of the entire executive entourage during the course of their term and thereby cause Congress to be dissolved and new elections to be held for all seats in Congress as well as for those making up the presidential establishment.[15]

The Finer plan is, of course, merely a somewhat modified and diluted version of the British cabinet system, sugarcoated by a show of respect for some of what the originator apparently regards as the more tolerable established American political mores and institutions to make it more palatable. Somewhat less revolutionary in its potential impact—in fact, it is defended by its originator as a return to pristine constitutional principles—is the panacea proposed by the late Professor C. Perry Patterson. The latter-day Patterson plan he advocated featured the establishment of a congressional cabinet, headed by a prime minister, all chosen by Congress from among the congressional membership. Reliance would be placed upon these "ministers" for furnishing the political leadership and energizing functions that have been usurped by power-hungry Presidents. The President would retain his present constitutional powers and duties, but inasmuch as his functioning as the head of administration and the initiator of policy would be channeled through ministers responsible to Congress, the legislative branch would be restored to its rightful place as the primary directive force in the governmental system.[16]

Radical departures from established ways of government such

15 Finer, *op. cit.*, Chap. VII.
16 Patterson, *op. cit.*, Chap. X.

as those just outlined are not likely to be given serious consideration by people who have responsibility for charting the course of American public affairs. History teaches that, short of some kind of dislocating upheaval of the sort that confronted the American people in the Revolutionary War period or the French and German people at the end of World War II, the processes of change in governmental institutions are evolutionary and gradual, not revolutionary. Nations simply are not in the habit of turning their governmental institutions upside down and overhauling them from time to time to satisfy the demands of theorists who would like to try out new models of their own devising. However much present-day would-be constitutional architects may yearn to make the nation the beneficiary of their erudition, wisdom, and discernment in things political, they are not likely to be heeded so long as the Ship of State sails ahead with reasonable smoothness.

In seeking to improve governmental institutions one must start from the here and now, in a social and political environment that sets narrow limits on what is possible in the way of new departures. The Framers of the Constitution did a remarkably successful job of putting together a sound, workable plan of government because they were, above all else, practical politicians, willing to draw lessons from the American political experience and apply them to the problem at hand. Blueprints for an ideal form of government imported from another political environment, another age, another society, were discounted by them because they knew their handiwork would be rejected if it was too remotely dissociated from the political habits and thinking of the people. For similar reasons America today is in no mood to accept radical changes prescribed by "experts," however well such innovations can be defended on the basis of what has been proved feasible elsewhere.

Reforms in the presidential system that do not involve a sudden break with past practice stand a better chance of being accepted, in time. In this category belong a number of suggestions that have been made by contemporary critics who set as their more modest goal the achievement of closer *liaison* between the executive and legislative branches without altering the basic outlines of the separation of powers plan. Their objective is to assure a greater sharing of responsibility by the two branches in the making of major policy decisions and thus, incidentally, relieve the chief executive of some of the crushing burden of fateful decision-making he is called upon to bear.

Professor Corwin, for example, who felt that the powers of the presidency had become dangerously "personalized" and too much dependent on one man's judgment and capacity, proposed that a new type of cabinet be brought into being. Its functions would be only advisory, as is the case with the present Cabinet, but it should be set up as an institutionalized element in the government on a more formal basis than is the case with the present Cabinet. It would be composed of members selected by the President from a joint legislative council to be created by the two houses of Congress and containing its leading members. To these would be added various executive department heads as the nature of the business under consideration dictated.[17] A somewhat similar proposal is that of Professor Charles S. Hyneman, who suggests the establishment of a central council to serve the President as an official advisory body. Its membership would be selected from among the congressional leadership of the President's own political party, but it would also include members of his own administrative staff and some individuals from outside the government in whose political judgment the President had confidence.[18]

Before one concludes that a suggestion of this kind should at once be formally implemented by statutory or constitutional provision, it would be wise to take into consideration what has happened at the state level with innovations of the same general character. Several states have established joint executive-legislative councils of the same general design as those proposed by Corwin and Hyneman. They have by no means proved to be an unmixed success. The first state to pioneer in this field, Wisconsin, gave up its experiment after a brief trial, but a similar scheme met with somewhat greater success in Virginia.[19] It should be noted also that while the National Municipal League's Committee on the Model State Constitution incorporated provisions in earlier versions of its model for a joint executive-legislative council, the idea has been dropped from the more recent versions.[20]

There are indications that a legislatively based executive cabinet may actually be in process of establishment on an informal, flexible basis. Regular consultations by Presidents and by governors with their party leader colleagues in the legislative branch have become so commonplace during legislative sessions in recent years as to be treated

17 Corwin, *op. cit.*, pp. 297–299.

18 Charles S. Hyneman, *Bureaucracy in a Democracy* (New York: Harper & Row, 1950), Chap. 25.

19 Cf. Leslie Lipson, *The American Governor: From Figurehead to Leader* (Chicago: University of Chicago Press, 1939), pp. 227ff.

20 Cf. *Model State Constitution*, 6th ed. (New York: National Municipal League, 1963). The 1963 edition also fails to include provisions incorporated in some of the earlier versions giving the governor and his department heads seats without vote in the legislature; permitting the governor to authorize submission to popular referendum bills recommended by him but not passed by the legislature, provided they have received a favorable vote from one third of the legislature's members; giving the legislature a similar privilege with respect to any measure vetoed by the governor and failing to receive the necessary two-thirds vote to override, but favored by a majority of its members; and authorizing the legislature to recall the governor from office by a vote of two thirds of its membership.

as routine. Meanwhile, the summoning of legislative leaders of both parties into conference by the President on the occasion of his having to make major critical decisions during the post-World War II decades—in connection with Korea in 1950, the Cuban crisis of 1962, the Chinese atomic bomb explosion in 1964, for example—suggests that face-to-face consultations by the President and members of the congressional leadership may become more frequent and more regularized in the future. It should be kept in mind that the institution of the Cabinet as a consultative body for the President developed in essentially this way during the early years of the Republic.

As for those advocates of change who pin their hopes on a revitalized, better-disciplined two-party system and the development of a strong party leadership role for the chief executive in his relations with the legislative branch, there is reason to believe that evolutionary processes are under way that point toward the goals they have in mind. During the first two or three decades of the present century there was a rather heavy emphasis in some academic circles, the "enlightened" press, civic reform groups, and other opinion-influencing elements on the shortcomings of partisan politics and the virtues of a nonpartisan approach to public issues. The "informed" public's attitudes of the day tended to reflect these views. Since that time there has been a change in public attitude on the question of the place political parties have in the functioning of democratic government. More general acceptance of the idea that parties play a necessary role in the governing process at the state and national levels has generated a climate of opinion in which exertion by chief executives of the functions of party leadership has become more widely understood, approved, and expected. There is accordingly an increasing likelihood that changes in party usage and practice having this end result in view will be put into execution. Unmistakable evidence that a vigorously functioning two-party system is coming into existence in the South and in other areas of the country where it has heretofore been lacking tends to reinforce this conclusion. Recent Presidents, such as Woodrow Wilson, F. D. Roosevelt, and Lyndon Johnson, have demonstrated that, in the right hands, the party leadership tools now available to a President can be used to produce remarkable results.

Critics such as James MacGregor Burns[21] who would like to see changes made in party organization and procedures in the direction of equipping the President with weapons to discharge more effectively his functions as the responsible leader of his party in the legislative

21 Cf. Burns, *The Deadlock of Democracy: Four-Party Politics in America* (Englewood Cliffs, N.J.: Prentice-Hall, 1963). See also his Edmund J. James Lecture on Government delivered February 19, 1964 at the University of Illinois, *The Embattled Presidency* (Urbana: Department of Political Science, University of Illinois, 1964).

branch are therefore probably in league with the future. Professor Burns advocates a program of reform directed more particularly at the mechanisms of party government rather than at the machinery of government itself. As was pointed out in Chapter 9, there are relatively narrow limits imposed on what can be accomplished in this way alone, without basic alterations in the governmental structure with respect to such matters as the election time table and the method by which the chief executive himself is chosen. The present state-block, electoral vote system for choosing the President is one of the features of the present arrangement that stands in the way of realization of this objective, since it emphasizes the coalitional character of the national party the President heads. There will always necessarily be a considerable gap between what is ideally desirable in the way of an executive-led, programmatic, responsible, nationally oriented political party and what is actually attainable, given the conditions under which a party must function in translating public desires into accomplished action under the present system.

As for those would-be reformers who preach the simple doctrine of a return to allegedly disregarded constitutional fundamentals as a way of salvation from the evils of an overextended, dominating executive authority, it should be observed that if their objective is to cut back the range of powers and influence of the excutive branch to nine-tenth-century standards, the answer is, it cannot be done. It is a condition and not a theory that must be dealt with. The functions of government as dictated by the twentieth century are here to stay, and with them the conditions that have brought about an enlargement of the role of the chief executive in carrying on the business of government.

If more zeal were displayed by such defenders of legislative prerogative in the direction of urging a restructuring of the legislative branch both in its composition and in its internal organization and procedures so as to give it a more popularly responsible character and a leadership more closely attuned to the political impulses of the times, their basic objective would have greater possibility of attainment.[22] Unfortunately, many who preach the gospel of the need to reduce the power of the executive by enlarging the legislature's positive role in the management of public business stand in their own light. There is too much mere negativism in their attitude. Too often they take the lead in the fight against reforms in legislative practices and pro-

---

[22] Thomas R. Dye in "Malapportionment and Public Policy in the States," *Journal of Politics*, Vol. 27 (August, 1965), pp. 586–601, presented empirical research results leading him to the cautious conclusion that corrections of state legislative malapportionment in line with the Supreme Court's rulings had not thus far resulted in any significant change in state legislative policies or product indicating a shift toward a more pro-urban orientaton.

cedures calculated to enable the legislative organ of government to devote a larger share of its time and attention to major questions of public policy and to give this branch a more representative character. The recent series of Supreme Court decisions barring unreasonable deviations from the principle of equality in popular representation in state legislative bodies and in the United States House of Representatives, which many such critics seek to reverse, may well turn out to have been the most significant stroke in a great many decades toward assisting the legislative branch to become a more effective part of the governmental mechanism. To the degree that the legislative branch in its collective capacity more accurately mirrors the state of the public mind, it is in a stronger position to challenge the chief executive's claim to be the "spokesman of the people."

PROSPECTS FOR THE FUTURE

It should not be concluded from the foregoing brief summary of critical comment about the presidential system that there is currently widespread dissatisfaction or alarm concerning it in the United States. It is in no danger of being supplanted by new arrangements that would alter its character in any fundamental sense. It has become too deeply embedded as an element of political life in America for that to happen. Many competent scholars and analysts who in recent years have examined this feature of our governmental system in depth have come up with a resounding verdict in its favor. They recognize that it has imperfections, remediable within the context of the system itself. But its contributions to the political stability, health, and strength of the nation have been so immeasurable that reforms which would seriously alter its character should not be undertaken lightly. Included among the many works in recent years that have found in the modern-day presidency a profoundly useful instrument for promoting the public welfare and preserving democratic values are those of Harold J. Laski,[23] E. Pendleton Herring,[24], Clinton Rossiter,[25] Wilfred E. Binkley,[26] Sidney Hyman,[27] George Fort Milton,[28] and Louis W. Koenig.[29]

[23] Laski, *The American Presidency* (New York: Harper & Row, 1940).

[24] Herring, *Presidential Leadership* (New York: Holt, Rinehart and Winston, 1940).

[25] Rossiter, *The American Presidency*, 2nd ed. (New York: Harcourt, Brace & World, 1960).

[26] Binkley, *The Man in the White House* (Baltimore: The Johns Hopkins Press, 1958).

[27] Hyman, *The American President* (New York: Harper & Row, 1954).

[28] Milton, *The Use of Presidential Power 1798–1943* (Boston: Little, Brown and Company, 1954).

[29] Koenig, *The Chief Executive* (New York: Harcourt, Brace & World, 1964).

To these could be added many other scholars who see in the development of the strong presidency one of the distinctive achievements of the people of the United States in the art of self-government.

This general approval of the institution of a strong presidency is matched by similar opinions about the office of state governor. The overwhelming weight of scholarly authority urges that the states take further steps to bring the governorships more closely into line with the national model. This is the import of the message that runs through the two most extensive studies of the governorship in recent years, the works by Lipson[30] and Ransone.[31] The 1963 version of the Model State Constitution, which reflects the views of a large number of authorities in the field of state government, points toward the same conclusion.[32] And in fact the states during the past four or five decades have gradually been adopting constitutional and statutory changes designed to enable the governor to provide stronger legislative and administrative leadership. The national plan of executive organization has evidently been evaluated and found efficacious at the state level as well. This readiness to follow a common pattern is all the more remarkable in view of the fact that, except for the provision in the United States Constitution requiring that state governments be "republican" in form, the states are left free to devise and adopt any form of governmental organization. They are under no compulsion to be mere slavish imitators of the national plan for the management of public affairs.

This is not to say that we are justified in being complacent about the presidential system as it now stands. It would be foolish indeed to refuse to recognize that there are weaknesses and even dangers in it. One may echo approvingly Professor Rossiter's warning to would-be tinkerers with the system, "Leave Your Presidency Alone,"[33] while at the same time conceding, as he does, that there are various aspects of it that need shoring up. Unquestionably, one of the keys to the general success the presidential system has enjoyed has been its flexibility. It has proved to be highly adaptable to the changing conditions, challenges, and moods of the times. There is no reason to believe that it has reached such a state of perfection that preservation of the status quo for every one of its current features should be the order of the day.

One valid cause for concern is the inadequacy of present arrangements for the succession in the event of the death or disability of an

---

[30] Lipson, *op. cit.*

[31] Coleman B. Ransone, Jr., *The Office of Governor in the United States* (University, Ala.: University of Alabama Press, 1956).

[32] See Appendix D. For critical evaluations, pro and con, of current trends toward strengthening the position of state governor through structural and functional reorganization, see Sherrill D. Luke, "The Need for Strength," *National Civic Review*, Vol. LIII (March, 1964), pp. 126–130, and Samuel K. Gove, "Why Strong Governors?" *ibid.*, pp. 131–136.

[33] Rossiter, *op. cit.*, p. 258.

incumbent President. Redefinition of the role of the Vice President in recent administrations and submission of a proposed constitutional amendment on this subject justify the conclusion that this potential source of trouble is in process of being eliminated. The mechanism through which the presidential selective process operates, both in the party nominating phase and in the final elective stage, should be subjected to continuing critical analysis with a view to the adoption of improved procedures. Here state experiments with various nominating and elective devices in the choosing of governors should be carefully evaluated for the lessons they teach. In the nomination phase, the goal should be the achievement of a proper balance between reliance on the judgment of those occupying high and responsible places in the party hierarchy and providing adequate means for taking into consideration the wishes of the rank and file party membership. Probably we should aim for a nationally regulated, genuinely representative party convention system somewhat on the order of the earlier "mixed" party caucus for reaching final conclusions on candidates.

So far as the final elective stage is concerned, the nation is unquestionably courting trouble as long as it continues to rely on the outmoded electoral college for registering the people's choice for President. As events in recent elections have demonstrated, the elector system can be manipulated by an uncooperative state legislature so as to deny to the people an opportunity to express their choice among the major party candidates. In the interval between the choosing of the electors and the casting of their votes there remains the danger that the electors, as a result of some untoward event or by deliberate design on their own part, may exercise their independent judgment in the selection of a President. Given the rule that only an electoral vote majority may control the outcome and that the two houses of Congress may have to act as electoral bodies, the possibilities for confusion and for thwarting the popular desires are serious. The principle that the President should be chosen through the suffrage of the people of the nation as a whole has been, in effect, the guiding rule for more than a century and a half. The goal of reform efforts here should be to sweep away the useless and potentially dangerous elector system and to substitute in its place some form of national direct popular election, eliminating all intermediate agencies of choice. An electoral vote system that operates as a kind of nationwide gerrymander in the choosing of the President in that popular votes are more crucial in some states than in others is no more defensible than any other kind of gerrymander; the possibility that an election may have to be resolved by Congress remains a frightening threat—and a real one—under the current system.

How the chief executive's office shall be organized and staffed to assist him in the discharge of his staggering range of duties necessarily continues to be a problem. It must be so set up as to enable him to devote his main energies to making informed decisions on the most pressing and important questions that come to him, but he must be safeguarded against being buried by the machinery of his own staff system. The chief executive must be left wide discretion to determine the organization and methods of operation of his staff machinery in the light of his perception of what his own role should be. He must be permitted to adjust the executive staff organization and procedures to accommodate his own views on how he can best utilize the talents and skills of subordinates. His ability to devise an effective operational procedure for handling the continually mounting responsibilities will determine whether the presidency as now constituted will continue to exist. If institutionalization of the office through the staff system is carried to the point where an actual fragmentation of its functions among the elements comprising the presidential entourage occurs, it will have ceased to be, in fact, the presidency in all that term has come to mean.

Nagging international tensions, shock waves emanating from other countries undergoing profound social and political upheavals, and persistent fear generated by the threat of nuclear warfare present grave problems that may affect the future of the presidency in a fundamental way. Foreign policy is a province wherein the executive has always had an unusually heavy share of responsibility. An unsettled world seems to require that a complex, expensive war machine be kept in constant readiness to meet any challenge from abroad. The resulting burden of responsibility falling upon the nation's chief executive has become heavy beyond measure. The search must therefore continue for ways by which he may share the burden to a greater degree with Congress and with staff advisers who are specialists in the political and military fields concerned, while keeping his office the pivot upon which the decision-making machinery turns. If the state of unrelenting emergency and quasi-war in which the nation now finds itself persists for a generation or longer, the impact upon the institution of the presidency will doubtless be profound and lasting. This nation conceivably may be in the grip of cosmic forces that leave it no choice in the course the development of its governmental institutions, including the presidency, will take. War, or the continuing imminent threat thereof, may transform the presidency permanently into an American type of limited constitutional dictatorship. The inexorable course of national and world events may long since have committed this nation to a path from which there is no turning back. Problems of foreign and military policy that will confront the nation in the coming decades may prove to be the Achilles heel of the democratic system this nation has known and cherished.[34]

In conclusion, one may say that on the record to date the presidency has served the nation well. It has helped to unite the people and to keep them united and strong. It has served as the rallying point in times of crisis and peril. It has played a major role in the struggle for human rights, human dignity, social and economic justice, and for realization of all the noble objectives of government set forth in the Constitution's Preamble. It has given voice to the hopes and aspirations of the masses and helped them to attain a sense of common purpose. Our governmental system may well be characterized as a "presidential democracy." On their more limited stage of action, state governors have played a similar role.

Yet, in the final analysis, one must always keep foremost in mind that the office of chief executive has been, and continues to be, only one of the several instruments of popular self-government in the nation. Its occupants have had no monopoly on civic virtue and wisdom. It has not been, nor should it ever be allowed to become, the sole avenue through which government by and for the people operates. The people by their suffrage and consent have given the office its form and being. Its successes and its failures have been those of the people themselves in the art of self-government. Democracy as a form of government is forever on trial. It never reaches its final stage of perfection. It is condemned by its nature to be forever tentative, pragmatic, and adaptive to the changing environment in which it operates. The manner in which the office of chief executive has evolved in the United States is a testimonial to the truth of that observation.

Gazing into the dreadful abyss of civil war, Abraham Lincoln in his first message to Congress posed the question: "Must a [republican form of] government of necessity be too *strong* for the liberties of its own people, or too *weak* to maintain its own existence?" The ensuing four years of turmoil followed by a century of unparalleled advancement in power, wealth, and prestige by a united nation supplied the answer to Lincoln's question. There are those today who, awed and

---

[34] For an interesting attempt to pierce the veil of the future by drawing a lesson from the past, see Amaury de Riencourt, *The Coming Caesars* (New York: Coward-McCann, 1957). His underlying theme is the parallel to be seen between the rise of Rome with its mission as a conservator and disseminator of Greek civilization in the ancient world and the rise of the United States and its similar role as the heir of Western European civilization. As the title of his book indicates, he forecasts the evolution of the presidency eventually into an American version of the Roman emperorship. In his view, the presidency underwent a fundamental, irrevocable transformation in the Jacksonian era, when it became an office deriving its political power and influence from the mass of the people. Also cf. Ransom, *op. cit.*, p. 252.

alarmed by the immense responsibility and power that have come to be lodged in the presidency, pose his question anew in terms of the maintenance of a viable system of responsible, democratic government of balanced powers. One feels impelled, as did Lincoln, to take a hopeful view of the situation. One may safely predict that, barring some cataclysmic upheaval in human affairs, the presidential form of executive organization will continue to flourish for years to come in this nation. New ways will be devised for dealing through it with new challenges as they arise from time to time; old ways will be quietly shelved. But the office will retain its fundamental form and functions. It will continue to serve as the primary organ for supplying energy, direction, and leadership in the handling of public business, subject to effective check by the other branches of government and ultimately by the people themselves.

APPENDIXES

PRESIDENTS OF THE UNITED STATES

	Term of Office	Politics	State of Birth	State of Residence	Age at Inauguration	Age at Death
George Washington	1789–1797	Fed.	Va.	Va.	57	67
John Adams	1797–1801	Fed.	Mass.	Mass.	61	90
Thomas Jefferson	1801–1809	Dem.-Rep.	Va.	Va.	57	83
James Madison	1809–1817	Dem.-Rep.	Va.	Va.	57	85
James Monroe	1817–1825	Dem.-Rep.	Va.	Va.	58	73
John Quincy Adams	1825–1829	Dem.-Rep.	Mass.	Mass.	57	80
Andrew Jackson	1829–1837	Dem.	S. C.	Tenn.	61	78
Martin Van Buren	1837–1841	Dem.	N. Y.	N. Y.	54	79
William H. Harrison	1841 (1 mo.)	Whig	Va.	Ind.	68	68
John Tyler[a]	1841–1845	Whig	Va.	Va.	51	71
James K. Polk	1845–1849	Dem.	N. C.	Tenn.	49	53
Zachary Taylor	1849–1850 (1 yr., 4 mos.)	Whig	Va.	La.	64	65
Millard Fillmore[a]	1850–1853	Whig	N. Y.	N. Y.	48	64
Franklin Pierce	1853–1857	Dem.	N. H.	N. H.	50	74
James Buchanan	1857–1861	Dem.	Pa.	Pa.	65	77
Abraham Lincoln	1861–1865 (4 yrs., 1 mo.)	Rep.	Ky.	Ill.	52	56
Andrew Johnson[a]	1865–1869	Un. Dem.	N. C.	Tenn.	56	66
Ulysses S. Grant	1869–1877	Rep.	Ohio	Ohio	46	63
Rutherford B. Hayes	1877–1881	Rep.	Ohio	Ohio	54	70
James A. Garfield	1881 (6½ mos.)	Rep.	Ohio	Ohio	49	49
Chester A. Arthur[a]	1881–1885	Rep.	Vt.	N. Y.	50	56
Grover Cleveland	1885–1889	Dem.	N. J.	N. Y.	47	71
Benjamin Harrison	1889–1893	Rep.	Ohio	Ind.	55	67
Grover Cleveland	1893–1897					
William McKinley	1897–1901 (4 yrs., 6 mos.)	Rep.	Ohio	Ohio	54	58
Theodore Roosevelt[a]	1901–1909	Rep.	N. Y.	N. Y.	42	60
William Howard Taft	1909–1913	Rep.	Ohio	Ohio	51	72
Woodrow Wilson	1913–1921	Dem.	Va.	N. J.	56	67
Warren G. Harding	1921–1923 (2 yrs., 6 mos.)	Rep.	Ohio	Ohio	55	57
Calvin Coolidge[a]	1923–1929	Rep.	Vt.	Mass.	51	60
Herbert Hoover	1929–1933	Rep.	Iowa	Calif.	54	90
Franklin D. Roosevelt	1933–1945 (12 yrs., 1 mo.)	Dem.	N. Y.	N. Y.	51	63
Harry S Truman[a]	1945–1953	Dem.	Mo.	Mo.	60	—
Dwight D. Eisenhower	1953–1961	Rep.	Texas	N. Y.	62	—
John F. Kennedy	1961–1963 (2 yrs., 10 mos.)	Dem.	Mass.	Mass.	43	46
Lyndon B. Johnson[a]	1963–	Dem.	Texas	Texas	55	—

[a] Became President by succession rule.

STATE PRACTICES CONCERNING

THE GOVERNORSHIP

State	Term of Office	Election Schedule[a]	Re-eligibility Limit—Terms	Elections Won Since 1900[b] Republican	Democratic	Others
Alabama	4	N, O	1	0	18	0
Alaska	4	N, O	2	0	2	0
Arizona	2	N, O, P	—	8	19	0
Arkansas	2	N, O, P	—	0	33	0
California	4	N, O	—	13[h]	3	0
Colorado	4	N, O	—	15	17	0
Connecticut	4	N, O	—	18	11	0
Delaware	4	N, P	2	13	4	0
Florida	4	N, O[c]	1	0	18	0
Georgia	4	N, O	1	0	29	0
Hawaii	4	N, O	—	1	1	0
Idaho	4	N, O	—	19	10	0
Illinois	4	N, P	—	11	6	0
Indiana	4	N, P	1	9	8	0
Iowa	2	N, O, P	—	26	7	0
Kansas	2	N, O, P	—	28	5	0
Kentucky	4	(N), X	1	4	12	0
Louisiana	4	April (pres. yr.)	1	0	17	0
Maine	4	N, O	2	25	7	0
Maryland	4	N, O	2	4	13	0
Massachusetts	2 (4)	N, O[c]	—	28	16	0
Michigan	2 (4)	N, O[c]	—	21	12	0
Minnesota	4	N, O	—	20	8[d]	4
Mississippi	4	(N), X	1	0	17	0
Missouri	4	N, P	2	5	12	0
Montana	4	N, P	—	8	12[e]	0
Nebraska	2 (4)	N, O[c]	—	19	14[f]	0
Nevada	4	N, O	—	6	11	0
New Hampshire	2	N, O, P	—	29	4	0
New Jersey	4	(N), Y	2	9	11	0
New Mexico	2	N, O, P	2	9	19	0
New York	4	N, O	—	13	13[g]	0

State Practices Concerning the Governorship (continued)

	Term of Office	Election Schedule[a]	Re-eligibility Limit—Terms	Elections Won Since 1900[b]		
				Republican	Democratic	Others
North Carolina	4	N, P	1	0	17	0
North Dakota	2	N, O, P	—	23	10	0
Ohio	4	N, O	2	13	19	0
Oklahoma	4	N, O	1	1	14	0
Oregon	4	N, O	2	12	6	1
Pennsylvania	4	N, O	1	13	3	0
Rhode Island	2	N, O, P	—	21	18	0
South Carolina	4	N, O	1	0	23	0
South Dakota	2	N, O, P	2	28	5	0
Tennessee	4	N, O	1	3	27	0
Texas	2	N, O, P	—	0	33[h]	0
Utah	4	N, P	—	9	8	0
Vermont	2	N, O, P	—	31	2	0
Virginia	4	(N), Y	1	0	16	0
Washington	4	N, P	—	9	7	1
West Virginia	4	N, P	1	8	9	0
Wisconsin	2	N, O, P	—	27	4	2
Wyoming	4	N, O	—	14	12	0

[a] Meaning of symbols:

  N—Holds elections in November at same time as national elections
  O—Governor elected at same time as off-year national elections
  P—Governor elected at same time President is elected
  X—Elected in November of odd year immediately preceding presidential election year
  Y—Elected in November of odd year immediately following presidential election year

[b] Includes elections held in 1900 and 1964, and also special elections in some cases. It should be noted that over a third of the states have increased the length of term of the governor since 1900.

[c] Will have all elections at same time as off-year national elections beginning in 1966.

[d] Includes four elections in which Democratic and Farmer-Labor parties endorsed same candidate.

[e] Includes one election in which Democratic and Populist parties endorsed same candidate.

[f] Includes four elections in which Democratic and Peoples Independent parties endorsed same candidate.

[g] Includes two elections in which Democratic candidate was endorsed by American Labor party and one in which Democratic candidate was endorsed by Liberal party.

[h] Includes one election in which the winning candidate was endorsed by both major parties.

C

APPENDIX

THE CONSTITUTION ON

THE PRESIDENCY

ARTICLE I

Section 3

The Vice President of the United States shall be President of the Senate, but shall have no vote, unless they be equally divided.

The Senate shall choose their other officers, and also a President *pro tempore* in the absence of the Vice President, or when he shall exercise the office of the President of the United States.

The Senate shall have the sole power to try all impeachments. When sitting for that purpose, they shall be on oath or affirmation. When the President of the United States is tried, the Chief Justice shall preside; and no person shall be convicted without the concurrence of two-thirds of the members present.

Judgment in cases of impeachment shall not extend further than to removal from office, and disqualification to hold and enjoy any office of honor, trust, or profit under the United States; but the party convicted shall, nevertheless, be liable and subject to indictment, trial, judgment, and punishment, according to law.

Section 7

Every bill which shall have passed the House of Representatives and the Senate shall, before it becomes a law, be presented to the President of the United States; if he approves he shall sign it, but if not he shall return it, with his objections, to that house in which it shall have originated, who shall enter the objections at large on their journal and proceed to reconsider it. If after such reconsideration two-thirds of that house shall agree to pass the bill, it shall be sent, together with the objections, to the other house, by which it shall likewise be reconsidered, and if approved by two-thirds of that house shall become a law. But in all such cases the votes of both houses shall be determined by yeas and nays, and the names of the persons voting for and against the bill shall be entered on the journal of each house respectively. If any bill shall not be returned by the President within ten days (Sundays excepted) after it shall have been presented to him, the same shall be a law, in like manner as if he had signed it, unless the Congress by their adjournment prevent its return, in which case it shall not be a law.

Every order, resolution, or vote to which the concurrence of the Senate and House of Representatives may be necessary (except on a question of adjournment) shall be presented to the President of the United States; and before the same shall take effect, shall be approved by him, or being disapproved by him, shall be repassed by two-thirds of the Senate and House of Representatives, according to the rules and limitations prescribed in the case of a bill.

ARTICLE II

Section 1

The executive power shall be vested in a President of the United States of America. He shall hold his office during the term of four years, and together with the Vice President, chosen for the same term, be elected as follows:

Each State shall appoint, in such manner as the legislature thereof may direct, a number of electors, equal to the whole number of Senators and Representatives to which the State may be entitled in the Congress;[1] but no Senator or Representative, or person holding an office of trust or profit under the United States, shall be appointed an elector.

[The electors shall meet in their respective States and vote by ballot for two persons, of whom one at least shall not be an inhabitant of the same State with themselves. And they shall make a list of all the persons voted for, and of the number of votes for each; which list they shall sign and certify, and transmit sealed to the seat of government of the United States, directed to the President of the Senate. The President of the Senate shall, in the presence of the Senate and House of Representatives, open all the certificates, and the votes shall then be counted. The person having the greatest number of votes shall be the President, if such number be a majority of the whole number of electors appointed; and if there be more than one who have such a majority, and have an equal number of votes, then the House of Representatives shall immediately choose by ballot one of them for President; and if no person have a majority, then from the five highest on the list the said House shall in like manner choose the President. But in choosing the President the votes shall be taken by States, the representation from each State having one vote; a quorum for this purpose shall consist of a member or members from two-thirds of the States and a majority of all the States shall be necessary to a choice. In every case, after the choice of the President, the person having the greatest number of votes of the electors shall be the Vice President. But if there should remain two or more who have equal votes, the Senate shall choose from them by ballot the Vice President.][2]

The Congress may determine the time of choosing the electors and the day on which they shall give their votes, which day shall be the same throughout the United States.

No person except a natural-born citizen, or a citizen of the United States

[1] Modified by the Twenty-third Amendment.
[2] Superseded by the Twelfth Amendment.

at the time of the adoption of this Constitution, shall be eligible to the office of President; neither shall any person be eligible to that office who shall not have attained to the age of thirty-five years, and been fourteen years a resident within the United States.

In the case of the removal of the President from office, or of his death, resignation, or inability to discharge the powers and duties of the said office, the same shall devolve on the Vice President, and the Congress may by law provide for the case of removal, death, resignation, or inability, both of the President and Vice President, declaring what officer shall then act as President, and such officer shall act accordingly until the disability be removed or a President shall be elected.

The President shall, at stated times, receive for his services a compensation, which shall neither be increased nor diminished during the period for which he may have been elected, and he shall not receive within that period any other emolument from the United States or any of them.

Before he enter on the execution of his office he shall take the following oath or affirmation:

"I do solemnly swear (or affirm) that I will faithfully execute the office of President of the United States, and will to the best of my ability preserve, protect, and defend the Constitution of the United States."

Section 2

The President shall be commander-in-chief of the army and navy of the United States, and of the militia of the several States when called into the actual service of the United Sates; he may require the opinion, in writing, of the principal officer in each of the executive departments, upon any subject relating to the duties of their respective offices, and he shall have power to grant reprieves and pardons for offenses against the United States, except in cases of impeachment.

He shall have power, by and with the advice and consent of the Senate, to make treaties, provided two-thirds of the Senators present concur; and he shall nominate, and, by and with the advice and consent of the Senate, shall appoint ambassadors, other public ministers and consuls, judges of the Supreme Court and all other officers of the United States, whose appointments are not herein otherwise provided for, and which shall be established by law; but the Congress may by law vest the appointment of such inferior officers, as they think proper, in the President alone, in the courts of law, or in the heads of departments.

The President shall have power to fill up all vacancies that may happen during the recess of the Senate, by granting commissions which shall expire at the end of their next session.

Section 3

He shall from time to time give to the Congress information of the state of the Union, and recommend to their consideration such measures as he shall judge necessary and expedient; he may, on extraordinary occasions, convene both houses, or either of them, and in case of disagreement between them, with respect to the time of adjournment, he may adjourn them to such time as he shall think proper; he shall receive ambassadors and other public ministers; he shall take care that the laws be faithfully executed, and shall commission all the officers of the United States.

Section 4

The President, Vice President, and all civil officers of the United States shall be removed from office on impeachment for and conviction of treason, bribery, or other high crimes and misdemeanors.

ARTICLE VI

Section 3

. . . All executive and judicial officers, both of the United States and of the several States, shall be bound by oath or affirmation, to support this Constitution; but no religious test shall ever be required as a qualification of any office or public trust under the United States.

AMENDMENT XII[3]

The electors shall meet in their respective States and vote by ballot for President and Vice President, one of whom, at least, shall not be an inhabitant of the same State with themselves; they shall name in their ballots the person voted for as President, and in distinct ballots the person voted for as Vice President, and they shall make distinct lists of all persons voted for as President and of all persons voted for as Vice President, and of the number of votes for each; which lists they shall sign and certify, and transmit sealed to the seat of the government of the United States, directed to the President of the Senate. The President of the Senate shall, in the presence of the Senate and House of Representatives, open all the certificates and the votes shall then be counted. The person having the greatest number of votes for President shall be the President, if such number be a majority of the whole number of electors appointed; and if no person have such majority, then from the persons having the highest numbers not exceeding three on the list of those voted for as President, the House of Representatives shall choose immediately, by ballot, the President. But in choosing the President the votes shall be taken by States, the representation from each State having one vote; a quorum for this purpose shall consist of a member or members from two-thirds of the States, and a majority of all the States shall be necessary to a choice. And if the House of Representatives shall not choose a President whenever the right of choice shall devolve upon them, before the [fourth day of March][4] next following, then the Vice President shall act as President, as in the case of the death or other constitutional disability of the President.

3 Proclaimed September 25, 1804.
4 Superseded by the Twentieth Amendment.

The person having the greatest number of votes as Vice President shall be the Vice President, if such number be a majority of the whole number of electors appointed; and if no person have a majority, then from the two highest numbers on the list, the Senate shall choose the Vice President; a quorum for the purpose shall consist of two-thirds of the whole number of Senators, and a majority of the whole number shall be necessary to a choice. But no person constitutionally ineligible to the office of President shall be eligible to that of Vice President of the United States.

AMENDMENT XX[5]

Section 1

The terms of the President and Vice President shall end at noon on the 20th day of January, and the terms of Senators and Representatives at noon on the third day of January, of the years in which such terms would have ended if this article had not been ratified; and the terms of their successors shall then begin.

Section 2

The Congress shall assemble at least once in every year, and such meeting shall begin at noon on the third day of January, unless they shall by law appoint a different day.

Section 3

If at the time fixed for the beginning of the term of the President, the President elect shall have died, the Vice President elect shall become President. If a President shall not have been chosen before the time fixed for the beginning of his term, or if the President elect shall have failed to qualify, then the Vice President elect shall act as President until a President shall have qualified, and the Congress may by law provide for the case wherein neither a President elect nor a Vice President elect shall have qualified, declaring who shall then act as President, or the manner in which one who is to act shall be selected, and such person shall act accordingly until a President or Vice President shall have qualified.

Section 4

The Congress may by law provide for the case of the death of any of the persons from whom the House of Representatives may choose a President whenever the right of choice shall have devolved upon them, and for the case of death of any of the persons from whom the Senate may choose a Vice President whenever the right of choice shall have devolved upon them.

5 Proclaimed February 6, 1933.

AMENDMENT XXII[6]

Section 1

No person shall be elected to the office of the President more than twice, and no person who has held the office of President, or acted as President, for more than two years of a term to which some other person was elected President shall be elected to the office of the President more than once. But this Article shall not apply to any person holding the office of President when this Article was proposed by the Congress, and shall not prevent any person who may be holding the office of President, or acting as President, during the term within which this Article becomes operative from holding the office of President or acting as President during the remainder of such term.

Section 2

This article shall be inoperative unless it shall have been ratified as an amendment to the Constitution by the legislatures of three-fourths of the several States within seven years from the date of its submission to the States by the Congress.

AMENDMENT XXIII[7]

Section 1

The District constituting the seat of Government of the United States shall appoint in such manner as the Congress may direct:

A number of electors of President and Vice President equal to the whole number of Senators and Representatives in Congress to which the District would be entitled if it were a State, but in no event more than the least populous state; they shall be in addition to those appointed by the states, but they shall be considered, for the purposes of the election of the President and Vice President, to be electors appointed by a state; and they shall meet in the District and perform such duties as provided by the twelfth article of amendment.

Section 2

The Congress shall have power to enforce this article by appropriate legislation.

---

[6] Proclaimed March 1, 1951.
[7] Submitted for ratification June 21, 1960; proclaimed March 30, 1961.

THE MODEL STATE CONSTITUTION

ON THE GOVERNORSHIP

ARTICLE I

Bill of Rights

Section 1.07. Political Tests for Public Office. No oath, declaration or political test shall be required for any public office or employment other than the following oath or affirmation: "I do solemnly swear (or affirm) that I will support and defend the Constitution of the United States and the constitution of the state of _____ and that I will faithfully discharge the duties of the office of _____ to the best of my ability."

ARTICLE IV

The Legislature

Section 4.04. Legislative Districts. . . .

(b) Immediately following each decennial census, the governor shall appoint a board of _____ qualified voters to make recommendations within ninety days of their appointment concerning the redistricting of the state. The governor shall publish the recommendations of the board when received. The governor shall promulgate a redistricting plan within ninety to one hundred and twenty days after appointment of the board, whether or not it has made its recommendations. The governor shall accompany his plan with a message explaining his reasons for any changes from the recommendations of the board. The governor's redistricting plan shall be published in the manner provided for acts of the legislature and shall have the force of law upon such publication. Upon the application of any qualified voter, the supreme court, in the exercise of original, exclusive and final jurisdiction, shall review the governor's redistricting plan and shall have jurisdiction to make orders to amend the plan to comply with the requirements of this constitution or, if the governor has failed to promulgate a redistricting plan within the time provided, to make one or more orders establishing such a plan.

Section 4.08. Sessions. The legislature shall be a continuous body during the term for which its members are elected. It shall meet in regular

The author wishes to thank the National Municipal League, publisher of the Model State Constitution (6th edition, 1963), for permission to print these excerpts.

sessions annually as provided by law. It may be convened at other times by the governor or, at the written request of a majority of the members, by the presiding officer of the legislature.

Section 4.16. Action by the Governor.

(a) When a bill has passed the legislature, it shall be presented to the governor and, if the legislature is in session, it shall become law if the governor either signs or fails to veto it within fifteen days of presentation. If the legislature is in recess or, if the session of the legislature has expired during such fifteen-day period, it shall become law if he signs it within thirty days after such adjournment or expiration. If the governor does not approve a bill, he shall veto it and return it to the legislature either within fifteen days of presentation if the legislature is in session or upon the reconvening of the legislature from its recess. Any bill so returned by the governor shall be reconsidered by the legislature and, if upon reconsideration two-thirds of all the members shall agree to pass the bill, it shall become law.

(b) The governor may strike out or reduce items in appropriation bills passed by the legislature and the procedure in such cases shall be the same as in case of the disapproval of an entire bill by the governor.

Section 4.17. Post-Audit. The legislature shall appoint an auditor to serve at its pleasure. The auditor shall conduct post-audits as prescribed by law and shall report to the legislature and the governor.

Section 4.18. Impeachment. The legislature may impeach the governor, the heads of principal departments, judicial officers and such other officers of the state as may be made subject to impeachment by law, by a two-thirds vote of all the members, and shall provide by law procedures for the trial and removal from office, after conviction, of officers so impeached. No officer shall be convicted on impeachment by a vote of less than two-thirds of the tribunal hearing the charges.

ARTICLE V

The Executive

Section 5.01. Executive Power. The executive power of the state shall be vested in a governor.

Section 5.02. Election and Qualifications of Governor. The governor shall be elected, at the regular election every other odd-numbered year, by the direct vote of the people, for a term of four years beginning on the first day of (December) (January) next following his election. Any qualified voter of the state who is at least _____ years of age shall be eligible to the office of Governor.

Section 5.03. Governor's Message to the Legislature. The governor shall, at the beginning of each session, and may, at other times, give to the legislature information as to the affairs of the state and recommend measures he considers necessary or desirable.

Section 5.04. Executive and Administrative Powers.

(a) The governor shall be responsible for the faithful execution of the laws. He may, by appropriate action or proceeding brought in the name of the state, enforce compliance with any constitutional or legislative mandate, or restrain violation of any constitutional or legislative power, duty or right by an officer, department or agency of the state or any of its civil divisions.

This authority shall not authorize any action or proceeding against the legislature.

(b) The governor shall commission all officers of the state. He may at any time require information, in writing or otherwise, from the officers of any administrative department, office or agency upon any subject relating to the respective offices. He shall be commander-in-chief of the armed forces of the state, except when they shall be called into the service of the United States, and may call them out to execute the laws, to preserve order, to suppress insurrection or to repel invasion.

Section 5.05. Executive Clemency. The governor shall have power to grant reprieves, commutations and pardons, after conviction, for all offenses and may delegate such powers, subject to such procedures as may be prescribed by law.

Section 5.06. Administrative Departments. All executive and administrative offices, agencies and instrumentalities of the state government, and their respective functions, powers and duties, shall be allocated by law among and within not more than twenty principal departments so as to group them as far as practicable according to major purposes. Regulatory, quasi-judicial and temporary agencies established by law may, but need not, be allocated within a principal department. The legislature shall by law prescribe the functions, powers and duties of the principal departments and of other agencies of the state and may from time to time reallocate offices, agencies and instrumentalities among the principal departments, may increase, modify, diminish or change their functions, powers and duties and may assign new functions, powers and duties to them; but the governor may make such changes in the allocation of such functions, powers and duties, as he considers necessary for efficient administration. If such changes affect existing law, they shall be set forth in executive orders, which shall be submitted to the legislature while it is in session, and shall become effective, and shall have the force of law, sixty days after submission, or at the close of the session, whichever is sooner, unless specifically modified or disapproved by a resolution concurred in by a majority of all the members.

Section 5.07. Executive Officers; Appointment. The governor shall appoint and may remove the heads of all administrative departments. All other officers in the administrative service of the state shall be appointed and may be removed as provided by law.

Section 5.08. Succession to Governorship.

(a) If the governor-elect fails to assume office for any reason, the presiding officer of the legislature shall serve as acting governor until the governor-elect qualifies and assumes office or, if the governor-elect does not assume office within six months, until the unexpired term has been filled by special election and the newly elected governor has qualified. If, at the time the presiding officer of the legislature is to assume the acting governorship, the legislature has not yet organized and elected a presiding officer, the outgoing governor shall hold over until the presiding officer of the legislature is elected.

(b) When the governor is unable to discharge the duties of his office by reason of impeachment or other disability, including but not limited to physical or mental disability, or when the duties of the office are not being discharged by reason of his continuous absence, the presiding officer of the legislature shall serve as acting governor until the governor's disability or absence terminates. If the governor's disability or absence does not terminate within six months, the office of the governor shall be vacant.

(c) When, for any reason, a vacancy occurs in the office of the governor, the unexpired term shall be filled by special election except when such unexpired term is less than one year, in which event the presiding officer of the legislature shall succeed to the office for the remainder of the term. When a vacancy in the office of governor is filled by special election, the presiding officer of the legislature shall serve as acting governor from the occurrence of the vacancy until the newly elected governor has qualified. When the presiding officer of the legislature succeeds to the office of governor, he shall have the title, powers, duties and emoluments of that office and, when he serves as acting governor, he shall have the powers and duties thereof and shall receive such compensation as the legislature shall provide by law.

(d) The legislature shall provide by law for special elections to fill vacancies in the office of governor.

(e) The supreme court shall have original, exclusive and final jurisdiction to determine absence and disability of the governor or governor-elect and to determine the existence of a vacancy in the office of governor and all questions concerning succession to the office or to its powers and duties.

ARTICLE VI

The Judiciary

Section 6.04. Appointment of Judges.

(a) The governor, with the advice and consent of the legislature, shall appoint the chief judges and associate judges of the supreme, appellate and general courts. The governor shall give ten days' public notice before sending a judicial nomination to the legislature or before making an interim appointment when the legislature is not in session.

ARTICLE VII

Finance

Section 7.02. The Budget. The governor shall submit to the legislature, at a time fixed by law, a budget estimate for the next fiscal year setting forth all proposed expenditures and anticipated income of all departments and agencies of the state, as well as a general appropriation bill to authorize the proposed expenditures and a bill or bills covering recommendations in the budget for new or additional revenues.

INDEX

603